THE WHEEL'S STILL IN SPIN

STARDUST AND COALDUST
A COALMINER'S MAHABHARATA

BY
DAVID JOHN DOUGLASS

The Wheel's Still In Spin
(Stardust and Coaldust — Part II)
First published in Great Britain in 2009
by Read 'n' Noir
an imprint of ChristieBooks
PO Box 35, Hastings, East Sussex, TN34 1ZS

Distributed in the UK by Central Books Ltd
99 Wallis Road, London E9 5LN
orders@centralbooks.com

ISBN-10 1-873976-36-4
ISBN-13 978-1-873976-36-4
EAN 9781873976364

British Library Cataloguing in Publication Data.
A catalogue record for this book is available from the British Library

The Wheel's Still in Spin

Acknowledgements

My deepest thanks go to the family of Eric Fraser, the late *Radio Times* illustrator, for their kind permission in allowing me to reproduce his dramatic drawing. It was one of his splendid illustrations accompanying the ground-breaking Radio Ballads transmitted by BBC Home Service in the late 1950s, and early '60s. The front cover is a copy of his Big Hewer illustration, which was transmitted on 18th August 1961. (A comprehensive history of the Radio Ballads and their brilliant creators Ewan MacColl, Peggy Seeger and Charles Parker, entitled *Set Into Song*, written by Peter Cox, was published in 2008.

The back cover illustration is a personal retirement card, photographed and designed for me by Adge Covell, technical director of the miners website *www.minersadvice.co.uk*. The top panel is a scene from the Durham Miners Gala at the Miners Hall, Red Hill, Durham by Mike Jones; the two women are Maureen Douglass and Alison Sharp, photographed at The Red Star Folk Club, The Spreadeagle, Doncaster, in 1978. The small pit scene cameo at the bottom — 'Testing for Gas' by Ted Holloway — is from *Shafts of Light. Mining Art in the Great Northern Coalfield*, by Robert McManners and Gillian Wales.

My thanks are also due to ny long time friend and comrade Stuart Christie for getting this work by the scruff and dragging it into existence, to Mark Hendy for getting the book on its feet and knocking lumps off some of the more distorted sentences and passages, to Louise van der Hoeven my fellow IWW member for proof reading this work, and to Dr Hilda Kean of Ruskin College, Oxford, for her careful reading and summary of the standard English confusions of the book and the need for some basic explanations.

INTRODUCTION
THE WHEEL'S STILL IN SPIN

The decade and a half between the end of the Sixties and the rise of Margaret Thatcher witnessed a massive and global revolutionary upsurge. In part, this was symbolised by the almost impossibly heroic struggle of the Vietnamese people against the naked Imperialism of the USA. Off the shore of the mass empire of capital little defiant Cuba sat within spitting distance. Nationalist struggles and class struggles rocked the world, liberation and resistance movements joined with the blowing winds of change. Within the belly of the US beast, the civil rights movement and the armed wings of class and racial justice were emerging to challenge the status quo in their own backyard. In Europe the urban guerrilla lived not in the evergreen but among the concrete jungles of downtown cities and finance capitals, as the Red Army Fraction, the Red Brigades, First of May Group and the Angry Brigade pockets of armed red resistance began to bring the rebellion home. In Ireland, the Provisional IRA was beginning its long war against the British state, winning increasing authority among the oppressed occupied population of Ulster. In Scotland, in Wales, even in the Cheviot Hills of Northumberland, armed teams prepared for the coming decisive clash which would seek to smash the United Kingdom state.

In Britain, the biggest industrial challenge since the Twenties was afoot as unions and wildcats unleashed the greatest number of strike days since the General Strike. Within the unions and despite the unions the rank and file sought to stamp its control on work and unions and communities. The National Union of Mineworkers which someone was to call the 'shock troops of the TUC' presided over the rise of the flying picket, and mass 'secondary' action, which would take a government by the balls. For a time it looked like the labour movement would take the whole system by the throat. Dockers, building workers, struck and fought toe to toe against scabs and police. Rent strikes, occupations, work-ins, and mass demonstrations posed old ideologies and old common wealth solutions of co-operation and solidarity.

All of these movements, tendencies and ideologies overlapped, inter-bred, and formed a loose but comprehensive movement. The Wheel was surely in spin, and there was no telling whom it was naming.

This volume, told through the perspective of one of its working class revolutionary activists, explains the history as viewed from the ground and a number of those turning points and crossroads. David

Douglass, a long time coal miner, union activist and revolutionary, joins up the dots, along with some telling insights into the hidden world of underground labour in its harsh and gritty reality. Throughout the whole story the air of sexual freedoms, which broke free of constraints in the previous decade, survive and prosper.

This was a time when the world was up for grabs, the earth resounded to the world revolutionary impulse. The genii were free from the bottle, and the music was up loud.

From where we all stand now, that distant period seems dim and becomes dimmer with every new law and every new brick successive governments have placed on the wall. Soon, they hope, no-one will remember how close we came, to finishing with the whole scumbag system of greed, privilege and power.

> *Don't speak too soon for the wheel's still in spin*
> *and there's no telling who that it's naming*
> *for the losers now will be later to win*
> *and the times they are a changing.*

COALDUST

When I was young and in me prime
Ee aye ah cud hew
Whey Ah wes hewin all the time
Nuw me hewin days are through-through
Nuw me hewin days are through
At the face the dust did flee
Ee aye ah cud hew
Nuw that dust is killing me
Nuw me hewin days are through-through
Nuw me hewin days are through
Av laid doon flat and shoveled coal
Ee aye ah cud hew
Me eyes did smart in the dust filled hole
Nuw me hewin days are through-through
Nuw me hewin days are through
Whey av had marra's and they were men
Ee aye ah cud hew
Whey they were men! and sons of men
Nuw me hewin days are through-through
Nuw me hewin days are through.
They say that work is made by men
Ee aye ah cud hew
But whey med dust ah dinnit ken
Nuw me hewin days are through-through
Nuw me hewin days are through
Its yon. That pit ney mer Ah'll see
Ee aye ah cud hew
Ah'll carry it roond-inside of me
Nuw me hewin days are through-through
Nuw me hewin days are through.[1]

DUNSCROFT

Dawn is thick with mists, rolling in from moorland,
vast tracts of empty peat bogs and moors,

Hatfield wastes, Thorne Moors. Thick dripping wet fog, enveloping everything in a silent wetness, and chill. Black slate roofs blur into pale grey outlines. Webs of wet fog envelope the rows on rows of silent pit houses, the odd surviving tree, and telegraph poles.

Eyebrows, lashes, nose, hair, drip with mist,

A chill from the silent bog seeps right into your bones. Air smells of peat and the odd wisp of wood smoke as three hundred early morning fires are lit and the house rises with the man. Returning from the night shift, spent and exhausted, such dawns are the gratuitous goodnight kiss before rolling into clean sheets, to snuggle down and drift into deep lang sleep. But this is 5 a.m. and day shift. The pit bus has gone, its distant lights disappearing up the end of Broadway, a two-mile gallery of pit houses, before I had got to the end of the street. Bliddy day shift, panting, heart pounding and every inch of bodily function resisting every motion. Stale alcohol rips through my bloodstream and sticks on my breath. My eyes strain to sleep, even while I hurry over the railway bridge as the pit looms up out of the mists. Mouth dry, the thick encroaching fog begs you to sit down right here, curl up and sleep, as you would have done, crouched in the bus shelter, donkey jacket lapels turned up against the wind, if you had got out of bed ten minutes earlier. The alarm, shrill and painful, stabs into your consciousness. You leave the warm bed, leave the warm shapely body next to you, roll, with eyes still closed, into the shock of the icy cold morning and ice-cold clothes. This morn you lay too long, pretending the alarm had been a dream, pretending you still had an hour before it actually went off.

'Are you up?' Maureen would prompt. 'Aye,' you would lie, then let the nothingness slide you back under. 'Dave, you'll miss the bus.'

Damn the bus, damn the pit, I want to sleep. But don't damn Maureen, not for me the shoot the messenger, outrage against the wife's urgent prompting. For it is her who has to manage the budget minus a shift's money if you knock. Stagger round the silent living room, taking the pit clothes from the fire guard and stove where they have hung to dry, still smelling of soap powder and coal dust. The bait made up in the poke.

Then out the door, into the sea of icy fog. Seven hundred men are rolling from their beds, clumping down from Stainforth, Hatfield or Dunscroft, silently sullenly heading for the pit. An army of cloth caps and Woodbines are boarding the buses at Moorends and Thorne. The army of underground labour is up and on its way and scarcely a sound. The canteen is almost barren of men by the time I arrive, identity check in hand; rush through the baths, envious of the naked bodies in the showers coming off shift, warm water and steam rising through the corridor, songs echoing with the steam. Then drift in, lamp bouncing, with the herd of humptybacks, jackets flying, baccy juice apostrophised, water bottles slung, climb the steel stairwell to the cage. Struggling with those last few steps—as the men said, if they would just get rid of those top two steps the stair would be no climb at all. Shuffling forward, forward, forward, draw dropping away down and down, then rising as hot air rushes up through the chains and gantries into the morning mist and the cage gate thrust up, in yee gaan, whammed up against the mesh, struggle to keep ya feet on the wet iron floor, this is the last draw, everyone must get on, or gaan away yem and be paid nowt for all that effort.

As the cage lifts off the keps, a moment's silence, then away with a gust of wind, down, down, shaft wa'ater slashing in, salty but refreshing, all lights off, blackness and the nearness of bodies, and the crack: 'So Ah seys to wor lass this morn, "Or Ah cannit gaan this morn, it's white all ower." She sits up, and she says, "Whey there's ney snow on the rooftops pet." "Ah knaa," Ah seys, "but a divind gaan that way."' A collective rock of laughter 'Aye, mine seys "Hey up, tha's put buets on wrong feet." Ah seys "Aye, Ah know they should be on your buggers!"' The laughs are louder. 'So Ah seys ti this bird with web feet, "Hey up, duck!"' Just laugh man; fuck it, just laugh. And the cage is slowing, slowing, and the lights from the pit bottom break into view, as we push past the late riders, black and bloodied, smelling of pooda reek, coal dust, and stale wa'ater. Run, with your battery bouncing into the small of ya back, and jump into the paddy, crush and wriggle your arse into the tight confines of the rollercoaster carriage and the paddy guard waves 'There's off' with his cap lamp. A shower of hot water and a cloud of diesel fumes spurt into the air and envelop the coaches as we set off. Prop ya feet up, but keep them inside the coach and don't nod off to the left, the coach skims the paddy road wall, with broken boards, and jutting rocks, and splintered iron sheets, nod that way and behead yesell. Nod to the right and this big hairy unshaven ripper will stick his tongue in your ear. So just sort of come out of gear but stay running.

Today I psych myself up: I will take whatever man or nature throws at me, I will do whatever they can do, I will make up in speed what I cannot match in strength. Am I on trial? Oh God yes I am. Sparrow's team—the most conscientious, hard-working rippers at the pit, some would say lackeys. I had been put with this team to make or break me; they intended to break me. I was an unpopular red-raggin little Geordie bastard. I had had the divisive inter-Union, anti-four-shift strike laid at my door. The Branch had voted on 5 January 1969 for the third time to reject four-shift working. We failed and got landed with four shifts per 24 hours instead of three. 6 a.m. day shift, this bastard, the one the stupid Yorkshire twats called 'a good shift'. 1.30. After you got back home, half-past nine, just time for your dinner and a pint if you still felt like it by then. 6 p.m. shift—get in just before 2 a.m., all work and bed. And finally midnight shift; you were going out to work while others were putting their lights off for bed. On a Friday men were staggering from the pub as we suckers slunk out to work. What a system.

It had been worth the fight, but the pit was divided, it was an unofficial strike, half the Union officials for it, half against. I had been in my element, me cloth cap with the peak turned up in what I thought to be a sort of Lenin style, with the red Mao badge on the front. For good measure, I was now wearing the regulation beard and my hair was long and bushy from the daily showering. Addressing the masses as they swarmed through the corridor to the token cabin. 'Comrades and Fellow Workers! We aren't the nuts and bolts, we aren't the machines, we have lives away from the pit, we work to live remember, we don't live to work!'

'What's that daft cunt on aboot?' I remember one of the fellow workers commenting.

I had worked tirelessly producing *The Mineworker*, the duplicated revolutionary miners' paper, and stood hawking its defiance to the boss and Union collaborators. To some of the older lads I was a sudden reincarnation of Aud Man Parkin and his Sylvester Rebel, and Butty Squasher, communist piss-taking papers of the 1930s—very popular, much more so than *The Mineworker*, which was heavy, political and jargonised. I hit the typewriter keys like a machine-gun, I machine-gunned the bosses' men, the deputies, the gaffers of all descriptions, the NCB, the state, capitalism, tap-tap-tap-tap. As the duplicator whirred and the piles of papers mounted in corners of the spare bedroom, I never slept. Not during a production run, and during the strike I was down for every shift picketing, I spent more time down at the pit during that strike than I did at work. Selling papers, haranguing the crowd about four shifts, about workers' control, I made enemies determined to cut me down before I became dangerous. Not least among the Branch; I had just survived a sacking on haulage when Tom Mullanny, the Union delegate, threw me to the lions.

I had stopped the pit along with the pit bottom lads, using the coupling block in a work-to-rule against the dire conditions on the pit bottom. It landed me before the manager. 'What would you do with him?' he asked Tom, the Union man with the left-wing reputation brought in to defend me. 'Ah would sack him,' he responded. The Union man I had earlier attacked in correspondence to Frank Waters, the Communist Party organiser in the coalfields. Frank knew a Trot when he saw one, and passed the correspondence back to Tom, so he had me, and my letter. On the occasion of the grand disciplinary hearing before the colliery manager, the moderate Union secretary Frank Clark, who I had also clashed with, stepped in and asked how many lads had been killed on that job. 'Two, I think,' said the manager. 'So we can't discipline a lad for protecting his own safety, can we?' It worked, and I learned a lesson about moderates and 'militants'. Before falling out with Mullanny I had confided my indecision between anarchism and Trotskyism. Mullanny was later able to publicly attack me as an anarchist Trotskyite! When we arrived from Geordieland, we set away as an outpost of the Toon political scene. Firstly establishing a Doncaster Youth Against The Bomb group, we campaigned on Vietnam, on the Bomb. We held folky socials at The George, fetched doon singers from up yon, preached peace and revolution in clubs and pubs. Held public meetings. Started to attract attention, not just the politics, not just the folky music and blues stuff, but the way we dressed, the things we said. Kids had shouted 'Gypsy' at us when we first arrived. We were, when we landed in this isolated pit village locked in a sort of forties–fifties timewarp, nothing short of a revelation. When we started painting political slogans on supermarket walls and bus shelters, daubing Ban The Bomb symbols on roads and signposts, the circus had really come to town.

There was a coterie of advanced thinkers here and there. One couple, Ken Terry and his wife, dressed like Sonny and Cher. His dad was a prematurely retired miner laid up with ill health. He looked scornfully on Ken in his shoulder-length hair and kaftan coat, her in her straight black hair and micro skirt, he heroically wearing the same outfit that Mick Jagger had for Concert In The Park following Mark's death. But for these two, right now, it was mixed up with village life; they still rode about on their bicycles, and still went out to the club, to listen to Frankie Lane and Sinatra stand-ins. Ken was to become one of our closest comrades over the years, evolving as we evolved through a variety of revolutionary organisations.

Art was the local hip character. He was the local reefer head, smoking, dealing, buying. He summoned me to his ma's house, when she was out of course. Remarkably she lived in our street, or rather we lived in hers since his family had been there since the pit was sunk. He stuck his hand out and grabbed my shoulder warmly.

'Tha's fucking ace thee, tha's just what we want roond here.'

A couple of his mates and a sultry chick sat on the best settee smoking a magnificent joint. Art had a ball of shit the size of a melon, I kid you not, a greet ba'al of dope, the biggest I have ever seen in my entire life then or since. He threw it to me. I was amazed at the weight. 'You must be a bliddy millionaire,' I suggested. 'Na, this is orders this. I take up the dosh, buy a big stash, all I gets me dope for free, I do it for t'lads like.'

By the time I staggered up the street with Art, to introduce him to Maureen, we had sampled quite a few tokes of his wares. I remember Maureen was making dinner at the time, and she offered us a beer each from our newly purchased fridge. Art couldn't say 'fridge' and got it mixed up with beer, so it kept coming out as bridge. It started one of those unstoppable bouts of manic laughter, which rocked me to the floor, while Art collapsed on his knees, eyes streaming. I was helpless with body-pounding laughter and begged for it to stop; it hurt like a bliddy kicking, but I couldn't stop laughing. Maureen as I recall rolled us outside onto the step, where we stayed until late afternoon and the laughter finally stopped.

Gradually we started to get together; we became something of the scene. At the pit I had formed the Haulage Workers' Committee which rapidly became the Young Miners Committee, militant, political, Syndicalist at first in its orientation. The young miners from this group were to stay in our political circle as the centre of struggle moved on to other fields, *The Mineworker* and also later the Revolutionary Workers' Party (Trotskyist) (RWP(T)) directly, who at that time we just worked with in a common front, but were being drawn closer to under their political direction and orientation. The group included Tom Minto, an apprentice underground fitter at the time, from a large mining family, and later his wife Trish, Norman Pugh from Moorends, and countless others, lads who joined at the beginning and stuck to it throughout the twists and turns of life.

The Abbey, a pub which hadn't been opened long, became our pub. This was to be our Bridge Hotel. Mind, the various landlords over the years didn't always appreciate being the informal hotbed of revolutionaries. We used to hang out there on a weekend, and gradually our gang grew. At closing time, arms full of bottles, we would set off for foot-stomping folk-singing arounds at wor hoose afterwards. These dos also were not too appreciated by neighbours, particularly those with whom we shared a dividing wall. It was the start of many frictional battles over our different lifestyles, which raged for a decade and more. In the back room disco at the Abbey we went round selling *The Mineworker,* and giving out anti-Vietnam-War literature. The CND badge was still cool then and most young'uns in there identified with it. For years before becoming known as Danny the Red I was nicknamed 'Ban The Bomb' and it stuck long after it became inappropriate.

It was one such night, when a big team of leather-clad bikers were in, all in their exclusive group. I came over to flog them a *Mineworker*. '"Mineworker"? Does tha think we're pit moggies like?' One of them asked, as if I had downgraded his status from gun-toting, Lone Ranger, leather-clad, speed king biker to a flat-capped pit yakker.

'Yi cud be.'

'Aye, we is actually, but not th'neet,' the same bloke explained. Pit work was for the pit, pit politics, whatever that was, that was for the pit, this was weekend. Still the discussion went on, to politics, to class, to authority. They joined us, both at the table, then in the house at wa folky party, and for much of our lives afterwards: Jim and Lynne Shipley and the other bikers—'reet folk' as they say in Yorkshire. They were fascinated by the songs, by the crack in general. Lynne was a straight-from-the-shoulder working-class lass who challenged everything and everybody. Jim as it turned out was a ripper, at Hatfield. Actually, it was through joint community mobilisations, particularly around rents, that we met Legay Shipley, Jim's Dad. Legay, in full beard and belt and braces was a Labour Party zealot.

GI ME A MOUNTAIN

So I had landed with the no-nonsense Sparrow team, so called after Keith, the chargeman and all-round star stoneman go-getter. This was a hand-bored, fired and hand-filled caunch. Every pound of stone which went on the chain lowered the vend and spoiled the run of mine, so it had to be packed, 12 yards of pack on my side and 6 yards on the other. The paddy stops at the meeting station amid a clutter of men unloading chains, shovels, bags of shot firing powder. For me is the long walk up 22's tailgate. It is miles long, and like a sauna. Clouds of dust and heat seep from its entrance and into the paddy road.

Stripping down to me hoggers and T-shirt, I have me bait poke and bottle slung around my neck. Dusk mask on for now—I won't be able to wear it long in that heat. Oil lamp in hand, I set off. Actually, Maureen made a little pencil drawing of me, on my way inbye, which is extremely accurate all bar for the shovel which she didn't quite capture. I do not wait for the meandering crew who walk a steady pace and stop for a minute on the way. Such would be fatal to me. A sitdown on this shift would mean a swift slump into deep sleep; and once the sleep is on you, in the sodden heat of the tailgate your body will give up any idea of work. Punch-drunk and sapped of strength you would be vulnerable to rockfalls, and stumbling, head injuries and much else. So dive in, drive on, build up the pace. It is a weaving, dodging, bending road, with low beams and sharp inclines where the earth has pressed down hard and the road has boiled up in uneven rolls and falls. The sweat streams freely now, and that's a start. The first real sweat alerts your body to the coming combat. Two other rippers are on my tail, like me thin to the bone. 'Like a Gypsy's dog,' someone commented on my stature, 'all ribs and dick'. We do not talk, we concentrate on the road, we concentrate on fast walking and keeping wa feet—breath is laboured. The dust mask tears at my beard and a thousand little ant-like drops of sweat run through it on my skin. It is wet and sucks at my cheeks. About half way in, I pull it off, and let it flop under my chin on its strap. I will wear it when the machines start up again as we seem to have a period of less dusty air. The noggin men working between shifts have obviously stopped cutting and will be cooling off in the main gate. As we arrive at the gate end there is time to flop for a minute. Grab a board as a backrest, squat on a chock piece, grab a bit bait (only a slice—its still early, the belly still feels like retching, and there is hard merciless slog ahead). Cheese and tomato, same every day, wouldn't have it any other way; it's like a piece of kindness in a world of cold hardness. By the time I get up, knee pads tight to knees, leave the bait poke in the gate hung up, and start to look under the caunch, the colliers are arriving and are stripping off before going under the rip. With me oil lamp in hand I dook under the caunch. Bliddy hell, they've cut out a football pitch. A huge expanse of ground stands exposed and unsupported. It sits like a monstrous slab, just waiting; another tickle of movement and the lot will be in. The cutters are supposed to stop cutting after one web width, to give us the chance to support the exposed ground, sling packs on, advance bull rails and props. But they haven't, sloppy bastards, they've just kept cutting. Meks them look like the big hewers, big hitters, just keep roaring it out like a great wave, never thinking of the weight being thrown on the tail gate end or the potential for disaster. As if to make things worse this is a flooded pack hole. Foul smelling black water covers everything, a foot deep, the water is already over me boots. This is going to be another good shift—welcome home! Another team of rippers would have ragged up at this. But not this team. If you moan, it's because you're scared or too lazy to meet the challenge.

There is a faint, musty, sticky smell in the air and I suspect firedamp has built up in the huge empty blackness of the gateside. I wade through the water, to the rear of the pack, lower the flame on the lamp to just a button. Turning off my cap lamp I am plunged into absolute blackness. I raise the lamp to the roof slowly, and peer through the glass. Faint strands of methane burn round the flame. Blue edging curls up its sides, the start of a square shape which given enough gas leaking from the seam grows into a clear pyramid shape and indicates 5 per cent, the explosive point of the gas. But this, this is about 1per cent, just perceptible.[2]

The bull rails need advancing from back in the packs under the exposed ground in front. These are big, heavy-section steel girders. With two of you, shoulder under each end, prop cupped in both your hands back and front, you strain to inch the girder forward, sitting it on the prop with each advance, not letting the weight of the girder pull the prop forward and fall—do that and the full weight will drop on your shoulders and you'll be down under it, worse, you'll drop the weight on your marra at the front, with his back to you, impervious of your error. But there is no such consideration here. Today Burt is under the lip with me. One of those characters who can only mek hissell look good by pulling someone else doon. So to wait for Burt to join me in the operation is to court public accusation of laziness. So against every judgement I ever had, I lower off the big girder, and hear the creak of the roof as it eases slightly. Facing the pack and away from the face, I lower the girder to my right shoulder, lift and pull at the same time, by lifting up on thigh muscles, then drop down in a crouch to lower the girder back on the lowered prop. Then, again, each time the weight at the front gets greater as the girder advances, the balance on the prop gets more tricky as it acts as fulcrum on a seesaw. Pump it up for now, find another prop for the front, rake around under the water for props fallen out as the girder is left behind and the weight came on. Drag it up, like a great metal cumbersome body. Wedge it under the girder nearer the front, then lower the back one off. Now the biggest weight is on the rear of the girder, so your shoulder takes more weight, as you lower the front prop again, just enough to jack your legs up, prowl it forward, forward, balance on the prop. At last you can pump it up and drag the rear prop to the front, but the water obscures the floor. Pump up onto a soft bottom, and just as you have the prop tight tensioned, the floor will yield, often unevenly and the prop will fly, oh yes they'll fly. Under hydraulic pressure it will shoot out and punch you straight in the head or face or body—it can kill you. So pain up the arse as it is, you dig out, thrusting the shovel under the surface of the water and dig up the coal and shale slush, till you strike a hard floor. Now the prop will sit in a bloody hole, which will be a darling to get out next time you have to advance the dam thing. Meantime Blabbergob has arrived and is making an effort to advance another bull rail. My instinct is to go to the front of the girder and let us advance the rail together—fuck him, this is a dog-eat-dog team. The gate men are dragging forward their sheets and fitting them one on top of the other, great flat metal sheets salvaged from other jobs or cut to order in the blacksmiths and sent underground, on the initiative of the caunch men themselves. These will form a solid floor when the full web of stone caunch is dropped on them. They will provide a solid base upon which to shovel the stone, flung back into the packs at either side, or filling out what surplus is left onto the face panzer. They will sit one under each other so the shovel glides from one plane to the next without striking a metal edge. They are part of the ancient Geordie pitmen's 'la'r', or Yorkshire colliers' 'nouce'—it is a pit sense learned of doing things the hard way, and the brain riding to the rescue of the struggling sinew to find an easier way. Without the metal sheets, the hard stone will force the shovel down into the softer floor, which will always fill in with more hard stone. It will force the edge of the shovel always to be pointing down and not flat, it will mean you always strike the hard sides of the stone and never find its edge. You will break your back in pointless endeavour.

To the sheets is added the 'scaffold'. In reality this collection of long planks and metal girders is to stand on after the shots are fired, from which to set the bow and then the legs of the new arch, tunnel support. But pit wit bends its existence to the task at hand. It becomes an inverted chute stretching right across the gate. It will prevent the stone flying off down the gate, and scattering the rock. It will ensure the stone will slide down onto the sheets. The sheets and scaffold were not invented by the gaffers; they were dreamed up from backbreaking, shovel-swinging, knee-aching toil by the man at the foot of the stone pile, kneeling stripped to his hoggers, in clouds of stone dust, powder reek and coal dust. My pack, for Burt was a spare man and this was my regular place, was infamous. At good times it was 12 yards long, and 3 foot 6 inches wide. This morn it was three times as wide.

In the opposite pack hole, which was a mere 6 yards, you could get a start by robbing stone from the waste and getting the rough outline of the back wall and side established. My side, the pack ran back to the cusp of the coal cut. There was nowt at the end of my pack but broken roof, leaking gas and the wet coal seam. Underfoot was the soul-destroying black lake, into which I would soon have to kneel to work. Emerging from the dark pool is a stack of rusty wire bags. These will act as wallers, when there are no big rocks left, or just now to make a start. We drag a rusted confused mass of wire over to the panzer side, and unravel and peel an individual wire bag from the fusion. Bastards—I hate them; they are full of bits of wire sticking out and sticking into your naked flesh. The chain is stood, Burt holds open a bag, I stand on the chain and shovel the residue of cut coal and gumming into the bag, we fill them and stack them, until the pre-start warning zooon-zooons and I step from the chain as it begins to move and drag the coal down the face.

We drag the sacks to the back end of the pack and start to construct the outline of the wall. Meantime the boring machine is voicing its angry presence in the gate, twisting its way into the reluctant rock to fashion the shot holes. Nowt to dey nuw but wait. Might as weel eat ya bait; after they fire we will get no time for a break. I drag a bundle of the wire bastards to the back of the pack, one lump to sit on, one lump spragged against the last pack wall to rest me back on. I turn me shovel over; it will be my seat on top of the bags, to keep me arse oot the wa'ater. More comfort yet, I take off me knee pads and position one under each cheek of my arse, slinging me shirt loosely round me shoulders to stop the wire sticking in me back, which it doesn't of course since the wire pokes through anyway. Now I can balance me bait tin on me lap, and with me feet under the water, I lean back and enjoy the taste of home.

Cheese and tomato sandwiches have possibly three occasions when they become more than themselves, when they take on a culinary transformation almost miraculous. One is at the seaside when you're a kid, and they have become squashy and salty and a bit sandy. Another is after climbing a high crag in the bitter cold, when every sinew is taught and your legs are like iron and your belly is fast in fear, your fingers hold your life in their dire grip, you emerge at the top and breathe and see the world around. Your body relaxes like a bottomless sigh while your belly released from its grip of fear is suddenly chasmously empty. Then to prop yourself against a welcome rock out of the wind and pull from your rucksack the bait—that is a banquet. The other time is now, doon the pit, with the dust from the cutting machine seeping toward you, and the noise of the boring machine. Bite it, and chew it, and feel like you are getting one back on the bastards: I can stand this, I can manage this.

But you don't get a chance to finish it. 'FIRING!' comes the cry and you grab your oil lamp from the prop, hang ya bag up out of line of the shot and, still chomping on ya bait, bang ya way through the chock line, some yards from the caunch. You just get sat when a dull thud tells you they've fired, and the air stops dead at your ear drums. The acrid taste of sulphur and stone grit finds its way doon ya gullet along with the last bite of butty. That's it; here we go; now it is time for combat. The grey, merciless rock now seals the exit to the gate; I've positioned my steel sheet atop some of the bags to give it a slight slant so the stone will roll toward me as Burt shovels it back from the edge of the pile. Kneel now into the wa'ater and feel the cold surround me knees. Soon the straps from the knee pads will bite into the backs of my knees and calves as I rock first into the stone piling up in front of me, then back as I sling it back hard to the temporary wall of bags we had erected. The rhythm takes time to get going; the stone is reluctant to move at the front as it has packed itself tightly together as it dropped under the blast. But soon it is coming flying, and I hold the shovel so the blade is inclined toward the stone in flight, to stop it hitting my knees. I scoop in one movement and fling. Again and again. You go into autopilot for forty minutes of hard slog, pulling the larger lumps out by hand, dragging them down the side to form the walls.

Slowly a dry stone wall construction starts to emerge from the floor to the roof, packed solid with rock, and anything else which needs disposing of. Old oil drums come tumbling down the pile as the first small exit back into the gate emerges; these can be wedged back into the pack and fill the space rapidly, but must be covered with rock as soon as possible—empty cans do not make good packs. Steadily the pack advances, four yards, five yards. Some huge rocks, which didn't break with the shot and wouldn't crack with the windy pick, slide slowly down the heap; the trick here is to catch the edge of the rock on the shovel which you will use as a ski, while you pull backwards and your marra lifts at the back and pushes forward. It moves, slowly, relentlessly to the pack wall, a gud'un. Solid as ... well, as a rock I suppose.

At the other side, the shorter pack is complete and the men prepare to fill out. One at the front digs stone and flings it back to his mate who catches it, like me, with the tilted shovel blade and then flings it around onto the chain. Two shovels are thus attacking the pile from two directions, while the gate men are trimming off rock with the windy picks to set the arch girder supports in the gate. The last piece of the pack takes skill, flinging the stone to the back of the closing space, without dropping it short and leaving a gap where gas can collect. If its not packed up tight to the roof, the rock will break and start falls which will spread into gate. So you don't fill the shovel up, just half fill it, gently. Then it's done. As soon as the last rock is in place and our massive 12-yard dry stone wall is assembled we get into the gate, and stand up. No time to admire any views, though—we are en route doon the gate to the stack of steel girders to assist the gate men in erecting the arch. The arches lie in three bits, a crown and two legs, heavy section, 14 by 12 feet. Heavy. Finding an edge to pull a portion free to get a grip is tricky; these are finger-trapping bastards as is everything doon the pit. Once you get a corner enough to prize up one edge, your marra does the same at the other and you lift the bow on its arch free from the others. The next bit is trickier and hard for a wee twat like me—this work is too hard for my frame really, but I do it. I do it because this is what I am, and I will do it.

'When you're mad!' shouts Burt. We face the arch sidewards to us, we lift up in one movement till it rests on our forearms, then twist and turn parallel to the girder as our shoulders now are wedged underneath it, so now it sits on our shoulders and we set off, over the rough ground, through the leaking oil, over the rammle laid about the gate. Don't drop it. No matter how heavy it gets, don't drop it. If you do the whole weight will leap onto your marra and put his back out or worse. If you slip your only chance is to try and fling it off your shoulder to stop it landing across your body or legs, but the pit being the pit, more often than not the bliddy thing just boomerangs back and smacks you with added momentum in the legs or buttocks. So you hussle forward, the pace determined by the weight of the thing which doesn't lend itself to a leisurely stroll. My aud marra in Wardley, Geordie Summerson the linesman, passed by in the gate by sweating caunchmen stooped under the weight of the arch, would invariably comment 'You just brought the one then?' The arch is passed up to the scaffold, consisting of just two big planks across the gate—too few really, but they know that, as they balance on the planks, side by side like circus acrobats about to do their stunt.

We pass up the arch from one end first. It comes from the floor, and scaffold man number one keeps it rising as he squats on the scaffold. Number two stands behind him and as the steel arch is fed increasingly upward he turns to take the weight on his curved back, and his mate turns and takes the bottom portion on his back. They raise themselves in unison, feeding the arch further up and over the horsehead, bit by bit, dragging it into the centre and over the left side horsehead, till it sits in place, a naked arch of steel as yet uncovered but up toward the bare stone of the tunnel.

The danger is quite not over yet; at this stage a rock fall will cowp you with the rock and the falling steel and smash the scaffold on which you stand, hurling you to the floor with battens, steel and rock flying around you. So you rush to secure the bow to the last portion of the tunnel and wedge it to the roof. Sheeting-in, which follows, is a jigsaw of corrugated steel sheets woven in confined spaced to fit in neat connections right round the arch, wedged tight to support the top and then the sides as the legs are bolted into position. We complete; this is a term of victory, since to complete is to do a full web of ripping, a complete arch and two packs. No mean feat in a shift. Usually this takes a noggin on top, two hours of overtime. It still will. As the deputy phones down to the gate to ask what the position is. 'A leg to complete,' comes the answer. A leg is one third of the three-part arch girder which supports the tunnel or gate. Actually it's already been done, but the deputy doesn't know that. This is a way of getting back more money for the work we've already done. 'A leg to complete' will earn a couple of the men two hours overtime; they will usually, 'just to be reet', advance all the steel in the gate, lay the sheets for the next team coming on, then flop exhausted to sit for maybe an hour, not asleep really but in a sort of blank, shell-shocked stare. The more totally conscientious will regard sitting down as a mortal sin, and will instead travel the gate looking for bits of wood which will serve as 'pinners' for wedging lagging and props in future shifts.

For us is the long steamy walk through the dust-filled jungle back down the gate. I refuse to go out 'the other way'. The other way means you go out by the main gate, it means you get to ride on the belts with the coal, dooking and weaving, sliding from one side of the belt to the other to dodge the low work and obstructions as the belt passes at speed along the tunnel. This is not a manrider belt, and getting off it while it is running is one of the most dangerous parts of the shift. Most just leap for a strut and swing themselves off, others leap for overhead cables only to find they are not secure and fall heavily to earth from some height; others still, catch great rocks or lumps of coal and shin themselves and graze their arms.

None of that is the reason why I don't do it. To get to the main gate means traversing the full length of the face, on your hands and knees with your gear, this is lowse and there is no time to dey that, so they ride on the blades of the scraper chain, their heels propped over the edge of the blade. At Rossington where I had trained they turn over their shovels and sprag the handle into the adjacent flight and sit down on the opposite one, feet wedged against the handle. The belt is dangerous, the face chain is suicidal. If an inspection cover is missing under the moving chain, you will not see it, until your foot goes onto it, and the chain slices it off, or your leg. So I march down the gate, in full flight picking up steam, while the dust from the men cutting between shifts and firing the rip in the main gate makes an orange fog of only a few yards vision. The sweat streams from my wafer-thin body, black and grey from stone dust and coal dust. Hair like Old Father Time's, wisped with stone dust like a rock candyfloss sticking oot from me helmet. Head down, get up the pace, legs are weak now, ankles buckle and I stagger like a drunk into some low arch, cursing and consumed with intense anger at the stunning dull blow to me head.

Christ what mun it o' been like before helmets? Some aud buggers refused to wear them, a couple o aud Northumbrians still wearing their leather caps with the clip originally intended for the carbide lamp, which they had also refused to abandon until the law forced them to. Stride out again, thick grey swirls of stone dust, bastards are cutting in the floor unless they're into a roll, the stone dust smells of burning, keep gaanin, keep gaanin.[3]

Thud. A broken metal strut, forced out at right angles into the roadway, digs me directly in the shoulder joint and throws me right on my arse. Yi fucking bastard! I leap up and grab the strut and wang the bastard back and forth back and forth in wild rage until the coupling bolt on the last arch starts to bend.

'Brek, ya bastard!' I shout as if the strut deliberately ambushed me and did me a great indignity. It did! My shoulder joint pulses in pain and I feel the faint trickle of blood under me shirt. Finally the bolt snaps and I seize the strut and fling the bastard as far up the gate as I can—and think that that probably wasn't very clever: what if some poor bastard was hoofing along after me and suddenly a flying broken strut came flying out of the darkness. He'd think he was in Indian country. Can't resist a chuckle at the idea though. 'I've been splonned, mate,' in a Goon Show, Peter Sellers voice—the thought kept me chuckling as I got the motor up to full speed again, lights aheed, distant voices, the afternoon shift is here. Quicken the pace, if them fuckers from the main gate are all aboard they tek off and bugger me, I can hear them saying it. 'Fuck that little fucker—he should ride doon chain like the rest of us.' I burst into the fresh air and cold of the junction, in a cloud of stone dust, and pooda reek, grey from dust, wet through, with a little splot of red soaking through me sark.

I grab me duds from the dog nail on which they hang, and run to the paddy. The loco revs like a spluttering pneumoconiotic bread van, slathering hot water and diesel smoke like a celebration bon voyage. I jump aboard the crammed paddy, and squeeze me arse into the throng of coal-black colliers. Picking me spot to stand and getting dressed as the manrider switches and clanks through low work and high, then dooking doon again, then up again, till by the time we hit the pit bottom area I'm dressed.

The men don't wait for the paddy to stop but leap from the carriages and charge toward the shaft like a D-Day invasion force. Not me, I will not do that, here and there bodies go down and others trip up in the mad excitement of getting to the front of the queue and out of this god forsaken pit. The crowd sways and surges, but there is neywhere ti gaan, the onsetter hasn't rapped off yet and the gate is firmly closed. If they keep fucking aboot he'll keep them here all bliddy afternoon. This onsetter took more clog than most. Clarence the men called him. He was named after the short-sighted, cross-eyed lion in the TV programme *Daktari*. When inspecting the men's water notes to ride up the pit early he would hold the note paper directly in front of his eyes, though how the hell he could read it like that I never kenned. Mind, he couldn't always; in a famous incident he inspected an unfolded large toffee wrapper, and allowed the man to ride the shaft on the strength of it. He often employed an aud wrinkled marra at lowse especially on days when the melee got dangerously close to men going down the shaft. This marra he got to impose a chain across the gap between the cage and the place where the men were supposed to stand in orderly queues. We knew it was getting near lowse when the aud figure loomed up from roond some turn chains festooned roond his aud wrinkled neck; he was christened 'Long

Chainy' at once. I get the third draw but me feet still are lifted off the deck in the surge of men squeezing into the cage, a final rib-crushing heave and the wire mesh gate drops. Rap three, and off with a jolt, up and up and that distant smell of tab smoke detectable about half a mile down the shaft. In the baths the voices crash, spirits are light, the cut in my shoulder turns out to be more bruise than cut, it looks like a giant love bite with a hole in the middle. As the water hits my head the stone dust clings on for one last time, clogging me hair. The shoulder wound stings; I try and soak it in the hot water and suddenly I am singing. Not just singing, but something about this situation turns you into your dad, I am singing Some Enchanted Evening! I don't even know that bliddy sang. Songs come to you, in the shower, you sort of subsume them from the atmosphere. Wrang words, someone singing No Milk Today The Cow Has Run Away, a Searchers number I do believe, and those who get two or three songs blended into one. Meks ney different I suppose. Call at the First Aid Room, just to get the accident in the book in case I need to fall off work sometime in the future, or in case it turns nasty of course.

I walk into the living-room. The room is a mass of light and a blazing fire in the grate, Maureen is there all in her aura of smiles, plus a couple of comrades from the Party. I wasn't expecting them. Despite being a revolutionary I do not like change, or so Maureen keeps telling me. 'What you di today?' Maureen asks, as usually there is some bodily mark or graze to show for the shift. I relate the story of the strut and show the big boil-like swelling on the front of me shoulder. 'So this is capitalism, comrade.' This is Kay—a small, dark French comrade. 'With socialism there will be no such accidents, oui?' 'Well, Ah think the pit will still be the pit, comrade,' I venture. 'Oh yes, but with the workers running the mine, accidents will be no more, nothing should be accidental at the pit, everything deliberate.' She had optimism. like all the comrades of the Party, a clear vision of what would be, no question. 'Well, comrades, I'm shagged. I hate to be antisocial but Ah'm gaan for a belly flop.' 'You do not wish to ear the news of the comrades in the International?' 'Aye, aye, certainly, but I have ney wish to fall asleep while the news is being telt, bonny lass. Ah'm away ti me bed a hoor.'

The rumble of voices below. French, and Italian—Luca was here too. Eyelids heavy with stone dust, eyes bloodshot, body spent, I just lay and drift into a sound, deep, sticky sleep. Coming down, the sun is still bright, the house a ferment of discussion. 'So, comrade mate', Kay begins, 'Our comrades in France, oose little dog keep watch when the team are flyposting and whitewashing slogans … the comrades in Brazil are facing hard repression just now … ' This is not the Party world analysis we get at cadre schools. This is the personal, day-to-day lives of our comrades, a sort of extended international family of communists. Those overseas too will be told of our daily lives. Doubtless my swollen shoulder bruise will be discussed in Buenos Aires within the week, along with the latest revelation from Comrade Jose Posadas, the leader of the Fourth International. [4]

The term 'leader' is chosen because he is not simply General Secretary of the International Secretariat, of the Fourth International, but is held by his followers, as Mao Tse-Tung is held by his, to have intellectually furthered the doctrine and philosophy of Marxism—to the point where the international blesses him by calling itself by his name, 'the Fourth International—Posadist'. So we didn't have 'P's and 'Q's in 'the Revolutionary Workers Party—Trotskyist, British Section of the Fourth International—Posadist' so much as we had 'P's and 'T's. Posadism developed as a fully formed split in the Fourth International in 1962. (The Fourth International itself had been founded by Leon Trotsky to unite the international Bolsheviks who supported the USSR and the world communist revolution, but opposed 'Stalinism'.) This division had been in the making earlier at the 6th World Congress in 1961, where Posadas emerged as the leader of a tendency. He led the Latin American Bureau of the International, and had began building his Argentinean Section between 1945 and 1951. Argentinean Trotskyism was indelibly marked by the movement surrounding Juan Peron who came to power in 1940. The early Trotskyists had sunk themselves into Peron's movement, becoming effectively the left wing of the Peronistas. Argentina had become a 'sympathetic group' at the second world congress on the Fourth International in 1948, and a section in 1951 at the second. A major division between the European leaders and Posadas had been growing for some time over the years. It probably came to a head with the arrest of Pablo in 1960. Pablo was one of the 'stars' of European Trotskyism. Posadas couldn't understand the lack of urgency and commitment among the European sections when he came to assist with the campaign to free Pablo. Some had continued with their holiday plans and others were only happy to fit the campaign into their personal lives where there was room. Posadas was to regard the whole crowd as dilettantes, whose vision of Trotskyism was as some academic theory to be pontificated over in the coffee-house. These were the part-time academic revolutionaries, not the professional, fully committed Bolshevik team which he deemed was essential for Trotskyism to have any relevance. So we had arrived at the RWP(T), BS IVth International (P) for short. But didn't it sound grand? Weren't its flags splendid, in revolutionary red, decorated with hammer and sickle and the '4' of the Fourth International?

But we weren't members, not yet. We operated in a united front through *The Mineworker* with them. We were doing a sort of apprenticeship and as such discipline was less stringent with us. Our lives however were night and day committed to the revolution, had been since before we met this team; but now it seemed we were organically locked almost irresistibly into the world revolution, in its myriad of shapes and forms, which we could see unfolding all around us like a mighty tide. I argued with the certainty of a born-again preacher predicting the second coming of Christ. Time was short; we had teams to build and the RWP was building them; embryos, cadres in industry, among the working-class communities and organisations. So we directed our impulses at the Labour Party and the Labour Party Young Socialists, which we seen as mass organs along with the unions, in which revolutionary perspectives would wrest the mass of the membership and its grass roots working-class support away from its bourgeois leadership and structure. The Communist Party too, we seen as misguided comrades—not rivals or enemies as many other Trotskyist groups did. Indeed Posadas had taken the position of Trotsky that the USSR and its bloc were degenerated workers' states, and stated that he saw 'a partial regeneration' among elements of the Soviet bureaucracy, especially the armed forces and Comrade Ponamariov.

There was in our view an overall 'world revolutionary process', multi-layered and operating in different dimensions and with various degrees of class consciousness and class composition. The arenas ranged from that of the armed struggle of what the Posadists called 'the putchists' through the Labour Party and the unions, through the national liberation struggles in all their variance and complexities, to the tips of the Soviet missiles. The overall 'world revolutionary process' interlinked all these aspects and connected them dialectically and dynamically.[5]

The bed was wet with my sweat, my mind a blaze of philosophy and random thoughts. I had to get up soon. I kept telling myself, 'Go to sleep; you're getting up soon. You'll be knackered. You are knackered. Sleep.' Time slips past: turn sideways, lie on my back, face the damn clock, only three hours left, sleep for God's sake sleep. The alarm is shrill and stabs me all over like I'm being thrown into a bath of ice. I kill it in a millisecond, and lie. 'No, no!' I think. 'It can't be! I must have set the alarm wrong. It can't be 4.30 already—it's too dark. There are no sounds. It must be set wrong. I hope to God, pray to God it's set wrong!' Drag myself out of the bed, leaving Maureen struggling to stay in sleep mode. I am convinced I will soon be sliding back in alongside, gently so as not to give the impression I want sex, just sleep—beautiful soundless sleep. Nip downstairs, check the clock, 4.35. Fuck! Bastard hell! I want to sleep. Sit in the quiet of the room, sup my last cup of tea, grab the bait bag and step into the dark drizzle of the morning. I see the pit bus coming up Broadway, walk quicker, or rather stagger. My legs are made of rubber, my breath smells of cans of beer and tabs. The baths are a cacophony of voices with light and steam, men bump into each other, jostle each other, get on with stripping off. Bare-arsed men are walking with their boots on and nowt else; they remind me of horses. They walk through naked holding a towel and bait poke and carrying a single tab and match. This the last tab, taken at ease in the silence of the morning when dressed in the pit duds. A silent aura falls on each man, at once solitary, steeling himself for the shift. In another part of the yard and en route to the shaft, the lamp beams bounce and boisterous voices sound their rebellion at the morning, 'Ha'way lads, up and at 'em!'

At the shaft bottom we stream off in different directions to different paddies, different routes to different seams and faces. As I hit the inbye end of the tailgate, I'm surprised to see lamp movement under the rip, and the sound of shovelling. Before getting stripped, I crouch on me hunkers and keek down the long expanse of the empty pack hole area, waiting, empty, the roof sagging already in unsupported suspense. At the back end of the pack, a kneeling figure is dragging bits of rock and big pieces of coal into a stud pack. It's Charlie. 'Huw dey, Charlie lad, what yee deyin here?' 'Thiv set is on, ti gi yee a leg up, Ah've to set yee away with a stud pack.' Thus the cusp on the machine cut and about two yards square of basic pack will be prepared in preparation for the main pack, to get the job completed quicker, and allow more ground to be cut out. Not that the cutters ever took any notice of the support rules; they just carried on cutting leaving grand galleries of unsupported ground for us to shovel into. Charlie was a happy-go-lucky bloke, a plodder, no hero. He joked all day. 'I just don't understand it,' he'd comment to nobody in particular, shaking his head gravely. 'What?' you would ask, like a fish on a hook 'Chinese, I just can't understand it,' he responds. 'Stud Pack Charlie is me name, Stud Pack Charlie is me game,' he sang. I wondered how the super ripping team would take to this ex-officio bloke infesting their working area. They wouldn't. Charlie wouldn't be hurried, wouldn't be upset, insisted on having his snap at snap time, whatever the gate men wanted, stopped the job to sit and have his bait. I was more than happy to join him. Everyone else stopped for snap, not these fuckers. Work was something to do with manhood.

'Eating a sandwich? Fuck me, we're at work!' they would bellow. 'We snap when we're stood!' More often than not that meant on the way back out after the shift was over. Snap time was a flashpoint, and became an annoyance to the team. They would get little sympathy from other teams for telling it like that, though, so they put it about that me and Charlie couldn't manage it, couldn't scrat stone with the chickens, never mind such ace rippers as these. Charlie, after finishing his stud pack, floated about helping out, he thought. He would wait till I started to wilt in the pack, and offer to give me a minute. He was not up to the constant slog of the pack, but tried to do his bit, at a normal rate of work. Not kill himself. That wasn't good enough, and the team wanted to prove it so, slinging back, shovel on shovel, giving him no chance to stop, they piled the sheets up, buried him in rock. Then banged their shovels on the floor, and shouted 'Waitin' on here! For fuck's sake shift that muck!' Knees going, sweat streaming, his eyes rolling, he had no power left; leaned on his shovel, his helmet slid forward over his face, he stumbled over his own feet, looked close to collapse and, to shouts of derision, handed the shovel back over to me. Charlie didn't reappear, took a job outbye. The bastards had won. But they wouldn't fucking beat me, I resolved. The following day I had a note on me lamp to go and see the undermanager, Mr Robson—a good bloke but not a man to cross. His outer office was full of overmen and deputies milling around, handing over, drawing with pieces of chalk the problem with the face alignment. They picked up tools, shouted down telephones to each other, spat streams of tobacco juice out the door or into the wastepaper basket. The office hung with smoke, the oil from lamps and coal dust, black men and clean men, big mugs of tea. 'What yee done nuw, yee little rag ragging bastard?' one asked. 'Nowt,' I replied. 'I divind need te.' I knock on the door. 'Come in!' I walk through the door, smiling, he stands in his pit gear, pit stockings on the outside of his lang 'uns up to his knees. Knee pads already in place, shirt open, his oil lamp in readiness hangs on a filing cabinet, giving off the sweet oil scent. 'Yee, yee little cunt, are fucking up me best ripping team!' he starts. 'If tha cannit do job, seh so, Ah'm not paying men to be lockers in the tub.' I thought of the graft and sweat and pure willpower I had been throwing into the job since they drafted me on it.

I exploded with indignation: 'Fucking bollocks!' 'You what?' 'Ya ta-alking fuckin' utter shite. I pull mer than my weight, Ah'll tell yee, its me in that 12 yard pack hole everyday, don't let anyone pillock yee.' 'That's not what I hear, what about all this bollocks about snap times then?' 'Ar so, that's what this is aboot is it? Well let's dey this then, should I stay out of the pit and see the Union and see if I'm in order getting me snap? If we're all in order getting wa snap? Because if your gaana dey away with snap times that's an issue for the Union and this pit could stand,' I said, banging his table and making his ash tray bounce off his mug.

It was suddenly silent in the outer office. We raged at each other, throwing in cutting out of distance, lack of adherence to the support plan, no timber, cutting in muck, excessive dust and heat. Finally we came to a standstill. 'What's tha want?' he asked. 'Yee sent for me, what de'yee want, me to kiss ya arse?' 'Ah want yee do ya job.' 'Aye well, yee dey your bugger. I want timber, props and chocks, otherwise that pack doesn't get put on, all reet. Oh Ah'll dey me job bonny lad.' 'Is that a threat? Are you threatening me Mr Douglass? I do not take kindly to threats,' he said, slamming his drawer shut and making a step toward me as if to punch me in the face. 'Yee are listening to some lying bastards.' 'The best rippers in the pit tell me you're spoiling their team.' 'Sooks and arse lickers. I work as weel as them but fight for me reets anahl.' He took a big breath, 'Aye lad, happen you do, and there's nowt wrang wi that, I'm a fair man.' 'Yes gaffer, I reckon you are.' We both had calmed down to a more conciliatory tone.

'Do you want to go with another team?' he asked. 'Not fucking likely!' I replied, walking from the office with my teeth gritted. I rode doon the pit, seething in silence, piled off the last draw and walked round to the boxhole where the men congregated and sat on their respective paddies waiting to set off. I spotted my team sitting almost in the middle of the manrider, which itself was standing in the middle of the throng. 'Yee fucking scabby arse-licking bunch o sooks!' I directed to them. Men stopped talking, started earwigging. 'I was sent to Robbo's office, I was threatened, I nearly got took off me job, why? Because yee fuckin' twats went telling lying spunking tales behind me back, because I dared to eat me snap at snap time, and yee big hard fuckers have got Charlie shifted an'ahl.' 'Huw wait!' Sparrow shouts, 'Yer not accusing me, yee little bastard. I never went to anyone, if I have something to say I'll sat it to thee face, and so will these,' he started to say and looked toward Chappie and Mitch, who shuffled about uncomfortably and Mitch started to stammer a response. 'You lousy fucking twats,' declared Sparrow, joining in the general hubbub of disapproval from the groups of men standing about. 'Bang oot o' order!' 'Gaffersmen!' 'Nor, nor it wasn't like that,' the spies started in stammering defence. But I didn't wait, I had repulsed a serious charge, a charge of idleness. I had been dropped in it for sticking to a Union principle, snap time, I had suddenly taken on a reputation. I boarded the paddy to acclamation.

I didn't know whether to hang back and give these two both barrels all the way inbye; I wasn't sure if they'd snap and attack me in the dark of the tailgate somewhere off inbye. So I set off at me normal pace and speeded through the dips and swallies, banging here and there on the roof and tripping over, me sleep-starved feet setting off in their own directions. A distant hug of voices carried from the face for further than their leets reached, then the distant beams dart to and fro. Activities at the tail end. Must be the fitters and colliers working on replacing the new motor since neet shift. There'll be mountains of rammle. Flop doon 50 yards from the rip, don't want to be in the way, start to strip, one boot off, one pants leg off, one boot back on, the other boot off, other pants leg off, other boot back on. A technique in case you have to run, you always have both boots on for the maximum time and never less than one on. Pads on, shirt off, feel the breeze, warm and foul, but better on the bare skin than against the sweat of the sark. Dig in the poke and drag forth a crumbled, soggy cheese and tomato sandwich, which I eat while weighing up the grunting, crawling bodies pushing and dragging greet lumps of metal and cogs aboot under the caunch. Their job is done, etiquette and fear of a belt roond the lug will not let them leave the place a shithole, and since they are on a noggin anyway, will try and make it actionable for the day shift. I wade in to seize what I can to start me pack off. Laying the metal sheets like giant railway lines, we edge, piece by piece great lumps of box end, under the shovel and with fitters and colliers pushing with shoulders and backs and heads, it scraps its way doon the back of the pack.

Then the return roller is lumbering down in my direction a little too fast. 'Danny!' they shout, and I wedge the shovel underneath the rolling drum in a stupid attempt to wedge it stopped. The roller sits fast on the edge of the shovel, which cocks up the handle still gripped by my hand and thuds it right into the roof and squashes it ever tighter as the weight comes to rest. 'Aagh! Me fuckin' hand!' 'Yee daft cunt,' they all laugh. Ugger, the big Neolithic Pole, is helplessly, soundlessly laughing with tears rolling down his face. While squatting his back to the abandoned box end, he brings both his feet up in a push squat, and forces the big roller back, so the shovel drops out and my hand is released.

Putting on a manly front I announce in what I hope sounds like brave understatement: 'By, that smarts.' 'Good,' says a fitter, 'then rub it on thy heed.' The roller is wrestled to its marra in the pack while the face side pack men start their work and the windy pick starts to drop rock onto the flat sheets.

Bags of old bolts and lumps of metal, together with ploughed-up lumps of floor and broken timbers used as wedges, are being flung back to me, while the stone mound starts its pile at my door. Handy stuff this; the back end is all but on, the rough outline of the base of a third of the side is on, and needs only wedging to the roof—this gives me an edge. A competition? By fuck, aye, this is a competition, and I am going to bury this bastard today. Mitch starts to throw back, but the rock is uneven, the floor holed from the dragging of machinery and improvised wedges; despite the sheets his shovel is not gliding anywhere. It rams up hard against the facing of the stone and he can pick up only small loads and they fall in pathetic tinkles while I sing 'Why are we waiting?', much to the amusement of the night shift gang now getting a blae. As the pile starts to build I whack into it, throwing the stone back in tight groups into the empty spaces left by the rammle, pick out good heavy wallers and wedge tight to the roof. I am on top of the task, I am not being buried, my pace is faster than his, I have been waiting for this, my sheet is empty in front on me, I bang the sheet with me shovel and yell: 'C'mon, Mitch, are yee asleep?' Bang! Bang! Bang! 'C'mon, give us a mountain.' His fluster and frustration only makes his efforts worse. He is taken off by Chappie, my other protagonist, but he can't find his pace in this to keep the sheet from becoming empty again.

We slog away, yard by yard. They take each other off, but I do not call for break or assistance. The sweat streams from me like a cloudburst. I snatch glorious water from me bottle, and let me gob fill and overfill and the wa'ater run over me face, me chest and doon my hoggers—then back into the fray. Shovel thrust, swing throw, shovel thrust, twist throw, the rock thuds back into the pack and slowly we advance filling the pack, back toward the gate side.

The chain stops, the cry on the tannoy is 'Snap Time, get ya bait.' 'Get your bread then, Danny,' says Mitch moving to take me shovel. 'Not fucking likely, yee think you're gaana steal the glory when there's only three yards to dey?' 'Whey Ah thought tha believed in snap time, Danny?' 'Aye Ah dey, but you're not getting the satisfaction of finishing this pack, when it's this near done.'

So they continued, throwing back to me, off both shovels at once, with a little help from the gate men, casting back. Shovel, shovel, shovel, shovel, wanging it up and in, tight as a box. At last, as the chain set off again, and clouds of dust billowed from the face, I was wedging in the last wallers, wet through, shaking with effort, when Robbo the undermanager appeared down the face line. He inspected the long wall of the pack, and the soaked pack rat, on his hunkers in front of it. 'Solid is it?' he enquired and attempted to push his yard stick into any holes, to see if it wasn't just an empty space with a wall built round it. Finding no fault, he stood up into the gate. 'How yee getting on with Danny the Red then lads?' This was in front of me. 'Nowt wrang with that lad,' Sparrow began, 'now that he's found his feet, is there Mitch?' 'No he's worked hard today.' 'He's like the gypsy's dog,' offered the undermanager. 'Aye, agreed, Chappie, but full of shite.' 'Right!' shouts Mitch, 'let's go get the arch leg.' 'Mitch, I am getting my bait.'

In the pit bottom the throng sways back and forth in a scrum to ride the chair. I sit, legs out, back to the wall, and just wait; the body is drained. I want to curl up here and just sleep; don't feed me, just leave me till tomorrow and wake me up on the way in. Tessa bounds down the path to greet me. A big ex-RAF police dog abandoned by her owners when they emigrated to Australia. She is a source of endless walking—winter, summer or spring, rain or shine, she must be walked. She rears up and bounds into my face off her hind legs, sending me flying backward while I attempt to take her weight like a big bairn. In the house the typewriter is tap-tapping, tap-tap-tapping. 'Maur.' 'Hello, love. Just finishing that Derbyshire article.' *The Mineworker*. Hard work: articles to tidy up, to get in, to type out onto stencils. We draw cartoons and pictures into the stencil with the stencil pen, primitive but effective. The duplicator should be whirling by Sunday at the latest, then we go flat-out to print the whole thing, maybe 30 or 40 stencils, 1,000 copies of each. The pages are piled in rows on a long table. We walk round the table, each one taking a page, and adding it the right way up to our bundle, page after page until we have the set, then we staple them together at the end of the table, then set off walking again. It takes hours, but as the typewriter hits the roller, this is our gunfire in our war against the system, as we tramp the table, round and round and the boxes fill up with incendiary material for dissident miners looking for political solutions; this is dedicated class struggle. Sometime the duplicator will whirr away into the night and be still at work, with the comrades ink-soaked and bog-eyed, as the alarm goes for day shift again.

Wednesday, thank God—day-release day. I can sleep, not just two hours langer in the morn, but actually at neet, knowing I'm not getting up in the middle of the night. To tickle one's own fancy with a dread that you're up at 4.30, and know really that you're not, you can sleep. An overture of luxury, aye and sex—what the hell. I board the train at Donny, meet up with the other mining students in the lounge. Fred Higgins, a member of the Communist Party, one of our *Mineworker* supporters, face worker at Bentley, earlier of the bonny Toon as a lad. He had thought our *Mineworker* too political and started *Link-Up* as an agitational paper, which we printed on the *Mineworker* press. Dave Noble, artist, quiet spoken, fitter from Goldthorpe, his wife a Dutch girl, Myrna, a supporter of *Mineworker* and a singer at our folky neet singsongs round the living-room fire. Ron Parr, non-political militant from Cadeby pit. Sid Weighels, moderate surface worker, who inspired by our *Mineworker* founded *The New Link*, a colliery rank-and-file paper. Aah—the crack was good on that train to Sheffield on a Wednesday morning. Never to hide whatever it is under a bushel, our loud debates often drew in many of the other commuters, blue- and white-collar workers. We attended Sheffield University's day-release class run by the extramural dept. This ran from 3 October 1967 for three years under the direction of Michael Barratt-Brown. Mostly the tutors were ex-workers themselves. The course had run for some time, and many saw it as the stepping stones to a branch position or the opportunity to go to full-time education. Certainly it was a sound grounding in the tools of the trade. The complexities of bourgeois economics, political theory, social history, maths, stats and English. To read books and learn how to use books, as tools not sacred objects. Learn what the index is for, how to use it with the contents, how to précis, how and what to footnote, what to nick and what not to nick. Using books not at random but interlinked, seeing a spectrum. No—I wasn't convinced just then, arguments were thick and fast and the tutors claimed me harsh and disrespectful. To the point where myself and handful of politicos were in civil war with the hardnosed wage militants who didn't want to talk about this Anarchism and Marxism bollocks; men like Bill Fearon from Cadeby, they wanted 'more about conciliation, consultation procedures, method study, time study, practical bliddy stuff, man'. The disagreements became personal. In the midst of a row verging on physical force, Karl Hedderwick, a Scottish economics tutor I had branded as a bourgeois lackey, called for calm; I told him 'Had ya gob.' 'You are in danger of being asked to leave this class,' he warned. 'Fuck it, Ah'll save yee the bother!' I said in my usual calm, collected way, and swept up me books and walked oot. Like many a protest since, it was cutting my nose off to spite my face, if for nowt else the two hours abed and not doon the pit, not to mention the study which I actually did to the small wee hours. A climb-down would be unthinkable. But Dave Noble, the calm voice of reason, persuaded me I was actually giving in by giving up. I should return. Which I did, and made a public apology to Karl, and the rest of the class, who applauded the gesture. Actually although I almost give Karl as much stick as some of my classroom teachers, over the years the notes I took from his class all that time ago proved sound. I was to return to them on every course I ever attended for basic summaries and configurations.

One of the Team

As days and weeks went by, my relations with the caunch team got better. I suppose I got into their stride of working. I was perfecting the fast shovel technique I needed to compete and stay relevant among much bigger men. At times the packs would be smack to the tash (up-to-date). With a full web of ripping still to shift there was nowt for it but to fill the lot out onto the face chain. This could be donkey work. Depending how far away the edge of the caunch was, three men would be filling from the heap, and throwing back to two men behind, who in turn would hoy back to me. But I had perfected this crack now. Strip off for action. With nowt on but me hoggers and boots, I would hang my belt with the cap lamp battery and respirator round the pump-up nipple on a prop next to me, still wearing my helmet and lamp, but without the belt and its load, so it didn't dig into my naked skin, so the battery and respirator didn't come together and nip me skin and me arse as I shovelled. Sometimes I would dispense with the helmet and lamp too; I wasn't gaanin anywhere, I knew what was in front of me, and I knew where to hoy the stuff. Without annoying encumberments I was light as air, and honed for the job. I would make a cushion of wire bags and me shirt and be set. I had perfected a throw straight over me head, crouching doon, legs splayed flat, arse on the deck, hips spread doon, in a low squat. Dig straight in, scoop it up and straight ower the top, body forward, arms thrust out, knees flexed, heed doon, thudding into the face and dropping onto the face chain. In the half light I looked 'like a mini Emco bucket', rocking forward and back, punctuated with a crash of stone. I could keep that rhythm going some time, then as the rock got too much and started to fill the sheet, just pull the sheet up, and sit it on, top the stone and start again, this time standing alongside the sheet, scooping the stone from front to back and tossing it on the chain. Sweat bathed me head to foot. I would frequently pour the precious water over my head and sit me helmet back on again, letting the wa'ater trickle through me hair, down me face, down me back, down me chest while legs bent and strained, arms tore into reluctant stone and rock. 'Gimme a fuckin' mountain.'

I think I began to see something of my protagonist workmates too. Chappie, at times, would cough his inside out, his whole body convulsed with gasping rasping gulps for air and racking, expirational coughing ripping his lungs to shreds. When the big fault was on the 22s, and the cutting machine made a total arc of orange sparks, as the picks hit the stone intrusion, we would put the lock on and crawl the other side of the machine to escape the worse of the dust, which folded down the tail end like a malevolent fog. Chappie would stay where he was.

'Ower late for me,' he would say, and stay, with his mask on, but sitting against the pack wall, looking at his adversary, which was already eating his lungs and consuming his life. If you have never seen a miner seized by the dust, you might have seen a cat in the throes of coughing up a fur ball or a dog after it's eaten some grass for the purpose. Its whole inside wretches and heaves and it's as if another living thing is coming out of it, as the hair is ejected. A miner with emphysema or pneumo is like that; the whole internal system is being sucked in and then violently out, in till he near turns blue and then wrenching and bloody he coughs his insides out. His thin body, the walls of his rib cage stark against his chest, his stomach pulled right in to his spine, then shot out again and again as the dust rips open his lungs and shreds his life. I was shocked rigid when I discovered Mitch went to the Bingo. It seemed to open my eyes, that he wasn't, couldn't be, a snarling, work-mad critic all the time. Even more so as he complained bitterly that a woman had stabbed him with her pencil for talking—it made me roar with laughter. 'What's up wi thee?' he asked, slightly annoyed since his tale wasn't meant to be funny. 'He wants to buy the woman a pint,' suggested Keith; actually I think I wanted to buy Mitch one. I think, grudging though it was, I had started to respect these blokes. What was certain was their work mode never left me. Whatever I did. But my absorption of the team's work pace robbed me of caution, made me impetuous. So it was that filling the pack on the open side with old Jimmy Dauber, locked me into my own world, my own thoughts. I had pulled a buried prop from its mire of clarts and oil and gumming; dragged it up from the soggy grip of the quagmire, with me legs and back straining. Stuck the prop key in the nipple and heaved down on it, to lower it off, to reset it. No movement. Pinched the barrel between me squatted knees, and heaved doon on the key, no movement. 'Yee fuckin' bastard!' Ah yelled and flung the useless iron object to the floor. Jimmy was meantime, on his knees, swinging up a large waller onto the pack wall. His hand, rock and falling prop all met in silent collision. The rock fell into Dauber's lap and rolled down his knees, pulling the skin and coal dust off as it slid to the floor. The prop fell with a thud and Jimmy fell back into the pack on his arse. He looked up at me with a look of betrayal in his eyes. 'You've cut me finger off,' he said quietly.

I looked to his hands which were gripping each other. There was no blood. 'Yee pillocking get,' I began. He opened his hand, and there gaping, open was a gash and a space and in his other hand the squashed remnants of his severed finger.

Tommy, the end gate deputy, sat him down, shouted into the gate for morphia, for the first-aid box. 'Man injured!' he yelled.

I just stood. It was like a distant memory of some drunken act deeply regretted and somehow not fully your own responsibility. My brain raged around looking for excuses, looking for ways to undo it, to rewind it, to replay it. He was jabbed in the vein with the morphia needle, a big bandage wrapped round his hand, the poor battered finger wrapped in another bandage, and off he went staggering down the gate. Him and another Jimmy, the fitter, sent along in case he fainted, and to carry the finger, refusing to have a stretcher so near lowse, which would slow the men up. Interviewed by the Frank Clark the NUM Branch secretary as to what happened, I was convinced he was out to get me, out to sack me. I blamed the prop, its very presence there, its brokenness, its uselessness, its stubbornness, its clartyness, slippyness. Not me, no not my fault. It was many months later, Jimmy came up to speak to me in the George. 'Eeh, Ah'm sorry Jimmy,' I began, tears almost welling in my eyes.' 'Ah'll reet Danny lad, Ah was mad as fuck at first, but it was time I came off ripping. Ah've kept me PLA[6] and Ah'm on taps,[7] Ah can handle that bugger, got a canny payout too, tuek me and wor lass off, and bought me a caravan doon at Fitties,[8] Cleethorpes. Poo, man, they think Ah'm a deputy!' We laugh, he puts his arm round my shoulder and asks if I want a pint. 'It did is a gud turn in the end lad, dain't worry.' I still do though. By fuck you've got to be careful in a pit. It could all turn so bad with just the slightest lack of caution.

Lyndon Johnson told the nation 'Have no fear of escalation
I am trying everyone to please.
Although it isn't really a war' We'll send 100,000 more
And help save Vietnam from the Vietnamese.'

Newcastle Haymarket. The crowd crammed round the Dirty Angel. A public gathering to prepare a Geordie intervention for Vietnam, not a preach-to-the-converted rap, the same old well-worn 'intervention' to the faithful, but tek the cause to the toon, to the kids, to the generation. The movement people, the city kids, the peaceniks and revolutionaries, the anarchists, class-conscious workers and socialist students, this along with Eldon Square was a mini version of Trafalgar Square, or we thought maybe Dam Square. The voice rings across the Haymarket and the bus station and the cinema queue.

'Peace? Peace? Aye, peace ... But also justice! Not Peace In Vietnam, the Vietnamese could have the sort of US-imposed peace tomorrow. That's not the peace we want, we want VICTORY to the people of Vietnam, DEFEAT for US Imperialism, that's the sort of Peace we want!'

The hippies are reet and wrang, reet when they refuse anti-social violence, reet to outcast the self-declared hard lad who nuts the stranger, who fears comradeship and tenderness. Reet when they say 'Be kind to the universe ... and be kind to each other.' Wor nature is not lang in tooth and reed in claw, wor nature is just what we wish it to be. There's nowt good, edgy or cool aboot fighting amang wasells, why bean a lad whey bumps yi, when a joke will dey instead? But tha wrang aboot fighting the state, aboot fighting that bunch of weirdoes who are determined to desecrate the planet and sow division and hate. They are the enemy. We will not save this earth for the gentle folk of Vietnam by letting the biggest bloated capitalist state in the world stamp all over the folks of South-East Asia. There is a war on ... nuw! We mun mek wor side clear; and gaan ti London, not with a petition, not with a protest BUT TO GROSVENOR SQUARE WITH THE PEOPLE OF VIETNAM IN A FIGHT AS THEY WOULD FIGHT.

If you want to stand in torchlight procession ... stand for us also for we will demolish that block of imperialism or we'll nay be comin yem! We carry this message to all who will gaan from this city ... from the county of northern resistance ... we are with you, Vietnam!

The days before departure let us remember ... we are not on an Aldermaston March ... we have not come for moral comment. We have not come in conscience. When wi gaan ... we will leave a mark in SOLIDARITY WITH the brothers, sisters ... our family humanity ... of Vietnam. Aye, some of us expect that we could die ... some of us think some of us should die ... as an act of retribution to what the West has done to the Third World ... Geordies dinnet believe in martyrdom mind. If there's a bastard, kill the bastard ... no yasell!

And so with all in mind, for Vietnam ... aye and for us .... We went to fight for Vietcong and the Geordie Cong.' The Geordie Cong. A joke when first perceived ... but as the time went on, no se much a joke. We had been so christened—us the anarcho-syndicalists, the anarchists, the revolutionary socialists of Tyneside Youth Against The Bomb, the descendent of the old Tyneside Committee of 100, the Geordie Cong—by the more conventional left, the old left as it was now called.

By the time of this demonstration the organisation (TYATB) has already been dissolved for twelve months, its members dispersed round the country to plant new seeds of rebellion in mines and foundries and colleges.

The offensive of Tet was for Vietnam ... the all-out, dey or die for an end to 50 years of oppression by the west ... to the world youth ... the subverted generation ... it was the culture shock ... the whack on the conscience ... how far did we believe? ... the march to Grosvenor Square would see.[10]

November 1967. Simultaneous bomb attacks against the Greek, Bolivian and Spanish Embassies in Bonn and the Venezuelan Embassy in Rome. Claimed by First of May Group in solidarity with the Latin-American guerrillas and against the fascist regimes in Europe. On the same day bombs destroyed the entrance to the Spanish Tourist Office in Milan and the Greek and American Embassies in The Hague. This was the month Ché Guevara was reported killed in Bolivia.

January. An explosive rocket is disarmed before it could be launched at Greek Embassy in London.

9 January. Got letter from Ralph. Les Cain is dead! Killed in a car crash. 27 February. Stuart Christie's home raided by police led by Detective Sergeant Roy Cremer with an explosives warrant on information received about forthcoming bombing action in London.

3 March. Six bombs damage the buildings of diplomatic missions in London, The Hague and Turin. These actions claimed by the First of May Group.

6 March. Incendiary bomb with timing mechanism exploded in the Moabit Criminal Court, West Berlin.

17 March. London was black with bodies and red with flags ... banners ... the Vietnam flag. This was not Aldermaston. We had not come in peaceful protest... we had come in solidarity with the struggle of the Vietnamese.

'The spirit of the age', wor Keith had called it. John Grell put it thus:

Well, it's two days after I split from Woodstock and the mud is still caked heavy and my pants below my knees are still shit-brown. Four days of constant tripping have still left an acid reality in my head and yeah, goddammit, I wish I was still the fuck up there instead of coughing my lungs out from too much carbon monoxide here in 'good old New York City.'

It sounds like that real old show on the tube, Naked City, but there was a million people together in the rock rollicks of revolution in one dinky cow pasture and every life holds a different tale of what their reality was like.

The land was once a few hundred acres of cow pastures and woods which for one weekend were turned into a swarming mass of hip humanity, and I caught a glimpse of revolution. I danced in the mud and the blood and the beer, baby we were in one cosmic entity —our unity was our power, we were the armies of the mojo-mutated rebels, choogling down the line to zap and be zapped by ourselves and our music. We were the social revolutionaries of hip energy, realising for once the dope entropic fantasies of post-revolutionary post-scarcity society.

We arrive like refugees seeking our places in the final Armageddon knowing that we would not be fucked with, arriving by any means necessary. For four days, doing it in the road was our reality, boogying to Canned Heat and Credence Magic music was in the hearts and minds and bodies of a million warriors of the rainbow. Our zonked, fumbling, dancing bodies brought us to enter the grounds for free, we were free, and for four days our microcosm of revolution was free, anybody who sold food was ripped off, anybody who sold dope was ripped off.

Yeah, baby, I saw what I was fighting for, I was with my people, like the Indian gathering on the plains to celebrate an annual peyote ritual, we were a people gathered in the greatest manifestation of our culture; our music, yeah baby, my dope was free, and my food was free and my clothes were free and my shelter was free and my water was free and my music was free and honey I was free and that's what we're all about, and that's what we're fighting for. We saw our revolution and we built it and we made it baby and I dug it so much that I'd kill to make it happen for ever. Monday morning, coming down to six or seven tabs of acid, just finished making it with a chick by the swimming hole, and it was almost dawn, and Jimmy Hendrix was just coming on and I stood with my arm around my old lady for an hour and Foxy Lady brought up a psychedelic sun to a now garbage-strewn and almost empty cow pasture, and Hendrix played and electric bolts of universal dope energy brought up the sun to a full clear day and Hendrix jerked off his guitar for hours and around ten Hey Joe brought in dark clouds from the west and the clouds gathered and it rained and people left to 'Hey Joe where you goin' with that gun in your hand?' and people trucked back to hip community and job and school, but they know and they feel and it's down so deep in their heads that, baby, this is where it's at, and they're gonna fight to see it in their lives, and they're gonna make it happen and one day soon Hendrix will play and no one will leave and we will be one for the rest of time.

Was there a path between Buddhism and socialist revolution? Was there a conflict between the world revolution and the Earth's revolution? Was it the same process? Was the movement to nirvana, from the lower planes to the higher planes, equally reflected in historical materialism in the process from the caves to the communist society? Was the hand of karma, unseen and determining, itself determined by the social conflict and contradiction endemic to class society? The two philosophies were becoming one in my mind but others saw it as desperate confusion.

What was sure was that the average public punter could see no distinction between the hippie proper and the urban guerrilla, between the advocate of armed revolution and the peace-loving, flower-giving, big-haired freak. Truth was we were a movement, which ranged across several schools of thought but overlapped in perception and attitude, dress and lifestyle.

Washington was burning and US soldiers patrolled their own streets. 'Burn, Baby, Burn!' was heard across the length and breadth of the United States.

The Vietnam Solidarity Campaign had planned a massive march and rally in Trafalgar Square. But the enemy wasn't in Trafalgar Square and, while the rally was still in progress, contingents in heavy, linked-armed columns started to do the Ho Chi Minh stomp out of the Square. The Maoists bounced forward and back rhythmically waving their shining red books. International Marxist Group in regiments with identical banners and the hammer and sickle imposed with the '4' for Trotsky's International. (There were at least four different and warring Fourth Internationals around at the same time.)

The RWP(T) would never be stuck in alongside this rammy, no. 'We will intervene in this struggle empirically,' they told me, which meant basically selling your papers while those not so empirically engaged gave the cops some clog.

'Ho Ho Ho Chi Minh.' 'Ho Ho Ho Chi Minh.' Hair in a forest of windswept branches. The Lords of Anarchy linked arm in arm, black flags gripped like battering-rams. From all sides of the square, greet wedges of humanity swept forward, and the chorus was:

HO HO HO CHI MINH.
HO HO HO CHI MINH.
DARE TO STRUGGLE, WE SHALL WIN.
LONG LIVE HO CHI MINH.
HO HO HO CHI MINH.

The International Socialists, who thought all the states in the world were capitalist, and therefore didn't 'defend', critically or otherwise, the degenerated workers' states or their leaders, countered:

Ho Ho Ho Chi Minh
How many Trots have you done in?[11]

(In the later October demonstration against the embassy the Welsh anarchists chanted 'Ho ho rubbish bin!')

But it did not derail the overall chant, which would dey for now, without political precision. For the 'Lords of Anarchy' with their bonny black banner, it wasn't a government they were fighting for, but the defeat of US Imperialism and a victory for the people of Vietnam. This was where the actual fight was, it wasn't about slogans and philosophy.

As there was no overall direction, but diverse direction, the warring factions of the revolutionary left were united on Vietnam, hated American imperialism, were touched by the high tide of revolt in America and the rest of Europe. The ball had passed to us now for Vietnam.

Towards Grosvenor Square from two directions, one step forward, one step back, three steps forward, a momentum of rage, building a unified wave of pressure.

HO HO HO CHI MINH
HO HO HO CHI MINH
WE SHALL FIGHT, WE SHALL WIN
LONDON, PARIS AND BERLIN.

The solid wall of police, ranks upon ranks, would stand to hold us out of the Square. When the red tide smashed forward into the black barrier a frenzied battle broke out. The police's sudden kicking wave and rake of punches into the demonstrators' faces, which for a decade had broken the ranks of peaceful protesters, did not produce the panic collapse. The front rank aye, lasses as well as lads, bloodied and fearful, held in place and was impelled into the police lines. The second, third and fourth lines broke the linked formation and dived between the heads to stick hard punches into the police mugs. Helmets were seen flying in the air, individual lines of police going under. The columns behind kept coming, relentlessly. I see the Merseyside Anarchists' banner amid the fray and one or two of their tall, hairy, street-hard comrades in the middle of the struggle.

HO HO HO CHI MINH HO HO HO CHI MINH HO HO HO CHI MINH.

They start to break, start to fall over one another, start to go down in a torrent of blows. Back ranks start to fall back. Pushed back, they break arms, start to run, start to run. And the lines of red, flying, bouncing ranks sweep into the square from the north side. The cops still hold the Audley Street side. Meantime the great park unfolds before us. The US Embassy looms large. Its great eagle mocks the surging, walking bodies, now laughing and breaking links, as they break into the square. There is a moment's peace and the police rush back into the great cordon they have thrown around the embassy. Our contingent, flushed and hearty, enter, seek a way to speak to all. Climbing on a wall:

COMRADES, COMRADES, DO NOT CHARGE YET. WAIT UNTIL EVERYONE IS IN THE SQUARE. THE NUMBER OF PIGS CAN'T INCREASE. WE HAVE THEM TRAPPED HERE. WAIT UNTIL ALL THE MARCH HAS ENTERED AND THEN RE-FORM.

But the Maoists, coming now into the Square and catching sight of the objective, renew the bouncing motion, bouncing on the spot just now. 'COMRADES, COMRADES, WAIT FOR A COMBINED EFFORT.' 'HO HO HO CHI MINH, HO HO HO CHI MINH.' Bounding now toward the police cordon, the police faces ashen as the pro-Chinese banner poles dropped like lances towards them. Then, in a diagonal, the IMG and others started to sweep toward the same point in the cordon. US EMBASSY BURN, BABY, BURN. US EMBASSY BURN, BABY, BURN. A confusion of voices, and now screams as the bodies rake each other. Truncheons rise and fall. In a frenzy banners rip to shreds as they cave and cleave downward onto the helmets. A police surge. The crowd responds. A volley of smoke bombs, and a huge cheer goes up. Geordie Cong, Geordie Cong ... Geordie Cong, Geordie Cong. We had met up, long-lost friends and comrades now back together, we were filled with a thrill of belonging, like the 'We are the Mods, we are the Mods, we are, we are, we are the Mods' of *Quadrophenia*, we revelled in bravado and the notion that we at least were the real McCoy. Banners became lances, every arm was linked, we stomped that road like it was Johnson and Nixon's heads.

The thinned rank of police left exposed to support against the main thrust steeled itself and was rocked off its feet as the northern horde crashed forward. A sudden confusion of bodies gaanin' doon, police trying to put the boot in and draw truncheons at the same time. Lads in a spinning, kicking, punching, head-butting, street fight; this wasn't the practice of post-war British demonstrations.

The cops had no order now: isolated, surrounded, we had no rank before us. All the police were to wor right. We had the steps before us. 'Ha whe, ha whe, form up, form up!', and the ranks started to come back, ten ranks bouncing in warm-up, while the cops quickly tried to drag bodies to form a line. Then the horses: two dozen horses brought up to stand behind the cops. Twenty ranks, drag in the strags.

Geordies, wa mental, wa off wa fuckin' heeds. Geordies, wa mental, wa off wa fuckin' heeds.' Not the polished, politically correct slogan of the cadre school, these were the chants of the football terraces, imported by raw working-class youth to wind the filth up and to infuse the adrenaline.

People started to drop in with us, seeing the weakness of enemy ranks and hearing the chant of determination.

'DO STOP THAT GEORDIE THING,' shouted a petty-bourgeois lass in a combat jacket. 'You're breaking the centralism of the demonstration.'

'Fuck off!'

'Geordie Cong ... '

We started forward ...

'Geordie Cong ... '

A sense of unified power swept the wedge.

'Geordie, Geordie!' Smash! We hit the thin ranks and at once broke, arms again flaying. Keith in a flying drop-kick. Bags of flour were raining forward, adding a mad comedy to the serious fighting. Real blood and red paint splattered the entire square. Cathy gave another famous heeder on a cop face, and the secondary ranks pushing forward, forward. Suddenly the massive height of mounted cops in full flight toward us. Night-sticks drawn like a cavalry charge ... grovelling aboot for stones or mud or owt to pelt.

'Stick the poles in the ground!' came the order. 'Stick the poles in the groond, hold them into the horse's gob.' My God, to hurt an animal, an animal! A massive greet beast under the control of a malicious one trying to ride wi doon. We must resist, resist. As the flaying, flying, falling bodies met, all fear had gone. We would never escape from this square. It was a final encounter, we believed, so fight like fucking fury. We will give this everything our weak and feeble and untrained physical frames would permit. For we had not trained for this day nor equipped for it. The movement was fresh from a thirty-year sabbatical in the mountains of pacifism and yoga.

A flying bike chain—a bike chain?—went whizzing ower heeds and made contact with a mounted cop neck. As he fell from the hoss so the renewed thrust began.

Now protesters, flags in tatters, covered in blood. Stretchers flying aroond and people screaming as the other ranks were pushed back from the Embassy. We were being herded into one corner. The police ranks, kicking and belting out with sticks, were turning us away from the Embassy steps. Greet volleys of pepper, bricks, paint and flour were being flung, in an effort to stop the relentless police surge. Then from off a building site a greet wooden plank was passed forward.

The Maoist students form up behind it in a rank 20 feet long. The plank will demolish the police rank. They start forward, gripping the plank across their chests.

'Dare to struggle, we shall win. London, Paris and Berlin! Ho Ho Ho Chi Minh! Ho Ho Ho Chi Minh!'

The police shuffle as the plank and wave of the pro-Chinese sweep towards them, then a crash as the plank strikes the police rank and all the bloody students fall over like so many skittles. Amid mocking laughter from the cops, and quite a few withered smiles on wor side, the plank is passed back to the building site.

For a full hour the battles rage, ney holds barred. But their order is better than wor spontaneous direction. Even the anarchists agree: coordination and planning are necessary—but only, mind, in the hands of the demonstrators and participating organisations: when the going got tough the unelected leaders had wet themselves, and subsequently dropped mass violent demonstrations like this one from their agenda. It was too big, too violent and too uncontrolled for the leadership of the Vietnam Solidarity Campaign.

In March the truth of what was really happening in Vietnam starts to leak out. The My Lai massacre is pictured live, and on film and in photos. A coldblooded, genocidal ruthless and murderous attack upon a hapless and helpless village. Females of all ages from children through to old wives were brutally raped and then many just shot to death after having been violated. Several hundred men, women and children, little tots and babies shot down, doused in flames, blown to smithereens. Close up, eye to eye, face to face—wanton, frenzied, hate-filled killing. Those scenes will never leave my mind. Those little bodies, barefooted, lying on their mothers, shot coldly and callously. We ought never to forget it. The napalm dropped from an aircraft, which couldn't even see the village or the forest, incinerated and destroyed everything human, animal and vegetable in its path, cruel and wicked and out of sight. The divebombers swooping in to drop their canisters on defenceless villagers, machine-gunning down the people trying desperately to flee or save their animals so that they might survive, shot to pieces with bullets big enough to blast rocks apart. The plastic shrapnel had been deliberately designed so it wouldn't show up on X-ray, and the victim would die a slow and tortured death while tying down their comrades to days and weeks of fruitless healthcare and attention.

Those things were cruel and barbarous, but this sustained and endless savagery, this showed where America and its army already was. The truth was this scene had been repeated time and time again across the country. This time the nice folks at home go to see it, though it had first been suppressed from the highest level down.

18 March. Plastic-explosive bomb attacks damage three US buildings in Paris: Chase Manhattan Bank, Bank of America and Transworld Airlines.

24 March. Inland Revenue Office, Cardiff, bombed; work of the Free Wales Army.[12]

25 March. US Embassy in Madrid bombed.

11 April, Easter Saturday. They shot wor comrade Rudi Dutschke.[13] In the multimillion-page press, the press baron Axel Springer had called for 'someone to take an iron broom to these students'. He got his iron broom in the form of Josef Bachmann (Tom Schilling), a Nazi. And the youth of Europe hit the streets again. In London, we charged the police ranks DUTSCHKE! DUTSCHKE! RUDI DUTSCHKE! and attacked the German Embassy. In Frankfurt and Hamburg young German workers and students attacked the Springer agency, and the quasi-fascist police showed us the weapons they were preparing for British demonstrations. Police swinging truncheons followed by tanks firing water-cannon surged into the young Germans, still holding the streets four days after poor Rudi collapsed in a heap with four bullets in him. The arrests built up, the Germans, chanting 'Revenge Dutschke', erected barricades and tore up the cobbles for ammunition, seizing trucks and turning them over ... A flying wedge of police dispersed the young workers in two directions but by now Brussels found the German Embassy under attack, and the list of European cities ablaze increasing. 'Springer murderer! Shutz fascist!'[14]

'Dr. Kissing said in a broadcast that the authorities would tighten their protective grip on the rioters to prevent them causing further damage.'

In St Peter's Square in Rome the Pope declared: 'The agitation in the universities has now passed the limit of legality and nobility.' It had passed in fact to the school students, who were occupying, demonstrating and building barricades.

In San Sebastian, Spain, mounted police guarded all strategic locations while foot patrols, jeeps and water cannon trucks manoeuvred. All public transport had been halted and the city sealed off.

In Denmark the office of the Education Ministry was attacked with tomatoes, toilet-rolls and smoke-bombs. Fifteen-year-old Brigitte Thomson, the school students' leader, struggled through the battling Danish cops to deliver a protest letter to the Education Minister. The banners read: 'IF SOLDIERS CAN TRAVEL FREE SO SHOULD WE.'

DAYS IN THE LIFE OF...

3–11 May. French Revolutionary students seize the bull by the horns and close down the formal bourgeois education system, occupying colleges and universities, declaring 'All Power To The Imagination'; it is the prelude to a real revolutionary situation. Demonstrations, barricades, bonfires. The sparks in the breeze were political, ideological and dangerous.

Paris was in the grip of the insurrectionists. Burnt-out cars and charred smouldering debris littered the streets of the student quarters, while, throughout the country factory gates and dock gates stayed shut, with workers occupying the plants. General strikes grabbed the state by the balls ... but kept letting gaan. The rags announce: "The university students no longer stand alone. Their pickets weary and unshaven, bloody but unbowed, still face police today in the ravaged Boulevard St Michel. But they have been joined by their teachers, by a junior but equally militant army of schoolchildren, by scores of professional organisations, by the trade unions, and finally by the two great opposition parties: the communists and the Socialist Federation of the Left. All the opponents of the regime are today engaged in feverish political consultations to coordinate their attack.'

The sound of exploding petrol tanks, like crashes from big guns, boomed across the Right Bank. Fifty thousand students and workers were in mortal combat with the riot police in battles around the Sorbonne on the Left Bank. A fusillade of tear-gas met a rainbow of petrol bombs across the entire continent. Workers and students asserted: 'Power to the imagination' and 'Better to die on your feet than live on your knees.'

12 May. Students burst into Strasbourg University and hoist the red flag, proclaiming the university autonomous and at the facility of the revolution.

13 May. One-day general strike of all unions in France supported by all leftist parties, even the Communist Party. Mass occupation of the Sorbonne University in Paris.

14 May. Formal end of the one-day general strike; mass unofficial strikes spread across France. Sud Aviation workers in Nantes lock up the management in their offices, form an action committee and occupy the plant. Next came Renault at Rouen, then 60,000 Renault workers in the company's six factories seize the plants. Managers, imprisoned in their offices, are given escorts through jeering workers to the toilet, after having to put their hands up to request leave to go, as the workers had been forced to do. Shipyards and hospitals followed. Then Citroen and the port of Le Havre and Marseille.

16 May. 50 French workplaces under occupation and 200,000 on strike.

19 May. 2 million workers on strike.

22 May. 10 Million workers on strike—two thirds of the entire French workforce.

25 May. Welsh Office in Cardiff bombed (Free Wales Army).

27 May. Lake Vyrnwy Reservoir: damage to Wales–Liverpool emergency pipeline.

28 June. Helsby Reservoir 60-inch pipeline broken, cutting off half the 80 million gallons of water a day supplied to Liverpool.

In July of 1968, me and Maureen loaded up the big blue canvas tent onto our faithful shopping trolley, and with rucksacks and sleeping bags on wa backs we headed off with pots and pans and stoves and God knows what else hanging off the back, to go camping in Wales, the first time we had either of us been there. We were at a little village of Newborough on Anglesey. We wrote ourselves a postcard home:

> We're camping here in North Wales miles from anywhere. The weather is beautiful but every morning we go through the ritual of curse of the flies—this consists of having half your face devoured by flies while spinning the tea towel in complicated Celtic circles while cooking the breakfast. This done you tuck your jeans into your socks don your sou'wester and mac and run Indian fashion round the field till you collapse, and the other side is eaten by mad Welsh nationalist flies and wasps.

Well at first the folk in the pub talked Welsh, out loud when we were in, though it always sounded like Welsh-English as we stood outside. Then over the days that followed, they discovered I was a miner and suddenly they all started talking to us. We were invited to take the village bus to Llangollen to the Eisteddfod for a long day out. This Eisteddfod was my idea of world humanity. Not that Melting Pot song: 'Take a pinch of white man / Wrap him up in black skin / Add a touch of blue blood / And a little bitty bit of a Red Indian boy / ... And turn out coffee coloured people by the score.' No—I liked differences, I like people getting together to be different but together. There is nothing wrong with native folk, colour and ethnic tradition, so long as it is shared and equal, and mutually appreciated. Through the streets walked a throng of people about our age, all dressed in national costumes, I think from the Balkans; they were a choir and as they walked along they sang and it was like listening to a heaven of angels, it just filled the town and the surrounding countryside.

The diary entries read:

Wed 10 July. 'Went to Llangollen Eisteddfod. It was about two hours to get a seat. We saw all the dancing. The costumes were marvellous and there was some beautiful scenery on the journey.'

Friday 12 July. 'Maddest day of all. Walked to Lighthouse thro forest four miles pursued by some monstrous insects—attacked by seagulls. When it was all over we laughed—but we were both scared at the time.'

Monday 15 July. 'Afternoons on 85's rip, only 3 ft high in the little corner where I was. Cracked me back a million times.'

6 September. Rolled the big blue tent up and the camping stuff and with Maureen and Tessa in tow headed for a camping holiday in Seahouses sandunes. Tessa, who loved camping, also enjoyed that strange doggy custom of rolling on dead animals to absorb the smell. She had developed a nice concoction of dead albatross and shark sunk deeply into her smell glands. She thinks she will knock all the boy dogs dead, which she might just do with that smell. Actually we all know the smell is to disguise her dog smell, so when she's hunting the prey doesn't know its a dog creeping up on them ... it's an albatross riding on a dead shark! So

that won't arouse any suspicions then.

I recall here that Tessa liked to rush around the sandunes, bounding along in lang strides; brought up short sometimes by the dune giving way to a big drop she would fall out of sight and land in a crump then pick up her bounding stride. Some portion of ancient connection between dogs and kangaroos seemed to fuel this mad steeplechase.

She bounds along happily; occasionally rolling heed ower tail doon a dune, only to regain her feet and turn in a shower of sand and bound off again barking at nothing in particular, full of endeavour and purpose which was utterly meaningless to us humans. It had me and Maur in stitches, until some poor unsuspecting bloke sat at the foot of one the dunes, laid oot reading his paper in blissful peace. In the distance and unknown to him a huge ex-RAF police dog was bounding along the dune above his head. Yup, then there was no more dunes and an Alsatian lands from several feet in the air right in the middle of his open newspaper and incidentally it seems also right in his bollocks. Mind, the dog looked equally confused.

14 September. We are invited to the wedding of my sister Veronica and Jim Feldwick at St Mary's Cathedral. It is a big wedding, with Veronica's Irish dancers[15] forming the guard of honour. Relatives are over from Ireland and across the coalfield, and a grand ceilidh is held at St Dominic's, New Bridge Street. Entry reads: 'Very lovely wedding and me and Dave looked lovely. Met all the relations. Uncle Thingy talked too much and gave me a headache.'

19 September. Big exposé of *The Mineworker*—'Take Over Bid Rebels'—in the *Doncaster Star*; silly buggers.

15 October. Imperial War Museum, London, gutted by incendiary device.

4 November. Department of Internal Affairs in West Berlin is attacked with 'Mollies'.

Time for a Stand

In Wardley's thin-seamed depths the memories of revolution and the Wobblies were vivid, particularly among the aud lads. But nationally the Union was a kind of living death. Coal was now unnecessary; we were in 'the white heat of the technological revolution' and it was too late to strive for decent wages and shorter hours. But the tune was wearing thin, and the revolutionism of the age shot through the new generation of miners, and the link to wider questions, to the whole world in struggle, was being made; it was time for the miners to stand, too.

Festive Gaff

Friday 27 December. South Tyne Folk and Blues; Country Hotel, South Shields. With 'The Colliers'. Wallace had come back upstairs with that beaming smile of his and eyes in orbit—he'd had a smoke. Amid the music and foot-stomping he mouthed 'bliddy hell' and waggled his head from side to side. I sneaked off down stairs and there in a tiny car sat big John Reevey, and about four others. The windows looked like a Turkish bath inside and when I opened the door, John rolled out on the pavement amid uncontrolled mirth. I was grabbed and pulled into the car, and John flopped in next to me, saying 'Hev a smoke a' that and shut tha gob'—normally an impossible command, but I got the gist, and ... bliddy ... hell ... the car was flying, we were on a journey. By the time I floated back up stairs, it was my turn on stage. I was on total autopilot and sang and glided round stage much to the amusement of the crowd who'd never ever seen Geordie pit songs performed Bowie-style and thought it hilarious.

Maureen wasn't ower impressed though: 'What song were you supposed be singing?' But I just sat there alang wi Wallace, stupid smirks on wa faces staring into space and stomping amid the cheer. It was Christmas man, and Ah was back up yem!

A Terrifying Encounter

I had explained I think that I came resplendent in Castroesque beard as well as a shaggy mane of hair. The helmet had to be sort of screwed onto me head, working the hair underneath it, till it was wedged. I arrived on a Friday to find we'd worked the caunch up to date, and a wee bit beyond. The tail end was now in front of the rest of the face and the bend on the face line necessitated holding us rippers off the tail gate. Right we now stand in 'the pool'—spare men again suddenly, awaiting fill-in jobs or other work. Of course strong Union negotiations had guaranteed our face rate was paid whatever we did; we were available for face work, so we got paid face money. This was day shift again, cursed cruel bastard shift; I could certainly dey with a easy one today. 'Danny, gaan chock cleaning, 85 area; there's been a fall of ground.'

Smashed fingers time. Bait bag slung across me shoulder, water bottle slung across me other shoulder, shovel in hand, crawl, stumble, bounce me way through the chock line, chock after chock, leaping onto the chain each time it stood and dashing a few yards doubled up along the face, before diving back into the chock line as the warning zong-zong-zong of the pre-start siren echoes down the face, then as I near 85 area, the stone and rubble begins to build up inside the chock line, leaving less and less and less space to travel. 85 must be made up tight. I unload and hang me stuff on the leaking chock handles, which ooze soluble oil from every joint; hope it doesn't seep through into me bait.

For two hours I dig, painfully, scratin in the restricted space, trying to find some sort of floor, and hitting buried hoggers and pipes, metal base and holes, and bolts, clanking and bouncing the shovel off, shuddering up me wrists and elbows, knocking lumps off my knuckles, jamming me fingers, and bits of hose that trap the shovel and drag it off you, and you tear it away, till you only succeed in tossing a few bliddy pebbles onto the chain. Finally you have a floor, you start to attack from a flat surface, start to drag the stone blockage from its pack, start to feel fresh air released. Nerves are tingling from exertion, from early morning rising, from late night sleeping, must be nearly snap time. Sprag me trusty blade upside down into the heap, do the old knee pad trick so I can sit me arse on them, work me back into the pile of stone and try and flatten it a bit, to lean back, relax.

What's in the poke? Maureen, God love her, has stuck a big lump of raw cabbage in a bag along with me cheese and tomato butties. A nice refreshing taste of daytime, tek the helmet off, put me lamp oot, and just eat in the dark and silence.

A chock fitter meantime was crawling toward me in the dark, his head pointing doon; he rarely looked up and I didn't notice him. Suddenly he reached my area and, alerted by a strange crunching noise in the dark, looked up and his light alighted on … aarrgghh! He was later to describe this monstrous gopher, sitting on its haunches eating a cabbage in the dark of the mine. My hair was now free of the helmet, my beard formed a whole furry frizzy with the mane of hair, my skin was black, my eyes shone red in the darkness, and ,true, I was chomping a raw cabbage held in two mucky paws. That wasn't the final straw for the beard, mind. No, that was an altogether more painful decision. I was back in my pack hole, splayed out, stacking the inoculating wire bags filled with stone rammle onto the wall of the pack. As the wall got higher, the trick was to flatten it out, balance it across your upturned arms and throw its not inconsiderable weight up onto the wall, where it should fall, like a basketball player's ball, straight flat on top of the wall, snug to the roof. Bag flattened, arms balanced, thrust forward and up with the bag. The bleeding wire fuckpig, sticks itself into me beard, held fast by a dozen wire strands, the weight comes back onto my beard and the bag starts to pull me to the floor by me beard. Benny, my pack hole mate that day, decides to liberate me. This he does by picking up his shovel, and before the bag has reached the floor, smacks it flat with his shovel, freeing the bag by pulling out handfuls of beard from the root. Pain, indescribable pain, made worse by the manic laughter of men falling over themselves in mirth.

The beard came off. What a disappointment I was. Suddenly this Danny the Red, with the ferocious flying hair and big beard, becomes a youth again, all chin and insignificance. 'Want to see some puppies?' they all mocked for days.

CLASH OF CULTURES

The weekend cadre school was at wor hoose this time—quite an honour, I guessed. All the former comrades from Newcastle, Sean Kelly, and new comrades from *The Mineworker* were invited. Dave and Myrna, Fred Higgins and Angus Martin from the Communist Party, comrades up from Derbyshire, Tom and Judy who were party members as well as lifelong friends across from Hull where they carried the message as I did in Doncaster. These, and 'the comrades': the Party PB, the political bureau, the British leadership of the world revolution. Comrades like Kay from France, and Luca from Italy. Mike, an Arab comrade. The car workers from Luton, the workers from London. We prepared as we would any other bash really, organised to have the singaround folk neet in front the roaring coal fire, ordered a huge barrel of ale, organised the menus for huge pasta fare on Saturday, and multisessional Sunday dinners the day after. Tom had warned that this isn't really the sort of fiesta the comrades normally enjoy at the weekend school. I hadn't realised they normally toasted the International with a glass of port or so, on the Saturday night, but really only meant a glass. Swaying, foot-stomping, beer-clanking choruses of The Wild Rover hadn't been their style, but we didn't know. This team were, well, a little like Raph Robertson, not mysticism and Sri Ramana Maharishi, but abstainers. We just didn't realise what a mutual culture shock this school was to be. The comrades arrived for early Saturday morning. The front room hosted thirty folk, sitting on chairs, on the floor, up against walls, spragged against the fireplace. The wall was hung with the red flag, glistened with the black of the hammer and sickle superimposed with the four of Trotsky's international. Comrades from the PB gave forth from their chairs; expositions we called them. Passing pit folk looking into the house, seeing the parked cars, seeing the flags, seeing the earnest talk, looked and knew the revolution must be at hand. Inside, each exposition went on, and on, and on, almost endlessly, like a sort of communist beatitude. Maurice began with a history of the Fourth International. It began with a description of the Marxist-Leninist theory of class struggle, the development of the dictatorship of the proletariat. This was not of course as it sounded, a dictatorship of the proletariat, that is a dictatorship over the proletariat, no this was meant to be the dictatorship by the proletariat, who being the overwhelming social class numerically is actually a highly efficient form of democracy. Although of course it wasn't, because it had become distorted by the bureaucracy—a self-serving caste which usurped the true soul of the revolution. So what had developed was a dictatorship of the proletariat, but that wasn't what we believed in, we believed in the dictatorship of the proletariat which was by the proletariat. Nonetheless, we called countries where this regime applied 'the workers' states'. They weren't actually states run, owned and controlled by the workers, but we believed they had either been so in the first place, or had set off to that end and become distorted and diverted by a self-interested caste, a parasitic bureaucracy which sat on top of the workers and controlled the state. However the nature of this workers' state, resting as it did on the might and authority of the working class, forced it to act, often against its own inclinations, on the side of the working class worldwide. Communist parties had to be internationalist despite themselves. In this sense we imagined them something like the trade unions. These had begun life as vehicles for the aspirations of the workers for simple justice, for better wages and conditions; then the conflict around those basic demands had led to a growth in political consciousness by the workers in those unions, who then saw in the unions a means perhaps to change the entire social system and at least challenge its right to govern. But unions, at least at the top echelon level, at the big table, with offices full of administrators and professionals, were not like that, did not share that theme or culture. The officials were a caste, which had arisen above the members, had taken on a different lifestyle, for whom social peace and industrial conciliation had taken the place of conflict or any designs in a war to the finish with the employers. Sometimes, despite themselves, they were forced to fight for their members, were forced to make a stand for the class, despite themselves as individuals or their lifestyles, because that was the nature of the organisation they belonged to. At times of course the ruling class might attack the organisation as such, with the officials in it; then they had no choice but defend their own social position and the actual objective, progressive role of the union. At such times the rhetoric would become harder and the old message got dusted off again—'Comrades, Fellow Workers.' So it was with the 'workers' states'—the necessity of both the trade unions and the workers' states wasn't in question; their progressive role despite the bureaucrats and ruling caste wasn't in question. It wasn't what we set off to create, it wasn't what we wanted, it was what was for now—fight to both defend them and change them. If necessary, at a given moment, smash them and rebuild them, although the Posadist, 'in this phase of social and class history', would see that as not necessary—we could capture back our organisations of the class.

The first, second, third and fourth internationals all express the continuity of Marxism, a synthesis of scientific analysis and direction of the class struggle. Marxism is a great instrument in the struggle for socialism, in assisting the masses to take power, although it isn't a requirement: the masses can still take power without it. The construction of Communism means the scientific organisation of life. The interests of all humanity are the same. Under the collectivisation of all production there will be no dispute, no cause for dispute as all collective interests will be resolved together. In this period we intervene in the process to help create forces which are of others, but not for others, essentially the Communist Parties worldwide. We aim toward the construction of the World Communist Party. At present the Fourth International is simply a tendency of the world movement, but it is only a transitional form on the road to a single Communist International.

We sit, listen in silence, almost afraid to cough, write notes, or doodles, head in hands, or eyes looking at ceiling, or the floor. Nobody interrupts. We absorb the collective view. At the end of the long session, the floor is open to us in turn, to basically repeat everything which has been said, to demonstrate that we understand the exposition. In this party there is no necessity to express some new expression or individual view. The party hails the nineteen workers' states, a view common on the Trotskyist left, but goes further and hails what it calls 'the revolutionary states'—usually countries making a stand against imperialism, the objective circumstance of which is that they will inevitably fall into the camp of the workers' states and therefore the world working-class and communist movement. We are a web, a connection, a strand of revolutionary thought at once linking the masses worldwide and seeing in every action in objective or conscious terms movements in the relentless world revolutionary process. If optimism was rocket fuel this party could have flown to the next galaxy. Which isn't too good a joke, since most of our comrades on the left thought that was where we came from. Some time later I was to see a TV adaptation of the Mad Hatter's Tea Party. The passage of time going on and on, the characters in trancelike state, the monotone lecture: it was us, and the whole Revolutionary Workers Party (Trotskyist).

The party was not a democracy, wasn't designed that way; the party was a vehicle with a task. Its task was to meet the shortfalls of the world movement left by the degeneration of the Communist Parties of the world. It wasn't intending to be a government, or a ruling body—perish the thought; its aim was to impel the masses of the world, the people of the world toward the capture of power, and the construction of the most democratic form of society, through elaboration of mass-membership, democratic workers' parties and more particularly workers' committees and councils in whatever form they arose and developed. The party therefore did not see itself in competition with any trade union or labour movement body of the class; wherever possible it strove to be a formal part of that body—although almost always that was denied it—and its members would always act within or toward the mass body.

Central in understanding the whole process taking place in the world and the developing world situation was Comrade Posadas, the General Secretary of the International Secretariat of the Fourth International. It was the wisdom of Posadas which passed from on high through the ranks to us cadres down below and out through us to the masses at large. The party was, self-admittedly, monolithically centralised. That structure was explained against the background of World War Two and the decimation of the Trotskyist movement in Europe at the hands of the Nazis and within the USSR and other parts of the world by Stalinism, or the atomisation of the party into sects behind Healy, Mandel and Pablo.[16] There had been a decision made, in the time of Trotsky, to put the party on a war footing, on a siege footing, to suspend democracy, and the party became monolithic. The impending nuclear war ensured it stayed that way (the Second World Congress of 1948 had agreed that capitalism worldwide was preparing to launch a nuclear war against the USSR).

The creation of teams of cadres, acting as self-supporting cells who could function as a party on their own, was ideally linked to regional bureaux or committees, down to the Central Committee and the Political Bureau. For every legal and open member there was a clandestine and secret member of the party, each legal cell replicated by a clandestine one. The comrades in the legal apparatus knew nothing of the comrades in the clandestine organisation. All comrades would adopt party names, to disguise their real identity within the party.

The purpose for such an elaborate secret structure was the second most central plank of the party's doctrine, namely the inevitability of nuclear war. Imperialism wouldn't give up the planet until it had used everything at its disposal to hold onto it, even nuclear weapons. These would be directed against the engine of the world revolutionary tide, the workers' states, and in particular the USSR. The forthcoming nuclear war would be the highest expression of the world class struggle. Prior to this final settlement of accounts the state would unleash 'the repression' upon all communist and progressive militants and basically try and ensure that no semblance of structure remained to orchestrate rebellion and revolution during and after a nuclear war. Hence the necessity of the clandestine duplicate structure. On a world scale, the war would devastate imperialism and capitalism, but the masses as such would survive and the knowledge of the ideology of communism would advance to cleanse the earth once again, and humanity would triumph at last. But, for now, branches and cells of the party would seek to establish a commune-type existence, not of the hippy variety, but as far as possible living to a communist social and moral ethos.

In a nutshell that was the Party. But Posadas wasn't simply a man of here and now in the hard practical material world: he mused and speculated on much, including flying saucers, folks on other planets and the deeply mysterious 'communist association with the object'. Which sounds rather rude, but actually is more existentialist than Marxist, or so many might think. It basically says you transmit to the world, animate and inanimate, your own cultural and philosophical level of understanding. Would a communist smash to pieces an ornament or piece of art she or he didn't like or understand? No: your level of cultural and material sophistication would ensure a more measured and reasoned response. The object would exist and continue to exist because of the external political consciousness of the human being—or not. Heavy stuff, though in a way I sort of dug this. When I was kid, if I saw a worm washed out of the soil in the rain I would pick it up and put it back on the soil, but then it wasn't just worms; once I kicked an empty can from Wardley garage all the way yem near, then suddenly felt sorry for the can whose life I had just disturbed, picked it up and carried it all the way back to where it had been. Maybe that wasn't what Posadas was talking about at all. With the lecture session over, the team, as we called ourselves, set about the tasks of organising dinner. Everyone had a turn. There was none of this 'she is better at it than me,' or 'I enjoy doing the dinner'; everyone had to have a turn. The host team would plan the meal, but everyone had to engage in its preparation. The party aimed at being a collective. It encouraged comrades to live in collectives, not of just anybody of course, but a collective of party cadres where we could live together, work together share wages, share food and daily tasks, learn together, intervene together. We were not supposed to have 'individual lives' as such—we were to aspire to collective lives and every feature of our life was subject to debate and discussion and collective decision.

The debates on vegetarianism were a case in point. It was breaking the collective, it was being individualist, it was sectarian and impractical. To which we countered with the cheapness, the nutritional value, the speed of preparation, the simplicity of the fare. We usually won, but this meant everyone ate the same. We had been at one cadre school in Nottingham where as a highlight at the end of the meal we were served with ice-cream, equally portioned of course. At the end of the serving Luca, an Italian comrade, asked if there was any more. More?! Like in a scene from Dickens, he was told no, he could not have more. 'Well, is there any left?' we asked. Yes. But not enough for everyone to have more, but the rest of us didn't want any more. This was not the point, however. This was individualism, and was anyway nutritionally not necessary. It got thrown away. The evening social was a splendid affair. Dave got the guitar out; we had some tambourines, and a bodhran. Everything was soon in swing, the beer flowed and we noticed not the raised eyebrows of the PBs as Tom and the other working-class converts drank heartily as they always had. The songs went round, and each in turn would fill his bosom and sing, a story of struggle, a story of history, a fun song, workers' songs, international songs. Then the turn fell upon Theo, the chief theorist. An intellectual in thick horn-rimmed glasses, his no-nonsense mode made his eye twitch as he elaborated without hesitation the line from comrade

Posadas. But here, called upon to sing, he fell back on his favourite, Joe Hill—one of ours too. Theo however was an ex-public school boy. He sang in the falsetto of the cloisters, with rolling vowels and 'R's. What made it worse was his fellow leading theorist from the PB had been taught to sing in exactly the same way and together they sang the chorus, rather like the choirboy in *The Snowman* sings 'Walking In The Air'. Still, we didn't mock folk's backgrounds; we could be big enough to ignore that, just. We sang, we drank, we stomped, the barrel seemed bottomless and it was quite unthinkable to go to bed before we had bottomed it. Some comrades passed out in their chairs, and we covered them over with blankets. Sean Kelly, a veteran from the old Young Communist League days and a bloke who had spent nights working round the clock with me producing *The Mineworker*, turn and turn about, was crashed out just about in his sleeping bag, sound asleep but alarmingly with his eyes wide open. He looked dead. Comrades were camped out in every corner of the house.

I thought it looked a revolutionary encampment. This was not however the view of the PB. The next morning we were all highly berated, for our 'downright conservatism', 'our petit-bourgeois individualism'; it was 'menacing and vulgar and lumpen'. Sean had been so taken aback, he stammered, 'But this is what its all aboot, a good piss-up, a good shout'. 'No it isn't, comrade, this is not what its about at all.' The lofty criticism left a mark, it stung, we—well some of us—resented it. Among ourselves we rationalised it as a culture clash, the party was dominated by intellectuals and middle-class folks, it would change as more workers joined. Of course, we weren't conservative, it was inconceivable that drunken foolishness and singing and stomping were anything other than revolutionary. The neighbours, with whom we did not enjoy the best of relations and with whom we also enjoyed a culture clash, however, would have agreed with the PB.

THE OLD FOX

As summer approached, the day-release class at Sheffield University offered the chance for an extended full ten days' study, mainly a research project. This would necessitate understanding how to use the university library and the others. Temporary membership tickets, and rapid schooling in the filing system and indexing boxes, opened us up to a world of books, and periodicals. As I recall we had two projects, one a group effort and the other an individual one. The group one saw Fred, Dave, Frank Parr and me research the question 'Is Scientific Socialism Scientific?' Now at this stage of my academic career I hadn't quite sussed out the real purpose of such questions, but we knew enough for it not to be sufficient to just say 'yes'. It required a correct analysis of such things as 'What is scientific anyway?' 'Is any science scientific, and why?' Then we came to Marxism's proposition of scientific socialism and a little canter through social science in general with a bit on non-scientific socialism, too. The piles of books we waded through mainly were in search of someone who could synthesise the answer better than us.

My individual project was on the forerunners, the earliest thinkers and actors in the socialist historic trajectory, beginning I thought with Spartacus, via early YCL notions and I supposed Kirk Douglas. I was to be later disappointed with Spartacus, along with many another of our socialist heroes, when the posthistoric gloss gave way to less than ideal idealists.

Forbye, John Halstead, one of the tutors had loaned us his Sheffield flat, which was roomy, swish, and near the university and did we plan a neet oot in Sheffield? Us young'un pitlad academic revolutionaries like, thought we'd sharp cut a dash and score; we were destined for the night life of Sheff. Fred tagged along, though we told him he needn't sort of hang around us, yee knaa like spoiling wa chances, and him being embarrassed or whatever as we strutted wa stuff.

After visiting a few hostelries, we descended on a night club. Oh, that Motown music, those spinning shinny balls (on the bliddy ceiling, fool) that atmosphere, jackets slung over one shoulder, hair tossed with wild abandon. Fred said 'See yee later,' and swerved off to the roulette gaming area, where we later glimpsed him with a cigar in one hand and a wee glassy with a lang stem, walking aboot like Maverick on a riverboat. Still, that sorted him out. Well, there wasn't many dancing yet, we should have to be careful—don't want to get blown out and start a chain of rejection.

Two real cool chicks there, micro-skirts, low-cut tops, dancing round their handbags, waving their arms over their heads and letting it all shake on down man (we'd had a smoke by then, but not too much, just enough to whey lowse off a bit). They'd dey us, me and Steve, one of Derbyshire lads, just dive up and start getting down, hey. They were cool, give them some chat: oh yes, we're at the university doing a course, yes, sort of sociology and a bit of political science, 'Oh I really enjoy politics,' mine says. 'Well ...' Suddenly Steve's marched over, grabbed her arm and they both took off, off the dance floor. Steve shrugs! 'What the fuck yee said?' 'Nowt, just chat, tha knaa's?' 'Chat?' 'Well I asked her if she believed in free love.' 'What?' 'Well its getting on a bit and I thought I'd just mek sure we were in like.' 'You bliddy puddin.' 'OK, it's OK. It's filling up now. Look,' suggests Steve, 'lets split them two up.' 'Them big fat lasses?' 'Aye.' 'Ah divind like them.' 'Na well I don't either, but we can like, start wi them and then go on't something better like.'

Well I didn't like this plan—what if she liked me? I would be stuck, I didn't like to hurt anyone's feelings. Never mind. Very publicly, we strode up: 'Yi's dancing?' 'Not wi' yor two, does tha think we're desperate? We like men,' they said, giggling. Well that was it, a public humiliation. A total crushing, not another lass would dance with either of us the rest of the night then. They had drawn the mark in the sand, and we were outside of it. The lads all cheered when they blew us out. Jealous bastards. So we just sat and drank and shouted a political debate, over the top of the music and the dancing, becoming more and more profound— we thought—with every pint, till every response carried the resonance of the Gettysburg address, or some socialist equivalent if there was one. It was depressing though, as it neared the last dance, all that smooching stuff, and slow waltzy stuff and deep snogging while moving side to side so slowly. 'Eeh, yi'd think they would grow out of that,' we all agreed. As we headed for the door, we realised no bliddy

Fred. Ner mind. By the time we got sorted out, as to where we were all sleeping, still no Fred. 'Fuck him, the bastard. I bet he's got off with someone.' 'Na.' 'Aye, Ah bet.' We locked the front door—let the fucker stop oot.

It was about 5 a.m. when Fred after climbing up the fire escape made an entrance through some French windows in the back, and came in, with his little trilby on the side of his head, his pencil moustache, his coat slung over his shoulder, a half-finished bottle of champagne. 'What about the old bastard now, eh? Ha! Who scored then?' 'Fred, yee didn't, did yee?' 'But of course,' he responds doing a little a dance and sidestepping across the floor. 'Won some money in the roulette game, then on the blackjack, ordered up champagne, a posh bird, out for the night, joined me, played some more, whisked away in a taxi to her hotel room, and I have just left, you suckers!!' We could hear him giggling to himself 'Old bastard, eh?', as he flopped down in a big armchair to catch some sleep before the morning lecture. Fred was to be an eye-opener as time went on. Though I thought him 'old' he was in fact only in his forties and Maureen and others had commented that he was a very attractive man, despite those years.

RETURN OF SPICEY

In the years of the great push, '68 and '69, the clans began to re-rally and Spicey, now of more mature years, wrote in serious vein. In later years, while he served a lang sentence for GBH, he wrote to me that he'd become a Buddhist. On reflection I supposed that kung fu and kicking people's Adam's apples oot while meditating must have made the conversion, rather than serene padmasanas. 'Oh yee of little faith,' reflected forebye on my cynicism, as I read a final letter from Spicey, en route to Japan to find 'the middle path', adding that he had brought a bag full of *Mineworkers*: 'No for the monks, pillick, for the Japanese coal miners.' I had a vision of a shaven-headed Spicey, saffron-robed, selling *Mineworkers* to the Japanese pit lads, 'LOVE' and 'HATE' tattooed on his fists. I put down the letter with the certainty that he would get there, and if he isn't the chief abbot by nuw, the Japanese Red Army must be telephoning its warnings in a Wearside pit twang.

3 February 1969. Unexploded dynamite charges discovered on the premises of the Bank of Bilbao and the Bank of Spain in London

9 February 1969. Bank of Spain in Liverpool bombed.

While we protested in London streets, past London commuters who had assumed the mines had lang since vanished from these islands, we passed the Agitprop bookshop on Gower Street, roond the corner from the NUM headquarters. They had hung out a banner of support. It was the start of an undying friendship with the bookshop and its trajectory against the state. But the march was a prelude to a mass unofficial strike wave, the first serious start at standing up.

15 March 1969. Alan Barlow and Phil Carver arrested after powerful explosion at the Bank of Bilbao in London.

We were preparing, I suppose, for the big leap into full-time academic study; the options were opening out now. In this regard our two comrades Len and Marian, former members of the Socialist Labour League (SLL; Healy's profoundly bureaucratic Trotskyist sect) but still human, had began working in Bulgaria, to growing disillusionment:

Bulgaria

6 May 1969

Dear Dave and Maureen

Sorry not to have replied sooner but I've been very, very busy here lately. Firstly there's my university work and a lot of tangles with Bulgarian bureaucracy about import tax, as well as school work of course.

Well my university work is coming on well at the moment, I have completed 5 papers at the moment and have received quite good marks for all of them. You said (Dave) that you might be interested in taking a BSc (Econ) if the course was politically OK. Well they'll allow you to say anything you like if you give a well reasoned argument for it. Of course they do require certain stereotype answers sometimes. Economics I am quite interested and surprised by. At the moment I'm finding it a little tough, reading works on modern economics casts a lot of new light on Marx's theories which somewhat outdate them. His basis though still cannot wholly be disputed. But a lot of Marx, which many socialists still use in arguments is somewhat dated and they would do well to study some modern works. It is a point of interest to note that incentives are being brought into practice in Eastern European countries—not an entirely Marxist idea, and even if can be rationalised surely it is a pragmatic approach to everyday problems.

I felt before I came here and even more now that the true socialist societies will be born in countries like Britain and to a lesser degree USA. These countries are no where near our standards and will take a long time to achieve them. I'm not dehumanising socialism by emphasising the purely materialist side of Dialectical Materialism but everybody here just wants to accumulate things. Everyday, more or less, I have people asking me for western money (banned here i.e. only available through certain channels) and records, clothes, books, literature—you name it. Somebody even asked if we wanted some of Carla's baby clothes. I'm just bloody fed up with it all.

Apparently they stopped Italian CP members going to Moscow because as soon as they returned to Italy they tore up their party cards in disillusionment and disgust. I don't care a damn what the Young Socialists or that bloody group of intellectual bourgeoisie playing at Revolutionaries, the SLL, think, patronising the workers and telling them what they don't want to know anyway—as far as I'm concerned once you had the revolution its the fucking beginning not the end! and that's so bloody obvious they couldn't see it from two yards.

Anyway simmering down a bit! As you can guess we are looking forward to returning to Britain. I don't know when you have your holidays, so if you could let us know when we travel up to Doncaster sometime in August probably, you won't be away anywhere as we'd like to see you.

Sorry the letters a bit short and touchy but it's just that I felt I've got to tell someone. Anyway, I've got you two volumes of 'Capital' and some posters and so well bring them up when we come.

Anyway tatty bye for now,

love Len, Marion and Carla (not Marx)

I didn't want to hear this sort of stuff, and accused them of being middle-class intellectuals who went to this country with rose-coloured spectacles.

12 August 1969. 'Battle of the Bogside'. This was the turning point in the latest sustained Irish uprising. Behind it lay the simple but determined civil rights demand for justice and equality for the oppressed Catholic minority living under British and loyalist occupation in their own land. It was the demand for one person one vote, for not all Catholic adults could vote. The democratic struggle was met with the utmost repression and murder. The Bogside would be the turning point in resistance. It became for a while an autonomous region run and controlled by the population directly.

> Steady on your aim with your petrol bomb
> Don't throw it son till the Peelers come
> You are the Bogside man
> Now the Bogsideman he's the man for me
> He's cut recruitment in the RUC in the Bogside
> Were all fed up with the midnight raids
> Every man to the barricades, in the Bogside

16 August 1969. House of Duncan Sandys, MP, firebombed. 'Well, good heavens again!'

17 August 1969. Ulster Office in London bombed.

19 August 1969. Bomb explodes in empty army recruitment office in Brighton.

15 October 1969. Imperial War Museum gutted by incendiary device.

In October 1969 a passionate anti-war, far-left group, a development from the Students for a Democratic Society (SDS) in the USA decided to 'bring the war home'. These were the Weathermen, their name taken from a line of a Bob Dylan song, 'You don't need a weatherman to know which way the wind blows.' The Weathermen took to the streets of Chicago in their campaign 'Days of Rage'. Thousands of their supporters in helmets and armed with clubs and bats charged through the streets attacking the buildings of the corporate cornerstones of capitalist America. The state cracked down hard with 284 arrests and mass clashes with the police; 57 of the latter were hospitalised so they didn't get it all their own way, and neither did the corporations who suffered millions of dollars of damage and bad publicity. The Weatherpeople, as they became known from this point on, decided 'Dinnet dey things be halves'. And went into clandestine armed struggle against the US state. A 'home goal' explosion in a Greenwich Village house early in their campaign was probably an accident caused by inexperience, but state propaganda would start to say the Weather people practised fratricide.

Between 1926 and 1969 there had been no national mining actions, official or unofficial, although of course nationwide at pit level and sometimes area level, the pits were a watchword of strikes and rag-ups of all descriptions. In part this lack of coordinated national actions was due to the defeat of the '26 strike and its aftermath, the leaders fearful of the fate of their forebears who not only had had their fingers burnt but their lives and reputations too. The miners at large were bitter and resentful at two major betrayals by the folk they had considered their allies (first the railway workers and transport workers in 1921, then the TUC leadership in 1926), then came the poverty and depression of the thirties followed by World War Two. In World War Two the government stepped in to rationalise and control the mines as they had done in the First World War, and the miners were able to have many issues reviewed. Up until the outbreak of war miners were placed eighty-first in the wages league table. Despite the virtual banning of the MFGB (Miners' Federation of Great Britain) in support of the breakaway Spencer union, in the Nottinghamshire coalfield, something like 20 per cent of Nottingham miners had stayed loyal to the national organisation throughout the decade following the collapse of the 1926 strike. During WW2 the Union leadership proved a valuable asset to the state's war effort in trying to suppress strikes and stoppages within the coal industry, although this largely failed and widespread unofficial strike action and strikes by branches and lodges increased as the war entered its last year. Following the war had come nationalisation and 'a new epoch', or so the miners had hoped. 980 privately owned mines were brought into 'public ownership' with a labour force of 750,000 miners. The Labour government of 1950 introduced the first Plan For Coal. Despite the Suez crisis of 1956 when coal temporarily was seen as a strategic block against an oil embargo, the closures of pits went on relentlessly.[17] Armies of miners were being thrown on the dole and a forest of mines closed. The Union leadership had argued for continued restraint and cooperation in the run-down. Miner's wages hit rock bottom as our labour seemed superfluous and redundant. However in the late Sixties this new generation of miners and a new attitude started to emerge. In addition a milestone in the history of miners' wage negotiations was achieved in June 1966 with the signing of the National Power Loading Agreement (NPLA). For the first time it set down a national day wage, so that a miner on any job anywhere in the country would be paid the same rate of wages for his work. This shifted the emphasis away from area and regional and local bargaining to the national negotiating table, an ambition of the miners' union since the 1840s.

In 1969 a simmering, bubbling, repressed feeling of anger in the coalfields burst to the surface in the first—albeit unofficial—national strike of the miners since 1926. There had been serious dissatisfaction with the Wilson Labour governments elected in 1964 and 1966, and what was seen as attacks upon the unions and workers' rights. The miners felt they had taken all they were going to take. Wages at rock bottom, the position the leaders of the NUM were often to occupy was seen by many a rank-and-file miner as indistinguishable from the NCB directors, and a close paternalism pervaded industrial relations. The miners had been told it was absurd to contemplate strike action. We were in Wilson's modern 'white heat of technology' age; coal miners were an unneeded anachronism. The technocracy was going to deliver the poor miners from those cramped, thin seams and dripping water and give us factory work to liberate us. For energy, we would have instead benign nuclear power, because of course uranium grows on trees and the condition of the poor black miners working in the uranium mine didn't occur to Wilson—it wasn't meant to: people hadn't a clue where their power came from when they switched on the TV or plugged in the kettle, and nuclear energy was something like that, we didn't need to know how it worked, it just did.

Something of the something in the air which was disaffecting the college kids was also catching the pulse of the young workers, miners included. Older miners too were starting to correspond to a rising chorus of discontentment. It was becoming a watchword, that if these pits were to stay open just one more day, then the miners wanted decent wages to work in them. The threat of closure no longer produced restraint; too many mines had closed already for that event to have any resonance among the men still in the industry. Shut them? They shut them anyway.

In 1969, the Doncaster panel had called for strike action on the issue of the eight-hour day for surface workers, which had been promised since Vesting Day, 1 January 1947, the day the government took over the mines .

Sam Bullough refused to accept the motion at the Area Council meeting and he was moved out of the chair. The motion was passed. Yorkshire took the decision that something had to be done about the surface workers—if they weren't getting their eight-hour day we were going to come out on strike about it. There was a strike in Yorkshire and most of Scotland and Wales followed them. In Yorkshire there wasn't a wheel turned in a fortnight in 1969—there had been no national or Area ballot, just mass meetings and masses of upraised hands and voices. Yorkshire, Scotland, Wales and Kent went on strike and Nottinghamshire and Derbyshire were picketed. After a two-week stoppage concessions were won.

The various parts of this unofficial movement were largely uncoordinated. They tended to be coincidental rather than linked. Broad Left, with its election slates, miners' forums, papers like *The Mineworker*, the *New Link*, the consensus growing from miners' day-release classes, more than anything in Yorkshire the semi-official miners' panels, co-coordinating the local branches in a militant alliance of miners' branch officials outwith the control of the Executive.

While official wage negotiations were still ongoing the strike broke. It had followed the initiative of the Derbyshire Area, who called a national miners' demonstration to the NCB offices. It was a totally unofficial call, and heartily supported. We flooded into London, much to the amazement of London cab drivers and station staff who assumed there were no coalmines left in Britain. This was the first big body of rank-and-file miners ever together, certainly with the tacit approval of some of the area leaderships and panels, but this did not come from above. While pay talks were still in progress, Welsh, Scottish and Yorkshire miners walked out demanding a reduction in working hours for our brothers on the surface. The strike burned hard round the edges of coalfields which had been solidly moderate for a generation, Durham and Lancashire in particular. Yorkshire, too, was feeling the challenge to its moderate officials. The strike though failing in its immediate objective of an agreement lowering the surface men's hours, extracted the largest ever pay award in our history and it led to a *de facto* reduction in actual hours whatever formal agreements said. It did another thing. Within days of the strike, industry started to scream; we actually were discovering we still had bargaining power. And it did more: it made militancy respectable, it made the militants sound practical and not just hotheads. It forwarded many a branch challenge, and later area challenge, so to it brought around a dramatic rule change. The current rule had demanded a two-thirds majority ballot vote nationwide to call a successful strike, the new rule called for 55 per cent. Without this rule change the subsequent history of the miners, and so too the nation, would have been completely different. For us, in *The Mineworker* team, we had managed to get our revolutionary brand of mining politics into the eye of the storm. The journal was carried away to Wales, Scotland and Derbyshire. By the time of the next edition we had regular distributors in those coalfields and lifelong friends. The movement of '69 put militancy, and the militants, on the agenda after it had been moved off that agenda by nationalisation and the joint-consultation and conciliation bodies. The action resulted in the best part of 2.94 million tonnes of lost production (other minor disputes that year made up the rest); at its height this involved 140 collieries, including every one in Yorkshire. As aud Jock Kane, the doughty Scots Communist Armthorpe militant was to comment later:

> In 1969 for the first time in the history of the miners, they got the complete award that they asked for. They asked for 27 bob—and they got it, for all the workers and the surface workers got their promise: 'All right—go back to your pits and make arrangements locally. You can do that without us conceding it nationally. Behind the doors you can go back and make arrangements for your surface lads to knock off at the end of eight hours.' Which is what was done on a nod and a wink.

Jock had been of that generation of Scottish and Northumbrian militants who set the Doncaster coalfield on its feet in the 1920s and later. He didn't suffer fools or self-declared heroes easily. It's a mixed metaphor but you'll know what I mean when I say he could cut through bullshit like a knife through butter.

In 1970, the Doncaster panel again called for action, this time on wages. An area ballot in Yorkshire rejected strike action but the Doncaster panel went out on strike and set about picketing the rest of Yorkshire.

The strike lasted three weeks.

Sammy Thompson the area vice president added, 'I believe that those two actions were the preparation for the national strike of 1972.'[18]

That year we went camping to the Stainsby Folk festival, down in Derbyshire in a field overlooked by a derelict mine's winding gear. The field was home to a big circus tent of a marquee in which professional folkies got up to sing. The beer tent was well stocked. Guests were the Ian Campbell Folk Group, whose path we would cross at regular intervals, the Grehan-Mathews group, the Grehan Sisters, part of whom we had met in Newcastle and later on at the White Hart at Bentley. The Yettis, Robin and Barry Dransfield and all sorts of Morris men, sword-dancers, rappers and folk in animal heads and bells on their knees. We were there in force. The miners, and pit lasses, from Donny, Derbyshire and South Shields, the lads and lasses from Dowses Bakery at Thorne, and Darleys Brewery. The fitters from Harvesters shopfloor, bench workers from Rockware Glass, train drivers and guards, lorry drivers, and bikers. We looked indistinguishable from folkies or hippies, except for those in leathers, but we felt something else. We were a force. Our bonfire lit the night sky and our songs were not the variety the folkies had sung. Ours were about struggle, about strikes and lockouts, riots and revolution, and sex of course.

Thursday 27 November. 'At work started ti carry an oil lamp as I suspect gas in the gate and don't trust the deputy to tell since the life of the colliery depends upon our unit. It's an uncomfortable object.' (Although in truth I had always loved them. No so much this big, nickel-plated 'Protector' lamp, as much as the old, thin-bonnet Davie lamp I had first carried down Wardley. Thick wick, matt black, awkward pricker, it smelt sweetly of lamp oil and was with me every day, rarely out of my hand. This round-wicked, big lump of a thing, shiny though it was, was a poor second, though I treasured it still. It was easier to draw down a test flame, and I could read it like a book.)

DONCASTER SOCIALIST ALLIANCE

In Doncaster, we had by 1970 established the Doncaster Socialist Alliance; it brought together, ourselves in various guises, mainly as the Mineworker Tendency, but also the International Socialists, and Doncaster Women's Action Group, together with most of the rest of the 57 varieties of socialist militants, with or without a particular group affiliation. People like Len and Marian, former SLL members and now teachers, brimming with enthusiasm. Quite a number of the group were teachers actually, and at times they introduced some of their older students to meetings to hear debates and views on current political and social issues. The meetings invariably took place at the Coach and Horses, on Scot Lane, where many of our folky music/poetry socials and public meetings were also held. Apart from public meetings at the Coach our specialty was the impromptu outdoor public meeting. We would simply walk into the middle of the marketplace or a corner of the High Street and start to stage a meeting. Surprisingly, people invariably gathered round, listened for a while, sometimes cheered sometimes argued. Occasionally we got the odd drunk heckler and the polis would move us on, but we were there, in the street, shouting our cause of resistance and an alternative slant on the news of the day. Sometimes we would take over the Museum and Art Gallery in conjunction with the Doncaster Film Society to stage revolutionary films such as *Battleship Potemkin* (Eisenstein) and *The Cranes Are Flying* (Kalatozov)

CAMBODIA

April 1970. The USA extends its war into Cambodia. This was illegal and covert and done without the knowledge or consent of the US population, but as they would say, 'Hell, what else is new?'[19]

People had always flowed freely between Laos, Cambodia and Vietnam, and not surprisingly the 'Ho Chi Minh trail', which kept the fighters in South Vietnam supplied with arms and supplies from North Vietnam, bypassed the US borders and blockades and ran through Cambodia. Now with the US invasion of Cambodia the maverick playboy ruler Prince Sihanouk, an outspoken critic of US imperialism and interference in the area, was rapidly overthrown and a pro-US puppet military government put in his place. The resultant rise in armed resistance among the Khmer (Cambodian) people themselves would give rise to the Khmer Rouge and their eventual coming to power under the eccentric and then monstrous leadership of Pol Pot.

Armed forces were moving right across Indochina. By February informed commentators were announcing that the North Vietnamese regular forces in alliance with the communist-led Pathet Lao nationalist movement had swept across the Plain of Jars in northern Laos and driven covert US 'guerrillas' out of the region. The 'purely internal' war going on within Laos between the Pathet Lao and the puppet Laotian government had been previously off limits to the US, or so they had always alleged, while the North Vietnamese communist government in Hanoi, other than pouring arms and equipment through the numerous 'Ho Chi Minh trails' through the country to supply its forces in the South, had more or less stayed uninvolved in the Laotian conflict, like a snooker player with a pocket already covered; Laos could wait. CIA sources were indicating however that it was Vietnamese forces which were taking the bulk of the punishment in Laos, in order to preserve the Pathet forces for their own major offensive further down the line. The US then decided to launch a new initiative and sent numerous blanket-bombing raids into northern Laos to both weaken and soften up Pathet forces and also disrupt the Viet supplies.

This wasn't working. The Americans had developed a 'secret' forward base at Long Cheng in Laos and poured in masses of sophisticated weapons and logistics to support government forces. A key portion of the strategy had been to try and stir up racial and ethnic resistance to the Pathet Lao, developing a guerrilla force of Meo tribesmen to pursue the Lao population fleeing the aerial bombardments and destroy any efforts to protect themselves in new cities and towns developed in caves and protected areas. This team was led by a Rambo character, General Vang Pao, and was entirely an invention of US Special Forces. In part it was an attempt to create a counter-guerrillas war within a guerrilla war; it could only work however if the Viet Minh stood aside—they chose not to and swept across the country with less than 400 troops, pushing the 'guerrillas' and their advisers back and the US camp off the map.

Mao

Somewhere along the line, I think in the earlier encounters with London during the unofficial 1969 miner's movement, and the birth of the Mineworkers' Internationale, I came across the Working People's Party of England. Actually some of my old comrades from the Newcastle YCL were already members of its northern branch. Dixie Deans, a militant lagger from the building trade, a leader of the Tyneside lagger's strike of the late Sixties, and one of the older Fitzpatrick brothers. This was one of the pro-Chinese 'Maoist' groups. It had actually been born out of the grand sounding Movement To Defeat Revisionism and Promote Pro-Chinese Ideology-Mao-Tse-Tung Thought. My theory is that they couldn't fit the title on a badge so it disintegrated. This was part of the pro-Stalin revolt, which followed the Khrushchev revelations of corruption and dictatorship, 'the cult of the personality' as he called it. The Soviet Union was to take a step away from the old red monarch's dynasty and allow a little more freedom into Moscow's monolithic walls. Many would think this small beer; not so the traditional Communist Party Stalinists, who hailed this as a betrayal, a sign that the USSR had sold out, while China, still basking in the glorious cult, hailed Stalin and Mao as the true leaders of the world communist revolution. For these people, Stalin was the fundamentalist bedrock of their faith, the saviour of the USSR, the hero of working people worldwide. Trotsky was an agent of the international bourgeoisie, his followers disrupters and dispensers of disillusionment.

What game these superheroes played wasn't clear; for Mao to hail Stalin despite his close personal contact with that despicable individual was peculiar to say the least-though this is not to suggest that Comrade Mao was Mr Nice Guy. Despite Stalin's disastrous instructions on how Mao should fight the duel battle against Japanese imperialism at the same time as the class war—well, mainly that he shouldn't fight the class war but rather should subordinate his forces in the Kuomintang and behind Chiang-Kai-Shek in a common patriotic front against the Japanese invaders. Good idea Joe; Sign My Cheque as we called him expended more bullets on massacring the reds than he did on Japanese invaders. One would have thought a brilliant tactician such as Mao would have concluded not only that this tactic is going to wipe out the Chinese Communist Party, but that that is just what Joe had intended. A rival superpower claiming the mantle of world leadership of the workers' revolution, perhaps with more credible democratic and left-wing credentials, perhaps with 100 million troops, perhaps with its own atomic bomb!! Too close for comfort. Despite the threats of US Imperialism, despite the Korean War,[20] Stalin resisted, prevaricated, and ultimately refused to give China the bomb. They were forced to develop their own, though we speculated they were working on a super-length giant catapult to fire it, since the Soviet allies wouldn't give them the ICBM to carry it either.

The hold of the Party upon our activity was obviously slack in those days, as shown by the records of my attendance for the miners at numerous WPPE functions in London, usually staying in the latest Cinema Action squat, or with WPPE people on St Giles High Street. I was there at their second congress in

May '69. Again at Gower Street, but at Student Movement House. I seem to recall a pooled fare system ensured most of my train fare was paid. Attendance sheets show I was present in September 1970 along with Fred Higgins, Dixie Deans, R. Ogilvy, who had been the wife of Sid, who first laid the RWP's wicked hand upon me with the revelation that they believed the nuclear war was inevitable and to some extent even desirable. He and Rasheda had gone their separate ways. Sean Kelly was also invited, though whether he came or not I can't recall but shows how despite political differences we were still capable of trying to keep a dialogue and joint actions together, the WPPE being great believers in uniting all who could be united on the broadest possible programme.

Meantime this new democratic Khrushchev revolution hadn't actually moved too far from Joe, for as Nikita exposed the cult of the individual, the show trials, the massacres, the starvation, the failures, the lies, a voice cried out: 'And where was comrade Khrushchev during all this?' At which he stopped in full flight and demanded, 'Who said that?'

Nobody moved. 'Let the man who said that stand up!'

Nobody moved.

'That's where I was,' continued Niki, with probably more truth than we will ever know.

I liked Khrushchev, sort of instinctively, certainly not politically, probably not rationally, but he had a sparkle and a wit, and when his little defiant frame stood up against the USA and all that, when he had banged his shoe on the desk on the UN summit while JFK was in full flight, you couldn't help but smile. 'We are spending huge sums of money on rockets and atom bombs—and they are not for slicing sausages,' he said. And 'If you start throwing hedgehogs under me I will start throwing porcupines under you.' He had the most amusing term of phrase: 'Give us time and we shall produce panties for your wives in colours which cannot be seen anywhere else.' 'We can supply anything except bananas. If you order the devil from us, we can also supply him—but you must specify what kind of devil you want.'

I was left with the lasting impression given me by Stan Wilks, the oldest YCLer in the business, Nogbad[21] as we called him for short. He told of the visit of Premier Harold Macmillan to Russia in 1959, the state procession, the grand black limousine that sped Mac through the Soviet countryside. Gleaming on a hillside a magnificent building had caught Mac's eye.

'This, you like this?' Khrushchev had asked, 'Well, it looks splendid,' announces Mac. They stop the car and walk over the hill to the gleaming building. On the oak doors, are gold knockers, one of which Niki bangs, bangs and pulls from the door, 'Come Harold' he urges, so Mac knowing that strange Russian customs, like supping back a glass of vodka and smashing the glass into the fireplace exist, bangs, bangs and bangs on the second knocker then wrenches it from the door, 'Come Harold' says Khrushchev as he flings the knocker he is holding through the nearest window. 'Really?' asks Mac in disbelief. 'Da, Da, through the window, so bash, Harold's knocker goes through the window, as Khrushchev's boots open the door. There inside, is a magnificent sight, a fountain, a sculpture, gold lamé curtains.

'Come on, Harold!' Niki is inside and pissing in the sculpture, then washing his hands in the fountain. 'Come on Harold!' So Harold, in need of a piss, pisses into the intricate folds of the sculpture then washes his hands, while whump! Khrushchev yanks down a gold curtain and starts to dry his hands on it. 'Come on Harold!' he says.

Harold washes his hands and face in the fountain then whump! pulls down a curtain and starts to get dried as Khrushchev starts running out of the building down the field and toward the car. Harold thinks this is really great, what an adventure; as he catches up he says: 'Nikita, that is a great place. What do you call it?' 'Oh this place? We call it the American Embassy.' Bureaucratic divisions aside, the impact of the real world revolution in all its forms was breaking down many a sectarian divide, even the unthinkable ones between Trotskyism and Stalinism. So it was that a joint conference was convened with the WPPE and the Mineworkers' Internationale. Like a many of our 'rank-and-file miners' conferences' we hosted it at the Bay Horse, Bentley. It was preceded on 15 May 1970 by one of our folk music socials with proceeds to the Mineworkers' Internationale. Getting tickets printed owt like proper was a challenge in those days, so we hit on a novel scheme. Norma and Mike were two of Maureen's colleagues from Newcastle Art College; they had gone into photography and opened a studio down at Whitley Bay. They often came to stay at weekends, taking photos of me and Maureen and the cats, the pit, the winding engines etc. In addition they took a photo of a ticket we had mocked up with Letraset on a pitch-black background. These Mike simply printed, 200 of them as I recall, so each ticket was in fact a photo.

It was some novelty, but then so was the social. Bentley Colliery was predominately Scottish, Scots miners having been shipped down wholesale, and the local lodge was almost entirely Scottish, indeed, the branch had a pipe band rather than a brass band. Our folk social struck a chord they hadn't heard for some time. The music was frequently Celtic, the songs of industry and struggle familiar, and when Maureen got up to sing *The Blantyre Explosion* you could hear a pin drop, until the end when she was met by a standing ovation. Many a collier in the audience came from the Blantyre districts and had grown up with the songs. We had coaxed not a few up to sing, and of course many of the local Scottish Communist militants came along for the crack and the sing. The following day's conference was chaired by Dr Alex Tudor Hart, the chairman of the WPPE. Doctors and medical folk populated their contingent while ours was almost exclusively the miners, miners' wives and folk like Tom, watchful I think, that we didn't become too overwhelmed by the spirit of bonhomie. Dr Paul Noon was chairman of the Junior Hospital Doctors' section of the Medical Practitioners' Union, his wife an Asian microbiologist. Also Sid, an animated Turk, with whom I often stayed, and a bunch of the lads doon from Newcastle ours and theirs and the miners up from Derbyshire. Tudor Hart's brother Julian was the chief chest consultant to the NUM, a man who had dedicated his life to the struggle against miners' chest diseases and for legal compensation for their slaughter.

Both brothers had served in Spain. Alex had actually been the chief surgeon to the International Brigade. He had also designed a heart valve, confusingly called the Hart valve, which allowed operations to be done in and around the heart. He too was a genius at what he did. Although driving was not one of them. Alex was bliddy aud, huw aud, Ah didn't like to guess, but like a many a genius he was forgetful of little unimportant things, and as he got older, more things became little and unimportant. This was never so evident as when driving his wee hippie Citroen. This was a very basic model, with seats like deckchairs in, which I don't think were even fixed to the floor. Alex in full flight of debate could do the most anarchist of things given he was a Stalinist, like going over the middle of a bliddy roundabout island and then rejoining his lane at the other side, or taking a short cut round the wrong way because his turning off 'was just here'.

THE RED BOOK

At this time, I loved all things revolution, sure I knew the parties take on things, I understood the process, I had no illusions about workers' states' bureaucrats, or I thought I hadn't, but on a world scale, it was our side versus their side. Fidel, Mao and Ho didn't see things as we did, but they saw them enough of our way for us to see them as on 'our side'. This being the case and having been equipped by the WPPE with direct ordering from China, I ordered up 1,200 copies of Mao's *Little Red Book*, one for almost anyone at the pit who wanted one. They arrived in boxes, and I went onto every shift, standing as the men queued for the checks, standing as the men queued in the canteen, or as they came off shift, or boarded their buses. Very few miners refused the book. One, it was famous; we had seen its magical powers as ranks of Red Guards waved them at adversaries and counter-revolutionaries of all descriptions, we had seen people go to their deaths in pits and in train crashes clutching their *Red Book*. Two, it was shiny and novel. Three, it was also free.[22]

One man had tried to rip it up, but the plastic cover had got the best of him and he threw it in the bin amid jeers of derision from the men who thought him ignorant, narrow-minded or anyway impolite; he should have done it when I wasn't there, some had suggested. Management were puzzled by the appearance on every belt drive and every junction of copies the Red Book. It was pulled out at bait stand, or when having a minute as colliers debated over Mao's encyclicals to the masses, as well they might.

One bloke insisted he would never support any such revolution because he wasn't going to live on Ambrosia rice. 'Well, comrade, first off, that's not the sort of rice they eat in China ...' In those days actually eating any sort of rice, or pasta even, would have been unheard of in most working-class homes—revolution or no, it was meat and two veg and Yorkshire puddings or they were staying with capitalism.

It was two months later the bill arrived, and my jaw hit the floor. I wrote off a hurried note saying I thought they were free. I had distributed them to every man at the pit. I would pay but it would take some years ... it was OK; they wrote off the debt.

SOMETHING IN THE AIR

The 'revolution' that swept the world in the late Sixties, reaching a pinnacle in May '68, had its storm centre in the selfless Vietnamese Tet offensive. But it echoed across the USA and Europe. Many thought they saw, in the Czech 'Prague Spring' revolt, struggles from within the 'workers' states'. Although there were bitter arguments as to whether the Czech revolt was a 'capitalist restoration', Dubchek, the first secretary of the Communist Party having dreamed of getting IMF funding and abolishing social welfare, not to mention joining NATO. The comrades in the party had ney doot; this was restorationism and we should welcome the Soviet intervention—given the bureaucratic mess both states were in, it was a progressive purpose carried through with bureaucratic methods. Others saw this as a struggle for real workers' democracy and an end to Soviet rule.

In Belgrade the students took to the streets and occupied the university, launching a renaissance of the Yugoslavian revolution, demanding 'Fewer private cars, more public education', hailing Tito, but believing the self-interested functionaries had lost the plot and were leaning too far toward capitalism.

We thought the so-called 'cultural revolution' in China was a fundamental struggle for control over the direction of the Chinese people's revolution. We did not think this was some scheme launched by Mao, indeed Mao was clinging to its coat-tails for all he was worth. Mao had been brought from the back of the cupboard and dusted off in order to contain it. This was a political revolution, not a 'cultural revolution' as the centrist state authority had christened it in order to tame and derail it. But the rank and file of China, those youngsters, were fresh with the wind of change in their faces and coupled with the wizened old men and women who had sacrificed titanic hardship in fighting this revolution, represented a new militancy, or perhaps the original old militancy was back on the streets. It was back in the fields, it was taking the armed forces by storm, it had the party apologists and careerists by the throat. 'Just who reigns here?' the young Red Guard demanded, 'What are we doing and who says so?' Factories stopped, peasants walked out of the fields, the airforce was grounded. The young insurgents demanded that these high-flying guys understand the lives of the people, the toil in the fields, the back-breaking work in the Chinese industrial power house, before they got back into their planes. 'Until you understand why you are up there, you stay down here with us.' The doctors, taken from their clinical and often cynical and cosseted practices, would be brought to work in the paddy fields, down the coalmines, in the mills. 'When you have bent and laboured ten hours a day you will know what these ailments are that your patients complain of, and perhaps be not as quick to dismiss them.' Here and there came reports of excesses, brutality and injustice but a largely spontaneous political workers' revolution, in a country bereft of sentiment and tenderness for so long, could be expected to throw up some harsh treatment. This was a country of hundreds of millions fighting for the life of its people, the standard of existence, the fate of its children and possibly the people of the world, yet the western bourgeois papers concentrated on the hanging of the British Ambassador's cat during an embassy occupation. Sad for the poor moggy and certainly infantile, but not actually what this revolution was about. Its aim was to take direct control from the functionaries, the party apparatus, the bureaucrats waiting their turn to sit at the big tables like their Soviet equivalents.

In the middle of all this Lin Piao, the old marshal of the liberation war against Japan, was seen to be a leading figure.

REBELS

4 May 1970. At Kent State University in Ohio an antiwar demonstration on campus was attacked by the National Guard, who fired into the unarmed and anyway retreating students killing four white middle-class kids who cared too much about the world, while two black kids were shot down during antiwar demonstrations in Alabama. This war was coming home, and some of the kids chose to fight.

June 1970. The embryonic caucus (Baader, Ensslin, Mahler and Meinhof) of what would become the Red Army Fraction began training with Palestinian and Algerian socialist commandos, having already launched an arson attack on a Department Shop in protest at the outrages being committed by Germany's leading NATO's ally the USA.[23] Baader and Ensslin, two comrades from the German SDS (Sozialistischer Deutscher Studentenbund), had listened to too much talking, had seen the writing on the wall with the shooting of the student Benno Ohnesorg during anti-Shah demonstrations in West Berlin in 1967. Had taken up violent direct action, moving to armed direct action. Sentenced to three years in prison in December 1969, Baader escaped in May 1970 and went on the run. While underground Baader had met journalist (on *Konkret*) Ulrike Meinhof, who with others assisted in his escape from prison.

July 1970. The official leadership of the NUM decided to come into the open and attack the developing unofficial movement and its emerging counter-leadership. Sidney Schofield, national vice president, made it the centre of his platform speech at that year's Annual Conference at the Isle of Man.

> Minorities in our union who are arranging unofficial meetings, printing and issuing pamphlets, ignoring the policies agreed upon at annual conference, have one purpose in mind, to try to undermine the status of area and national officials of our union and to incite our members into taking unconstitutional action ... We must not allow the minority who are already holding unofficial meetings, to formulate policies that undermine the whole concept of trade unionism ...[24]

The NCB too was bemoaning the loss of £8 million in the Yorkshire coalfield as a result of the action ... At a press conference following the publication of the Yorkshire Area Annual Report, regional NCB chairman John Brass had described it as 'disastrous' and then went on the complain that it had been followed by Xmas and then a flu epidemic! 'Things in threes,' we reasoned. Meantime our comrades in Sweden had launched an unofficial action inspired by ours. 1,200 miners walked out on a wildcat and started to spread the action demanding a 21 per cent pay increase. The formal action had ended with much bitterness in February. The leadership had called off their eight-week strike so negotiations could take place; now they had management's offer of 11% and greatly increased divisions and bands and differentials. 'They are trying to divide us as well as insult us' was the view of the unofficial miners' movement, which had been developing alongside ours, and staying in touch through *The Mineworker*.

RETURN TO AMSTERDAM

In July 1970 me and Maureen were all fitted up to go to Russia with Progressive Tours—got our visas, passports, the lot, paid it all up. Then a week before we were due to go, cholera broke out and the company wouldn't send us. We desperately tried to find ways to get there on our own, but it wasn't to happen. Maureen cleverly fixed us up with a holiday to Holland instead, which although it wasn't Russia saved me from my misery. We visited some of my old dens in Amsterdam. A new centre and movement De Oranje Vrijstaat housed the hippy hordes, with their wild music, anarchism and protest. We were soon at home, oh yes, well I was a veteran. I ordered up dope, rolled joints, toked and passed them round, drank beer. Then suddenly, stupidly of course, the world started to lose its substance and go like a regression scene in an old Hollywood movie, all swimmy and out of focus. I started to get up; didn't want to pass out here, leave Maureen vulnerable and alone and, my head was flopping like a rag doll. Maureen tried to help me to the door, where my knees buckled and I collapsed. I felt like the verge of a faint, fading away, drifting back. I lay helpless in the alleyway. Voices asking Maureen if we need help. 'No, it's OK.' 'Smashed?' 'Si—er, ja—smashed,' she confirmed. First she tried to heave me to the tram stop, but I could neither stand nor sit, so lay unceremoniously on the pavement. Incredibly the tram stopped, and the driver helped Maureen drag me onto the vehicle and prop me in a corner, but it wasn't too many switches and turns along the cobbled route to the Stadium before I started to feel something begin to retch down in my stomach, the pills to swish, the dope to fire up again. I made a dive for the doors. Maureen held on to me until we reached a tram stop. As the doors opened, so did I, and a huge spurt of spew launched from the tram platform; it was certainly a good job no poor bugger was standing waiting for the late evening tram to arrive. I followed the spew out of the door, and the driver shrugged at Maureen and then went off into the night. As I tried to regain some control of my head and my legs I staggered along the Amsterdam outskirts. It was early morning and the milkman had just set about his deliveries. Good! I snatched up a bottle of milk, and downed it in one; this should help put me together. It was in fact that sour, curdled milk the Dutch drink. If I had drunk a pint of salt water the effect couldn't have been more dramatic and I shall spare you graphic and sordid let alone assorted details of my guts turning inside out for nearly an hour, with me kneeling by the gutterside like a Japanese disgraced person committing hara-kiri, except I didn't need a sword to spill my entrails on the street. I wouldn't mention it, but somehow this incident stayed in my memory for some reason. As I recall I even took time to join a riot— what else to do in Holland while on holiday? It was a demonstration against the

CIA puppet Suharto, who a few years previously had been installed in Indonesia, the former Dutch colony, against the heavily communist-supported Sukarno along with much blood and repression—hundreds of thousands of Sukarno supporters were slaughtered in the coup and its aftermath. When the police horses appeared though I made my excuses and went. One, Maureen was in the tent up at the Stadium on her own waiting for me to come back; two I was actually on holiday; and three, following my experiences in Grosvenor Square, I was not inclined to get involved again in a game of chicken with charging police horses.

3
Hippies In Uniform

Our house was most certainly a revolutionary centre. A network of contacts, comrades, rebels of all descriptions at one time might be staying there. Comrades and friends down from Newcastle, or en route to different political and industrial flashpoints. So it was one stormy night, when the big battered van of Cinema Action rolled onto the path in front of our house. This was a revolutionary film-makers' team, an inspired group of worker film-makers who put their knowledge and equipment at the service of the class. Mainly they covered trade union actions and left political events, but the makers of history were given the chance to make their own films with the help of CA. These films were then shown by the workers in their plant, workplace or community as part of the struggle, part of the alternative to the bourgeois media and its pro-bosses slant on things. Most of the group were German or Portuguese but also Cockney, raw working-class Cockney, or middle-class Anglo-Germans. They were down from Upper Clyde Shipbuiders in Glasgow were they had made a tremendous film on the occupation and work-in at the shipyard, the UCS film. The film caught that momentous moment, the first workers' occupation in Britain. The seizure of the yards by thousands of shipyard workers on 30 July 1971 was followed down the line by the occupation of Plesseys at Alexandria in West Lothian in September and then a knock-on with strikes and go-slows all over, as well as mass solidarity meetings nationwide. This was the stuff of our dreams. The crew had got the big projectors out and shot the film onto our living room wall, which it filled and spilled over across the ceiling. The house was filled with a silver glow, beaming out into the street, and many must have thought the aliens had landed. Here on our wall, big strong, solid-jawed and strong as concrete was Jimmy Reid, the UCS convener, addressing thousands of boiler-suited Clydesiders, hanging off cranes, cramming along gantries and sheds, like a scene from one of Eisenstein's films. His voice boomed out, clear and strong: 'Today the Clyde speaks, today Scotland speaks, no the Scotland of the Lairds and the lackeys, but the Scotland of the working class.' From UCS, occupations as a tactic spread over the border and throughout Britain. It posed a challenge, not simply to the status quo, but also suggested more, that workers could themselves take over the means of production and run them for ourselves. Cinema Action made films, produced films, then humped them round the country showing films, living on a shoestring, touching the rich and famous of the theatre and film world for donations, living in squats all over London, living the real life of communist communards. They debated, nay argued and yelled at each other, they elaborated positions, they filmed brilliantly, they worked into the dead of night cutting film, splicing film, they shared all their food, and all their money, which was next to nowt. They were poorer than town mice, raw and red. We were at once absorbed into their collective. The state was terrified of them, what with their revolutionary reels, and that they were German: the Red Army Faction had clearly crossed paths with them from time to time, and all sorts of mysterious European revolutionaries were staying with them. Police raids, when they could find where the squat had next decamped to, lock stock and barrel, were frequent pains up the arse.

BEAUTIFUL PEOPLE

Meantime, we, Tessa and Maureen and me, and our tent, and pots and pans, and stoves and sleeping bags, set off back up yem, camping. We would take the train from Donnie, up as far as we could get, to Berwick, then sneak, as far as is possible with two weeks' camping gear on your back and a massive dissident former RAF police dog in tow, aboard unsuspecting buses further north. This time two weeks at St Abbs. Buses were never very keen on having a big Alsatian on board, but I usually distracted the driver by asking for the key to the boot, and having him come round the back to park wa gear; meantime Maureen would dive on with the dog, and once installed she would lie if not happily at least quietly under the seats (the dog of course not Maureen). We were dropped in the village, just up the road from the official campsite, na, not wor style that. We walked on doon a long winding road toward the St Vedas hotel and the beach, over the dunes and in a quite cove we pitched the tent. We always just camped in the dunes or backbye somewhere. We had chosen a grassy sand[25] dune near a winding path through the grass overlooking a splendid rock outcrop and pebbly bay. Night times we would walk down to the St Vedas, and lay into bar meals, while the dog became the life and soul of the party; she could be relied upon to clear everyone's plate, if invited of course—she was a most polite beast. It must have been early in the year as the weather was stormy and the surf was high; night times it would come crashing up the bay and a time or two I thought it would reach the tent, which was weighed down with more rocks than Hadrian's Wall. Tess had learned to come and go throughout the night, and had taken to hunting rabbits while we slept. This she apparently learned from watching the big hotel cat do likewise. The cat was a truly massive creature and would sit atop a big abandoned gatepost in the middle of a rich cornfield. Silently she would wait the approach of a rabbit, then drop like a stone, crunch. Deed rabbit. Otherwise, she would suddenly come to life, alert from heed to toe, and fling herself into space, landing more often as not straight on the back of the unfortunate rabbit. Now Tess up until this time scarce ever thought where her dinners had come from. As strict vegetarians we didn't like the idea of buying meat but we had landed the responsibility of this carnivorous animal so what we couldn't scrounge we had to buy, usually greet sides of mutton and other cheap stuff from the supermarket. Tess thought of this, up until now, as some sort of manna from heaven. Watching the cat hunt and kill the rabbits rekindled some old instinct in her, and she suddenly realised you didn't need a can opener or a human in order to get fed. Mornings would find her fat and happily exhausted. The cat had also taught her to catch fish. I kid you not, like a great American bear this cat would sit patiently by the side of the stream[26] which fed down to the sea and waited for the salmon and other fish to come upstream, leaning forward, silently straining on three legs, the fourth poised in readiness for the strike and the poor fish suddenly whisked from the water and onto the bank where it was soon pounced on. Tess couldn't do this flick-of-the-wrist bit, but soon learned to belly flop into the water at the appropriate time and come up with her teeth wrapped around some big fish. Na we didn't like it, but somehow it was far more appropriate than us, vegetarians, buying bloody meat for the dog to eat when we didn't eat it wasells.

This place was geology sliced open, naked anticlines and synclines exposed on massive cliff faces, in our little bay a tall rock abutting the cliff, from which Maureen, a powerful swimmer and fearless diver, dived, in perfect rhythm, deep into the bay and emerged like some beautiful sea creature. Just lying about as evening came in, the crash of the waves and the sea running strong up the shore and meeting the fresh water streams en route to the ocean in great crashes of foaming confusion, we sat by a fire of sticks and flotsam, still and quiet, breathless at the world. It troubled us, this beauty, this stillness, this near religious joy at life; it contrasted with the grey world of social realism, of industry and scientific socialism. Our natures rebelled against our reason. We regarded ourselves as hippies in uniform, we too were stardust and golden, but we couldn't just wait for the world to change, we couldn't just drop out and reject the world, we had to intervene to change it, and change could only come through the mass action of millions of workers and a political programme for seizing back the planet. But secretly we felt as they felt, though the PBs would never have understood that, so we didn't speak of it, to speak of it was at once to court ridicule and venomous accusation of petit bourgeois idealism.

Speak of the devil, from behind the winding hillside a trio of the beautiful people glided towards us, a strikingly beautiful girl with big hair, a cheesecloth bodice with embroidered red flowers, her bum fitted neatly into her faded blue jeans, Scholl's sandals and coloured beads around her neck. A tall blond boy with spiky hair and a necklace of shells, a collarless white shirt, a pair of tight blue jeans and sandals, was followed by the third, a mass of hair encircling chin and head and blowing out behind him like an ancient guru, a little pair of thin rimmed glasses, a ganzee Tom would have been proud of, a pair of army shorts and tanned strong legs, he carried a wee knapsack over a shoulder. 'Hi. We've come to share your fire,' the girl said in what I took to be an Australian accent, which she giggled at and playfully went to strangle me in defence of her New Zealand ethnicity. The tall boy sat beside Maureen and started to roll a joint. 'You smoke this?' Maureen suddenly in her blushing confusion of smiles and hand movements started to explain: 'Well, yes, but it's a waste of stuff because it doesn't affect me.' The hairy took from his knapsack a huge bottle of wine, and two big galvie cups. Tess came round and carefully inspected each new arrival in turn, sniffing and reflecting on the flavour rather like a wine connoisseur, before flopping into a heap over everyone's legs. We blended, we merged into each other, we smoked joints we supped wine, we roasted tatties, we became inseparable, for now. They were staying in the Youth Hostel up the road, whence came the galvie cups. He came from Denmark; the hairy was a Canadian of Scottish parents, Gerry Dunne. She a wealthy farmer's daughter, we an artist and a coal miner, together we got the nick name The Coldingham Gang. Our gang expanded to include Bob Campell, an anti-war yank as he described himself as soon as we met and heard his accent.

A surviving beer mat signed by everyone at the time records 'August 28 1969. St Vedas Hotel Coldingham Bay "Coodly-coo, Ky-ke-le-ky"' (the Danish interpretation of a cockerel). We walked miles upon miles on windswept cliffs around St Abbs, we read poetry, we picnicked on raw veg bought from the gardens, we swam, we ran, we chased and tumbled. We embraced each other warmly, we hugged each other with real sensuous pleasure, it seemed the most natural thing in the world, it felt like we had always known each other. We didn't move onto sex, though, that never seemed appropriate, yet. This was the other side of the revolution sweeping the world, a revolution the PBs would be totally alienated from, and yet it was tied to that struggle in the bowels of the earth, the pounding mills and car plants, the farflung fields of Indochina and the sweat of Africa. We could feel that. Humanity needed to be free from work, if not work from sold labour, to discover its alienated true self, love, beauty, freedom.

Though Tess came in our tent at night with us, she was oft out of a morn doing her born free bit, romping through the grass and whatever; she usually came back wet, tired and happy, flopping onto our sleeping bags in the dark.

Half way through the last week of the holiday, we were making our way back over the dunes and cliffs in a force nine gale, the sea spectacular with mountains of white crashing foam. Good job the tent was in the lee of a big grass covered dune and weighted down with a ton of rock. Tessa was bounding on ahead, oft out of sight. We crossed the stream, which was by now raging and crashing, and filling most of the beach. Tess didn't catch up. It bothered us, but we knew she was well used to the place and knew where we were. We shouted but our voices came back on the wind, and our torch beams fell uselessly after a few feet. We were soaked, got curled up in the tent and expected she will return when she's finished thundering around in the storm, barking at the waves. Sometime in the dark of night, a wringing wet hairy mass flopped itself on my sleeping bag and my hands reached out and felt the soggy hair and gentle soft mouth. As dawn broke, my face felt sticky, my hands were sticky, and as my eyes opened I became aware of blood, on me hands, obviously now smeared around me face, I thought at first 'my nose'. My eyes catch site of the bleeding whimpering Tess, she had obviously gone off a cliff at Milldown Point and battered against rocks and shore had fought a huge battle with the seas to survive. She was clearly hurt inside and out and her tail had been ripped up from her backside, which was oozing blood, her nipples were torn and severed. Bliddy hell Maur, wa dog. Maureen was desperate, poor Tess, poor dog, Oh Dave she won't die will she? She pleaded. I didn't know, but not without a fight anyway. I set Maur off over the dunes and sand running like hell for help. Meantime, I tried as well as possible to patch her up, immobilise, and pad whatever I could. Wrapped round in a blanket, I heaved her up, and carried in front of me, with me arms breaking under the dead weight I started to carry her down the dunes, through the waves, up the dunes and over the rocks to the pub. Maureen had miraculously organised us a lift to the nearest vet, which was in Berwick, no mean feat as I recall—this was about 7 a.m. on a Sunday morning. The bloke, a local fisherman, at once took pity at the plight of the poor animal awash in the sea and struggling her heart out to live in the crashing waters. Me and the bloke went for a walk around a deserted Berwick; to be honest I couldn't stand the idea of Tess in pain, and I knew at the very least she was going to need stitching, if she could live at all. When they emerged about 90 minutes later, poor Tess, was like an Egyptian mummy, her arse had been sown back in place, her chest was stitched, her paws which had all been split open had been sown up and wrapped together and three of her legs now sported bright white socks covering tightly bound plaster. It was weeks before she would eat. She cried out in pain every time she had to shit, and she slouched off up the beach at the mere sight of a gentle wave splashing on the shore, but she lived. Lived and enjoyed the fame: she would sit under the table of the pub of an evening until sympathetic voices and patting hands coaxed her out to limp dejectedly and be comforted by all and sundry.

4
MILITARY COUP

For the miners the movement of '69 put militancy and the militants on the agenda. It had been moved off that agenda by Nationalisation and the joint consultation and conciliation bodies. Wilson's overall assault on the workers' movement, with proposals to introduce incomes policies and restrict the right of strike, had come up against a barrier of trade union resistance and a nationwide unofficial one-day general strike of ninety thousand workers. It was a small shot across the bows. The big cannon was fired a little later at the general election of 1970. Wilson was to be swept from power against all forecasts and predictions, not by any swing to the hated Tories, but by a mass abstention of Labour voters. Labour voters staged a strike at the ballot box and stayed home. This was not the Labour government they had expected or been promised. Whereas the first government in October 1964 with its wafer-thin majority was hogtied, Wilson's second coming in March 1966 had opened up the opportunity of the most radical labour government since 1945.

Indeed expectations of far-reaching socialist inroads into wealth and power were so great that elements of the state started to plan for a military coup against Wilson. If that sounds fanciful, it's well documented and an assortment of bankers, newspaper owners and military heads had come to Lord Mountbatten to head up the provisional government and seek the approval of the Queen. They had been working night and day to undermine his government since it had come to office, with the promise of a strong assault on privilege. Not only that but the fools had convinced themselves that Wilson was working for the Soviet government: the British prime minister, not a particularly left-wing one by our standards, was supposedly working to bring the Soviet fleet to Portsmouth and send the Yankees and NATO packing along with international capitalism. The plotters believed it to the extent they were already testing out the organs of dual power, i.e. their power over the government's. The manoeuvres at Heathrow Airport and elsewhere were mini interdepartmental coups, over which neither Wilson the prime minister nor the cabinet had had any consultation or veto.

They need not have worried. Wilson was already backing down in the face of the powerful threats from the City. As time has gone by, though, it has become clearer, and apparently less and less fanciful, that he may actually have been considering his neck in physical rather than purely political terms. He had had to choose a side with the gun literally at his head. His working-class supporters then decided to administer a bullet of their own design, at the ballot box. On the far left we had been preparing for the coup, readying our side of this forthcoming civil war for a direct takeover of industry and general strike, not so much 'in defence of the elected government', although objectively that would have been I suppose the popular slogan, but in defence of and in furtherance of democracy. How far our side had managed to subvert enough sections of the armed forces wasn't tested, how far there were well-spoken civil servants and secret agents on our side never yet came out, but the massive abstention by regular Labour voters at the polls in the general election of June 1970 may have saved Wilson's life and certainly allowed Ted Heath to lead the Tory Party back to office and become prime minister.[27]

The incoming Tory government decided to build on Labour plans with attacks on welfare benefits. They also took the unusual step of bringing in the so-called Fair Rents Act. This compelled local councils to implement huge rent increases. It was to have the knock on effect of encouraging mass private landlords, like the National Coal Board, to also implement 'fair rents', in line with those imposed on neighbouring council tenants. The assault was to lead to the most bitter community resistance since the end of World War One, and in at least one council, at Clay Cross in Derbyshire, it brought about a stand by the municipal-socialist elected Labour members against central government dictates.

If Heath had thought he had come to office on the back of an anti-union tide he was to be proved mistaken and the mass strike wave and discontent rife during Wilson's period carried on regardless, into Heath's first couple of months, beginning with a dockers' strike which squeezed substantial payrises. A few months later in autumn of that year the pitmen launched a new offensive.

In the mines productivity had soared from under 25 cwt (1,270 kg) per man shift in 1951 to 45 cwt (2,286 kg) per man shift in 1970. Despite this, wages were steadily dropping in the national wages league for all industries. Taking the average weekly earnings for manufacturing industry as 100 in 1967, the miners' pay stood above average at 107, but by April 1971 this had slumped to 93. The position was absurd: productivity at that period had risen 20 per cent but income had actually fallen. A few months later in autumn of that year the pitmen launched a new offensive. They were substantially near the bottom of the pay league and as the wildcat action in the previous year had shown they wanted radical change. A 10 per cent payrise was all the NCB had come up with, a long way short of the substantial rises the miners were looking for. This led to a national strike ballot, but at that time the rule still required a two thirds majority in favour for official national action. Although a majority (55 per cent) was gained it was not enough to meet the terms of the rule. Following the 'failure' of the wages strike ballot came a backlash in the form of an unofficial strike of Yorkshire, Wales, Scotland and other pits in other areas, lasting a full four weeks. From the striking coalfields flying pickets were dispatched to all the others. The action, which was destined to stop the country, was derailed by a further ballot which accepted the NCB's revised offer of 12 per cent. The Union's National Executive Committee, which was badly unrepresentative of real and relative area membership strengths, voted to accept. The increases were taken however as demonstrations that twice in as many years higher pay awards had been wrung out of the Coal Board as a result of strike action or the threat of strike action.

Many other issues were proving flashpoints and miners were striking and picketing in many coalfields. Major industrial actions over issues central to miners were being launched. Tonnage lost through disputes exceeded 3 million for only the second time since Nationalisation, with the highest rates of loss in the

Doncaster area, South Wales, Scotland and Kent.

Fall-back rates for face trained craftsmen were disputed in Doncaster, as were fall-back rates for 'market men' in South Yorkshire. Even North Yorkshire, the more moderate of the areas, was at the forefront of this movement, launching unofficial actions, led by Kellingly's new Scottish secretary the communist Jimmy Miller. Jimmy had come down from Scotland with a fiery reputation, having been lodge secretary at the Michael pit, and his brand of communist activism, deploying flying pickets all over North Yorkshire and bringing collieries to a stand, must have been some shock to the more conciliatory Yorkshire comrades. .

TV DEBATE

I was contacted by another group of film-makers, this time the BBC and their radical filmmaker Philip Donellan. Philip was part of that oldtime, wartime, Communist Party team of actors, playwrights, radio journalists and TV documentarists. All of them great comrades of Ewan MacColl and their lass Peggy Seeger, rarely out of touch with Charles Parker, the great radio documentarist and inventor along with Ewan of the radio ballad. These were educated blokes, most of them spoke what I would have called posh, but their commitment to working people verged on reverence. Philip wanted to make a series called *Where Do I Stand*, an insight into the hotly held views of working folk, and he asked me, as editor of *The Mineworker* to be the subject of one of the key films. *A Man And His Ideas On Film*—that was the subtitle. It was 1971; Maureen, although wor bonny lass, still spoke with the distinctive twang of the Tyneside Grammar school. She was passionate socialist feminist and turned from bonny dimpled smile and those wonderful teeth to the snarl of a polished courtroom QC, cutting down all futile argument before her. By she was hell of a bonny, she'd fetch ducks off wa'ater, the lads at the pit said. For some days we shared the living room with cameras and crew, as they recorded dialogue and shot the drafting and production of *The Mineworker*. They were up with me for the day shift; it was most disconcerting to have folk around in wee hours, bad luck in the extreme as they were also there last thing. Frustrations became more frequent as my partyfied speech dumbfounded attempts at simple explanation of things. Phrases which were simple common sense to me, talk of 'the class', 'the bourgeois', 'capitalism', 'feudalism', 'surplus value and social labour' poured from my throat, like a tap turned on. It made perfect sense to me, but even Philip, once a disciple of the doctrine himself only now understood pidgin Marxism, so we talked to each other in a foreign tongue. The programme was going nowhere. On site Philip had managed to secure the confidence of the Hatfield management. He didn't tell them about me, and managed to get great shots of the lads going to work, the shafts, the lamp cabin, the baths. He had made great strides too with the local officials, Frank Clark and the Branch delegate Tom Mullanny. He was trying to set up a debate between the officials and the management, with me thrown in. He'd kidded them on that I was a bit part—a promise made when we had met at a conference to include me in a few shots of the film about the coal industry. All was set for the on-site debate, with the steam of the winder and the hoot of the buzzer and our debate, when Frank discovered they had been filming at my house for a week. Then the shit hit the fan. 'You can't pillock a pitman, lad,' Frank stabbed at the stammering producer. 'The BBC? And we are suppose to admire people like you for your honesty?' Oh he had them on the run. Mullanny chipped in: 'I'm too big a gun for the crowd scene!' Tom saw himself as national presidential material, and he was too. Oh dear, now it was a BBC Trotskyist anarchist conspiracy to seize the TV screens. To resolve the dialogue dilemma the crew ordered Phil and the co-producer (Sarah Boston) out for a pint while we, just the crew and me, discussed what the bliddy hell I was talking about. It worked, because of course, doon the pit I wasn't prone to lapsing into unintelligible Marxist-Leninistspeak and spoke to men, worker to worker, in images and sentences which resonated to reality. Without the producer present, relaxed over some beers and a pipe of baccy (which was still cool back then in 1970) we tossed it around, and came up with a viewable dialogue at last. The debate, after being banned from the Miners Welfare by the Branch secretary, actually took place in The Harvester, a new redbrick pub on the outskirts of Stainforth. My protagonists by this time were Billy Matthews and Danny Doneghue, local long-time members of the Communist Party. Our relations with the CP had been stormy to say the least. From our first arrival with slogan-splattered walls, to our declaration of the unofficial Haulage Workers' Committee, the appearance of *The Mineworker* and my presence at their left front meetings with Labour leftists, I was 'the Trot, loose cannon'. Worse of course I had blown the gaff by writing about Tom Mullanny the leftist Branch delegate, as a bosses' man, to Frank Watters. I didn't know Frank Watters was the influential 'kingmaker' on the fringes of the NUM, spying out 'the party candidates' for branches, for the Area Executive Committee, for the National Executive Committee and area and national leadership positions. He ran the CP in Yorkshire; nothing happened anywhere in the coalfield he was not aware of. My early attempts to do the party's work within the CP was foiled from word go, as left labourites and CPers closed ranks to repel the ultra-leftist hairy from up north. I had tried to demonstrate my ideologically sound past by telling them I was a former Newcastle YCLer, but the bastards wrote back and denied me existence! Mind they could have told them they expelled me and about a hundred others for dalliance with Trotskyism or in my case anarchism. Mullanny still called me an Anarchist-Trotskyist, a term which would have confused them back at Kronstadt in 1921, but had a certindiviknaawhatyeknaa? aboot it. I was widely known anyway as 'Danny the Red' so it was hardly some undercover work, what with the paper being sold every two or three weeks round the canteen and at the wages office.

So the debate took place. A clash of visions, a clash of generations, a clash of optimism and analysis, it stands to this day as a monument to my absolutely conviction of the correctness of our line. Politically correct by no means, not in modern terms, I talk of black men and slant-eyed peasants, but I talk of them as beloved comrades not in terms of abuse. I talk of the rallying of the class worldwide as well as the party line on the pre-emptive strike; oh, yes I had become a convert to that perspective. That at a crucial stage in the international class war played out between 'the workers' states' and imperialism, the workers' states should move to the final settlement of accounts, and launch the nuclear war against US imperialism and all its nuclear allies. I had gone from mortal fear of the bomb, from paralysis at the very threat of its use, to embracing it as simply one more step in the class war. 'Our nuclear bombs' would of course devastate the cities and military targets of imperialism, millions would die, millions of our fellow workers in the belly of the beast, but humanity would survive, humanity would be freed from the crippling yoke of imperialism and capitalism, and arise blinking into a new dawn, a planet in the hands of the workers, who would sweep aside the bureaucrats and remnants of capitalism in all its forms and install a new age for the earth. An age of communism. The film was to cause a storm, not least from irate complaints to the BBC from the Branch officials and the NCB, and then when the rushes were seen old Beeb decided the programme was just so red, it needed extra balance. So instead of three episodes it got four, the fourth one being my antithesis, a forelock-touching gamekeeper who voiced such thoughts as 'It's not for the likes of us to question the likes o' them', and 'There's some that's bred for wealth and some that's bred for toil' or something to the effect. It would be a good two thirds of a year before the film hit the TV screens. Much would happen in between.

This was 1970; the left was on the ascendancy. This had been illustrated by the election of my mate, the left Labour Lawrence Daly as NUM general secretary, but we weren't having it all our own way. Joe Gormley defeated Mick Magahey for NUM president. The pitmen thought Red Mick, communist, and leader of the Scottish miners was a step too far. They thought Joe would balance our Lawrence, perhaps. As it turned out Lawrence was more Labour than left, but we weren't to know that just then.

The NUM HQ stood in London at 205 Euston Road, round the corner from 160 North Gower Street, which as it happened was the home of the Agitprop Bookshop. I encountered the two at the same time. What I think none of us realised, although I am certain they did, was that this was opposite the HQ of the state's secret political service, MI5, although none of us discovered that until decades of surveillance later, they probably had extensions to our phones, in fact needed only to open their windows to earwig on the NUM and the urban guerillas. Lawrence had recently been elected our leftwing general secretary. He was the start of a wind of change that would blow away the cobwebs from the Union, and in the process bring down a government. Lawrence was an intellectual, a man thoroughly well read. He knew his literature, he knew his political theory, he was a lover of art and poetry. On the TV book club intellectual discussion programme, given over to a panel of writers and critics, Lawrence was a regular member of the team, analysing books, plays, poems, prose. That he was a coalminer, and leader of our Union was a great source of pride for me. But he was a fish out of water down here. At the end of his shift in the office, he would stroll round to the pub on North Gower Street and after a few jars regale the scattered commuters with fine renditions of pit songs and rebel songs. The Foggy

Dew, commemorating the 1916 Easter Rising, was one of his best performances. Head back, standing up, arms outstretched he sang: 'While Britannia's sons with their long-range guns/Sailed in from the foggy dew.' An unlikely team we made: the comrades from Agitprop, militant, anarchist, some to be the bedrock of armed struggle, me and Lawrence. By, we solved some problems around that table. Lawrence was a most undogmatic and open-minded man, but he was lonely for Scotland and the company of miners. London kills Union officials we always said, and it was eating Lawrence alive. On one occasion Lawrence dragged me back to his house, rather our house, since it was one which belonged to the NUM. He had called it Glencraig after the pit he worked at in Scotland. As we staggered through the leafy suburb singing 'Red Fly The Banners Oh!', the curtains twitched and one got the impression Lawrence was not the kind of resident by any means who usually abided here. Their lass was non too pleased. I was one of a number of mining waifs and strays he brought back from time to time. While Lawrence was having his ear thumped upstairs I was sitting, in the lush wood-tiled floor of the sumptuous living room, all wood and ticking clocks and books and souvenirs of delegations and trips. An old raggedy dog stood at the entrance to the room, wagging its bum in joy. 'Come on then,' I called, and it skidded in its excitement trying to gain traction on the polished floor, sliding across to me, and nuzzling into my hands for a big pat, when Mrs Daly arrived down stairs.

'You devil!' she cried. 'You know you are not allowed in there!'

Both me and the dog stood up at once, though it was the poor old dog who got bollocked. 'Ee,' says I, 'he just come in.'

'Traitor!' telepathed the dog.

Actually, breakfasting with the family the next morning they were all fish out of water, they all missed Scotland and all missed the company of pit folk and being where real life was. One of the lads was a left Scot Nat at that time, and I couldn't blame him for that; his politics were not exactly going down a treat at the comfortable southern school he was at. I must have stayed for the weekend because I recall our loud conversations in the country pub, about strikes and rebellions and history, drawing down disdaining remarks about 'full-time well-paid troublemakers'.

'That's us,' said Lawrence.

'Na, that's you,' said I.

The wage or the house we paid Lawrence wasn't in question. Lawrence was a Scottish communist collier through and through, and a sudden change in income and venue wasn't going to change his side of the class line. It didn't, but his isolation and class loneliness probably cost him his health. Lawrence did in the end move to the right; on the crucial issue of 'the social contract' he and Gormley switched the Union's stated opposition to the collaborationist scheme to one of support and threw the Union's votes behind the Labour government's project. It was to draw a withering criticism from me in the pages of *The Miner*. Lawrence responded in person in the next edition with a double-page defence against the criticisms. That the national secretary had deemed to cross swords publicly with me, a person of no particular position, demonstrated just how deeply he felt the critique. He was more than aware that it was the rank and file who had put him there, through a combine of unofficial agencies represented by people just like me, and, it might be said, in opposition to Gormley. That movement had not yet finished its work. Lawrence chose the wrong side in the end, and was as far as his health was concerned in the wrong place. He became caught in that pincer, but I actually didn't discover to what extent he was a casualty of it until nearly the end of my tale.

RIGHTS—WHAT RIGHTS?
15 July 1971. First of the Red Army Fraction Petra Schelm[28] dies in shoot out with German police, following attacks upon banks, and the judiciary.

9 August 1971. The mask of democracy is ripped away, internment introduced in the six occupied counties of Ulster. The British state give the go-ahead to the Northern Ireland prime minister Faulkner to take any semblance of democratic rights from 'the Province' and brought in detention, arrest without charge, trial or guilt. In the early hours of morning the armed police and British troops in full military occupation regalia swarmed into republican and mixed areas and lifted hundreds of men from early teenagers to the middle-aged. They were out to break the back of the People's Democracy, which was campaigning for full civil rights for the Catholic minority, and to emasculate the Civil Rights Association in particular. They wanted to stem the tide of democratic struggle by taking away the 'rights' that so far existed or at least were thought to have existed. But what are 'rights'? Are they enshrined on some old lump of parchment in a wooden box with a gold key? Can you go to this box and take out the 'rights'? You can't, and if these rights can be taken away, without your knowledge, your consultation never mind your consent, did you ever have them? Who can take them away if they are truly yours? It was clear these 'rights' did not belong to us, any of us, in Ireland or Britain. The internment camps, the barbed wire, the sentry boxes, the knock on the door in the night, the scream in the street, the body being bundled into the police vehicle or the British army truck, it was a scene visited on many parts of the Empire previously. Now it was in our back yard. 450 'suspects' were rounded up, the explosion of protest on the street was matched by the Angry Brigade's explosion at the Army Recruitment Centre, on London's Holloway Road.

COMRADES
By the autumn of 1971 news was coming in that Lin Piao, the old diehard leader of the left of the Chinese revolution and an inspiration to the so called 'Cultural Revolution'—in reality a real workers political revolution—had died under mysterious circumstances. Mao, to whom Lin had been apparently devoted, suddenly was accusing him of 'Trying to halt the adoption of a new foreign policy.' The USA had surprisingly, in the middle of its life-and-death struggle in Vietnam, started to make overtures to China. We wondered if the two were linked. The internal revolution had posed in stark, red terms real workers' and

peasants' democracy; the party apparatus was loosing control. Mao, although an icon, was loosing actual control, and turned to the centre of the party for assistance. The Red Guards were stood down and disarmed, the red communes of Peking and Shanghai modelled on the Paris Commune were dissolved, Lin became 'a running dog of Soviet imperialism' and the purge started, in the process of which, having used the centre to defeat the left in outright struggle, Mao then dissolved the centre through use of the apparatus and bureaucratic strangleholds. In 1972 Richard Nixon visited China. Nixon—the man most vilified among progressive Americans and the antiwar movement. China's foreign and domestic policy started the road to the right. What Mao's role was during this time was unclear. We could never believe at first swallow that Mao could betray the workers' revolution, few could believe Stalin would, even fewer would ever believe Lenin could. Some never would believe it, even yet. Years later at the TUC Conference in Blackpool, we were having a long drinking evening in one of the hotels on the sea front. In our company was Lo Chia-Huan, the first secretary of the Chinese Embassy in London and two of his assistants. Me and Lo had had long discussions on the Cultural Revolution, on the Red Guard, on the turmoil, and Lo emphatically denounced the whole thing as a ultra left deviation, a distraction from the great tasks of the Chinese revolution and its standing in the world.

Later as he got a wee bit more drunk his true thoughts developed: 'They make me come back to China, make me and family work in fields, I am administrator not farmer, I work in water up to knees,' he said bitterly. 'Ah-ha,' I says, 'So here is why you were against the revolution, they took you from your nice London office and flat, the big cars and nice meals and brought you home to the people who were paying for it all and demanded that you too contribute.' My opinions didn't go down well as I recall, but the junior staff laughed heartily and nodded vigorously.

THE TROUBLE WITH TED

The biggest source of conflict was to be Heath's plans to hold down wages and set limitations on advances of pay and conditions. The 'state', through its massive nationalised industries, was the country's biggest employer. In 1970 for example there were just fewer than 300,000 miners in 300 pits. If the pay restraint strategy was to work, wages in the state sector had to be screwed down to set an example to private industry.

As the biggest employer they would have to set the firm example of holding the line. They prepared themselves for a head-on confrontation with the big well-organised sections of state industry, confident that after the thrashing the press and TV had already given the power workers in the electricity generating industry, 'public opinion' could be mobilised behind government barricades and inflict a defeat on the state-sector unions. As luck would have it or otherwise, the postmen were first to walk into the firing line. They were already low-paid, and although well organised had no tradition of militancy. In line with local-authority manual workers the UPW put in a 15 per cent pay demand. The local-authority workers had won. The postal workers however were offered a stinging 8%. In the January of 1971 they called an indefinite strike. Forty-four days later it ended with a marginally improved pay offer. With that one down, car workers backed off from action and Heath lined up another group of state employees, this time the miners.

Over the previous fifteen years miners' wages had dropped by 25 per cent. Academics had demonstrated what we already knew in our pockets. Calculations which involved price movements, taxes and social benefits showed the average mineworker with a wife and two children had in 1957 had a net real income 22 per cent above that of his counterpart in 1969, who in the latter year was paid 2 per cent less than an average manufacturing worker.

Over the previous three years overall productivity had risen by 15 per cent, but miners' wages were lower in real terms in '71 than in '67. Every miner would require a £5 per week rise just to get back to the 1967 position. One miner in ten was earning less than £20 per week GROSS.

The Union's paper *The Miner*, which printed thousands of extra copies to distribute to the public, reproduced a miner's paynote across its inside pages showing a gross payment of £18.00 per week. It showed a take-home of £15.54. 88,000 mineworkers were taking home wages in the same category.

EWAN MACCOLL AND PEGGY SEEGER

John Reevy was one of the toon characters, a former heavyweight boxer, with the squashed nose and bullet head. He had starred in *The Fight Game*, Ewan MacColl's radio ballad. The radio ballad was a new artform elaborated by MacColl, Seeger and Charles Parker. People's voices were recorded, then the recordings were placed in the context of their lives and illustrated with songs written from their words and set to music. Most famous for us was *The Big Hewer*, the dynamic story of the miners, but this had led us on to other works. *The Fight Game* was about boxers and John sang and talked. John struck a menacing though playful stance on stage, always with a risqué sang, always with some pithy political satire. He had opened a folk club in one of the most unlikely places in Newcastle—the Victoria and Comet, nicknamed the Spit and Vomit, and not just because it rhymed. Though once a major luxury hotel, its bar clientele tended to be drunks and down and outs positioned as it was fernant the Central Station. The floor of the bar was laid with marble which contained small groves for swilling the spilt beer out at lowse, often as not blood and ale ran along the little lanes as the barmen brushed the place out. John's club was on the very top floor, maybe seven flights of stairs. The room must have been a luxury suite at one time: chaise-longs and armchairs still adored the place and one could relax in magnificent splendour and take in the crack. Top of the bill were Ewan MacColl and Peggy Seeger. This I couldn't miss. MacColl had been an inspiration to my political development, the background sound to visions of class, history and progress. Our struggle glorified in verse and the power of voice. And what a voice. They called him 'the red megaphone'. Me and Fred Higgins agreed to hitch up, since we never ever had much coin; Maureen poor soul who also loved them, didn't fancy the prospect of the long hitch hyme. We had done it von nie every weekend when we first moved down, but the novelty of standing in buckets of rain for hours had worn off. We managed actually without a deal of problems. This was the first time ever I had seen these live, and they were actually larger than life, an odd couple though, Peggy—a wee doll of a girl with red rosy cheeks, and a tiny miniskirt. Her legs crossed, she sat strumming with perfect precision a dulcimer. Ewan—braw, buff, solid, bearded; voice resonating like a bass drum through his body and out through the room.[29]

Spellbinding. Peggy had come from one of the most famous 'folk' families of the USA. Peter her elder brother had written most of the songs which dominated our CND youth, though we didn't know it then. Peggy was however a musician in her own right.[30]

At the interval, I of course set off round the room selling my revolutionary literature, *The Mineworker* I think. Ewan straight away called me over and took a paper and talked avidly about the miners and making *Big Hewer*. They were genuinely pleased that we were present and had actually hitched all the way up to see them. They promised to take us back to Donny in the morn on their way back doon sooth. True to their word they did.

We never stopped talking from getting in the car. The Soviet Union—Ewan and Peggy's experiences were eye-openers, not because I didn't know in theory what had happened there, but because Ewan painted the scene in colour not black and white. They had been guests of the Soviet Writers' and Artists' Union. Politically Ewan had thought Stalin a genuine and dedicated revolutionary so he wasn't overimpressed with the post-Stalin situation as it was. The longer they stayed, the more they heard and seen the worse it got. Sholokov (*Quiet Flows The Don* etc.) did not impress, though he tried to. He took them back to his dacha, somewhere on a cliffside. Not only was the entrance to it via a liftshaft hewed through rock, but there was a permanent lift attendant to operate it, just in case the famous people's writer felt like an odd visit to his coastal retreat. The walls and floor were panelled in rare Russian woods.

Sholokov was keen to show off his wealth to a very unimpressed Peggy. He took a little fur coat from his wardrobe and showed it to Peggy, thinking she would swoon with excitement. 'You don't know what that is do you?'

Peggy had confessed that she did not.

It had been made from the pelts of some rare Siberian creature (whose name I can't recall). 'It takes a generation of Siberian fur trappers to trap enough of these animals to make this jacket,' he said with a flourish.

Peggy and Ewan were horrified, not at the slaughter of the wee furry animals—Ewan hated that kind of liberal sentiment—but at the wage labour exploitation of so many hardworking people engaged in a lifetime of toil and misery for such crude bourgeois vanity.

When it came to the last day of the conference, foreign visitors were allowed to speak. Ewan strode to the platform and give them both barrels. He told them they had less in common with the people than many bourgeois writers in the west.

Sholokov countered that British artists couldn't understand how close to the people Soviet writers were. 'We are forced to work among ordinary workers for at least three weeks in a year,' he had said with pride.

Their tales and encounters went on and on—Cuba, China, revolutions in which they thought they'd seen the honest transparency of genuine socialist construction. We argued over the theory, which I had described as 'mad', of renewed inter-imperialist rivalry leading to war. Ewan thought this no so mad. I ventured the Party line, that all imperialisms were subsumed into US imperialism, which represented capitalism on a world scale. The threat facing the world was world nuclear class war, with imperialism on one hand and the workers' states on the other, an inter-imperialist war was unthinkable in this period.

So it went on, history, economics, unions, Stalin, Trotsky, Hitler, the war, fascism, Spain, the anarchists, the IWW, US imperialism, coal mining, Salford, theatre and art until we arrived in Donny before we knew it. But more than that, when I told them about Maureen and not being able to get up to see them, they dropped Fred off and ran me all the way to Dunscroft. I couldn't believe it when they came in with me, carrying all their instruments, but there, in our living room, Ewan and Peggy sang and played highlights from their show, just for Maureen. That's how genuine they were. Maureen and Peggy became correspondents and Ewan and I debated politics from that day on. I was proud to have made such wonderful and genuine friends. We wrote almost every week, on great events and small, and our paths were to cross time and again as the guns of the class came to bare in the rolling sea of humanity.

5
PIT WORK

Down in the dusty roadways of 22's long and unloved tailgate a new contraption was taking form. For the first time, machine mining was coming to caunch work. This was the dawn of the boom ripper. There was a cutting head like those on the coal-cutting machine, but smaller, on a long extended arm, which pushed forward, or ranged across the rip. Hydraulic legs on the back propelled it forward. No more boring the rip, and greatly reduced jiggering. Oddly, we felt, sort of cheated. Rippers had long believed they ought to be back on contract. We weren't power loaders, we were hand fillers, pack builders, tunnel makers, arch constructors, borers and drillers. We were not machine men. We felt our effort was disproportionate to the tasks of colliers. We should have an added financial incentive, perhaps be on contract. I confess that I missed the beneficial effects of the National Power Loading Agreement (NPLA) completely. I didn't see the worth of the national pay-bargaining it engendered, the centralising and solidarising impact of making all face men's wages dependent on national negotiation and national union unity. Instead, at this instance, we felt they were giving us this machine instead; we would rather have the money. I felt so aggrieved about it I even wrote a poem about it and stuck it up on the union notice board. I submitted it for *The Mineworker* too, but the comrades in the party who always reviewed its content thought it didn't correspond to the high political motivation and orientation of the journal. Just as weel really; history would ultimately have made such an article a political bollock and a half.

So here we were with this monster in the gate, all teeth and tearing power. Sparrow was taking his deputy's tickets. Mitch and Chappie looked at it suspiciously, as if some wild beast had just been let loose in their back gardens. Driving it would fall to me. It was pure trial and error at first since nobody had seen one; even the crew who put it together had never fired it in anger and were not caunchmen. Within a week, this was MY job. I could let the bugger rip, which of course was its job, but I mean let it loose in the belly of the caunch, no more pulling my arms oot with that jigger yee bastard. The problem with it was the dust—thick massive clouds of stone dust in a great continuous wave, streaming from the yielding strata. Within days, I had fitted 'a wander hose', a separate high-pressure hosepipe with a mass of spray cans on the end. Another bloke would walk up to just outbye the cutting head, which also fired massive jets of water into the rip, and direct the spray straight into the dust, deadening it and at least making a path of clear vision to see where the head was operating. Together we would stand (sitting reduced concentration somehow), in waves of fine spray and fogs of stone dust, till within two hours we and everything else were covered in fine layers of concrete. Though we wore plastic goggles, they soon clouded over, and rapidly became caked in muddy stone.

We were real stone men now. Though I had resented the machine coming I made it my own; I heard an overman comment I could cut the top off an egg with it. Once, the shift before me had had a heavy fall of ground, and big rocks jammed the arms of the machine. It seemed crippled for a time by the rocks which had felled themselves before the teeth could deal with them. I now knew this machine. I could coax it to ease the great wallers back up the side, and bit by bit by pulling the head back, and shortening the turret, to drag them back over the arches, much to the surprise of the gathered ranks of gaffers. In April 1970, the High Hazel 69s unit was finally shedding its fault, which had moved down the full length of the face choking everyone, whilst the chock legs were being changed bit by bit, to provide shorter legs in a thinning seam. The management were looking for 7500 tons a week from this face. My old diehard 22s had been shortened to 180 yards to loose the fault, working two shifts. Down in the Barnsley seam B04s was proving a disappointment, with bad roof; the massive modern chock system was to be supplemented by wooden roof bolts. The face gradient was 1 in 2, with the massive chocks being provided with 'anti-topple rams'. Just by way of good news H21's in the Hatfield Colliery newsletter of April 1970 the manager Mr I.C. McGregor reports:

> This unit has negotiated some of the most difficult faulting ever worked at Hatfield and is currently working an up throw fault parallel to the face varying in throw from 3 ft to 7 ft. The roof conditions in the hade of the fault are extremely difficult, timber and steel canopies having been erected as the strata is worked through. The geological evidence now available suggests that we have normal fault free coal beyond the fault now being negotiated, if this is the case the face has a life of 500 yards, approximately 6 months. The replacement unit H23's is on schedule and should be ready for production about October of this year.

Meantime H68s, which was meant to be a bonus or sneak development, was encountering faulting which would delay its opening for a further ten months. What all of this illustrates is that mining in the seventies was mining. We mined the reserves we had, through difficult conditions of faults and throws and steep gradients. You didn't walk away from millions of tonnes of coal, or write them off as 'too difficult'.

In August 1970 23's opened up. Through the sheer luck of the union's job rotation priority system I land as the first man on the first team of the tail gate; I'm the chargeman now! This will be my team. Wonders of all wonders, Jim Shipley is on with me. With this version of the boom ripper, they had tried to develop 'a slusher'. This was a greet lang wire rope, attached to a kind of metal sledge, back and front, via a motor under the machine, which fed out from one side, down the open pack hole, round a pulley wheel and back via a return wheel in the other pack. What a contraption. Its aim was to save the backbreaking toil of packing, well not really, its aim was to ensure that the rips kept pace with the machine cutting coal on the face, by speeding up packing operations. You had to cut the rip with the boom, and while lumps were falling, machine number two would throw levers which pulled the bucket, with its snow plough front, through the pile of stone, and ram it yards down the pack into an anchor chock. Then you reversed the levers and it came back out again, sliding through the accumulated stone this time, by means of a big hole in the bucket at its other end for the return run.

I well recall nearly killing poor Barty Croft, the Sunderland chock fitter with this contraption. When the anchor chock was broken, perhaps the hoggers snapped with all the whamming too and fro. He had to dig all that end out, make a space big enough to work in, drag his tools along and get working. He was several yards down the end of the pack, while we had been stood for a time and debating the ongoing slaughter in Vietnam and the resistance of workers, manning anti-aircraft guns even though the murderous bombers were miles out of range. Jim had been saying that if the USSR was serious it would be equipping the Vietnamese with missiles and radar which could detect the bombers and blast them out of the sky.

Suddenly the slusher man rapped 'off'. So I shouted 'Here's off!' and pulled the power button back out. So Jim jumped to his handles and charging down the pack hole came the slusher. Barty watched in horror as a mini-mountain of stone and rocks started to advance toward him. There was no safety device, no lock-out in the pack and no way out. Through abandoning everything he had and squeezing himself to the size of a stick, and projected by the force of the rock, he was pushed, cut and bleeding, through a space in the anchor chock and out the other side. Too late, the shouting and waving of lamps was seen, and realised with ashen faces. 'What must have befell Barty?' we both said at once.

We didn't have lang to wait, as Barty clutching a big spanner with death in his eyes, tore through the chock line, and emerged screaming into the gate. In truth, there was not time to stand and reason this out, and me and Jim retreated some steps down the gate backwards, pronouncing our deepest apologies.

'Thou's did it di-liberate!' he yelled. 'Nor we didn't, why would we?' 'Yee fuckin' red bastards, Ah'll kill tha.'

Fortunately for us, his knees were knackered, and he was quite a torn-up mess, and was forced to sit down just where his energy finished, and was even unable to stop us helping him, and getting him a drink. I think we also were forced to get him another pocket watch, as his was crushed in his waistcoat which he had hung in the path of the bucket.

I never liked the damn machine. For a start, each turn over, as everything was rammed forward, you had to unbolt the wire rope, full of broken threads and sharp pieces of metal, from the slusher. Then when the ram over was complete somebody had to crawl down between the completed pack and the chock line, dragging the rope with them, several yards on their belly, though an obstacle course of rock and stone, then thread it through the return wheel, and crawl back up again. Only I was small enough to get down the bliddy pack hole. Barty was a character, heart of gold, broad Wearside dialect. Like many a northerner not only did he often get the English wrong;, the logic often came out arse side up as well. He loved the crack and would set the conversation away. 'Eeh lad, did thou see that black Ford Zeppelin in the car park?' 'Alsatians? Alsatians is the most vital dog there is man.' But his masterpiece of mis-thought I will never forget. In a heated discussion on crime and punishment he ventured 'Yee knaa, the snap in them prisons these days, is that gud, anyone whey bracks oot, wants locking up!'

Mind, he wasn't the only one with the northern aptitude to get the English wrang. Les, a native of Chester-Le-Street, member of the Branch Committee, militant and amusing, could none the less coin the wrang phrase. His new neighbour had moved in and leaning over the fence assured them, 'And yiv ney need to worry aboot yer strawberries. I deen like them and wor lass is anaemic to them.' He later described his efforts at putting together 'one o them sexual sheds in the garden'.

'JE SUIS BELGE'[31]

The party comrades were establishing a similar united front in Belgium with the miners to the one they had here with us. The party in Belgium was quite strong, especially round the industrial steel and coal towns,. They were running in elections, and the walls of the cities screamed: 'Pont 9—UNIQUE DES PARTIS OUVRIERS REVOLUTIONNAIRE P.O.R. (TROTSKYSTE).' Me and Jim, who was now my number one Mineworker member, were invited on a speaking tour of industrial Belgium. Jim was young, long frizzy hair, bearded, now smoked a pipe, dressed in denim from heed ti toe, wore pit boots. Hard uncompromising Donny twang, never been out of Yorkshire in his life let alone the country.

Among the party comrades things were tough; they didn't speak English and we didn't speak French or Dutch. But it wasn't long before we were in the midst of miners, chemical plant workers and steel workers; here communication was direct. Jim in a crowded bar in Charleroi, workers had crowded in from factories and foundries across the way to hear me speak. The banner of the Mineworkers" Internationale was draped across the fireplace, and our comrades from the Belgium mines were to start the meeting talking about their struggles and ours, and international solidarity.

Jim was busting for a piss. 'Dain't start yet, pal,' he urged. 'Where's bog?'

'Ah deen knaa Jim, ask some bugger.' 'Aah excuse me, pardon'— he thought that sounded a bit French but didn't realise most of this crowd were Dutch. 'Toilet?' He hunched his shoulders to show this was a question. Blank expressions. 'Piss?'

'Aah piss!' they all roared, and cheered and pointed to the bog.

Not for the first time I discovered common Saxon words were the best way to communicate with the European workers, the Germanic ones anyway. In Holland I usually filled any gap in my Dutch with a Geordie dialect word, which nine times out of ten worked. I was on. I spoke of the recent unofficial struggle in the mines, the struggle to recapture the union for the members and for action, the need of rank-and-file committees, the role of the Mineworkers" Internationale, the struggle worldwide against imperialism, the common fight of workers across the globe, the unity of the European workers, for a socialist workers' Europe based upon democratic workers' councils and committees, a Soviet Socialist Europe! The translator, a tall Dutch miner turned academic, spoke as I spoke, shouting as I shouted, looking round as I looked round; he was a mirror image. It certainly struck a note with the audience who leapt to their feet and cheered.

We ended with a spontaneous rendition of the Internationale, sung with such gusto and pride it near made me cry. The bar room rattled to the refrain: 'So comrades, come rally/And the last fight let us face/The Internationale unites the human race.' After the meeting, crowds milled round. I sat with Desire, the leader of the Zwartsburg–Limburg Miners Federation. 'I affiliate to your Mineworkers' Internationale,' he says. 'You'll affiliate to us?' 'Ya, all the Zwartsburg–Limburg miners.' 'How many's that, like?' '25,000.' 'Hmm, the Mineworkers' Internationale is an idea at present Desire. Maybe we should affiliate to you.' 'How many members you have?'

'Well, all together, hmm, 24.' '24. 24,000?' 'Na, 24, but lots of miners read the paper.' They laugh. And say in Dutch '24. We affiliate when you have thousands of British miners, ja?'

Meantime, Jim was wading through the same half-pint of yellow sparkling Amstel beer he had had all night. The landlord asked what's up, didn't the bearded comrade in blue like beer?

Na its not that—he only drinks Guinness at home and he's lost without it.

'Guinness,' they say, 'Guinness,' and out of a special cabinet in the bar comes a big old-fashioned bottle of black-as-night Guinness. It had been a point of speculation and mystery for the whole bar for many years, surely nobody could drink beer so black and foul-looking? Jim could have this bottle, this one surviving bottle. It was opened with majesty, and Jim looked in anticipation as he poured it into a glass, and the crowd looked on.

He took a deep swallow, and I could see his throat stop in mid-gulp. His hand steadied, and he slowly brought the glass down again, the crowd all cheered.

'Gud, ja?'

'Ja, good,' says Jim.

'Drink it then,' says I.

'This needs time to drink,' he announced as I noticed his face going an odd colour. The bottle had been got as part of a special consignment to give to the troops as they liberated Belgium from the Nazis, so this was a special thank-you to any British troops who might come by. This was the only survivor. Except it hadn't, really. Half the bottle had crystallised and turned to sugar.

Still the crowd looked on, so Jim, hardened pit lad that he was, downed the bugger and waved as we marched to the door; he was retching slightly. Driving back to the party's house that night, Jim had another shock, he had fallen asleep in the passenger side of the front, and awoke on the motorway in what looked like the driver's seat, the wheel being on the opposite side of course. He woke with a start and thought he was driving the car.

6
RUSKIN COLLEGE

On the academic front there were a number of routes to go. First off was the Joint Matriculation Board exam. This was to establish you as as good as the kids from skuel with their various passes and papers. Pass these exams and you could apply to all the universities on the Joint Mat list. The other was to try for Ruskin, and do your two years' diploma course which would then gain you entry almost anywhere with a year knocked off the university course, thus taking four years for a degree plus a diploma. Very good for those who liked collecting awards. Or you could just apply direct to some of the universities as a mature entrant. I was to try all three.

The Joint Matriculation Exam was a nightmare. I had intended to do Politics and Economics for a BSc, and hopefully get into Sheffield. The economics paper was, whey, the drawing kind of economics, formulae and graphs and all that silly code which really I had only touched on. Nowt in there about surplus value (the fact that your wages only account for a fraction of the value of your contribution to the production process) or anything else I could wax lyrical about in Marxianese. Politics? Sure I had strong views, but these were constitutional questions, and questions of procedure, local government reforms. Ney idea really. The maths paper I expected to fail, and, well, English? I still didn't know what half the terms meant, and I still didn't know the alphabet, not straight through in succession. The interview board was also very smug, very harsh. I think I rubbed them up the wrang way. I didn't really need telling I wouldn't be gaan to Sheffield. I had also applied to Hull. Hull offered a course in Politics and South-East Asian Studies. Wow, what a combination and right up my alley I thought. *The Mineworker* had established quite a correspondence around the world. One of these had been with the Publicity Department in Hanoi; they had been sending me their excellent *Vietnamese Studies* publications, and as they went along other Vietnamese stories, histories and cultural books. This was personal too; they often put in little notes 'To Dave and the comrade mineworkers' and some other remarks which just added that human touch and made us feel living touchable comrades across the world. I had also been taking *Peking Review* as they called it then, a shiny Chinese publication showing the wonders of the Chinese people's revolution, and the changing state of politics if only by implication (for example, the individual pictured on the front cover as 'Close comrade in arms Lin Piao' becomes in later issues 'A running dog of Soviet imperialism'). Anyway between the two, and the countless overlaps into Laos, Korea and Cambodia whose governments' publications I also occasionally got, I guessed I knew at least as much as any school-leaver. The interview was a great success.

We talked and talked and talked. This wasn't staged, not what they had actually planned, but my being a coal miner, a communist, an activist took us off on tangents all over the place. The South-East Asia side had opened up with my review of the current US invasions and activities across the continent, but when they told me we would be doing more cultural questions and religious areas, well that opened up my deep interest in Buddhism. Our discussions were friendly and sound, to the point where they looked at each other and just said 'OK—you're in; we are giving you an unconditional acceptance.' My heart near burst, I could have cried. The smile never left my face throughout the journey from Hull to Stainforth, retracing the journey I would be making every day now for three years. 'God, I will be studying Thai, or Vietnamese think of that.' Maureen was ecstatic. This was ideal. I could live at home, travel to university, work all my holidays at the pit, supplement my grant. The best of all worlds. The joy didn't last. A week later I received a letter apologising but rescinding the offer. I was 21, too young for a 'mature student' entry. The logic was I was still young enough to go and sit A Levels and get in like the rest of them. I was devastated.

My interview for Ruskin took me on the long, convoluted train journey to Oxford and then in a taxi up to Headington Hall, the college's first-year building. A great manorial edifice with some ancient and modern outbuildings which were the student accommodation. Here I had decided to study history if I got the chance. My interview took me before the college history tutors: Henry Pelling, whose books we had used on the day-release class, Victor Tredwell, and, beaming at the end, with his rook-black hair flopping across his face, Raph Samuel. In the chair was the principle Mr Billy Hughes, an ageing kindly-looking former Labour MP (although I didn't know that at the time or I might just have reacted to questions about parliament and constitution with a wee bitty mer restraint).

Competition for these places was tough; the interview would be no pushover. Despite this my politics blurted out at the rate of a machine gun, and suppressed any suggestion at liberalism, or plurality, or parliamentary importance. The political process was a manifestation of the international class war unfolding around the globe, obviously.

On history Mr Tredwell asked me, 'Have you ever read any formal history?'

'Hmm, no,' I confessed, feeling rather dejected, I didn't think I had. Then it struck me: 'Oh except, *The History of The Russian Revolution* by Leon Trotsky.' Raph was delighted and sat his head on one side like an interested Labrador. 'Gosh, Dave, all three volumes?' 'Whey, aye.' Then it started to come back, my day release stuff: 'Oh, and [E. P. Thompson's] *The Making of the English Working Class*, and Cole and Postgate, *The Common People* ... ' On reflection I had read quite a lot of history. 'Anything not connected to the class war?' asked Victor Tredwell now puffing interestedly on his pipe. 'Well, only various histories of the Royal Navy, and Nelson.' 'Well now ... ' And we jawed away about battles and boats, until Mr Hughes announced: 'Sorry gentlemen we've gone way over the interview time. We have to let Mr Douglass get his train.'

I walked out of that room feeling in my heart, I had cracked it, and I had. Raph told me later that the dogmatic RWP spiel had nearly lost me it: like why would I want to go there? I knew it all already, and why would I study bourgeois politics when the class war was braying on the door? Actually they were good questions—I had asked myself them, I had been challenged by Tom and the other Tyneside comrades as to why was I going? Good God we were on the verge of a nuclear war, the final settlement of accounts with imperialism and I was taking a sabbatical to Oxford? At the pit too, but only among certain cynical and hostile Communist Party members, they warned that I would sell out, and we wouldn't see me again. On the contrary, I had counselled, in line with other class fighters before me, Geordie Harvey for one, I would study, learn what I could and return to the pits to continue in whatever capacity the miners wanted me, that had been the tradition of miners who went into full-time education, you came back, to the community, to the Union, to the pit, to put whatever you had learned back at their disposal. I did not know at that time how stormy George's years at the college had been or the means by which he 'graduated'.

I was accepted. Actually it was the second time I had been accepted. The first time Follonsby Lodge had put me forward, and I had been selected by the Durham Area of the NUM as their potential student, I was 17, and it was right in the middle of our plans to elope to Scotland, so I had withdrawn. Would it all have worked out still, if I had went to Ruskin then, and Maureen had gone to art college, perhaps nearer home? Would we have stayed in love though apart at that stage, in the middle of the sexy Sixties with all that temptation and my all-absorbing jealousy? Who knows. I oft time reflect on it. But this was now. I would enter Ruskin, while Maureen would man the base at home, and distance would never separate us, that was our absolute conviction. Amazingly Fred and Ron Parr my fellow miners off the day-release course were also accepted, so we were three pit moggies in the City of Spires. I received my acceptance letter on 15 May 1970, to start on 6 October.

I was to be based at the Rookery, right in the front of the building upstairs, overlooking the entrance, the little field, the trees. A massive though ancient bedroom, in a massive old mansion, which smelt of books and furniture polish and occasionally the dinner cooking down in the dining hall. My first memories of the place were being awoken rudely by the clatter of buckets, and cacophony of the female cleaners, who had the most bizarre knack of being able to send and receive speech at the same time and all together. They all talked, out loud as if to themselves, at once, but then also in conversation all at once, no turns, simultaneously. Every morning was the same. An alarm clock wasn't needed with these ladies around at 7.30 a.m. without fail.

In the big lecture hall at Headington this year's intakes were gathered for the AGM of the Ruskin Students' Association. It was also by way of an introduction of students, to each other and to the various student committee and bodies. Each student in turn announced his name where he was from and his trade union if relevant. I remember when it got to Dahan, he announced that he was from 'Occupied Palestine' amid cheers from the students. There were many African students, from all over that continent, while my room neighbour Don Daloney was a member of the Detroit Black Panther Party. I recall quite a lot of miners though most of them in the second year, and mostly members of the Communist Party.

Lots of political irons were in the fire during this period. There was a rise of black consciousness, and a number of black students from England had taken to going back to their roots in terms of African shirts and tops as had the women, platting their hair in the traditional style. Knight Marupee was a Zulu prince and world traveller who also did spells as a miner. Edgar Moyo was a former Zimbabwean miner from Shabani Mine, also a journalist and liberation fighter. Dave Marsden was almost as big as Knight. A Hull docker, Dave Merrick was a long-haired hippie who spoke like an Oxford grad, but smoked joints and spoke peace and revolution; his constant mate Terry Houldsworth ('The Heap') was a dishevelled mass of hair and a walking air of a rock concert, with a broad Barnsley accent. Many of these people were to become close comrades.

A guy I christened The Larch became my constant companion. He bore a passing resemblance to the Monty Python actor Eric Idle, who in one of our favourite sketches repeated the slide show presentation of 'The Larch—The Larch'. It was an improbable friendship really; he was a Brummy for a start, a former car worker fitter, and a member of Militant. Even Maureen noticed and commented: 'You especially seen to have hit it off with Larch. Its strange to see because you've never really had a strong personal relationship with anybody have you? You've had so many casual friends but with him its something different and I'm glad because I like him very much.' It was true—despite all of the negatives we just hit it off from the start. Larch had brought his wee Arial motorbike which was handy, though as time went on I had developed certain antisocial habits. Thinking perhaps I was in Amsterdam with the Provos, I used just to pick up any bike that was left standing and ride it to wherever I wished to go, then leave it, and get another for the way back. How come? Something like the gallawas when they are let oot the pit and run around crazy for days, kicking their feet and running wild and free. I had suddenly been freed from all restraints, this was the territory of the alien offspring of the ruling class and I owed them nowt by consideration.

Though actually that concept was immediately challenged. The first Oxford students I met were picketing the Radcliffe Hotel in solidarity with the striking dustbin men. Me and Larch and a few others from the college went to join them. They stood there in their donkey jackets, lang unkempt hair, and that jolly-jolly hooray Henry public school boy accent. They were members of the International Marxist Group, although one was in the International Socialists, they hadn't yet become a party. A little later Ted Heath would arrive as a guest of the Oxford Union and we joined the picket of the approaches we thought he would take. The streets were flooded with rich young girls in evening dresses and blokes in evening dress and dinner jackets; this fare got my goat and drew some venomous remarks, but none which the Oxford students standing alongside would join in with. It dawned on me later, they didn't object to the dress at all, it was just as they themselves would be garbed on another occasion. To me it was flaunting your wealth and privilege in the face of the plebs, but to them, it was just clothes. One of the more daring comrades, with his flat directly over the route to the Union, played continuously 'Street Fighting Man', in defiance of Ted who he must have assumed would recognise at once the angry strains of the Stones, and realise he was not approved of. I tended to think an actual street fight against the prime minister and his entourage would have had more of an impact, but hell, I was told later members of the Oxford Labour Students had gone all buffed up to hear his speech and make some constructive points.

Things got a bit livelier with the invitation of Enoch Powell. Quite a push and shove took place up and down the alleyways leading to the Union, but I don't think he actually showed up. I have a vague recollection of a bomb threat.

Maureen wrote:

Do you remember I said we saw Christy Moore on Monday and then we were going to see him in Scunthorpe on Tuesday? Well we had a really good time. He is definitely one of the most potent (that's the best word for it) singers I've heard. Anyway the whole club was good. Afterwards we went for some chips with Christy—I didn't mention that you'd sent him a *Mineworker* in case he'd forgotten, but he mentioned it and said he thought it was great. He then offered to come and sing for us any time as long as we give him good notice. Free too!! Well I think that's pretty good. I thought with him singing the songs he does that he must be a socialist. So we will have to organise a social for the future and get him along. He gets packed audiences—we could get £20–£30 clear profit.

Again Maureen writes:

Not much news except one marvellous episode on Calendar yesterday. There were hundreds of miners picketing a delegates' meeting at Barnsley. They had a megaphone and were singing The Miners Lifeguard. It was really militant and inspiring and good old Noble was there with his painting of the two miners with card pinned on top saying 'And all we ask is £22'.It was really effective. At first I just saw this painting rising above the heads of the crowd and I thought 'hey I know that' and then what should appear with open mouth (shouting) but his big bearded body. I must write and tell him.

I can't really explain the fantastic sense of inspiration I got from it but I know you'll understand what I mean.

And later:

Had you seen Frost. I don't suppose you did but you must have read or heard about it. It was fantastic. Jerry Rubin of Chicago 8 (conspiracy) and many friends. Smoking pot on stage —they offered it to Frost and he was really put out. He was in an absolute panic and the studio was so overrun they had to change to another for the 2nd half of the programme. Oh I did enjoy it.

The Chicago 8 was a trial arising out of the famous 1968 Democratic Convention in that city, and the mass mobilisation of revolutionary working class and black youth against the war. The Chicago 8 had been put on trial for conspiracy and riot. Un-American, communist, untamed youth, our generation on trial before the US state's most bitterly reactionary, not to say stupid judge, before the eyes of the world. Every mass movement and real revolutionary upsurge throws up its own leaders from within its own body of rebellion and protest. Rarely do they resemble the custom-built models of the professional revolutionary vanguard builders, who have patiently copied the blueprints from Lenin and the Bolsheviks or the Spanish CNT. Cometh the hour cometh the man or women, born of the particular nature of that peculiar and specific time and circumstance. So it was the Chicago 8 represent unlikely looking leaders of the Sixties revolutionary upsurge in the USA, but truth was, along with Jerry Rubin, George Jackson, Eldridge Cleaver, Stokely Carmichael, Davis and others this was the true colour and stamp of the movement. Some were moving toward us like Malcolm X, shot down in the process. Some moved away from us as time went by and comrades were shot down, murdered, jailed and framed. Some stuck defiantly to their guns, literally or ideologically. Abbie Hoffman must be recalled as one of the heroes of our generation and that movement. He was in many ways the brilliant visionary of the 'the happening' . Asked about his politics he was happy to be 'A long haired hippie revolutionary freak,' but when they tried to nail him down to something specific declared 'nothing that ends in "ist" not a socialist, a Marxist , or dentist.' They shouted once to a big rally with Abbie in the lead, that they should 'grow up'. Abbie responded that they didn't want to be grown up, because 'We know what being a grown up in America means.' He was to declare that nobody should trust anyone over 25 ! At the time we'd have said 21 probably. After doing its best to beat Abbie to death they switched to using his lifestyle and morality as a way of public character and reputation assassination. Let's be clear here, it wasn't that Abbie didn't engage in sex and drugs on a grand scale, it was an adjunct to the culture of many in the movement. The point was, these activities, private sex lives and orientations, personal drug use and hedonism were used by the state to discredit a political movement. They exposed them, after frequently setting them up, with the sole purpose of creating a moral panic and a right wing moral backlash. Their aim was to turn public support for the deeper wider aims of the movement by misinformation and slander on the side lines.

On 12 April 1989 Abbie is found dead, an alleged suicide, another awkward leftist revolutionary disappears. Five and a half years later on 28 November 1994 Jerry Rubin gets run down and killed by a car. [32]

Teamed up with me and The Larch as often as no was Big Chris Green, broad, ruddy-faced, Cockney, ex-railfootplateman. They two being six foot, me a wee yin, I think over the two years of our constant friendship they mun hae gettin stiff necks, ney wonder they always sought a table when oot, so's we could sit doon. The chief cook up at Headington was an ex-army sergeant (another one), his sense of cuisine limited at best. His idea of cooking vegetables started off from the proposition that they were inherently bad and needed to be purged of everything nutritious in order to make them edible. Thus it was that every vegetable was rendered into a mush. Each day we lifted the lid on the vegetable dishes and guessed the contents. The colour of the mush was normally a clue, but mushy sprouts devoid of shape look much like mushy peas or cabbage also devoid of shape. I had explained my status as a vegetarian which had him puzzled for a while, but he agreed that at every meal a vegetarian meal would be provided. Sadly his ingenuity at the veggie meals followed much the same track as his vegetable philosophy. All egg substances ended up the same, a gooey yellow mass on the plate, sometimes three times a day. Most days he provided an omelette, but his range of contents was again limited by his culinary experience so he frequently served up sultana omelette. You would penetrate the outer shell of the omelette and thousands of sultanas, looking like rabbit droppings, would spill over your plate. In Knight Murupee, the Zulu prince, he had my opposite. He would only eat meat, and what he called 'real meat'. Queuing up for breakfast, they drop two pieces of bacon on his plate. He put down the plate and between finger and thumb holds up the offending article. 'What is this?' he says in loud voice. 'Pieces of skin? I eat meat.' Whether Knight was a Muslim or just thought bacon was beneath him I'm not sure, but he actually got steak for breakfast from then on. On occasion I would drag the hard-working Knight out for a drink in early evenings, especially when we got down town in the second year. It didn't take much to make Knight merry and start dancing, the way Zulu's dance! On the plains of Africa it must be a colourful sight, in quiet, middle-class, simpering Oxford waterholes it was far more so. Gently grazing couples at tables, with their little glasses of wine and whispered conversations, were suddenly confronted by a huge smiling black man, stamping out his war dance. 'This is how we dance in my country!' he would proclaim and advance on them, shaking his imaginary assegai, in a threatened lunge and throw, and singing one of those clicking chants. Alternately he would assume the female roll, cupping his imaginary breasts and bouncing up and down: 'This is the way the young girls dance in my village.'

But what used to really get him going, and what scared the rice out of the middle class and aristos most of all, was his reaction to 'Mona Lisa' (that is the song not the actual painting). At first I just didn't understand it. You would walk into a pub or one of those posh hotel type places with the bar open to the public, and via the piped music system the tune of 'Mona Lisa' would start to fill the air. Then he'd be off, bobbing and jabbing, ducking and diving, punching out. Knight, it seems, was also a very good heavyweight boxer. Every morning for years he had followed a punishing schedule, part of which was hours of shadow boxing. His gym had very few musical accompaniments for this rhythm, but one it did have was 'Mona Lisa'. So it was that Knight would time his skips and feints, his thrusts, his counters, his jabs, his uppercuts to the tune, to such an extent that as soon as the tune started playing he went into autopilot: 'Mona Lisa, Mona Lisa men have named you,' Thud-Thud-Thud, 'You're so like the lady with the magic smile,' Jab-Jab-Thud. Odd the number of times we ran into that record while taking a stroll round the Oxford taverns.

I only truly saw Knight get angry once. It was at a showing of *Zulu* at the cinema in Oxford. I can't remember which part of the film, set him off. He enjoyed earlier bits of it and joined in the Zulu singing, but I think it was the battle of Rourke's Drift. I recall he stood up and shouted very loud and very clearly, 'This is a lie! This is not true!' and we decided to leave.

As a student of history it was required that I learn a foreign language. I chose Dutch, though it was not one of the recommended three, namely Spanish, French or German and I had to argue my corner for it. 'The purpose of the foreign language in history, David, is to appreciate another nation's development and culture,' I was told by Billy Hughes. 'Don't the Dutch have history, and culture?' I had asked.

Although not setting out to sound cheeky, it must have smacked a little of that. I went on to explain my passion for the developing youth revolutionary culture in Holland and its impact upon my formative years. They nodded sagely; I had good enough grounds, and I never even mentioned Patats and Lumpia. The college paid half of the fees to a young Anglo-Dutch girl, with whom I began taking lessons. Dutch fascinated me, surely because of the influence of my hippie colleagues in my early teenage years, but also just the wonderful sound and resonance of it. I found much in the Northumbria dialect of similarity, which suggested to me a common root in the twang, probably via the Angles. My trouble in learning the language was I had no knowledge of the science of English. I had never been taught about nouns, pronouns, tenses, and all that stuff so it was doubly difficult. I confess to this day to still not knowing what they mean, and have never ever mastered the English alphabet right through.

My enthusiasm was such however that I rendered my room and much of the college bilingual in so far as I had made numerous little stickers with the name of everything—doors, windows, rooms, tables—in Dutch. Chance is a fine thing, and evening time, having a drink out on the open-air tables of an Oxford summer evening, we came across a group of stunning female Dutch tourists; Ah, ney piss taking nuw, they were most impressed at my efforts. Apparently only very old folk talked the version of Dutch I was attempting. It was full and formal, and they thought it sounded 'so cute' and giggled delightfully. It was to be the start of a near lifetime friendship with Moni, an exotic looking Dutch-Indonesian. Her oriental face, her slim and sexy form coupled with her Dutchness were just fatal combinations for me. She gave me a tiny little Dutch–English dictionary which I still have. Sadly, although Chris occasioned many enthusiastic nights in bed with one of the girls, and Larch too, we never actually got to human contact outside of a wee kiss. This despite the fact that she arrived to stay with me unannounced at Ruskin after I had left, then followed me down to Raph's, but he couldn't accommodate us, and we ended up, well ended, at least so far as physical contact was concerned. We have stayed in touch though only by post ever since. My attempts at 'lerende Nederlands' were to continue sporadically over the years.

GENERAL STRIKE (FOR ONE DAY)

The Tories were in the first flush of their election success to start a serious redistribution of wealth and income, from the poorest to the richest of course. They were also to implement a policy of creating high unemployment levels as a whip against high wages and militancy.

They decided to dig in when the hitherto musclebound power workers who operated the power stations took limited action in December of 1970. They implemented a simple work to rule. The press responded with a virulent hate campaign. The press virtually encouraged the public at large to attack the power men, which one guy did on the Frost programme, knocking the power worker to the floor, while a farmer in audience shouted that if he had his shotgun he would have shot all the power workers on the programme. Did Mr Frost condemn the violent attack on workers explaining the poverty level of their wages? No, he beamed. 'How very exciting,' was his comment as I recall, and I nursed a desire to punch him likewise the first time I ever saw him. The green light was given for the rabidly anti-communist leader of the union (ETU) Frank Chapple to call off the strike—in the face of public opinion as he called it.

The Tories' Industrial Relations Bill was to be the gauntlet they would throw down to the organised labour movement, not so much the solid institution of Transport House and the TUC, but the wildcatters, the quasi-official and unofficial bodies of shop stewards, panels and committees. The vast majority of strikes were not over wages as such, but over areas of job control exercised by workers and their representatives, the eternal challenge to 'managerial prerogative'—that being management's right to manage. It was also crucially aimed at stopping solidarity action. The TUC though publicly opposed to the bill refused to take action, and an unofficial general strike was called for one day, 8 December 1970. I was up home from college. I was in fact due to be setting off back down but the movement was actually moving. Trades councils, trade unions, unofficial teams, rank-and-file bodies, and at centre the Communist Party's Liaison Committee for the Defence of Trade Unions. They had managed to build a respectable left alternative to the TUC General Council, with links to left bureaucrats in the van of most of the big unions; they also linked with many Labour Party leftists and fellow travellers. Many trade unions were affiliated to this body, including Hatfield Main; in fact, I was one of the delegates to it. The one-day general strike was massively respected, and demonstrations took place across the length and breadth of Britain. In Doncaster, workers of all descriptions downed tools. We paraded not simply up the High Street as we did on May Day and the miners galas, but around Wheatley Hall Road, past the big factories, most of which were at a standstill—Harvesters, Pilkington's, Compton's, the Railway Plant Works. Banners came out on that march from unions I didn't know we had in Doncaster. Workers of all descriptions, some marching off the job and out of the factories in their boiler suits. Gangs of lasses from the tailoring factories—Stainforth Fashions, for example—were getting quite a militant reputation, 'manned' by many a collier's, mother, wife and daughter. Often they just ragged up, and walked out in the style of the miners. They were great: noisy and militant lasses who could shout down the biggest foreman and trade union official. Another great clump of women were from the chicken factories and all their heartless, brutal, alienating, backbreaking toil, free at last of the military and arbitrary constraints of the bloody production line, marching in the sunshine, feeling a great surge of power. We were the workers. 'We are the working class, this isn't a slogan, this isn't a gospel.' This was an intense realisation and something we could tangibly feel. The miners' bands blasted out their martial chords, the workers of the region, men and women, old and young, white-collar and manual, filled the streets.

'KILL THE BILL! KILL THE BILL!'

I had made a big poster with a scalded Wobbly wildcat leaping bolt upright in the air, his tail up like a poker and his legs rigid and claws drawn, together with the slogan 'Long Live The Wildcat!!' We marched into the great theatre, one time a motion picture hall, and now a mass bingo hall, to a depressingly boring meeting. These minor windbags certainly knew how to throw great buckets of cold water on the ranks of bristling workers, come to hear the good word and the call for insurrection. Well, maybe not insurrection but when and how we would defeat this legislation; what was the plan? Down in Oxford a hastily called meeting of the students and academics had seen John Hughes, the vice principal, genuinely angry, march down to the front of the hall, throw his jacket to the side and in his shirt sleeves tell us he was going to 'expose this hateful bill'. John and many another liberal socialist academic felt betrayed by this bill, it was a breach in the post-war pluralist consensus on how to deal with the working class. In his speech he destroyed the bill line by line, page by page. On the streets the student unions, and the local trades council, the car workers and the public employees, marched, shouting 'Kill The Bill!' and 'Workers! Students! Unite And Fight!' On the TV screens, Tommy Steele, the beloved heartthrob of my sister, announced himself a scab; he would not join the strike of the actors and musicians, even for one day. 'Don't worry, kids,' he said, as if he was in one his stupid films, 'You'll get your panto.' Ee, these heartless unions, eh? Trying to stop the kids watching their Christmas pantomime? How they tell it, but many of them couldn't, because the TV and radio technicians had joined the strike too. The strike event needed developing into a campaign, the formal TUC needed movement, needed to crank its old ancient muscles back to life.

The bill was to become law in the following year, 1971. In June of 1970 the new Tory government had been elected, in July the NUM conference resolution was for a minimum wage of £21 underground and £20 on surface or we strike. In September they offer £2.10 and we reject it; going to a national ballot in October we achieve 143,000 yes votes and 115,000 no votes. The no votes win, because we require not a majority to call strike action, but a two thirds majority. Pits all over the country strike anyway, and many others implement work-to-rules and overtime bans. The NCB remarkably found another ten bob which was then accepted. The coal industry is crying out for men—3,000 short in the North East mines, which makes me ask why I was working in Yorkshire? The government now withdraws all restrictions on importing coal to Britain, and in January the first coal in 12 years from abroad starts to flood in, its obvious intention is to lessen our bargaining power.

I met John Malvos, I think, at the Institute for Workers' Control conference at Sheffield University. I had spoken from the floor, about *The Mineworker* and job control, and the struggles against supervision. He wrote to discuss things with me and comment on *The Mineworkers* he had bought at conference in November 1971. John was an Australian, belonged to some tiny Pabloite group, though not Militant, who incidentally though nicknamed 'Pabs' were most un-Pab in their politics.[33]

He circulated a theoretical journal called the *International Marxist Review*, which he was producing the English translation of. He was actually a lecturer and researcher in physics at the University of Bristol, but also I knew he was some sort of academic in Oxford. His contribution to the revolution as it landed on our doorstep was that he bought old duplicators, did them up and passed them on to revolutionary groups of workers and class fighters. 'Let a million blossoms bloom, let ten thousand schools of thought reign' —had been Mao's slogan, would that he had meant it. But John meant it, and we got a free working duplicator. I later met John down in Oxford where he was working. He wore his customary donkey jacket with his hands plunged deep in the pockets, which usually contained some revolutionary pamphlet with an in-depth article on this or that feature of the ruling class's plans for us. Turned out he was a bliddy nuclear physicist, not just that, but one of the top five or six in Britain. He was working on a nuclear project now in the nuclear research establishment. 'Do they know you're a communist?' I inquired. 'Too right,' he said.

It seems the work John was doing had no military application—yet—but because it was at the cutting edge, they not only permitted it to be carried out— even by a communist—they actually funded it. Seems they couldn't allow the Ruskies to get ahead and then find it had some military application and they had fallen behind. Having communists at the centre of nuclear research wasn't any big sweat for them anyway; it was US Commies who had developed the first atom bombs, albeit after being conned into believing the Nazis were about to nuke the Soviet Union. The deal had been that the Soviets would be given the bomb by the Americans after they had successfully developed it; after all, we were allies weren't we? Oppenheimer was utterly betrayed and refused to work on the H-bomb. By 1953 he was forced to retire from any political or public pronouncement on threat to his life and those of his family by the shadowy thugs who keep America 'safe for democracy'. John's project was to work on a tiny particle of a neutron, or some other 'on. He had to produce these tiny features and that meant getting the nuclear reactor up to full power, till all the elements, atoms and things are fleeing aroond in a sort of giant wall of death; then when they get up to the right velocity, they fire one off down into his experiment which is functioned with the main reactor, it then collides and smashes up and for an unrecordable portion of time this tiny feature breaks off. How does he know its there? It passes over a film of mercury, which records its trajectory and life span. Infinitesimal particle science I think they called it. The object of the exercise was to discover the very smallest particles in the universe, in order to reconstruct the big picture, unless we had all the building blocks, or in this case, invisible tiny particles of matter, you can't build it up into the overview. I visited John on numerous occasions at the nuclear research centre. Fascinating. First off I couldn't quite get away with the big burly security guards on the gate, dressed in what looked like a cross between police and Gestapo uniforms, with belts and chains and peaked caps. As we drew up to the big mesh gate the big feller steps out, holding up his hand and peering from under the peak of his cap. John winds down the window. 'Afternoon comrade,' says the man in the Gestapo uniform.

'All right, yi fat bastard,' John replies.

'Who's this, and a new student?' 'Na, he's from the revolutionary organising committee, come to look the place over, ready for the glorious day comrade.' 'Ah—well, just so long as you're not crawling up any management backsides then,' he says and waves us through. I am speechless. 'He's the site NUPE shop-steward. Most of the technicians are in Clive Jenkins's mob, ASTMS. He's a good comrade, and I don't think he's in any group.' We near the plant, like something off those old fifties sci-fi films, except the technicians are outside playing football.

'He's back,' they shout disparagingly.

Apparently, this nuclear generator is very temperamental, it needs hours of coaxing to get it up to speed and make the atoms behave in the way they require and rolling round the nuclear circuit in the right way. It takes hours, and once you start work on it, you can't just say 'bugger it', you have to stick with it. So cooperation from these guys is vital. Without them on your side, your experiment is gaanin neywhere. 'How's she cranking?' 'Be ready by 8 tonight,' they respond with some evident modesty—this apparently was after pulling all the plugs out, or sweating under a hot nuclear reactor, or whatever you sweat under, for some time. 'Good fucking lads,' he says, and opens the boot. He unloads two crates of the broon dog! 'Now that's the stuff,' they say, walking over as John hoys them a bottle opener. 'A little thank you, you know.' We go through a wee door, cut out of a big warehouse-type door, in front of us on the wall a massive poster of Mao, in his grey uniform, raising his hand in a wave, big red cheeks and brighter-than-bright Chinese colour print. Below his image some slogan about uniting the technicians, the academics and scientists and the workers for humanity.

I get fitted up with a radiation detector, in case there is a sudden leak. The tab turns yellow or something—about three minutes before I turn into dust, I think. 'Na,' says John. 'A minor leak. We could scrub that bastard outtaya.' He leads me through this giant structure—why all the height I wonder? He takes me to his work area, and a great wall of metal cabinet-like objects; it reminds me of the left-luggage lockers at Kings Cross. 'What's this?' 'Ah that's an old computer I built sixteen months ago.' 'You built it?' 'Yeah, for the experimental data, its fucked now, too old, this is ma new one.'

He points to a console of winking lights and buttons and screens. 'This one will hold ten times the information of that big bastard, and download it in a hundredth of the time.'

This I reflect isn't the experiment, it's a piece of equipment he built to assist his experiment, and he constantly updates it as he goes along. This takes us into our ongoing discussion on Soviet nuclear technology. John is not a guy who can be fooled by big rockets on May Day parades: 'The Soviets are twenty years behind the Americans in miniaturisation. Their microchip technology is stone age compared to the Yanks. Everything they build is massive. It limits their horizons. They have only so much further they can go with the technology they have.'

I didn't like to hear this, but John was not a man I had any reason to doubt, and his words sounded all too true. 'What about space rocket technology?' 'Ah well, that's their edge, it just so happened that they are experts at what they have got, and that's big heavy machines and big thrusting rockets. They're probably built by big women with giant spanners and rivet guns.' 'But aren't the Soviets likely to put a space station up there and have a jump-off point for the solar system?' 'Well, maybe, but they'll be building it in a shipyard somewhere, out of steel. No doubt if you have a word with them Dave they'll doubtless make it coal-powered too. At this particular stage in the space race, the Soviets are ahead. American basic engineering could learn from the Soviets—they seem to have missed a phase in their technological evolution, or abandoned it. But that phase can't last, it will be irrelevant in ten to fifteen years' time They've got the technology for the steps after the ones the Russians are making. Soviet technology will only allow them to stay in front in very narrow areas.' Well I wasn't too happy about this stuff. My knowledge of Soviet military equipment seemed to suggest it was as good as anything the Yanks had and better, but John should know. About the nuclear war?

John just shakes his head. 'You fuckers just don't see the necessity of science and knowledge in building communism. Posadas thinks that if we all take turns at throwing nuclear missiles at each of the big civilisations and cultures in both blocks, we win in the end because there are more of us. That the ruling imperialists are therefore defeated, and we, humanity, emerge triumphant. Into what Dave, a devastated, dying planet, with all the means of putting it right, and all the accumulated science of our evolution wiped out? What will we have, the primitive communism of the Stone Age tribes? I just don't get it, Dave.'

'Yeah, well, I don't think its a matter of picking what road we would rather go down to communism, John. I think Posadas is trying to be realistic and say imperialism will never abandon the planet to the communists. They would try and destroy it first.'

John used to scare the rice out of me, talking about the effects of nuclear bombs on cities and other nuclear sites. Not that I expected we would survive it anyway, if the state's special forces didn't bump us all off in what the party predicted would be a phase before the war called the repression, then the comradely bombs of our Soviet and Chinese comrades would.

What I loved about John was his down-to-earth Australian working-class crack coupled with his obvious intellectual genius. He went up to Balliol I think it was, to interview the top students who would study with him. The dean introduced one young lad, saying how attentive and studious and quiet he was. John said, 'Yeah, well I'll soon knock all that bullshit out of the bastard, get a few beers down his neck and sleeves rolled up.' Science was work to John, it was like car mechanics, or coal mining—work, just with different muscles. He changed my appreciation of science and scientists.

OXFORD

I had just come out of the Social Studies Library with an armful of books. I had a big box folder under my arm containing the foothills of my notes on early unions and miners' strikes. The sun was blazing down, and I was walking down St Giles, the main street in Oxford. Students were pressing into cafes for breakfast, others sat leaning against the wall loudly debating questions of logic and mysticism, and I wanted to stop and listen. You know, I suddenly felt great, felt I would grow to love this place, its learning, its access, its fairytale spires, and toffs or no toffs, academics in their silly corduroy pants and bow ties or not, I felt happy. The strains of 'American Pie' were drifting out of some bar doorway, and the whole scene started to take on the air of my teenage fairgrounds. Oxford just dripped with privilege, fruit hung from the trees, apples and pears and cherries littered the streets approaching the city. Ney body was hard pressed enough to want to gather them all up, well until I got there and embarrassed everyone it seems. The streets of the city were frequently deluged by floods of students in their gowns, pouring from one lecture to another, often in squads of bikes, making off to a distant lecture. The Marxist students carried a poly bag in which to stuff the offending article whilst out in public, though wearing them was not an option in the lectures and at certain ceremonies. Jack Gannon, an Irish graduate of Ruskin, admitted to Magdalen, was duty-bound the wear the gown on the ceremonial procession through town. He carried a poster stating 'I have been coerced in to wearing this ridiculous get-up, or I won't be admitted!' The poster drew mixed responses; he was spoiling the ruling class and their offspring's nice day, he was challenging tradition. As he came to a wall, the bulldogs (university-hired thugs) jumped on him, knocked him to the floor and pulled the poster off him. Oh, yes a fine intellectual tradition is the gown.

The colleges were fed by streams and rivers, the trees lapped the water and the meadows around the whole place twinkled with wild flowers. The punts made their silent way through the canals and waterways, pushed by tall, handsome boys, carrying girls in their flowery frocks with lacy underskirts and little straw bonnets, their skin clear and unblemished, their teeth perfect sets of gleaming white, their bodies the neatly kept product of years of privilege and good living. Aroused to sex they were fully functioning—full-on working vehicles of sex and sensuality; virginal innocence abstinence and ignorance was not something which went with the kit and why should it? Thank God. Oxford itself was an ancient monument to study of all descriptions, to scholarship and learning. Suddenly we too were a part of it, part of its fringe at least. For the men and women who worked in the town, in the shops in the bars, on the buses, in the grounds of the colleges, in the kitchens, cleaning, building, repairing, manning the services of phones, and gas and electric and water and everything else, they too were part of this city. Though at times there had been trouble between 'town and gown', scratching the surface revealed both more and less. Just along the road, maybe a half mile from Headington was Cowley car plant, which teamed with proles. They all lived in estates like Blackbird Leys, some wee distance from the town. They were self-contained with their Headington football ground just the front of our annex, and the dog track and pubs up that end.

Attacks on students tended to come not from militant class-conscious members of the working class out for a bit of class revenge on the offspring of the ruling class, but from Oxfash. Yes a pun on Oxfam, but real enough. The skinhead tribe of NF supporters, hated the students because they were supposed to be Marxists and communists, because they were degenerate, because many of them were black. Not all skinheads were fascists of course, but in any group you'd almost certainly find the core that were. Ruskin students were not above having a go at the 'Henrys' themselves at times, but usually from a comic view point. I recall at one of the many watery events, where the students turn out in their best, with their blazers and boaters, the lasses in their bonny shawls, and lacey tops, punting along with skill, a rogue war canoe, constructed from canoes and lashed together, speeding through the water and ramming the punts! Then making off into the leafy undergrowth overhanging the banks. On another occasion, some lads from the town dropped a paving stone over the Magdalene Bridge which was aimed at the passing punt below, which, holed through the thin deck, sank by the bow. Some Ruskin ravers had likewise bought a couple of old gowns and painted on perfect Hell's Angels symbols complete with studs and chains and the legend 'Hell's Angels, Oxford Chapter'. With these, they would parade in processions of the Oxford students, and hang around prominently during the photography at graduation days. That is until the bulldogs knocked the piss-takers down and ripped the gowns off their backs.

Mind, Ruskin had access to punts too, but none of us really could manage it, someone always did the Norman Wisdom thing and got stuck on the pole as the punt took off; more than likely it wouldn't take off at all and just went round and round. Now while this might seem mildly amusing elsewhere, to Oxford malehood it is regarded as the height of incompetence and effeminacy not to be able to punt. To see a bloke floundering around with the pole, overbalancing in every direction was a common insult to manhood. 'You're bloody hopeless, sir,' they would shout, as if I didn't know. 'Poor show, sir.' 'Ah, get fucked off!'— as if I cared. But I cared. I wanted to be able to sit the lassie in the punt with a chilled bottle of wine and box of strawberries and expertly and intellectually discuss the Fourth French Republic while effortlessly gliding through the water. Couldn't do it, actually did the unforgivable and smashed a pole, the bliddy thing got wedged under one of those little Chinese bridges and fast in the mud beneath, as current and punt went one way, and me and the pole stayed in the middle something had to give. It must have looked la'ry from the bank, punt pole and boater disappear under the bridge, then a loud crack, and little Indian boy comes paddling punt out the other side like Hiawatha. Hmm, very poor show. I guess you have to be born to it; rich kids probably can't make sliddies. Actually, we hadn't been at the college long, when we were attacked ourselves. We were in animated discussion and a great state of jollity, coming back up the hill to Headington after a night round the town—Larch; me; Bill Adams, a Cornish polis; his Cornish ex-polis wife; Jennie, a girl with a noticeable figure, and intelligence too of course, with large glasses to match and a southern accent; and wee Margaret with whom I had established an almost immediate liaison. Down in the opposite direction came four or five surly looking lads. As we came to meeting as it were, I suddenly moved to the outside of Margaret, protective like, in case one of the lads should grab her and that would start some problems. As it was, my move was misunderstand as an attack on one of their mates and suddenly boots and fists were going in. Larch took off, the big ex-polis seemed to be taking two sets of thuds, the littler assailant, who I think threw the first punch, tried to kick me and slipped on the wet ground and went down with a thud, and I pretended I had laid him out, though actually my blow had more chance of catching flies than his clock.

Margaret had shouted 'You bastards! We're working class students!'

But it was in that sort of middle class educated voice, and it drew the response 'You bastards! We aren't any sort of students.'

But Jenny was suddenly a mass of blood. She had determinedly dived into the fray to save Bill and pull the other two off him when someone had elbowed her in the face, smashing her glasses into her nose and cheeks. The lads took off, and we waved down a passing polis car, which was highly reluctant to stop as I recall. Well the whole sorry mess ended up in court. We gasped as their pathetic wages were announced, they all worked for the local authority as gardeners' labourers. They blamed us, indeed two of them said I thumped them, and another blamed Jenny for kicking him in the bollocks, which she said in court she hadn't, but she wished she had. Another explained that when he felt her arm pulling him away, he thought it was a bloke and he wouldn't have elbowed her otherwise. We all began to feel a bit stupid really, and began to see their point of view, although they did confess to having had a lousy night and then missing the last bus and seeing what they thought were posh students living it up.

QUALIFICATIONS

My course was to be the college history diploma; I would follow the regular route and rules, lectures, essays, seminars. Of course, a number of other subjects were to be studied at the same time. It was an indescribable thrill to explore the college library, a treasure house of information and knowledge, and the bigger one down at Walton Street. Then we had access to the social studies library, and the town libraries, and even some of the more prestigious Oxford libraries like the Bodleian and the Radcliffe Camera. In the Bodleian, we swore an oath not to draw our swords or kindle fire nor ride our horses up and down the stairs, which apparently had been a practice of earlier Oxford students in the middle ages, sufficient to keep the oath intact by the time we got there. Just as well really. At night when the college slept, I would oft times just sit in the Headington library and listen to the silent wisdom of thousands of books, soak in the silence and smell of wood polish, feel history all around you. Mind I also tried to steal the knowledge, carrying armfuls of books away to my bedroom, to just sit there, somehow feel I suddenly had accumulated their knowledge like a conker absorbs the titles of its defeated opponents. Raph was founder of the History Workshop movement. I was soon a recruit although to be honest I really did at first want to do the history diploma and win one of them. Increasingly, however, research work for the workshop, preparation of research papers, and the aim of getting the work published started to take up more and more of the course time, and then all the time, and then more than the whole two years. But at this stage I was managing the two. It was clear, though, that there was two views of the role of the college.

Apart from the staff view, there were at least two student views. There were those who seen the college as a custom-built rung on the ladder out of the class and into the enemy camp, or as a staff training college for the ranks of the union bureaucracy and parliament. On the other hand there were those of us who seen the college, its facilities and its research as weapons in the class war.

To this latter end, we could find little use for diplomas set by Oxford University. We could see little justice in outside examiners from the University accrediting college theses and awards. Why should the intelligentsia, the brainbox of the ruling class, judge the worth of the working class at understanding its own history and theory? That is at least the way we seen it. As time went on, and as the student movement overall began to challenge exams anyway, we too began to think the unthinkable, that we should use our time here to study, to learn, to advance the efforts of the working class to liberate itself, and bugger exams and curriculums.

In truth, as my efforts sank more and more into primary research there was little time for the laid-down guidelines of the course.

But for now we, or rather I, was still on the rails, more or less. The wild coursing freedom and lack of restraints coupled with class revenge justified numerous scams on the children of the rich. One of the lads had discovered a list of new residents pasted on the notice board of the porter's cabin just inside the gate of Magdalen College. He would borrow the poshest-sounding name, walk into one of bespoke tailors or outfitters, and purchase himself shirts and jumpers, shoes and jackets 'have it put on our account'. Only once was there no such account, when he with genuine embarrassment, though fake tears, threw everything down on the counter and in his poshest weepy voice cried 'Oh beastly Daddy, I hate you!' and fled the shop, to the sympathetic nods of the shop assistants, not for the first time encountering a public school boy being thrown to the wolves by daddykins. Much better than being arrested of course. Actually, on reflection he nie got caught before that, when he asked in a shop where 'his' or rather his nominated benefactor's credit was good, if they 'had any John Wesley Harding shirts' and his accent lapsed to broadest Barnsley. A combination of the outrageous request and the less than au-fait manner of its delivery cautioned the butler-like shop assistant to go back behind the counter and check the name.

'Do we have your signature on account, sir?' he asked. 'Oh yes indeed, would one require it again, I love signing away signatures,' he countered in gay abandon. He could too, though from whence he had perfected the signature with the borrowed name Ah dinnet ken. For me, apart from the bikes, I developed a pernash for stealing packets of cigs from college junior common rooms' tab machines, the wooden kind that hung on the corridor walls. A bent coat hanger, a half-open draw, snick the coat hanger in the overhead cig packet and pull it down onto the lower deck. I could empty a column in about ten minutes and then flog the cigs. Also of course, the great book club scam. Give yourself a name, give yourself a college, and wait for the post. Usually this was delivered before the registration and clerical offices opened of a morn. So just collect your parcel of books in your assumed name, and no one was the wiser. Scams got better as the time went on. Fred, too, had suddenly been rejuvenated, and why no? This was somewhat easier than rising at 4.30 to shovel coal on his knees stripped to his buff in Bentley pit. The wild freedom of the pit gallawa was affecting Fred, how did I know?[34] We were in the big army and navy store along from Oxford rail station. Fred and I mused round the shop. Fred discovered a pristine 'Digger' Australian army hat with the brim folded over on one side the way they do. He tried it on— my he cut a dash in it with his moustache and all.

The lady behind the counter says: 'Oh yes, you're going to have that.'

And to my utter astonishment Fred replies: 'How right you are,' and runs straight out of the shop leaving us all gaping.

'I'll, er, just try and stop him,' I suggest, backing for the door, and running for it.

Fred had soon found a soulmate, a little Jewish girl, and not to be one for deyin things be half, they moved in together more or less. One day, Fred and his new woman were sitting round the long dinner table, on one side. One of the piss-takers suggested, 'Aren't you a bit old for free love Fred?' To which the girlfriend, usually a thoroughly quiet sort of a girl announced, 'Well I've got no complaints,' to cheers from everyone else.

Like me Fred, found the essay questions hard, in so far as we tried to convince the tutor of some argument or another, as though the tutor didn't actually know the answer the question he was setting. Our essays at first came out as political manifestos or left leaflets; on one such essay, the tutor had written VIVA at the end of Fred's poetic and enthusiastic flourish. I wrote to Maureen:

> I got here and got settled in fine, Monday we got stuck into the work with a vengeance, Fred turned up here and is getting on OK. Well it seems that Doncaster Socialist Alliance has linked up with Fred and Angus in a conscious alliance to print a broad sheet for Bentley (colliery) to stir the place up! I'm a bit Jealous because Granville[35] supplied the paper and stencils for free ... Had a good night out last night, I feel a bit guilty about it because you must have spent a rather lonely evening. Try and enjoy yourself if you can pet don't be too lonely.

The college hosted regular discos and ceilidhs, at which I would perform me Geordie pit lad repertoire, and Larch would do his filthy 'Maraldo-Maraldo-Maria'. I recall that Gimpy, the Lancashire Chairman of the Commercial Branch of the TGWU, so called because of his gammy leg, would wade in with 'The Hole In The Elephant's Bottom'.[36]

Or together we would boom out the chorus of 'Oh there's none so fair as can compare to the lads of the RSA (Ruskin Students Association)', after '"Toss your balls in the air" said the juggler, "Fiddle as you widdle as you widdle," said the fiddler, "Slap it up and down up and down," said the painter, "Slap it on the block, chop it off" said the butcher,' in the college's version of 'Old King Coal'. None of these songs would be allowed houseroom in today's climate, but then they were thoroughly working-class fare and quite acceptable, actually more than that, they were bliddy funny. At History Workshop socials, crammed with the front-line troops of the Women's Liberation Movement, I would sing old Jack

Elliott's 'Little Chance', with the verse about the mother-in-law, and letting her drown, quite impervious to the place of mother-in-law humour in the hatred of the women's movement. Raph said anybody else would have been strung up from the ceiling. In the first few months of the first year we were like kids let loose in a sandpit, well me and Larch were anyway. Headington Hall and later the main college building were warrens of ancient cellars and hidden nooks and crannies which we were always poking about in then emerging in unexpected parts of the buildings. Having discovered a large collection of Morris Dance stuff and having come back roaring drunk about 1 a.m. we donned the bells and sashes and took off up the stairs to dance around the corridors. I recall playing tennis after another drunken binge, around the staircases and corridors. Larch, having gone off to the bog, found on his return we had gone, but so had his bed. It was a mystery. He looked out of windows and in libraries but no. Actually, we had lowered the whole thing, out of his window and then suspended it from ropes, where it hung against the side of the wall. We were having a whale of a time, but other students complained constantly. Boring bastards. Me and Chris, minus Larch for some reason, after attending some drunken do down at Walton Street were then faced in the early hours of the morn with the long trek back up Headington. We decided to borrow one of the rich folk's cars that littered the streets round Walton Street. Chris picked out a bliddy Mark VIII Jag. 'Bliddy' because although the doors were open and he did something underneath the bonnet it still required me pushing the damn thing up and road to get it going. Such trials of strength were no problem to me; they allowed me to demonstrate that I was a pitman used to hard tasks of toil, though this would be equivalent to pushing not so much a tub as a mine car. We drove in cosseted luxury back to Headington, but then left the Jag outside the front entrance to the college, where embarrassingly it stayed for a couple of days until either the cops retrieved it or someone else nicked it to drive it back into town. Did we ever contemplate the consequences of such actions? I don't think it crossed any of our minds, and none of mine – I was often occupying more than one at that time.

Oxford has a high Irish population. It had given rise to a great Irish folk music community which me and Larch were soon part of, together with a strong smattering of Oxford students. It didn't take too long to see that some of these students, well, they were OK, socialistic, sympathetic to all the causes we espoused, intelligent and witty. Some of them were poorer than us, and as for being up for a laugh or making a stand, they made as strong an intervention as many a working-class kid. The only thing was, the cynics would say, was that this was just a fad for them. In the end, they would all join the rulers and the enforcers of the rules. Was it true? I don't know about them, but many a former raggy-arsed working-class student was to do so. Mind, to be right, most of the working-class students weren't raggy-arsed at all. Most of us had come from well-paid work, most of us had decent grants. Not so many of the children of the public school system; debating whether to have beans or chips at a dinner time pub was not a fashion for them, it was a necessity. One of my first memories of Oxford was walking past the rugger pitch of a private primary school and seeing the poor little buggers being tortured in the name of making them men. It was howling a blizzard, the kids were in their rugger kit, their legs and knees red raw, and the pitch was an ice-rink with pools of muddy slush.

There in the middle was a big bastard with a whistle, walking about, commanding the charge and counter-charge, crying 'Oh do come on Mathew, you little girl, stop whimpering!' Blood-soaked socks, eyes blinded with hail, they were forced into wet, stubborn combat with a ball like concrete.

'No wonder they grow up cruel, bent and heartless,' I thought. Many of their older brethren of course were loaded, with more bit than sense. These we could con with impunity, mainly because they didn't know they were being conned. A little dope dealing round the colleges was a trade to make you cut a dash, have money and be popular too. Even if you were selling the silly twats moistened Oxo cubes re-wrapped in silver foil. We even sold them the bliddy tablets from the steepy peas, as giant purple hearts. The daft thing is they all seemed to work. A time or two our hearts turned over as the Oxo cube was sprinkled expertly on a joint, and re-rolled, then passed round the room; no wonder it gave them the munchies! But what the fuck—it got them high, it bought wor beer, it did ney harm. At the student fair, a myriad of clubs and societies hawked their wares. Although Ruskin wasn't part of the university structure or the student union(s) at that time, the fight for a single representative body was engaging the Oxford students anyway. They had the Oxford Union, but 'union' didn't mean union as in the Student Union, it meant a sort of 'welfare' like a miners welfare, with bars, and a famous debating club and other activities.

The student fair covered everything from riding—'Do you ride?' the young thing in jodhpurs asked. 'Aye but not on a horse, bonny lass.' (This was what Chris called my 'tourist Geordie', i.e. done for effect. Certainly, we wanted to manifest our working classness, though not hopefully as boorishly as our skinhead colleagues from Cowley.)

The Oxford Monarchist Society had also set up shop. 'Do you get to be king if you join?' I asked. 'Oh no,' they replied. 'Not much point joining then really is there?'

The colleges themselves had JCRs, junior common rooms, and college representation was college-based not university-based. Although our Ruskin Students' Association was actually affiliated to the Mature Student Federation, later on in our year we affiliated to the National Union of Students. Anyway, most student societies allowed Ruskin students to join. The choices and the exiting possibilities were unlimited. Me and Larch decided that we would join something which would be of use to the class struggle, so we joined the University Gun Club, and in particular the pistol section. Of course, we kept our politics secret. Especially on army camps and establishments, the club was actually under the wing of the University Officers Training Corps, but we kept wa gobs shut. Putting accurate holes in a card with a pistol is actually extremely difficult, far more so than with a rifle, which we had also had a go at. In Oxford v. Cambridge athletic competitions, whereas the others competed for 'blues', in pistol shooting the best you could aim for was a 'half-blue'. We enjoyed our pistol training, practising putting bullets into the bellies of the bourgeoisie, although Larch was on a limb politically since Militant and its clandestine Revolutionary Socialist League didn't really believe in armed struggle, but rather a more militant version of *The British Road To Socialism* as perfected by the Communist Party of Great Britain. Our cover was sound, until the time at a folk night down one of the pubs in Oxford, tanked up from foot-stomping, we recognised a familiar face and hailed 'Huw comrade?' And Larch carried on 'All right, comrade?' It was a confused president of the Gun Club who shook our hands that night and realised we were perhaps engaged on another agenda. The college was in the middle of struggle, a hive of Anti-Apartheid activism through the Kitson Committee (Kitson, a white communist supporter of the armed struggle in South Africa and former Ruskin student had gone back to fight and been banged up with many another freedom fighter). The Vietnam war still daily filled us with pride and grief. Angela Davis was sat in the dungeons of the US state. The Tories were drafting under the authorship of Robert Carr their hated Industrial Relations Bill, aimed at ruthlessly restricting the rights of unions and workers in the unions on the point of jail. All unofficial strikes would be rendered illegal (95 per cent of all strikes were unofficial), official strikes resulting from unofficial strikes would be made illegal, official strikes not in the national interest would be illegal. All rules would be vetted by the State Union Registrar, who would decide what rules should exist and what rules shouldn't. Any strike for political purposes would be illegal.

British troops were playing an increasingly partisan and brutal role in Ireland. The struggle for civil rights, for One Person One Vote, had been met with ruthless Loyalist repression. The republican communities had spawned the Provisional IRA in response, and the state introduced internment, arrest without judge, jury or trial or charge. Alongside the Industrial Relations Bill came an assault on student unions, introduced by the newly emerging figure of Mrs Thatcher. This was aimed at stopping political involvement and activism. As things were, the autonomy of the student unions rendered them independent organising bodies of the students. Now the government wanted to bring them under the control of the university authorities. Strikes, boycotts and occupations were the response of the students. But within the college too the debate and argument as to the role of college, the nature of our study, the form of assessment raged as it had done since inception. We founded The Ruskin Dissatisfaction Committee, and had had some success in liberalising the exam system, but the following year we produced a joint draft under the title of their Students' Minority Committee on Examinations. 'The Rusker's Boating Song' (to the tune of the Eton one—'Jolly boating weather ... '—what else?) lampooned our more conservative and acquiescent colleagues.

> We are all working class students
> We come from the great unwashed
> Filled with reforming fervor
> But now this has all be squashed,
> For we are at Ruskin College,
> Away from the common herd

So Hurrah for the English method
And Marx is a dirty word.
We used to be revolutionaries
Once built a barricade
Nationalised the means of production
The ruling class was afraid
But now we're at Ruskin College
We believe in going slow
So three hearty cheers for Oxford
And hurrah for the status quo
We're learning to call dinner 'luncheon'
We all take tea at four
We no longer spit in the ashtrays
We knock before opening a door
For now we're at Ruskin College
We cheer for the best of schools
We think of our mates in the factory
And we laugh at the bloody fools.

We ended up with a position not only that there should be no exams, but that we shouldn't take the existing exams; although quite a number of us made that pledge only one person held to it. Later, in the second year, we were to draw up our own alternative set of lectures, seminars and booklist. The struggle over purchasing them was to be the most bitter of all clashes with the authorities, who were usually represented by John Hughes, the college vice-principal.

RAPH SAMUELS

Raph Samuels—somewhat eccentric. How? Well firstly his appearance, a wafer-thin person, very Jewish with a great swathe of jet black hair which came across the front of face and perpetually fell in front when he was talking, only to be swept back over his head as he got animated in his theme. Invariably when out and about he would be on his bike, with his corduroy pants tucked into his socks. He oozed enthusiasm and was always in a rush, with never any notion of time or place or appropriateness of venues for his tutorials, which were given sometimes on the hoof. We had one en-route from his Oxford flat back to the college as he rode his bike slowly, looking about and threading my ideas in and out of his vast historical knowledge. Entirely dedicated, scholarly, anarchic revolutionary communist. You could list his attributes like a shopping list. A good tutor would tell you, you had to have faith in your own abilities; Raph would actually give you that that faith in yourself. Pose you with tasks impossible to contemplate, throw you in at the deep end, and if you didn't swim, tell you 'Write about the experience of drowning.' He founded the History Workshop, in its fifth event by the time I was being installed at Headington. These were heady days with the new left challenging all aspects of life and culture. This was the assault on conventional wisdoms in social history and how it is learned and taught

This perspective would ensure that as a first-year Ruskin College history student I would skip the years of apprenticeship supposedly required by such original research and go straight for the sacred scrolls and primary sources. Within months of meeting Raph, I was housed in the reading room of New College library rubbing shoulders with the postgrads and PhDs. The Bodleian Library and even the British Museum Reading Room were to grant me membership.

I had been set two great tasks, one to explain and discover the origins of 'cavilling'[37] in the Durham and Northumberland coalfields, and two, because pits were my life, some other field of study, which in fact evolved into a massive, almost lifelong study of the Liverpool dockers, seamen and related trades and culture of the seaport. I was soon immersed in the nineteenth century, in the daily papers and daily lives a century and a half before. And this wasn't simply reading a history, this was going back in history, indeed this was discovering history like an archaeologist and dragging it to the surface.

The research would lead me to stay at Raph's Whitechapel (Spitalfields) house in the East End of London. From the ancient gas lamps, to the cobbled streets, to the barrows trundling up and down to the markets and the shouts of the market traders, from his house untouched inside for two or more centuries on walls and stairs wound round with massive monuments of books, this was a journey through time. The house, the streets, Raph himself creaked of Victorian London. In fact, his companion at the time, Anna Davin, spoke like a character from *Jane Eyre* or *Pride and Prejudice*. Fascinated, I was spellbound and totally betwixt.

So deep did I throw myself into the original research material, reading nineteenth-century newspapers daily for many hours at a time, that on numerous occasions I caught myself recounting 'news' from 'today's newspaper' only to realise the stories were over a hundred years old. Buried as I was in the 'Tardis' of Raph's home, buried in the nineteenth century while listening to the rumble of the market stall barrows over the cobbles outside—sounds changed little over a hundred years—that on my rare emergence from writing up this research work I fully expected to see horse cabs trotting through Whitechapel. The massive vegetable market and warehouses, and the daily passage of truckloads of fruit and vegetables, meant that for about two hours after closing and the corporation sweepers coming around a veritable Garden of Eden abounded. Boxes upon boxes of abandoned fruit, some a little worse for wear, some perfect. Crates of vegetables, tatties rolling round the streets. I would take a walk with Raph and Anna and collect up loads of free stuff. They only took the exotic stuff though, thought the staple things should be left for the down-and-outs, those sleeping rough or the poor families who came to fill their baskets up as the night fell. Bliddy hell, where was the disgrace here? This was good stuff; the urge to pick up boxes and crates of tomatoes and just horde them was a strong one to resist. Still, loads of it went into the dustcarts and refuse vehicles—what a waste. The exotic stuff Raph took was like crates of little brightly coloured peppers. I had never seen them before and didn't have a clue that they were quite inedible to working-class palates at the period. It was more middle-class food; Raph's kitchen was full of it—nothing to eat, only this stuff. One trip, when Maureen was down and we went on a crop-gathering sortie, they collected up big green looking things, which again I expressed my total ignorance of. Raph expressed his utter disbelief that I didn't know what an avocado was. I didn't, I wouldn't have known what the hell it was, nor what to do with it. Maureen had to intervene and explain that truly, very few working-class families, up north anyway, she couldn't speak for anywhere else, would have seen, let alone eaten an avocado. And after all the fuss, was it some succulent, sweet little delicacy? No its a very confused beast that doesn't know what it is, it sort of tastes like egg to me, it's coarse, hairy, and they cook the damn thing, but they still think its the fruit equivalent of caviar. Working-class people had obviously let this particular middle-class privilege pass without much argument. Mind, I felt exactly the same about garlic. Often Raph would say, 'Just let yourself in, and make yourself something to eat.' I would rummage the cupboards looking for tins of beans, or tatties, or yer knaa, basic bait like, but what was there? Garlic, ranks and ranks of herbs, them avocados, even funnier yet the aubergine; God must have designed that while he worked on the platypus duck. Bread, oh aye, bread, flat, hard, bricklike German bread, like a sort of old Christmas cake. Poor Raph. Apart from my vegetarianism was my working-class conservatism which made his delight in cooking for folk a task. 'Cauliflower cheese?' he asked expectantly over the phone before a visit. 'Whey aye, nowt wrang wi that, bonny lad. Beautiful.' But then what, as my eyes bulged and sweat streamed from my brow? He had laced the whole thing in garlic. Spoiled a perfectly good nosh. Sad to say the march of that poisonous little bulb has been unabated and today it occupies many a working-class kitchen too, though not in the numbers and frequency of those middle-class folks. Strange, people middle-class people, don't you think?

THE BRITISH LIBRARY

I became a reader at Collindale's British Library newspaper archive, and the British Museum, privileges I dearly cherished. By the second year when not staying at Raph's I was installed at Oxford House, in Bethnal Green Road, or else hitch-hiking from Ruskin down the M40 to London and back, day on day, week on week, month on month. The best-quality lifts in the country, Rollses and Bentleys. In one, I was actually to be given my first real chance of selling out. After messing around as to what he did and who he was, John Bulmer, of the one-time family cider firm, before they 'went public' he told me, now the thrusting young top sales executive of the company. We discussed socialism, and the family Quaker tradition from whence he and his company had come, and the ethics they worked by. Although I seem to recall they didn't have a union in his firm, 'because we don't need them'. John, was on the crest of a wave, he was taking the company from back-of-the-shelf plodding product range to a young, dynamic and male customer. His adverts were bringing cider back to centre stage (though not in my range; I had never recovered from my 14-pint massacre while in the YCL at the age of 14). He was fairly taken with me, and offered me a job then and there, when I finished at Ruskin, in personnel or PR:

'A new field just opening up for people like yourself,' he enthused. We corresponded for a while, he even invited Maureen and me down to his country house. Although we enjoyed the crack, we never took him up on the job offer or the trip to the country. Still, it heartily made me feel wanted, though we soon lost contact.

PETTY CRIMINALS

Back home for a lang weekend, I discovered that Ken Terry and Cher had split up not very long after they had got married. Not an earth-shattering event, but for the knock-on effect. A young married couple, they hadn't even unpacked many of the wedding presents, indeed some stuff was still in their boxes, new and unused. I don't know if that was true of them two as well, but that's aside the point. Ken was now living in his house at Thorne not far from Dowes's bakery where he worked. He had also become chair of the LPYS and was drawing closer to the party. Just over the bridge in Stainforth was a bric-a-brac shop which also bought and sold second-hand goods. Ken had taken along a number of the unwanted and often duplicated and triplicated presents—three alarm clocks, two canteens of cutlery etc. The bloke had paid him for the things, but then phoned the police and described his suspicions as to how a young lad had all these unlikely things. Obviously stolen or being fenced. Ken was at work when the filth rolled up, and finding nobody in, forced an entrance through the back and then ransacked his house. In the process they found all the Young Socialist gen, all the Revolutionary Workers Party materials and much else. When Ken arrived back, his front door was open, and sitting in his armchair, copying out a list from the LPYS address book of all the socialist and communist activists in the area, a rather fat and scruffy cop who carried on writing, and explained that they were acting on 'information received'; actually, he told him, it was Stovin's who had phoned them. Ken had no need to explain, it was obvious what had happened. Well it would be after you've read through all the diaries and letters in the house—the stuff wasn't stolen so it was OK. What about breaking in? Not us mate, someone must have forced an entrance in the back door and we disturbed them just as we arrived; good thing, eh? Well, later that night we had been at a late party somewhere over Thorne, and Ken who drove a Triumph Herald at that time drove us back. Drunk? Quite well drunk, I would say, people would think nowt of driving with four five pints in them. Anyway tanked up and coming towards Stovin's Ken says, 'That's that bastard's shop.' So I say, 'Alreet stop then, lets have a look.' He stops; suddenly, I have a building brick and wham, straight through the plate glass window. Ken decides he had better add one too, then we dive in the car as little brass bells start to tumble from the shop window, those daft little brass things of women in crinolines and little fat men with a dinger up their arses. Anyway we spin around and gather up these stupid bells and nick a few more out of the window while we're at it. Why? I haven't got a clue. At the time it was a drunken act of revenge, with bells on so to speak. Anyway, as we drive off we notice some workers standing in the shadows of the bus stop waiting for their day shift bus to take them to Scunthorpe Steel Works. We think nowt of this—they'll see it as an act of resistance to capitalism, and wave a clenched fist salute out the window as we roar off into the night. Well Ken drops me off, I get the bell collection and stick them in a bag and stick them in the kennel at the bottom of the garden and collapse drunkenly into bed alongside Maureen. Meantime, a little later, the squad cars roll up to Ken's door.

He feins, 'What the hell yi talking about?'

But a search of his car reveals a couple of the bliddy bells on the back seat. 'Lets go and collect your mate who lives on Broadway,' they say and bang-bang-bang in the night, they come for me. Revolutionary and thinker, bell thief. It was the morning of 14 March 1971. On 3 May we faced a stiff talking-to by the magistrate, who convicted us, and charged us with entering a building and stealing and criminal damage. A local Labour Party bigwig who actually knew us, but he didn't jail us or have us shot; we were fined a total of £19.96 each but the humiliation is there with the record. Humiliation, not for breaking the law for God's sake, but for breaking it in such imbecilic circumstances. Of all the daft things I have done in my life, this is one which curls me up in self-hatred, when my subconscious is in 'torture me at the stake' mode.

THE DEATH OF WARDLEY COLLIERY

In March of 1971 my old Lodge and that of me Dad and Grandad and the famous coalfield revolutionary George Harvey, Follonsby, closes. It is a sad and sorry day; the men still say there was coal to get—'The Victoria seam, lad, is 5 foot thick, it lies 60 yards below the 1480'—but our own mining engineer says it isn't. That old smoky shaft still sits there, open these last decades, and way doonbelaw its we'ttor filled depths lay miles upon miles of magic and mystery and backbreaking toil and ghosts, and my adolescent thoughts still prowl the endless roadways of Monkton, still struck with awe at the big silver 3s twisting on their lang legs, spewing wa'ater, making the falling staindust fines mix into pure plaster at the leg as they ream into the caunch, still climb the wind torn staplepit, crawl the thin seams, explore the path through the hundred-million-year-old forest which we had cleared, though Geordie doubted, and remember the rebellion, the mock, the crack, the pain. They are trapped there since my young spirit first descended the old shaft into its ancient aud seams. This old shaft that ties us through time and space to a millennium of Northumbria pit work, Tyneside coal work, The Geordie pitmen, the birth pangs of wa character, ethnicity and class, but it sounds too damn romantic and precious, these strange feelings, like some sort of wormhole in space. Though yee'l ken weel what Ah mean, if yee'v felt it.

Into all the boiling industrial strife comes the plans for entry into the European Common Market which it was hoped would greatly assist the ruling class across Europe to control wages and resistance.[38]

July 1971. Maureen gets to star on TV again. This time it's Calendar Sunday and the debate is about the forthcoming decision of whether to join the EEC or not. Maureen had been invited to do the housewify bit, and talk about shopping prices. Of course she didn't, she wanted to know about the creation of a super state, which would intervene into respective countries and put down workers' rebellions. She wanted to know about the drafting of troops from one country to another. Incidentally, a young Arthur Scargill was also on this programme. He was later to tell me: 'I thought I was to be the left wing slant on the programme then Maureen came on, and I thought who the hell is this—she's worse than me!'

LIVERPOOL

The material I was uncovering about Liverpool at this time was groundbreaking stuff, and I was accumulating acres of it in all directions: labour, the poor, housing, education, strikes, unions, and politics. Raph frequently confiscated boxes of Xeroxes and ruthlessly cut pages of unfocused research to try and keep my tub on the rails. This to me, though, was one big voyage through time, a voyage of discovery and jealously guarded treasure stolen from the past. When I presented the original draft as a paper in 1971 at the History Workshop in Oxford, Raph had to twist my arm to include references to footnotes. Indeed a question from the floor as to my sources drew a response from me that 'I had made it all up.'

Raph showed me techniques which stayed with me all my life. The use of *Palmer's Index To The Times*, illuminated fascinating and hitherto moments of the miners' history, my Wardley history lang since buried and forgotten. Day by day I was scanning the newspapers from a century and a half earlier, page by page, resisting the urge to read the whole thing, eyes tuned to Dockers, Seamen, Strikes. Searching County Records Offices. My own technique on the miners' stuff was searching the gravestones for the miner's tombs, village by village, taking photos of each one. A little girl in Heworth cemetery was to report to her Mam that she had seen me, and I 'was taking photos of the dead people', as indeed I was, and recording their lives, I hoped.

The original work was written as a portrayal, yes, of the waterfront, but also of general strikes in the city itself. This was a novel discovery: in the nineteenth century and before, whole towns would turn out together in collective action regardless of skills and trades. It is a feature which up until that time, anyway as far as I could tell, was, largely ignored by labour historians, mainly because these 'unions' were not unions in their, or rather the Webbs', definition, not being continuous associations of wage-earners and, more often than not, were lacking the fine minutes and middle-class parliamentary procedures, were unlike the associations the Webbs *et al.* considered real *bona-fide* trade unions. So their history went unnoticed or anyway unrecorded. It seemed the height of cheek, perhaps but I dared to say the Webbs' huge, 'pioneering' work on unions was flawed, like that of many other subsequent observers, by their petit-bourgeois preconception of what they were observing. Because they came from the world of learning and literature, of written records, of accounts and consistency, they judged the development of workers' organisations by how far they conformed to such precepts of organisation. With the top hatted artisans and craftsmen, the educated aristocrats of labour they found kindred souls developing trade unions on models of the craft guilds, with formal ceremonies, minutes, written records, statements of accounts and educated speech. The unskilled, untutored, illiterate labourer on the other hand had to wait until ideologically motivated artisans and craftsmen carried the message and model of trade unionism down to the labouring classes in the 'New Unionism' of the 1890s. It was a canny tale but utterly untrue! Thousands of labour history students have been misled into following the trail of the mythical creature 'New Unionism'. In the process they ignore and are taught not to see or perhaps 'exceptionalise' decades and centuries of unionism among seamen, dockers, miners and labourers of all sorts who had existed, fought, won and lost monumental battles, without the needs of minutes, bank accounts, fixed organisation or continuity for hundreds of years before the so-called 'New Unions' emerged. On the day of my presentation, the first chapters of the forthcoming Liverpool work, from the big hall down in Walton Street to the mass crowds of students and accomplished academics, I set my research in contradiction to 'the Webbs, Hobsbawm, and whole concept of New Unionism' to a 'hoorah' from the floor both cynical and supportive.

Maureen was down for the Workshop, and I basked in the glory of just being here, standing on my hind legs, addressing a mass ensemble of Oxford students and professors and students and tutors from colleges and universities nationwide, together with pockets of trade unionists and class militants come to seek the holy grail of our class history. The disclosure of amassing features of history, dug from time for the first time is a thrill only those filled with the fascination and continuation of times lang syne will appreciate.

Incidentally I had suggested to Maureen that she should come along to the Gun Club to have a go. Normally, you begin, and indeed continue for years, on a single-shot pistol. Correcting you aim, seeing how the gun pulls. On this occasion, I learned another reason. I passed Maureen straight onto a semi-automatic, and she at once blasted the target area and much of the wall to smithereens. She never hit the card, though she would certainly have put to flight a regiment of the master race and possibly a few low-flying aircraft.

The History Workshop agenda for 1971 reflects that most carnival (and sometimes carnal) of history events, speakers on their hind legs like stump orators, giving it some welly to mass crowds of workers and students. Ernest presentations of work long in research, and unfolding pages of yet undisclosed history like a seat on a time machine. Raph had once explained that the Workshops had begun in 1966 'as an attack on the examination system and the humiliations which it imposed upon adult students.' Rebellious young socialist feminists were digging their way from under the history where they and their sex had been buried, rediscovering the massive and important intervention of their sisters throughout history, hitherto unrecorded and or largely ignored by historians. Nartub Kettle was to say (in *New Society*):

> When Samuel gives a paper he does not read from a prepared and refined text, or even from closely argued notes. He delivers an argument from his head, summoning up supporting facts from an avalanche of papers, each of which contains some reference ... there is something of the professor from Conrad's *The Secret Agent* about his sense of subversive certainty.

And something infinitely appealing about his diffident benign, peering expression, the constant restlessness, the sharp movements of the head, the Bobby Charlton haircut and the almost childlike unpretentiousness of his manner. He disdains and yet demands individual attention.

Corridors jammed with stalls of 57 varieties of anarcho/Marxist/Leninist/Trotskyist groups, the crèche resounded to children while the evening bars bounced to stomping folk music and fiddle tunes in one common room, the disco strobe highlighted Motown in the other. The sniff of wine, booze and good stuff could be detected and the evening sleeping bag accommodation offered the chance of historic encounters by other means. These History Workshops had a great deal in common with folk-rock festivals and demonstrated most vividly that education and scholarship really could be fun. Mind, the radical feminists scored an own goal with their graffiti attempt. A massive wall near the big Oxford bus station bore in huge white paint the slogan WOMEN IN LABOUR KEEP CAPITAL IN POWER. Bliddy Oxfash or the Tory club in one of their brighter moments altered the entire slogan and scored a lasting success by adding one word, it then became KEEP WOMEN IN LABOUR KEEP CAPITAL IN POWER. The damn thing stayed on the wall for decades. I met Alun Howkins, as a great History Workshop enthusiast and contributor. A former Ruskin student, then studying up at Oxford, he nonetheless frequented Ruskin, a regular visitor at the bar when it opened and an excellent singer at the socials. Alun was an expert on farm labourers, and a great exponent of songs and music from that tradition. He spoke in the traditional Oxfordshire dialect, not the 'Queen's English' as spoken by HM and all the hangers-on, not the ultra-posh of Oxford's public schoolboy undergrads, but real Oxfordshire. Alun came from a part of former working-class Oxford called Quarry for the most obvious of reasons, the area from whence the stonemasons and quarrymen since Middle Ages had hewed and fashioned rock and stone for their gleaming towers and spires. It was an 'oo-arr' accent. What was so totally annoying for Alun was the fact that it was the accent that 'folk singers' who didn't come from anywhere themselves chose to sing in. It was a folky voice accent, which people transported to all songs. Very annoying for Alun, who actually came from the place from which all their adopted voices had originated. Alun was to become a great friend and comrade, and accompanied me back to Donny to experience pit life and culture. Doing the folky night in the aud lad's hooses, playing his wee squeezebox while they played the big piano accordions and I improvised with lethal-looking cutlery from the kitchen, a rapper dance. He was a frequent guest at our regular folk nights in clubs during and after my stay at Ruskin. Jim Shipley was like many of the Hatfield miners—also something of a fieldsman, out with the dog, poaching, walking, picked up a bit about fields and agriculture himself. On one of our early morning rambles over the fields of Hatfield, I pounced on a field of snadgies. 'Ha, ha! Turnips!' I said, cutting the skin off and about to eat the beast raw. 'Its sugarbeet, Dave,' they both cautioned. 'Bollocks sugarbeet, it's a turnip!' And I bit into the sugary spongy mass—sugarbeet! Phwett!

In heated debates over meanings of history, aspects of class war, political events

Alun would for years afterwards counter my certainty with the response, 'Sugarbeet, Dave!'

STRANGE ENCOUNTERS

I was still corresponding with Robyn, who was at University in Edinburgh now, and I took the opportunity of staying with Cinema Action to invite her down as she was interested in getting involved with revolutionary film. She had resisted my suggestion that she should join the YCL, as 'they were just kids.' She was being drawn towards the hated International Socialism group. I had also suggested that we could explore 'our relationship', which was a bit hamfisted. She wrote back that she thought our relationship was just political, 'but we'll see.' Which set me heart racing. When we met up we were a novelty of newness, a sort of rediscovery, a wealth of uncovered knowledge and experience. We mutually poured into each other. Every now and then, we would get to passionate necking, but Schlacke, Cinema Action's director, kept coming in, or sending us on some errand. I think he thought he was protecting Maureen's interests. We went to some arty cinema that evening and watched Mick Jagger's *Performance*. It was excellent we thought; the sexy scenes were very erotic and put me in mind of the trim form which probably lay beneath this combination of cheesecloth shirt and tight blue jeans, though of course I didn't try and put my arm around her or snog her in the pictures—good God no, she'd think that far too juvenile—just have to let things take their course, sort of evolve along those lines. When we at last looked toward time for bed, it was obvious we were sleeping in the same bed. I assumed, of course, that that meant sex. I took the chance of her going to clean her teeth, to whip clothes off and dive into bed. I think I even put a condom on.

She came back in, fully clothed and went 'I'm not sure I want to have sex with you Dave.'

Oh, Oh. 'Well, that's OK. I always sleep with nowt on anyway.'

'Yeah,' she says, 'so do I,' and pulled her shirt off over her head, revealing those firm pert tits and bulging nipples. Jeans and knickers off in one go, and I watched her slim little body and tight bum walk over to the light switch and put it off.

Well somehow, as soon as she got into bed, and turned toward me we just sort of melted together, I totally ignored what she had said previously, and just started to pet her, which she responded to. Rolled over and started to shag her. Her body, the tightness of her vagina, the feel of her ribs and firmness of her belly her arms suddenly around my neck. I was coming already, much too soon. I began to say 'I can't hold it,' in order to come and then get on with bringing her off orally while I built up a new erection, but she thought I couldn't perform or something. I started 'I can't ...'

She cut me short: 'Well that's OK, Dave, it's been a hectic day.'

Crunch. That was it. Penis shrank to the size of a small slug, and the Durex fell dejected from it. I wanted to explain, I wanted to make her, well make her.

'Lets sleep,' she said, and I didn't want to seem uncool or anything, so that was it.

To say I felt incredibly foolish the next day was not resolved by the impression given to everyone else in the squat that we had shagged. This situation had to be put right; my self-respect depended upon it. A few months later there was a big Women's Liberation conference in Edinburgh, and Robyn invited me up for the weekend. I resolved to hitch. The lifts to Doncaster were not usually too bad—going up anyway; coming back, because it was a Sunday, was usually much more of a problem. But I figured if I landed a big lorry headed north I could do OK. Wrong. Although I stood out on the big roundabout at Headington, from early Friday morning, nowt stopped. So I set off walking, to get to the other side of Oxford, thumbing all the way. Nowt, it was winter and as I inched my way north in ten thousand small rides the snow began to fall. I had on only a thin jacket. By about 9 p.m. I had reached ironically enough just outside Eyemouth, and stood on the desolate roundabout. On the opposite side of the road a forlorn hitchhiker told me he'd been trying to hitch to London and this was as far as he'd got. He suggested that at this rate it would take me 'three days, man'. It sounded like Arlo Guthrie at Woodstock, so I echoed, 'Three whole days, man,' which he repeated and we laughed. I left him walking south to a better vantage point. The snow came down thicker and thicker and the sheep in the field were now standing in a huddle to keep warm. My body began to freeze, my face was ice, my eyes were frozen. Should I get in the field and sit among the sheep till I see some lights coming? Did I in fact end up doing just that for warmth? I cannot recall, but I do remember the welcome lights of a pub some distance from the road, and I set off walking. Inside the pub a roaring coal fire was stacked up the chimney and I entered dripping snow, and couldn't speak for some time. The jolly jack tar sailors in the pub assured me that I would never get a lift at this time of year at this time of night, and true, it was a long, long time since I had heard a lorry. I thawed out and near closing time, cast myself back out into the night. Fortunately for my survival the bus stops in the Borders are proper closed-in sheds with windows. I was able to stand in there and peer into the night for signs of a lorry, or a car, but the odd car that did come was only going home, round the block or up the road. Then I seen the lights of a bus. It was however gaan the wrang way headed back to Berwick back the ten or fifteen miles I had just painfully advanced. Shit, I'll catch it and get the train from Berwick. I landed on Berwick station cold wet and forlorn. No trains to Edinburgh tonight, only one from Newcastle in the morning, at 5 a.m. OK just give me a ticket and I'll wait for it. Sorry, sonny, the station closes after this last train to Newcastle. What? Back on the streets of Berwick and looking for a place to kip down, a warm doorway, a bus shelter, anything. Well, Berwick must be pretty keen to repel all vagrants as not a crack or a crevice big enough to shelter me from the blizzard now blowing could be found. What did I do? I went back to the poxy station, which they close at night, and bought a ticket to Edinburgh, but then jumped on the Newcastle train. I was now unpicking my journey, by another 60 or 70 miles in order not to die from hypothermia. Once at the Central I could sit for a draughty few hours and await the Edinburgh train, which I duly caught. It was turning 7 a.m. when I staggered up the winding metal staircase of Robyn's tenement flat. She had told me where the key was, and I opened the door.

She was just stirring in bed. 'Where yi been?' she asked sleepily as I undressed, and naked rolled my exhausted, frozen body into bed beside her.

'You're like a corpse,' she said. 'Soon warm you up!' and at least one part of my body found the blood from somewhere to mount a rock-hard erection, mind I'm not so sure it wasn't frozen solid.

With no more ado, I rolled over and entered Robyn.

She looked at me, just like that, straight in the face. 'I don't want sex with you Dave,' she said.

There I was, up to the maker's name as they say, which I just assumed was one of the reasons I had just hitched the entire length of the country in a blizzard, and she was saying, na.

'Oh,' I said a bit stupidly. 'We are comrades and friends Dave, you know when the chemistry just doesn't work, even though you want it to, it doesn't feel right, I feel like you're my brother or something.'

Brother, blather, a quick withdrawal was in order. 'Is that OK?' she asked.

'Hell whey aye.' I suggested it was my fault for presuming we had something sexual.

'Do you always assume relations with females are sexual?' she asked. 'Well not all females,' I answered, adding on reflection, 'But mostly.' I thought, 'I mean, why not?' The conference as it turned out was the biggest ensemble of middle-class ladies I had ever come across. One woman was arguing with me that all women were all more oppressed than any man. She extended the logic to say that Queen Victoria was more exploited and doubly exploited as a woman more than a Victorian coal-mining man. At some other point in the conference, a women announced: 'Why go on about working class women? We are all exploited, we all suffer from poverty. I am struggling to pay for the hay for my daughters' ponies!' I kid you not, and would I lie about such things? It stuck in my memory like a fish bone in a cat's gullet, and I have after all reason to remember this conference.

The road south on Sunday was dismal and I was shattered, my head rolled about and my eyes strained to stay open. It's bad manners to sleep when someone picks you up, but at last I just couldn't stay awake and slept slumped against the window, to the other side of Newcastle, passing all the bonny Northumbrian coast and the scenes of our first encounters with the Coldingham gang. Boy did I feel stupid. This was not a story to share with Larch; God knows what he'd mek of that.[39]

August 1971. Internment introduced in Ireland. All pretence at 'the rule of law' and 'due process' is ended. 'Justice' is dropped by the state as its armed bodies of men arrest all males in the Six Counties likely to be rebels, without charge, without evidence, without trial, and put them into concentration camps.

21 August 1971. George Jackson one of the founding theorists of the Black Panther Party is shot down and murdered in prison.

We invited Lawrence (Daly) up to speak at Ruskin. He came back to a flat party we had at Chris's. We were all there, Larch and Fred and others, and having a sing around. Chris said that he thought Lawrence would be the last secretary of the NUM.

Lawrence said 'No, I wont, HE will be' and pointed at me without laughing. Fred giggled a bit, and then went 'Could be, could be.'

I can save you the suspense. I wasn't, although on a couple of occasions I think I got near to the start line. I think I always underestimated the block of forces in the higher echelons of the NUM who would turn heaven and earth to ensure I didn't get in the race, ner mind the finish line. November. One of my early encounters with TV, *Look North*, was doing a programme about the closure of the North-East coalfield which was going on unabated: *Close The Coalhouse Door*. They wanted to feature people who had been ousted from the pit but managed to survive anyway, along with men on the verge whose pits were on the verge. I think the idea behind it was that there was life after coal mining, but I wasn't quitting the industry. They correctly identified that I was at Ruskin College now, but then said I intended to go back to work at Wardley when I finished—a bit wet as many people were to later comment. The interviewer had done a preliminary interview with us, so he knew who had to be stopped from long political interventions. I came with a sheaf of notes about fact and figures and the economics of the industry, but he wouldn't let me get more than a sentence in. Actually I was on with one of the Fitzpatricks, whose pit was closing; he ended up in Coventry Colliery, I think. Me Dad was laid up in hospital having his hip done. I went to see him before going onto the TV studio on New Bridge Street. He had been through hell and said he didn't think he would have the other one done. A month or so later, he was jigging aboot like me Ma at a ceilidh. Sometime around this time, we went to a big disco, a social at an all-women's college, out in the sticks somewhere. We cut a dash in Larch's sports car. Trouble was, he scored and I bliddy didn't. So I was the spare prick, crumpled up like a rear gunner in the back of the two-seater car, while he and some posh totty he had pulled headed off back to her house, actually her old man's. Oxford and its inhabitants are rather like the miners in one respect. The stereotypical view of both is largely accurate, I mean miners did wear cloth caps, keep pigeons and greyhounds or whippets, did get drunk, did beat each other up, did go on strike, did speak strong dialects etc. As for Oxford, this pad was a case in point. It was actually a mansion, set in tree-filled grounds, with huge wrought-iron gates and big wooden doors. Inside, in the hall they would call it, stood suits of armour and a grandfather clock, while up the wall of the stairs were portraits of upper-class twits and colonel blimps, obviously the family gallery.

Larch pulled the giggling thin rich young thing up the stairs.

'Daddy sleeps in the other wing so we won't disturb him,' she said confidently 'and anyway, he's quite cool about cheps. Help yourself to drink,' she offered, before I heard them disappear down what must have been a very long corridor.

'OK then.' I set off to finish getting plastered and then crash oot. The cabinet houses all kinds of shorts and whisky and that sort of thing. Ney beer, in the fridge, any beer? It's that bliddy middle-class thing again isn't it, oceans of spirits but ney bliddy beer, not even puke-inducing, smelly Southern beer. Ah, a mini cellar, and racks of wine, hmm I bet this is all real posh and real ancient wines, ner mind, just pick the one with the least dust on. That'll dey. Whey, why waste posh stuff on me, I just want to drink it.

I finish the bottle, and then after a fearful exploration of rooms and corridors in the dark looking for the bog, during which times I passed a number of suits of armour and peered inside just to be sure, I curl up on a greet settee, amid the clump ... clump ... clump ... of the pendulum

They two get up around 11 a.m. and I'm rear gunner again. We drive to the local. Rich country folk in tweed jackets, and bear-stalker hats, ladies in woollen cardies over flowery dresses, upper-class girls in their bonnets and Laura Ashley dresses, drinking and talking around the pub tables in the sunshine. We order sandwiches and as we start to eat them a spuggy comes hopping on the table, straight up to me, and I offer in jest my sandwich, which it springs forward and starts to peck at, without the least fear.

'Look at this, look at this bird!' I say loudly and excitedly, and the girl, without sarcasm, in all genuineness says 'Don't they have sparrows in Doncaster?'

I am speechless. Larch says, 'I think he was talking about how tame it was.'

The bar at Ruskin was downstairs in the cellar; upstairs was the games room with two big snooker tables and a table tennis table. Some students would night on night come here have a quiet pint and play pool and then go neatly off to bed. They had done this for two years or whatever its equivalent had been up at Headington, they never ventured into the town, never whooped it up. That tap: long pause, tap: long pause, tap of those snooker balls, rolling almost silently across the big tables and into the pockets. Walking round, bending, tapping the ball with the stick, walking round, tapping the ball with the stick. It was like some dream stuck in a groove, like those misty English cricket greens and mind-numbing distant thud of cork on willow, only without the sporadic and restrained clap from the terraces. Well it takes all sorts. I and a couple of very drunken undergrads from the university were playing our own stupid version of pool, which I recall involved whanging the balls in fast succession at each other. This progresses to batting them across the table tennis table, and eventually as the pool balls ricocheted off the floor and walls, one went through the big plate glass window, with a deafening crash; the other student, because it was his serve, then whanged the other ball through the remainder of the window, which came down with a resounding crash. They dropped everything and headed for the front door, as stampeding feet were heard charging down the stairs from the rooms above. I delayed slightly, but standing there with a bat and a new open-plan games room, I didn't seem to have any immediate excuses to hand and took off down the corridor. I thought to make my escape through Chris's kitchen, past his bedroom and out through his front door back over to my place. But they were upon my heels, I could see his front door was locked and I wouldn't have time to open it, so I did a sharp turn left and ran into Chris's bedroom. I could hear the feet pounding down the corridor, so I leapt into the bed and under the covers.

Under the covers already were Chris and a sweet smelling naked girl. Chris looked at me through the gloom. 'Any particular reason why you're in my bed,

Dave?' he asked in his Cockney accent, though with his long-suffering, 'bleedin Northern person' inference, not the deliberate and slow, Michael-Cain-type 'I ... Am Going ... To Kill ...You!' voice. 'Shhhh.'

Then there was a loud knock on the door. Chris got up to answer it, and for some unknown reason I thought it would allay suspicions if I started necking with the girl, who, totally confused, didn't quite get into the part. Chris opens the door, bollock-naked.

A voice comes, Gimpy I think: 'Is bliddy Dave Douglass in there?' 'I bleedin well 'ope not!' replies Chris, not lying really.

As the feet receded down the corridor I made a dive to get out, but they had turned round and spotted me, caught me getting the key into my front door opposite. Then they accused me of smashing windows in the games room!

'Me? You set of bastards!' I came storming back over, where a small crowd of students were angrily discussing the smashed windows, and my name was in great frequency.

'Yee fuckers blaming me yee fucking bastards? Want to see some damage?' I yelled. I pick up a chair and go to smash it over a table, in a demonstration of rage, that I am accused of smashing the widows, and to prove it, if your gaana accuse us, I'll start smashing other things. Had a certain logic at the time.

Calm was called for, and a student court of inquiry called in the common room the next day's dinner time. Oh, the evidence was stacked high, but ney body had actually seen who did the act, only that someone thought they saw me, disappearing stage left, then acting suspiciously in the residences.

Dave Merrick leapt to my defence: 'A number of us have been horrified at the flimsy cases made out for criminal damage at the army recruitment centre during the occupation, and the indiscriminate nature of those identified as having been responsible. It seems to me there are people here who have a lot less evidence prepared to make the same kind of leap to accusation.'

I was called upon to speak and taking centre stage burst forth:

> Since I was young I've always been keen on judging others.
> I used to practise flagellation on my younger brothers.
> From there my path was straight and true.
> My school was right, my college too, I've joined the most exclusive clubs and I mingled with the noblest bloods.
> My views are strictly of the right and quite above suspicion,
> In the art of legal strategy, I was soon a skilled tactician.
> And so today above the fray in my exalted state,
> I judge the crimes of mortal men a messenger of fate.
> Give that peasant 50 years me livers bad this morning.
> Cut off that lying peasant's ears and let that be a warning. That punishment's the only way to teach you plebs crime doesn't pay, and every day is judgment day. Hey, ring-a-ding ding I love the spring the pretty birds sing so gaily, I don my wig and dance a jig and delve out judgments daily, in ordinary robes I'm an ordinary man, but dressed in my regalia, I punish every lawbreaker and chastise every failure....

It was sung in a judge-like imitation and went down a bomb among some though not all the students. The decision of the court was 'Not Proven'. But I was still called to office of the principal, Billy Hughes, who asked me to pay towards the windows. 'Pay, me? I'm broke and innocent!' which at least was partly true, so that was that. I never saw those middle-class Irish twats again. If I could have remembered who they were I would have gone round to their JCR and repaid the compliment, if they hadn't already done so themselves.

It was during this time that the comrades at home started to plodge in distinctly muddy water. Maureen was going to bite the bullet and have 'the meeting' with Legay Shipley, the Keir-Hardy-style Labour man, with a passion for the people and the cause of the poor as he put it. 'All you young people ought to be in t' Labour Party and Young Socialists,' he had pestered. Maureen wrote:

> As you know tonight was the meeting with Jim's dad. He's a great fellow, I think you'd get on with him very well. He's an old type LP Member, a bit like your Dad. He really believes in socialism but not Communism (really what he thinks Communism is is the USSR type police state). However he's a very good militant worker and said that all that's really wrong in Russia is the bureaucracy. He's also branch secretary of the National Union of Public Employees who are on strike of course.
>
> Anyway he's keen to see a YS Branch formed because he believes that's one way of keeping the LP Bureaucracy in check. We discovered that all official members of the YS have to be members of the LP. So as a means to an end I've had to put my name forward, along with Jim and Ken to join the LP. in order to start a branch. As you can imagine there are certain channels to be gone thro! Jim's dad also suggesting setting up a branch of LP at Hatfield so we'd also have full voting rights at the actual big conference. However we intend to concentrate on the YS And Jim is going to write off to Area Organiser of LP.

None of this stuff was at first been something we relished. The Labour Party was after all part of the problem, not part of the solution. Throughout the Vietnam War we had charged the Labour leadership with providing support and aid to the USA. We were convinced it had only been the depth of our hostile reaction to that war and to the role of the USA which stayed the hand of Wilson from sending troops, perhaps even of reintroducing conscription, something we were already preparing mass resistance to. Labour had launched Britain's nuclear programme, Labour had gone ahead with bringing US nuclear submarines here, and testing atomic and hydrogen bombs all over the place, in preparation for nuclear war against the Soviet Union. None of this the subject of permission from Cabinet, or Parliament, let alone the people.

So Labour, at least the leadership, was not exactly our cup of tea. Even at local level, those dreary parish pump councillors were almost to a man right-wingers despite being almost to a man miners. When there were big public meetings at the Miners' Welfare at Stainforth, of the Communist Party together with the Labour Left—Len Caven, for example, chairman of Hatfield NUM Branch—I always got up to denounce the so-called Labour Party and dispute that they were socialists or ever had been. This greatly rankled with Frank Watters and the local Communist Party activists; not the line at all—it couldn't have helped my clumsy attempts to join the CP. Forebye, the mass of workers actually still saw the Labour

Party as a means of change, as an expression of working class politics, as our side. Inside the Labour Party and the Labour Party Young Socialists was a desperate fight for direction of the party and the whole movement. The whole of the Young Socialists had been expelled and the organisation closed down and disbanded. It had fallen heavily under the control and orientation of Gerry Healy's Socialist Labour League. They were kicked out, but retained the earlier Young Socialist title. The Labour Leadership had relaunched the Labour Party Young Socialists as a cleansed and sanitised body.

It wasn't to stay like that, as the other non-Healyite Trotskyist groups reorganised. It wasn't long before the Militant tendency became the dominant group throughout the LPYS, making heavy inroads into pockets and constituencies of the Labour Party itself. Could we actually be so simon-pure as not to want to get our hands dirty in that struggle? It felt almost embarrassing to even discuss it. Then to agree and sanction joining the damn organisation was like wading in shit. But we had seen it as a platform too important to be left to the quasi-Tories and traitors who had taken over the party since its earlier more sincere inception—as an alliance of socialist bodies and ideas rather than a fixed and proscribed social-democratic bourgeois party infesting and dominating the class and limiting its progress, which it had become. In or out of that party, we couldn't pretend it didn't exist.

Would that we had ever seen the day when we thought we would be in that organisation. However it wasn't our own choices or being in the most sexy sounding revolutionary group that mattered, but standing with the masses in their camp. It was a fact 'the masses' were by and large still standing in Labour's camp despite the mass growth of groups, parties and alliances on the revolutionary left.

Joining the Labour Party for 'entrist' work wasn't joining a serious political party, this wasn't a party of our views, this was a party of the class, through which to express our views. We had the perspective that we revolutionaries could not off our own bat walk away from a platform around which the masses still clustered. Besides which the battle inside that party was far from lost. From time to time, particularly in opposition, it swung sharply to the left and all sorts of fearfully socialist and downright revolutionary ideas might be advanced and debated in conference.

So first Maureen, Ken and Jim and then others joined the Labour Party itself, and applied to form a branch of the LPYS. They were instead informed they should form a Constituency body since no other LPYS branch existed in the constituency. Well, Goole was the local Labour Party constituency, not in our knowledge a hot bed of revolution, but we didn't know its stormy history then. So the Goole LPYS was up and operating. In a short time it was to become the biggest LPYS group in the country and certainly its most revolutionary. By the time Peter Doyle and myself addressed a public meeting of the group on 20 February 1971 at the Miners Welfare, Stainforth, we had close to 100 members.

Within the LPYS we became a sensation. The working class credentials of our members, indeed the rough and raw nature of our delegates, never mind our members at large, and the crimson red nature of their politics, together with a constant sense of fun and having a party, set us aside from the Militant grouping and put us in alliance with other Trotskyist groups on their left, like the Chartists. Goole Constituency LPYS was to become something of a Tyneside Committee of 100 in terms of its standing among young folk, and its epicentre for parties, camps, outings, folk and disco nights. 'Gooleys'—that's what our abbreviation looked like (Goole YS), so we stole the Boy Scout song: 'Ging gang gooleys gooleys gooleys watcher ging gang goole ging gang goole, ging gang gooleys gooleys gooleys watch out we're from Goole we're from Goole!' The YS had links, mutual friends; we shared the Abbey as a centre with the Abbey footballers, so we turned up en-masse to cheer them on, and they invited all the young politicos to their dos, and oddly, the same happened in reverse, at least as far as raffles, socials, and stuff like that were concerned. It wasn't so odd really, all the football lads worked at the pit, on building sites or in related jobs, lived round the same streets, faced the same political system.

In the village, we were, we thought, preparing the all-round revolutionary cadre; they were a large and honed-to-perfection Bolshevik leadership. Then Art's faction upped and moved en mass to St Ives; they were still more hippy than the steely-eyed Marxists we'd endeavored to become. St Ives was the scene, man, groovy. Dozens of young workers just upped and left, squatted flats or shared them, worked the hotels, worked the bars, worked the restaurants. Set up mutual trade-ins, so that nobody ever charged anyone of the group for food, or booze, and frequently hotel rooms. They sat on the beaches, smoked dope, made love, listened to the music, were still right on, still into revolution, but t'old Labour Party and the grey streets of Dunscroft and Stainie, Thorne and Moorends were far far away. Truth was they were nearer to the heart of the revolution sweeping our generation than we were.[40]

Pete Thompson a local self-employed businessman–socialist was the ever popular organiser par excellence of everything in the area, football, football fixtures, leek and veg shows, racing pigeons, and into the bargain was the local gunslinger. Pete was a hell of a street fighter, maybe it was from being small, or from a big family, but Pete could knock them dead when called upon. In the days before we landed there, lads used to turn up, just to have a look at this Pete Thompson, and if they felt up to it, have a go at him, like the sort of gunslinger legends. I am told three carloads ambushed him one night on Broadway; Pete took a thumping, but nobody got back into the cars, and they say the cops wiped them off the pavement. But Pete was a cultured and quiet man. He came from a great socialist tradition. His family in all directions were miners and his brothers and sisters were born-again working-class activists. It wasn't odd at all that the footballers et al. were linked closely to the LPYS and the general socialist circle, including the RWP and *The Mineworker*.

The 11th National Conference of the LPYS was held in April 1972. Goole Constituency LPYS in true uncompromising form submitted a resolution on LPYS organisation. It said that it saw in the Charter and Programme of the LPYS the essence of the transitional programme of the Trotskyist Fourth International 'as a fundamental part of the world revolutionary process in its European aspect'. It called for the LPYS to carry that programme into the Labour Party itself and the movement as a whole. It called for joint Labour Party and LPYS conference and national and regional level, and similar conferences 'in unity with the Communist Party and Young Communist League as well as the Trade Unions and Trades Councils.'

Alison Sharp was our delegate and the resolution drew quite a debate, with three amendments, mainly rendering the resolution less explicit.

We camped at Scarborough, the whole team—miners, RWP comrades like Tom, the LPYS; we brought our guns too, at least four big shotguns. Peter Doyle my fellow Gateshead Tynesider was national chairman, and he knew me and our team well. He astutely avoided drawing any of our comrades from the floor of the conference into the debate of the resolutions, particularly those on Ireland and world affairs. So we kidnapped him outside the conference hall on the pretence of giving him a lift back to his digs. He got into the back of the van and at once faced four shotgun barrels.

'Right, now, Doyle,' I said. 'Either you allow wor delegates to speak, or we march down the floor of the conference with these guns and take over the platform!' 'You mad adventurous bastards,' he smirked. 'Luek Davie, I give yee me Geordie word of honour. I will not overlook your delegates the morra.' We shook on it, and took him back to the camp for one our campfire singarounds. That night, some big bastard shouted for us to shut up, actually, since it was only 10 p.m. on a Saturday night, we thought it was the content of the songs not the noise that was bothering him.

'I've told you lot, shut up!' he yelled. Then he charged across the field and into the big bell tent where we were having wa folky session. I think he thought there were a couple of little wimpy hippie types in the tent, because as he burst through the flap, and seen five bikers in their leathers, a number of shot guns, a group of variously sized miners and some determined looking females, he changed tone completely. 'Yee want to settle this ootside bonny lad?' Tom offered. 'No, no, just em, don't go on too long—OK lads?'

That was it as far we were concerned, until we came back that night and found he'd smashed up all the tents, smashed the poles, ripped up flysheets etc. The bastard. We had to spend a couple of hours in the rain tying things back up and strapping broken poles together, before we resumed another singsong. As for Doyle and his promise, he kept it right enough. He wasn't in the chair the following day, and the female stand-in, obviously also from Militant, also ignored all our delegates right throughout the conference.

June 1972. Comrade Baader of the Red Army Fraction was captured in Frankfurt by 150 heavily armed police using armoured cars and snipers. They next raided the 'safehouse' and captured Ulrike sitting on a mountain of guns and explosives. 'It wasn't me' didn't swing it. It was clear both these captures were the result of some inside informer.

June 1972. The push on the streets and the headlong rush of the unions' rank and files, particularly the miners and railworkers, was matched by a push in the party, no not THE party: the Labour Party was infused throughout its apparatus by the Labour movement, at a bureaucratic as well as rank-and-file level. It responded to impulses within the industrial and working-class sectors. The victory of the miners was to mark victories for the left within the Labour Party too. A whole programme of nationalisations—land, banks, finance, oil, etc. without compensation and under workers control—were being advanced, it wasn't Labour Party policy, let alone a government commitment, but they drew millions of votes from constituencies, wards, and affiliated trade unions. One could hardly pretend this wasn't a progressive trend no matter how one viewed the history of that party and its bourgeois leadership. The NEC itself started to reflect left currents within the party, although there was no danger of a sudden call for the workers to seize the land and the banks and take back industry. Many looked to the days when it would, foolish though that proposition seems now; there were those among the armed men in the state's repressive forces who feared it was a possibility too. Well in 1973 I took the poison chalice, and in order to affect a pincer movement within the wider Labour Party constituency I joined the bliddy Labour Party. Old 'Bant' Hardy, the local Dunscroft/Hatfield secretary, was a bit surprised. 'But tha's a revolutionary in't tha?' he asked in his Old Wearside mixed with Donny twang dialect. 'Aye, Bant, but there's nowt in the rules against ideas, marra.' I omitted to mention I was a member of the Revolutionary Workers Party at the time. Well once a member, the local NUM Branch at once put me forward as a member of the Trade Union Section of the GMC of the Goole Constituency. Maureen and Alison and Ken were already on it from the LPYS. Legay and Jim were on it from the local ward, so our ranks were starting to swell. My membership needed endorsement and this caused quite a storm in the local party, a classic battle between the right-wing old guard and those committed to what they seen as genuine radical socialism. My own speech addressed solely the question of what sort of vision we should have in the party. A platform for the working class and socialism in all its varieties and forms, an end to all bans and proscriptions in the Labour Party, the right for the communist and socialist parties to affiliate to the Labour Party in the way they had at its inception. I reminded the miners from Hatfield in the ward, of which there were a few, mostly moderates, that Hatfield Main NUM policy was for an end to all proscriptions in the Labour Party and that it should become an all-embracing party of the left and working-class movement for socialism.

Someone got up and said, 'That means we could allow Tories to join the Labour Party!' which caused great cheers and laughter. 'That is the point comrade, while Tories already are members of this party, and they go under a variety of names and associations, there is no ban on them, they may not be card-carrying members of the Conservative and Unionist Party but they agree with everything in terms of British imperialism in Ireland to supporting US imperialism in Vietnam and expansion of Britain's nuclear armoury. At home they believe in wrecking the social gains of generations, attacking our benefits system our health service, the lot. Have you listened to these people at conference and in here? Tories are already in this party—we have had a few lead it. Its time to take down the barriers against the left, against the real socialists.' Well I had made them pick a side, and with NUM Branch policy on my side and their nomination to GMC twisting their arms, we won the day. For now. No sooner had I arrived at my first GMC meeting through at Goole, the following Sunday morning, when up jumps aud Matt Busby, a veteran right-wing miner and plague of the left in the Union and the Labour Party, clutching a copy of the bliddy *News of the World*. *The News of the World* in those days was nicknamed 'The News of the Screws'. It was actually a pornographic publication at base. It sold titillating stories of forbidden sex, as much detail as they could cram in about rapes, and, far from the recent 'Scourge of the Paedophiles' scams they have run latterly, this was the paedophile's gazette. In those days unlawfully consenting children were called 'wayward' and their exploits in rude and naughty encounters with grownups were spelt out in lurid and erotic detail in the paper every week. In the postwar years the *News of the World* was something like child porn on today's internet. If one were to compile all of their lurid and puerile stories into a single compilation of underage sex encounters and tried to publish it today you would almost certainly be done not only for obscene publications but under a whole range of anti sex legislation brought in by Mr Blair, and if you don't believe it, look them up at the British Museum Newspaper Library. Most men bought the *News of the World* as a substitute for the girlie picture books which their wives and families would have condemned them for, but a newspaper, well it just looked like a newspaper so must be OK. In among the salacious rapes and unlawful sex was the popular outrage, whack 'em and bash 'em type tirade of the right. Unions, commies, students, strikes, all that sort of blustering Colonel Blimp stuff. As luck would have it, they were running a campaign exposing the militants in industry and they had found me! They had taken a photo of me with a long distance telephoto lens. My beard was a bit daft-looking to begin with, but photographed from a distance blurred and black and white, I looked like some early version of Peter Sutcliffe, indeed me Ma, always proud of any publicity about me,—'Its me son, he's in the paper, he's an urban guerrilla you know?'—sent it off 'back home' to Ireland to show to the family. Me aud Granny with her fading eyes looking at the blurred long-distance shot and cried, 'Its the Divil, me grandson's the Divil!' It was a coup for the right wing. Aud Matt Busby, the former Hatfield Main NUM Delegate and leader of the now deposed Gaitskell wing of the union and the Labour Party, still sat on the GMC and the EC, ironically representing the NUM Branch. We would have to sort that out in the next selections. Meantime he was up on his feet quoting from the paper: 'Meet the man behind the slogans: "Seize the supermarkets! Distribute the food free among the communities! Organise armed detachments of workers to defend communities and picket lines! Occupy the mines and the power stations under workers control!"' While the old guard's eyes popped in horror, our Young Socialists and our few allies in the adult party cried 'Hurrah!' at the end of every slogan, which wasn't exactly helpful given the circumstances. I was immediately suspended while an enquiry could be held. As luck would have it, that was the very evening we were holding a mass meeting of the Kirk Sandal tenants to bring them into the anti-rent-rise struggle. We had toured the area for weeks and I was pride of place on all the leaflets which had been dropped through every letter box. The meeting was planned for Rockware Glass Social Club. How would the tenants of Kirk Sandal and Edenthorpe take to the invitation to listen to an exposed red wrecker? By the hundred as it turned out! I wanted to believe it was because nobody with guts enough to participate in the struggle would read the News of the Screws, or that having read it, they thought sod it, I know what side I am on. But truth was many of our militants couldn't even read the damn paper properly; more than one tenant came over to congratulate me 'on your article in the *News of the World*'. One bloke said he had read it 'and I agree with every word you said'. I signed at least two autographs on the edition of the paper which folk had brought along with them for that purpose! We decided after discussion with the Party to run a left slate in the forthcoming DMBC elections. We would stand as 'True Labour' candidates to challenge the local councillors because of their collaboration on the Tory rent acts, and the failure of 'Labour' to be 'Labour' at least as the working class perceived what that label meant. Of course it is an automatic rule that if you run against Labour you are automatically expelled from that party. With our home support and the strength of the tenant's resistance, the experience of mass rallies on the estates and the rent strikes we were confident of victory. Candidates would be me, Ken Terry, Len Caven the NUM Branch president, Bible John (as he was nicknamed) a wily Scot, militant and piss-taker, and I think Big Harry the anarcho-copbasher, an extremely well-read, world-travelled, self-taught travelling agitator who had tried to wipe out the entire Doncaster police force, not single-handed but double-fisted. The announcement attracted lightning interest and outrage, and not only in the establishment ranks. Our comrades on the left, the Revolutionary Communist Party (the Chartists), Militant of course, the Communist Party and many NUM branch militants from other pits thought we were wrong. Wrong because, it buggered up our fight within the Labour Party to fight the bans and proscriptions: we couldn't claim to be 'on the side' of Labour while running candidates against them. We couldn't claim to be against bans and proscriptions and yet leave the party to contest those whose views and actions we opposed. The Chartists in particular were furious. They had mounted a big campaign against Militant within the LPYS and wider Labour Party for their failure to defend myself and Gooleys from expulsion and exclusion; now here we were giving Militant the bowl of water and towel to wash their hands of us. The Party, who had at first argued 'against this sort of thing' then argued for Party candidates running on the Party programme—although we couldn't see 'Vote RWP for Nuclear War' being a catchy slogan on the doorstep—then they had come round to the idea so long as we declared our party membership under the True Labour banner. Now they too were having doubts again. In the end, after pressure from close comrades, not least Derek Blunn (the Larch), who Militant had brought in to dissuade me, and a visit by the Peter Doyle, the national chairman and Gateshead LPYS en-masse, who debated with us in the bar of the Abbey like a celebrity quiz night before the local drinkers and footballers. We relented—well me and Harry and Bible John did; Ken left it too late to withdraw his nomination and we instead circulated a leaflet, explaining why we weren't now running and asking voters not to vote for Ken. Ken made the point that with a split vote the Independents, who were Tories but didn't wear that badge round these parts, could sneak in. We were able to reach quite an electorate in the long run and our meetings were packed. We also got to appear on the official Labour ones too, where we belted the right wing of the party for all it was worth. Len stood, and was elected as True Labour. Quite a number of other such candidates quite independently of us also stood around the country. Mind, there were a number of 'Democratic Labour' candidates who had broke from the right believing the Labour Party too left-wing and socialist! This was the wing which successively would first become the Social Democratic Party and then merge with the Liberals to become the LibDems.

My spot at the Labour Party Young Socialists conference that year, as the delegate from Goole, and for which I had planned a barnstorming speech, was now also suspended despite protests from the floor of conference, and mass fringe meetings at which the comrades to the left of Militant, mainly the Chartists and also the small team around *Workers Fight*, spoke forcibly in my defence. Graham Bash, one of the central; leaders of the Chartists, white-faced, intense, his group some descendant of the Ceylonese Trotskyists, the Revolutionary Communist League I think, did likewise with great passion. Militant were split, between apparent opposition and apparent compliance. Their problem was the way the party had deemed I fight this suspension. I had been suspended on the basis that I belonged to a proscribed organisation, in this case the Revolutionary Workers' Party; they would suspend me while they investigated the accusation. The Party's position was that unlike Militant and their Revolutionary Socialist League, whose existence they totally denied, I should admit that I was a member of the RWP, but there should be no bans and proscriptions on working-class parties and organisations within the Labour Party. I should fight this all the way, to the floor of the national Labour Party conference, which was duty-bound the hear my appeal. The fight against my expulsion would be a fight against their proscriptions; it would be a rallying point for the whole movement to end the bans and proscriptions in the party. It badly exposed Militant's 'deep' entry in the Labour Party and the LPYS. It forced others like the Chartists out into the open too. They were damn good comrades: for the lobby in my support and against my expulsion they put buses on, leaving London at 7.30 a.m. and travelling from their strong holds in Norwood, Vauxhall and Cricklewood. Peter Doyle, my erstwhile Geordie comrade and president of the LPYS, addressed a stormy national conference, riven with shouts and counter-shouts around the room: 'Of course we are against bans and proscriptions within the Labour Party, but if Dave Douglass is determined to put his head on the block, he can expect to have it chopped off!' This was said to a mass conference, in which sat the National Youth Officer of the Labour Party, the great headhunter of 'Trots' and lefties, Burt Twigg. He sat with veteran witchhunter Harold Simms. These two had been cardinal in the expulsion of the entire Young Socialist organisation a few years earlier. In those days the Young Socialists were dominated by Gerry Healy's Socialist Labour League. Militant were the inheritors of Labour's pristine new youth organisation, the LPYS, to distinguish them from the old YS which continued as the SLL's and then the Workers Revolutionary Party's youth wing. To stand there on the stage of the national conference, before the eyes and ears of the hatchet men, and tell us all Dave Douglass was asking to have his head chopped off, to us sounded like Pontius Pilot washing his hands of Jesus and handing him over to be crucified. Twigg didn't need any encouragement. He had been targeting the Goole Constituency with a vengeance; our opponents had been collecting evidence on cine cameras, photographs and tape recordings of our speeches and rallies.

The 'Defend Dave Douglass' campaign swung into action. The NUM in Doncaster at once became active supporters, Hatfield 'branched' Bushby and his associates from 'over the bridge' in Stainforth, Tom Mullany telling them: 'Dave Douglass argues for this branch, mister (always a sign he was loosing his temper), and this branch stands for socialism.'

'But what sort of socialism?' a red-faced Bushby demanded to know.

'Well, not the sort that supports atomic bombs, NATO, and capitalism, Matt,'[41] Tom replied. Thorne and District Trades Council, of which I was the secretary, had of course won over the Doncaster Trades Council and was calling on the Yorkshire Region of TUC to support my reinstatement 'unconditionally'. Militant on every platform hedged its bets and never once came off the fence; they were scared shitless we would force them into the open. Well the comrades of the local Communist Party were none too comradely either, as the following shows:

> Thorne/Moorends Communist Party,
> 12 Pine Hall Rd, Barnby Dun, Doncaster
> Wed Nov. 14
> Dear Mrs Sharp
> Your appeal for support for Dave Douglass was heard before our branch meeting last night. It was felt that bans and proscriptions were a hindrance to progress in the Labour movement But that the case of Cde Douglass involved neither a ban nor a proscription according to our evidence. We felt the matter to be of concern of the internal (i.e. Labour) Party discipline and as such felt we could not actively busy ourselves with it.
> Yours Bill Carr (Jnr), Chairman, T/M C.P.

Red Flag, our Party paper, in its 14 November 1973 issue, carried a big inside feature, calling for my reinstatement and elaborating their line that this is part of the inevitable confrontation between the right and the left in the L.P. And raises the whole discussion of the right of tendency and the necessity for the complete transformation of the structure of the LP. 'But we do demand the right to be members of the LP at any level, whilst being Posadist militants and the right if we so choose to join the LP as a tendency with our own independent functioning and press ...'

November 1973. The Socialist Labour League left its cocoon and became the Workers Revolutionary Party! It drove the RWP to the point of temper, which was very rare. They called it a provocation and a deliberate act to confuse the masses. Meantime my appeal to the NEC of the Labour Party took place in Goole in November.[42]

It was met by a hundred of my supporters chanting 'Reinstate Dave Douglass' and 'Socialism not a crime!' and 'End the bans!'

Harold Simms, a regional organiser and witchhunter of the left, had at an earlier hearing, from which I had been excluded, advised the GMC that I shouldn't be admitted or heard. They had suspended me in my absence. He declared that the regional Labour Party was investigating the whole of the constituency Labour Party Young Socialists with a view to expulsion. He had been making a tour of all the constituency bodies, local wards and branches outlining the case against the Young Socialists, pre-empting any appeals, preventing any counter-arguments. His biggest challenge came at Hatfield and Dunscroft wards, where he couldn't prevent the people involved as members of that branch being present. He met some stiff resistance at Stainforth too. At the Hatfield Branch he said the Constituency Young Socialists were 'a national embarrassment'.

My appeal was presided over by Joan Maynard, a wonderful comrade and genuine socialist, a great comrade of the left, Ireland and the miners. I didn't leave her much room to support me, but she said she would investigate the matter further and report to the NEC. This was a bit of a stalling tactic to try and get me to leave the RWP or at least say I had left the RWP. She tried, God love her. That's not the way we were fighting this rule, though. I was supposed to have my day at National Conference where all appeals can ultimately be heard. It would force the issue among the Labour Party's 'broad church' of labour movement affiliates to debate the question of bans and proscriptions; we would ensure all the delegates and bodies knew all about this appeal when it came.

When my appeal came before the sub-committee of the NEC, Joan was the investigator. She virtually told me, 'Dave, if you say you are not a member of the RWP, they can't get you out, they must reinstate you.' But I proudly proclaimed I was a member and that shouldn't debar me. It left poor Joan in an impossible situation. She could only report back that I was the chosen delegate to the GMC from the miners, although I was a member of the RWP. In the meantime the entire Goole Constituency LPYS was under investigation.

Twigg arrived at the bookshop door early one morning, unannounced, strode in, and demanded from Alison, who was in on her own, all minute books and documents related to the group. She phoned me in a panic, and I in fury set off over the field to the shop.

By the time I arrived Twigg was standing in the living room, which was amply covered in a huge poster with the hammer and sickle, emblazoned with the four for Trotsky's international, and the words Goole Constituency Labour Party Young Socialists on the top and RWP(T) on the bottom. Posters announced a victory to the IRA, to the PLO, to Cuba. Portraits of Ché looked down from every wall, the duplicator and stacks of leaflets sat in piles, while the bookshop carried every form of incendiary pamphlet book and poster your average urban Marxist guerrilla -could wish for. He stood sternfaced.

'Oot!' I shouted.

'I am here ...' he began. 'You are trespassing in someone's house, a women on her own, afraid, alone, and if you do not get your useless form out of this building in two minutes flat I will knock you through that door.'

'I am here at the request ... '

'Not our request. Not her request. This isn't Labour Party property. You are not our landlord. Your special political patrol doesn't rule here. Now get!' He started to leave, muttering that he had been sent by the constituency chairman, Mr Bill O'Brian, to collect all the Labour Party Young Socialist material.

'Oh!' Bill O'Brian was the NUM branch secretary at Glasshoughton Colliery. I got him straight on the phone and while Twigg paced about outside, I gave him all barrels. He finally told me he had ordered no such thing, and not told Twigg to come round on a raid, but said that he would be requesting from the LPYS that they hand over the minute books, if they agreed, so the EC could see what sort of activity the Young Socialists were engaged in.

I brought Twigg in so O'Brian could tell him to get his snout out of where it didn't belong. He left, and between the formal request and the agreement to hand over the minute book, Maureen had written out, page by page, line by line a new sanitised version, with different inks, and signed pages etc. Mind, it was still based on the original and highlighted talks from all our Black Power, Irish Republican, Civil Rights and Palestinian comrades, not to mention guest speakers from the RWP and the Chartists. Bill was later to declare it was very interesting reading, and some of the meetings looked very interesting too. 'But I couldn't swear to its authenticity. It was too neat,' he declared. It wasn't, though—he didn't know how absolutely perfect Maureen's minute-taking and handwriting was, a legacy of the grammar school education. In the midst of all this Goole Constituency LPYS submitted their resolution on Ireland. Ireland was a battleground in the LPYS between genuine anti-imperialists who saw in the rebellion a people's war against British Imperialism, and those like Militant who thought it a murderous distraction. The 'social imperialists' we called them, socialists in name, imperialists in practice. It was not that they manned the Pigs (the army's own nickname for armoured Humber trucks), or patrolled the streets in khaki, but that they de facto cheer led from the left the anti-republican struggle. They called the soldiers of the British army 'workers in uniform'. They flooded LPYS conferences with their resolutions. Invariably these would suggest that the Irish working class was like the British working class except it had been divided along religious grounds. They called for the two religious communities to get together to fight for the same set of trade union demands as the rest of British workers. The IRA they saw as sectarian terrorists; they borrowed a phrase from the Marxist-Leninist handbook to label them 'individual terrorists', never really comprehending what the phrase meant. To the rest of the left it was a reference to individuals and atomised teams who took it upon themselves to wage war or retaliation against the state on their own behalf unconnected to the mass of struggle of the people. (It was never a pure formulae anyway, since such actions were rarely if ever just 'out of the blue' or unconnected to the overall class war being waged, but we got the point.) Militant looked not at whether the IRA was a genuine and mass-based militia of the working class, but instead what sort of military tactics they used. Had the IRA chosen to wear uniforms, and march up the middle of Belfast singing the Internationale with red flags flying, they would no longer be individual terrorists. They would all be instantly wiped out of course. The size and scale of the British army and its occupation necessitated guerrilla urban warfare. They were, however, hidden, housed, fed and staffed by the working-class communities of occupied Ulster for whom they fought. Militant's programme was for nationalisation, housing, minimum wage, indeed all the things a united working-class force in the contemporary political situation of Britain should be advancing. They had drafted an anthem to the tune of 'Land of Hope and Glory', which we sang along with, heartily too:

> We want nationalisation. We want workers control.
> We want full employment and the Tories on the dole.
> Higher old age pensions, a full free national health.
> For the workers of the country we'll use the nation's wealth.

But they missed and ignored the main issue—the occupation of Ireland and the partition of Ireland by British imperialism. The people of the republican communities were resisting that occupation and partition, guns in hand, engaging Britain in the biggest, most bloody conflict since World War Two. All that other stuff doesn't answer the question as to where you stand on that issue. The division between the loyalist north and republican north was festered and fostered by religious divisions, but that wasn't the issue that divided them it was the issue of where you stood on British occupation and Irish independence. The religious aspects were largely a ploy by the British establishment to keep the North divided. The fundamental issue for socialists in this period was to demand British troops out of Ireland. If Militant ever called for it, it was a very muffled reference at the end of some demand for Socialism as a precondition to progress in Ireland. Crucially though, they would never take a stand with the forces in Ireland actually fighting to get those troops out of Ireland.

> I looked over Mountjoy what did I see coming for to carry me home?
> A helicopter coming down for me
> Coming for to carry me home
> Swing low, sweet helicopter, coming for to …

Veteran Irish republican fighter Kevin Mallon, along with Seamus Twomey and J. B. O'Hagan, were plucked from the Mountjoy Prison exercise yard by a hijacked helicopter and flown to safety. (August 1973)

The above parody became my favourite warm-up song while it was still topical. For many just singing the words became a very daring and subversive action, God knows what the bloke at the controls felt!

Goole Constituency Labour Party Young Socialists proposed to the 12th National Conference of the LPYS at Skegness in 1973 the whole programme of Provisional Sinn Fein, Eire Nua, as our resolution to conference on Ireland. Of course they didn't say whose programme it was, and Militant were so insular, so isolated from the politics of republicanism they didn't know what it was. We submitted the entire Sinn Fein manifesto to become the policy of the Labour Party's youth section and nobody noticed! The only objection which the standing orders committee made was that, it was so long, we would have to publish the entire document, sufficient for every LPYS branch in Britain, and then they would circulate it. Nay bother, bonny lad. Done. Eire Nua became Goole Constituency's resolution to conference and the Labour apparatus distributed it. Brave Jimmy Shipley drew the honourable task of moving it, since I had become suspended then expelled.

This conference was at one of the Butlin's holiday centres; we were all accommodated in the holiday chalets. Jim and I worked on the speech, the most radical ever to be heard in this organisation, a speech actually in support of the political programme of the IRA. Although we considered this a master stroke and a political coup, the Party, when they discovered it, were not amused. Although technically the YS was not under their direct control and we could arrive at positions different from theirs, we were actually under the political sway of Posadism. If, when they started to lean on you, with their much-esteemed and - valued opinions, you reflected too long they started twisted arms, not literally, but in a sort of huffed political hurt way. They argued that the resolution 'was too restrictive'. It wasn't opening out a broad enough platform. In truth the Party little understood Ireland either, and like Militant tended to see the struggle for Irish independence as a distraction from the real struggle of winning the workers of the whole of the 'British Isles' to socialism as a joint goal. They ignored everything I had laid before them in an extensive Irish Commission report. They ignored the face-to-face retelling of my experiences, following their pedestrian list of questions, against my better judgement; I had tested their homespun theories. By September 1975 *Red Flag* was still calling for a joint Labour conference of unions, social-democratic parties 'and both wings of Sinn Fein'. Their line was that British imperialism was responsible for the bombings of Britain, not ultimately, or politically, but literally. For revolutionaries they didn't actually like armed struggle. Violence was not in the party agenda; doubtless, we intervened, if at all, 'empirically' into the process. The clarion cry was 'For a United Ireland of 32 Counties as Part of a United Socialist Britain Within the System of a United Soviet Socialist States of Europe'. Some time later we were drafting the introduction to what would be the Irish Document of our new tendency; it revisited this period:

> The Goole Constituency LPYS at the 12th National Conference of LPYS moved the following resolution in order to contribute to the growth of solidarity struggle with the Irish Republican Movement. Coupled with the need to elevate political and class consciousness within the Labour movement was the equal need to combat the social chauvinism of the

majority tendency Militant (R.S.L.)

Because the bulk of the debate on Ireland always revolved around the Provisional IRA and the Provisional Sinn Fein; because the debate always portrayed a complete ignorance of Provo policy, it was decided to move as our resolution Eire Nua (the IRA policy document).

The NEC of the LPYS refused to produce it as a resolution along with the others 'because it was too long'.

Although they did not rule it out of order, so Goole Constituency LPYS produced it themselves, in hundreds, and took them to Walworth Road, where the NEC circulated them, to every LPYS branch in the country as Goole's resolution.

However between the submitting of our resolution and it coming to the floor of the conference we realised that we had pinned ourselves down too tightly in simply calling for 'Full support to the programme of Eire Nua'. We realised that we had not made our own disagreements with the programme clear, nor had we put forward our own belief in the development of 'soviets' (workers' committees and councils) as the key organ of class power etc.

The beauty of the eventual withdrawal of this resolution from the platform was we got to circulate the document and Jim got to make a tub-thumping, ear-rattling speech which made conference sit up.

Jim made the point, that while we were withdrawing the resolution.

[We] do not withdraw our support for the Provisional IRA or Provisional Sinn Fein. We find both these organisations amongst the most dynamic and confident sectors of the anti-imperialist forces in Ireland.

We do not, as Luton YS does, join in the chorus of liberal lefties in repudiating armed struggle. Armed struggle is a legitimate method of working class progress—the armed struggle of the people of Ireland against decaying imperialism is one of the highest contradictions of European capitalism. We must seize upon the contradictions of capitalism and ruthlessly exploit them.

The limitations of the Provisionals' programme and therefore our resolution are the inadequacy of its anti-capitalist programme ...

We also failed in our resolution to make it clear to the conference, that it is not the role of the LPYS to criticise one or other sectors of the anti-imperialist forces, anti-capitalist forces. It is this horrible arrogant attitude which the Goole constituency LPYS so hate about this conference. It is the idea that you can manufacture resolutions in this room and hand them ready made to the people of Ireland, which prompted us to move this programme. We were wrong, comrades, for being impatient with the conference— but on the other hand your tablets of wisdom handed down from the lofty heights of English social democracy to the revolutionary vanguard, completely refutes common sense, to say nothing of Marxism.

The chair had shuffled uneasily as Jim's voice, hard, Yorkshire, and working class filled the conference room. Jim was no shrinking violet despite this being his first conference speech. The chair's finger hovered over the 'shut up' light switch, but Jim had timed this speech to the second, and we produced in literature and in the platform appearance and speech everything we wanted to say to this conference. We went mad when Jim had finished speaking. As he stepped from the platform and people asked 'Who?', and the reply came 'A coal miner from Doncaster,' there was no doubt that this was the authentic voice of the revolutionary British working class. Not the working class per se, of course not, if he had been we would lang syne since have stopped debating imperialism and capitalism would be a subject of historical research. Jim's consciousness and almost revelationist understanding of the way the world worked had come about from seeing his own life overlaid and shadowed by workers' struggles around the world and seeing himself in their shoes, and knowing his own reactions would be much like theirs. In the unlikely Dunscroft streets and colliers homes, Jim had met Palestinian fighters and sat in awe at their stories and their life struggles. Young Irish fighters had sat by his fireplace and sung songs with him and walked the moors telling of their daily experiences and those of their forefathers as Jim had told of his. He and his wife Lynne had sat down to dinner with tall, beautiful and proud black people, silent at the resonance of their almost poetic speech, honest working folk who had experienced the thick end of the wedge for too many generations.[43]

Born-again Christians talked of 'their revelation', 'the hour I first believed'; for Jim, and each and every one of us, we too had experienced such 'revelations'.

8

THE ANGRY BRIGADE

Twelve comrades were arrested for bombings between January 1968 and August 1971—the actions of the Angry Brigade. Really the police evidence rested simply on these being the kind of people most likely to be angry enough and politically motivated enough to have carried them out, i.e. they had a motive. The defence tried to line up a string of people who likewise had motive and plenty justification for carrying out bombings, but actually hadn't. I was asked if I as a young miner, would be one such person and of course I accepted the offer, but I wasn't actually called. Ian Purdie had been found not guilty, and so was my old comrade by proxy Stuart Christie, while Jake Prescott was handed down a 15-year sentence. Agitprop with whom they had been linked were forced to move from Gower Street to a new address, 248 Bethnal Green Road – actually just across the road and under a railway arch from Raph's place.

> Other political people began experiencing police pressure on a political activity to a degree unknown to any before. What were innocent activities casual acquaintances or remarks became distorted and related in ways that made them appear criminal. Agitprop's house was raided after the bombing of Carr's house in January and again after the bombing of the police computer in May. On the first occasion a member of our collective was forcibly taken for questioning and our duplicate copy of our office addresses photocopied. On the second visit the [Metropolitan Police] Special Branch removed from the house even more political and personal papers. – Agitprop

In among the arrested had been our old comrade Stuart Christie—you will recall from our 'Free Stuart Christie' campaign in Newcastle. We had campaigned often violently against the Franco government; the Spanish consulate was a frequent visitor of our outrage with sabotage and graffiti. Our fellow anarchist Stuart had been so clearly framed by Franco's agents. This comrade had been en-route to an anarchist camp in the South of France. He was hitch-hiking, wearing a kilt, which he thought would get him better lifts, he would hardly be so attired to try to get over the border carrying bombs in his rucksack to assassinate the Spanish Fascist dictator, now, would he? A Scottish anarchist, wearing his kilt, and a baggy gansie, hitch-hiking with a rucksack full of explosives, over the border into fascist Spain where they are known to love that political current so much? Whey lad, it was clearly obvious the whole tale was nonsense. He wouldn't dey that. Actually, yes he would, daft bugger. When he was released, the true story emerged, all bar the kilt bit had been true, and even then he was carrying the kilt sticking out of his rucksack so folk would know he was Scottish. Stuart tells us some hilarious details of this adventure, although let's face it, at the time this was almost a suicide mission. He had in fact been given the money for his rail journey into Spain, but thought he would be much more likely to attract attention and be searched than as a tourist hitchhiker. He did however reason that some customs man on the border would doubtless search his rucksack, so he came up with the idea of actually sticking the explosives around his body.

In Perpignan I found the public baths and paid for a cubicle. After a hot soak and still naked I unpacked the slab of plastique and taped them to my chest and stomach with elastoplast and adhesive tape. The detonators I wrapped in cotton wool and hid inside the lining of my jacket. The bag of potassium chlorate, the base of the chemical trigger, was too bulky to hide on my body, so I emptied it into a packet of sugar with a layer of sugar on top, and left it in the rucksack.

There was one tense moment when the lady attendant came in unannounced with clean towels, opening the cubicle door with her keys. She appeared surprisingly nonplussed by the sight of a naked, skinny young man from whose chest and stomach were protruding what appeared to be either full colostomy bags or brown paper poultices. Not realising she was in the presence of a Glaswegian kamikaze, she muttered something in French, presumable apologising for intruding on someone so modest and afflicted and quickly backed out closing the door behind her.

With the plastic explosive strapped to me, my body was improbably misshapen. The only way to disguise myself was with the baggy woollen jumper my granny had knitted to protect me against the biting Clydebank winds. At the risk of understatement I looked out of place on the Mediterranean coast in August.

There is a hilarious sequence where he gets picked up by an eccentric British person driving an eccentric car; the quid quo pro for the lift is he is expected every time it stops to jump out and push it. Which is fine on country lanes, but when it happens in a heaving Spanish city centre, in the rush hour, under the blazing sun while all the explosives start to slip and the sticky wraps come undone, he thinks, not surprisingly his number is up.

When the poor bugger actually gets to Spain and books into a rat trap of a room he is so exhausted he falls onto the bed, and fully dressed and wrapped in explosives he goes to sleep.

Stuart was an odds-on 'person most likely to' for the police roundup in 1971. Although he and three others 'most likely to' were found not likely to and were acquitted, leaving eight to go down for the bloody front door, mardy bastards.

The Angry Brigade meantime carried on its activities.

Time marches on, and the back room of the Bridge saw a meeting of all the revolutionary groups, outraged at the introduction of internment in Ireland: the International Marxist Group, the International Socialists, the Revolutionary This And That, many of them students and middle-class kids. Sitting at the table in his combat jacket was David O'Connel. The talk went on and on and back and forth.

Dave jumped up: 'There's ower much bliddy talking. Ah want ti dey something.' And with that he pulled a greet hand-gun oot of his coat. The room fell silent. Then wham, whoosh, it emptied in an instant as the middle-class revolutionaries realised the thing in his hand was a real gun.

FELLOW REVOLUTIONARIES

We have sat quietly and suffered the violence of the system for too long. We are being attacked daily. Violence does not only exist in the army, the police and prisons. It exists in the shoddy alienating culture pushed out by TV films and magazines; it exists in the ugly sterility of urban life. It exists in the daily exploitation of our Labour, which gives big bosses the power to control our lives and run the system for their own ends. How many Rolls Royce's ... how many Northern Irelands ... how many anti-Trade Union bills will it take to demonstrate that in a crisis of capitalism the ruling class can only react by attacking the people politically? But the system will never collapse or capitulate by itself. More and more workers now realize this and are transforming union consciousness into offensive political militancy. In one week, one million workers were on strike ... Fords, Post Office, BEA, oil delivery workers ... Our role is to deepen the political contradictions at every level. We will not achieve this by concentrating on 'issues' or by using watered-down socialist platitudes. In Northern Ireland, the British Army and its minions have found a practicing range: the CS gas and bullets in Belfast will be in Derby and Dagenham tomorrow.

OUR attack is violent ... Our violence is organised. The question is not whether the revolution will be violent. Organised militant struggle and organised terrorism go side by side. These are the tactics of the revolutionary class struggle. Where two or three revolutionaries use organised tactics to attack the class system ... there is the Angry Brigade. Revolutionaries all over England are already using the name to publicise their attacks on the system. No revolution was ever won without violence. Just as the structures and programmes of a new revolutionary society must be incorporated into every organised base at every point in the struggle, so must organised violence accompany every point of the struggle until, armed the revolutionary working class overthrows the capitalist system. COMMUNIQUÉ 6. THE ANGRY BRIGADE.

The north and the south were meeting, as comrades, in London's East End—those up against the English law, those from the sooth in exile, Scots and Yorkshire folk, us doon from the north. While a dinner cooked, 'a reet Yorkshire Sunday spread', the guy from that which we shall not speak of, Geordies and armed fighters mixed the gravy. While two young lasses cuddled and hugged on a couch in the living room, and two not so young men embraced and hugged in the kitchen, the debate had flowed.

The armed action was premature. The unit should not be in service, but rather should be an armed training unit at the disposal of the proletarian vanguard, not the parties but the sections of the class itself engaged in struggle, or likely to be in struggle: such units should enlarge the tools of the militants' trade.

We needed surely the duplicator skill, the YCL skill of street oratory, the manner of welfare assistance and legal rights, but at the end of the day na, always, the tools of violently resisting the state and organising for insurrection.

It was the first of the fault-lines opening up within the Party: between those of us advocating preparation, armed preparation, building a revolutionary militia, developing the ability to respond to the state's armed bodies of men; and Party petty-bourgeois intellectuals who would call such visions putschist, Blanquist.

But with these comrades, we were the ones calling for restraint, calling those with a view of building an ACTIVE armed group putschist. We advocated preparation, building the means: 'That is the role of "The Brigade", not to take up that task for yasells.'

'NOT FOR WA BLUDDY SELLS ... !'

'Sorry, by yoursells.'

But the team had had enough already. They would not be the leaders, nor the vanguard. They were the victims of the state already. Their response was credible and achievable. They were not in trade unions, though they respected trade unionists. They were not in political parties, although they had seen good revolutionaries in many left parties. They had read Marx, but Marx did not answer the burning insurgency in their souls, NOW. A vision of the future was gratifying. A prediction of the revolution was rewarding. But for NOW the state must be made to realise that it is only MEN yes, mainly MEN, and resistance from people would follow their repression.

Explosives from the pits?

'Whey aye, but its ney gud ti ye, comrade.'

'Ney prevari-fuckin'-cation.'

'It wadn't bla' the top off a dustbin.'

'Nevertheless it's usable.'

So the word gaans oot, for 'Pooder for the Brigade'. Pit by pit. 'Pooder against the state.' Some was raised for the IRA, some for the Angry Brigade. Did they ever get it ? I really don't know, I am told it was sent on its way via people who were trusted.

I am told the bomb runners came close to life imprisonment.

Durham Big Meeting: the bands, dignity and message of two centuries. And booze aye, plenty booze. Folks wi' bits o' bait and pooder in bait bags, ex-loaf packets 'Gi's a pint here's the bait ...' Until a collection from east and west, from pitmen and colliers, Scots and Yorkies, Geordies and Cumbrians, Lancs and Staffs, Notts and Welshmen, the word had gone to those who stood with us, th' want pooder for the cause, th' get pooda for the cause. Three sheets ti the wind, the host stands ti deposit the 'bait'.

'Here's the key for the car ... put it in the boot.'

Then, after the boot is locked and a couple o' late arrivals from the Valleys land with two dozen pills more, and the daft buggers were so pissed thi couldn't be fashed to open it again, so it gets hoyed on the floor in the back.

As beer and crack ... the speeches and heckling ... the roll in the riverside fields ... the sing-sang, the sangs of the ancestry flow ... and the broon dog flows ... This is the Meetin' Day ... a sunny day.

'Lowse nuw, lads,' stagger back to the car.

'What's ahl this ahl ower the floor?' as the back-seat lads rolled in.

Some of it sat and sweated ... leaked from its sausage rolls ... crept in icy blue stuck ti each other, made a reet mess ... mer nor less encased in Mother's Pride packets ... but the sang was live:

> COME AHL YE CANNY TYNESIDERS,
> HERES A SANG AH CERTAINLY LIKE,
> AH'LL WHISPER A WORD BRIGHT AND CHEERY
> TI THE MANY POOR FELLAS ON STRIKE.

Cop cars, cop cars they're waving at wi. Wind doon the windows: 'FUCK OFF BASTARDS.' 'FUCK OFF FASCIST PIGS.'

'Hey, steady up, lads, Ah's weel ower the limit. Dinnit encourage them.'

'Ah, fuck 'em fuck off, bastards.' Then a deadly shock. 'How the stuff, ye silly bastards.'

'What stuff, I haven't smoked nowt th' day. Ah'm not carrying, are ye, like?'

'Nor, ye silly bastards the explosives.'

'Fucking hell under wa feet if the cops stop wi.'

'Fucking hell, gaan back. Ah'll get oot and say wi wes joking ... just havin' a crack ... let is oot nuw.'

But the cops didn't follow, didn't pull them over, didn't find the odd collection of TNT sausages in their Mother's Pride bags. But it actually got worse (or so I am told).

Robert Carr, Minister of Employment, director of Securicor, inventor of the Industrial Relations Bill which was to jail the dockers and try and cripple the union militants, was abed in slumber with his likewise haughty wife. The English upper-class art of understatement and coolness was reflected in her statement to the TV, live before the cameras, in her dressing gown, her front door blown off with a bomb.

'Well, we were lying in bed, when there was this frightful bang. "Good heavens, Robert", I said, "They've blown our front door off!"'

A proper little English tea at Mike's with angel cakes, cups, and saucers. Then, suitably refreshed, we hit the Bridge. As laughter rocked the back room and the crack fuelled on dinner time's broon, suddenly the Bridge hit me. The ceiling came doon and crushed me ti the floor. I shrank to the size of a moose. Simultaneously everyone grew. Their faces enlarged, their arms ever-growing. I scuttled to get out, but fell from the enormous chair on which I was sitting, falling forward right over the end of the bench seat and hitting the floor a great distance below. Murderers grabbed each arm and dragged me to the river ootside. I was helpless. Me limbs were jelly, me belly in a grip of fear, of loathing of terror, naked terror ... breath was laboured ... couldn't breathe ... constant state of fainting ... monstrous folk towering over me ... looking doon on me. It was two hours before the whispered knowledge: 'Dope in the angel cakes.' It had affected neybody else. 'Just yee, sorry, Davie ... sorry, Davie.' But the paranoia continued. Convinced they wanted to murder me, I ran to be alone ... ran to escape whoever was waiting for is ... had set a trap for is ... staggered, walked, fled, aye, fled in wild terror vornie to Shields. Then the panic started to subside. 'Phew, man, that was some rough ride', Ah telt mesell all the way back to Gateshead. 'Stupid bastards I could have panicked, done mesell some injury. Never eat that stuff again. Crazy bastards, should have telt is.'

I am told that elsewhere another scene was unfolding. The boys in the car, trusted with the stuff that gaans 'bang' had stowed it in the boot of their car and then they smoked dope, ate dope, some dropped acid. While their car radio was being robbed in the street outside the window.

One of the trippers waking to a dazed and fussy world next morn peers out of the window and asks lazily 'Where's the car?', noticed it not ootside. 'The haven't fucked off withoot is have th'?'

'Len got up and foond some bastard had broke into the car and nicked his radio,' came the reply.

'Cheeky bastards.'

'I sent for the cops. They come and had a look then said to take it doon the station and they'd give it a gaanin ower for fingerprints etc.' I am told a full ten minutes passed until the two looked in shocked realisation together.

'WHAT THE FUCK YEE SAY?'

'THE STUFF. Bluddy hell, how lang's he been gone? Het te try and stop him.' Feet kick, started aching bodies forward. Threw up all the way doon the street. The prospect of imprisonment loomed large.

'We'll get life fucking life.'

Ootside Gateshead police station Len's car sat with both doors open. A lang pair of cop legs and cop boots stuck oot of one side. Len stood by the open door. Getting closer disclosed a cop lying along the front seat dusting the dashboard with fingerprint stuff. A quick glance at the back seat disclosed the moist-looking bread packets all ower the floor.

It took half a dozen grimaces, nudges, foot-kicking and nips before it dawned on Len just what the crisis was. The cop chirped away and dusted his dust and yammered. Len's face went grey, visibly. As the cop got up from the front seat he caught sight of two trembling, grey-faced, lang-haired kids with bleary eyes, a slight hesitation, a 'will Ah, wint Ah' smile on their lips.

'By, yee two look rough.'

'Aye,', 'bit of a rough neet. Had a bit of a party.' Legs were turning to jelly.

'Wasn't one of them pot parties where yee all smoke dope and shag each other's wives was it?' he jested. 'Mevie Ah should check the car for dope an'ahl, shud Ah?' (Fucking hell!)

'Well wi wouldn't likely bring it doon the cop shop if the boot was full of dope would wi?' (Why'd he mention the boot, the bliddy idiot?)

'Nar, Ah suppose even yee lot's not that daft' (Wanna bet?) 'That'll dey lads, Ah'll put the word oot. But yee can bet it's sold nuw ... been a special order and they've come across yours forst. No respect for people's property these days.'

'They haven't', they agreed. 'Let's bliddy gaan but quick.'

The time of the 12 February 1972 Workshop on 'Childhood In History, Children's Liberation And Youth Culture', I had been commissioned by Raph to write *C Stream On Tyneside*. Really this was the first time I had started to write down my own history, it was to become not only the core of my contribution to History Workshop publications on patriotism (in our case the non-patriotism of the Tyneside-Irish secondary school) but also of *Geordies Wa Mental*, the first part of my autobiography. This second part, more than 30 years later, shows what a long road I was starting down. It was in preparation for this workshop that Dave the big Hull docker had made his wonderful discovery of children's school strikes of the nineteenth century: a nationwide strike wave of schoolchildren from the poorest state school to the richest public school, which swept the country. Another feature of people's history which had laid dormant and hidden for so long. He discovered their manifestos, photos of the period, and even their anthem (Fall In and Follow Me). Fascinating.

7 May 1972. The History Workshop on Children's Liberation was held on at Ruskin with overflow venues all over the town. I spoke on 'C Stream at Wardley', Larch on 'Selection and Authority', Chris Searle on 'Divide and School'. There was History Workshop Theatre with David Selbourne presenting *'Three Class Plays'*. The following day my colleague Edgar Moyo presented his *Big Mother and Little Mother in Matabeleland* and Dave Morgan talked on 'Gypsy Family Life'. Jenny Kitteringham spoke on 'Country Girlhood 19th Century and Today'. Peter Burke of Sussex University spoke on 'Origins of the Idea of Childhood'. And Dave Marsden gave his paper on 'Childhood Strikes in 1911'. On the Sunday Sheila Rowbotham was talking on 'Women's Liberation—Children's Liberation and Socialism'.[44]

Dave Selbourne was a tutor of political theory. He was a lawyer by profession and had that cultured, pure English pronunciation and semi-growl of a tone perfected before the bench. Tall, black curly hair, 'a libertarian' flirting with anarchism and the revolutionary left. He was the hero of my year for his stance against the college authorities and in support of attempts to bed the course in the direct struggles of the working class. His partner was best described as 'a young woman' since she was too old to be 'a girl', not of the teens and twenties years, and yet not 'a woman' in the sense of being all grown up and sensible. She was blond, short and strikingly attractive, given to dressing in mod middle-class gear, a leather Beatles cap, a suede waistcoat with fringes over a jumper, miniskirt and high boots. Everyone fancied the bum off her. In my final year, she began at the college as a student.

Dave went off to China in the midst of the aftermath of that glorious cultural revolution when much was still in turmoil. He took his slide camera and began an extended sabbatical down among the emerging Chinese revolution. He had taken photos of demonstrations, mass crowds, folk at work in the fields and in the factories, on the construction sites, and the mass slogans and posters which punctuated every view from every angle. When he returned to Oxford, he at once presented his talk on Revolutionary China, illustrated by a dramatic slide show, about which students, cramming the great hall, asked questions and made points as they went along. A party of Chinese students sat at the front. One asked, 'Why you take this photo?' The photo, on a peasant collective, shows a large revolutionary slogan in those evocative Chinese symbols. 'I thought it captured the spirit of the revolutionary upsurge and new found proletarian zeal,' explained Dave. 'It says, 'Do Not Tip Pig Shit Against This Wall,' said the Chinese student, much amused.

He had also been lecturing in Italy and came back to ask me about where he could deposit donations to the IRA. His eyes twinkled and he stroked his beard. 'A delegation of shop stewards from some large Italian factories have agreed to an ongoing levy of their workers, to the IRA. I don't know whether these are small donations or large ones, but they are coming.' I asked around some of the forces involved with the Irish struggle and eventually Gerry Lawless, a one-eyed Irish pirate, who always wore combat fatigues, and spoke strongly in a Dublin accent for the Irish armed struggle, volunteered that he was in the IRA and he would channel the money. He was a well-intentioned bullshitter and journalist, no doubt was very close to the republican movement and many people loved him and others feared him because they thought he carried a revolver and could call on dozens more at his command, but it wasn't true, although it took me some time to fathom that out. He was, though, passionate in support of the Provos though they, I am reliably informed, did not appreciate him purporting to speak in their name. The IMG had no doubt a commission whose purpose was indeed to channel funds to the IRA. One poor hapless comrade was found viciously tortured to death in his Dublin flat, nailed to the floor in fact—literally. He had been a fundraiser and some criminal gang had concluded he had access to large sums of money, which he didn't, doubtful if he handled a quid of any of it. Our comrades in Ireland had concluded the murder was by criminal criminals and not the state or the Orangies, though my suspicions would have fallen on the latter two. It was a dangerous game this speaking up for Ireland, though in the hallowed halls of Oxford it sounded dangerous in a cool groovy manner. I suspected later Gerry basked a wee bit in this latter glow, although I am informed that arriving back in Ulster and having ordered a car to be waiting for him to transmit his vital communications the car duly turned up and escorted him to a lonely place and with a gun in the back of his ear hole cautioned him on being such a twat. Mind I liked Gerry and as time went on, I began to see his act as both useful and comic. That he scared the liberals amused me no end.

Dave was a great lecturer. He exposed all the bourgeois political theorists and ruthlessly demolished their theories. From time to time he would discover fascinating new forces, like the bloke from *The Black Liberator*. This was a radical black journal, expertly printed and presented, none of your old duplicated stuff, which he wrote had printed and then carried around on his back from action to action selling it. I remember the front of his first edition, which featured an African child princess, whose striking carriage, dignity and demeanour I couldn't describe in words. However although that was the end of my contact with Dave Selbourne it was not the college's. Dave's ideas of 'liberty' and 'freedom' clashed harshly with the class consciousness of the students during the 1985 Wapping printers' dispute.

Dave remarkably continued to write a feature article for *The Times*, which the unions and the working class en masse were boycotting. Dave pleaded that this was about individual freedom, and liberty. The students argued this was about class war. He refused to stop submitting his articles and of course being paid for them, while outside the gates pitched battles ensued between printers, the folk from the East End, workers from all over Britain against the mounted police and riot squad. A picket, Michael Delaney, was run down and killed by a scab lorry. Dave was himself then boycotted and nobody attended his lecturers or spoke to him again.

One long weekend me and Larch hitchhiked back to Donny. Larch was at once a considerable attraction to the women. He was tall, dressed in gear which was all the rage down south but you wouldn't really see a bloke wear up north. It was like middle-class southern blokes' gear, like you'd see in a glossy mag odd times—or so I am reliably informed. Like cardies with a belt on, flowery, open-chested shirts like the bloke off *Saturday Night Fever*, white flared trousers, high heel shoes. His long hair was cut and shaped. He was a sensation all right; it scared me rigid as the blokes nudged each other and went 'What the hell is that?' But pissed and working class, if a Brummy, and just as impervious to the fact that his form of arm-waving, hip-swaying dancing just wasn't seen here, he just carried on. He got away with it, and a number of the women I believe. When Sunday afternoon came and the time to hitch-hike back, the hard slog began. No traffic or very little on a Sunday, no big lorries, which seemed to work a six-day week these days. It was just tortuous, little, few-miles lifts, till we landed in Oxford, wet dejected, hungry and, worse still, after closing time. I was standing by St Giles steeple, while Larch went off to the public toilet which is down the steps and under the road somewhere. There was a gentle breeze blowing, and in among the leaves blowing in clusters was a roll of paper, someone had abandoned a toilet roll. Might come in handy. No, its too grey-looking. Its an old map rolled over. No it isn't, its a wedge of ten-pound notes! I kid you not, £100 in rolled up notes. Larch come out of the bog. 'C'mon!' I says, grabbed his arm and headed for the Chinese restaurant. Wined, dined and a dozen bottles of beer later, the waiter was urging us to leave. (We could tell because they were wearing their hats and coats and had put all the lights off.) We took as I recall a crisp box full of bottles of beer and rode in a taxi back to Headington. Ee—the perfect end to a perfect day.

By the time of our second year, we had moved down to Walton Street. The college year clearly didn't coincide with the date year, because our second year began on 5 October 1971.

Because of our noise, and complaints from fellow students about our nocturnal shenanigans, we were allocated one of the houses outside. It couldn't have been better really. Here we were free to come and go as we wished. Also, we had got approval for the opening of a bar, down in the cellar under the college. A bad mistake really, as this would become more of a nightclub than a drinking establishment with fixed hours. Fred became the bar steward and at once was at home behind the bar, pulling pints and dispensing shorts. This became the in-place for Oxford radicals; none of the JCRs uptown could match this joint. More often than not the Irish crowd with their fiddles would descend on the place, or

Howkins with his squeezebox and all of us with full voices. One aud wild Irish fiddler, playing the increasingly furious 'Four-Poster Bed' which involves striking the four corners of the fiddle, faster and faster as the tune picks up pace, was so drunk and so successful each time he got up that he played the same tune three times in succession and neither he nor most of the crowd noticed. At the dead of night, patrolling policemen would hear voices seeming to rise from under the ground, and then stop without trace. This was due to the little skylight which betrayed their presence and caused an immediate blackout and silent rig.[45]

It was at one of these folky dos where we met Alison. Middle-class, minute, Oxford accent, blonde, and beautiful in a big combat jacket. She was a totally passionate and sincere person, and looked right into your soul when you were talking; 'Oh gosh!' she'd say. Almost at everything you said—'Gosh!' Her laughter was full and genuine. We none of us got near her, not sexually; somehow it would be like trying to shag your sister, your very little sister—no that can't be true, because we, me and Larch at least, lusted after her something chronic. She was though fascinated by politics, class struggle, the working class, people in general, her course work, singing, drinking large amounts, smoking dope, and being so full of life and interest, sex just didn't seem to find a place. She sang rude songs about seamen and girls on the shore, and female highwaypersons, and border ballads in much the accent I suppose they were originally sang in, in some high garret in Northumberland by the daughters of the northern aristocracy—though she was obviously of southern middle-class lineage. She hitch-hiked everywhere, indeed had hitched in Africa on locations where only one lorry a day came down the road. She believed so intrinsically in people she never felt danger, though her naivety and her lack of understanding of working-class accents brought her near to bother from time to time. She was hitching up to Doncaster to sing at one of our folky dos after she graduated, when the big Somerset lorry-driver asked her, she thought, what she thought about sax. Alison, a big lover of both modern jazz and trad replied that she loved it, which brought the lorry to a screeching stop in a lay-by, as the driver started to move over to her side of the cab. A hurried and very ruffled explanation brought around the revelation that he had said 'sex' which in Somerset was 'sax'. She quickly assured him, oh no, no, sex didn't go with hitch hiking, and anyway she didn't. Mind there were also shades of the Fiona Scott-Batey, the youthful mystic hippie of my early teens. We were singing away round the room 'Roll The Old Chariot Along', a sea chantey:

> We'l roll the old chariot along
> We'l roll the old chariot along
> And we'll all go rolling home

Everyone added their own verse:

> A weekend in Liverpool wouldn't do us any harm
> A weekend in the 'Pool wouldn't do us any harm
> And we'll all go rolling home

I sing:

> A bottle of Newcastle wouldn't do us any harm
> A bottle of Newcastle wouldn't do us any harm

A bottle of Newcastle wouldn't do us any harm
And we all go rolling home

Then Alison:

An eternity in Nirvana wouldn't do us any harm
An eternity in Nirvana wouldn't do us any...

and the sea chantey men voices drift away leaving Alison's singing away in gusto in her beautiful upper-class English with her eyes twinkling and her long blond hair swinging.

She stood on our picket lines in '72, in the rain, in the middle of the night, drenched to the skin. She hitched up to the miners' socials, she sang in our pubs, and centres. She spoke at street rallies. When it came to her graduation, she applied to Goldsmiths College, and she asked me to supply her reference, which I did. She wrote in 1974 saying the reference had stood her in good stead with the college selectors 'and in fact one of them said it was one of the best references they had ever had for anyone wanting a place on the course.' She got in.

In March of 1976, she wrote to me again, guessing correctly that I'd be surprised to receive the letter. She had last written from 'the States' over a year previously:

The whole experience of being there was very valuable: so much of what we come into contact with here is simply watered down or modified versions of things over there, that actually being there was an opportunity to view both reasonably objectively. That means the bad things like American politics, foreign policy, general manipulation as well as things which I'd generally approve of, like certain cultural movements especially amongst young people and minority groups, things which largely grew out of the 60s' peace movement. We stayed with some Party members in Berkeley (near San Francisco)—the Party in the States is pretty hard-line and dogmatic (I guess it has to be for survival) but we did meet some good radical blacks.

I came back to Bristol on my return which was a chance decision though I'm glad now that I've made it. I'm still in the Party and as I develop my own theories more I find myself becoming more and more active. I'd like to talk to you about the Party sometime. I'm also working on a Community Newspaper called *Bristol Voice*—its broadly socialist (the people running it include IS, CP and various non aligned people) and seems to be important political work. Since Christmas, I've been teaching too—in a crazy 'blackboard jungle' comprehensive school serving a huge post war panic council estate on the edge of Bristol. The estate has nil social facilities and not surprisingly, most of the kids have as their main interests vandalism and Bristol City in that order. Its a pretty exhausting job...

Yours In Struggle
Love,
Alison

SEX AND THE PETIT BOURGEOISIE

While the first year had afforded few real chances of sexual encounters, other than inter-college ones, and I recall those yet, being in the town opened up online sex. Larch became maniacally proficient and rarely had a night abed alone. I was frequently visited in the night or early morning by naked females looking to borrow coffee or tea.

I had meantime scored with an upper-class lass, married, posh and pushy. She was a regular visitor, and frequently stayed over. Liz they called her, and I don't think she actually liked me, not out of bed anyway. She hated me talking politics and was given to smacking me round the head, which would normally have caused me to knock her off her chair, but for the fact she was not only highly sexual, she was also sexually tuned to my bit skin and bones. She was given to the most pompous and snobby comments on just about everything. 'God!' she said first time we actually fully stripped, 'It's the biggest thing on your body', which could be taken as in praise of me cock but struck me as more critical of my slight and bony frame. By the second year, I was down to around 7 stone. I had developed a sexual technique which set the benchmark that the girl had to reach two orgasms and a shag with or without an orgasm. With Liz, I never failed to meet my own target. She would comment, 'You've got so much nervous energy haven't you?' This again, might sound like praise except it suggests it's illegitimate, unreal energy. Her smooth skin and thick bushy flowing hair, her immaculate teeth, her flouncing lacy underskirts and black lacy underwear, in the end could not blind me further to her upper-class mannerisms and overbearing upper-class arrogance and I stopped seeing her. She actually cried when I told her, which shocked me. Strange folk these bourgeois. Larch was prolific, virtually every night a different women. I have never before encountered a man who on walking into a crowded pub and surveying all the lasses in the room could pick his choice and say, 'That's the one,' and always end up getting her, but he did, honest to God. Was he handsome, well, I suppose, he was tall, that was the trick, both he and Chris were tall and lasses seem to favour that above much else. I have known the ugliest-looking ignorantest blokes, who are blessed with nowt more than a 6-foot-plus structure, to draw lasses like moths round a lightbulb. Mind, neither Chris nor Larch were like that—they were personable, intelligent, kind, and full of blather, which also didn't seem to gaan amiss in Oxford. Other than Liz there were some choice encounters, the first though survives only in outline sketch. I was down at my daily spot in the Collindale Newspaper Library of the British Museum, deeply enthralled in nineteenth-century Liverpool. It wasn't my custom to waste time eating during my periods of study in this place, since desks were on a premium and much in demand. Next to me was a very interesting young academic, a postgrad, in one of those strange Victorian flouncy dresses and shawls worn by feminists at the time. She wore big-rimmed glasses on a little chain around her neck and behind the lenses two of the deepest brown eyes peered into your soul. Her hair was in pigtails which reminded me of Gigi, that French girlie in the Maurice Chevalier film. Although cagey and secretive, as we all were in that dark hive of discovery and personal archaeology, fearful that someone might steal your academic coup before you could launch it and claim it to the world, she told me she was working on poorhouses and guardians, and I confessed to looking for pre-New Unions in Liverpool. Anyhow we decided to work through till closing time then go for something to eat. We walked along, more or less aimlessly with our folders full of Xeroxes, and her with a shoulder bag in which her uneaten sandwiches and flask of tea were still intact. They were 'just in case'. We talked, walked close, I wanted to put my arm around her, but felt a bit like I had with the B stream girl when I was 14, thought she would think me stupid or something. She kept doing a sort of half turn toward me, which implied she wanted to stop, her breasts kept coming into contact with my arm or chest, and I kept missing the cue, which I thought was a cue to stop and hold her, and kiss her. So the walk went on, ostensibly looking for a cafe, but in reality leaving the built-up area and heading off away from the houses and shops. We came to an abandoned suburban rail station, and walked down the steps, from the road, down toward the platform. I guessed, we were going to sit and she could have her bait after all. At the bottom of the steps I caught hold of her hand, and she turned and smiled, and did the most delicious schoolgirl smile accompanied with a naughty glance to the floor, which if it wasn't flashing green lights all over the place I didn't know what was. That combination of looks has remained one of the most sensuous I have ever encountered and stays with me still. We walked to the waiting room, which had lost its door, but not its walls or boarded-up windows. She snogged enthusiastically though without skill. As I preceded to grope up her skirts she became highly passionate and to be honest I got a bit scared, as she started to rip at my pants and grabbed my cock with such force I had to grab her wrist, and whisper 'Gently, it doesn't go all the way down,' referring to my poor foreskin being pulled from my penis. We ended up squashed against one of the wooden benches, her with her legs drawn up and feet on the bench, me in a back-breaking semi-squat, with me knees begging to kneel down or stand up, and instead forced to bounce off the bench while my flat hands took the weight. Remarkably, she had been a virgin. Even more remarkably this was the second one I encountered since coming to Ruskin and I do believe the first I had ever in my life. Not that I thought virgins were particularly attractive or desirable, indeed I would ordinarily have avoided contact with any sort of sexual virginity in the belief that changing that status was too much of a responsibility and too fraught with potential pain and discomfort. That had not been the case here. We wondered at last from the station, and at the top of the stairs, I decided to put my arm around her; mistake—she shook it free and I kicked myself inside as I reflected this must look like I suddenly owned her and she was now my possession. 'I can get a bus here,' she said. 'I'll wait with you'— here I was going again, but I couldn't really just walk off could I? 'You don't need to suddenly protect me, Dave, is it Dave?' I felt daft, 'Well OK, then,' I said, 'Probably see you in the library' She just smiled, a normal smile this time, and I never did. Hitching back up to Oxford I kept on reflecting on what had just happened, and turning it over and over in my mind, oh, and later on in bed as well. When I told Larch, he said 'Bliddy hell, she must have been desperate!' Bastard! Now he was at it, diminishing me memorable sexual encounters.

9
IRELAND

In the October of 1970, the university Socialist Society invited a speaker from People's Democracy over from the occupied Six Counties. I think this was the first time I met Frank Murphy, a founder member of that heroic organisation. Frank and me would become close friends and comrades. Around August 1971 Bernadette Devlin was invited to speak in Oxford. She was on a barnstorming tour. She was still at University at Queen's and had thrown herself into the civil rights struggle at the end of the Sixties. She stood as an Independent Unity candidate and was elected the youngest MP since William Pitt at the age of 21. She could be a fiery and impassioned speaker, but at the time we saw her in the big Irish pub over the Magdalen Bridge, in a bar crowded with Irish workers, many in their muck having just come from work, and loads of Irish families there with their children, she was adopting a different style. A small girl in stature, she sat informally on the speaker's table, literally on the front of the table with her little legs dangling over the edge and spoke in a quiet, though clear voice. I thought she overdid the 'ordinary Belfast girl in a big world, talking home truths and common sense' presentation, but hell, the audience loved it. She had been demonised in the press and obviously thought the image needed calming down somewhat. Which all went out the window during the Battle of the Bogside when in the van of the barricades and petrol bombs and the bricks, up to her armpits in RUC and Orange thugs she stood her ground and urged her neighbours to do the same. She was sentenced to nine months in jail. Me and Bernadette met for the first time in that Oxford bar, but our paths would cross on numerous occasions after that. It should be said perhaps at this stage, that the struggle in Ireland was not by and large understood by the British, particularly the English left, and then by proxy of the same blurred vision was likewise not understood by the left across the world who took their information from here. Preformulated ideas and inflexible thinking had assumed the split in the republican movement to be a left/right one all right. But this was seen as a politically conscious orientated divide, with the right-wing nationalists in the Provo break away and the Marxist progressives in the Officials. The bitter shooting war, which followed for a time the political split, was seen as 'fascist terrorism' against the left. The British left was on autopilot and it must be added were being misled by the Officials' propaganda and through their influence within the CPGB and the unions. *The Internationalist Newsletter* (USA) for September–October 1972 was somewhat typical of the period perceptions. Under the headline 'Provo Kamikazes Versus the Irish Revolution' we read:

> It is impossible to comment on the struggle in Ulster without some mention of the curious, tragic and sinister phenomenon of the Provisional Alliances, one would that it were possible to say less, and from recent developments it looks like we shall be able to speak less of 'the Provo's' in the near future. Briefly as we summed it up in Common

Ground (1) the Provo's 'claim to be waging' guerilla war' (and are played up for this in the yellow press), but in fact leave the hard, grueling job of defending the Irish working class ...to the hard pressed 'official' IRA units, while they devote their time to planting bombs in offices, shops and even workingmens' café ... [A] mixed bag of pseudo-nationalist religious bigots and short-sighted but sincere patriots, the Provo's claim to represent 'THE' IRA whereas in fact they comprise only a small minority of the Republican Movement concentrated in the North (where the imperialist enemy is ever so much more obvious, and the problem so much simpler) and above all in Belfast where a generation of classic 'old men with guns' were frustrated by their own isolation from the campaign in the fifties (as the IRA command scaled down offensive action in this especially tense and precarious center ... Now the Provo's grope with increasing desperation for a cynical deal with the British ('MacStiofain' and others traveling under safe-conduct to London in RAF aircraft on at least one occasion to contact top officials) their ultimate bankruptcy becomes ever more obvious, even within their own demoralised ranks, and a sharp split, if not complete disintegration, is clearly looming on the horizon.

Meanwhile the steady progress of the Irish Revolution continues under the increasingly confident and competent leadership of the 'Official' republican movement. In the Provo's the puppet rulers of the Free State manage to create a tragedy for Ulster and stumbling block for the Movement as a whole, but they failed abjectly to halt the inexorable march of the people toward the reconquest of Ireland.

In retrospect one could scarcely credit how such self-appointed commentators and analysers of world events could get it so wrong. Peter Anton, a man and an organisation I had yet to meet, edited *The Internationalist Newsletter*, organ of the Revolutionary Socialist League–Internationalist. The article was written by Bob Henes, who Peter says was quite ill then. We understood I think neither quantity nor quality of what was happening over the water, only that a war was developing. That there was confused armed resistance, that there was police repression, that there was religious bigotry and sectarianism. The Civil Rights movement, and People's Democracy seemed hearty attempts to unite the working class on basic democratic demands. The Civil Rights Association was non-violent, and modelled itself on Luther King and the black civil rights movement. Nobody here and few people there realised the depth of bigotry and anti-Catholicism and entrenched loyalist supremacism, nor the extent to which the British state would tenaciously hold onto that Provence and preserve the status quo. The Civil Rights Association, inspired by the black struggle in America for 'One Man One Vote' to win votes for all Afro-American adults, incredibly in 1969 Ulster was fighting for the same.[46]

Not all Catholic adults had the vote! The vote was based in part on property proscriptions, so voting was based upon the property you controlled. Many Catholics in joint occupancy of a house were excluded from voting, while

Protestant property-owners might have more than one vote. This coupled with the gerrymandered borders and boundaries gave a disproportionate voting power to Loyalist areas than Catholic ones. 'Ulster is British,' they had claimed, but unlike anywhere else in 'Britain' only certain members of the adult population were allowed to vote. The Civil Rights Association was demonstrating, marching, protesting around this issue. At first it drew in middle-class academics from Protestant areas and traditions, but the weight and fury of the Orange backlash forced all but the most determined to run for cover. Marchers were attacked by Orange gangs, or police officers who were members of Orange gangs and loyalist military organisations when not in uniform. There was something of the Ku Klux Klan in the whole bigoted setup. Many Catholics in the traditional republican areas had mellowed their demands at first and sought now only common justice within the UK designation, but now they were brutally and clearly denied even that, an old full-blown demand for complete and total independence and total control of their own island as a whole started to come back to the fore. Frank Murphy was a founder member of the People's Democracy movement. Working class, Belfast socialist. The PD had started in October of 1968. It had moved from a radical movement for people's democracy, votes, social justice etc. to one of an entirely socialist perspective. For a time it had not worked within broad fronts like the Northern Ireland Civil Rights Association. But it moved back from sectarianism and by the time I met them, was a well-balanced revolutionary socialist organisation fighting on the democratic and republican socialist front together. Frank had paraphrased Jim Connolly's words when I asked about their relationship with the Provos. He said you couldn't and shouldn't avoid the armed struggle in the north, but they hadn't fused with the Provos because their aim wasn't simply flying the tricolour from North to South; they wanted a workers' socialist republic. That couldn't just be won by militarily defeating the loyalists in the North. They required a struggle in the South against the southern ruling class. 'The trouble is neither wing of the republican movement is waging that struggle. The Provisionals are concentrating too exclusively in the North while the Officials are too dominated by the CPI (Communist Party of Ireland) strategy of winning over sections of the Southern middle class. We cooperate with the IRA volunteers though. The vast majority of them want to go the full road down to a workers' republic.'

He reminded me what Connolly had said on the eve of the Irish rebellion (1916) 'In the event of victory hold onto your rifles, as those with whom we are fighting may stop before our goal is reached. We are out for economic as well as political liberty.' Frank had thrown down the challenge, for me to come over to Ulster and see for myself what was going on. So I decided I would. The Party sanctioned the visit formally; I was given a 'commission'. They drew up a set of questions; crushingly naive, they reflected the poverty of information, which the so-called vanguard of the class had about the struggle in occupied Ulster. What was the source of the split between the Officials and the Provisionals? Was this a reflection of a Stalinist v. Trotskyist schism, was it Nationalist, Catholic versus revolutionary Marxist, could the factions be united? Along with the information

I was to draw from the struggle on the ground I was to take a bag full of the works of Posadas, some of which mentioned the Irish struggle in very general ways. I packed little, a small brown suitcase I had found in Oxford. I brought my bank book, since I didn't know how long I would stay and this was the only money I had, my passport, since I needed ID to draw any money from what was really a savings account. An address as to where I was going, and that was it. I wore my short white Gurney Slade raincoat, and having kissed Maureen goodbye with a promise not to get killed, I set off, from Oxford, to Manchester/ Heysham for the ferry across to Belfast. I had bought a few bottles of beer for the journey and was opening them on the buckle of my belt, a knack I had picked up of necessity somewhere, and was reading with my knees up on the seat in front. A youngish lad came to sit opposite and asked me to open his bottle. From there we chatted, what was I doing, why was I going to Belfast, I responded with tales of the world revolutionary struggle, the struggle against British imperialism, the fight of the miners and the workers in general. He said he was a student who hadn't got things worked out just yet, but probed me here and there on all sorts of subjects. About three stops before Manchester he gets off, wishing me well. I thought nowt of it.

After Manchester the trains heads for Heysham and the ferry. The chill of the dark night was closing as we halted at Heysham. The smell of the sea, the cry of the gulls, and that icy cold which comes off the sea grips me, with the excitement of going on a ship again, going to Ireland again. I set off down the platform, along with the rest of the folks from the train, some squaddies, Irish folk, men and women, some kids. Suddenly two tall thugs in raincoats with crew-cuts come either side of me, and walking quite briskly along, without stopping, say 'Mr David Douglass?' Not a lot of point saying no, they knew who I was. 'Come with us, sir.' Here and there, plain clothes cops have some blokes by the arm, and some women with their kids are being escorted into an office just off the platform. Inside it are uniformed policemen, in a crush of bodies, some leaning over desks, others held against the wall. In offices off the main room, the door is open, a woman being forced to undress shouting 'For God's sake can yee no keep the doors closed?' Officers ignore the semi-naked women and walk in and out. In another corner a man is standing in his underpants. I am got by the arm and pushed into a small office. Behind the desk is a tubby, middle-aged, ugly-looking balding man, with a most unpleasant air about him. He wears little glasses. He reminds me at once of portrayals of the Gestapo and I wonder if this is an image he hopes to promote. I see on his desk D.S. Danby. He clicks open the latches on my brown suitcase, which has been laid across his desk, opens the lid, and lets it flop backwards off the desk, unclips the elasticated straps inside, then empties the contents of the suitcase on the floor, some shirts, my jumper, some underwear, socks and washing stuff, together with handfuls of Posadist pamphlets, their red spines gleaming, the hammer and cycle emblazoned on each one. He moves the stuff about the floor with the toe of his shoe, looking alternately at me, and then the stuff on the floor. 'By you clever lad,' I said with restrained anger. 'Fucking cleverer than you,' he responds and looks straight at me. He has in front of him my passport, my bank book and the daft bloody letter from the Party with its list of questions: '"Unite the factions?" You want bigger bombs- and more murders?' he says. 'Ideas are more dangerous than bombs' I responded, which I thought seemed quite pithy and solid-jawed.

He jumps up. 'Yi think I don't fucking know that? You're just a little shit-stirring twat off on a mission aren't you?' 'No.' 'What were you doing in Belgium?' 'Visiting the miners' 'The fucking miners! Oh, they'll be involved here somewhere, I have no doubt. Is Mr Scargill paying for this trip then, unite the factions?' He pulls my jumper and my jacket out of the suitcase. 'Now get your stuff and fuck off on the ferry.'

'What about my stuff?' 'You've got about six minutes and the gangplank goes up. Doesn't bother me which way you go, lad.' 'Do I get a receipt?' 'Yes, my boot up your arse,' he says as two cops push open the door and grab me arm, pushing me toward the exit and toward the ferry.

One bloke staggers along in front of me, blood streaming from his nose; he looked like a farm labourer, in a big old overcoat. Two women, in their thirties I guessed, are struggling to hold their stuff together in a holdall which had been bundled closed again. Both had been crying, one carrying her cardigan and coat, as if she'd been strip-searched. We went up the gangplank. I didn't feel so happy now.

I lug my suitcase down the stairs to the bar, which is sullen, filled with smoke and in separate hostile territories bordered by non-aligned individuals like myself who didn't know anyone. Groups of squaddies sat round tables, talking loudly, playing cards, drinking, smoking. Huddled men and women and a few children had closed areas off with their suitcases. I pushed through the crowd to the bar and bought a pint. The ship was now dipping slightly and rolling, the smell of diesel was everywhere. Spying a spare place along the long bench-like seat which ran around the back bulkhead, I sat down, put me pint between me feet and surveyed the room. It seemed nobody was looking at anyone else. Just I get up again to go the bog a bloke with a rolled-up paper sits down next to me.

'Hoy!' he says suddenly, loudly and smacking me with the paper, which I resent hotly and turn toward him feeling like I should punch him. He points at my case. I look in non-comprehension. 'Don't leave that.' 'Ah'm gaan the bog!' 'Your gaan nowhere,' he said mocking my dialect, 'without that,' he said with a point of his foot. 'You fuckers have just searched that case inside bliddy oot, there's nowt in it.' 'Case,' he says looking straight at me. 'Fuck it,' I think, 'I will not just do as I am told', and plonk myself back down again and pick up my pint. He meantime unrolls his paper, and starts to look at it, as if he is reading the crumpled object. I take a sup of me pint—manky beer, smells horrible as well, I won't be getting drunk on this. 'Got a copy of *Red Flag* in the case if you want to really read something,' I say out loud without turning toward my flat-footed companion. At least the headlines were usually catchy.

He stands up and leans toward me, 'You're not in England now,' he threatens and slowly walks away. Hmm, now I go to the bog, lugging the bliddy case, which although not big, is a pain to get into a cubicle when you want a crap. I doze a little and then a certain excitement emerges through the gloom of the bar, which is now closed and sorrowful looking. We are nearing Belfast and I go on deck; it's bitter cold. I open my case and drag out the one remaining jumper I have and put it on. Odd that—they took my jumper and jacket. As the boat nears the dock, and then the gangplanks run down, officials and obvious plainclothes cops stand either side of the gangway at the bottom, waiting I presume to pull people out as they land. Well nothing ventured, I set off breezily down the gangplank swinging my case and expected to get pulled, but no, either they don't want me, or else the new jumper has thrown them. I come down the plank, through the customs, out into the street, where queues of people wait for taxis, rapidly rolling up and then away. Suddenly a phalanx of soldiers, in twos, SLRs at the 'port' position about a dozen strong are doubling toward me, their boots resounding. Toward me. I freeze to the spot, put down the case and stand. They stamp off by me; they are escort for the soldiers on the boat. I stand in a queue for a taxi, and just before I get to the end people are asking each other's destinations so as to share the taxi and share the fare. Folk are jovial and joking; they ask me where I'm heading, then a women in a headscarf shocks me rigid: 'Not in this fucking queue you're not,' she says, looking round the queue all standing in commonly held disbelief. An aud bloke gets me elbow in a friendly fashion and says: 'Sure, these cabs don't go there son, you need the Falls taxis over there.' I join another queue, mystified. Belfast is a divided city, years of rebellion and pogroms and murders meant that buses did only basic routes; they didn't go on estates or off the beaten track. When they did they were stoned according to their destination, or hijacked and used as barricades, Catholic drivers in Loyalist estates were shot dead and left hanging from the bus. Taxis wouldn't venture onto Loyalist-dominated estates; if they did they were hit by Loyalist gunmen and the same tended to be true on the other side: local kids might recognise them as non-Catholics and stone them. So no taxis either. Car ownership was negligible on both sides, and who would wish to drive around Belfast anyway? So the republican areas developed their own fleet of taxis. They were a co-op, they operated a door-to-door service, took folk shopping, took folk out and about and knew everything and everybody. They were the eyes and ears of the community. 'Frank Murphy, aye, sure he's a good lad. Is he in?'

I bliddy well sincerely hope so, or what the hell is Ah gaana dey nuw? The driver waited. There was a note on the door: 'Tied Up Meet You At "The Crown"'(I think it was—some big non-sectarian, old-fashioned bar in mid-city). Shit Shit Shit! The driver said: 'No sweat, I know it.' He dropped me off at a minor street adjacent to the main drag in city centre Belfast, and pointed me down the High Street.

It's hard to explain my impression of Belfast then. A bustling modern city, streets full of people, shopping, bars full of people. Laddies with long hair like my own and girls with miniskirts. Yet here is a city under occupation, around the streets armed soldiers walk, Pigs—the aptly named armoured trucks— and Saracen armoured cars roll along in traffic, the machine gun on the turret of the cars turning this way and that as the gunner surveys his potential targets. Off the main drag are the split communities. The republican wall art is like a huge lodge banner, each end house with a depiction of struggles past and present. The world revolutionary struggle—not simply this aspect of it: Palestine, Vietnam, South Africa, South America, peoples of the world in armed insurrection. Slogans hailing the Provisional IRA. There was no doubt that these Provisionals had the ear of the graffiti artists and their finger on the pulse, if nothing else. I am stopped in my musings by someone grabbing me by the top of my hair and collar of my coat. 'Fuckin' gerroff is!' I yell and drop the suitcase and try with pain to turn my head and twist my neck round.

Out of the corner of my left eye, I see a soldier, combat fatigues, sleeves rolled up, rifle butt in the crook of his right arm, from behind me a Liverpool voice: 'A Geordie!' He lets go.

I turn round eyes blazing, he's a big fucker, stocky, broad, squat. 'Does it mek a difference like?'

'Yis,' he replies in broad Scouse, 'yi'd be in da doorway on yi face udderwise.' His mate says 'Open the suitcase.' I kneel down to open the case. They both take a step away; the boy with the gun starts to lower it toward my level.

I open the case. 'Step away!' no. 2 shouts. I stand up instinctively with my hands in the air like I'd seen on the cowboy pictures. Then he grabs me by the collar again and with his hand forcibly on my right shoulder spins me round and pushes me up against the glass of the shop window. 'Spread dem arms lad,' he growls. I spread my arms out, and he kicks my legs out and pulls them back so I fall with my face against the window and my arse sticking out and my legs splayed out behind me in both directions. His mate is kicking my stuff around in the case, with the toe of his boot, that fucking case, I wish I'd come with nowt. He is meantime feeling down my back and backside, my legs looking for bumps and bulges that might be weapons. 'Don't move an inch!' the stocky one shouts. So I stand, and listen and wait, the sound of traffic, the sound of people talking passing by, the clip- clop of female shoes, the car horns. I drop my head and look round, they've gone, leaving me standing up against the wall like an idiot, leaving me bag open and stuff flopped out on the pavement. Nobody says nowt—it's an everyday occurrence. I restart my walk and quest for the pub and Frank. It slowly dawns on me: nobody ever carries a suitcase through the streets of Belfast. I find the bar, it's near jammed to the gunwales, Stones music, hippie-like folk, Sixties-like folk, young folk. I get to the door, with the suitcase, I walk in and for a moment I feel like every pair of eyes in the bar surveys the man at the door, in the short white Gurney Slade raincoat, carrying a brown suitcase. The barman, in mid pull of a pint stops and looks up. I try to spurt it all out together 'Avjustcome off the ferrymeanttibe meetingsomeone thanot inso I've ti meethim hereyou can check the suitcaseif yiwant.' I go to open the case on the bar, and he looks in. 'Not worth carrying that I wouldn't think,' he correctly observes, and allows me, remarkably, to leave it behind the bar. It is only about 11 a.m. or maybe earlier, but by fuck I am going to murder a pint, which I do in just about one. I soon get on talking with everyone, having the crack, talking in hushed tones about the current situation. I am sitting next to an Irish folk-rock band, and rabbiting on about folk and folk singers and songs, I believe I even give them a few verses of wor Geordie sangs. I think the band was called Barleycorn; they had been responsible for a rip-roaring hit throughout the Irish communities of the world, 'The Men Behind the Wire', about the implementation of mass repression via internment, rounding up men and boys and teenagers and putting them into concentration camps, without trial or jury or charge.

Through the little streets of Belfast in the hours of early morn
British soldiers came marauding, wrecking little homes with scorn
Heedless of the crying children, dragging fathers from their beds
Seizing sons while helpless mothers watched the blood flow from their
     heads
Armoured cars and tanks and guns
Came to take away our sons
But every man will stand behind the men behind the wire.

It was some song, it caught the truth and resentment of the moment. The band were off on a tour of the USA on the strength of it. I recall the big hippie lad, who I think played bass guitar, wanting to buy some knee-length boots for the tour and we set off round the shoe shops of Belfast to find some. On the way, we had bought a few snacks for back at the bar. I was starving, and had bought a little wedge of cheese, and put it in me pocket for later. Shopping with the Irish rebel hippie, for a pair of knee-high boots in occupied Ulster, seems a bit incredulous, but somehow, because everything else seems normal, the buses are running, it's raining, folk are out shopping and going about their business with umbrellas, it doesn't seem strange at all. We actually found a shop with just the thing he was looking for in the window. Well actually as it turned out, there was only just this one in the window. The other was on another side of town. The shop girls phoned through to have it sent over and we just started what seemed to become a long wait. I was browsing mesell for some non-leather item of footwear when the door opens behind me, the bell tinkled, and a sort of hush fell on the shop. Two soldiers with SLRs had walked in. 'Against the wall' they command.

Me and the hippie walk over to the wall and following his example I spread my arms out leaning on the wall. One stands gun at the ready, the other squats down and starts to frisk me, moving down my back and inside my coat, and down the outside of me coat.

'What's in the pocket?' he says loudly. Pocket? Nowt, nowt I'm sure. 'Nowt.' 'Sarge!' he calls, and the other one comes over and points this gun right at my head, whilst his mate starts with two fingers to extricate the package from my poke. 'Ah,' I remember, just as the package is drawn out. 'Its cheese, its cheese.' He places the packet on the floor. 'Open it' he commands, the gun pointed at my head, the girls in the shop staring hard at the packet.

I start to open it. 'Slowly!' he shouts. 'Its bliddy cheese, man,' I reply indignantly and this bastard kicks me right in the ribs as I am bending down to pick up the package, I drop to me knees and groan. 'You'll be fucking cheese, man!' he shouts. 'Open it slowly.' I open the packet, unfold the greaseproof paper, and reveal the lump of Edam, which I break off a piece from and start to (painfully) but I thought defiantly, eat. He knocks the cheese to the floor and then thuds me with one flat hand into a chair. 'Why are you here?' he begins and the hippie lad is dragged out into a back room and thudded up against the wall. 'I'm just visiting.' 'Visiting who, why?' 'A mate.' 'Who, why?' 'Just a mate I met at Oxford at college, and I came over to surprise him.' 'Name?' 'I don't know his name, I just thought I'd drop over and drop in on him.' 'Where are you staying?' 'I don't know yet. I've just arrived. I thought a hotel.' 'I don't trust you, son,' he said. 'If I were you I would get the next ferry back to Geordieland and leave well alone.' I thought I was going to be rounded up, and taken away, but, glaring at me, he and the sergeant who had come back from the back room, backed toward the door, and out.

The big hippie came weakly forward, a thin trickle of blood from his nose. 'Good job I didn't sing them a song,' he joked. A little later, amid families coming into the shop and kids trying on shoes as they would in any British high street, the other boot arrived. We walked back to the pub, through streets crowded with traffic and army vehicles, sitting in awkward spots and presiding over the scene, making a point, that they controlled. Back in the pub I was very, very pleased to see Frank, poring over a newspaper. 'Get here all right?' 'Well ... '

Frank took me on a tour of the loyalist estates and houses. It was at once a culture shock, nowhere had I ever seen working-class people appear to embrace everything which was alien to my politics and culture and background. The butchers apron, the Union Jack, was a flag I had despised since youth, even when I was in the Cadets. I knew its history. Knew it to be the flag of the ruling class, the flag of our enemies. This was the rag pushed in the face of exploited people across the globe; it marked the sign of the enemy, even for British workers, on streets of Liverpool or Shields or Newcastle, it had headed up the state's repressive forces against miners, seamen and dockers. Then the St George flag: I never seen anyone fly this flag who wasn't a fascist, it was in the standard parties of the National Socialist Movement, and then the National Front. Here it was painted on every wall and hung from every house. The walls bore the slogans 'No Surrender', the old lie 'Home Rule is Rome Rule', 'British Till Death' and the various regiments of the loyalist murder gangs, the UDA, UFF, UVF. There were other more obscure armed groups, which Frank informed me where often just British Army fronts, used to assassinate republican militants, or awkward politicos who they targeted. Sometimes they would shoot down Loyalists too, for many reasons, not least to stop them getting close to the republicans in anything which could be seen as a dialogue. We ended up in a mid city bar, a bar which still housed lots of young people laughing and flirting and listening to the latest sounds on the pub taped music, lots of students, lots of discussion, a progressive bar Frank told me. Here were some young thinking Protestants, but they were taking a risk, though not from the republicans, he hastened to add—the future of this conflict was tied up with winning Protestants back to their republican past—but from the Orange ultras who would think nothing of beating them up, or worse, just for visiting a bar like this. This wasn't a political pub, though, it was mixed in so far as ordinary folk out shopping could still pop in and have a pint. It hadn't been targeted by either side. Frank surveyed some of my literature while I talked to people. 'What a load of aud bollocks!' he would cry out from time to time as he read through the sacred texts of Posadism. 'The people of Derry are inspired to their revolutionary struggle and heroic resistance to British Imperialism by the courage and confidence in the future by the masses of Bangladesh,' he read out loud, to laughter from everyone who heard him. 'Dave, the folk here understand imperialism because they see it everyday. Everyday in discrimination and denial of basic human rights, a job, housing, votes—for what fucking good they are, we should still have them—the right to worship who you want or not without being shot for it, the right to control our own streets ner mind our own country.' Posadas was wont to make such comparisons to see the entire world struggle not simply figuratively linked but organically. This was one of the embarrassments I spoke of above. Even the ordinary day-to-day 'orientation', a kind of blessed guidance given on this or that, was embarrassing. The word of Posadas was so pure it wasn't allowed to be translated in kind, or in estimation of what it would mean in English. Instead it is translated literally from Spanish to English and becomes Spangle, utterly meaningless in English. We sold oceans of newsprint like this. In Spain the word for 'white-collar' as in 'white-collar worker' was 'stiff-collar', so Posadas is translated literally and from everywhere come cries of 'What the fuck's a stiff collar?' The party got into the habit of never questioning what a damn sentence meant—just translate it and print it. We, the northern working folk, had led a mini revolt over a pamphlet titled We Must Study the Texts of Our Masters, Marx, Engels and Lenin. We baulked at being told we had masters of any sort —not just those of us from anarchist pasts, but solid working-class experience was 'against the masters'— maisters in dialect. They were the coal maisters, the mill maisters, the shipyard maisters. We hated the masters from long generations; we couldn't sell any document, which told us to study them. The party wouldn't agree, but allowed us to reprint for Tyneside purposes only the title page as Study the Texts of Our Teachers, which is what the damn sentence meant in any case. We were told that Posadas in Spanish was a poet with much of his wisdom contained in his phrase; we couldn't just render it practical and English, so we rendered it nonsense instead.

Off on my own for a wee while, I had set off down a busy side street to visit one of the lads I had met in the pub. I called at a corner shop to buy some tabs on the way. I was lighting a tab, and then setting off, when I bumped into Frank. 'Where yee been?' I explained about the shop. 'Fuckin' hell!' he says and gaans fleein back up the road, while I stand in complete non-understanding. He comes running back. 'C'mon yee!' 'What's up?' 'That shop is a Provo spotting post, looking for squaddies just like you, buying tabs, another few feet and you would be in some cross-wires.' 'Squaddie?' I said outraged. 'You're a fuckin' Geordie, most of the bastards who maraud about this place arresting and beating folk are Scots or Geordies.'

'But me hair?' 'They don't even see that, or if they do they just think you must be with special intelligence or some murder squad. And Dave, get rid of that fuckin' white coat! Nobody wears a white coat in Belfast, You might as well paint a target on it.' I was a bit rattled, but I knew at least what he meant about the coat. I should have binned it then and there but it ended up back in the case. My Durham Area NCB St John's Badge was the next best thing in those days to a miner's badge. 'An' don't put that fuckin' thing back on again either. It looks like a UDA badge.' 'The boys are a bit trigger-happy, aren't they, shooting someone because they have a non-Irish accent?'

'The boys, Dave, started out not shooting the bastards at all. They thought about working class solidarity and appealing to the Brits to go home, and trying to explain what our fight was all about. It didn't work. They had a strategy of kidnapping soldiers on patrol, blindfolding them taking them back and giving them a telling off, basically explained to them what the fight was about, then let them go. It was only weeks before SAS men were posing as ordinary squaddies to get captured and memorise the route, the time and background noises, the voices and then on release steam back tooled up and murder everyone. The gloves are off, comrade. Yet still nobody here blames "the English", nor "the Protestants"; this is a political struggle and most of the boys although they don't have your political sophistication ken weel what's the world revolution and imperialism is all about.' On another occasion, we are walking down the main street in early evening, when a line of Pigs and jeeps bristling with armed troops travelling on past us suddenly turns in a U-turn across the other side of the road, forming a semicircle, and blocking both traffic and pedestrians in both directions. As the troops, guns in hand, start to jump from the vehicles, Frank suddenly shouts 'Run!' 'Run?' 'They'll fuckin' shoot us!' Frank was off down the road shouting 'Run!' over his shoulder and as I set off I heard the thud-thud of bullets hitting walls, and the sudden silence of traffic halting. There was some small machinegun fire, as we swept round the corner into a bar. I was red-faced, sweating and my knees were shaking. We both gasped for air. The barman had turned the TV down and the customers were listening to the gunfire. The barman flicked his head and smiled. 'Ours,' said Frank to me as we walked to the bar. 'What will you be having me fine young gentlemen? Are you just in out of the rain?' 'Oh, we are,' said Frank. He sat on the bar high stool, and I stood up with me back to the door. 'What?' 'I could tell it was an ambush. Too good to miss, when they started circling the wagons, if we hadn't run, we could have been caught in the fire.' 'A road block?' 'Aye and searching for young internees or more suspects to stick behind the wire.' 'The bastards' I was volunteering to all and sundry when the bar fell silent.

I felt a wind on my back, and a voice shouted 'You!' I turned slightly, although I noticed everyone else just carried on drinking or looking around, not speaking. There was a squad of soldiers. Riot sticks, short round riot shields, about eight of them, two with rifles. 'You!' the NCO was shouting and pointing with his club at an old bloke in a big cloth cap, who got up slowly and walked toward them. The sergeant grabbed him by the collar of his jacket as he drew parallel and spun him round to face the wall. 'Spread!' he shouted. The old chap started to lean shakily against the wall. 'Spread them legs!' the English voice shouted. 'I'm an aud man sure, I can't spread ...' And with that the soldier whacked the bloke on the inside of his legs with the club, smack, smack, side to side. 'I'll spread them for you!' he yelled. My belly went over and I knew I was going to dive in, and fuck the consequences. Frank gripped my arm with a grip like iron and stared right into my eyes, so much suppressed anger along with a sort of look of contempt for my arrogance that he stopped me in my tracks. After searching the old bloke they spun him round and let him slide down the wall onto the floor. The two soldiers with guns stepped into the middle of the bar and cocked their weapons with a mechanical chorus. I thought, believed, they were going to spray the bar with bullets, but having scared everyone shitless they walked out, leaving the door banging in the wind. Frank's house was like an ordinary terraced house at Gateshead, the streets were 'Coronation streets', the area thoroughly working-class. At night time though there were no lights. The streets were in total blackness and the curtains were heavy and drawn with little light escaping. It was dangerous and hard finding the way back at night from the pub, as I walked along, discussing the nature of the war and the resistance, ever seeming to stick me feet in it. The expression 'the republican socialist movement' had scarce noisily left me lips when down by my side, in the dark, invisible until that point, I saw a soldier, his face blackened, crouched in a gateway, his rifle pointed in our direction, then through the gloom, more outlines, soldiers squatting, lying, standing, waiting their chance to shoot 'the enemy' however they defined it. Frank filled me in about the way in which the state used the armed Orange forces coupled with their own special forces to carry out murders and bombings to combat the republican movement. There were many, perhaps the biggest outrage was the bombs in Dublin in which 33 people had died. A warning no doubt of London's frustrations with the Dail for lacklustre efforts to combat the Provo supporters over the border, or to relinquish the claims of that body to sovereignty over 32 counties of Ireland not just 26. It was a punishment shooting carried out not by the militias of either side, but the armed forces using undercover operators and linked to the Loyalists for cover. Frank always told me he wasn't a part of the Provisional movement. I knew him to be a founder member of PD, but whether this precluded involvement in the former I began to doubt. For a start, when we were out, in a café we never paid for a meal. This I discovered was one of the ways known republican activists, engaged full-time in struggle of one sort of another, managed to live—nobody charged them for food or provisions or drink. Each time I reached in my pocket, Frank would offer 'This is mine,' but then simply nod to the waiter who would nod in return. Mind it could have been he was just a popular chap, which he was.

Over the course of the next few days I got to meet men and some women who were clearly members of the armed wing of this Provisional movement. It became very clear to me that the old IRA had given up the struggle. 'The Officials' they became known as, among the youth of Ulster, the 'old rusty guns'. As the repression against the emerging Civil Rights movement had intensified to raids and riots and pogroms, attacking demonstrations and well-known speakers and activists had given way to raids into Catholic republican areas, petrol-bombing houses, murdering helpless people for no other reason than their surname. The RUC, entirely partisan and bigoted, had often led the charge, and certainly turned a blind eye, in much the way the southern local establishment of the USA was embroiled with the men in the hoods. The communities had looked to their armed force for defence, only to find the IRA had been wound up for all intents and purposes under the political direction of Sinn Fein, which in turn was following the path of Euro-Communism and former members of the Irish Communist Party. 'Reform not revolution' meant work within British and Irish parliamentary set-ups, in alliance with social democrats and liberals—not an outright quest for revolutionary republican socialist independence. They would endeavour covertly to call themselves the National Liberation Front, never seeing the irony that they were in fact abandoning armed struggle and resistance. As the murder gangs and thugs had attacked at will, old IRA slogans had been lampooned: 'I Ran Away' (IRA). Something had had to give, and the young, exploited, downtrodden youth of Ulster rose in self-defence, to re-form the IRA as the Provisionals. In 1969 they had started with a couple of handguns and shotguns and loads of petrol bombs and spunk. They hadn't worked out the world programme for the socialist revolution but they hadn't needed to. They could see, eat and breath repression and that consciousness bred resistance and history was relearned on the hoof. There was lots of confused politics in those early days, certainly the language was misleading. Sinn Fein had split, along political grounds, the Officials tending to have the best-sounding slogans and talking of Marxism and socialism, whereas the Provo split had supported the struggle on the street, and tending toward a more nationalistic outlook; they were given unfortunately to describing 'the Stickies' (the Officials) as 'ultra-left', as 'communist extremists trying to set up an extreme Marxist dictatorship'. Although they were in fact engaged in nothing of the kind, to the kids on the street this sort of language was meant to express their hatred for the bureaucracy and autocratic 'Stalinism' of the Officials' leadership. Unfortunately it made it easy to misrepresent this struggle as being between genuine socialists and a bunch of catholic nationalist bigots. The Provo armed militants tended to be mainly young working-class militants from the cities, while the politicos were the old diehard wing of Irish republicanism. It would take years for the politics of the northern working-class fighters to stamp itself on the more green conservatism of the southern-dominated Provos. It was to be an ongoing struggle for a generation and more. But right now a movement was re-emerging, its sharp end was undeniably working-class, revolutionary socialist and internationalist.

THE PROVISIONAL IRA: A PHOENIX EMERGING FROM THE ASHES

It wouldn't take the world's best Marxist to detect less than a perfect perspective in the early publications of the Provisionals. These were not written by Marxists, in fact even in the opening couple of years of the Provos, this literary expression was to the right of the average Provo IRA volunteer or their young supporters on the streets. Freedom Struggle, an opening salvo, an illegal and much prized declaration of war announcing the arrival of the Provisional IRA, was a case in point. Although it was illustrated with defiant photos of armed insurgents it talked about fighting for democratic socialism on the basis of Christian principles. It rejected 'atheistic Marxism', as it called it. It needed no 'foreign' movement, or philosophy. It saw itself as the embodiment of the principles of 1916, and the two wings of that movement, socialist and 'Christian' nationalist. It betrayed, such as it was, a profound ignorance of that movement and the Marxist wing of it at least, the one represented by the leadership of James Connolly, an international revolutionary communist, thoroughly imbued with 'foreign' doctrines and notions, if not totally atheistic. However the people at the core of anti-imperialist struggle, the people in the van of the risen working-class republican areas were the Provisionals, warts and all. Utter crap though the draftsmen of the early publications were, this was an emerging anti-imperialist, largely working-class socialistic organisation. Such organisations are not developed in the social science laboratory, but in the fire of struggle and contradiction. Those to whom the task of writing up the early perspectives of the organisation fell, or who claimed it for want of anyone better, or even for want of anyone else at all, tended to be drawn from the hard republican fighters who had been in severe political and sometimes physical battle with their ostensible 'left' under the sway of the Officials. It was the 'Sticky' ('Official') brand of Marxism and socialism which had coloured the old green republican view of what both were meant to be. 'Eurocommunism'— an accommodation with the current system using parliamentary means—had come to dominate the European Communist Parties. In Britain the notorious *British Road to Socialism* had been accepted since the 1950s. It conceded that socialism in Britain would be won through parliament, and through a left Labour government working in conjunction with CPGB MPs. In Ireland the remnant of armed republicanism in 'the IRA', now dominated by the Irish Communist Party, stood in (largely theoretical) contrast, and was everywhere under political attack within that movement. Its conclusion had been the abandonment of the guns and the armed struggle. (Ironically, some of the weapons had come to the Welsh Free Army insurgents.)[47]

The armed struggle was replaced by work within the existing structure of bourgeois society, the civil rights protests, the unions and community-based actions, within the confines of the recognition of Stormont, partition and the border. Those old republicans who had stood for continued resistance, anti-imperialism, continued armed struggle and a Thirty-Two County Ireland came to associate the new politics with a confusion of unacceptable ideologies. On the one hand was the politics of accommodation and surrender to 'Britain' and the concept of Six-Counties Ulster, at least in the foreseeable future as part of that political and geographic landscape. On the other hand was 'Stalinism' and single-party dictatorship, with all that meant in terms of deprivation of freedom and state terror. This was 'communism' as they understood it. The Officials saw the reform of Stormont as it stood as the most pressing issue. They strove for 'the unity of Protestant and Catholic workers' as an economistic unit within the confines of the occupied province. When the Provisionals brought down Stormont, the Stickies seen it as a reactionary step and actually stood with the loyalists on the issue. They had nailed their colours to the mast of a united community and trade union campaign to reform Stormont and win a Bill of Rights within the six counties. 'The old rusty guns' remained in existence and under the weight of the loyalist backlash, against the fear of total loss of credibility in the nationalist community, were forced to actually 'defend' the community with arms. However they made it completely clear that their guns were not offensive and would be used only defensively. This limited operation too was brought to an end by 1972, via a statement from their Army Council declaring all those still under active arms to be 'fascists', 'murderers', 'criminals' etc. The blundering language of the early Provo spokespersons denouncing 'the communists' helped spread the lie that the Provos were fascists. This 'line' was fed wholesale to the CPGB in Britain and through them into the upper and middle echelons of the British TUC and movement. It was a line heartily endorsed by Militant and through them the bulk of the LPYS and large swages of the labour and trade union movement. I recall a stormy confrontation in the Bridge Hotel backroom, following a meeting of the Newcastle Branch of the CPGB. We had drifted in there following their meeting and suddenly a loud and public argument began over our literature in support of the Provos. An aud CP bloke at length announced 'De yee knaa lad? the last time I argued with a bloke in black shirt sounding like you was in 1939.' 'Yee mean yee think Ah's a fascist, whey man, its bliddy obvious Ah'm a socialist?' I responded somewhat taken aback that my shirt colour would suddenly become my heart on my sleeve. 'Aye, that's what they said then an'ahl,' he countered.

The split had developed largely around the dynamic of the resistance emerging through the process in the North, and the vacuum left by the poverty of the Officials' 'new realism'; and those charged with developing the political rationale of the new movement did so from the stand point of 'anti-Marxism' as they understood it. In reality it was a pragmatic and subjective response to Stalinism and social pacifism/social imperialism. It was a further irony that the process on the ground within the Six Counties was fuelled by ideas of 'the new left' and world revolutionary struggles linked cheek-by-jowl to left-Marxist ideologies. Ulster had caught the 'something' which was in the air sweeping round the world. It had nothing to do the Marxism of the old Stickies and Rusty Guns, and everything to do with revolutionary Marxism and revolutionary socialism as ideas, if not organisationally at this time. There were those still within the 'old IRA and Sinn Fein' who posed a potential 'left' break in terms of conscious expression as well as physical force; these would bide their time and emerge later. When they did emerge as the Irish National Liberation Army and its political wing the Irish Republican Socialist Party, in 1974, they were perhaps already too late. The bulk of the alternative bus had already left in the shape of the Provos and most of the republican population would either already be on board or boarding along the way. Had they left as a strong revolutionary Marxist tendency, as part of the Provisional break at the time, they might have been in a position to consciously underwrite and synthesise the empirical and uneven left political development taking place.

I could see clearly now where the Provisionals fitted into the total war against imperialism and capitalism. No, it wasn't some empirical process, some objective fact, which put them in the camp of the world socialist revolution. It was, whey aye, the nature of the struggle; but also their ideology was developing fast and to the left, becoming within a year or so of the first publications avowedly socialist, certainly far more so than the British Labour Party for example. They called for an all-Ireland socialist government of small farmers and workers. They recognised the necessity for the complete separation of church and state, that all peoples would have the right to worship or not worship how and what they wished, or not: a fully secular socialist society. They recognised the problem of nearly one million Protestants in four and half counties of Ulster, understood damn well, or correctly bloody well, how loyalism had been wholeheartedly embraced by the bulk of that community, how they identified as a people with its reactionary current. They knew too well also that the Irish history of the Protestant people had militant republican traditions, radical and socialist traditions and anti-imperialist traditions. These had not disappeared, they had been suppressed and buried; they had not died but had been ruthlessly murdered. They recognised that the Protestant section of Ulster from both those traditions had to be won again to some form of recognition of Ireland as an indivisible people united in one country. Indivisible that is in terms of nationality and ethnicity, not class; the enemies of the Irish workers Protestant and Catholic was capitalism North and South and imperialism and neo-colonialism. To try and hold out a branch and make some effort to win those workers the standing policy of Sinn Fein was Eire Nua, a new Ireland. It promised four semiautonomous traditional provinces in a federal socialist Ireland. Ulster would be united once more to nine counties, but the former loyalist communities would be a hefty lobby fighting for the interests of their religion and 'culture' as they seen it. I stand back now, decades further down that road, through twists and turns as the Provisionals fought and died, starved and jailed, killed and were killed, tried every which way in the book and made it up as they went, carrying a heroic people with them, and I am proud to say they were heroes and heroines one and all. They took the UK state by the balls and they hung on for grim death taking all that sophisticated and brutal apparatus could dish out in terms of murder and slander and torture. They were to take the British army to an eventual 'no win' if not defeat.

When I returned to Oxford I joined Sinn Fein, something of which I was (and am) immensely proud, as was my Mam when I whispered it in her ear whilst me Da was making tea in the kitchen. She took me by the hand with both her hands, and whispered: 'I am so proud of you, but please be careful.' I assured her I was not in the IRA or ever likely to be, but I am not sure she believed me. She wrote:

> Well David, you took me back to my very young days. When my poor mother had a rotten life with the Black and Tans, they had her held up at gun point made us little kids lie on the floor while they raided our home. Pulled all our beds up, emptied all my poor mothers things out on the

floor looking for arms and guns just because our name was Nelson. My poor mother was due to have her babies she had all her clean clothes for the bed and baby's little clothes in a trunk, they emptied them all out on the floor and walked on them, my poor mother went to pick them up to put them back and she fell behind the trunk and her baby was born there. I was only six years old at the time I had to run for the nurse, she nearly died and my Dad was out fighting all over the world for the B'King and England, so was Uncle Hughie that was Johnny Nelsons father. My poor mother suffered over them so and so.'s. Well you see its a funny tale we are more like sisters and brothers than first cousins, uncle Hugh and my dad was two brothers and Aunty Rosie and my Mam was sisters so that was two brothers and two sisters got married, so them Nelson's and us Nelsons was more like sisters and brothers than first cousins. Johnny Nelson my first cousin would make you 2nd cousin. My Aunty Mary, Nurse Bradley was Mary Nelson my Dad's only sister. Its your great aunt Mary. She was a grand women for the cause, great rebel, She fought, went on hunger strike, she fed Johnny underground in the Milking field on the Kilmanham Road, Kells ... they had a song out and every time they use to see us they would sing 'Nelson's on the run today, whack for the diddle de da.' Poor Johnny was a great IRA man. He is dead now ... I even remember our Jack was only nine years and they took him out of bed, put him in a lorry in his bare feet and took him to their hut to force him to tell them where Johnny Nelson was hiding, poor Jack was too young, they would beat him, he did not know anything. Only we were scared stiff. Our house had bullet holes when they use to fire, saying we had Johnny Nelson in our house.

I had joined the McAdorey–McCusker Cumann in Oxford, with old Jim Reilly as the runai. Although I think Pat Reynalds had been the first man I had got in contact with, he was a Cowley car worker and sold *Republican News*, which I collected from his house in bundles and sold round the college. I had discussed things with them many times before and taken copies of *Republican News*. Not as good a paper as *An Phoblacht*, but defiant by its very continued existence. It was sold around the Oxford car plants among the many Irish workers and Oxford Irish workers and their families.

10

Clydeside, Bogside, The Miners' Side

Just before I had started back for the second year at Ruskin, I had been as usual working back at the pit. The decks were being cleared for action. We had submitted the biggest pay demand in the Union's history (increases of between £5 and £9 per week for underground and faceworker groups respectively) On 21 October 1971 a special conference of the Union had agreed to reject the NCB's pay offer of £1.75 and £1.80 and implement an overtime ban and an end to conciliation (which effectively meant NUM branch officials would no longer sit on or try to settle local disputes and would instead just let them rip) in preparation for a national strike ballot. This time round, though, only 55 per cent was the required majority and not the two thirds which had damned us the previous year. The miners were to ballot in November. The result when it came was touch and go. Some areas including Durham and Northumberland had voted heavily against strike action, but the weight of Yorkshire, Scotland and Wales ensured the pits would stand from January of the new year. The press screamed that we were demanding a 47 per cent rise, the government absolute strict deadline being 7.9 per cent. Our wages were actually near the bottom of the pile and some men and their families lived in poverty while working every day at the mine with a take-home pay of less than £14 per week.

As mentioned earlier, in 1957 the net real income of an average mineworker had been 22 per cent above that of an average manufacturing worker, but in 1969 it was 2 per cent below. Of course, we didn't eat averages, but we knew damn well we were not getting value for wa toil. Over the previous three years overall productivity had risen by 15 per cent but miner's wages were lower in real terms in 1971 then in 1967. Every miner would require a £5 per week rise to get back to the 1967 position. Miner's wages had dropped by 25 per cent in the preceding 15 years. One miner in ten was earning less than £20 per week GROSS.

The Union's paper, *The Miner*, produced thousands of extra copies to distribute to the public, reproduced a miners pay note across its inside pages. it showed a gross payment of £18.00 per week. It showed a take home of £15.54. 88,000 mineworkers were taking home wages in the same category.

> My husband's take-home wage is now £13.60 this is causing argument and is breaking up the family. I cannot go out unless I do some knitting for a few shillings. Our daughter is going to a higher school and I have to buy her a new school uniform. I can't see how I can do this on the kind of wages I get from husband.
>
> On a Wednesday I go and get my groceries from the supermarket so that I can get double green shield stamps. These stamps help me to get household utensils and are a great help as this saves a little money for the kids' luxuries such as fresh fruit and ice cream.

In 1972 the miners put their case for a payrise and were turned down, not by the NCB, who were their employers, but by the government, who had instituted a statutory incomes policy.

A radical adjustment was on the cards or let the pits stand idle. The the second week of January was regarded as a bad time to start the strike. Winter was mild and anyway now passing, stocks of coal were at record highs, and the government was regarded as tough and resourceful. I was back at college, and it wasn't long before the phone rang—Comrade Daly on the line. I was needed to coordinate college accommodation and picketing for the Oxford area and in particular the Didcot nuclear power station, just then nearing completion. I was to ensure it didn't come on line to break this strike. It was as though I just been given a commission in some special forces unit. The Ruskin Students' Association had been poised to occupy the college and take it over for use by the miners, requisition it as it were. As it was we didn't need to because the college agreed voluntarily to open its doors to the miners. Accommodation was arranged both en masse in sleeping bags and in residence, and free meals provided for the pickets. Most of my academic work, both formal and informal, now went on hold, as I took over the organisation of picketing at Didcot. The Labour Club up at Headington farmed out pickets to families and the Oxford colleges took up the cause of the miners with enthusiasm.

Trainloads of oil and supplies were blocked at the rail station outside Didcot by railworkers' sympathy action, but we didn't trust them. Not their gaffers anyway, and we prowled the lines at night, jamming points and erecting rail blocks in line with any train that might try and sneak through. The plant itself was guarded by round-the-clock picketing headquartered on a huge old army tent. Oil, fuel, oxygen and gas was banned from the power station. I stopped everything, including a shipment of toilet rolls. An irate plant manager asked me if I was trying to shut the power station altogether. 'Yes,' I replied without hesitation, although really that was beyond my brief. All the Ruskin students and many of the lecturers turned out to man the picket lines on shifts round the clock, including Knight, who frequently stood in the centre of the road, one massive man, with one massive hand held in the air; the lorries stopped all right. The station wasn't producing power; it wasn't even completed. Construction workers were still working on site but had promised us we need not worry; they weren't going to do too much.

Massive support came in from workers and their families of all descriptions in terms of groceries, booze and money, which was passed on to the lads on the lines. Mainly these were the single lads who would get nothing from the benefits agencies, and precious little from the Union. When I wasn't standing on the line I was addressing meetings, around Oxford and at colleges further south, raising money for hardship funds, gaining support from students and encouraging them to join the lines and stand with the miners. Many would contrast this with 1926 when students drove the blackleg trains and buses.

In the midst of the miners' strike, the students themselves were mobilising for a huge demonstration against Thatcher's anti-student-union bill. She had earlier become infamous by abolishing the little kids' free school milk: 'Thatcher!

Thatcher! Milk snatcher!' was her first public heckle. The Student Union Liaison Committee, which had organised the demonstration, was however cleft down the middle between the International Socialists and the International Marxist Group, both of whom had belonged to a united Socialist Student Society. This body would not agree to making the links and joint solidarity action between the miners' strike and the students. The IS for reasons I didn't understand were agin it. That however was grist to the mill, and the IMG had signed me up to front its 'Students–Miners–Unite–And–Fight' platform. I was to do a tour of London colleges and universities including the LSE, which was under occupation at the time. I was assigned a young female comrade, whose job and brief clearly was to ensure that I arrived on time at each scheduled venue.

From time to time she would say things like 'Right, comrade, you can eat here, you have 20 minutes. I will pay for the meal.' Or a bit further down the road and a college or two later, 'OK, you're allowed 15 minutes here for ONE pint,' and then she would whisk me out.

I was landed at the pad I'd be crashing in (I had picked up the student twang, ney bother) too late for any further drink, and she made sure I was in the door. 'You're not coming in then?' I suggested. She turned on her heel and announced 'I will pick you up here at 8 a.m. tomorrow morning,' got in the car and drove off. The IMG was efficient in those days and had obviously in commissioning this comrade for the task of being my driver and guide briefed her on the dangers of alcohol and sexual activity while on duty so to speak.

The student ranks began to gather. I was given a loudhailer and introduced as Dave Douglass from the NUM. I was making the point for the student demonstration to march past the NCB offices, and demonstrate the united front of students and miners against the Tory government. Did we have memories of May '68 in France? Of course. Could the miners' strike be a catalyst for a general strike with students in support? But of course. Was the miners strike political? Hadn't they always been, for both sides? We succeeded in heading off with an army of students, and the chants 'March Past the Coal Board. The Miners' Strike Must Win!' and 'The Miners, The Students— One Fight, We Shall Win!' Arm in arm, we bowled the few blue-coated guardians of law and order aside as despite all our public preaching they hadn't realised we were actually going to march off other than where they had agreed to. Following a mass rally outside the Hobart House (NCB HQ), where again I did some stump oratory from the steps of the building, we set off to take the official platform of the NUS assembled in Hyde Park. Mind they hadn't actually put it like that to me; they told me I would be speaking on the platform. Our army surged onto the field crowded with students assembling around the platform. We wheeled perhaps three, four thousand strong, linked arms in ranks of ten abreast, advancing on the stage. 'They know I'm speaking, do they?' 'Well, we asked.' 'And?' 'They said no.' 'Do they know I'm here?' 'They do now!'

And into the crowd we surged relentlessly, like a Roman unit, right up to the stage, where a yelling match began, and then someone jumped up and grabbed the mics from the stage, and the stewards on the stage jumped into our ranks and a general melee started with vicious punches and kicks being exchanged while the mics were lost and the speakers smashed and the wires ripped out. By the time we assembled enough of our forces, in enough defensible space, to speak with a loudhailer, most of the crowd was dispersing and swelling eyes and bloodied noses were the fashion accessories of the day.

In February I appeared on *Late Night Line-Up*, a late evening TV current-affairs do for the BBC, slightly tipsy and exuberant, animated in support of the miners' claim but actually there to discuss my book on the Durham miners. I set us off on a great number of tangents and for a time the interviewer loses his thread. It comes over very powerfully despite this. In a way it's a bad thing; the next time I go on TV I think I can do the same, only this time the interviewer sticks strictly to his brief and the whole thing comes over-contentious and vexed. (I can't remember the name of that programme but it was a disaster.) In the UCS occupation, the Joint Shop Stewards Committee was restating its intention to stay in occupation until the four yards and the whole labour force were saved. It is almost impossible to convey what that occupation meant to us. We thought when the workers had taken over the yards that they were demonstrating that workers could run industry and society. That this was some prelude to a mobilisation which could take the system by the throat. That was the perception. The notion of workers' occupation spread like wildfire; from being 'unheard of in British history' it became the number one tactic for workers faced with redundancy and closure. But it was not just so, not at UCS anyway. First, the workers were 'working in' they were going to work as normal and just doing their usual jobs without pay. The receivers were in office and were going about their normal business looking for a buyer. They seen the work-in as a demonstration of good faith to a future employer, not some vision of soviet Clydeside. The stewards ran the action with a tight grip. By contrast, down the road at Plessey, the occupation was a real occupation. Nothing came in or out without the say-so of the workers. The workers held daily mass, noisy, confused meetings. Everything and every tactic was discussed at length. Receivers from this yard were allowed on and off site escorted by delegates of workers. They held the plant, and had elaborate devices set in place to repulse any attempts to take the plant by force. Outside the communities based on the plant were fully involved with support groups and supplies to the plant. The communist stewards down at UCS called the workers at Plessey 'the anarchists'. For five months, until the end of January 1972, the Plessey workers stayed in occupation, day and night, fed and watered by the folk of the town. But such differences and divisions were not perceived at the time, nor have they been since, to any degree. On New Year's Eve of 1971 the Allis-Chalmers factory in North Wales was occupied, followed five days later by the Fisher-Bendix works in Liverpool. UCS was an example of what could be, even if it wasn't actually itself!

FLYING PICKETS

The miners' pickets were a military operation, not centralised, but coordinated actions criss-crossing the country and reaching out to every sort of major industrial enterprise which was fuelled by the miners. Branches, panels and areas selected targets and supplied pickets. Area co-coordinating bodies kept lists of targets being covered and by whom, and then sent out allocations to panels or branches for targets not covered. Double-decker buses stood outside the places where we signed on, and filled up daily with pickets being bussed in to fill some gap in our preparation. Miners' wives and daughters often joined the dads on the quieter picket lines, which in actual fact were the majority. There were few gaps, what with the miners' navy on the Thames and the floating pickets on estuaries and inlets. From wharves and coal depots, power stations and steel mills, picket lines mean 'Do Not Cross.' The TUC had sent out an instruction to all affiliated unions not to cross the miners' picket lines. Here and there workers strained at the leash to get into the action, and be picketed out, even with only the slenderest of causes. Up at Cowley the car plant was heated by coke. A pile of coke sat by the boiler house, and the shop stewards asked us to mount a picket on it. It presumably would then not be moved, the plant then not heated and the car workers would then be out with the miners. We declined this picket, but put one on the gate to ensure that the pile of coke inside the plant, which was kosher, was not replenished by scab fuel, which was not. I am told the coke stock was burnt with more gusto than it would have been in a smokestack steamer crossing the Atlantic in order to rapidly run it down. For most workers, the miners' strike was a line in the sand. The fate of the postmen and the power workers before them was clear. The overall plan of the Tories was clear. The miners had to win this fight. Workers and students and activists of all the left hues joined the picket lines.

Although there had been great reluctance to get into this strike, once it started it was a cork from a bottle. The miners by and large refused to allow safety cover, which was something quite unprecedented. It meant this was really a fight to the finish, a game of chicken with the survival of the colliery and most of the coal industry itself in the balance. The denial of safety cover at most pits shocked the NCB, whose director went public to state that this action could close pits and loose jobs. 'I would have kept that back,' mocked the lads on the picket line. 'Are they trying to threaten us, that they might shut pits? Shut the fuckers then, you do anyway. We only went to work in the mines to earn money, not because we liked wet dark holes in the ground.'

I remember the saying of one aud lad: 'If we're not going to get paid for working in't pit, gi the hole back to them, so farmer can have his field back.'

Mind, it wasn't all militancy—something outside observers will not comprehend. Men who totally disapprove of the strike, or, previously, an overtime ban, will all the time push at the margins of the action to make it so extreme the whole thing is abandoned. I don't know if this strategy has ever worked, but they have certainly made industrial action harder to sustain. At some pits, a call for safety men meant some men would be getting paid while the others were on strike; this would at once cause resentment among the men who disagreed with the strike and didn't want to strike. 'Na fuck 'em, if we're on strike we're on strike,' they would charge, the logic being that we couldn't let the mines fill up with water and gas, so we would be forced to call off the strike. It was a bluff which was called, against moderate workers and NCB chiefs as the men responded with 'no safety cover'. 'You've got NACODS [the deputies and under-officials] and BACM [the managers]—let them do the safety work, they're getting paid for doing nowt. Let them have a try.' The pickets moved rapidly to seal off coal stocks at pitheads and depots, and isolate the power stations to stop them being resupplied. We on the left warned that to counter this the government would have to move the stocks by force, which would mean large numbers of cops and then perhaps the armed forces. Were we ready to confront the armed forces? The leadership might not have been, but the rank and file were increasingly readying themselves for such an eventuality, and we were hammering away at other workers' ranks to prepare them to get involved if this happened. Solidarity was near total. Lorry drivers and train drivers refused to move coal, dockers refused to unload it, some power stations were trying hard not to burn it. By the second week of February electricity nationwide was rationed; one and a half million workers were sent home.

Impromptu debating societies flourished up and down the country around the braziers. For *The Mineworker* this was our swan song. We went to proper printed format in standard newspaper size. The bold black banner read *The Mineworker*. For Workers Control of The Mining Industry, organ of the Mineworkers' Internationale. The headline, a third of a page long, shouted out VICTORY TO THE MINERS.

SMASH CAPITALISM.

TAKE CONTROL.

Maureen reported that it was a joy to sell, and well recognised everywhere they went.

There were scabs, rogue lorry drivers mad with greed, coal and coke depots defying the pickets. With these we tried to deploy force. But down at Keadby Power Station at Scunthorpe we had only a minimal team of Hatfield pickets. On 3 February a scab fuel driver had announced he was going through the picket lines and if anyone got in his way, he would run them down. As he swept round a sharp bend into the plant, Fred Matthews, one of our supporters and a workmate of mine, was crushed beneath the back wheels of the vehicle and killed.

On the streets of Derry on Sunday 30 January 1972 an unarmed civil rights demonstration, called by the Civil Rights Association, supported by Peoples Democracy, and republican groups and a big chunk of the beleaguered catholic population, men women and kids, was attacked before the TV cameras of the world. The Paras, famed for their hatred of the republican community, shot indiscriminately into the demonstration, killing thirteen and wounding many more in a bloodbath of innocent civilians. The Paras were later to say they had come under fire from the city walls, but since those walls were manned by their RUC colleagues, and the IRA had anyway demilitarised the area of its forces in response to a request from the marchers, the story is either untrue or the state's forces were shooting at each other. In any case the people on the ground being shot where they stood or fled were not shooting at them but were totally unarmed and helpless as the bullets tore into them.

As the events unfolded on the evening news, my eyes burned in tears and rage. I met Dave Merrick on the stairs; he too was streaming with tears. Within minutes the army recruitment office in Oxford was windowless and smoking, a message read: 'The Miners, Clydeside, Bogside, Join The Angry Side'. In the Commons, young Bernadette Devlin, the comrade from the Civil Rights Association and a witness to the shootings, crossed the floor of the commons and flung herself on Reginald Maudling the Home Secretary when he insisted that the Army had fired in self-defence, calling him 'a murdering bastard'. A few days later a team from Ruskin stormed the Army recruitment office and occupied it, pushing the recruitment sergeant out and nailing up the door. Meantime our comrade back up north thought it was time to do something too, a little more dramatic than break a few windows.

'Yee alreet ti give is a lift?' David O'Connel had asked his marra.

'Where ti, like, a demonstration?'

'Not exactly. This is my special protest against what the bastards are deyin in Ireland. Yee with is or not? Ah want ti gaan to Otterburn.'

So it was till they arrived at the massive army barracks, and the living accommodation. Incredibly enough, without restraint and just the way Davie did things, Dave gaans up and knocks on the door he's been looking for. It opens.

'Yes, what is it?'

'Oh, are yee the base commanding officer, like?' 'Yes, I am.'

'You're commanding officer?'

'Yes, yes, what is it?'

'Well, this is for Ireland,' and the massive old hand-gun is pulled out. Bang, the army officer fell dead on the floor, and Dave ran back to the car.

'What the fuck yee done?' his marra asks. 'Ah shot the bastard. Now Ah think we'd better fuck off.'

The Party produced a leaflet in immediate response. Wading in with enthusiasm it yelled: 'Avenge the Massacre In Londonderry By the Organisation of the General Strike To Throw Out Faulkner and Heath and Impose a Left Labour Government On An Anti- Capitalist Programme.' Well their hearts were in the right place, but what a cringing embarrassment. Nobody who had any resonance with the Irish struggle or a remote understanding of the history of Derry ever calls it 'Londonderry'. It was the term of the imperialist; it at once betrayed the remoteness of the authors of the leaflet from the reality and history of the struggle.

THREE-DAY WEEK

On the industrial front the railways cancelled more than a thousand trains nationwide per day. 20,000 firms were now on the three-day week the government had imposed. Power cuts hit homes, but still the bulk of the class did not turn against the miners.

A little later a mass demonstration was held in London in support of the miners. The streets were black with marching columns, NUM banners, bands, the TUC and all its affiliates, all the students and leftists. This was a growing force to be reckoned with and one now growing increasingly angry. Maureen arrived in a big van from Doncaster with the comrades, just as I was thinking they weren't going to make it. 'There was a hitch,' she said without explaining. We unveiled the Mineworkers' Internationale banner complete with black drapes. The young Hatfield miners and some of our LPYS comrades marched with us, as did for a time a group of Belgian miners carrying Belgian miners' flags, which unfortunately nobody recognised. We chanted 'Victory to the Miners, Victory to the IRA!' It caused consternation among the conventional trade union marchers, but we wanted to make a link, in case the state didn't already see it: objectively the miners and the Irish resistance were allies—not that many miners would have seen it like that, despite the fact that we were reliably informed the Provos had blown up a scab coal lorry in Ulster. In Trafalgar Square, as a five-minute silence was held for Freddy among the hundreds of thousands of marchers, and banners were lowered and a hush fell across the centre of London, the bird-scarers installed somewhere on nearby buildings rang out, with echoing booms, at scheduled intervals; it sounded for all the world like a volley of salutary shots over the coffin. I had journeyed home for Freddy's funeral, and was abed when a bang came on the front door. Looking out of the window I saw it was Gareth Jones, one of the Mineworker comrades from Wales with Martin. 'Oh I'll be reet doon, Gareth.' 'No don't bother Dave there's four ...' 'Four—that's all reet. Come in and we'll mek some breakfast.' 'No—four coachloads, Dave.'

There they were, having driven all night from the valleys of Wales. The Regal opened up the club at 6.30 a.m. and served them free food—well it was pie and peas, which was a bit strange for a breakfast, but perhaps not so for a funeral. The Mineworkers' Internationale had flooded the villages of Dunscroft, Hatfield and Stainforth with a leaflet explaining who and what we were, in preparation for marching behind the coffin of our comrade with the banner draped in black. However his mother had asked that only Hatfield Branch banner, and then that of the Lady Windsor Lodge from Wales, be borne that day, in order to keep a sense of discipline and centrality. Mrs Matthews was a lifelong activist of the ILP, a native of Washington, and the mother of a family of communists and revolutionary socialists. Fred had died however, not because of that, but because he was a miner, standing on a picket line in a collective endeavour with his mates, fighting for a wage increase for all, for a better life for his kids, and because another bloke who seen only his personal bonus and individual greed, and thought it a dog-eat-dog world, ran through picket lines and sod everyone else. The BBC commented that there had never been a funeral like this, outside those of IRA activists in Ulster. They had made the link and posed the objective connection. But as our pickets flanked the coffin, and the Lodge banner draped in black silk followed our band with muffled drums, and a sea of miners, with grit and anger slowly paced through the village streets packed with every man women and child in the district, it was clear that this was no ordinary death and no ordinary funeral. The temper of the pickets changed after this. The gloves were off like never before. At Saltly coke depot in Birmingham a haemorrhage of non-authorised coke was being bled from the body of the struggle, weakening the strike, oozing away strength. It was one of a number of strategic stockpiles; this was a trickle through the dam wall. The Union had been pouring more and more miners onto the streets, and the police had responded with increasing numbers. Violence started to break out regularly in the rugby scrum at the gates, with the police determined to get the strike-breaking lorries in and out. Reinforcements were requested and Arthur Scargill, a man with his eyes on the prize of forthcoming elections and national publicity, picked up the call at the Barnsley HQ and led 600 Yorkshire miners to the gates with an attendant number of TV cameras and journalists to hand. The gates were shut, but only for that evening; they opened again the next morning, to columns on columns of marching police. Increasing numbers of other workers were joining the miners' lines—building workers, delegations from factories, and students. Police snatch squads were seen in action for the first time in a labour dispute, and it seemed for a time that the police would face down the picket line however big it grew by sheer weight of numbers and licence to use what force was required. I like the way the writer Anthony Burton put it a little later in his book *The Miners*:

> The government stood on a point of principle—an uncomfortable position and one from which it is notoriously difficult to shift anyone, least of all a government. So in many ways it was a return to the old days of direct conflict and the scenes that, in the days of television, reached every home were often violent. The pickets were determined that the coal should not reach the power stations; there were arguments, scuffles, fights. It was ugly to watch, but it marked clearly the way in which the mood of the miners had become embittered.

On Tuesday evening, 8 February, the Birmingham East District Committee of the engineering unions in Birmingham called a mass delegate meeting. Arthur Scargill addressed it in typical barnstorming, inspiring and explosive passion, demanding that the engineers stand with their brothers from the mines. They agreed, voting for a solidarity strike and march to Saltley depot gates. It was the stuff of legend. On Thursday 10 February 40,000 Birmingham workers from factories and foundries and mills downed tools and 10,000 of them, banners flying, marched to Saltley. The chief constable took a deep breath and ordered the gates padlocked in the interests of public safety. 'Close the Gates! Close the Gates!' had been the chant. The gates were closed. There would be no more haemorrhages.

Arthur Scargill did not 'plan' the action, did not conceive of it, organise it, or 'win it'. Frank Watters, the influential Midlands area organiser of the CPGB, had arranged for Arthur to attend the engineers' meeting, where his speech was like a sudden infusion of adrenaline, making what sounded like the most obvious and common-sense of propositions and gaining a unanimous vote of approval for action. The picket however had been a formal NUM Midlands and South Wales operation, which had been ongoing. The solidarity of the workers in the Birmingham mills, forges and factories was achieved not least by the mass influence of the Communist Party, and Frank Watters probably was more influential than anyone else in bringing off the action, together with the gut class instincts of the workers themselves of course. Arthur was in the right place at the right time, and deserves his moment of glory, but the achievement was collective and his involvement almost entirely incidental.

The government was now faced with approaching generalised solidarity strikes. The layoffs ordered at coal-fired powered plants across the country had not turned public opinion against the miners; where workers hadn't taken advantage of the extra holidays they had joined the miners' picket lines. The government started to look for a way out and came up with 'an independent third party', Lord Wilberforce, a name from British constitutional history. Five days after Saltley the Wilberforce Inquiry on Coal Miners' Pay was set up, being given the task of looking at the whole question and giving an objective judgement on the mines and the miners at work. Meantime Derek Ezra, the chairman of the National Coal Board and its chief negotiator, upped the pay offer to 9 per cent. Wilberforce, who had discovered that the miners were 'a special case', came out with something a lot better: 19 per cent, some way better than the government's strict 8 per cent pay deadline. The TUC rushed to the media to declare this a breakthrough. Vic Feather, general secretary of the TUC, accepted it, and the NUM's NEC started to shuffle their feet. The branches replied emphatically however that this dispute was their property and its terms of settlement must be acceptable to them. In any case the NCB were only prepared to offer 12 per cent, and thus the deadlock remained.

The government then covertly went onto the offensive to see if it could free up the captive stocks of coal. The Attorney General, reporting on the Saltly debacle, concluded that only by use of the armed forces could the picket line be breached and coal stocks released. This would almost certainly produce an unofficial general strike—the worst kind, outside the control of union bureaucracies and the TUC General Council. In any case, once the coal was freed the army would then have to transport it itself, and also burn it itself, since workers would never process fuel released in such a way—not at this time. Mr Heath then called for a deputation of the miners to meet him, and conceded wage rises of 20 per cent and 22 per cent, with other outstanding issues to be investigated. The area leaders stood respectfully in a line outside Downing Street; Ted walked down the line being introduced to his protagonists and all respectfully nodded and shook hands, except the piss-taking Joe Whelan, who couldn't resist offering his hand and saying 'Hello, Sailor!'[48]

For the first time since the Union had started almost 100 years before, this could be seen as a clear national victory for the miners. The old miners who recalled the defeat of 1926, and the bitter years of hardship which followed, felt vindicated, as though this was the second half of the same game—this time they had won.

On 15 July that year at Durham Miners' Gala the platform speakers leaned more to the left than was customary, with the leftish Michael Foot and Tony Benn balanced by the NUM president, Joe Gormley, who although an entrenched moderate was seen as the leader of the miners in one of their most glorious victories.[49]

Walter Malt, too, the general secretary of the Durham Miners, seen as every bit as right-wing and moderate as Mr Gormley, made a most forceful and clever speech. He reflected upon the leaders and 'friends' who had told us the industry was dying, and asked: how could such an anachronism justify improved wages and conditions?

> Know-alls shook their heads and murmured of industrial suicide as the strike grew. They are still at their chantings, although the grave tones are receding. I cannot think what they expect of us. Even if we do accept that the industry is old and dying this ought not to lead to fatalism. As Dylan Thomas wrote on the death of his father—'Do not go gentle into that goodnight, old age should rage, rage against the dying of the light.' It ought to be a controlled rage, a looking back in anger, and a determination to alter things where we can. The timing of the action was bad, our detractors said. Coal stocks were reputed to be plentiful. The weather was almost benign. Yet, by some peculiar throw of the dice, the men were back at work on the same day as the Industrial Relations Act took effect. Under the creeping paralysis of the strike, the 'loud mouths', who had talked of a dying industry stammered then lost their tongues completely.

My work on the Durham miners, cavilling, red villages, and miners' job control, titled *Pit Life In Co. Durham*, was published, datelined Didcot Power Station, Oxford, February 1972, by the History Workshop. It was dedicated to my fellow Branch member and picket Fred Matthews. It was an absolutely outstanding achievement for me. Me Da was just so taken with it, he just kept looking at the book, with my name, well his name too, on the front. He must have shown it to every miner at Wardley and walked to every club in the district to show everyone how proud he was of it. I think he had just had the first of his hip operations done at the time and was recovering in hospital from the great pain it had put him through. Me Ma and him had moved up to Nursery Towers in the Felling, a high-rise block of flats though they were given a ground floor apartment. Someone thought they had done them a good turn. Me Ma became me book distributor as folks far and wide tried to buy one. She wrote:

> Got the books OK if you had left the end open on wrapping you would only have paid book postage. Otherwise you have to pay parcel post. Well David I was up again at Westgate Bookshop and Percy Street Book Shop sold out again, young lads have been coming to me for your books. I already sold 12. So I have orders for more and I hope they don't be long in coming. While I was in the shop on Westgate Road a gentleman came in from Kings College wanting 12 of your books, then John Oxberry from Wardley came in for 20; so you see they are in great demand. I don't know why Ruskin is so slow in sending the orders. The man in Felling Library said he is sick of waiting. Dad feels a bit better only in pain. Well dear all the best I am ready to go and see him, it's a

long bus ride.

God Bless from Mam and Dad

Publication of *Pit Life* got me interviews on a number of TV programmes, a *Late Night Line-Up* shot with Joan Bakewell (*Late Night Line-Up*, 16 February 1972), another on the opposite channel. Around this time me and Larch, and the whole male population of the college, probably the world, were avid fans of Pan's People. The common room would be crowded to capacity for Top of the Pops, and the Pan's People number. I was going to say they were years ahead of their time but that would be wrong. They were of their time. No other time would ever have allowed a group of women to perform in such a totally sexually explicit way—mind, without actually revealing anything. Not that you would know that often—the skin-coloured body stockings left little to ponder on. Today they would not be allowed. They would not be PC; they would be denigrated as sex objects. Well they were sex, if not objects, then priestesses. Queens of the carnal. I mention all of this because as me and Larch were blundering down a corridor at the BBC looking for the hospitality room, we passed the girls ready to go on, body stockings, crochet string dresses, and those faces. We drooled as they passed us by without noticing our presence. On another occasion, I think, they left me so long in the hospitality area I had supped a good bottle of wine before being brought in to the live interview. I had been rabbiting on to Larch about Brigitte Bardot on her million-dollar private beach, enjoying the secluded nakedness of being a rich bitch. (Though one I had always fancied the arse off since being about 11.) The interview went from the book to miners' history to class struggle and capitalism and the rich and suddenly I was talking about Brigitte Bardot naked on her private beach. Larch, watching the show in the hospitality room, buried his head in his hands and went 'Oh, no!' He thought the line of drunken thought would take me to tits and nipples and God knows what else, but thankfully, I was distracted off to a different random thought. My fame as a mining/student/historian/author suddenly got me called upon again to do a live debate. This would be on the 'I'm Backing Britain' Movement. A sort of Spencerite, anti-union, work-for-nowt scheme to get British workers to put more effort into it and beat Johnny Foreigner. Some workers down at the Imperial typewriter factory down on Humberside somewhere were working two hours a day overtime for nowt, to 'Back Britain'. We certainly gave the class-collaborationist, make-yourself-skint scheme short shrift. A few years later, the firm upped pegs and moved its manufacture to India.

This was the day of another scam. One of the hire drivers on the gate suggested that we should tell the programme we had to be back in Oxford that night. Which I did, so he got the job of driving us to Oxford and a signed cheque to take us there, pay him and get his fuel. He took us round the corner, gave us £40, dropped us off, and went off home with a day's pay and expenses. Ee, them were the days. £40 was enough for a canny crack in the big smoke, before touching any of wor ain bit. Mind, closing times were a pain. You could only get a drink in one of them bliddy strip places, and the beer was about £5 per bottle then, which was silly money. But shit, it wasn't wors anyway. We slept at the Cinema Action squat.

UNION JUGGERNAUTS

The miners had won, and on the backs of our victory, a little later so did the rail workers. The wall of pay restraint had just had a hole knocked in it and two juggernauts had just gone through. The genie was out of the bottle. Workers in all sections across the country felt the wind of change and the power of the unions. 1972 was to record the most days ever lost from industrial action in a single year except for 1926, which had been greater of course but had included the General Strike and the nine months of the miners' strike. But the greatest numbers of actions were yet to come. Class-consciousness among workers nationwide and across industry was plain common sense; many felt deep ties of internationalism too, which affected their approach to all kinds of domestic and international affairs. My Da wrote on 23 February 1972:

> This is just a few lines to say how pleased I was that the miners have won a good rise for themselves also extra holidays, although I feel that this government might make them pay for it by closing pits and using oil and gas wherever possible, I hope that I am wrong ... Your Mam and I got surprised with a lot of people telling us they'd seen you on the Telly BBC2, well David I am sorry to say we didn't see you as we never have that station on, we were very disappointed that we knew nothing about it. I was talking to Wilf Robson and he said you were very good and one or two other men from Wardley also seen you and said you were smashing; young Terry Lamb enjoyed watching you. I received the papers that you sent me, and read your article in *The Mineworker* it was very good and well put together, but David with all due respect don't send me any more of the other paper, you see I don't believe in it.
>
> You will find enclosed one or two cuttings that I have been keeping for you one concerns the Goose Pit and one about William Jobling, also one about your Granda Nelson which you're Mam had published in the *Gateshead Post*. Well David I see your new book is costing £3, it is very dear. Well this is all for now David, stick in and learn all you can while you are at Ruskin, your Mam and I are very proud of you...

18 March 1972 Moira and Des, two great friends of ours, got married. Moira had been working with Maureen at Loversal Hospital; they were nursing assistants with a brief for art therapy, helping the mentally handicapped. Des was a real bonny lad, tight curling hair, a great singer. Looked a bit like David Cassidy.

17 June 1972. The Yorkshire Miners' Gala was at Wakefield, with Comrade Daly as the guest speaker and on the crest of a wave. This was Lawrence's finest moment, though the rest of the platform in Yorkshire at that time was decidedly right-wing, with Roy Mason MP and Sam Bullough the hardline moderate chairman of Yorkshire. A little while after the success of our strike the dockers are

in mass action across the country. Their flashpoints are the same as ours, the damned unregistered non-union ports, Neap House on the Trent and Grove being the major culprits. The men want the strategic gap closing with the registration of these docks, and to bring them within the National Docks Scheme. Jack Jones himself, the general secretary of the TGWU (the union that then included the dockers, among more than a million workers in the transport industries, though not shipping or railways), is given a rough ride by the men, who are not in the least happy with his level of commitment to their cause. Scenes of dockers fighting with cops and pulling down fencing on mass pickets are quite inspiring. We see this as the crack battalions of the working class moving into action.

THE RENT ACT

On the home front, the Tories had waded in with their Rent Act. Around the same time the Housing Finance Act came in. The two pieces of legislation affected council tenants, ostensibly under a different law and regulation than the NCB tenants, but in the same way. That is, they were putting our rents up. As mining tenants, we had always had the advantage of being organised industrially and communally in the same body. A set of repairs not done could produce industrial action. The Tories, through the clause in their Industrial Relations Act, had now rendered any action we cared to take against the Act illegal by virtue of it being political. What they had done was actually to unite the council tenants and the NCB tenants into a single opposition, since we now faced the same rent increases by virtue of the same or similar Acts. Tenants' and residents' committees (TARCs) had been active in many villages for years, but they had usually not included NCB tenants as we had recourse to our union branches for action. Now the branches were affiliating to TARCs or setting up new ones. In our patch Hatfield and Dunscroft Tenants Committee was chaired by Ken Terry and Maureen was secretary. A similar committee was established at Thorne and Moorends. Our committee was under our political leadership whereas Thorne and Moorends were under the direction of the CPGB, as were a number of others. But on this issue we had a sound common front. At Thorne, the old diehard communist pit community, which from the fifties had had CP councillors sitting in the town hall, and communist union leaders sitting in the NUM branch office, it was old Bill Carr of Thorne, the CP stalwart who had the reins, while overall the whole NCB tenants' action was being coordinated by CPer Percy Riley. We had this thing down to a system whereby every street had a committee and an elected representative. They all met in the Regal club with Ken Terry on the concert secretary's desk mic, like the bloke on the Wheeltappers and Shunters Social Club on the telly. Rank upon rank of tenants organised right across the district. This was a people's assembly; to us it was microcosm of how proper socialist democracy would function after the seizure of power by the working class come the glorious day. These were 'soviets' in our eyes. We held street rallies marching with fiery torches, had assemblies at the end of every road. This was people's power. The decision was made to withhold the increase. For the council tenants this was a big step; being able to pay your rent was an act of pride and principle for many of the women in particular. Being in arrears with your rent was something considered somewhat of a disgrace, like you were a bad housekeeper. Such a scandal today might not cut much ice, but in those days, it was a point of working-class dignity. For the NCB tenants, since we had our rent taken off our notes, each man at the pit filled in a form declining permission for any increase to be deducted. The pit villages and communities around Hatfield and Thorne pit struck solid. Not a single tenant, other than the councillors themselves, was paying the increase. In Doncaster, Percy reported 5,000 council tenants withholding the increase within the first two weeks of the action beginning in Barnsley and the picture was similar elsewhere. Just in case anybody got any ideas about authorising evictions, we held mass pickets at the gates of the councillors' own houses, and warned them: 'Evict one tenant and we shall come in here and evict you, first from your house, next from your seat as a councillor and then from your job.' Nobody doubted our ability and willingness to do so.

Some of the councillors stuck to their guns and refused to sanction the workings of the law, risking not only debarment from office but also sequestration, i.e. having to make up the lost rents from out of their own pockets. These included Bill Carr at Thorne, and Nev Nickles, a left Labourite and Rossington coal miner. Nev like me had gone to Ruskin College and then on graduation had returned to the mine and the coalface, it being a tradition among miners in higher education that you always returned to your men and community. Other councillors refusing to sanction the rent rises were Len Caven at Stainforth and George (Bant) Hardy at Hatfield/Dunscroft. We marched on council offices at Thorne and Doncaster, banners flying, at the head of some real angry working-class women and their kids. Quite a few of the councillors, of all political persuasions, took some stick and the odd kick. Meantime through party-political pressure we were demanding that Labour-controlled councils refuse to collect the increase required by the Act, and many stuck to their guns and did so, until the threat of legal sanction made them back down. The lasting exception was at Clay Cross in Chesterfield, Derbyshire, where the councillors refused to back down and were all sacked and surcharged .

For the NCB tenants we flooded the appeals procedure with so many demands for millions of repairs, all of them genuine, that the rises were delayed three years or more. For the NCB, one avenue around our action was to re-register the whole rent by altering 'the superficial area of the house'. This was done by bringing the toilet, which was outside, inside the parameters of the house, mainly by bricking up the netty door and knocking a wall through from the bathroom. Many folks thought this a godsend and conceded an added 50p per week to save going out the door in the dead of winter, but it secured a new rent. For council tenants, although we delayed the increase for a long time, and won many concessions in terms of repairs and upgrades on windows and doors, etc., I think with the collapse of resistance by the councils themselves our people were forced to pay the increased rents, though they were able in many cases to spread the backlog of debts over years.

MINEWORKERS' INTERNATIONALE

May Day 1972. Our comrades from the Belgian miners, Desire Dylse—the president—and his executive officer and translator, repaid us a visit and marched with the Mineworkers' Internationale Banner. There was a deluge, which caused the trades council to cancel the open air May Day rally. We staged an impromptu rally in the grounds of the museum at the end of the march. Stan, my fellow Ruskin student and long-suffering first-year next-door dorm mate, and member of the merchant navy officers' and engineers' union, grimly holds onto one pole, while the rain washes his face as if he was back at sea. Jim, in denim heed to toe, steelies on his feet and a woollen commando hat on his heed, stands at the other side. I stand addressing the milling crowd, suddenly leaderless and pointless. I am wearing my Gurney Slade shorty white coat, my sideburns curl up to the sides of me mooth. My hair is lang, wet, and dragged across me face. I stand on a bench and preach the gospel of revolution and class struggle. My Belge comrade joins me next and his wonderful, ancient mining Netherlands echoes across the thinning crowd, while Matt his translator speaks almost simultaneously; they have rehearsed this speech for days. We decide we have time to shoot across to Sheffield and join the later- scheduled big Sheffield Trades Council march and rally. They grant permission for the Belgian comrades to speak to the crowds from the steps of the City Hall, their voices carried across the city via big speakers on the columns. Our Mineworkers' Internationale banner acts as a backdrop, and for a brief period the Communist Party thinks 'the Trots' have taken over the rally. But the touch of internationalism is well received.

That night we had one of our public May Day Red Star Folk Concerts, this time at the Coach and Horses where the regular folkies also met. The singers were good and Desire got up to sing a couple of rousing Flem nationalist workers' songs, getting hot and passionate and waving his arms around. Matt jumped to his feet to join in and the Doncaster throng stamped out the rhythm without a clue what we were listening to, but it sounded good.

'ONE IN THE DOCK, ALL OUT THE DOCKS!'

The next big flashpoint and again one which teetered on the verge of an unofficial general strike came over the Industrial Relations Act and the legal paraphernalia that had been set up to give it teeth. The dockers were in dispute over containerisation, a process aimed at displacing their labour, a third of which had gone in the preceding five years. The containers were not being handled by dockers, but by general workers working for far worse terms and conditions. The picket of the Chobham Farm Depot in London's East End led to the summons before the Industrial Relations Court of five of the dockers' leaders. They refused to attend and were to be arrested in the midst of a picket line and hauled off to court. Outside the Midland Cold Storage depot, 300 dockers stood in a defensive block to protect the men and the first cops to arrive could well have been killed. The stewards however decided to allow the law to run its course, while organising to smash it. The five were arrested. The slogan at once was 'ONE IN THE DOCK, ALL OUT THE DOCKS!' Meantime massive numbers of dockers started to picket the prison. Pickets were now being deployed and poised to stop not just the docks but the whole country. The first out were the Fleet Street electricians and SOGAT, the machine-minders' and newspaper handlers' union. By the Sunday, all papers were at a standstill except *The Times*. The Doncaster NUM panel was being convened to call out all the Doncaster pits, which in turn were already poised to picket out the coalfield. At the same time the TUC General Council remarkably was talking about calling a general strike. Jack Jones was telling every union official who would listen that if they didn't take the initiative the rank and file and countless unofficial bodies would take it for them.

The Tories were against the wall. They could see this strike spreading like wildfire and out of any control of 'official leaderships'. They knew the left and the far left in the unofficial movement was getting stronger every day, and they dared not risk this general strike despite having comfortably won the last one. With the miners, they had conjured up a legal get-out, in the shape of the Wilberforce Inquiry, which duly found in favour of the miners. Now they discovered a chap at the bottom of their legal wardrobe, the 'Official Solicitor'. His job was to plead the case for those who would not do so. Within a further five days the dockers were freed. But somehow in the process the leaders, the officials of the official trade union movement, had reasserted control. The actual dockers' issue, the demands they were on strike for in the first place, was sold far shorter than could have been achieved. Guarantees were secured on jobs and redundancy pay, which were sharp advances on what they had before, but the need to concede something to the other side meant that they like the miners earlier didn't get agreements set in concrete and nailed to the floor.

At the end of the summer a massive building workers' strike broke out, marked by flying pickets and militant picketing in scenes reminiscent of the miners' strike. Heath, unbowed by all this, forged on to try and make some incomes policy straightjacket fit over the heads of organised labour. Given the way the TUC seemed to be bending over backwards to accommodate him, he might have had reason to believe this could be done through cooperation. But when this didn't materialise Heath then moved to compulsion. A strict limit for pay awards was imposed. Numerous challenges were mounted by unions, but only by those which were weak and/or non-strategic. Heath was succeeding in holding the line.

Back at Ruskin, the exam days were upon us. Off they went to examination rooms in Oxford, dressed in dark suits and ties, or dark smart skirts and white shirts, the poor crowd's equivalent of caps and gowns. Sam wore his merchant navy uniform and larked about sticking a breadknife in the belt, as the stipulation had said students wearing uniforms were allowed to wear ceremonial swords. The folk taking the college exams were likewise brushed, washed, and fresh, like little kids going off to a new school. Me? I sat on a high stool at the bar of the Picketer's Arms as it was now called, and contemplated whether this stand against exams had had any point at all; where was the principled resistance? It took me back years to the Committee of 100's 'Fill the Jails' campaign, about which me and Davie Arrowsmith, sitting in nick all on our own, had commented that maybe it needed rethinking. Could I, should I, have backed off and taken the exams at that stage? I often felt I had dropped a bollock, but truth to tell I had thrown myself so thoroughly into the strike organisation in Oxfordshire and beyond, and sank myself so deep into the research and analysis of the Durham and Liverpool material that I hadn't followed the course curriculum. Sure, I knew just as much as there was to know about the area likely to be in question, but exams are not about that. They're about demonstrating that you had read the books, heeded their words and wisdom, and taken the points they thought you should be making. Ten thousand interesting anecdotes over the development of this or that feature of the industrial revolution wouldn't answer the question they had set, because the answer was specific and not general. So I didn't take them. My term didn't end, despite the exhaustion of my grant, and increasing poverty now from lack of funds. I was still hard at work down at Spitalfields, still trying to meet the publication deadline for the Liverpool work. I was fast losing patience with it, and Raph was fast losing patience with me. All that is Anarchy is not total freedom. Raph as a tutor was a hard taskmaster, and as deadlines approached for the completion and publication of this work loomed large, we arrived at an impasse. I had discovered that during the time of the 1850s waterfront strikes a sea monster had been caught by an American whaler off the coast of Liverpool. Naturally, in my historical Dada mode, I included it in my text. Raph promptly removed it. Every time I resubmitted the draft, the monster was back in. Raph began to lose patience.

'How can we have a bloody sea monster no matter how fascinating it may be, emerging in the middle of a social history pamphlet on dockers and seamen's strikes?' he would plead. To which I would answer: 'These were folks bred and born on the sea, they would all be talking about it wouldn't they?' 'It's a hoax,' Raph would insist. 'It's a sea serpent and they took it to America,' I would respond. Finally, after cutting the text out, he confiscated the original newspaper copy.

Sometime about now, we actually formed the Doncaster Region RWP(T). Maureen's terrific eye for art along with my knowledge of lodge banners meant we would emerge onto the Doncaster streets with the most magnificent of banners. In red satin, with the huge black hammer and sickle emblazoned with the '4' of Trotsky's international, and our title in thick white capitals of white satin, 'Revolutionary Workers Party (Trotskyist) Doncaster Regional' in a semicircle around the hammer and sickle, and 'British Section Fourth International—Posadist'. It hung in a drape from the central crossbar like an NUM banner. We also now started to take active steps to try and proletarianise the Party, try to wrest it back or perhaps take it for the first time into the world of working-class realism. Stop doing the things they always done without question, start forcing through changes to the things we had questioned and got nowhere, drop the things which weren't common sense or at the very least explicable to working-class people in working-class terms. Along these lines I was hurriedly elected to the Central Committee of the Party. But the 'communism' of the commune, the collective social control over the Party by the 'whole' began to take on a sect-like, almost mystical discipline. A little of this can be demonstrated in the 'orientation' of Posadas's The Revolutionary Militant Function of the House We Live In. Some comrades had moved into another house. The house of party members of course was also a revolutionary cell, a new locale of the Party. Posadas had been invited to inaugurate the house. After a reception and meal Posadas outlines the qualitative transformation, almost like the wafer and wine into body and blood, which had taken place here.

This change of home must mark and increase in your revolutionary activity.

The change of itself is unimportant. What is important is to use new means—even if they are same as before—which will make it easier for you, and make you determined to increase your militant capacity, will and discipline ....

It is fundamental that before any action there is preparation. You have to take this place as a place of discussion, of study of fraternal life, of communication, in which the most capable, the most elevated, can communicate with the rest and live together, relating to one another and elevating the militant relations and human relations too. There is no difference between human and militant relations within the party. .. In the party there is no separation between militant and human, it is militant and human militant.

So you have to inaugurate this new house with a plan of theoretical, political and organisational progress. Begin by living together in a very profound way, in which the relationships are elevated in such a way as to construct fraternal relations and a fraternal atmosphere, a fraternal preoccupation, fraternal communication and concrete activity, conversation and discussion ... Homogenising the preoccupation, to be preoccupied that all progress and all discuss, that there is a level of preoccupation with others, with the dignity of not thinking of oneself, without the indignity of thinking of oneself.

The order of the house has importance, but it is established very simply. Order is not just the way things are left, but how things are used. How they are left comes after this. And beginning with things of the mind. This is the main thing. This is the principal object: how things are left in the mind. If they are left badly then time cannot be found for what has to be done.

As in the street, as in the factory, as in the trade union. The house too, without formally being a cell, the house is a cell. A place where comrades living together is a cell. Independently of the fact that each one of you militates in different cells. It is a cell here. Isn't the prison a cell? And isn't the moon a cell? The three Soviet cosmonauts made a cellular meeting on the moon. And they communicated what they had been discussing on the moon to the party. Any place of meeting, gathering, living together or existence in the same place is a means of political life.

Time has to be organised to sleep as much as necessary and the rest dedicated to study. The entire epoch leads to a shortening of the amount of time dedicated to eating and sleeping. All future history leads to this. The human being dedicates a lot of time to food and unnecessary sleep. It is the product of a conservative constitution of the organisms and a still very limited utilisation of the brain. We can already do this. Organising sleeping in order to sleep quickly and in four hours you can sleep a lot and so be able to dedicate a minimum of time to sleeping and the maximum time to reading and discussing. Not just one reading, but discussing with the others, exchanging ideas, asking things.

This is the way to live together, without subjection, in the most gentle, sweet and harmonious form of communist thought in the march of history. You have to organise to do this. And to have the confidence and security that this is the best and fastest most complete way to progress. Take the necessity that one has to study and one has to have a plan of progress. This is one of the most important consequences of the inauguration of this beautiful house. Not because the house is beautiful. The atmosphere is beautiful, the sentiment given by those that live here. The house itself is just stone and walls. It has no importance. If it were a factory here, it would just be a factory, it is unimportant. But on the other hand, Trotskyist comrades live here and give the house a structure, of harmony and fraternity, in which the essential basis is the scientific decision to gain knowledge to accomplish the tasks which you have to fulfil. As a cell of this house to elevate the communist life to communicate and organise the communist life.

I recall one of the cadre schools at Cherrytree. Young Ron had gone off to a disco with a mate he had met. Boy was he in for a scolding next morning. He was carpeted during the 'balance', a thoroughly embarrassing and excruciating verbal and mental flogging. Why had he abandoned the Party? He assured them he hadn't abandoned the Party. What was wrong with spending the evening with your comrades and not off with people who were not in the Party? 'Well, I'm young, I wanted to meet some girls.' 'Girls?' they replied, 'What's is wrong with the girls in the Party?' Tom was later to caricature it as the traditional Jewish mother demanding 'What's wrong you want gentile girls? There are no nice Jewish girls now?'

Mick and Lynda Terry tendered their resignations from the Party. They self-criticised their lack of understanding, their lack of perception and admitted they were not made of the stuff required to be cadres of the Fourth International. Mick and Lynda were honest, dedicated, communist revolutionaries. Mick was a factory worker at Harvesters, Lynda an enthusiastic member of the LPYS. The two of them had thrown themselves into the struggle, and made banners and armbands and flags for the May Day march; decorated the Doncaster LPYS float; accepted the internal library at their house; would work all night making posters, hosted cadre schools and parties. But they couldn't understand what the hell Posadas was on about or what was actually required of them in his Party. So they resigned, and dedicated themselves to the LPYS and the struggle in the Union. Around June or July Maureen wrote me the most fantastic news that she was pregnant. We were expecting a baby. I resolved that yes, by God, gore or no gore, I intended to be there for the birth of my child. Ewan and Peggy who were almost weekly correspondents by this time were also pregnant. They had written about the Donnelan film which they had just got to see. 'Let us know if you have a moment what you get in the way of a baby—if it is like its parents it will come out fists first.' Peggy's baby was born on 2 December: 'No name and no chin.' And, encouraging Maureen, 'It does come to an end.' No name became Kitty as I recall.

Maureen writes to me, while I am still working my eyes out at Raph's and feeling very much trapped:

My Dearest Dave

I got your letter and post card and you seem so miserable. Never mind my love, it will soon all be over and you can come home to me. Then we will have a lovely time together, wont we? Of course, I'm waiting here for you—always! Don't get too upset about all the work Raph is making you do—put your foot down. Tell him to 'allez au feu' and that means 'go to hell' in French. But probably he will understand so you had better not.

I sent you the dates to remember but seeing how busy you are, never mind about the Frank Murphy meeting if you can't make it. But please try and get up for the gala on the 17th. That is very important and I want you to be there.

The Rockware lads (GMWU) are out on strike and have got pickets on the gate but they aren't getting many. John said they only had 50 men all together on four shifts and that's out of 1000. Isn't it terrible? They are going to try and get around all the other Rockware factories and get them out. Its for a payrise 15p per hour.

Our little baby is due on Dec 30th. Poo Poo, I might miss New Year if it comes on time. Mam and Dad are really thrilled especially me Mam.

She sent me a letter. I have been to the doc's and had all the necessary poking abouts and bloodlettings. I've got to go to the ante-natal clinic on 4th July that will be my first visit. Lynn probably is pregnant too but she hasn't had her test yet. I think she's taking her sample in today. I get ever so excited sometimes just think if its a little bit late it might come on your birthday. Wouldn't that be lovely?

I think the Party are coming up on Sunday and will probably stay until the Ireland meeting. I doubt very much if they will send Mike. Ken met John and Margaret at the Bakers Conference in Torquay last weekend and they said they knew about the 'difference' we'd had and that Mike was relatively new to the Party and put forward the old, very strict views. That's probably true but in that case, I don't think they should have sent him as a representative do you?

Let me know darling when your going to Liverpool and I'll send letters to Veronica's place. Take care love and I will see you as soon as you get home. O by the way Agitprop called to see me yesterday but I wasn't in and they pushed a note thro' the door. They are travelling round with pamphlets etc. I would have loved to see them. However. Be a bit happier.

I love you Mau (She illustrates her letter with a drawing of a pregnant self.)

29 July 1972. Our informal folk nights dotted around the town and in our living room became the Red Star Folk Music Club, and were to be held every Friday night in the Bay Horse Bentley. We had quite a crowd over in Bentley, what with the Mineworker supporters from the pit, the people we knew in the Communist Party, as well as all the tenant activists and various rebels. Doncaster had a great folk scene, and we were rarely short of singers, who just came along and sang.[50] By 4 August we were installed right smack in the middle on town at the Spread Eagle. This was the old Buffs[51] room upstairs. From now on, it was associated with the folk-singing communists. We had twelve regular singers who turned up most weeks without fail, as well as the occasional guests whose fares we managed to pay, like Alun Howkins from Oxford; he was a regular visitor, as was Tom and the crowd over from Hull sometimes with the Watersons in tow, or Ian Manual, one of the finest traditional Scottish singers anywhere. Down in the bar, a noisy group of West Indian bus drivers and their girlfriends and wives on occasion would rumble or maybe rumba up the stairs after their darts games and regale us with powerful calypsos and rude Jamaican songs, some of which we couldn't understand but had us in stitches at the contortions and gestures which went with them; then they were off down the stairs and round the market pubs.

Groups of Doncaster art students would occasionally visit with their bearded whispering and eccentric tutor. 'The coolest company around,' he would assure his students, though they weren't always convinced. I remember in the dim light of the crowded room a young lass was on her feet singing in a powerful voice James Connolly. There was some shuffling and murmuring from the area of the room where the students, unseen in the semi-dark were sitting. The song got to

'Where oh where is the Citizen Army?' 'They're in the bar downstairs!' came the shout out of the dark, 'Why don't you join them, then?' I shouted. The girl carried on singing. The rest of the room remained hushed. 'Clever, what do you do for an encore?' came back. 'I smash your fuckin' head in!' I shouted, diving out of my seat, as the students jumped up and headed down the stairs followed by two or three of us who chased them right up the road. When we tiptoed back up the stairs and back into the room the singer was just concluding her beautiful song. We gave her a standing ovation as she explained, 'I just didn't know what else to do but carry on.' Our club was not the normal Arran sweater, country ditty type of folksong club. It was rough.

In August of 1972 the fascists planned to take over the steps of Leeds Town Hall to hold a rally. This was to be a protest to demand their right to hire halls in the city which up to press had been denied them. The antifascists decided to occupy the steps first, and hold a continuous meeting all day. I think they must have thought I liked talking because I was invited to speak. We were a crowd of about fifty I suppose. We had the Goole Constituency Labour Party Young Socialists banner there, which doesn't sound too revolutionary except that attached to the bottom of it was a billowing red flag and hammer and sickle. A platform had been constructed of two sets of stepladders as far as I could tell. Most of the folk standing around looked like retired workers, old communists and socialists. There was the odd likely lad in amongst, but I wouldn't call the crowd the phalanx of the red detachments.

It was my turn on the platform, when suddenly from across the road a rush of bodies charged individually towards our assembly, and before I could get off the ladders, some thumps and headlocks were being exchanged. Some bodies were on the floor, and most of the antifascists stood about in confusion. It was hard to tell who was who; the fascists might at least have worn swastika armbands so we would know who to kick. Suddenly this member of the master race takes a flying leap up at me, clutching a sheath-knife. Well one of the lads must have seen some films because he had wrapped his coat around his arm as a shield, parried the lunge and scored an ace right hook on the lug of the fascist, who dropped the knife and let out a savage kick, which connected all too badly. Then another fascist joined in. I jumped from the platform but missed the last bloody step and fell backwards like a fool, mad with myself as well as the boneheads. I was in a perfect position to bang both the ladders over onto the two fascists who had backed toward the platform, when they went down. People by this time had regained some focus and were wading into the struggling bodies. The original knife bloke then charged off across the road with the determined would-be knife fighter taking flying kicks at him as he fled.

For a moment we thought that was it. It wasn't. The escaping fascist then charges into the butchers shop across the road, and dives over the counter, grabbing up all sorts of big choppers and cleaving knives, a couple of which he flings at the pursuers. Everyone starts trying to get out of the shop; as the butcher is trying to grab him he is stabbed. The fascist then barricades the doors, and the cops finally arrive. No, its still not over. He smashes his way through the glass door and, bloody and screaming, he stands with this big meat cleaver taking swipes at the cops who look totally terrified as they wave their ineffectual-looking truncheons at him. Finally two of our lot decide enough is enough and risking a beheading they rugby tackle him to the floor where the plod dive on every conceivable bit of struggling body they can locate.

In all this time the buses were standing still, the traffic had stopped, other minor skirmishes were taking place with hit-and-run blows being exchanged. As the fascist loony is lifted bodily in the air and carried overhead by about four cops, the area starts to return to normal. We re-erect the platform. I suggest a body of stewards be stationed around our platform, facing outwards so we can see incoming attacks, and we restart our speeches. By about four o' clock we call it a day. We set off with our banner rolled up down the main road to the station. Fuck me, in the opposite direction, with their flags rolled up, come the bloody fascists, four of us about six of them.

We pass each other but neither of us has belly for any more. Ken whaps one of them with the front of our banner which we are carrying one at each end on our shoulders, so I reciprocate with the other end, Charlie-Chaplain-with-a-plank style. 'Yi bastards!' they shout, and one tries to hit us with his rolled-up flag but misses by a mile. We keep walking away, they keep walking away. We comfort ourselves that they backed off, not us. Mind, had this been the beginning of the shift it wouldn't have ended like this, in fact, its doubtful whether all of us would have been able to walk away from the encounter.

CUT AND PASTE

Back at Raph's Victorian living-room, or in the kitchen of Oxford House off Bethnal Green Road, my back bent over the gluepot (in the days before PCs one literally 'cut' and 'pasted' text onto the page) and volumes of nineteenth-century newspapers, the deadlines were upon us. We made an attempt to cut down on the text and make it simply about dockers and seamen, cutting out all the other joint and independent actions. But we still failed, and the sources, in a wholly disorganised fashion together with bits and pieces of disassociated text, have sat atop my wardrobe unattended and unloved for years.

It's a shameful thing to say, but as later and much later other researchers have come along and started to uncover all those fascinating things I had planned to reveal to the world, piece by piece in labour histories and town theses, more and more of the industrial social and political archaeology is being uncovered. Sheer vanity has made me jealous, when I thought that if I couldn't get the bit of paper with Ruskin or Oxford on it, I at least would have credit for the dedicated years of research. You vain fool, as if history belongs to anyone!

I needn't have worried. In February 1973 my second pamphlet, *Pit Talk In Co. Durham*, came out, published by the History Workshop, so I had two pieces of worth published which at least demonstrated some of what I had been doing all this time. It had also set me down a road of discovery and writing which would be somewhat of a never-ending story. It was pointed out to me that few academics, even tutors, ever got anything they wrote printed and published. This was some achievement.

The experience of Ruskin had on balance been priceless in itself. I now wrote to the colliery and asked when I could sign on. I was not expecting the answer I received.

Although I didn't succeed in getting an actual NUM grant, I was still considered an NUM student. As such, certain provisions had been agreed. One, I would work all my holidays back at the pit. This would make a great difference to our actual year's finances since it was invariably tax-free, and there was loads of overtime if I wanted it. On the odd weeks I didn't start at the pit I was eligible for dole, since I had the required NI contributions and was in theory at least available for work. I qualified for a ton of coal every five weeks I put in at the pit. This too made a colossal difference, especially to Maureen managing on her share of the grant. The NCB would hold my student period as actual paid employment and pay my pension for the period. Most important, they agreed to re-employ me when I finished. So after the slightly messy end to my Ruskin period, and some months of no money whatever while I struggled to finish Liverpool, I was keen to be back established at the pit.

Within Party circles, there were a few notable privileges. One was 'a commission'. This was where the Party delegated you to a task. It was a sign of high regard and trust and in an organisation where all truth and light flowed from above, it was a rare chance for meaningful input. Another was 'an orientation'. This was where your fame had been brought before the eyes and ears of Posadas himself. He then looked at whatever intervention and role you were doing so weel on behalf of the class and the Party and orientated you. He gave his sense of direction to whatever it was you were doing. He fitted you into the world scale of things. It always reminded me of a line from Christopher Robin: 'Do you think Posadas knows all about me?' / 'Sure to, dear, but it's time for tea,' / Says Alice.' I was due an orientation, the PBs had told me, but just now I was bestowed a privilege almost as rare. A little later in 1973 I was authorised to write a Party pamphlet! Most pamphlets were translations of Posadas's view of the world. The odd other was written by the PB. For me to write this one was rare indeed. Of course, it wouldn't say I had written it, not even my Party name would be on it. It was a collective work, it was the input of everyone in the Party and the influence of the masses which wrote it; I was the mere cipher. *The Need for Workers Control in the Mining Industry*: well it was with great pride I viewed its splendid visual presentation. The red stripe down the left side with the Party's hammer and sickle and figure four and our title. I was a little less pleased and then quite rattled when I started to read it. I had been away in Cuba when the Party decided to print me; they therefore were not in a position to actually ask me what things were meant to say. First off, I had part-typed the draft, bad spelling being my speciality, poor ribbon being another; in parts I had hand-written it. Also, it was of necessity highly technical; it referred to many mining machines and operations which would be unknown to non-miners. The task fell to Maureen and Alison, having some knowledge of the mines and miners, to put it into print form. The Party was also trained not to question too hard whether something made too much literal sense; translations from Posadas had to capture the essence of his flowing and poetic Spanish turn of phrase and, sadly, the comrades seemed to apply this to my illiteracy. They didn't know what a 'worler' was; it sounded like some kind of rotating machine, but actually it was supposed to be worker, not worler, as in 'Worlers of the World, Unite!' An image of rotating workers, spinning at the workplace, lodged itself in my mind. I had used the expression 'laughing stock' but my bad spelling and a brainstorm later had ensured that this would translate as a launching pad. Referring to the industry as a milch-cow left them totally confused. They again assumed this to be some sort of machine which was translated as munchker—they imagined some big beast of a cutting machine munchkering down the gates. Ee, well, I at once started to go through the neatly stocked piles of printed books and correct them in felt-tip, which earned me the disciplining by the PB. That was not my role; the pamphlet had been approved as it was; it stayed as it was; it was to be sold as it was. Fine, fine! Any folk who didn't know one end of a coal seam from another just took it for granted—this was all technical stuff. But what about the miners? These were the folk the booklet was aimed at; what the hell would they make of it? No argument, the book went ahead as it was. Well it didn't, because I managed to nobble quite a few reference samples and correct them— brutally, OK, but at least it would prevent some poor researcher being utterly misled and perhaps drafting into further literary mythology my technical twang. It didn't matter that these didn't have my name on; it was my work so it troubled me badly, though we, Maureen and Alison and myself, laughed ourselves stupid as I went through the book and explained what it was supposed to say. The first BIG advert for the pamphlet *The Need for Workers Control in the Mining Industry* appeared in *Red Flag* for 30 January 1974; didn't it look grand? I winced when I saw it. Actually by the end of March the PB was congratulating us on the sales of the booklet and telling us they too were now sold out of it. I longed to rewrite it, but as events turned out that wouldn't be within the Party. Our great enthusiasms for the Party's enthusiasm, their boundless optimism, their finger-touch knowledge of the world revolutionary process from the global conflict down to the factory in some obscure (to us) Italian or Brazilian town, their apparent deep understanding of how this mass complex jigsaw all fitted together and where we fitted into it—all this had for years washed away all doubt. We rarely challenged within ourselves let alone publicly the misgivings about Posadas. This monolithism, his almost papal dominance, his visions were all interesting, all new; but time and again they confronted our earlier concepts of what this whole Marxist formula was about. In June of 1974 he drafted a major 'orientation': *The Relationship with Children and the Unity of Humanity*. I couldn't help feeling this was an orientation about the PB comrade who had gone off with her husband, a bit like Adam and Eve, and conceived of a child without discussing the process and necessity and desirability with the rest of the PB. It was, they said, an act of selfishness and individualism and betrayed a lack of faith in the Party. Both comrades ultimately accepted this motivation and resigned from the PB.

Here Posadas was discussing the development of the child, within the communist family. The Party was big on 'families' despite what Marx and Engels had said, and our earlier anarchist hostility to monogamy, bourgeois marriage and the family as cornerstones of the whole capitalist system. Within the Party, the Party family was a ready-made cell, not only a unit of the revolution but a microcosm of communism, especially existing within the extended Party commune, which was the favoured means of living. Here all political and social tasks could be shared with communist consciousness.

From custom and method we say 'the education of children'. In reality, it is not the education of children, it is the relation with children. Education is a form of relation with children established by private property, to submit the child to the experience of the adults, imposing what capitalism imposes on adults, on the family, to prepare the child for exploitation. What relation do we have with children? Instead of being a relation of father, or adult, with the child, based on imposition on being bigger, and with more strength, there must be a relation of persuasion, of identification with the child and then the child sees it's simply a question of not possessing the strength which we have. Then it is possible to transmit experience to the child and organise his development ...

It is necessary to integrate the children in all tasks of the house, with explanation, and persuasion; to have the object of speaking to them, not to take them as a secondary aspect but to do it with most elevated passion. The child feels thus integrated in the life of the adult, sees that the difference between the adult and the child is through experience, capacity, means, muscular development, intelligence, but now he assimilates experience and regulates behaviour as part of humanity. He does not develop the egotistic sense, the competitive sense which is the product of class society, transferred into family life. It is necessary to integrate him in everything, talking about everything, talking to him with the utmost consideration as you would with an adult ...

What they call childhood has been a creation of private property. If the stupid doll exists, it is because private property and class divisions still exist. The children in Vietnam don't need dolls any more. Life helps them to realise that is more useful to be interested in life than in dolls. Dolls and other toys are a form of stupidity created by private property and today by the capitalist regime ...

The stupid toys alienate him from the life that he sees developing in the class struggle and to which he is attracted to intervene. This stage of history is very fertile for this.

For children, logical behaviour from the father and of the mother is fundamental. The child soon learns to see when the behaviour of the parents is the product of a mood, or arrogance or superiority. He has to see a logical behaviour in everything. Including with objects; it is necessary not to throw them around, or treat them roughly in temper, be logical in everything. Then, the child will develop with the capacity to think logically and he will find bad behaviour stupid. The child is not bad, no children are bad, they may behave inadequately, but no children are bad. They cannot have sentiments of perversion when they develop in that way it is because they are educated in that way by capitalist society ...

We raise our understanding and we develop with our companion, with the children, a communist relation and communication. In such a way that the family thinks as a whole. By thinking as a whole it elevates the capacity to think because they will save energy and preoccupation that now they must dedicate to family problems created by capitalism, they will therefore think integrally. This gives an enormous human solidity that transmits confidence, and feels the most important conclusion, that we are not like this because we are born like this, but because we are the result of the forms of property, of the forms of production, of social relations determined by this.

It was true childhood, like 'teenage', as a separate identity and social mode was an invention which suited the social system of capitalism as it developed. There was no 'childhood' for the kids working in coalmines or in the mills of the early nineteenth century. Children worked alongside older folk from their families and down their street without any notion that they were somehow in a special phase of their lives. But Posadas in his earnestness referring to the 'stupid doll' appears to believe that all things associated with childhood, perhaps like play and games, were also irrelevant inventions. In fact before the 'childhood' distinction everyone, adults and children, played games, together; children were just small adults and vice versa as far as fun was concerned, albeit increasingly confined by the strictures of industrialisation as it developed. Along with the stupid doll, the reference to 'perversion' also jars on modern nerves. In those days the belief that homosexuality was a perversion of repressed healthy sexual relations, caused by the capitalist system and destined to be purified by socialist free relations, was common. This was a standard Marxist-Leninist-Trotskyist-Stalinist-Maoist conclusion. Certainly it was the standard view of Militant and our view too, though we boldly, or what we thought was boldly, defended the rights of the homosexuals and defended them against discrimination and repression. I recall Theo describing with disdain the 'bourgeois feminists, the lesbians and those types' who were undermining the force of socialist women. It should be added that the 'far left', despite its subsequent absorption into the mix of the swinging Sixties was not uniformly in favour of heady heterosexual hedonism either. Some Maoist leaflets condemned 'all forms of unchecked sexuality'! The RWP was positively puritan, while Militant made up for its grey conservatism on issues of armed struggle and revolution by being rampantly sexual. I guessed if you've got poor politics you can always make up for it with an uninhibited sex life. Mind, Militant were not as sexual as the IMG, which was, contrary to the Maoist proscription, up for everything going, and also whose politics were quite good, so that theory didn't leave the drawing board. Some years later as we developed politically from the Party, we reconsidered the whole prospect, but still hadn't taken on board the idea that homosexuality was really as kosher as heterosexuality.

I remember a weel drunk conversation with Paddy Prendoville, a bisexual Irish revolutionary from London. The conversation was going nowhere. I voiced in desperation 'Luek, I just like tits, alreet?' to which rejoined so did he, but also thighs, and in any case under a developed communist society there wouldn't be any tits! 'Whaat?!' Paddy elaborated on his theory that tits were simply mammary glands, male tits were a biological dead-end, and in the future women would no longer have to actually bear children or physically feed them from their own bodies, babies would be born in laboratories and so tits, like the state, would simply wither away for want of necessity. This sat like a bombshell for a moment, then the logic phased through the booze haze. 'Wait a minute! Sex organs are biologically simply reproductive organs, if we don't need them for child procreation, they too will wither away, so there won't be sex of any description!' Paddy mused for a moment then conceded: 'OK. We need to rethink the laboratory thing,' amid mutual laughter and piss-taking. It had actually been the realisation that sexual activity had stopped being purely or even mainly procreational decades ago that made us realise that all sex was purely for enjoyment, so whatever turned you on was OK with us no matter what 'nature' had designed the bits for in the first place.

BANGING ON THE COAL BOARD'S DOOR...
LIKE A TURKEY ON THE OVEN DOOR

The personnel officer's reply via a letter made serious reading. It said, basically, that 'Although we had been happy to employ you before,' on this occasion there was no work I could usefully do. I assured myself that the fool personnel officer thought this was another holiday-period, short-employment job, not my actual job we were talking about. A hurried phonecall established however that he was not mistaken and that he wished me well for my career now that I had finished my studies. I was soon battering the door of the Union office down. Tom Mullanny on this occasion was prepared to make a stand on it, rival and political opponent or no. 'There is a misunderstanding,' the manager Mr I. C. McGregor informed us when we attended a first-stage meeting at the pit, together with the Union secretary Frank Clark and the personnel officer. The area office of the NCB at St George's had a position for me, in the Industrial Relations Department. 'Ee, there you go, lad,' said Frank Clark in all sincerity. 'You've made it.' 'Made what?' I asked. 'Made a success of yourself lad, you're out that bliddy pit, in a job where you can excel, there is a place where you can offer real justice for the miners, because you will have seen it from our side too.' I stopped short of knocking Frank off his chair, because I realised he was being genuine, and actually me Dad might have said something similar; neither of them seemed to grasp what I or it was about.

Mullanny detected I was close to tears, which I was. I felt like I was being made an offer I couldn't refuse and felt utterly alone and full of guilt and betrayal. 'Would you like a few minutes to think things over, lad? This is a lot to take in just out of the blue.'

The manager too decided to be sympathetic 'I know, and I apologise. Dave should have been invited up to St George's to discuss his future when he finished, but I understand there was some kind of a delay in when he did finish, and he hadn't returned home or something to that effect. Otherwise we would discuss it all formally.' 'There's nowt to discuss', I said, throwing me head back, and feeling my blood starting to boil. The manager's remarks suggested that they were fully aware of my situation, and maybe had been in touch with the college about which course I had actually completed, half expecting the threat of withdrawing the pension contributions, but what the heck? 'My job is down that pit, you agreed I should have my job back when I finished.' At that, the manager jumped up. 'It appears to me lad, nobody can help you enough, but just for the record,' and he started to speak very slowly and deliberately: 'We did not offer you your job; we promised you a job.' I got up. 'It's time for a Union meeting I think.'

'Dave lad, what yee deyin?' said Frank, putting his hand on my sleeve. 'This is victimisation, Frank.' He laughed. 'Whey man how can it be victimisation when they are offering you a better paid job, better conditions, better holidays, working in the fresh air and daylight in a white shirt every day?' 'It's selling out Frank and you know it.' 'Dave lad we need people like you in that office,' he started.

I had had enough, I turned to leave. But the manager beat me to the door, and breezed by me: 'If you think I have time to mess about with bullshit like this ...' he said to anyone who would listen and stormed off to his office. Now what was I going to do? Well another trip to the unemployment benefit office was a start; I might as well pretend I was looking for another job in order to get some money. After a short wait, and a brief discussion with the normal clerk on the desk, she went off, and after a somewhat longer wait was relieved by a senior-looking bloke. 'Mr Douglass, I understand you are trying to make a claim for unemployment benefit, and you don't qualify for that benefit.' 'What?' 'Its come to my notice that you have been offered full-time work, and you have refused it, you have rendered yourself unemployed.' Well the balloon did go up then. I tried to argue that I was in dispute with my employer, but they pointed out I didn't have an employer, whichever way I tried to shout and storm my way out of it, the personnel office at the pit had queered my pitch and no mistake, with even more vindictiveness than I ever recall. Now we had nowt. For a week and then into the next week, I was kicking my heels on the cobbles. I was down the Union office every day, men at the pit were starting to hear about this, blokes would come up to me in the street and stick £5 in my hand 'to keep me going', and embarrassing though it was, I had to accept it. Things were starting to move at the pit. Johnny Sadd, well known and dignified Union committee man, got up at a Branch meeting and said it was shameful if any face worker, ripper or heading man was working overtime at this pit when a bloke in this room can't get any time at all. 'That's right,' agreed Tom Mullanny, and Monday day shift were going down to that pit and tell everyone that. Feeling a bit foolish, I was ushered into the canteen first thing, as the day shift assembled in their hundreds.

Len Caven, the president, called them all to order: 'Right lads, lets have a word.' Tom Mullanny rose to speak. Now me and Tom might not have got on, but I had to take my hat off to him as a public speaker, and boy did he give it some welly. 'We aren't going to have one our workmates out on the streets, having to accept handouts, because that set of bastards over there don't like his politics, or the fact that having had an education he dares to come back here to share it with us, rather than them. This lad is an example to the management, that there are people on this side of the street who can't be bought!' And a big cheer went up, there was a surge of men wanting to strike then and there, but Tom didn't want to go that fast that soon. From this day on there would be no overtime for NPLA workers until I have been reset on.

Behind the scenes, Tom had contacted Scargill, and Scargill had contacted the area director and the phone wires were red-hot. By the Thursday of the following week, Mullanny, Clark and the area agent met the area director, the manager, and the personnel manager. The area director was I believe Mr White; he had said, 'And its not him,' pointing to the manager. 'The bastard over in them offices' (referring to Tom's canteen speech which some yellow dog had duly relayed to them) 'is me, I am the one who has stopped him getting set on and I'll tell you why. The IRA,' he said banging the table. 'Dave Douglass's wife has been down at this pit selling communist papers, and supporting the IRA, how can we put him in an underground environment where he is dealing with explosives, it wouldn't be responsible, and I, this bastard, has that responsibility. Second, NACODS have told me if he comes back here they walk out, he has gone in print, humiliating NACODS members, advocating men to refuse authority and discipline, and threatening violence against NACODS members. So there are the reasons, why I have told the manager not to employ him, and those reasons stand.' The steam was coming out of Mullanny's ears by the time he rose to his feet: 'Last week, you lot were offering that IRA supporter and potential bomber, he could pick his own office, you wanted him on your side, so that's enough of that rubbish, and as for NACODS determining which members of the NUM shall work at which pit, you have lit the blue touch paper mister—watch me.' The area agent, in a quiet controlled voice, wiping his glasses, said: 'Well I have to say, Mr White, I know you to be a very belligerent member of the management team, and I wasn't expecting anything very constructive from you today, and you haven't disappointed me, but I must say, your words have added a new gravity to this situation and a greater dimension. I have also to tell you, the Doncaster panel, is taking this matter back to all the Doncaster branches, with a view to resolution or action. You could have Doncaster on strike, Mr White.' 'Threats I do not submit to; you know me.' 'Just putting you in the picture Mr White.'

Following that meeting, as if it wasn't enough for them to consider, I am led to believe Mr Scargill phoned the area director in overall charge and told him this wasn't a Doncaster matter anymore, and the area EC had instructed him to convey to you that the Yorkshire area could stand, yes, the Yorkshire Area.

Sunday evening they sent for me to start on Monday morning; go and see Mr MacConicky and he would tell me what was required. Tom Mullanny had been a branch official and senior member of the Yorkshire Executive for some time; he had been tipped to become area president, before Arthur launched his publicity coup by leading the charge of Yorkshire miners down at Saltley gates. I don't think Tom ever forgave Arthur; nor in the bitter infighting which preceded, and followed, did Arthur ever fully forgive Hatfield. That forebye, Tom's commitments at area and up top meant that apart from the regular inspections he carried out as the senior s123 inspector, he was rarely at work as such. He was reputed to have a back rip, although few had ever seen him deployed to it, and its progress must have been deathly slow. I know it existed because I had a shift with him on it. During my spell of absence at Ruskin, there had been a number of bomb threats at the pit. Anonymous phone calls, usually on hot sunny days, and, strangely, more frequently on a Friday. The management and the Union were in a cleft stick with it—you couldn't not pass on the message to the men, and you couldn't dare say it was a hoax, even though everyone and their dog knew it was. To try and calm nerves, the management agreed that instead of everybody just going home a detailed search would be made of the surface and the underground working areas.

The deputy manager stood in the canteen and asked, 'Now then, if you were going to plant a bomb at the pit, where would you plant it?'

Some wag called out: 'On Tom Mullanny's back rip, because nobody knows where it is!' to laughter. Monday day shift, I was ushered into Mr McConicky's office.

'Now then Dave, the pit has to be fitted with Whitticar manriding cars, to comply with new regulations. These as you know must be closed in vehicles and they require more clearance than some of our major roadways have got. I want you to head up a team, back-ripping those roads. Now, there isn't much point starting before 7 a.m. because the night shift has to get out and the day shift get in. You'll have an extended snap time because the day shift paddy's coming out and the afters paddy's going in. So we can make up a couple of hours overtime between shifts. You can pick three or four mates to work with you, and you'll stay on that shift.' I looked at him.

'Well, this an ideal job for a lad like you,' he urged. 'You're offering me Tom Mullanny's back rip aren't you?' I said. 'Put me back on face rips!'

He looked at me exasperatedly. 'I blumming well give up with you. Go on, get down pit.' Some days later, as I rode my way inbye, on a belt which weaved up and down the arch sides, and through low work which would cut your head off, to the most inhospitable main gate rip, with arches much too big and much too heavy for my slight construction, with a gate chargeman who was an absolutely born-again psychopath, another man with a mission to break me, or kill me, I thought, 'Well, I hope this is hurting the management, because its bliddy killing me!'

When I told Jim and Ray and a couple of my other former mates, that they could have been in my team on that shift, they went daft. 'You stupid fucking twat!' was the congratulations I gained for the firm stand against further 'victimisation'. 'They can victimise me like that all my working life,' Ray had complained. 'I shall think of you and your principles when I'm getting out of my bed at crack of dawn for day shift and leaving 'owse at midnight for nights. Twat!' Or as wor Bob had said: 'Twenty years of schooling and they put you on the day shift.'

We had started our regular Friday night folk club in Doncaster and I had tried to get everyone in the vicinity, singers especially, to come along. Tom had written saying he couldn't make it and

> I saw Johnny Mac and Sue (his wife) this afternoon, so they may come over to the premiere. By the way, your constant references to Johnny's 'women' would give any self-respecting women's lib militant the screaming willies. Anyway, good luck with the folk-song club and remember—don't overdo the medieval allegorical ballads, there isn't the audience for them that there used to be. RG, Tom
>
> PS I'm glad to hear of your success in getting back down the pit. I hope you didn't have to eat too much shit. Right On! (An American revolutionary phrase of encouragement, now gaining popularity in this country. It's often followed by the word 'baby'.)

I was in the main gate pack, something of a doddle after the tailgate 12-yarder;

this was only six yards and it was left-handed, so you hoy your muck back without tying yourself in a knot. You could also get the back end on smartish by using rock from the waste and give yourself a start. Trouble was, Brad, the gate chargeman, was stark staring mad. He had injured his 'mate' in an argument over pigeons, knocked him clean off the scaffold. So I had now landed in the gate. Brad would urge you to hold the arch leg while he connected it to the bow, which we had previously fitted over the horseheads in the gate or tunnel. You had the weight of the leg, you had to balance it in place while he connected the huge fishplates together to clamp it to the arch. For reasons best know to himself, he would drop a plate or both plates on your back, or he would kick a waiting arch strut, a strip of metal which braces the tunnel arches apart, onto your shoulder, sometimes he might throw it like a spear and pretend it had fallen on you.

'Why?' I once asked him outright and just as outright he replied, 'Because I don't fuckin' like yee.'

On one occasion, we had lifted the heavy-section arch up onto the scaffold, which although constructed of three planks and not the usual two, was raised higher on one side as against the other. I am 5 foot 5 or so, he is 6 foot plus. So he, the awkward twat that he is, goes to the high side and I am left at the low side. This means when we come to lift the bow up and onto the horsehead girders running forward I am on my tiptoes, while he without much effort has it on his shoulder. My shoulder will not raise the arch high enough, so I am forced to squat beneath the arch and extend my arms as far in the air as they will go, struggling under the weight and wobbling, with every muscle straining and my back and neck being electrocuted with warning pins and needles. It still doesn't quite get high enough to reach the horsehead, so he throws it down off his shoulder. The whole bow, on its way down to the scaffold, twisting as it goes, has my hands and arms attached to it, and it spins painfully from my grasp and then tries to wallop me in the head as it glances by, then thuds on the scaffold and makes a rapid twist round, catching me in the back of both legs and near knocking me several feet onto the moving metal scraper chain below. My legs looked like they'd been mauled by a giant tiger. I was torn from arse to ankles.

Another little point of amusement was general shit-stirring. We were making our way inbye, on the rope paddy, when he says: 'And you yi little cunt, you've got our water note stopped.' 'What?' I ask. 'We always get a job and knock on that job on a Friday, but because you're with us you little commie bastard, they've stopped it.' As soon as the paddy stopped, I launches into Alan Barras, the unit deputy. 'Why?' I demanded after screaming blue murder at him, 'punish them if you're trying to get at me?' 'Dave,' he replied quietly, 'I haven't a clue what you're talking about. The arrangement stands as it usually does.' The men are milling around, afters going on, day shift coming off, listening to the heated argument and this little Geordie twat always the centre of bother running up and down, for now I confronted Brad: 'He says there's no change, he hasn't took any concession off you.' 'What yee on about, you daft little twat?' 'You telt us, Barras had stopped wa note because I'm with yee.' 'Ah haven't spoke to you, tha crazy little twat.' 'What?' 'This is the first time I have spoken to you,' and he walks off, with a few of his silent partners. Oh yes, even sharks I am led to believe have little fish which they don't molest and swim harmlessly in and out the great killing jaws. Brad had a couple of 'mates', or rather people who he didn't pick on, they kept stoma on all they seen and he did. He never had witnesses. He was a killer looking for a victim and anything could be the circumstance. I recall once Alan had told him the arch was off-centre, and from the scaffold where he stood he hurled the pinch bar, a long steel chisel about 5 feet long, straight at him; it just missed his throat and disappeared through the metal sheets lagging the arch beside which he stood.

Alan's face drained of blood, and he said, more as a plea of disbelief to Chick, Brad's gate mate, 'Did you see that?'

Chick let fly a stream of baccy juice and went 'See what?'

As Alan walked wobbling up the gate, Chick laughed and said 'I thought he was goin't say "and tha hasn't packed that arch reet well either."'

I had an Australian communist mate who worked down the NE part of the pit. He used to have an expression 'You wouldn't read about it.' Well, some years later I got to write a book on contemporary pitwork and Brad you're in it, so maybe you actually will 'read about it'. Fortunately for all concerned they needed a Dosco driver down the tailgate, and I got some fool to swap me. In the tailgate, I landed first off with Jimmy Mason, and his sidekick 'the master ripper' Phil (Wardle I believe). Phil swore he had trained under a master stoneman, and studied all sorts of junction, heading and caunch work, like a sort of City & Guilds certificate, so we honoured him with the title. He was almost blind, his eyes screwed up into slits; he had been hit by the burst of a cordite shell one time and it vor nie blinded him. He was a tall man, a strong plodder, good with a jigger and had the reach and power for the windy pick and the boring machine. He loved the crack, but rarely came up with original tales of his own, he just sort of added a bit on to some one else's story, or went one better. I recall the discussion was on 'cunt books' and films.

Jimmy was describing a film in which a solitary women had taken three large penises in her orifices—her backside, her vagina and her mouth.

Phil chipped in with 'I just watched one and she had four dicks up her!' 'Four?' 'Hmm, aye,' says Phil. 'She had another in her ear!' A Wearside lad, Dave Walters, six foot tall, skinny, could turn anything round, says, 'Whay was she a ghost like?' Phil says, 'How'd yi mean?' 'Tha knaa's—one of them eerie fuckers!'

Priceless.

A little later I lands once more with Jimmy Shipley. It wasn't long before a dispute was flaring again. What needs to be understood is that both me and Jim like mining, and we were good at what we did, and we did it properly. But there were things inherently conflictual in the modern mining ethos. There was a lang syne rejection of supervision among face men the country over. The NPLA, as well as benefits for the face men, had carried penalties, one of which was the abandonment of that opposition to supervision. Whereas the old lads refused to work with any gaffers around, the current generation pretended to work while they were around, and the gaffers knew this so left them alone, having made the point that they could if they wanted to. With me and Jim it was a principled and articulated resentment. Likewise, we would not allow production to come before safety, our own in particular. Finally, we expected that we got a snap time. That minor programme of principles was an ongoing flashpoint. We were going through some bad ground, and the stone top was breaking well above the height of the arches we were setting. This necessitated us getting up, on top of the arch and timbering, with wood blocks and half tree trunks, a trellis of wood from the arch up to the heaving roof. At any point a slab of rock could silently lowse itself free and fall on your unsuspecting back or head, the roof could spew forward its deluge before you got it secure and the whole wooden stack would go flying, and you'd have to start over again. Between the wood blocks and tree trunks, we would wedge bags of stone, filled 20 feet below and thrown up and up to the man at the top—back-breaking, fearful work. Jim had put the lock-out on the face chain, so the rumbling, clanking metal ensemble and the cutting riving coal-cutting machines wouldn't rock the roof and vibrate the gate end. The deputies were going mad, the overman was going mad. 'What the fuck has the tailgate rip got to do with our coal cutting?' they yelled. We were too busy to answer. The manager, Mr Deeming, like a voice from God booming out from the control room, asked that Jim be put on the tannoy. Jim, soaked in sweat and cut from small rocks, climbed down from above the rip and knelt by the tannoy. 'Listen, Mr Deeming, you're gaffer up there, I'm gaffer when my back's concerned. We are trying to get this gate end supported before the lot comes in, the machines and the face chain are vibrating the top, do you understand that?' 'I am aware of how the pit works Jimmy. But can you leave that now, and let the machines cut, then during snap time get it timbered up while were all stood?' 'Mr Deeming, if I take lock off now, an't leave work we just done t'last two hours, an' t'cutting fetches roof in and collapsed gate end an' t'face is stood for days, do tha think 20 minutes snap time will put it all back? Or if I get clobbered because your advice has made it more dangerous are you going to tell our lass it was your got me back brock or got me killed? You might worship coal Mr Deeming, but I worship me health marra.' There was a silence. Then 'I guess we carry on, Jim.' Me and Jim landed an apprentice—well, a lad doing 'close personal supervision', on the rip. Walking out with him, Jim had gone off ahead, whistling down the tailgate like a rocket, until his light was completely gone. Presently we came to the loop, a return in the road which was as far as the mine cars could advance. An empty mine car was standing, on the rails, and as we drew up next to it, out jumped Jim with his light off, and scared the young 'un half to death. A couple of days later, me and Jim were walking out discussing resolutions to the forthcoming LPYS conference and the position of Militant on Ireland, when steaming up behind us came Pickles, the senior overman. As he catches us up, he spots a big rock in the roadway. 'Come from up there, Bob.'[52]

'Aye, the sheets are rotten. How yee fixed for a noggin on that tomorrow, lads?'

'Aye, we should manage that, Bob.' 'Right, let's have that in the tub,' he says, and me and Jim get one side each and sling the rock into a tub standing on the rails. There is a dull thud and limp cry like a cat being squashed, and a very bloody CPS lad emerges from the tub. Bob thinks he's been sleeping in there all shift, and we have to explain that he was trying to return a bit pillock. Poor bugger.

He was a darling, this lad. I had given him the trust of clamping the ring plates onto the arch leg and the bow, while I held onto the leg, while Jim waited with the heavy mell to knock it back. The lad shouts 'All right—bang it back!' I look up briefly and scream 'Stop!' The fool has his finger through the bolt space in the fishplates and is urging Jim to knock the leg back so as to line up the plates. He had seen us do this, only we used a pigtail bolt tightener or an extra long bolt, which of course came to no harm as the plates and arch girders ground into place. A finger? Certain amputation. The resentment about NACODS actions rumbled on. In particular it came to a head when management insisted that the check office would close 15 minutes before the start of the shift, and any man not underground by the shift start time would be sent home. There had been a practice at the pit of allowing deputies, overmen and other miscellaneous management and professional staff to ride up the pit on the first draw; sometimes these von nie filled the whole bottom deck. We demanded an end to this practice and instructed our onsetters not to allow anyone to board the cage from the back and that everyone should stand in the queue and ride on a first come, first served basis. This led to the onsetters being sent out of the pit, and the pit struck again.

Part of this dispute was about what exactly our hours of work were. We had long complained that our time didn't start until we reached the pit bottom: we were expected to get our checks, get changed, pick up our gear and travel down the mine in our own time. It was a running sore that our comrades who died in the Markham Main disaster in Derbyshire, when the brakes failed on the winding engine and the cages plummeted down the shafts, weren't even being paid at the time of their deaths. So if that was the case then at lowse nobody had the right to go in front of us in time we were no longer being paid for—that was our time and not at the disposal of management to allocate. The defeat of the 1926 strike had inflicted extra hours and a winding time. The agreement actually referred to 'one winding'. That was clear to us: they got one draw in the pit or one draw out of the pit in our time, but they couldn't have more than that and they couldn't have it at both ends of the shift.

The area agent persuaded us to go back to work while they discussed the question. 'Trust me lads,' he had said. A month later they came back with an offer of half a shift payment for each day we had lost in dispute and no resolution to our stand about winding times. But management would not stipulate when you got your checks out, but you would still be sent home without pay if you weren't actually down the pit by start of shift. The men were furious and told the officials to stuff the money up their backsides. The dispute and issues remained unresolved to this day.

CANAL TAVERN, THORNE

In September of 1972 we took our folk concert to the Canal Tavern at Thorne, and in the process opened up a whole new world to loads of people who had never encountered music like this first-hand, the wild fiddle tunes, the hearty singing of the chanteys, industrial stories to music, comic tales and songs, and a vision of a struggle which was tangible and growing all round. We had at that time just met a former RAF bloke, Steve Walker, who had just started work as a fireman. He tended to have RAF-type arrogance when we first met him, but his wife and our company, and his love of the folk world, took him to studious, though not always successful, attempts to master the fiddle. He was better on the banjo, and his political stuff started to grow, especially the Scottish nationalist stuff.

29 October 1972. Tom wrote to tell me he wasn't dropping out of political activity despite the fact that we hadn't seen him for some time:

I am not stagnating quite so much as you fear. For example, we've finally got the engineering side of my firm unionised—the first time in half-a-century that the union has had a foothold in the firm. Trade Union work takes up the bulk of my political time. My last contact with any lefty group was an encounter with the SLL. It was not a debate. I simply lost my temper (I'm a mercurial little fellow, you know) and slammed one of them against a wall and foamed frightening oaths between my yellow teeth. It must have been fairly effective, for I've never seen them since.

On Friday 17 November Jock and I will be coming across to the folk club, with a lad called Brad ... I hope this doesn't clash with any bookings you may have made—if it does, then possibly we could squeeze Jock in somewhere in the evening.

Congratulations on the rent strike comrades! Its splendid news! I can envisage the area becoming an English Ulster, which cleverly brings me to the subject of the IRA. I'd like to discuss the IRA with you next time we meet. By the way it's not a one way line from Doncaster to Hull if you and Maureen fancy coming across here for a weekend then do so. We can discuss things here as well as Doncaster.

As for the child, I honestly can't see the need for a naming ceremony. I'm becoming a surly swine these days—I never bother with birthdays, anniversaries celebrations etc. I tend to regard them as fripperies that young folk indulge in, and I feel that I'm getting too old for such fol-de-rols. Needless to say though a good solid mature drinking bout would not go amiss. I think that a stern debauching is completely different from a ritualistic ceremony, and as such I would welcome it. See you on the 17 or before.

RG Tom Kilburn

Ps. I see some prancing sodomite in Tin Pan Alley is playing an electric set of Northumbrian small-pipes. It will end in blood being shed. PPS Churlish though it sounds I'd forgotten to write about Judy. I imagine that Maureen's mother, or yours will be down for the birth, but if Maureen wants it, Judy could come across for a few days to show Maureen (as an old experienced hand) the best way to thrash the bairn ... if you fancy a species of twins, Judy can leave ours with you—we're becoming bored with her, for the little cretin still can't talk sensibly.

Good Luck to you both — TK

5 January 1973. Before my very eyes, my daughter was born. The whole thing wasn't bloody or messy at all, until they decided to cut Maureen to make the birth easier, then there was blood. Poor Maureen, she's exhausted. She asked 'How much would that shift have been worth then?' And I conceded it was far harder than any 12-yard pack I had put on. My little girl was born, alive, well and healthy. I was ecstatic. She is most precious, our love and friendship would grow from this time on and never be broken. Maureen wrote the following day (because I was on shift) 'You were lovely with me. It was hard I will admit but I'll never forget the look on your face when you saw her.' Actually it wasn't all that optimistic at the time. Maureen couldn't breast feed and was deeply upset at all the milk having to be taken away and pain. Poor Emma was a blue baby, with Maureen being rhesus negative, and had swallowed lots of mucus so was constantly being sick. Maureen wrote 'Anyway my pet however long it takes we'll have her and she is marvellous. I love her so much my heart could burst.'

Tom was to write on the 19th congratulating us on the birth, which had been somewhat delayed owing to Emma deciding it was much too comfortable where she was to come out into this hard cold world of lights and noise.

> No doubt you're both wallowing in the luxury of sleepless nights amid shrieks and wails (from Emma of course). A vista of excrement, stale vomit and indescribably soiled nappies will open up before you, and I sometimes think that you richly deserve it ... we thought that Emma had decided to do an extra fortnight's bird.

Actually, the hospital staff induced the birth in the end, something I was really mad about, but they needed the bed, and Maureen was becoming exhausted at being on the brink for days and nights.

Out from the Ashes

27 January 1973. In Derry a mass ensemble of the people of Ireland, North and South, of the British left, of the republican and social democratic parties held a mass protest procession to mark anniversary of the repression on Bloody Sunday. The Party had intervened here, as had most of the left from Britain. Following their instincts they lined up on the official march, with the Social Democratic and Labour Party (SDLP; then the majority Catholic and nationalist party in the Six Counties), such trade unions and trade councils as had principles, the Official republican movement, the Civil Rights Association. The drums were muffled, the banners draped, the sullen mood descended with the rain. Then bursting from a side street, with a mass band playing Chief O'Neill's Favourite, an army of uniformed 'Fianna' republican youth surged forward, followed by the lofty banners of the Provisional Sinn Fein. The city was behind their banners, it was anger and confidence which fluttered on their poles, not depression. To anyone undecided as to where the allegiance of this risen populace stood, the contrast in support and demeanour couldn't have made it clearer. The Party comrades were deeply touched by it, but then went on to totally misunderstand it; it just got wedged into the shape they wanted it to fit the foreign formulae elaborated under different conditions.

The Party had meantime relayed the desperate news of repression in Brazil, a roundup of every sort of dissident and progressive across society. Murders, beatings, closing down of all the left, Christian and democratic papers and organisations. Our comrades were among the first to be rounded up and in some cases shot down. We at once started to campaign on the issue of political prisoners in Brazil. We spoke at union meetings, trades councils, political parties and lobbied where we could to raise the news across the world. We planned a big folk music social to raise money and awareness. This was to be held at the Park Hotel in Doncaster, just down from the racetrack, and was scheduled for 27 January. I dug out the battered but tried and tested address book. I had written to Eddy Pickford of the Northern Front months earlier, really to plan the concert around their availability—they were to be the stars of the show. Eddy had written back: 'Maureen must be delighted to be in the club. Ted Heath is no doubt equally displeased at the thought of another Douglass on its way to "bore holes" in his "sinking ship". I trust it is kicking well.' The Northern Front, which I had always tried to add 'liberation' into the middle of, were a trio of Geordie singer-songwriters and performers. Unique really. Mike Elliott, Eddy Pickford and Nick Fenwick had actually broken up as a team but reformed for a barnstorming evening of humour and song and music-hall theatrics. Just how much of their stuff you would get away with today is uncertain—little, I suspect: sexual jokes, jokes about nationality, sexuality, politics, religion, the pope, the queen, queens, nothing and nobody was sacred. I cringed and looked around the room with one eye peeping out from hands clasped over my head in expected uproar from the mix of right-on left politicos, normal working-class folks, and rip-roaring likely lads, but it went down a storm. A battered but surviving tape of the evening is still around, 31 years later and records the devastating applause and football-crowd-like choruses. That was some neet. The stage was star-studded and I had brought together friends and comrades from everywhere.

Alun Howkins, up from Oxford, with his waistcoat and collarless shirt, his belt and braces, his neckerchief at his throat, sang his agricultural songs and gave the rural humours full blast. Ian (Jock) Manuel, the most famous exponent of 'bothy ballads', author of 'The Frosty Ploughshare' and others, held us spellbound in full Scottish dialect. Larch and Chris organised a bus full of students down from Leeds University where they were now studying, and Fred, likewise, had a wee party down from York.

Our baby was only two months old, and we used to divide up our time between her and our political work and social activity. Because I had the biggest gob, and was the organiser, I did the MC. But we had planned a big reception/party at the shop afterwards, so Maureen minded Emma, and Tom stayed with Ruth their bairn during the concert. Then I minded Emma, while Judy, Tom's companion, took over Ruth during the duration of the shop party.

DISASTER

At 2.30 a.m. on 21 March 1973, men were working on the south 9B coalface at Lofthouse Colliery. Terence Cotton was working feet away from his Dad Charles.

The seam, not untypical in Yorkshire, was three feet high. It was as it turned out Charles's fiftieth birthday but he had come to work. Moments later a wall of water and coal slurry burst through the coalface. Terence escaped, along with eight others off that face; nobody else did. His Dad and six others were trapped by water which rushed down the tailgate, and beat them to the air doors in the main gate, sealing their fate. Six weeks of hard slog by the rescue party found only Charles's body. *The Yorkshire Post* had reported:

Early today six Coal Board frogmen brought in from Cannock Staffs, slid into the dark water on what was called a 'feasibility exercise'. Their task was expected to take up to four hours. To make a rescue attempt they would have to swim more than half a mile along an undulating passage 750 ft underground taking an airline with them ...

John Craner head of the team said 'It's black, filthy and visibility is nil down there. The real object was to see how far we could get. We managed 25 yards into the water.'

Keith Stone, a young fitter, who after surviving the inrush went back with the rescue team said 'I was in the loader gate about 20 yards from the coalface when suddenly I felt the air 'turn'. It felt strange and it was so unusual that I knew something disastrous was happening. I turned and ran hell for leather up the gate away from the face. As I did so I heard the water break through the face with a roar. As I ran I could see other men's helmet lamps bombing about on the roof of the loader gate. At one time the water was only five yards away but we beat it.'

The face was working in the vicinity of old mine workings. Nobody had read the old Victorian geological notebook which plainly described the depths of the shafts. The coalface was on a collision course with two shafts which by now contained 3.5 million gallons of water and sludge. The coalface reached the bottom of the shafts and cut out a yard of coal, unplugging the seal. Gravity did the rest.

On the Doncaster May Day march of 1973, we cut a dash with the magnificent Doncaster Regional banner of the Revolutionary Workers Party, which Maureen as the gifted banner maker had excelled herself with in crimson satin. We were a family of families, with all our kids marching at our side or riding on their Dads' heads and shoulders. For all our iron discipline it is an aura of scarce concealed mirth and abounding optimism which enveloped us as we stride along singing and chanting. That's to say, you couldn't fail to notice us, and this was just us 'in uniform'; elsewhere our Young Socialists marched with their own banners and placards or sat aboard the float we had constructed, in among the marching ranks of miners and factory workers many from our periphery. We even brought up the rear with a couple of transit vans bedecked in red flags and slogans. The Yorkshire Miners' Gala of June that year was at Wakefield. The splendid Red Theatre were guest performers, in top hats and on stilts, with painted faces and in cloth caps they lampooned the capitalist system with much humour and wit. Our contingent, marching off initially behind the Hatfield band and banner, became increasingly left behind and we couldn't help thinking some more moderate colleagues were walking rather fast with the banner away from us. It didn't matter—we had our own band and banner. The Ovalteenies, a juvenile jazz band based at the Oval in Dunscroft, led our party, in their red trews and white shirts, while we followed on with a huge slogan banner: 'Launch The Unlimited General Strike, To Overthrow the Tories And Impose a Left Labour Government on a Socialist Programme'. Behind the banner marched the red pit men of *The Mineworker*, the Labour Party Young Socialists, and members of the RWP not in either of those other two. Again we struck quite a dash and raised great cheers as we marched through the thronged streets, our banner readable from a block away. For Emma sitting in her pushchair and waving her tiny hands to the thud of the bass drum this was her first miners' gala in a lang, lang line of miners' galas as she grew up in the politics and culture of the miners. Following the gala we held our traditional folk music party, this time at our shop in Dunscroft. The walls beamed down in benevolent revolutionary instruction and illustration, the fire still roared up the chimney despite the summer sunshine, and the room rocked with the voices our friends and comrades. We are tanned, canned and happy. We felt we were advancing on a wide front. A mass public meeting of 'Miners and Tenants, Workers of Doncaster, and Labour Voters' was called by the Labour Party Young Socialists at the Stainforth Miners Welfare. It was a meeting full of the authority of our tendency in this area and witnessed Maureen address a room packed to capacity with tenants and union activists, members of the CPGB and loads of young people we'd met from discos and socials and the neighbourhood. She gave an analysis of the current state of the working class nationwide, the loss of social gains, the falling standards of health and wealth against the rising wealth for business and the individual rich. She talked about the past betrayal of the last Labour government and the mass abstention of Labour voters which allowed the Tories to take office again. She talked of the struggle within the Labour Party for socialism, and described some successes.

The picture locally is not so bright however—from the start the LPYS linked up with the socialists in the Dunscroft ward and started to fight for socialism.

We were instrumental in setting up of the Tenants Association to battle against the implementation of the Tory Housing Finance Act. The tenants were behind us—we signed petitions, lobbied councillors, went on demonstrations. But all except five councillors voted to implement the Act. They said that they considered it better that a Labour council should demand the increases than a Tory one. As far as I can see a rent increase is a rent increase whether Tory or labour and the working class still has to pay it.

To continue in this reactionary role the L.P. then dropped the five anti-Act councillors when the next election came up. If we want councillors who represent the people we must go into the Labour Party and make sure that they are selected and tie them to the will of the people by demanding that they be recalled if they do not do this.

Time and time again, we put forward resolutions to end the bans and proscriptions within the LP. These were introduced I believe along with clause 4, part 4, the alleged socialist commitment of the party, and sought to keep members of more socialist parties and socialist groups from joining the party or affiliating to it. At Labour Party meetings, we have constantly discussed political issues instead of concentrating on discussion about streetlights and park benches—there are bodies to deal with these matters.

Eventually the Labour Party became annoyed (to put it mildly) with our activity—they are now in the process of an investigation into the activities of the Young Socialists with a view to getting rid of us. They have already suspended one of our members.

We are socialists—that is why we are not liked—and I point out I am talking about the reaction in our area. As far as we are concerned, the L.P. is supposed to be a socialist party and therefore we have every right to be in it. What we want is more socialists in the party and this is why we have invited you here tonight—to show you how important it is that we all join the party and to get every other member of the working class in the area to take an active part in it too.

What we do not want is for everybody to join and lash out in all directions without knowing where we are all going. We must be co-ordinated, we must work as a socialist team so that we can plan our interventions, we must start to form and function as a regular tendency, with regular meetings.

Between 22 and 24 June there was a major conference in Leeds on Indochina, a teach-in-sing-in, a sort of combined education school, rally and social. I had been invited along to sing. Myself and Jim and John M. from the IMG came along together with some French comrades in his old Morris estate. First off was a film show on Vietnam, some of which was a bit graphic. John fainted, outright, straight off his seat. It was an odd event. The place fair bristled with feminists—bristled? Because the agenda was class struggle, the agenda was Vietnam and the fight of the Vietnamese people, and somehow they couldn't find an edge, though throughout the conference they tried. One of the Vietnamese female delegates at one point made a remarkable attack on them. She declared that the women of Vietnam were not at war with their husbands or with Vietnamese men, but US imperialism! That they were fighting alongside the menfolk 'in solidarity and comradeship for a better future for everyone.' I may have cheered too loudly. Later in the evening I got up to do my spot, and started off with the songs from the pit and stories of the mine. A disgruntled female voice shouted out: 'What do the women of the mines sing, Dave? Are there any songs for women in there?' This caught me attention. 'I'm not a woman, so I tend not to sing the many women's songs from the coalfields of Britain or other parts of the world; its better if women from the mine communities do that, but since you ask ...' I gave them 'Union Women', Ma Molly Jackson's famous song, and 'The Coal Owner and the Pitman's Wife'. Both were well received but not by the group who asked for them.

It got worse; we made the mistake of going back from the conference to a student party. Mainly Leeds students—Big Chris was studying at Leeds and so were a couple of other ex-Ruskin students from the Maoist wing of the movement. Well, the drink flowed and the feminist bristling somehow led to a big argument between me and them or the other way round. In the course of this heated exchange I made the mistake of saying there were some 'despicable tendencies' in the women's liberation movement and I certainly didn't support that movement as a whole, 'only the socialists and working-class elements in it.' 'Despicable?!' How dare I?! I think they tried to make out I was talking about the lesbians. Actually I wasn't, it was them—the middle-class, stuck-up, superior, anti-working class, reactionary cauldron I had meant, but I didn't say so, though I should have done. I was savaged from all sides, by wailing, screaming banshees, and the comrades from the Maoist tendency wilted in the furore and demanded I apologise and give unconditional support to the women's movement. I wouldn't and it got worse. Big Chris demanded to know what was wrong with the word 'despicable', and what did they think it meant? Jim squeezed himself further into the shadows of a corner in the hope nobody would notice him, reflecting on the fact that I was the most pro-women, anti-chauvinist worker he knew, so what might he say if he opened his trap? He later described the scene as being something from a film in which a lone fur trapper had held off a huge pack of starving wolves with a chopping axe. It was nice. I think I developed a reputation as being a male chauvinist pig over at the Leeds campus which lasted many years as a traditional belief. The fact was that the political struggle within the women's movement, which was dominated in its early years by revolutionary socialists, was being eclipsed by a vociferous, reactionary minority who would come to dominate the agenda. Some of the conclusions of this tendency were indeed despicable and ultimately would find themselves in the political bed of ultra-conservative and repressive forces. Worse, they would take women back to a state of victimhoood with separation or calls for more and more draconian repressions from the state. From women asserting their own sexuality, recognising their own sexual demands for and of men, as well as in same-sex relationships, we went now to seeing heterosexuality as almost de facto and of definition unequal and repressive. Male attraction to female was predatory; every male was at base a potential rapist; heterosexuality was in essence a kind of rape. This was a trend which was deeply opposed to notions of sexual freedom, free sex, female sexual promiscuity and adventure. Whereas once militant women would assert the defence of women prostitutes to ply their trade like any other, to demand health and safety regulations, trade union membership, legality, and protection now they would see prostitution solely as abuse. The sexual act between a prostitute and her client, no matter how relatively freely chosen, or how well paid, was still essentially a class transaction; however, it would, according to this viewpoint, be an act of male 'violence'. The right-wing feminist view which came to dominate seen things differently from our female comrades of the early years. It posited that women's social subordination was due to her sexual position and not her economic, class position. For many it meant that the sexual relationship per se between men and women ensured sexual subordination and therefore economic and class subordination. Lesbianism became a political action, a logical and moral conclusion based upon this viewpoint. From these conclusions much else followed. Whereas revolutionary socialist women had defended female nakedness either for money or art or the sheer fun of it and stood boldly against all forms of censorship, now the cry would be that 'pornography', a term which would come to cover almost any representation of a female or females in anything which looked like a position or pose which could be attractive to men, was 'violence against women': 'Porn is the theory— Rape is the practice.' All sexual images of women, no matter how freely entered into and for whatever motive, were miniature acts of rape against females in general. Right-wing, evangelical born-again Christians, repressed and repressive organisations and notions of all sorts found themselves in alliance with feminism, a cause with which before they had only ever clashed with and confronted as the enemy. From images to words in books and themes in plays, cinema and theatre, and on into language. Language became the subconscious desire to rape and oppress women and revealed hidden thoughts and desires. The language, particularly that held and spoken in solidly working-class areas, had to be ruthlessly analysed and purged of all implication— real, imagined or quite mad. Deeply repressive features of 'fundamentalist' religions, aimed at repressing sexuality, found strange new defenders in the shape of the 'radical feminists'. The Islamic veil and the full hejab have become 'liberating' in hiding the female form from the predatory gaze of men, and are defended by this tendency, whereas the militant socialist feminists of the Sixties would have been burning them in the street. With each and every step along the way of this right-wing repressive journey they have called for new laws and new punishments, new prohibitions and new banishments to be implemented by the state, the law and police. They have become the cheerleaders of many deeply repressive measures restricting social and individual freedom, indeed they have to some measure been their initiators.

Witness new laws brought in 2006 which make any sexual relationship entered into while the woman is under the influence of alcohol, such that she cannot remember if she consented to sex or not the night previous, an act of rape. We are not speaking here of an unconscious female and a clear-headed male which clearly would be rape, but to a drunken lady who in the course of her evening has gone to bed with someone. No such law applies to men in that condition, or when both parties are in that condition equally. Such a law is de facto confirmation that the sexual act itself is male-orientated and male-led, the women an unequal and basically reluctant partner, it being inconceivable that she would consent to a one-night drunken stand if she couldn't remember doing so. The fact that thousands of men have experienced exactly the same situation is not legally recognised because a woman cannot 'rape' a man despite doing no more or less than the man. I know from nights when 'the lads' have dragged me off round town with them and on to the local nightclub at Thorne or Fishlake how totally undiscriminating and blindly impervious they became not only to the looks but also to the shape and size of the females they ended up snogging and going home with. I myself have never ever been so drunk, and usually exited stage left into a taxi when it got to that point. I was frequently berated for not having 'scored'. When I pointed out that the women they had scored with had came out of a bearpit, the lads were genuinely shocked. 'That bad?' they asked in genuine amazement. I boasted 'I have never ever been to bed with an ugly woman!' Big Harry was quick to counter: 'Well neither have I, but I've woke up with a few!'

We had produced a Mineworkers' Internationale leaflet for the Durham Gala of the following month, but the Party caught sight of it, and, in the 'comradely' way that they did, they systematically took it apart. 'Yes, yes comrades, the leaflet is lively and is full of knowledge of the mine, and the miners will recognise it, but this is not what is required at this moment of history by a miners' cell of Trotsky's party, a world party of leadership cadres and world experience.' I can hear Kay's French accent even yet, as she sat with her comradely/matey arm around my shoulder . It seems the non-Party people could offer a 'lively' leaflet like this, but we the Party members in the mines must as always 'elevate' our functioning and offer a political lead, not a rank-and-file agitation. So it was that the Miners Cell of the Revolutionary Workers Party (Trotskyist) British Section of the Fourth International–Posadist put out its first leaflet. It was produced at Proletaria Bookshop, Dunscroft, and in typical hectoring fashion demanded that 'The Miners must intervene in the struggle in the Labour Party for the revolutionary programme and leadership.'

Some time before, we had broken contact with our friends and old comrades from the Geordie Cong days—Brian, Irene and Ian. About 1966 they all had become Mormons. Irene had been a Mormon when we first all met her. That church had sunken roots on Tyneside as part of its mission to save the industrial folk of northern England from the ways of wickedness. We were shocked rigid when Brian and Ian, both professed atheist anarchist communists, announced their conversion. They were both Gateshead lads and seemed right enough. But when they went, they went head over heels into the conversion. Gave up drink and drugs, tabs, and coffee and all forms of artificial stimulus. We argued to the point of violent shouting. They told the story of the famous *Book of Mormon*, brought down to Earth by an angel revealed to Ben Smith, who got the whole thing printed up, the original having been on tablets of gold it was a bit too weighty to cart round. 'And where are these sacred tablets now bonny lad?' I asked of Brian. 'Well, David,' he had started saying in a calm voice, with a slight American accent as all Mormons do, 'You won't believe this.' 'Try me,' I suggested. 'The Archangel Gabriel came and took them away again.' 'You were right.'

Ultimately we just ended up slagging them off and being quite nasty, I suppose. 'Never darken our doors again until you abandon this foolishness,' we scolded. And they didn't. But unbeknown to us, they sank themselves deep into the Mormon Chapel and started to climb its hierarchy. Meantime Brian and Ian, who had sung together in a sort of Everly Brothers style, but wrote most of their own material, had discovered that Irene had a wonderful voice, and together they blended the most resonating harmonies. One stormy night we were surprised by a knock on the front door, and there stood two bedraggled hippies—frizzy lang hair, Afghan coats, headbands and guitar cases. It was Brian and Ian. 'You told us not to show up again until we had recanted the religion.' Just looking at them it was clear they had done that all right. What a story they had. They had been welcomed into the Mormon faith, went to live in America in Salt Lake City, became very knowledgeable and got sent back out to preach the revelations. 'We were having five thousand convertions a day in London,' Ian told me. 'Five thousand? Surely not!' I said in horror. Ah, but Mormons can convert deed folk! They take on the identity of any number of corpses, and put themselves through the conversion and confirmation. Their hands are thrust through a gold curtain, and grasped at the other side by one of the church elders—scary stuff. The convert is then a Mormon, not that they know it. This can happen all day, with the same guy standing in for any number of deed punters. 'Wait a minute, you bastards,' I say in sudden realisation. 'You haven't converted Karl Marx have you?'

Mind, *The Book of Mormon*, for those that haven't read it, is somewhat of an enigma. I mean where did it come from really? The whole thing reads exactly like what it purports to be, lost gospels of the Bible. Some modern comedian could make up a fake version of the Bible if he had loads of knowledge and loads of spare time and was an expert on Bible contexts and philology, but some dumb bloke back in the sticks in 1840s America? If it is what it says it is, and say he just found it, not on tablets of gold, but in a trunk somewhere, how and why did it get to the USA? I certainly can't accept that Gabriel hid it like a Xmas present for this Ben Smith to find; if it's a hoax it's one hell of an obscure one. Mind a cynical voice in the other ear asks: 'How much money has this Mormon Temple made over the years, how much money, power and control for the elders of that church?' So maybe the motive wouldn't be too obscure, and for someone raised from the cradle to read nothing else but biblical texts, making another chapter or two in the same style may not really have been that impossible. Anyway, I digress. They passed many an hour giving us the lowdown on the Mormon tabernacle— fascinating stuff. They believe in heaven as a real get-to place, as is hell, and the angels are all real; more than real—they have factions and politics and are of this dimension. The Mormon story of Lucifer's fall from God's right hand is worth retelling. It seems he was kicked out of the heavenly kingdom because he got too big for his boots. He thought he should be God, having served as number two for too long. After his fall with his followers, he began designing an alternative heaven. A place where folk only worked if they wanted to, where an abundance of wealth and goods existed, where laws were nonexistent, where folk kept all things in common, where there was equality, and wars and violence had ceased. Start to recognise it? Communism in its ideal form. Lucifer was a founder of the communist ideology; it was an attempt to challenge God in his heaven, by trying to create and advocate a heaven on earth without all the fawning and preying and giving up to God his due. The communists were the physical agents of the devil. 'Kill a Commie for Christ!' began to take on tangible meaning. Volunteering to fight in Vietnam was to join God's war against the devil and all his legions. It wasn't here that the Deel was the absolute other than God, the opposite, but that he tended towards similarity; it was the sameness that was the problem, a fake copy, not the real thing, which was the danger which had to be rooted out. I was to come across left versions of this 'too similar to exist' theory as I went on, usually in some deadly variation or another. The Red Brigades in Italy, given a choice of which judge to shoot, would shoot the Communist Party judge, and not the rabid right-winger, for reasons similar to Mormon logic. Of course it could be said 'communists' shouldn't be part of the judicial system at all, maybe not the parliamentary system either; that was one view, while others had reasoned that until such time as we change the damn thing it's better make the most of it for the working class.

Still, I was fascinated by the idea of there being factions and tendencies in heaven. I recalled something St Paul had said that 'Even now in heaven there are angels carrying savage weapons.' It brought you back to von Danikin's notion that Jesus had come down from space, and maybe heaven was 'the heavens'. One could see the notion of 'angels' coming from unearthly creatures beaming up and down from some orbiting star ship maybe, and it made sense of a lot of stuff that was otherwise nonsense in big J's sermons—mind it would also have done if he'd taken a pan full of magic mushrooms too, which is also not impossible.

The trouble with the whole Jesus trip was we can't verify a single damn word of what he was supposed to have said. Most folk including me had thought the apostles who wrote down the story had done it contemporaneously, but they hadn't. They came along long after Jesus was gone. None of them actually met him. It was all hearsay, a number of times removed. Worse from the point of view of historic fact, the Jesus movement had been a dangerous rebellious movement. It was important for the authorities to draw its teeth, and perhaps coin the real message into something safer, even supportive of the system rather than subversive to it. The Jesus movement, like many of our communist ones, became subsumed by its opposite, in this case the Roman State. Constantine used it to build an empire and sign God up for his side, repressing his enemies who clung to their ancient Roman pagan gods, and also to suppress both the new and growing cult of Mythras and the secularism they had all previously agreed to, while Jewish Christianity was replaced by Roman Christianity and in all probability lost all but the vaguest outlines of its original cause and purpose.

The Jesus movement was originally a sect of Judaism. The 'true' Gospels which were written by people who knew Jesus and were at his side were all ruthlessly repressed. The Gospel of Mary (Magdalene) for example would have been a fascinating revelation. It survives in the merest fragments, and is based upon revelations which Jesus made to her after his death as well as a record of the man's words and movements when he was alive. Mary is the centre of a huge historic polemic and a number of conspiracy theories. She very clearly was a senior member of his team, if not his wife or close companion as well. Some ancient histories would say they were married and had a son, Judah. Peter bitterly opposed her and wouldn't accept that Jesus would place the spiritual hand upon her rather than him; his gospels were also suppressed, regardless of the fact that he is seen as the earthly head of the church after Jesus, and after successfully defeating Mary's right to accession. The approved Gospels would either write Mary out of history or else present her as prostitute or fallen women, which was cruel and ironic. Peter's gospel is hardly less controversial and too dangerous to survive, arguing that Jesus was never a man but always just God. He never suffered or died on the cross because he couldn't, although he allowed the earthlings to put him through the spectacle—unlike in the accepted version, in Peter's gospel Jesus never demonstrated any pain and never spoke at all during the crucifixion. The Gospel of Philip I believe argued the opposite, that Jesus was just a clever bloke with lots of wonderful ideas but wasn't a God.

Others, like Thomas, also thought Jesus was just a man, who was inspired by God; he had a wife and was born of Mary and Joseph and was just a bloke, no virgin birth, no Gabriel visitations and no resurrection ... Thomas's gospel ought to have been destroyed like the others, but his followers put it in an earth pot and hid it in a cave where two thousand years later it was found, intact at first, until the treasure hunters, thinking it was worthless, had lit at least one fire with some of the precious pages. Thomas was a Gnostic. His gospel, which is the oldest gospel of them all, contains little or no narrative and simply records the word and saying of Jesus. Most of these are like Zen riddles. Your average punter isn't supposed to understand them. It is a creed for mystics and wise men, not everyone and anyone. Another group, of ultra-orthodox Jewish Christians, had said 'Hey, wait on a minute! This was Jesus, he was the Jewish Messiah, he came for us, not you lot, he was a saviour of the Jews and no-one else!' No less than twenty gospels, most of them contemporary were suppressed and the majority utterly destroyed. We only know they existed because the Romans kept a list of the 'heresies' they were suppressing and cleansing from history. Quite fascinating. All we can be sure of is that whatever was left of the story was a sanitised and relaunched version of the truth robbed of any subversion and revolutionary intent and destined to maintain the position of the rich and powerful—something we can say with utter clarity it was never intended to do, whatever its view on sex and virgins, God and heaven was at the same time. All that forebye, Ian and Brian had split as the generation got on down to its thing, shagging in the sunshine and dropping acid and singing rock and roll. Whatever the lure of the tabernacle had been, the glory of Babylon shone stronger, so here they were. Teamed up with Irene, they went on to a storming top of the hit parade, with Neil Young's After the Goldrush, as prelude. A tight-harmony, folky rock sound. Mind, try as they would that was their only number one, but we were so proud of them I actually cried with joy when I seen them performing on TV. Me and Maureen could actually say we used to sing with them, well we did round the fire and that, but also before they formed, as we put on Geordie Cong socials at the Bridge and me and Maureen and Viv Steward got up with them to sing Seekers songs and other folky pop stuff.

Before all that, though, we all descended on Durham Miners' Gala in the July of

1973. We took a busload up from the folk club and stayed with Brian, Ian and Mick, dossing on floors and chairs across the toon. The Right Honorable Harold Wilson was the main guest speaker, with my mate Lawrence Daly. Walter Malt the moderate general secretary dived in with both feet this time, declaring

> I see no reason why the miners should become the storm troops of the TUC. We achieved a great deal by the strike of 1972, but it was a long struggle and the recent voting showed that miners were in no mood to strike again. We must not think that we can do a 1972 every time we take industrial action. That was a once and for all effort—a surprise attack which caught a lot of top people asleep at their posts ...

PIT TALK

2 August 1973. *Pit Talk* is printed. I am thrilled to wee bits by it, though it is not without mistakes. Raph pressed me on definitions and meanings of words, and to try and simplify them I got the technical descriptions and mining operations wrong here and there—nowt like the Posadista bollockses, but still mistakes and spotted at once by me Da and his marras. Still, they enjoyed patiently explaining descriptions I had got wrong, even though their descriptions were the same complex portrayals I had tried to avoid. For all that, my two works, *Pit Life* and *Pit Talk*, were real achievements, I felt. I was left, though, with a mountain of nineteenth-century newspapers, from Liverpool and Durham works, which I refused to abandon, in case they contained some hidden truth, some hidden history I had never yet found. Mouldy and mouse-eaten they remained crumbling away in the remains of the netty ootside until the day I finally left Doncaster, their secrets still unrevealed.

Mick Magahey, probably the most famous communist in Britain, was elected vice-president of the NUM. The national conference of that year passed a resolution for a wage increase of 35 per cent regardless of any government guidelines. A unanimous resolution called for the election of a Labour government committed to a 'true socialist policy', including nationalisation of land and all key monopolies. Lest anyone should doubt which way Mick seen the approaching contest, his statement to the full NEC of the NUM on 28 November 1973 was that: 'It is the miners' intention to smash the government and its pay policy and send Prime Minister Heath on his way down the road.'

In August 1973, international work brigades were being raised all over Europe to go to Cuba to help assist build the country and the revolution. It would be a three-month stint; this year it was the 20th Anniversary Brigade. It was twenty years since the attack on the Montcada Barracks, by Fidel and a couple of carloads of guerrillas. Fidel's car broke down, just round the corner from the barracks. Foolishly, the police started to help them fix it, and they might well have got it working and got away, but the other car full of guerillas came round the corner and that was it. They were arrested and Fidel made his famous 'History Will Absolve Me' speech in the court.

We would receive no wages, but we would be fed and housed and given a fortnight's holiday at the end. We would meantime study the development of the country and visit just about everywhere to see what was going on. Although I like many of my generation were fascinated and thrilled by Cuba, the Party warned of being too spellbound by it. There was for all intents and purposes a legal branch of the RWP(T) in Havana; it was listed on our public literature. But relations with the Fidelistas were often vexed and dangerous. The comrades had been arrested and jailed. The RWP Cuba press had published *Voz Proletaria*, but in April 1961 the press was smashed and the comrades arrested by the 'Official Communist' Partido Socialista Popular. However around the time of the conference of leftist guerrillas and revolutionary movements throughout Latin America, called by the Organizacion Latino-Americana de la Solidaridad (OLAS), Fidel and the others were forced to recognise other complexions of the revolution. MIR in Chile had a Trotskyist tinge but was respected. Mexico was of course the place of exile of Trotsky and his life and murder there had left certain indelible marks on some of the leftist forces there. The relations of Fidel and the others to the Communist Party and the USSR had in any case been complex and stony. Fidel began with his team of armed guerrillas to free Cuba of Batista, the right-wing dictator and friend of the Mafia. He was essentially a democrat; as such for a time he had the backing and support of the CIA. He inclined towards a form of social democracy but with capitalism under state guidance. His guerrilla team however didn't replace the internal movement of the people at large; there were movements among the peasants and within the city working class. Fidel had charged the Cuban Communist Party of the period of being corrupt and collaborationist. However as the revolution progressed, as the influence of Ché and the others came to bear and most importantly the demands of the people impacted upon Fidel, he started to evolve toward the concepts of Marxism and socialism, but he was to be far from orthodox. Cuba had been a revolution of youthful enthusiasm of long hair and beards, of Western-European-looking people, not the grey scriptures of Moscow and Stalin.

However, the greatest impetus to drive Fidel and his team to the left was the overreaction of the CIA and the US state, which imposed stringent boycotts which could only be challenged by closer links to the USSR and its political influence. Ché had come to speak with the Posadist comrades in jail, and had long discussions with them, some of them heated and angry. Ché concluded they were wrong but weren't counterrevolutionaries; this is how inter alia he described it:

> That did happen (the jailing and the smashing of the press); however we consider the Trotskyist party to be acting against the revolution. For example they were taking the line that the revolutionary government is petty bourgeois and were calling on the proletariat to exert pressure on the government and even to carry out another revolution in which the proletariat would come to power. This was prejudicing the discipline necessary at this stage … Let me give another example. They have one of their principal centres in the town of Guantanamo near the US base. And they agitated there for the Cuban people to march on the base— something which cannot be permitted. Something else. Some time ago when we had created the workers' technical committees, the Trotskyists characterised them as a crumb given to the workers because the workers were calling for the direction [self-management] of the factories.

He conceded a little later they had worked for the revolution. They were freed.

Now later when Ché had turned up dead in Bolivia the Party had floated a disturbing set of notions. They denied that it was Ché. For a start, the body had had its hands cut off, the only real positive form of identification. The hands were reputed to have been sent to Cuba where they were buried beneath a monolith. His brother was not allowed to touch the body, and could only view it from some distance. The body was cremated, despite Bolivia being a strictly Catholic country. The comrades had argued that the tin miners, who were the vanguard of the Bolivian people's struggle, had not seen or heard from Ché. The circumstances of his capture, on an open plain, seemed dubious. 'So where is he now?' we asked. 'We think he is dead, but he wasn't killed in Bolivia.' What the comrades didn't tell me was that this was a revised line. In Cuba our comrades had circulated leaflets saying Fidel had had Ché murdered, indeed the suggestion was that Ché was moving politically in the direction of Trotskyism and Fidel had to halt the process. I wasn't to discover this till later, too late, to stop me coming out with the theory that Ché didn't die in Bolivia, and that his hands were not under the memorial. The Cuban officials knew the conclusion of this tale, but I didn't. It was actually little wonder that the comrades giving out the leaflets had been rounded up and jailed; they could well have been lynched for such a suggestion. I knew nothing of this, as I volunteered and was accepted to go and work in the micro brigade in Cuba. I had no idea that the party I was a Central Committee member of had a history of bad blood with the state I was volunteering to entrust my safety and life to. The Union got me leave of absence from the pit. There were two of us, me and Ron Macabe, a branch official and painter from Carcroft workshop. Emma, in a different and future time frame asks, how could I go and leave her, my little daughter, and go off into the shark-infested custard of Cuba? Was it selfish? In these days, we lived for the revolution which was real and imminent. The world was faced with a choice, the continued inhumanity and greed of capitalism, the injustice of imperialism, or humanity, socialism and a world held in common and respect. The world wouldn't change unless we changed it. Emma had become the most precious thing in my life, together with Maureen, but we couldn't be so selfish as to put our own circumstances and loves and preoccupations in front of the plight of humanity. Our comrades were fighting and dying across the globe, other poor souls in their millions, who loved their children too, were dying of basic needs and starvation. We could not close the door and play happy families, shutting out the truth of life in the real world, life outside our doors. We knew too that our trajectory was taking us into greater and greater dangers and soon we would come to a code, that if either one of us got killed in the struggle, the other would then withdraw from revolutionary struggle and devote their time to Emma, because it wouldn't be right for her to give up both parents for the revolution. I can hear her saying, 'Well, that was big of you!' But it did in fact trouble us, and we had discussed it, to make the best choices revolutionary parents could make. In other parts of the world—there but for the grace of God—the choice of who lived and died was either the death squad or the long-range missile. We were lucky to have choices, though we weren't always sure that that state of affairs would continue anyway.

I had never flown before. We had missed a connection flight from Italy, I think, and instead would have to catch a flight in Spain. I was not keen on flying; and the idea of landing in Franco's Spain appealed to me even less, much less. Never mind—it wouldn't involve leaving the airport, I was assured. My first flight was dreadful. I was sick as a dog. The stewardess brought me tea, but then put bliddy cream in it, which made me even sicker. At Madrid airport the flight to Cuba was delayed. In our party were me and Ron, two Irish building workers, and a well-spoken member of TASS, the white-collar section of the engineering union. Accompanying us also was the entire Hungarian weightlifting team. No flight, so because we were to be delayed by 28 hours they were to accommodate us in Madrid. No sir, I did not like that idea at all. Franco had long tentacles and his agents were all over the world. I had been part of a campaign against Spain and the Spanish government; if it is all the same to you comrades, I will sleep on the airport. An official of the Cuban Embassy in England travelling back to Cuba took charge of the whole plane party. He assured me, he could guarantee I would be OK. He collected up everyone's passports into a big bundle, with mine in the middle, and, flanked by the weightlifters, I headed for the passport control. The officials flicked through the pile of passports. Then they pointed to me, indicating that I should step aside from the rest of the party. This led to a big argument with the Cuban diplomat. The officials waved everyone else through, but those who hadn't already gone through wouldn't move, and blocked the aisles up; those who had gone through likewise wouldn't budge. What was said I do not know, but that it was about me was certain. Eventually a senior official arrived and leaned over the passport desk. He looked frequently up at me then down at my passport. Then eventually he waved his hands in the motion, 'All right, all right, go through.' I think I thought I would be whisked out of the group and dragged off somewhere, but I stuck close to the rest. We boarded a bus and headed for a hotel in Madrid. 'So what was all that?' I asked the diplomat. 'Nothing. A problem with your passport maybe,' he said, not very convincingly I thought. That evening everyone headed out for a night round Madrid. 'I am staying put in this hotel,' I told them. The diplomat thought this a good idea, and warned me not to go out, which seemed strange if his passport story was true. By the time we boarded the plane to Havana, I was so keen to get going, get out of Spain, and get on with it, that I positively willed the aircraft to take to the sky. My fear of flying was over.

As we flew over the island in the dark, the evening lights criss-crossed the little land mass in the dark sky and ocean. A revering buzz fell over the plane, as everyone—including returning Cuban fishermen, incredibly learning about deep-sea and coastal fishing from the Spanish because Cuba had not had a proper commercial fishing fleet under Batista, and visitors and us El Brigadistas—peered out of the windows. We landed into the pitch-black stillness of Havana. The heat and steam was rising from the runways, into the cricket-clicking night, and there was the rustle of trees nearby. The main team had landed the day before with a great plane all to themselves. They came down the gangplank with a banner which read 'We Come Not As Tourists But As Fellow Workers'. Unfortunately a number of them fell down, as they rushed with their cameras to get in front of the non-tourist banner and take a photo. Me and Ron headed for the barrack-like building which housed the terminal. Inside it hung a huge photo of Ché in his beret, smoking a cigar. People were milling around, including the returning Cuban fishermen with armfuls of things they couldn't get at home—radios, fans, tape-recorders. Customs were pulling folk over and checking their imports. A uniformed man beckoned me and Ron to a side door. We went in and there was a reception for us late-arriving 'comrades', with a little Cuban band singing Guantanamera. We were handed white rum, in crushed ice served in coconut shells, and although we were knackered and it was late, we supped gladly as the cigar smoke and laughter and music just filled very molecule with excitement. I felt like I had arrived at home. Cuba—who could believe it? Cuba!! Next we were taken onto the campemento bus through the sleeping countryside, toward our camp. Telegraph poles made from unshaped tall trees, wobbly and higgly piggly. Cuban telegraph poles—why should they be perfectly round? Through the little villages; people were still awake, watching TV, and because of the heat of the night they sat in their front gardens, in their armchairs, watching their tellies through the open windows of their own houses. We arrive at the camp, to find it sleeping an exhausted sleep from the day's labour, which we have missed. We are told where are bunks will be. There are no lights; it is pitch black. I find my bunk, but then need a piss and need to find my way back into the outside, to the toilet bay. I grope my way to the door and my hand lands on a fat, slimy, cold splat stuck on the wall, which then splats on my bare foot and I stifle a cry, but then realise it's either a lizard or a giant fat frog and I am not actually hurt. Soon I am drifting deep, deep in sleep and still feel the flying sensation, still smell the cigar smoke, feel the heat and the humidity, deeper into sleep.

TRABAJO

I was awoken by the sound of revolutionary music being blasted over an intercom system, the first word I learned in Spanish, *trabajo*. This song would call us to work every morning, *blae-blae-blae trabajo*, and we would fall from our bunks singing it, although we never made out the other words. Something of my early years in the cadets came back to me, as we were fitted out with boots and lined up for work. The whole camp comprised young people and workers from all over Europe. Ours, the 7th Brigade, was a mix of north Europeans and Scandinavians, mainly because there wasn't enough of us to form a national brigade, and also because as it turned out we were very similar. So the 7th included two Swiss, tall bonny lads with long, flowing locks at whom the girls would shout 'El Beatles'. There were two Dutch, one of whom we christened Yo-Yo, because of the apparent number of times he made that sound, the other an Indonesian, who was to work with such ferocity with the machete felling the tall grass around the citrus trees that the Cubans called him 'El Samurai'. There were two Irish building workers, one of them a giant of a man, a Cockney building worker, a chippy called Malcolm Baxter, a fat Brummie YCL bloke, the long-haired, quiet-spoken TASS lad from the IMG, us two miners, Austrians and Germans. There were three Italian work brigades. The contrast between the brigades couldn't have been more clear. The Italians by and large with exceptions were students, there we thought more to enjoy the view than support the revolution. They had been given the job of working in the fields with the machete, felling the elephant grass which would otherwise have blocked out the sun shining on the citrus trees and groves. The girls wore little headscarves tied back, bikini tops, short shorts and boots. As we lined up the Cuban behind the desk would ask 'Ocupación?' The reply would come 'estudiante/a' and they were given a machete. 'Ocupación?' 'Studento.' Machete, go to the fields. Then me: 'Ocupación?' 'Coal miner—carbon minero.' They hand me a shovel—building site truck.

The big Irish labourer behind me says 'Studento'; they give him a shovel anyway, to laughs from the queue. Yo-Yo gets a shovel too. It came to Ron's turn: 'Ocupacion?' 'Painter,' says Ron, and they hand him a shovel. 'No,' says Ron doing an up and down motion of a paintbrush, 'I a painter.' The Cubans laugh. 'Companero, you are here for the mineros sindicato, I do not think they paint the walls in the mineo,' and he is pushed towards the truck protesting.

We got to the building site. We had seen the housing, some not too bad; others, the poorest, straw shacks with mud floors. We were building modern flats and modern houses. This would be the battlefront in the revolution we had joined. The trucks were old Soviet army wagons, and we stood up in the back, hanging on to roof rails and side rails, singing. I knew the song Ewan and Peggy had written as guests of the OLAS conference, 'The Compañeros', depicting the struggle of Fidel and Ché, mentioning all the epic battle scenes and place names. This one went down a storm: On Compañeros, Against Batista. Our comrades from Switzerland sang a cuckoo song, which had the refrain 'Cuckoo, cuckoo!' and a bit of yodelling in it; we all joined in with that one. The building of collective towns in isolated areas was a phenomenon of the revolution. They replaced the peasant shacks miles from everyone else, ending the isolation of the peasant, even the individual family tenant farmer. Now communities of land workers were being born, performing collective toil on collective land, with rationalisation of field work, so the peasant would work as a proletarian, side by side with others like him, sharing tasks.

The building site in the first early rays of the sun cast long shadows and reluctant bodies started to lift wheelbarrows, set going the cement mixers, start to shovel in the great mountains of sand, pebbles and lime, run with the wheelbarrows full of cement, carry the prefabricated steel rod frames onto their benches, and shovel the wet concrete over the rods to cast reinforced concrete for the buildings. It took a while to realise that speed here wasn't the most important thing. While I worked like hell slinging the wet concrete into the bays, it was invariably splashing down the sides and onto the floor. The Cubans came and told me 'No rapido!'—slowly. They would rather have half the blocks completed without spilling precious materials, than twice the number with waste. Of course the US blockade was biting all over the island, and materials were scarce. I worked often in the sand heap, digging the rock-hard sand into wheelbarrows for others to carry away. I tried with real effort not to keep anyone waiting.

People would run with the huge wheelbarrows, up the ramp to the concrete mixer and throw the handles up to tumble the sand and pebbles into the tumbler, up and down, hours on hours in the sun. On one occasion one of the Austrian female comrades just collapsed running up the ramp and her wheelbarrow fell over to the side. She was dragged into the shade and we tipped water over her head and put a wet kerchief round her neck. While she recovered another comrade took up her wheelbarrow. On the third-floor or fourth-floor roofs of the building the concrete would come flying up the scaffold lift in a wheelbarrow. The roof toppers, working in the blazing sun without a wisp of a breeze, would grab the barrow and run with it, tipping it out, and others with rakes would spread it, liftful after liftful after liftful. On the rock floor the foundations were being laid, inch by inch with, jack hammers—big old Russian jack hammers probably constructed for the Stakhanovite programme. Drills were my business, but with these I was like a dwarf playing a piano. I would bind the starter trigger with wire so it kept going and I could use both hands to hold the bloody thing, lifting it up horizontal to try and find breaks in the rock.

I used to say 'You know, comrades, you can get little drills just as good as these.' 'Good drills, Soviet drills.'

Our production meetings would allow us to put forward complaints, suggestions; 'Si, si. Good ideas.' But they rarely went anywhere. I tried to introduce some pit wit into the process on the building site. Every day I worked in the sand heap I tried to find a hard floor from which to shovel; all you ever came to was soil on which the sand had been laid, so you bent your back digging into the middle of the heap. Every production meeting I would suggest we lay metal sheets on top of the grass and soil, and then tip the sand and other minerals on top of them. No sheets? OK, then let's lay large planks of wood into a wooden raft and drop the stuff onto that. 'Good idea!' But still every day the sand and gravel would arrive and be dropped straight onto the grass and soil. Regarding the rock areas into which the foundations would be hewn, I suggested they map them all out in advance, then bore and fire them to break up the rock. It would speed production up 600 per cent at least. Good ideas. All noted down. Never materialised.

As we worked we noticed things which could be improved; as workers we couldn't help it. After two weeks, we asked Jose what he did.

'I am the compressor man,' he replied.

Right. What does the compressor man do?

'He works the compressor, for the picks and compressed air machines.'

Very important it was, but all he actually did was turn it on, then he stood all day leaning on it. It was not a happy comrade who heard us suggest to the production meeting that after turning the compressor on and making sure it was running, he took a turn or two with the big drills.

On the completion side of the site, scores of comrades worked with buckets and brushes whitewashing the buildings. Our comrade Mike from TASS suggested: 'Look, why don't you spray the whitewash on the houses, pump it on?' 'Si, si, good idea, but we have no pumps or sprays.' Frustrated, Mike said: 'I'll make you one.' He set to with drawings and a simple plan started to emerge. I think it revolutionised this part of the building process. He got one huge diesel drum, and cut the end off it. Then from the centre of the end, he chiselled out a circle and attached a plunger to it, a hole in the bottom of the drum with a pipe and crude spray attached, and: 'Comrades—we have a whitewash pump!' You pressed down on the handle, which depressed the inner circle into the liquid which forced the whitewash out of the spray—and eureka! The Cubans were delighted. Copies of his drawing went all over the country, modified a little so it all fitted snugly and didn't leak, and all bar one comrade could now be released to work further down the production line.

Mind, the production techniques were crude, for want of materials. The scaffold was built of wood spars and trees, in many cases tied together, and the lift carrying the wheelbarrow full of concrete up the side of the building was precarious to say the least. All the wood shuttering had to be salvaged from the concrete as it set and all nails saved, hammered straight and used again. You never saw a new nail. This wasn't choice of course, this was the Yankee blockade.

But some things, like refusing to work in the rain, were cultural and antisocial. At the first sign of rain, off they would go into shelter for the day. Our comrades actually picked up one of the Cuban building workers and carried him up the ladder, putting the hammer and nails in his hand, while the gentle rain fell on him. After a while he got the joke, and urged all his comrades to join him. 'Work in the Rain!' was the new revolutionary slogan, but it was greatly resisted. Part of Cuba's revolutionary problem was it was an agricultural economy, but revolutions were supposed to be based on the industrial proletariat—that was what comrade Lenin had said. Indeed there were Trotskyist groups all over the world who denied Cuba's socialist existence because it was based upon the peasantry, yet here it was. Part of the reason for the international work brigades was to infuse proletarian traditions and experience into raw Cuban workers taking up industrial toil for the first time. One day a big articulated lorry with a large trailer in tow pulls up laden with cement in great heavy sacks. We form a chain, marching forward. Two on the lorry lift the sack and drop it onto your shoulder, amid a cloud of cement. Like a fireman's lift the weight falls across your shoulders and back and you set off at a pace, to throw it off, and drop it as soft as you can, letting it drop first on your knee and then your foot, and then to the floor. One after another, forward and forward, bag and bag. Many of the comrades from other teams watched in a mixture of astonishment and respect as our 7th Brigade, men and women, boys and girls, took this punishment for hours, some simply wilting by the side and collapsing in a heap exhausted. Our number diminished, our ranks thinned, we carried on, covered in cement, hair matted, eyelids red raw, noses blocked with cement, stripped to shorts and boots. It was like two or three shifts in succession on the tailgate rip. We would not yield, though. This was our battlefront in the international class war. We stuck it out until the last sack was stacked, and a great round of applause was raised from everyone on site. Then with our skin peeling and burning off our faces and backs, we sprayed ourselves off with hosepipes. I filled one of Mike's drums with water to the brim, stripped off naked and got into it, totally immersing myself under the water two or three times. I could see this stuff being the crudest available and doubted it had ever had any health checks . At one of the production meetings, Raul Castro and the site committee turned out to tell us we had broken all site records for amounts of concrete laid on one week, indeed although this site's scales were lower than the ones in the rest of the country, we had matched many of them too. They actually mentioned me, for my speed with the shovel, and other comrades' non-stop toil with the wheelbarrow. This was supposed to be congratulations at the end of our stint on the rough work, on roof tops and construction as such. The system allowed us to take a turn on something less arduous. Following this high-level praise, murmurs were heard among the ranks, saying we should volunteer to stay on this work two more weeks: 'I propose that the 7th Brigade stay on construction and roof top work for a further fortnight.' 'Viva!' shouted the team, 'Viva!' and we stamped and cheered. Three days later in the blazing sun, they were muttering 'Which daft twat proposed staying on this game?' And I would counter: 'Which daft twats didn't suggest letting other people have a go as well?'

The principle organ of popular power in Cuba was the Committees in Defence of the Revolution (CDRs). More than half of the population belong to these. Originally they were local defence units. In these committees the whole population—50 per cent of the membership is female—children, young people, and men intervene. Established on an area-by-area basis, they cover such things as public health, sanitation, care of the communities, sport and culture etc. They elaborate the national plan and administer its implementation. On the other hand, Fidel was general secretary of the Cuban Communist Party, the head of Cuba's armed forces, president of the Council of Ministers and the president of Cuba; his brother Raul is his deputy in each of the positions. Just which way the view of the CDRs roll to or from the bureaucratic head is a question of hot conjecture.

I had gone to Cuba resolving that I wouldn't mention my vegetarianism. I reasoned that they had enough to do, trying to construct a socialist society and feed themselves in the middle of a blockade by the USA and its allies, without having to take care of my particular choice of diet. I had also figured I could manage whatever the food was like. I had not banked on the paucity of the diet. Breakfast time I usually managed with dry bread, sometimes jam, big mugs of Cuban tea and sugar. There were always oranges. Lunchtime we would come back at 12.30 and usually just collapse from sheer exhaustion on the bed; hunger is soon purged out of you with hard work and constant heat. Most of us would grab a shower in one of the open bays, men one side and women the other, before climbing back into the trucks, and that would be it. Others would queue, stripped to the waist, waiting for a turn before going off to grab something to eat. On one occasion as I came up to the end of the queue and stood before the shower. The occupant turned round and I was presented with a statuesque bronzed Cuban woman, naked of course down to her bare feet, long black hair down her back, rubbing herself with a sponge and smoking a big cigar.

Seeing my surprise and widening her eyes, she says 'You want the cigar?'

'No, compañera.' I much admired this comrade as she slung her towel over her shoulder and walked stark naked and wet across the yard towards the huts. Around 4 p.m. would come *merienda*, fruit juice and cake. I figured I could eat the cake but there was never enough of it for me to stock up on.

We would arrive back from the site at 6 p.m., ravenous, and resolved to eat whatever the hell was poured or dropped onto the metal dish as we lined up. The meat-eaters were struggling almost as bad as me. Shark soup didn't appeal somehow. The black beans swimming in a black soup might well have been highly nutritious, but they looked like the numerous cockroaches which seemed to share our toilet and bathing space. I had resolved that shite! I would eat this black bean and convince myself. I would comment on how good they were. Then I took a bite into the hard shell, and a white gooey substance poured out. It was still cockroaches, and I couldn't eat that in a million years.

The Cubans used everything they had as efficiently as they could, so bananas were a staple food, thank God. Crisps of various sizes were made from them, fried up like sliced tatties, dried out like dates, sliced on bread. I think they saved my life, as my weight began to fall. We used to trade: one bowl of ice-cream could be swapped for three bottles of beer with the Italians, so we usually ended up with four or five bottles. Also, each morning you got a big cigar and a packet of cigarettes as you got in the truck. A big cigar could go for two bottles of beer, so we managed of an evening to put together a bevy. One morning, news went round the 7th Brigade and especially the British contingent that we were to have potatoes for dinner; the news was greeted with jubilation. In fact, it wasn't a tattie as we knew it, but a big, misshapen, stringy object, though certainly of the genus spud. We wolfed it down coated in Cuban butter, and then set off trading for everyone else's; this time we traded beer for food, a switch which baffled everyone. Weeks later as we toured the isle on an educational and cultural study, and visited folk in remote rural and mountainous and coastal districts they laid on the best they had for us, which was usually chicken and boiled rice. I ate the boiled rice. Sometimes it would be chicken and boiled rice twice a day, but this we recalled was a feast for the Cubans and they were giving us the very best of what they had. I frequently would take the plate with the chicken on, and then wrap the bird up in a serviette and give it to one of the women serving or working in the kitchen, 'por los ninos'. I was aware I would contaminate some of the rice with the chicken juices, but shite—I had serious choices to make here and, anyway, how much bliddy dry boiled rice could I consume? At other times I would pretend to have a bad belly, something which was growing increasingly not difficult, and just take a plate of oranges and bananas. On one glorious day we descended from the mountains to some holiday beach where they prepared 'lunch' for us. Troughs of ice-cold beer lay in a bath of ice cubes and my God, it was chips, real potato chips. I stood in the queue slavering and impatient, as a group of middle-class English tourist girls in their little bikinis walked up and started talking to us. I was implacably dedicated to the task at hand—getting fed, and with chips. As I got my tray of chips one of the young pretty things reached over to take one.

'Fuck off!' I screamed, and held my fork in a manic grip as if to stab her eyes out. I think I ran off like Ben Gun in Treasure Island and found a secluded spot in which to devour the lavish fare with haste and appreciation.

I was told the girl had asked: 'Is he a bit crazy?'

And one of the lads had responded: 'No, I think he's starving.'

If my memory serves me right, whereas at other times we would have hogged the beer trough, and snatched handfuls of bottles, this time we gathered around the chip serving dish and waited for leftovers. The cook just handed us the big metal bowl and we piled into it like a flock of seagulls. Me and Ron climbed back up into the mountain, a steep hike and climb up, up, until the bay and the swimming pool and the bar are like distant postcard photos. In the cool of the forest by a spring, we strip back down to our trunks and lie back for a bit sunbathe. I have smeared myself like a chip from heed to toe with sun oil so as not to get burned if I doze off. The toils of recent days and weeks start to drift by. A warm feeling of sunlight on my face and my body. That orange, friendly glow through closed eyelids. Muscles relax. I am drifting off. I hear in the distance a rhythmic buzz of Ron snoring. I also, on the fringe of consciousness, hear sticks breaking, wood breaking, branches breaking, all growing louder, then suddenly it darkens and is suddenly cool. I hear a slight whistling noise and open my eyes to see two great buzzards, with colossal wingspans, swooping down in their bombing run, after having crashed their way through numerous branches in their descent. They are coming in for the kill on two Gringo bleached white emaciated bodies obviously on the verge of death.

'Wa!' I yell, jumping up, 'We're alive, we're alive!'

'Wa!' Ron jumps up and then dooks doon again as the buzzards peel off to the left and soar a little higher, before coming back again to be sure we weren't really on our last legs. Ron joked that they must have smelt me cooking, and thought this a sacrifice or something. Bastards. I'm sure that fucker was licking its lips as it swept toward me. Back on the campamento, our 7th Brigade had some exotic members, besides the two Dutchmen, 'Yo-Yo' and 'El Samurai', mentioned earlier. A Venezuelan girl called Lopey was particularly beautiful, with huge brown eyes and big glasses. There was also a moody Spanish girl, with an amazing figure squeezed into a T-shirt with long black (obviously) Spanish hair, who was the daughter of one of the colonels. I never figured out how that worked, since she was here with the approval of Franco's government. I had foolishly brought some Posadist pamphlets in Spanish with me to show to the Cubans. I had given her one, and from then onwards she considered me with grave suspicion. Raul Castro, who oversaw the camp, sent for me and asked if I had more copies as he would like to read them too. I gave him what I had, and of course never saw them again, although I think he must have read them, but then maybe he had read Posadas before. Two German blokes were both communist factory workers. Tania, six foot plus, was a Russian Belgian, quietly spoken, but fiery, thin and sexually explosive. We were a brigade but we welded into a gang and became close friends, choosing each others' company, or most of us anyway. Ron had not been long in getting a companion. After the first two weeks we held a fiesta on the camp, with great traditional drum bands and Cuban music, and lashings of rum, which the Cubans of course call 'ron'. Ron was a great source of amusement for that reason. He got dragged off into the female hut that night. Next morning, as he rolled out of the girl's bunk, he ran a gauntlet of women trying to drag him into theirs. 'Eh, Ingles!' they shouted. Ron fled, but returned the following evening, and the following evening. I don't know how many bunks he got through but he never seemed to expend as much energy as we did on the site, saving himself for the service role in the evening, or so it was alleged.

Every evening at dusk we went through the meticulous ritual of searching every inch of the bunk, and its mosquito net, for the little stingers. Then we would fold the net down round the bunk and tuck it in, for later when we would return in the pitch black, then make as small a space as possible, to crawl under into the bunk and hopefully leave them outside the net.

One night we had been abed about two hours when one of the big Irishmen was heard jumping around and shouting 'A scorpion, a scorpion in the bed!' Well, we rolled out from under the nets, and with a couple of torches patrolled the bed and bunk and floor and pillows and everything else we could find where a scorpion might be have scuttled, but we couldn't find it. And we all returned to bed. Next morning in the full light of day, there, squashed to death on the Irishman's mattress was the biggest, nastiest ugliest looking creature you ever saw. Like a giant cockroach, but brown and oval with huge mandibles sticking out in front. 'Did it bite you?' I inquired. 'Bite me? It kicked me up the arse!' he replied. Apparently this thing eats coconuts and eats its way from the outside in, right through that shell. Once we knew this, the Irishman's skull became the centre of scrutiny until he got sick of the same joke, and started to stick his chin out, a sure sign he was about to thump you. I decided to keep this sleeping beauty and bring it home. Knowing how the customs were about importing odd-looking insects, deceased or not, I cut the top off an empty body talc bottle, stuck the dearly departed in there and then sat the top back on. Stuck back in a little poly bag it looked like a talc powder container.

On site we were cracking on. One of the English building workers, a Cockney sparrow character, had taken over the steel-fixing on site. He had brought a pair of pliers with him, as opposed to the bent piece of steel the Cubans were using to nip and twist the wire round the steel rods. On one day he did more steel than 130 Italians together. This had more to do with commitment and skill and perhaps the pliers than with country of origin, but relations between us and the Italians were not good.

We would sneak off the base at night and head for some little scruffy cantina, where we would sup owt they had available. It was like a scene from one of those old black-and-white westerns—the ghost town, with the wooden shacks. One big lang, dusty shack was this cantina, severely depleted in most things. I chose a bottle of wine; it's warm, and tastes of blood. You also have a speed game with the flies. Keep your thumb over the neck of the bottle, then throw the bottle up to your gob and take your thumb away to get your mouth over the top of the bottle and take a long, disgusting swig before the flies dive in. You think you have succeeded, then you take the bottle away from your mouth with your thumb over the neck again. Inside the neck of the bottle, a cram of about five big flies. Next time you take a swig, they all sail to the bottom, and when you take the bottle from your lips again there are five big flies floating on the wine, and another five big flies sitting in the neck. When half of the bottle is flies and half is wine, you have to give up—the volume of the flies afloat in the wine blocks the exit of any more wine. They have won. You leave them the bottle, which is then squatted by every crawly flying thing in the vicinity. The companeros suggest putting the cork back in the bottle for revenge, and this starts a huge argument about justice for bugs. Meantime the others have chosen gut-rotting, head-bursting hooch, made from something like aniseed, but we always got up in the morning no matter how rough we felt, and we usually let the hard work and sweat drain it out of us.

Many Italian comrades would either booze it up in the huts, or sneak out and head to distant hotels, but then lie abed in the morning and not work. The bunks were double bunks, side by side, line on line. One morning, a whole hut near enough of Italians were knocking; their trucks stood empty and waiting to go. One of our big Irish builders charged into their hut and shoulder-charged the nearest bunk which toppled over and started a domino effect, with bunks falling over all over the place. 'Get out of your beds, you're in a socialist country!' he shouted. It was a bit of a strange message, but I think the Italians translated it OK.

Meantime, just to show there was no nationalist element in this division I had taken up with a young Italian girl called Maria. We had got to grips on the back seat of the bus taking us from some farm visit, then I ended up in her bunk in her hut. Quite regularly as it turned out. Until that is, I came down with the Cuban crud as we called it. Terrible wicked stomach cramps were accompanied by sudden flushing diarrhoea which emptied your bowels and half your intestines in one fall and almost without notice. You just ran to the nearest bush, normally because you wouldn't make it to the toilet, which anyway was just the hole in ground you squatted over. It was no good—a trip to the strict-looking, mirthless-looking nurse was inevitable. Cubans were in the first full flush of antibiotics, and they used them for everything, always administered with a needle. I might have known it would be a needle. 'OK,' she says, 'drop the pants.' So I pulls down the pants and bends over. I am waiting for the stab, and pain, and am trying to think about something else. There is a silence, and nothing happens. I look around, and she has her arms folded and is looking curiously at me.

'Why you do this?'

'What?' 'Why you bend over like this?' 'I don't know, I thought that's what you do.' 'No, no,' she says, and while I am standing up, still with my shorts round my ankles, she stabs me in the buttock with the needle. Why did I bend over? I thought that's what you did when you got a needle in your bum. On reflection I think she must have thought I thought some sort of bizarre sexual practice was about to take place. The estate we were building, Los Narangjos, was a model housing estate, set in countryside. It was certainly better than the houses and flats we lived in at home, and of course much better than the accommodation most of the Cubans were living in. Troops of them would come on an evening, with their families, and tell us they were going to live here—this was the house they were getting. Could you slack, when you knew that? The houses would be built with everything complete—wardrobes, kitchens, TV; it was part of the education programme that every Cuban family would have a TV. The floors were tiled in little wooden blocks.

One of the easier jobs we got after the double stint of the roof tops was laying the floor, and better still just clearing the splatter of cement from the wood. This I was doing with a young Austrian girl, kneeling down in me shorts, on hands and knees, with the trowel, just painstakingly crawling along, filing the hard cement off the floor. I became aware that girl was now standing up, and was suddenly speechless and staring in shock. I followed her line of gaze, and there about one foot from my leg was a scorpion in full charge, antlers raised and in a nosedive for me leg or further up the shorts. Instinctively I hit it with the trowel, and instinctively its tail whipped up and stung the handle of the trowel just above me fist. It kept stinging the handle as I released my grip and let it fall to the floor. It was dead—most of it; parts of it still twitched and stung. It was a reaction which I would not have chosen to make, if time had permitted me a choice.

A Cuban worker came in, and told me: 'No, its not aggressive, it sting you, your throat swells up, you cannot breath, you go unconscious, we make little hole in your throat, so you can breath, then you OK again, its not aggressive.' Boy was I relieved, though I think he meant lethal rather than aggressive.

In the evenings after work we would have visits and lectures. On the camp in the big assembly hall the roof was supported on brick pillars. Huge windowless chest-level squares of space interspaced the brick trelliswork. In this place, the whole Brigada 20th Aniversario was assembled to hear the veterans of the guerrilla campaign. They spoke in stirring terms of the struggle, and at regular intervals people felt moved to leap to their feet and shout 'Viva! Viva!' Until that is a large Cuban frog leapt through the windowless space and splatted around the revolutionaries from Europe, who leapt on their seats or screamed and ran, until the dissident frog, having amused himself enough by panicking much of the assembly, left back into the evergreen. The veterans looked on unmoved by this; one presumes they had encountered European revolutionaries before. One Havana visit to the National Museum of the Revolution was very enlightening. In the room devoted to Jose Marti was a revelation. Marti had been a great revolutionary and poet, probably one of the finest writers in the Spanish language. His poem *Guantanamera* was banned by the government, although a simple though beautiful love song about that island, had, set to music, become a great symbol of the Cuban revolution. He was one of the authors of the great anti-Spanish colonial uprising of 1893 but was killed in the Battle of Dos Rios. In a glass case were some of his possessions; his pocket watch was made in Goole! Two amazing things strike you about this. One, that there were watchmakers in Goole, which of course was an important seaport in the nineteenth century. But two, the great poet and revolutionary had in all likelihood, some time on his travels, been there. My delighted exclamation broke the silence of the museum, but nobody else could see what the excitement was about. I had earlier discovered that Goole was the centre of a number of serious port rebellions and revolutionary ferment, although it had retired to quiet obscurity.

Another discovery in the Natural History Museum was in the butterfly room, where the Swiss lads confided that their image of an Englishman was one in a tweed jacket, and corduroy pants tucked into checky socks wearing brogue shoes, with a trilby, and a butterfly net, catching butterflies in green meadows and flowery pastures. An eccentric sort of chap, who probably smoked a pipe and in the heat of argument would say things like 'Now steady on there, my good fellow.' I told them they had been reading too much Sherlock Holmes. In the succession of trays we found boxes and boxes of the most unbelievably beautiful butterflies, which illustrated, yes, the beauty of nature and how diverse its forms, but also the selfish idiocy of fools who would stick a pin through it and try and render it an inanimate stamp collection.

That evening we walked around the city, the pitch-black still night a backdrop to a sea of colour and noise, car horns, the smell of crude petrol fumes, wisps of cigar smoke, cooking, overhead balconies where shouted conversations and laughter echoed to the streets below. This is a living city, poor and collapsing for a lick of paint and plaster, but a vibrant old bastard with a fire in her belly. Overhead the one-time electric adverts for this or that product now carry revolutionary slogans. This one hailing the Twentieth Anniversary, and that one the heroes of the revolution Martí, Ché, Castro, ... O' Higgins! That drew a loud shout from the Irish contingent. In surviving little cafes, and in the little bars, stood great big flagons of golden beer, which required a sort of coalman's twist to lift it from table up to your elbow to support it then hit your mouth or the glass with the poured contents. Cerveza grande. We were travelling back from a visit to a nut-and-bolt factory, and I was in avid conversation with the dark and sensuous Tania, who I fancied the arse off. I had tried to casually drape my arm along the back of the seat and round her shoulder, but given the respective height difference it wasn't going to work. I was encouraged by the fact that she had slumped down into her seat and pulled her knees up onto the seat in front and so was at the same sort of head height as me.

'Dave,' she says, 'what you call it when two people ...' She makes a gesture of her two hands interlocking and clumping into each other. 'Oh,' says I hopefully, 'well, fucking.' 'Ah,' she says, 'I like to fuck this man Ron very much!'

I stands up. 'Ron!'

'Si, senor?'

'It's for you,' and we swap places on the bus. Ron and Tania became regular camaradas, although politically we continued to talk the hind legs off all the donkeys in Cuba.

One of the industries abandoned by the fleeing capitalistas as Fidel took over the country was a huge crocodile farm. This now did little else than pose as a swamp full of wood for the tourists, until a lump or two of meat was hurled into the mire, when a chorus of castinets chime out as teeth gnash and bodies roll. The thing originally fuelled the vain and mentally impoverished in the handbag and shoe departments of the depraved. With the rise of hippyism and general awareness of unnecessary cruelty as well as widespread anger at lavish displays of wealth, the business had hit the skids. Nobody wanted the skins of these ancient creatures, thank God. But since they were still an asset, here they sat, just basically lazing around like their owners had done before the revolution. I asked, in an attempt to be Bolshevik and hard-nosed, if the creatures couldn't be eaten by hungry peons. I was told the meat of the crocodile was an acquired taste, which indeed was something I could weel believe, and even then only the middle section of its tail area could be eaten. This I was told, de-boned and sliced like an eel, could be grilled, for a very long time. Coming away from the swamp we were puzzled to see a crocodile standing surrounded by a host of Italian brigadistas, who were having their photos taken posing by the great beast. It was clearly very much alive, though rooted to the spot. It snapped its jaws and tried to lift its head. We looked at each other in bewilderment. I was with one of the big Irishman*, and my guts were starting to heave at the spectacle. I assumed its tail was manacled to a tree or something—its back legs were clearly immobile, maybe shackled. Nothing would prepare me for the shock as we came upon the crowd and their trophy. The great crocodile was nailed to the floor, with a big circus tent style wooden stake, which had been hammered through its back and into the ground beneath. This for no other purpose than to entertain the visitors and have them take photos. As the horror hit me, a big Italian lad posed with his foot on the stake and his hands on his hips. I lost my temper in a blaze of anger, and grabbing his crooked arm flung him from the beast. He didn't know how to take it at first, thought perhaps I was having some joke, but he soon realised I wasn't as I fucked him up and down dale as all the cowardly torturing bastards in Gods heaven. He ran at me, and I squared up to thump him, but the big Irishman give him a firm thud in the chest with both hands in a violent push which took him off his feet and onto his arse. Soon there was a melee of bodies pushing and shoving, kicking out and thumping thin air mainly, rolling in the mud and wrestling in headlocks and throws, as the resentment of months and the horror of the scene combined into an explosion of pent-up frustrations and temper. A few bodies came close to the crocodile, but weakened and obviously dying it didn't think it appropriate to snap a little vengeance as arms and legs and heads came within eating distance. On the buses, lined up to take us on the next stop, the fury continued. The Cubans were quite angry and genuinely mystified. 'Its just an animal!' they kept saying. 'But its not a human, just an animal.' They even suggested a crocodile couldn't feel pain. Only life and death. This was not one our happiest memories of Cuba.

One special evening we were to visit the famous Tropicana Club in Havana. This was the spectacular 1930s big Cuban night out which time had left behind. It was a sort of social museum, a monument to the mildly degenerate, a huge nightclub, with girls with big bunches of feathers sticking out of their bums, or stuck up on ceilings on swings, a cabaret of colour, a Busby Berkeley spectacular, like a Sunday night at the London Palladium but five times bigger. To middle-class eyes, the proletarian custom of dressing up in suits and shirts and ties to go out is an odd one, but one which was dominant during this period. Knowing we were off to a posh nightclub for the evening, we prepared as we would a Saturday night at home. Perhaps it was the filth of the workplace, the rags or overalls during the working week, which made us transform in our own time into different people, dresswise anyway. Perhaps in addition it was to mark the end of that alienated self, the work self, and the freeing of the weekend self. In Doncaster when we first landed, there was little tradition of folk going away on holiday; instead the men would wear their suits every day, even though they visited much the same pubs and streets. It marked out a difference, at funerals and weddings too; it was the free self who attended. Also, at union meetings held on a weekend you were expected to dress as smartly as others did for the chapel. So we readied ourselves and rushed about to the showers. However, two things were happening. One was a torrential tropical rainstorm, magnificent in its deluge and cleansing power, which as it rushed downward in a torrent it dragged cooling air with it. Forked lightening crashed down from the skies, and advanced on us like an army from the gods. In fact there was much god-like in the whole thing—or we thought that until the power went off: no hot water then no water at all. We sat on the beds in the nude, or with towels wrapped around us, waiting our turn. Some, half-shaved, cursed and swore at the heavens. Darkness fell on the camp. 'Sod this,' I says, and 'spaghetti bolognaise.' I took me soap and walked out into the downpour. A few feet from the block, I started to get showered. The soap didn't foam too well, but the water was warm and lashed me with urgency. I was starting to put the shampoo on me lang locks, when the hut door opened and four or five others joined me. As soon as we were noticed from the girls' huts, then the Italian huts, a big cheer went up. Some came out with umbrellas to watch us, some took photos. But in a short while quite a huddle of brown and off-white bodies were engaging in the mass bath-in. The girls, too, were squealing and tossing their hair, but more sensibly had rigged up a shower from a fractured drainpipe, so the roof water poured in a torrent into a pool then down onto their heads. It struck with such force its a wonder it didn't knock them out. Naked, soapy and laughing, they revelled in the freedom of the rain.

As we boarded the buses, in our suits and shirts and ties, wolf whistles went up from the students. Man, we were in Cuba—wearing suits? But then the biggest surprise of all: the Cuban workers, who were coming too, they too were all dressed in suits, not quite like ours, a sort of 1930s/1940s version of them, but European-style workers in their suits for sure.

We were treated to rum of all varieties, and anise, and fruit concoctions. My attentions were totally engaged with a thin willowy, American girl, with rich, long, brown, thick hair; big freak-out hair, man! Thin little sensuous arms and long thin neck and little bitty ears that set off the back of her head and neck and cried out 'Kiss me!' and legs that went on and on to the sexiest little bum. Usually she wore shorts and a T-shirt; tonight was dress-up night and she wore a sort of shiny lamé evening dress, cut low, which clung like you knew she had nothing on underneath. But this was a talk-only relationship. She was a comrade, a fellow communist, from the belly of the beast. I confess to having thoughts of other bellies and beasts, but she was spoken for, she had a comrade/companion in the States. Despite this, it was clear we clicked. I know when we touched the hair didn't just stand on my neck alone, I mean all sorts of things stood everywhere, but I mean it affected her too; I knew that. 'Hey, Dave, comrade,' she said in that pleasing American way. 'Can't we just grab a beer or so, I'm not with this Ron.'

'Good idea, me too.' 'Compañero,' I said calling to a white-jacketed waiter.

'Si?'

'Dos cerveza, por favor.' 'Cer-vi-asa?'

'Si, cer-vi-asa, dos.'

'Dos?'

'Si.'

Off he goes, looking mystified. 'Gee,' she says. 'That's pretty impressive, two beers, ha?' 'Yes,' I admit. 'I can order beer in just about any language,' I boast.

Then back comes the compañero, carrying two cardboard boxes of 'serviettas' and lands two packs of serviettes on the table and walks off. We both laugh, then get up to dance. While we were rumba, mamba, rock 'n' rollin' we were just having fun. Then some late smootchy dance came last off, and boy did that generate some heat. We fairly stuck together. The heat from our bodies, sweat running through our clothes, her wet hair on my face, that neck—I could feel her every movement through that little dress, and she cupped my bum into her. The passion between us, as we scarcely moved, just hugged and radiated heat and sensuality. As the light came up, I pulled her away slightly and looked at her, she just looked down a bit and then back at me, and said 'We can't, Dave.' 'Phew, well, OK, I understand,' but I was panting and sweating as if we had. Indeed that mad dancing and that last half hour of intensity was more sexual than some of the actual wham-bam-thank-you-mam shags I had had previously. We walked back hand in hand; I think everyone thought we were lovers.

One afternoon off, I set off to find the Posadist comrades. They advertised the Party paper quite openly; it was on the back of the all the Party publications, *Voz Proletaria*. I had their address, Montes 12 Apt 11, Piso 2, Habana. I had some 'English' tea and various presents from the comrades in England, and word that Posadas himself was going to visit, I think under the name Carlos. I was also told to convey to the comrades that the Fidelistas should not be condemned, and they shouldn't be calling for their overthrow as they had done hitherto, it seemed. The line had changed. Mind, I had no idea what the line had been. I had no idea of the history of bad blood between the Fidelistas and the Posadist on the island. I had filled in the entry visa saying I was a member of the British Section, for God's sake.[54]

I took the wawa, the Cuban nickname for the old Spanish buses (the British Leyland double-decker buses had been stopped en route on the high seas by US gunboats, who claimed they could be of strategic value—a new use for a London bus and no doubt), to Old Havana. I found the crumbling old Spanish apartments, called Old Monte. I went up a flight of stairs and knocked on the door. A youngish women with a house full of children came to the door. 'I am looking for Alfonso. I am from England.' The women shook her head ruefully. 'He doesn't live here?' 'Si, Si.' He obviously lived here, the kids wailed, she looked harassed and afraid, I looked on a bit bewildered. Then she made the sign of two hands in manacles, one hand gripping one wrist then the other hand gripping the other. 'Carcel.'

'Carcel?' 'Trotskyista!' Right, he was banged up again then. This set me in a dilemma. It was clear that unless I dispatched this information to England, Posadas could walk into a jail himself. I rushed back to the camp, where there was a telegram facility. I would have to address it to Maureen and assume she would know to pass it on to the Party and they would know what I meant. I had to do this, too, without saying anything which the Cubans might decipher and block. 'Cancel visit of Carlos, Alphonso detained.' It arrived and it did the trick. Meantime my comrades from the 7th who knew I had gone off to find 'my comrades' in Havana, were surprised to see me back so soon. I explained the comrades were in jail. This at once started a furious row, as the members of Communist Party always claimed there were no political prisoners in Cuba. The debate got more heated, on the nature of the revolutionary struggle and accountability and freedom of political viewpoints within the socialist movement.

Of course the debate came to the ears of Comrade Castro, Raul that is. He again sent for me. He was with a party of Cuban camp workers and some from the brigade. The female German translator, young, blond and dolly, smiled with her head on one side. Comrade Raul want to know, 'What you are accusing them of?' I relayed the story of Alfonso. But really he could understand most of what I said anyway; you could tell. 'How did you get there? You can't speak Spanish.' 'Wawa.' 'How did you know where to get off?' 'I asked the driver for Old Monte.' 'What number did you say it was?' '12.' 'The street doesn't go up to 12.' 'Comrade, I have been to his house. I know he is in jail,' I said, starting to shout now.

He went quiet a little while, then pointed his finger and tapped his nose. 'Ah. This Alfons, I know him. He was CDR (Committee in Defence of the Revolution) chairman for Monte.' Raul had even voted for him. 'You know, comrade, when someone dies in a house, and nobody else lives there, it is the CDR chairman's job to seal up the door, and make sure everything is intact, so we can contact relatives, or dispose of the contents to people who need them if there are no relatives. The committee does this. We find that comrade Alfons was stealing clocks from premises; this is why he is in jail.'

'Yi see,' one of the Communist Party builders, who had tagged along and was earwigging, butted in. 'He isn't a political prisoner, he's just a criminal.' I jumped up. 'Yee daft fucking bastard!' I said, shouting at my comrade but making it clear I was addressing more than him. 'Alfonso was imprisoned and tortured under Batista. He led strikes against Batista, he supported the revolution and risked his life and the lives of his family, and you think he's going to steal clocks from his deceased neighbours?' 'You say I am lying?' Raul says. 'You're lying,' I says, and walked away. Well whatever went on in the minds of the bureaucracy, nothing more came of my outburst and I applied to see the comrades in jail. They told me it would be considered but events intervened. If Raul had said 'Look, your barmy comrades gave out leaflets calling for the overthrow of Fidel and the government and saying he murdered Ché with his own hands, of course we locked them up, go and talk some sense into them,' I'd have understood. But clocks? And stealing?

Dr Salvador Allende had been elected the Marxist president of Chile in 1970. They had called Chile 'the England of Latin America' because it had parliamentary democracy and a tradition of constitutional government. Allende's Socialist Party came to office without guns; it had hoped to stay in office without guns. Others would have other ideas. The Posadists termed Allende's Chile 'a revolutionary state'. That was a state where capitalism hadn't yet been expropriated or the workers weren't yet in direct control, but where the process was leading in that direction. Allende was a genuine enough bloke; he nationalised, i.e. confiscated, the command heights of the economy including the strategic copper mines formally belonging to RTZ, and ITT, the American-based multinational concern. He began a Marxist programme of education, sanitation, literacy and equality between sexes and people of the countryside and towns.

In the Pentagon they had other ideas. By September 1973, during our spell in Cuba, the US Eighth Fleet was off the coast of Chile and a military coup launched. Allende died defending the presidential palace and his socialist government. The repression was widespread, the resistance brave but hopeless. Allende had not armed the people; they fought with sticks and stones against tanks and guns. Allende had always argued with Fidel and the revolutionary movement about tactics. My German workmate, who could speak no English, furiously said 'Tactica, Tactica!' (Allende making the speech), then 'Tactica-tactica-tactica!' (the sound of a machine gun mowing down our comrades). Exiles were arriving in Cuba with news of resistance and repression. In Chile there was another miners' tendency, Miners Voice, and a section of the Party who ran a press office that sounded something like 'Prensa Alertena'. I asked how they were faring, and the Chilean journalist said yes, he had seen comrades from the press agency. Meantime armed resistance was being mounted by the Trotskyist guerillas MIR who had never believed the Chilean state would roll over and let itself be expropriated. Comrades from the communist and Socialist parties were linking up with them. A resistance front was being forged. We were all comrades again. But we wouldn't get the chance. The football stadium in Santiago was used as a mass detention centre, trade unionists and socialists of all descriptions were being rounded up and detained, beaten, tortured and murdered, some of them right there in the stadium.

Millions started to mobilise on the streets of Havana and across the country. We joined the mad demonstration in Havana on 13 September. Everyone was mobile and mobilising on anything which would move, battered tractors towing carts full of peasants with ancient-looking guns, men on donkeys and horses with sombreros carrying machetes, buses of armed women, marching children, cops carrying placards and slogans, soldiers in the throng. Marching choirs, and armed CDRs. We expected a Cuban expeditionary force to land in Chile and put some steel in the resistance. All of us from Britain at once went to see Raul and volunteered to join this force, we meant it too, as deeply as we had ever meant anything in our lives. This would be our Spain; Chile must be the Latin American stand against US imperialism. Raul told us it was too late for that; if we had been warned even two weeks before by Allende they would have dispatched teams of guerillas, but would Allende have sought such assistance given his principles, even had he known? No; coups and counterrevolutionary attacks were taking place across the continent. It looked odds-on that Cuba would be the main target next, and Cuba must prepare for a military attack. They talked of evacuating the camp. We had meetings among all the brigades and voted we would stay, and fight if necessary, this could only put international pressure on the US if they did invade; they might end up shooting down many of we 500 international citizens and create a storm. In Havana, the crowd was a million strong. We had been given translation earpieces; you could hear Fidel in full voluminous thundering voice in one ear, and the almost simultaneous though American translator in the other. Fidel said he had given the nickel-plated AK-47 to Allende as a gift, saying 'I know your way isn't our way, but you may need this one day.' 'I know now,' boomed Fidel, 'that had I given him 500,000 of those guns this coup couldn't happen.' It struck me in a way that it had not done so before, that the people of Cuba were armed, the masses themselves, directly were armed. There was no standing army to speak of—at any one time most of the army, such as it was, was abroad, assisting in other peoples' liberation struggles.[55]

I had been amused when they told me how Fidel had offered Cuban fighters to join the NLF in Vietnam, but been told by Ho, they didn't want foreign soldiers, even friendly ones, on their soil. They were fighting for genuine independence, not just socialism. So Fidel says OK, can he send the Cuban Camera Corps, to film the liberation war and show the Cuban people what the Yankees were doing? This seems OK, and a big old Soviet ship docks from Cuba

Follonsby (Wardley) Colliery

Hatfield Colliery 1982
(photo Adye Cowell)

Hatfield Main Colliery and Club

The author with Hatfield Pithead in the background

The author, pictured at Hatfield Main Coliery, 1967

Roadheader: LH1300

Roadheader: Mk2B

The author — 1967

'The Jaws of Death'
Hatfield Colliery — a massive
cave-in with giant rocks falling
all around

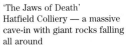

1878: that was then....

View of 'Pack Hole' before starting to stow

Oswald Bage, **'The Tunnel'**, Ink, 1945
© *Beamish Open Air Museum*

My 'Marra' and neighbour 'Bingo' operating chocks

The author: Hatfield Colliery, 1970

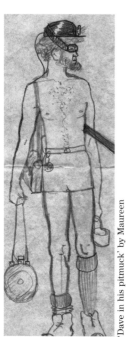

'Dave in his pitmuck' by Maureen

In many pits there was a long and, for the uninitiated, back-breaking walk to the pit face

A low seam combined with a wet pit produces the most appalling conditions

Drilling by hand

Easter 1983: Aldermaston/Greenham Common.
(Maureen and Emma on the left of photo)

Bernadette McAliskey

Ewan MacColl

Peggy Seeger

John Dowson (right of picture) being shot at point-blank range by an RUC officer

Civil Rights march to Dungannon

'Rough Music' warns 'the boys' of the patrol while the women and kids block their route

Life in Northern Ireland in the 1970s
and 1980s

Top and below: 'The Battle of Saltley, 1972

On Westminster Bridge, 1972,

Scunthorpe, 1972: dockers scuffling with police

Trafalgar Sq., 1972: Belgian miners show solidarity

New York, 1972: solidarity with British miners

Mick McGahey, Joe Gormley and Lawrence Daly

1972: Police in the dark

Miners' wives protest

Feb 9, 1972:Funeral of comrade Freddie Matthews

1980: The Red Star Folk Club

1982: the author delivering the graveside oration at Tommy Hepburn's funerall with Arthur Scargill looking on

Oxford — miners' strike 1972: the author fund-raising with Didcott pickets

1981: Emma and Stephan at the People's March for Jobs

The Hatfield Main Lodge: Yorkshire Miners' Gala, 1979

Beetham miners: Hells Angel - heavy rocker pitmen. Tweedy, a Hatfield miner, is in the foreground rolling a cigarette

1981: Peoples' March for Jobs

May Day! Doncaster Region RWP (T)

1972: tenants demo during the miner strike

Solidarity strike action in support of the nurses

May Day, 1978: Socialist Union banner

April 20, 1982; unveiling of the new banner: left to right - Albert Lovell, branch president; David Douglass, branch delegate; Dick Kelly, ex M.P. for Don Valley; Jack Taylor, president Yorkshire miners; Sammy Thompson, Vice-President Yorkshire miners; Peter Curran, branch secretary; far right, Johnny Sadd, branch committee

The Proletaria Bookshop

The Proletaria Bookshop

The Mineworker editorial desk

1972 Yorkshire Miners' Gala: 'Mineworker' team

Full employment meeting

New York, 1976: Founding convention Nationwide Unemployed League

May Day, Doncaster, 1972

Sheffield 1983: Anti-Thatcher demonstration

First EMC survival course, Easter 1975

Training for the Revolution

Preparing for the Revolution

Joel Knieger and Ken Terry on EMC map-reading course, 1976

EMC 'Special Boat Squadron', Scotland, 1976

Tenants demonstration, 1971

IWP Xmas Party, 1975

Maureen and Alison(Red Star Folk Club, Doncaster, 1982

Abbeyfield Road, 1969

Glasgow, 1976: Maureen

With Uncle Peter, Aunty Kittie, Emma and cousin

Bill Quay, 1968: Maureen

Whitley Bay, 1983: Jason, David, Chad and Emma

So-fa, so good: Emma, Dave and Maureen:

1973, Yorkshire Miners' Gala, Maureen and Emma

1971: Raph Samuels house, Spitalfields, London

1978: relaxing in Dennistoun, Glasgow

1979: Graduation

Editorial meeting, Ruskin College

1976-8: Strathmates (top, bottom and left)

Dave's dad, still in his 'pitmuck', congratulates his daughter, Veronica, on winning the Northumberland/Durham Irish Dance Competition in 1954

Dave's Anti-Common Market drive

1982, May Day: Emma on L.P. Young Socialists float

1976: Emma and Dave with Snow Duck

1982: Dave, Arthur Scargill, Dave's dad and two other Durham miners' officials

Institute for Marxism-Leninism Mao-Tse-Tung Thought (bookshop and office)

Tessa: former RAF Police dog

1971: Raph Samuels house, Spitalfields, London

1979: Graduation

Editorial meeting, Ruskin College

1978: relaxing in Dennistoun, Glasgow

1976-8: Strathmates (top, bottom and left)

Dave's dad, still in his 'pitmuck', congratulates his daughter, Veronica, on winning the Northumberland/Durham Irish Dance Competition in 1954

Dave's Anti-Common Market drive

1982, May Day: Emma on L.P. Young Socialists float

1976: Emma and Dave with Snow Duck

1982: Dave, Arthur Scargill, Dave's dad and two other Durham miners' officials

Institute for Marxism-Leninism Mao-Tse-Tung Thought (bookshop and office)

Tessa: former RAF Police dog

Dave's Hatfield 'Marras' on 'the way outbye'

Ted Holloway, **'Testing for Gas'**. Oil, 1950s

Oliver Kilbourn, **'Miner Setting Props in Lower Seam'**. Oil, 1950
© *Trustees of Ashington Group Collection*

Ted Holloway, **'Miners' Heads'**. Oil, 1954

Bert Sangster, **'Drilling the Caunch'**
Oil. 1970
Courtesy of Durham learning Resources

D Wharton, (Gedling Collier), '**Gedling's Record Breakers**' (First Prize, Paint-A-Pit competition)

George Sawyer, '**Restless Waters**'. Oil, 1965

1982, strikers, including 'flying pickets' from Corby, are pushed aside at the steel stockists John Lee & Co., in Grantham, Lincs — Mrs Thatcher's home town

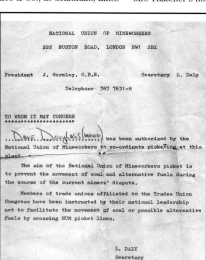

NATIONAL UNION OF MINEWORKERS

222 EUSTON ROAD, LONDON NW1 2BX

President   J. Gormley, O.B.E.   Secretary L. Daly

Telephone 387 7631-8

TO WHOM IT MAY CONCERN
****

....Dave...Douglass.(Windo)... has been authorized by the National Union of Mineworkers to co-ordinate picketing at this plant ....

The aim of the National Union of Mineworkers picket is to prevent the movement of coal and alternative fuels during the course of the current miners' dispute.

Members of trade unions affiliated to the Trades Union Congress have been instructed by their national leadership not to facilitate the movement of coal or possible alternative fuels by crossing NUM picket lines.

L. DALY
Secretary
National Union of Mineworkers

1974: picket authorisation

1971, Whitehall: Sinn Fein supporters protest against internment

1981, Long Kesh, Lisburn: marchers rally in solidarity with the IRA hunger strikers in the Maze Prison

1983, Doncaster: People's March for Jobs

The morning shift off to work

'An attempt to answer some vexed questions on the bonus scheme, Dave Douglass, Branch Delegate, Hatfield Main NUM

The slaughter of the miners by the pro-capitalist NCB and the need for workers' power in the mining industry, Dave Douglass

Irish Solidarity Movement meeting calling for the release of the Guiildford Four and the Birmingham Six and the Maguire Family.

Home from work

Moscow: miners' visit to Lenin's presidential home

Red Square, Moscow: interview on Radio Moscow

Bulgaria: with Sammy Thompson; area VP, NUM

Bulgaria: miners' delegation

Bulgaria — fraternal meeting

Bulgaria - Sofia: visit to a nursery

Havana, Cuba, September 12, 1973: spontaneous demonstration in the streets of Havana following the news that the government of President Salvador Allende had been overthrown by the military in a coup d'état.

Cuba, September 1973: mass meeting to listen to Fidel Castro's speech on Allende's overthrow

Cuba: on site with the work brigade

Havana: street encounter

The author and other members of his brigade attend an on-site workers' committee meeting

The author and friends unloading cement

and down the landing flaps come a line of tanks. Out of each turret pokes a Cuban with a Kodak round his neck. 'Back on the ships, comrades!' 'But we have to defend ourselves while taking the photos, si, this is Cuban Camera Corps!', They went back to Cuba, but the intention was there. Fidel had announced that the Cuban revolution started in the mountains of Cuba and would 'end at the tip of Africa.' The 'Cuban revolution' was 'a revolution of all the Americas and Africa and Asia'. The power here in Cuba was in the hands of the working people; at least in so far as if they had ever wanted to, they could turn out Fidel any time they put their minds to it. But now we stood on the brink of defending Cuba not with bricks and mortar but with guns. I hoped anyway that if the Gringos came we should at least be given guns. On the platform alongside Fidel was Madam Allende, the good Doctor's wife. Fidel said that in deference to her loss he would only make a brief speech. He spoke for an hour and three quarters, then Mrs Allende in a ringing, impassioned voice spoke for nearly three.

Next day in the Hotel Nationale in Havana we called in first off for a drink of Coke. 'Is no coke, is Cubacola.' Whey, it's in the Coca-Cola bottles, it tastes like Coca-Cola, and it was Coca-Cola till Fidel took over the plant and nationalised it without compensation, so now you have to be careful to ask for Cubacola. Two English engineering contractors, staying at the hotel were put out that there was no staff in the kitchen to make them breakfast. The barman explained that with the coup in Chile and the mass rally last night, nobody went to bed until late morning. However he would open the kitchen and they could make themselves some breakfast if they wished. A very Cuban and socialist answer to the problem, but they were outraged; good job we hadn't asked them to sling us a bit toast while they were at it. We needed to do something. So we borrowed the camp bus, with approval. They thought we were going for some British diplomacy and set off for the British Embassy, ostensibly to convey our displeasure at the non-reaction of the British government at the murderous coup. We discussed the occupation of the embassy if it seemed achievable; that should get some publicity and demonstrate an act of solidarity. I had visions of my earlier attempt at an embassy occupation, but that was the American Embassy in Grosvenor Square, London in 1968 and the task had been rather fraught with difficulties. As it turned out, we arrived at the embassy, a humble little construction with a metal gate across the door. We leaned through and knocked on the door. A Cuban security official in his blue shirt with the sleeves rolled up peered through the glass of the front door. We shouted out the first name of the ambassador. The security man opened the door, and looked puzzled. 'Si?' 'We are here for an important meeting with the ambassador.' 'No, not here.' 'Si here, he is coming.' 'He is coming here?' 'Si.' He starts to unlock with his big bunch of keys, muttering away in Spanish and English: 'He say nothing, I not know.' 'Its OK, its OK,' we all start to say, and most of us feel sorry for him. Downstairs is his little office, upstairs the ambassadors office and suite. We all start up the stairs; the last one through locks the downstairs door and the security man downstairs. We have the building. Upstairs, there is a magnificent view of the bay and the city. The office meanwhile is poky and functional. We start to search through files and drawers and anything which looks like it might give us the drop on British involvement with the coup, or spying on Cuba, or us. We find boxes of slides, but they're all like ours, of sun sea and sand, bliddy holiday slides, what kind of spy is this bloke? Downstairs the security man still doesn't grasp it. 'Señores?' he says, knocking on the door ' Señores, I think you should come down now, the ambassador is not coming.' 'Si comrade, he will be coming we are going to get him on the phone now.' 'No, this phone is to his house, he will be very angry with you.' 'That's OK comrade, he knows us.' Well he would soon. We lift the phone, a line buzzes and clicks, then a mystified very upper-class British accent, says 'What the blazes is happening?' And starts to speak in Spanish.

The big Irish labourer has the con: 'Excuse me sir, we have to inform you that your embassy is under occupation by representatives of the British working class.' Loud reaction at first, then silence. I take the phone; the voice says 'Well, go on then, what?' 'We have seized the embassy in protest at British complicity with the military coup against our comrade Allende.' 'Don't be such Silly Billys. Come over here to my house—its far more comfortable than the office. We can have a spot of lunch and discuss your concerns.' 'What's he say?' 'He says do we want to go for dinner at his house.' 'Bliddy dinner!' we all start to say, then a voice: 'Ask him what sort of dinner?' 'Dinner' started to take on real meaning, as in real food. 'We are considering your suggestion, em, do you mean British dinner, or is that just an expression like "Come up for coffee?"' He says he is having beef and new potatoes and vegetables which he has sent over. He says he will send his car over. So we go, having satisfied ourselves that no British spy base or military cell operated from this office. We bade goodbye to the security man, who was still baffled, even when we boarded the big black car to be ferried to the ambassador's huge house in tree-lined grounds. Mind he got both barrels, when we got there. Not literally, but verbally, though he denied any British collusion, or involvement or knowledge. He agreed to pass on at once our concerns to the Foreign Office that Britain condemned most wholeheartedly the coup against the democratically elected Socialist government of Allende and warned of the carnage which would follow if this coup were part of wider plan which included the invasion of Cuba. We sat on the terrace and ate dinner, new tatties, vegetables and beer; my compadres ate British beef. Of course news of our adventure had got to Cuban authorities, who congratulated us on our protest, though any mention of an occupation was dropped. On the camp, the whole camp was to draft the same statement of condemnation and condolence and eulogy for compañero Allende. The whole camp would read in one language after another, with a different national representative, the same message. The trouble was, while the flowing and flowery and exotic Spanish translated well into Italian, it didn't work in Austrian, German, Dutch and English. We just didn't speak like that. When we tried to redraft it into English it more or less came out as: 'We're sorry the comrade was murdered.'

Well, the Americans and the Mafiosi must have found out that the British workers had a delegation in Cuba, because they decided not to invade at this time. We weren't called upon to fight after all. Joking aside, we were all ready to put our money where our mouths were, though we were all of us relieved the swine didn't invade. The cost in lives could have been phenomenal judging by what we had seen of popular preparations for resistance.

SIERRA MESTRA

We resumed our visits and studies to the four corners of the island. Up in the Sierra Mestra is rich cattle country, and real-looking cowboys ride in cowboy gear herding cattle back and forth across the large areas of grazing land. In a little village we had stopped in a cloud of dust announced a storm of young vaqueros, galloping hell for leather into the town for their dinner break. It was like something off a Hollywood film. They hitched their magnificent ponies to rails and trees. The big Irishman says to me, 'Wouldn't it be grand now, to just borrow a couple of horses, and pack a couple of sleeping bags and just set off and travel the mountains and valleys, just stop when you felt like it and go where you wanted to?' 'It certainly would,' I agreed, though my comrade was talking at some point in the future. He was overheard by an older cowboy standing, I kid you not, rolling tobacco Clint Eastwood style. This bloke thinks we want to have a ride on the gallawas.

'Si,' he points at two quietly grazing ponies stood under a tree. And gestures for us to mount up and have a ride. So OK, the big lad with a few steps and the thing taking off on its own manages to swing himself into the saddle and sit there, looking a bit top-heavy I thought. By now we had a small crowd. 'Oh God,' I thinks. I take hold of the reigns and swing myself into the saddle. I lean forward in a mock pretence to whisper in the gallawa's ear, to tell him to go, when whoosh in a leap forward he is off, galloping like the wind, my bollocks smack-whack-whack-whack on the hard little saddle and I think they've gone up into my stomach. At first I am still leaning forward over his head somewhat, but then the momentum throws by body back into the saddle. Suddenly wham! he stops dead, and I am catapulted forward again, just managing to hang on and not go over the top, when whoosh! he is off again. And my balls take another merciless pounding. As the fields and hills in front of me loom closer and the voices and laughter of the village drift far away, I realise how to drive this thing. This pony doesn't respond to reins, but to weight movement. I lean back slowly and he slows his pace. I lean over the left, he wheels to the left. By the time I canter back into the village I can wheel to left and right and sit like a big aristo, high in the saddle. I get a round of applause from the brigade as I ride in, though I confess to feeling guilty at having made the poor gallawa work through snap time. Mind I have great trouble getting my legs to work, and my testicles have locked up somewhere in my groin. They all think the funny walk is for a laugh. Some time later, the two Swiss lads spot a patch of marijuana growing in a field, over a fence. The big Brahman cattle are down the far end of the field, and although they are usually docile, we are told this is the time for calving, so the big bulls are very wary of anything on their patch. So the lads have climbed over the fence and are picking stems to deleaf them later. They are excited and babbling away in one or more of the Swiss tongues and occasionally shouting to me that you can smell the resin as you pick the plant. An old Cuban is sitting under a tree, unnoticed by us as first. He is in the classical Cuban in the shade, sombrero tilted forward, knees up to chest, hands-on-knees position. He observes for a while the two lang-haired lads, gathering up the sacred crop. Then he gets up and strolls to the fence. 'What they do?' he asks. 'Well, they pick these plants.' I describe all this in sign language and talking very slowly. 'You can dry out the leaves.' Then, making a rub-together gesture, and rolling out a cig, 'Then you can smoke.' 'You smoke thees?' 'Si.' 'What you call this?' 'Well in England, we call it marijuana.' 'Oh,' says the Cuban nodding his head. 'In Cuba we call this tomato.' For two glorious weeks at the end of our work period we were taken on holiday; lots of visits, but based mainly on the Isle of Pines, an idyllic island once the haunt of Batista and his entourage. Those who were couples got a double room. They called accommodation for young couples 'posadas', which was amusing, although it wouldn't have amused him. Most of the secondary boarding schools, which many were through the week, had accommodation like this for serious young couples, not the one-night-stand varieties, but those who went out together regularly. A student committee vetted the application for these posadas, which were allocated at weekend dos or through the week in boarding schools. Cuba had had a great reputation for sexual freedom, though it and the women and girls of the island had been greatly exploited by the rich American tourists and gangsters in the past, and an unsteady set of compromises hung in place. The struggle against 'machismo' attitudes was a serious political struggle in Cuba, and a struggle among communist males in self-discipline and consciousness. I agreed of course; my reverence for my American comrade's tiny ears and lusciously sexy neck was surely not in conflict with those higher aims? The apartment kitchens had those big old American fridges, stacked with beer, rum, and Cubacola. Only problem was the cockroaches and mosquitoes. This being a special occasion, for the first time. I smeared myself all over with mosquito repellent, before drawing the blinds and jumping under the thin sheet which covered the bed and a naked Maria. I had not, of course, covered my penis with mosquito repellent, mainly because most of it wasn't there at the time, but anyway I wouldn't have thought anything about it if I had. Now I don't know what they put in this stuff, it was the first time I had used it the whole time I was there. As my erect prick fell backwards onto my belly, it made contact with the repellent. I was in a heavy, deep-throat snog with the Italian bombshell. Well the burning pain started to spread down my cock and up into the spout. OOhhhhh! I slipped off the bed, grabbing tissues and toilet roll, rubbing the damn stuff off, and grunting in pain. I think Maria at first thought I was having a super premature ejaculation, till she followed me from the bed into the shower, where I sat, on the floor with the spray nozzle directed at my nozzle, wiping it with tissues and rubbing soap over it to try and get the stuff off, which as luck would have it, was of course water resistant. Maria rolled about on the floor, hysterical, which was a novelty since mainly she was one of those permanently serious-looking girls, who only smiled on rare occasions. She was smiling now, OK.

'Hold onto it. I get the camera,' she says.

'You bliddy won't!' I shut the door, and finished my rescue attempts.

Mosquito repeller? Does it say penis repeller? Does it say do not spray near your dick unless you want to ruin a passionate moment? By the time I re-emerged Maria was back under the sheet, nearly dozing. The air was hot, the ceiling fan whirred, the room was in shadows and you could hear a gentle breeze outside making the coconuts in the palm trees knock together, in rhythm to the crickets' whirr. The room smells of perfume. Relaxed again, erect again, I pull back the covers. Her brown body projects up at me, breasts large and nipples erect. She's been waiting for me. Her hand falls across her forehead and she smiles.

I roll over and slide into her with ease. For a moment there is an intensely sensuous excitement, and I just stay still inside her.

Then suddenly she jumps up nearly knocking my teeth out with her forehead, and pushes me away as quickly as I had arrived. She rolls off the bed, shouting in Italian, 'Stupido Inglese! La mia fica e' infuocatta sta bruciando!' And gripping herself between the legs, she rushes for the shower.

Now it's her turn to sit open legged on the shower floor, shower nozzle directed up her vagina, trying to doosh the bliddy repeller out. No, I didn't laugh—you mad? Seemed a little poetic justice like, but I felt guilty.

I picked the spray up. 'What a-you do now, spray it again?' 'No, I'm looking to see if its made by the Vatican.' We both laugh, then go outside naked under big white towels, to lounge in the hammocks swinging between the coconut trees, overlooking the beach. 'I wanted to ask you anyway, Maria, do you take anything, any contraceptives?' 'Why a-do you ask?' 'Well, I haven't been using anything as you know, and I haven't really been withdrawing when we climax.' 'So a-why does this concern you?' 'Well, yee might have a baby like.' 'So? That's my business.' 'Whaat?' It was the start of a terminal argument. It seems when all was revealed she wanted a bairn. Well me and Maureen had an open relationship, but making another women pregnant I think probably overstepped the terms of that understanding. She was emphatic; she would not have raised this, and was mad as hell that I had. The bairn would be hers—nothing to do with me—if it was conceived. She wanted the bairn herself, just for herself, she didn't want a father, just a sperm donor. Apparently a committee of her female comrades had decided that the bloke whoever that turned out to be should be English, and I fitted the size and shape and looks requirements. Hmm.

We never had sex again, and she scarcely talked to me. Just because we were having sex didn't mean she had to talk to me. As it turned out Maureen was sympathetic to Maria's idea: 'If she doesn't want a man, that's fine, she can live just as happily and bring up a child without that unnecessary encumberment,' was her comment as I recall. Still, I felt a bit used, and at the same time I had voluntarily and as it turned out quite unnecessarily given up the opportunity of wild, irresponsible bareback sex. I wasn't sure which was worse. We left the sacred little island, with its waving palm trees and glistening beaches, its revolutionary posters wall-to-wall, praising the revolutions of Asia, Africa and Latin America, its identity with the toiling peoples of the world. Its backbreaking task of breaking the island and its people from the concrete straitjacket of poverty and low life expectancy which its huge imperialist neighbour had placed upon it. The sweat-soaked peasants and building workers toiling in the blazing sun to find a new man and new times in Cuba. Si, also the elements of bureaucracy, the leech that sits in the soul of all our revolutions, the power-crazed egotism of the leaders who will not trust the people to their own direct charge. This too, but this is largely cross-eyed paternalism rather than well-heeled hypocrisy. A piece of my heart stayed in Cuba, perhaps a piece of my soul too. I had gone with an orientation given me by an organisation far more bureaucratic than the one I was judging, but I had gone as a comrade and fellow worker too. I was later to deeply regret that I had gone in there full of Posadist formulae rather than a clear vision. I was later to write: 'In thinking about revolution we must understand that not only is a socialist revolution something that needs to be fought for in order that it begin, but most important it consists of an ongoing struggle, whether in Cuba or elsewhere. Whether or not the Cuban revolution has achieved the ultimate goals of socialism cannot determine our judgement as to whether or not a revolution has occurred at all. The crucial point when discussing Cuba or any other socialist struggle in general is that revolution must be viewed as a continuously evolving dynamic process, and not a static, already finished event: as a concrete series of events based upon real conditions, not in terms of an abstract prescription of how it is supposed to happen. And although it is part of our national heritage to reject the idea that a non-European, non-'great' (colonialist) country can provide us with some significant lessons and examples, it is necessary nonetheless to rise above our conditioning in the interests of adding to our understanding of revolutionary process.'

Our comrades on the plane home took out their souvenir machetes, which would hang in pride of place on their walls, a proof of their devoted toil in the cause of Cuba; then they noticed, stamped on the blades, 'Spear & Jackson' and thought 'Nobody will believe me.' I had left all my clothes in Cuba. I returned with a suitcase full of nothing else but cigars and packets of Cuban cigarettes for the lads at the pit. In the hold, wrapped up with jeans and towels and all sorts of packing, a case of Havana Club ron which in the absence of food, I had developed quite a taste for. I had lost my camera at the airport but had boxes and boxes of slides. We arrived at Heathrow and the customs workers, knowing we were a party of trade unionists just back from helping the Cuban revolution, waved us through—rum, cigars, the lot—and never touched a bag or a box. By the time I arrived back in Abbeyfield Road, I was tanned, a skeleton, an alcoholic and severely wrecked. Emma, me wee bairn, was toothlessly smiling up at me, smiling with her wonderful eyes, Maureen was tearful and warm and familiar, and comrades were round briefly, lads from the pit, and their lasses. It was like, we were real, in this revolution. The world was our world, and getting smaller by the day. The ron flowed. In among the maracas, the T-shirts, the badges, the sombreros, I took forth the talc powder box, and unwrapped the Sellotape, and took out the deed bug. It sat, in the middle of my hand, taking up the whole palm. Maureen was Urring, and 'Great God'-ing at it. 'Aye,' I boasted, 'yee het te get used te these things,' and looked away as something caught my eye. Unseen by me Maureen blew at the beetle to dislodge the talc, which had become stuck all over it. Suddenly I thought it was alive, and thought the wisp of breath on my hand was from this creature and not Maureen. Bravado had gone. AHHH! I shouts and up shot the beetle into the air. Maureen now also thinks its alive and jumps literally on to the settee. It falls still on the floor. 'Its alive,' Maureen suggests. 'I felt it breathe,' I exclaim. 'Well, that could have been me, blowing on it,' confesses Maureen as we creep up on the dearly departed brother or sister from the insect nether world. From that day to this, the thing stays in a box, secured by an elastic band. I know somewhere in the back on my mind, that these things can hibernate for generations, and I just don't trust its demise. I always open the box with caution and the preparation that it might fly, scuttle or leap off back to Cuba. I have now resolved that next time I return to Cuba El Beetle comes with me for a Christian burial in its own soil! When I came in off afters now, me bairn would be just in her carry-cot, but looking up at me, and smiling her smile; Maureen would get to go out and leave me eating me dinner. I then would take little Em, cradle her in my arms and lie down on the settee till we both dosed off. Sometimes I would wake and tip toe up the stairs to lay her in her own little cot. Other times we would both be fast asleep on the couch, when Maureen re-emerged from her evening in the pub. Usually she would take her book or else the latest article or paper that needed reading for the next meeting. People thought us odd, going to a pub to read or write reams of paper, but they got used to us. We were 'the odd couple'; now 'hippie revolutionaries,' the 'Gypsy' tag, had fallen away, but 'murdering IRA terrorist supporters' had taken its place among others.

18 November 1973. I am back from Cuba, emaciated and brown and full of fire. We organise a big public meeting on Chile at the Nelson. I decorate the walls with Cuban and Chilean posters. The Party object, and while I am downstairs getting in the beer, remove the Chile Solidarity posters because they have displayed on them an AK machine gun. I can't take this on just now since the hall is filling up with people from unions and the labour movement. Even the CP have turned out in numbers and the International Socialists et al. 'The gun is not our symbol, this is not the way we organise.'

'What?'

My speech was straight from the horse's mouth, straight from the escaping Chileans, the workers, the journalists, Madam Allende herself and *Gramma* (the Cuban daily paper). I retold the last 30 minutes of Allende's life. How he died with the assault rifle Fidel had made a present of to him some time earlier; he died fighting. There were many tearful eyes in that room that night, and I too had difficulty in holding it together. Allende was a good man, a mistaken man, perhaps brutally simple, but a good man who didn't deserve to die because of US corporations. Allende, though, was lucky; the fate of tens of thousands of trade unionists and socialists was to be bloody and cruel and ongoing.

* I regret using the term 'the Big Irishman'. I had hoped this much loved comrade's name would come to me before publication but it hasn't. Neither has that of his smaller mate. No disrespect is intended and I will doubtless kick myself when I remember their names later.

The Union NEC had urged rejection of the NCB wages offer of 1973 and went back to the membership once again for permission to call unlimited strike action if a satisfactory improvement was not made. Given the proximity of the previous national strike the favourable yes vote was remarkable: 82,631—against 143,006. The NCB and government saw not a massive vote of discontentment, but a sign that the miners had now exhausted their will to strike and were in conciliatory mood.

Satisfaction over the 1972 wage settlement was short-lived; although surface men had made real progress face workers and other underground workers were soon being left behind again.

By October 1972 the average weekly earnings in coal mining were only 5.5 per cent above average male earnings for all manufacturing industries and the ratio of face workers' earnings over average male manufacturing earnings was only one percentage point more than it had been a year earlier.

By October 1973 average mineworkers' earnings were only 2.3 per cent above the average for all manufacturing industries, which was about 10 per cent less than had been thought appropriate by Wilberforce. The ratio of face workers' earnings to the average for all manufacturing was actually lower than it had been in October 1971. So within two years most of the gains from the strike and the Wilberforce recommendations had been eroded. The sense of unfairness which had aroused so much militancy in the winter of 1971–2 had been allowed to return, with the chance to arouse it all over again in the winter of 1973–4.

We were not being let to 'get away with it'. Behind the scenes a plan was being unfolded which would be something of a industrial relations neutron bomb; in 1973 it was still on the drawing board.[56]

PROLETARIA BOOKSHOP

At this time we moved to cement our place in this community. An old lady's fruit and veg shop at 289 Station Road had become vacant. It had upstairs accommodation and big windows downstairs. John and Alison Sharp had not long been married and were looking for a place to live. We agreed we would rent it, with John and Alison living upstairs and a bookshop and socialist centre downstairs. The Proletaria Bookshop. Kitting it out was a joy. Maureen was along there every day with the bairne in her carry-cot, painting and cleaning, along with Lynne Shipley and Alison. The blokes went in their spare time, resuscitating all the ancient fireplaces and ovens. With donations of coal from the pitmen members the shop was soon gleaming in cream and red, with blazing fires in the back-room living-room and in the kitchen. It is amazing how Maureen managed all this together with the task of bringing up a wee bairne. The books show the most meticulous eye for financial detail, every copper in and out. Book suppliers, books on sale or return, books for purchase, what we owed to who, who we had paid, a mail order business, book orders, invoices. The works. She was a brilliant administrator.

CONSPIRACY

In October 1973 we were offered a trial of building workers, arrested and jailed for conspiracy. The charge of conspiracy was the state's catch net, for subversives and resistance fighters of all descriptions. The struggle of the building workers had been incredibly hard. In part it was a struggle to secure trade unionism over casualisation. An attempt to achieve what the dockers had won decades before, an end to casualisation, 'the lump'. The tyranny of the foreman and ganger. Construction firms were determined to keep the industry from unionising. Gangs of bosses' thugs had confronted the builders' flying pickets. The battles had been hard, bloody, out of sight of the cameras, not mass battles like Saltley Gates. The lads had told me they had killed guard dogs sent to attack them or keep them off sites. Our organisers had been severely beaten, homes attacked, cars attacked, sites had been wrecked. The strike though had been the previous year. It had been allowed to subside. The laws used were not 'anti-union' laws; they had been chosen to avoid the threat of generalised strikes and a general strike against the law. These charges now were brought under the conspiracy laws and 24 good men stood in the dock.

The trial was held in a quiet rural backwater, Shrewsbury. The two who got sent down with savage sentences were Des Warren and Rick Tomlinson. They were stitched up by their own side. The union leadership ran scared of the charges of violence, and riot and conspiracy. UCATT the men's own union instructed branches not to contribute money to financial support of the men. Solidarity action within other unions came to grief on this rock.

The NUM militant leaders boasted that if these men had been miners they wouldn't be in jail now, implying that we would have shut the country down from stem to stern in solidarity action. 'Why do they have to be miners?' we demanded. But action by the miners when the builders weren't themselves taking action was impractical. We suspected anyway that this was a shot over the bows of the NUM steaming into what seemed a new theatre of operation. In the autumn of 73 the Middle East war broke; the oil pipeline taps, if not turned off, steadied in their flow and prices rose. Coal was looking valuable. Heath was proceeding with Phase Three of his Incomes Policy, a new round of pay restraint. The miners' pay negotiations became blocked by the government's impositions. We were, many years later, to discover that Gormley, who had more than a nodding acquaintance with MI5, had warned that the miners could well strike with widespread support from other unions. The civil servants had fell out with Heath and thought 'fuck him'; they didn't pass the message on to Heath.

The NUM moved towards a total overtime ban. It began in November of 1973. The aim was to seriously cut back on stocks of coal, by greatly reducing the amount mined, while at the same time still allowing the miners to earn a living—albeit a reduced living—since they rarely got five shifts in. Allowing the mines to work smoothly and allow one shift on as the other went off demanded overtime and work between shifts. The overtime ban meant that work normally done in overtime to ready the pits was held over until normal shift time, which meant the main shift didn't work, or only worked half a day. The action, though costly to the miners' wages, was more costly still to the Coal Board and its productivity. The objective was to get four shifts in, but cut production by half; the odds would shift in the miners' favour.[57] :

The miners' all-out overtime ban, beginning in November 1973, succeeded in its goal, shifting the odds in our favour. The ban stayed in place until January 1974 amid screams from the government. Heath moved to isolate the miners from their vital allies in the rest of the organised working-class movement. Privately he had decided he must defeat the miners. Behind the scenes the TUC and the big unions, especially those who hadn't the clout or the independent bottle to take on Phase Three themselves, vowed to give the miners every support should it be called for. The media, the TV and the press, marched to the side of the government, hoping to let loose some of the venom which had eaten the soul out of the power workers earlier. The people at large still thought in terms of social classes. They had not voted for Heath because they ideologically agreed with his programme. He had come to power for the opposite reason—because the Labour voters wouldn't vote for Wilson, who they concluded had abandoned any semblance of a socialist programme and abandoned them in the process. They had abstained, but a socialistic-thinking majority was still prevalent in Britain no matter who had won the election. The miners were seen as the clarion of the working class; these were boys who could do the business if called upon. It would be an uphill climb to swing the majority of British opinion both against the miners and for Heath.

The Miron Plan was a hefty reposte following our spectacular defeat of Heath's incomes policy in the preceding year. It had been drawn up by Wilfred Miron, Midlands Area director of the NCB. It thought the unthinkable. Its central plank was full utility of technology and the reintroduction of the contract system as a way of dividing the NUM and winning workers from the union. It was to strike a chord with the future Labour government and be rehashed as part of its 'Social Contract' class collaboration scheme. Myron wished 'to ensure that of those employed in the mining industry the maximum number be outside the NUM'. The plan was covertly though widely acclaimed. Derek Ezra the NCB chairman convened a special meeting to discuss its application.

In December 1973 Heath called his fifth State of Emergency. Ashen-faced, he appeared on TV and told us how the whole country sat on the brink. The whole of industry was drafted onto a three-day week. The fuel shortage caused by those bloody Arabs and the miners was to blame. Petrol rationing was introduced. To save fuel, power cuts were enforced across the length and breadth of the country. The TV shut down at 10 p.m. Pubs had no light or power to serve beer! We thought the treatment dished up to the power workers had been bad; now Heath was throwing every piece of slander and shit he could find. Unpatriotic, back-stabbing, greedy miners. All those poor victims in industry forced to live on three days' pay, losing as much as forty per cent of income because of the already overpaid miners. Mind, some industries already had minimum-wage agreements and in many areas the three-day week simply meant less work for much the same money, so 'Thanks, Ted!'

The action demonstrated very vividly that these clashes were indeed conflicts of class war, in political and ideological terms, not simple economic equations as the bourgeois academics would have us believe. The three-day week lost Britain 800 times more national income than the full cost of the miners' pay claim.

But it was a game, a propaganda exercise: coal stocks at power stations were at record highs, so there would have been no immediate need for power cuts for some months to come, never mind a three-day week.

My membership of Sinn Fein and my association with comrades in the struggle in Ulster took me to the pulse of the developing movement in the six counties. The ordinary members of the Provo milieu, working-class lads and lasses of my generation by and large, seen their struggle as part of the world socialist revolutionary movement. Although the political break around Provisional Sinn Fein was far from as progressive or politically clued up as the lads now wearing the masks, or even the lads and lasses tossing the petrol bombs on the streets, it was being heavily influenced by them. An odd amalgam of old-fashioned Fenians, Irish nationalists, and working-class socialist youth was engaged in a struggle as to what sort of political process and organisation would emerge. It was like two or three different grubs in the same cocoon, but only one butterfly or in their case phoenix was supposed to emerge. It became a matrix of different ideologies and different versions of history. Eire Nua was the newly developed united Provisional Sinn Fein manifesto. It had been a compromise but marked a great victory for the revolutionary socialist fighters, mainly from the north. It talked of the task of building a united Socialist Ireland, not a unity with the Catholic-Church-dominated insular south, but a New Ireland north and south. An Ireland based upon the four historic provinces of Munster, Ulster, Leinster and Connacht, and owned and controlled by the workers and small farmers. It was to be an Ireland of Catholic and Protestant, it was meant to enshrine religious freedom and the separation of Church and state for a truly secular, socialist Ireland. It was federalist because some concession, some accommodation to nearly a million in the loyalist communities had to be made. Indeed the programme had been hammered out during constant consultations and dangerous liaisons with some of the more progressive individuals from the loyalist ranks and their militias.

> The terms being offered by the Republican movement are the most generous ever offered by a Nationalist Ireland in the sense that we would see four self-governing provinces in a federal Ireland and that would mean that, at all-Ireland level the Nationalists would rule, while at Ulster level the loyalists [originally loyalists—DJD] would rule. But then beneath that we would have regional government: West Ulster, East Ulster etc. but at local district level rule would go according to the majorities. Andersonstown, and Falls would be Republican Councils, while

Shankhill etc. would be loyalist ones.

This was real power sharing Ruairi O Bradaigh was referring to:

The Ulster Protestants would rule themselves and the Ulster Catholics would also rule themselves. Tyranny is prevented by a system of checks and the loyalists say that down on their list of priorities this is pretty high up. They sometimes ask us can we guarantee that this will last into the third and fourth generation but we say this is no transitional stage, this is our final system and this is a point we made in Fealde and we showed them similar plans for Munster and Connaught ... that was inclined to bring them along.

Ruairi went on to talk of the world process which demonstrated a demand for greater decentralisation and a move away from high government, to communities of communities cooperating together. He said the working class of both communities had been conned and their future was a united one. (*IRIS*, 18 April 1975)

As described earlier, Goole Constituency Labour Party Young Socialists, proposed to the 12th National Conference of the LPYS at Skegness in 1973 this whole programme as our resolution to Conference on Ireland. Of course we didn't say whose programme it was, and Militant were so insular, so isolated from the politics of republicanism they didn't know what it was.

THE NOTTINGHAM CONFERENCE

Thursday 10 January 1974. Miners and trade unionists, public meeting, Albert Hall Institute, Derby Road, Nottingham. Organisers were A. Palmer (NUM) and Brian Walker (Newstead Branch NUM, Notts), the speakers myself and Dennis Skinner MP, not yet 'the Beast of Bolsover' as he was to become, but still a hellfire preacher. Arthur Palmer, a Notts NUM militant and leftist Labour Party supporter, was in the chair. This was part of a matrix of meetings crisscrossing the country, intersecting the left, right and centre of the Labour and trade union movement, gelling the far left through to the moderate Labour folk; it was preparing a political summary of the impending industrial clash of titans. The Notts Area NUM does us the favour of writing to all its lodges to tell them not to come.

The Revolutionary Workers Party had called this mass meeting of the Nottingham miners. This was a rare event; 'the Party' rarely felt at ease addressing the class directly. On this occasion the miners from Gedling and Bestwood were there in fair numbers together with workers and shop stewards from Stanton's iron and steel works and Raleigh Cycles. Other engineering workers had sent along representatives. The Party would tell us this was not their role. To be right they didn't speak, I did, the hall was packed, about a thousand workers, trade unionists, miners from Nottingham, left groups. Part of the success, as I said, was due to the Nottingham Area of the NUM having sent round the circular telling branches not to publicise the event or attend. It was a revolutionaries' meeting, with this David Douglass, from Hatfield pit, speaking 'unofficially'. What an invitation, a revolutionary, unofficial, miner from Yorkshire on a platform not authorised or approved of by the Nottingham Area who were telling them not to attend! They turned out in their hundreds. Speakers from the floor reflected their frustrations with the grip the leadership had on the pickets, but actually, we didn't have targets. Ken Terry marched down the isle with a swagger, which he was wont to do at times, and announced fraternal greetings from the bakers' union, amid cheers. He warned that bakers weren't as revolutionary as miners, but they kneaded the dough just the same (to groans) and he foretold of a forthcoming strike by bakers across the country! Joe Marino who was to go on to be the president of the Bakers Union was a member of the Party and with Ken published *The Bakers Voice* which was gaining the ear of many in that industry.

21 January 1974. 'The Miners Fraction: Revolutionary Workers Party (Trotskyist)—British section of the Fourth International (Posadist)' issued its own leaflet 'Vote Strike'. This wasn't *The Mineworker*—this was the miners who were members of the RWP, acting as a political cell in our name. 'We urge that this colliery, the centre of our work have the highest recorded vote in favour of strike action.' We predicted a pitched battle on the streets with Heath.

Our picket lines are going to be attacked, and possibly by armoured vehicles, in this case we must prepare for the building of barricades to keep stocks of coal in the pit yards or out of power stations. This is simply one practical defence, but the main defence must be the united action of the whole of the working class, the same as we achieved at Saltley ...

On the payment of Social Security benefits, it's said that any money paid out will have to be repaid. We state categorically that any social security paid out to our members WILL NOT BE REPAID. There will be no return to work whilst that threat hangs over us, NO REPAYMENT OF ANY MONEY! In the event of Social Security NOT being paid at all, then we demand that the Union issues strike pay and that in the event of shortages of food, the supermarkets be taken over and under joint control and foodstuffs distributed.

This strike will be won! THE GOVERNMENT WILL BE SMASHED! But the control of the strike MUST be kept in the hands of the rank-and-file and not left to bureaucrats in the Union 'leadership'. We will say how the strike is run. We must have regular MASS PUBLIC MEETINGS which will be open to our wives and all fellow trade unionists ...

The leaflet first hit the local press headlines and then the national ones, and in the process revealed the fact that we had been given our own squad of 800 police, a rapid response unit to move into action against our picket lines and any militant insurgency. The bookshop got a mention, and *The Mineworker*, as well as the Miners Fraction RWP. We were informed by the press via the special squad that a special watch was being kept on our activities and a unit was ready for any trouble. The police were determined to be in far readier state this time than first time, but they, and us incidentally, were about to be outflanked by total Union solidarity which would render redundant all picket lines except purely token ones.

24 January 1974. The NEC of the miners held a national ballot for all-out

strike action. 81per cent voted yes, with votes of nearly 100 per cent in the militant areas of Scotland, Wales and Yorkshire. The strike of 1972 had scarcely secured the ballot, 58 per cent just 3 per cent over the minimum. The NUM had made great strides with that victory, to bring miners back to an earning level commensurate with the work and risks at work and from disease, but most felt they hadn't quite got there yet. The NUM demanded £45 for the power loaders, £40 per week for elsewhere underground, and £35 for the surface workers.

	Total Votes	Voting Yes		Voting No	
		Number	%	Number	%
Yorkshire	54,570	49,278	90.30	5,292	9.70
Nottingham	28,284	21,801	77.08	6,483	22.92
South Wales	26,901	25,058	93.15	1,843	6.85
Durham	17,341	14,862	85.70	2,479	14.30
C.O.S.A.	15,368	6,066	39.47	9,302	60.53
Scotland	16,587	14,497	87.40	2,090	12.60
Midlands	12,309	9,016	73.25	3,293	26.75
DERBYSHIRE	10,679	9,242	86.54	1,437	13.46
NORTH-WEST	8,637	7,084	82.02	1,553	17.98
Northumberland	8,420	7,075	84.03	1,345	15.97
DURHAM MECHAN	5,937	4,590	77.31	1,347	22.69
Group no. 2 (Scotland)	4,834	3,929	81.28	905	18.72
Cokemen	4,583	3,076	67.12	1,507	32.88
Power Group	3,981	2,239	56.24	1,742	43.76
South Derbyshire	2,604	1,827	70.16	777	29.84
Leicestershire	2,519	1,553	61.65	966	38.35
Kent	2,360	2,117	89.70	243	10.30
Northumberland Mechanics	2,191	1,816	82.88	375	17.12
North Wales	1,200	952	79.33	248	20.67
Cumberland	800	775	88.07	105	11.93
Power Group no. 2	1,164	681	58.51	483	41.49
Durham Enginemen	896	543	60.60	353	39.40
Yorkshire Enginemen	370	316	85.41	54	14.59
Totals	**23,2535**	**18,8393**	**80.99**	**44,222**	**19.01**

There was talk that the army would be used to run coal from pitheads and stocks and maybe even man the power stations themselves. Mick McGahey, the Union's vice president and leader of the Scottish miners, a Communist from generations of reds, made an impassioned speech. He said that if the army was called in against the miners, they would call upon the soldiers to disobey orders, to stay in the barracks, or join the miners on the picket lines. As the two sides in this conflict lined up for a battle which would embrace far more than miners' wages, this sounded like a call for revolution. At once Labour dignitaries started distancing themselves from the speech. One hundred and eleven Labour MPs signed a statement attacking Mr McGahey. Mick responded with the classic retort, 'You can't dig coal with bayonets', although just to set his politics straight he announced that yes he did want the downfall of the Tories, but we would achieve that through the ballot box. He didn't add that the miners in fact weren't waiting for any ballot box to arrive and this strike would determine whether the government fell or not.

The Union was playing actions in support of the strike close to its chest. The leadership of this strike was determined to hold control over pickets and flashpoints, and the foot soldiers were not let loose en masse as they had been in 72.

I was picketing down at Keedby; this was Hatfield's pitch. I was where two years previously on 3 February 1972 Fred had died picketing on the very same spot. Six of us sat in a wooden shed, beside the traditional empty barrel stuffed with smoking logs and drifting smoke. For excitement we watched the boats go by on the Keedby canal. One of the pickets was what you might call 'slow'; he was thick actually, the walking embodiment of the computer-animated character of Gollum in the subsequent Hollywood blockbuster Lord of the Rings. The power station drew in its water for cooling from the river, in huge draughts. All of the flotsam and jetsam were filtered out by a big boom net and grid, into which also were drawn numerous fish. Gollum here was permanently wet, with a fish in each hand, and fish in his pocket; he stood hour on hour over the brazier cooking his fish on a stick, his gob permanently full of the stuff. Every time I see Gollum with his 'fissss', I think of that picket hut.

We never saw a lorry. The story was true everywhere. The unions, or at least the leaders of the unions, had agreed: don't breach the miners' picket lines, don't use any scab produce, shut the country down tight as a box. Their members needed no special encouragement; this was a fight for organised labour, and many were happy to allow the miners to be at the sharp end of it. Not that it was particularly sharp in terms of action.

I was in big demand as a speaker right through February in Surrey, Lambeth, Ealing, all over the south. Students were straining at the leash to become involved and at least send money to the miners. Because of new regulations and restrictions on students donating to political causes, I was paid lavish sums of money for expenses for speaking and directed this back to the branch 'Hardship Fund' which I had fought hard to establish. At Guildford, John Mason, a member of the IMG, had invited me down to talk to the University of Surrey . The place was alive with cops, and surveillance, spot checks and searches. The IRA had just carried out the famous Guildford bombing. The press had said it was a defenceless pub full of innocent victims. Actually it was the army's favourite watering hole, and although soldiers wives and girlfriend's went there, it had not been an indiscriminate target by any means. The message to those who didn't do so by choice, was, keep the company of the army and you might be caught up in the target. Mind, most garrison towns had strict delimitations between soldiers pubs and civilians pubs anyway; your average non-soldier resented the squaddie, for numerous reasons, most of which were only casually political. Soldiers were by and large still out of step with their generation, who were still courting revolution and rebellion. In dress and hairstyle, pay, attitude and patter your average squaddie was most unlike the average working-class kid on the town.

At Surrey I had spoken to a mass ensemble of the students, on the proposition that the student union should donate £500 to the miners' support fund. The Tory students argued that such a move would not have popular student support, that only the left political students had turned up to the meeting. They put forward a rival proposal, that the Student Union would match whatever the students themselves donated that week, and nothing more. They counted on the idea that students were too busy studying, drinking, dancing and shagging to be bothered with giving money to these greedy miners. The proposition was carried. I was in an instant whisked around the college campus, then and there, making impromptu speeches to surprised mass-eating venues of students, in their refectories and cafés, in the TV lounge, in the games room, and on the stump, outside the libraries. I stayed for the weekend, and by the time I had finished the students themselves had donated about £800, which had to be matched from the funds. So we actually raised more money anyway as well as awareness among the students who backed the miners to the hilt.

The last shift before the start of the strike Charlie Palmer was killed in a rock fall, at Markham Colliery, Derbyshire. He was due to have his forty-second birthday that coming Friday, and his wife was waiting at the end of the pit lane in their car to pick him up; he never arrived. He was the 7768th miner to die in the pits since Nationalisation. His gross pay as a tunneller was £36.79.

5 February 1974. The result of the strike ballot was announced. The government's response to the strike was ill considered. Only two days later on the 7th Prime Minister Heath announced that he would call a general election on 28 February, the main issue being the strike itself, and the question 'Who Rules Britain?' In retrospect one wonders at the sanity of the move. One is forced to ask whether the rumours of bad blood between Heath and the Government intelligence forces referred to earlier weren't true, that they had sailed him out into the wild blue yonder. The strike was scarcely two days old; the government had a working majority and was under no constitutional pressure not to continue. The miners were seeking actually a return in real terms to a financial position the government's own enquiry had actually conceded just two years earlier. In fact the government's own Pay Board reported just prior to the election date that the miners' case was basically sound, publishing figures which purported to show that the miners were entitled, even under existing Phase Three of the pay policy, to significantly more than had been offered. Heath may have been victim of his own propaganda in the belief that 'the public' were sick of strikes and unions and would give him a decisive new mandate; if so, it was a disastrous error of judgement.

By sheer luck, we had called a public meeting of The Miners Fraction of the Revolutionary Workers Party, around the title "The Miners Strike—Is It Political?" The meeting had been scheduled for 7 February 1974. The speaker was

David Douglass, Doncaster Regional Committee of the RWP(T), Secretary of Thorne and District Trades Council. It was held at the George Hotel, Stainforth. On the same day as our meeting Ted decided to call a general election, which shows how scared we obviously had him.

The strike was now being run in concert with the election campaign although the rank-and-file miners insisted no deals other than a wage deal would be made with any government, Tory or Labour. There was a determination not to allow scenes of mass picketing, no riots, no mass scrums. An orderly quiet picket, which no one passed through, was almost everywhere achieved with total TUC cooperation. It was aimed at minimising damage to Labour's election chances. Despite this, APEX, the clerical union which had muscled its way into colliery offices and pitheads and displaced the traditional NUM white-collar section COSA, refused to join the strike and earned barely subdued resentment. When Joe Gormley went public to request the miners to call off the action during the period of the general election, the response was loud and clear. Seaham Lodge in Co. Durham immediately dispatched a telegram to Gormley demanding his resignation. Seaham had been a hot bed of rebellion in the preceding century and into the 1920s but had moderated somewhat with the advent of Nationalisation and Labour governments; these last two strikes would ensure that moderation as a political and industrial creed were exorcised from Seaham evermore.

In the villages we held mass stormy meetings, not least at the George in Stainforth, where, packed to the rafters, the miners heard me warn of attacks upon our picket lines to break the fuel free. The army had been moved into strategic camps near power stations, and a special surveillance squad was keeping us under close scrutiny. Somebody somewhere took the decision that sending in troops to move stocks of coal would precipitate a general strike. A general strike not in the teeth of recession like the last one, but with workers on the assent. They decided to back off the physical confrontation and take an ideological and parliamentary route instead.

At York university where Fred had gone from Ruskin, I had sang to a mass audience, again for a massive sum, all of which went back to the funds. I was touring the country, addressing mass meetings, urging support, but also letting the cat out of the bag about the grip the bureaucracy had round the throat of this strike, not just the strike, but the solidarity action too. The money came back to Hatfield's hardship fund, but the Branch officials didn't like it; this wasn't supposed to be happening—it was only the rank and file, now flocking to their Branch meetings, who thought the student solidarity was great. At the end of the strike a celebration big night out was organised at the Miners Welfare in Stainforth. Representatives from the Surrey and York university students were invited, and during the night the Branch chairman took to the mic to thank them, and they were asked to stand, and a standing ovation was given to them. John was there, beaming away, as well he might as the miners covered the tables with pints and shorts of all descriptions. The Hatfield miners would never hear a word against the students again; they were our friends and had did their best for us.

We had total solidarity, we were winning the strike, but was that the point? Without rank-and-file action, joint action on the streets and at work, without politics and class consciousness, debate and elaborating a strategy forward for socialism, we as activists were being robbed of the fruits of this victory. We lost the chance to draw out the deeper lessons of the strike and mobilise as an independent class force in direct rather than proxy control, as we had done in 1972. Mind, when the pressure came on for the miners to return to work, pending the outcome of the general election, there was widespread rebellion. No way were we going for that one; election or no election the miners were on strike, and would be on strike whoever was elected until we got justice, or if not justice at least what we had gone on strike for.

I later considered that this had been a sort of joint trade union bureaucratic coup in favour of a Labour government—we will give you solidarity up front, no need to march in and demand it, no need to erect those mass picket lines, only keep your troops off the streets, so we can persuade the nice voters not to be scared of a Labour government elected on the back of a violent strike. And Heath lost the election, Labour won, the NUM won much of its demands, we gained a reputation. So what am I moaning about? It wasn't controlled and managed by us. We were bashed on the head and kept below decks; it was a bad sign. We still didn't control this NEC and the leadership, despite Mick's presence in it, or Arthur's command of the Yorkshire area.

The election result was a crashing defeat not in numerical terms, for actually no party achieved a clear majority, but it was a slap in the face for Heath and the Tories, and their sense of themselves as 'the true voice of the people'. It was too for all those right-wing tabloid papers and biased radio and TV reports which had pilloried the miners cause. The *Mirror* however had given unstinting support, and the election edition carried hundreds and hundreds of crosses on its pages, an illustration of the numbers of miners who had been killed wining the country's coal since Nationalisation. The paper urged: before you use your cross, remember these crosses, it was strong stuff. Mind, if it had given a cross for every miner who had died from lung disease as well, the whole paper would have been filled with crosses. Deaths from pneumo alone were running at 300 per year and we had in March of the previous year submitted claims to be heard in Newcastle Crown Court for 44,000 current victims of the disease.[58]

It was a milestone victory in the history of the miners and a monument to working class solidarity, which had been 100 per cent throughout the strike. But there were misgivings. The leadership of the Union had quite off its own bat, and obviously in secret, decided to exclude the rank and file from initiatives and control. They quite consciously restricted the numbers and control of pickets. They actively stopped other workers and especially leftist students intervening in any platform the miners might try to create. The only pickets allowed had to be authorised by areas, each one identified with an armband and sticker 'official picket', and to keep charge of those few souls was a 'chief picket' to make sure things didn't get out of hand. Victory or not, we put down a motion of censure on the NEC for the bureaucratic way in which it had sat on the strike, and for allowing the Labour government, pledged to settled us the full claim, to get off before settling all of our outstanding grievances. The resolution, clearly initiated by us in the Revolutionary Workers Party, and supported by Billy Matthews and the Communists, caused outrage. Mullanny, who had been heavily involved in the Area and national hold on the strike and tactics, lined up with Frank Clark and the other officials to defend the leadership and hail them as great visionaries who had steered us through a great historic victory. 'The victory is ours not theirs!' I shouted in the clamour of the battle, 'The betrayal is all theirs!' Betrayal was a hard word really, and there were massive strengths in our victory, but we were peeved to say the least that the leaders had robbed us of greater politicisation, not necessarily conflict and action on the street, but direct measures of control from which we would demonstrate our vision for rank-and-file control of the industry as a whole and of this union of ours. The new emerging 'left leadership' was to demonstrate over the next twenty-odd years that they were just as keen to grab the poop deck and steer the ship as the moderates had been, but that wasn't the point of the mutiny.

The strike of 1974 gave conclusive proof that mining was still a vital part of the British economy. The oil sheikhs of the Middle East had suddenly announced a staggering price rise for their oil—something which a couple of decades later would not be tolerated by the consuming superpowers, even to the point of war and occupation of the oil fields. Now, though, with the counterbalance of the Soviet armed forces, for whatever reason, such a solution was not available and coal, still available in Britain, had seldom looked more attractive as a fuel, and the mounting trade deficit did nothing to reduce its allure. So following the defeat of Heath came a sudden realisation: 'The coal industry is needed after all, the miner is needed.' But a little caution would have warned us. We had been to this point before. Just for now, though, we were invincible and we had nowt to fear from anyone.

Miners' Pay Claim Settlement 1974, £ per week (basic)

	1973 (Actual)	Claim	Settlement
Minimum surface	25.3	35	32
Minimum underground	27.3	40	36
Coalface (NPLA)	36.8	45	45

Source: National Coal Board Annual Report 1973–4.

Although the Tories were crushed, and with them everything they stood for in terms of anti-union laws, worker-bashing, and attacks upon benefits, Labour did not ride to office on the crest of a popular tide. They had won the most seats, but polled less than at in any election since 1931. In part perhaps the working-class socialist voters were still not ready to vote for a Labour Party they couldn't trust, perhaps much of the Tory propaganda and Red Scare had sunk home, and some sections of the class, although they wouldn't vote Tory, were scared to vote Labour. This schism in the working-class electorate in turn was to colour the kind of 'Labour' government we would see emerge.

For us, this was our finest hour in terms of wringing concessions from the employers and the government, but we should have nailed all our demands to the floor and insisted we sort everything out here and now. We didn't; £45 was conceded for the face men, but only £36 for underground, and £32 for surface men. The offer should have been put to ballot but it wasn't; instead it was sent out for branch votes, with a recommendation of acceptance from the NEC and the area offices, and the bulk of the branch officials too. It was accepted. They got off cheap and those unresolved issues were to come back to haunt us, despite the fact that we had won, Heath had gone, and the miners could now walk on water. In the wings, our enemies slunk off to prepare for the next confrontation, resolving that these miners had to be slapped down and slapped down hard. Labour and Tory in their respective academic think tanks went off to plan how to disarm and defeat the miners. As mentioned earlier, Miron, an NCB chief in the Midlands, in consultation with Derek Ezra the NCB chairman, had drawn up the outline of dynamic plan to wrest the industry from the NUM, essentially through denationalisation, decentralisation, rundowns, contractors and financial carrots. Now the Tory advisers under the chairmanship of Nicholas Ridley, Mrs Thatcher's close confidant, were to draw up sophisticated plans and strategies which would engage the miners and defeat them come the earliest chance (more on this later). Mr Wilson, elected to the strains of 'Hello Dolly' ('Hello Harold ... nice to have you back where you belong,' they sang in the first year or so of office), was to close 36 pits with a drop of 7 per cent of our manpower.

No sooner was the ink dry on the agreement than the NEC approved salary increases to Gormley, Comrade Daly and 50 other full-time officials across the country. It put Arthur and Joe on £7,000 a year, and area agents on £4,600. I don't know if the leadership considered we'd be so highly delighted with our payrises that we wouldn't mind them taking what in many cases amounted to a 50% wage rise, but mind we did. There was another explosion from many of the militant branches, including Seaham again, who dispatched another resignation telegram.

At Usworth, the last of the Washington collieries, the men went back to work but under the cloud of closure. The NCB were deeming the pit exhausted while the NUM mining engineer had said there was Top Busty coal for another 12 months. The men were certain there was another bonanza somewhere. The same had been said at Wardley; the Victoria seam was said to be beneath the 1480 and to be 6 feet thick but our safety engineer had said it was more like 6 inches. What of the Monkton shaft, which postwar Nationalisation had started to sink between Follonsby and Monkton? They had won a third of the way when they abandoned the project. Surely they were after a rich block of coal between Wardley and Hebburn? Suddenly there was no seam. Washington Glebe were I had trained and me Uncle Ned worked closed just before the strike and the great 'F' pit in the centre of Washington, dominating the whole town with its high head gear and steam winder, belching clouds of white smoke and shrieking away at shift turns, closed in 1968. The closure of Usworth would end 700 years of coal mining in the town of Washington, and despite the preservation of Fanny's headgear (though minus its magnificent winder), the town would become a 'new town' divided into zones and numbered districts like something out of 1984 or the TV series *The Prisoner*.

Meantime Schlacke and Cinema Action were finishing off their greatest film to date, *The Miners' Film*. It had set out to record the 1972 and 1974 strikes, but the miners and their families had pulled the focus back to 1926 time and again. Many an old lad seen 1972 as round two of 1926, or at least a revenge for the beatings they took in that period. People like my Da seen in Heath a new Churchill, a right-wing, old-fashioned, push-you-in-the-dirt Tory. The victory for the miners in February 74 was to be like a year of Xmas celebrations for him and his old workmates up at the British Legion Club at Palmers Hall, or down at Hebburn Working Men's Social Club. Pit communities, many long since deprived of an actual pit, couldn't hide their glee.

I had hoped to do the talkie bit, the political overview, but Schlacke, with clear perception, knew when to confine me to the crowd scene. I got to sing the songs on the sound track, unaccompanied and off camera. But they come over powerfully against the grimy black and white background of the scenes of pit, pit village and strikers, 1926, 1972 and 1974. Where and how Schlacke had got the old archive film on miners in the Twenties and Thirties at work underground and in the villages I never discovered, but they were and are unique. He cut these with underground working scenes from the Sixties and Seventies in what was probably the most extensive presentation of miners' work ever presented up that point. It has location shots from villages in South Wales, Kent and Dunscroft and Stainforth, classic pit communities, in the shadow of the pitheads. The film rings with the chants of strikers calling out the scabs, in 1926, in 1972 and in 1974, actual voices of the period, actual scenes of the tanks on the streets, the mass rush of workers, the army in lorries, mounted police, mounted soldiers, the streets black with bobbies, and bodies. It showed the strange movements of tanks and armoured cars around Heathrow, and armed cops on the streets, supposedly a demonstration to the IRA, but we thought it was to all of us.

A COLLAGE OF STRUGGLE

Although technically the film is rather dark in parts, its professionalism, its sheer bloody raw facts of life on screen had not been seen before. It was to win awards all over the place. It was years ahead of its time, not least because Schlacke had won the trust of the NUM at all levels of the Union. He had managed to get his camera above and below ground, he had men in their muck and miners' wives in the shops against the backdrop of the headgear. People in Britain didn't know anything about the miners in those days, neither above nor below ground. This film was an amazing documentary, this was us talking directly to other working-class folk. They followed the process of that struggle, talking to miners at work during the overtime ban.

Here we had the leaders of the time, a youthful Arthur Scargill, Lawrence Daly, Joe Whelan, Jack Collins, and a silent, sidelined Joe Gormley. Joe Whelan was a charismatic Communist leader of the Nottingham miners, of Irish ancestry.

As I mentioned earlier, he had lined up with a delegation of miners leaders to meet Ted in '72 for negotiations. While all respectfully shook hands and said 'How do you do?' Joe had taken the hand and said 'Hello sailor!' I was to have many an amusing encounter with Joe over the years. He was never one for holding very well to the formal party line. During one of the mass rallies during the 74 strike, he was asked about the struggle in Ireland. Of course the Communist Party was lined up with 'the Officials' and dead against the Provisional rebellion. 'Well,' says Joe, 'I can't agree with the IRA, but if I were in Ireland and there were foreign soldiers walking about in my street armed to the teeth I know what I would do!'

Actually Joe will live in mind for his terrific speech at the 1968 conference in support of a South Wales resolution calling for withdrawal of US forces and British complicity in Vietnam and the unification of Vietnam north and south to a single self determination. The resolution had been condemned from the platform as one-sided and a Mr Kit Robinson, an Area official of the Durham Area, still right-wing at that time, on behalf of the NEC, condemned 'the terrorists, of the NLF'. Joe in a bomb blast of a speech added:

> You talk about democracy, you talk about the right of nations to have their independence, and some people talk about the atrocities and the terrorist activities of the South Vietnamese. Let me tell you a little story about terrorists, because I come from a family of terrorists. My family were fighting for their independence, and what happened? My two uncles who were fighting for the independence of Ireland, one of them was shot in O'Connell Street, and one was hanged in Mountjoy Gaol in Dublin. They were accused at that time, Mr Chairman, of being terrorists, of being militant. What were they fighting for? They were fighting for the freedom of Ireland against British Capitalism and British Imperialism.
>
> The same thing is taking place in Vietnam. The North and South Vietnamese are fighting for their independence against outside interference, and I as a Trade Unionist and Socialist, stick up for them and say they have got the right to have it and I am prepared to fight for them to have that right ... I am doing it as a Socialist, and every Socialist who has got a conscience must stand by the National Liberation Movement, not only in Vietnam, but in every country in the world where this is taking place ...[59]

Also recorded on this film is a glimpse of our own local political milieu. Faces from the past include the wild and anarchic young Hatfield miner Tony Larner,[60] singing and playing the penny whistle which was also used as a background theme; Dave Howes, an IS member and a great singer; Susan McQuire, our pouting and sultry babysitter, whose folks Pete and Margaret were activists in the Tenants Association, the left of the Labour Party and regular visitors to our house, demonstrations and socials. She was beginning to take a keen interest in politics. The sensual and sultry Susan was, though, off limits.[61/62]

In the crowd in the film are the faces of Hatfield miners, and lads from the local fire brigade, at first mistaken for cops because of their hair and boots. It is one of our Red Star Folk Socials, this one to celebrate the 1973 Miners' Gala, and held at the White Hart, Barnby Dun. The pub was owned and run by a Cockney ex-heavyweight boxer. He liked us, and we liked him; he was a fighter all his life and seen in us a related fight, and one he identified with. Mind, I nearly blew it; as we turned up early to get the electric and camera stuff in place, he blew his top. I had placed an advert for the social in the local paper. I had also announced our intention to charge admission. His licence didn't cover performances, the big upstairs room didn't have a fire escape and technically he wasn't allowed to charge admissions. So he was none too chuffed, but after a beer and some heartfelt apologies we were clear to go ahead.

We had operated the Red Star Folk Music socials at various venues around Doncaster. The Drum at Bentley had held a massive May Day social there in 1973 with Des Jones, Pam and Alan Bishop, the Hogshead, formed by the Donny fireman and foremer RAF man Steve Walker, who having married a Scottish lassie, became honorary Scottish, with songs of the rebellions and the heather and the whisky. To these regulars came the Tyneside Irish, the rip-roaring Beggermen, who were becoming regular guests at wor dos. The Spreadeagle was our regular venue and club, although that was superseded by the Bentley Hotel, the Drum which hosted our big concerts, and on occasion here we were at the White Hart. We hand-made posters, half imperial size, and stencilled our Red Star Folk Music Society heading and the forthcoming attraction, then flyposted these right through the town centre, the market, the shops, the pubs, the bus shelters and stations. You could never not know when we had a folky night organised. We had quite a membership. Our membership card had a bonny red star and a preamble about music of the people and class struggle.

One of our regular singers was the deputy editor of the Doncaster Evening Post, who also as it turned out was an international clay pigeon shooting champion. He had his own bullet loading gear, which Jim quickly copied. Jim's bullets were the only ones in the district made from corrugated green and blue plastic, which he stuffed with varying amounts of shot himself. Jim had a beautiful over-and-under, extra-length Russian 12-bore, and an odd 10-bore which he got from somewhere. I had an old, side-by-side, hammer-action 12-bore which Maureen had bought me; it must have belonged to some rich bastard in its heyday—it was magnificently carved along the whole barrel. My favourite though was a bolt-action 410; most of our members had 410s but mine was the only bolt-action. At this stage, though, it was for fun, targets, clays, tin can hoys. That forebye.

We carried a big periphery of local singers who normally turned up for everything we organised. Many of these we nicked from the Bay Horse folk club at Bentley. They ran a hugely successful Saturday night club, which we invariably went to en masse. I was the top guest singer myself there on more than one occasion, though they tended toward the folksy, country ditty songs rather than my red-raw, proles-in-struggle stuff.

Our venues took ages to prepare; we decked the place in banners, old and current, together with posters and flags. The tables were all given wine bottles with

candles, and when these were lit and the lights turned off the place and the crowd
and the power of the music and the collective hearty singing made a heady mixture
of emotions—taken with copious quantities of beer, it must be said.

But these were the days of pioneering legal changes, to swing some justice back in
the direction of the working people. The Equal Pay Act 1970, followed by the Sex
Discrimination Act 1975, the Health and Safety At Work Etc. Act 1974, laws
against unfair dismissals consolidated as the Employment Protection Act 1975—
these, coupled with the now confident stride of the rank and file and the partial
adaptation to the winds of change by the well-heeled union bureaucrats, made
many an employer and gaffers in general feel under siege.

Around this time, I am told, Mr MacGregor the colliery manager was on a
joint inspection with the Union secretary, on a surprise late-afternoon visit, when
they came into the empty canteen and peered into the kitchen only to find a
surface worker up to the hilt in a canteen lady laid on a bench.

'Sack her now!' shouts the irate manager.

'Whey, nor lad, you can't do that. If you don't sack him too, that's sex
discrimination, gaffer.'

'Well, sack him then!'

'Can't dey that either, gaffer. He hasn't been given a warning, there has been no
exhaustion of procedures and his behaviour hardly constitutes a serious breach. Its
unfair dismissal, gaffer.'

The manager stands fuming for a few impotent minutes then shouts: 'Well get
rid of that bliddy bench!'

The story also went round about our future victory in securing the one-day
week.

Arthur addresses a mass heaving crowd of miners. 'Right lads, a great victory.
From now on you need only work Wednesdays.'

A great cheer goes up, and then a murmur; someone shouts out: 'Hey-up
Arthur, tha doesn't mean every bliddy Wednesday?'

The formal *Plan For Coal* is published. It commits the country to coal power as
the cheapest form of generation, to developing the country's coal reserves, to
protect the industry.

One of the first actions of Mrs Thatcher when she assumed leadership of the
Conservative Party in 1975 was to establish a committee under Lord Carrington
to covertly collect information on militants within public sector trade unions, with
the aim of countering their influence. These were later developed by Nicholas
Ridley MP. *The Ridley Report* classified all the public sector industries according to
their vulnerability to industrial action. The plan outlined the setting up of
financial targets for nationalised industries and their preparation for softly-softly
privatisation. Coal in particular was seen as being the most likely area of resistance
by militants; a future Conservative government should adopt a political strategy
that could crush any such opposition. The report detailed building up the stocks
at power stations, plans to import coal, recruitment of non-union drivers,

conversion of coal-fired power stations to oil firing, the mobilisation of a large nationally co-coordinated police force to deal with pickets and non-payment of benefits to strikers and their families. The Tory response and that of the Labour think tanks, also behind the scenes, of trying to devise means of derailing future united action by miners (in particular plans to break the unifying impact of national pay bargaining and reintroduce localised bonus schemes)—these two responses, by the two major parliamentary parties, uncoordinated though they were, would impact together.

Meantime came the M62 coach bomb. An army coach, usually carrying soldiers coming back from leave, but this time carrying some families going on visits too, was blown up on the M62. It wasn't long before the press was crowing they had captured the female bomber. It was Judith Ward, a hapless fantasist, looking for fame. She had tattooed 'IRA' on her own knuckles, in the obvious sign that she was an undercover IRA agent. She told a tale, a version of the Tania The Guerilla story. (Tania had reached the world attention of the media, by telling everyone she had been Ché's girlfriend, and he would roll up for her, hot-rod style, in his jeep, and whisk her off to jungle pads.) Judith said she was dating the chief commander of the IRA army council. She didn't know who he was, but he used to take her to discos in Belfast and Dublin. Then pop back for a quick shoot-out with the army, before coming home for his tea.

The life of an IRA volunteer was not however as the comic press presented it, and poor Judith was a headcase. She had tried to join the IRA, and they guessing the girl had a reality problem sent her to the UDA, who in turn phoned up the IRA to tell them to keep their loonies to themselves as they had enough of their own. Apparently joint communication between the two groups did take place, and not always at the point of rifle. The thing was, Judith had owned up to the coach bomb, when she knew absolutely nothing about it. The state and the press and the politicians however wanted a victim. She was custom-built.

A statement from the IRA made clear she 'was at no time a member of the IRA and was not involved in any action carried out by the Provisional IRA.' ... 'It is evident from the course that that trial has taken to date that the English authorities are using a person who obviously needs medical treatment in a manner designed to satisfy a lust for revenge on the part of the British establishment' (*IRIS*, 18 October 1974).

A little later Ripon Army barracks went up, in a straight military attack upon the army. It wasn't Judith either.

Around the same time Ken's bakers' strike was launched to mass panic, and people trying to kill each other to get bread. The country couldn't function without bread. We began to think that maybe we should have picketed bakeries and not coal stocks. Down the pit, I pulled cold potatoes from my bait tin, coated in butter and salt, marvellous. Others had scallops, which were fat cold chips basically. Maureen also gave me flasks of hot vegetable soup. All quite novel, but not cheese and tomato butties.

A RUSH OF DEATH

1 June 1974. We hadn't been long back at work, when the night sky lit up in a red, yellow fiery glow. Across the 40 miles of moors and fields, on the horizon we could see the blast and fire of the Flixborough explosion. A chemical works which ignited and killed almost everyone on site. At Hatfield men on day shift turned up and went home. The management demanded to know from Union officials why miners, were going home when there was an explosion at a chemical works? 'Good God!' I thought, 'are they blind?' Seventy to eighty fellow workers blown to kingdom come, the works demolished, the town blitzed, you could see the bodies burning on the horizon, a number of the men went to work there from these villages, and they ask, 'Why don't you just proceed to work as normal? Nothing to do with you.' They just don't understand, do they? Other than which it was our rescue men, the Mines Rescue Service, who mobilised to go into the death of the storm. Nobody in the fire service had seen anything like this, and the miners' equipment and experience seemed best suited to enter the charred site. As it was, all the rescue men could do was find charred, twisted fragmented bodies, which they faithfully recovered, risking life and limb and their own sanity .

Across Yorkshire nurses walk out on wildcat strike, overtime ban, and demonstrations. They are joined by the miners and the local TUC's demonstrating in support—more pay for the nurses. At the end of the year, the Gaul, a modern, big fishing vessel disappears without trace. MI6 operate a command centre from Hull docks, and station RN undercover personnel on board fishing vessels. Fishing boats are took into Soviet waters to spy. *The Gaul* goes down with no distress call, no survivors, and no messages and no wreckage. Older boats in the fleet return, no one sees anything. 'Who sank the Gaul?' Becomes a political question and an embarrassment to the secret state.[63]

My life for some years had consisted now of almost non-stop political activity: my work in the Central Committee of the RWP and all that involved in terms of every waking hour, the vigour with which I thrown myself into the strike and picketing and speaking all over the country, plus demonstrations, marches, writing pamphlets, articles; reading, arguing and fighting. In the meantime I was working on the rip, driving an Emco bucket, a machine like a mini-bulldozer. I'd been getting out of bed at 4.30 a.m. shattered and shell-shocked, having managed at best three hours' sleep. (Other shifts, I kidded myself, were better.) It wasn't as I didn't sleep—I wouldn't sleep; too much to do.

Something was starting to impact. My face was becoming gaunt, white, eyes either squinting to stay open or round and full and wild. My body could never find time to eat, or, if I did, digest the food. Bottles of stomach medicine and pills rowed the windowsills, and I was frequently seized by stomach cramps and intense pain and vomiting till there was nothing to puke but bile and blood. I was wafer-thin. Inside me trembled.

I was making my way to the shaft, on a miserable day shift, hot flushes spreading all over me, pulse racing, stumbling along over me own feet, when suddenly my brain went blank, like everything got turned off—sudden deafness, blackness and no recollection. 'What the fuck was that?' I thought. I got on the cage and all the pushing and shoving and cramped, smelly atmosphere suddenly started to—what? I tried to analyse what was happening, I was near to fainting I think, my brain was spluttering. As we surged from the cage to the paddy, a sense of dread, or mortal fear, gripped me from head to toe. It's impossible to describe. I boarded the paddy with a reluctance verging on terror and I tried to think of ways out, ways not to do this; what was going on? As the engine started and we set off, and the warm air and reek of the mine started to flush past me, I started to panic. I couldn't breathe, I had actually stopped breathing, my heart was going like the clappers, I was starting to feel no life in my legs other than manic trembling. Me belly was as tight as a box.

'Hey up!' someone said and they shone their lights on me.

'Dave, Dave!'

'He's going over, him.'

'Dave marra, is tha alreet?'

I couldn't answer, I couldn't pick me head up, I started to feel a tingling, numbing sensation all over me.

Next I remembered they had lifted me out of the paddy, and I sat squatted again a wall, with two officials, as the paddy made off into the distance. It took some time before I was able to stand of a fashion, and although we hadn't proceeded far inbye it took some time to walk back out again.

I went to bed, and we sent for the doctor. In between nightmare spells of sleep, and sweat which bathed me in a drench, I cried, deeply and wretchedly, for no particular reason. The doctor, Dr Waters, with whom I had discussed many things over the years, came into the bedroom. It didn't take long to establish that I was suffering from nervous exhaustion and I had had some sort of mental breakdown.

We discussed the whole thing some days later in the surgery. I had filled my life to full and overflowing with politics and activity, and then tried to fit the pit and work and being alive into whatever space was left. The impossible physical and mental equation meant that I had subconsciously started to resent the pit and then hate and fear it. This I rationalised later, because between then and sorting it all into place, I had months of trying to get to work, months of collapsing en route, months of mortal, bone-chilling terror. Eventually I fell off work altogether and started on a course of brain-numbing tablets Dr Waters had promised I would not become addicted to (he was wrong). He also posed me with an impossible choice. My health would not allow me to continue work in the pits and to have a full-time preoccupation with politics. The Central Committee of the RWP, the Secretary of Thorne and District Trades Council, the NUM, and work on crucifying shifts through the early mornings and throughout the night: it couldn't all continue. I was on the club at present, and taking these brain-killing, fear-killing tablets, but I was still boozing, and using the time as a means to fuller political involvement were it possible.

This wasn't going to answer the question. Abandon the pits? Aye, well, there's a happy prospect in abstract, but in reality what? The pits were my post in this class war, my comrades around the world couldn't leave their positions because the going was getting tough, and more than that, I was a coalminer through to my bones, this was not only what I did, this was what I was. How could I abandon myself?

Angie wrote:

Winkcolbank.

Sheffield

Dave I was really worried to hear about your nervous breakdown. I'm glad to see that even you admit you need some form of break, but a stop gap wont be sufficient. No I'm not going to go into it via a letter you must come over. I'm sure I can't be much help, but I'll have plenty to say. I know well the pressure of being an active revolutionary. I'm sure the experiences are different but it can lead to such brutal results. This especially for the most committed. I can see how much worse it is for you since your political positions lead you to view any other course as a scab move. But enough of this—I insist on a discussion at least! ... I shall want to know what day(s) you will be here from 28th July to end of following weekend. Be Sure To Contact Me!....Look forward to seeing you next week.

Love and revolution

Angie"

Angie was a curly bundle of revolutionary energy, with freak-out big frizzy hair, she wore the latest fashion of her years, those clumpy thick-soled shoes, and checky shortish skirts with blouses. She was I guess 22 or 23. She had a wonderfully sexy perky face and was bright as a button. She was one of the IMG's 'planters', intellectuals on their way to university taking time off to gain experience of the class through factory work, which she did working on shifts at Sheffield. I fancied the arse off her. We did actually, whisk away in a taxi, from a pro-Irish social, on the back seat, chatting like crazy, and on into her living room which she shared with her flatmates, all abed by the time we got there. She sat on the settee, I sat on a chair opposite. I was staying, I knew; she had directed me to the spare bedroom earlier. I assumed all other things being equal we were on for a sexual encounter. I am hopeless at getting over the first step; from the time Maureen Scott stood hovering in the doorway waiting for me to come and kiss her, my ineptitude had got no better. I had managed after nearly three quarters of an hour to sit before her on the floor, in front of the settee. I suppose I expected her to join me on the floor, I don't know if she wanted me to just get on and kiss her, but I couldn't scale that distance between us. I was shite-scared. Of rejection I suppose, or starting and not being able to continue because fear and tension wouldn't let me get erect. I usually just started and then the reciprocity caused the penis to do its stuff, but it was all on physical autopilot wasn't it? Until you could actually relax with someone, and get to know them sexually until this first encounter was all over with, usually quite mechanically I had found at first. But this time, na, I just couldn't pluck up the courage and I stayed on the floor before finally surrendering. 'Whey a'hm off to bed,' I announced then kicked myself for not saying 'Are yee coming?' I was still waiting for her, to hold her hands out, or put her arms round me, or something. Had I mistaken the messages? Who knows.

Twelve years later I ran into her again by chance. I was giving a lecture to the media students at Edge Hill College, and Angie was a media studies lecturer. I didn't recognise her at all—she had changed completely. She had to tell me who she was, and then I saw the very distant reflection of the girl she had been, and reflected myself on what might have been that night. No, not the last time either; there'll be lasses reading this who'll think, 'So that's the reason.' Especially you in that holiday chalet that night, me on the floor, you on the settee, trying to make the move, not daring to. Rats! At times I am consumed by self-hatred as sudden memories of total stupidity, timidity or cowardice come flooding back tiv'is. But should that girl in the holiday chalet waiting till the TV finally turned itself off, waiting for me to actually make a move, read this, yes I sorely did want to and have kicked myself ever since that I didn't. Mind, on the other hand, in later years I tended to seize the opportunity without any thought of the consequences or the likely repercussions and these have tended to cause more grief than the rabbit-frozen-in-the-highlights syndrome of earlier times.

A CHALLENGE FOR LEADERSHIP

Following the Nottingham miners' conference, it was clear some of the comrades, particular the more northerly ones, wished to push me forward to challenge the leadership of the RWP, to try and bring it, not back, because it had never been there, but closer to the working class, and a clearer orientation of their struggle. The episode of the extra ice-cream seemed a little extreme, the scolding of Ron for his dalliance with non-Party girls was worse, but then we had Barbara and Brian's unconstitutional baby. Worse than this, both of the comrades were members of PB. They were instantly resigned from that position. Barbara was pregnant, they had planned the baby, they had never discussed the plan with the Party, the baby needed Party planning, Party approval. It was a dereliction of duty to the class, it showed an indulgent and selfish preoccupation. Barbara admitted her desire to have the baby showed she didn't have enough life with the PB and the Party; Brian also admitted his weakness and individualist outlook, putting their own family unit before the collective family of the Party and the class struggle. We were outraged and sent a letter of protest, in fact we rejected the report of the PB and sent it back to them telling them to rethink it and redraft it. which drew a ferociously strict reply: there was no procedure to debate this matter, and regional committees could not send in resolutions criticising the decisions of the PB. This was a disciplinary matter and both comrades had accepted their weakness; they were both busted to the ranks.

> The whole struggle of the Vietnamese masses against imperialism, its resistance to the equivalent of 50 atomic bombs which have been dropped on them. They fight because they feel, as Cde Posadas says "life has no meaning without the struggle for socialism" that "human happiness consists of struggling for incessant progress". There is no superior way to live today, no satisfaction to be gained outside this. If we do not feel this satisfaction fully, and seek it in other ways, even in ways which in themselves are not wrong but are inferior to this, it is because still our internal structure formed by capitalism, our individual interest, egoism prevents us feeling it fully. When we must write this letter to say that C.L. is expecting a child, we feel that is another expression of our weakness, of our resistance to fuse ourselves fully with Posadas and the International, to function completely as leaders of the International with the highest and purest human sentiments as they are expressed by the Vietnamese masses or at the same level but in a more scientifically organised way by Posadas and by Su. And the Brazilian section constructed by Posadas. How can we not derive satisfaction superior to that of having a child, from Vietnam, from Chile, from the process which develops today in the LP and TUs in Britain? We know and accept intellectually the position of the International in relation to children; for the leader it is better, more convenient not to have children. It is clear and obvious; if we are guided by intelligence and reason alone, CI would not be pregnant but we have not been.

The comrades' self-criticism was biting:

> We accept all the criticism made of us by the comrades of the PB, on the wrong way it was communicated outside any organism to the Party which caused difficulties and complications with the new comrades; particularly we accept the criticism for the failure to discuss it previously with the Party and the slowness and reluctance which we felt to make a self criticism afterwards. We thank the comrades for the severity of the

criticism and at the same time for the fraternity which has not wavered ... There are comrades in the Party, couples who have no children, who show in this way a greater understanding and dedication than we do; we make a profound salute to these comrades. We end by reiterating our determination to better our functioning and understanding, elevating our relations with the Comrades, constructing ourselves and Matt. And the new child, being constructed by the Party in the life of the Party, because there can be no worthwhile life outside it.

But other things would come to a head meantime. The conference was in Derbyshire, in February 1974 as I recall. The special guest was Adolfo Gilly, a great Mexican revolutionary and leading figure in the Party. Adolfo had been one of the political prisoners who *The Mineworker* had highlighted and who we had exchanged correspondence with when they had been in Mexico City jail. *The Mineworkers* and myself had been features in the 1971 BBC-TV documentary, produced by Philip Donnallan, *Where Do I Stand? A Man and His Ideas*. It had voice-overs of our correspondence with the Mexican comrades. Adolfo had translated sections of *The Mineworker* into Spanish and circulated them among the political prisoners, to whom our letters were also read out. It was the first time we had met. We embraced warmly and never stopped talking. He was in the throes of writing a book on the Mexican revolution, *The Unfinished Revolution*, but since he had never had formal academic training of any sort, he just wrote it as he remembered it and considered it—no footnotes, no other sources— so all the academic and bourgeois press had rejected the book. We were looking forward to having the Party publish it, but as explained they didn't do named authors, that position being reserved exclusively for comrade J. Posadas.

After a great flourish of everyone getting to know everyone and talking to everyone the conference moved on into the evening fiesta. We set off to the off-licence to get some beer and wine. Kay at once attacked my individualism and lack of centrality.

'How come?'

'Well, so what do the other comrades do, while you drink your beer?' she asks.

'Well, they can drink some too.'

'They may not wish to drink like in a bar room—at a Party conference, mate.'

'OK. They don't have to.'

'So there we have your individualism—a few comrades drinking to themselves and others not drinking.'

'We can make a big a collective bowl, comrade, and pass it round it turn if yee wish, bonny lass.'

'This is no the point, Comrade Leam (my Party name). This is an individual sectarian activity. It is not a collective activity.'

'You saying I can't drink?' I say.

'You should not drink, but I cannot stop you, you should stop you.'

Others started to join in:

'But this was supposed to be a fiesta.'

'Si, a drink which everyone takes, as a toast perhaps, but not this lumpen drinking.'

'OK, I won't drink." And I flopped down in a seat in a real sulk.

'OK, we start the singing,' Kay announces, and calls upon Adolfo to start, which he does—a long boisterous peasant revolt song from Mexico, which has the comrades in full song, but I am not now in the mood; I divind feel very fiestery. Me and Ken go for a walk, to the nearest pub and down a couple of pints, feeling like guilty schoolkids smoking behind the bike sheds.

'We live in different worlds,' I suggest to Ken, before coming back with a large bottle of wine. This we share out to everyone, who all then decides to have a glass, awkward sods, so we didn't get to sup the residue of the bottle as planned.

'Should we gaan an get another bottle, then?'

'No, comrades, stay, sing, be with us.'

So we set off with a few foot-stomping songs, like 'Red Fly The Banners-Oh', and 'Which Side Are You On?' But it was noticeable that only our working-class comrades from here and there actually join in our efforts. Must be they don't know these songs.

As we got ready for kipping down that evening a second problem arose, one which fuelled a furious argument. Adolfo asked, as people started to sort out sleeping bags and settees etc., what was going on. Male comrades and female comrades, together? In the same room together?

'What?' we asked, incredulously.

Maureen started: 'Many of these comrades are companions, they live together or are married.'

'This isn't a hippy festival, we can't have mixed sexes together, all together, this is degenerate.'

'What, you think there is going to be an orgy because we are all in the same room? We are comrades at a conference, not a love-in.'

'You know,' says Kay, 'when comrades 'ave been apart for some time, and some comrades they 'ave 'ad wine ... '

'One glass!' we all shout.

' ... then passions can arise, and it's not good, it inflames other comrades not with partners and create jealousy and then some lusting, and all the elevated work of the Party is lost, the cadre is destroyed. Save your passion till you are alone, not together.'

Adolfo and the PBs applaud, and I think I want to hit them.

Maureen suggests: 'This sex, then, which I am sure nobody here was thinking of engaging in anyway, it breaks the centralism of Party, I guess? Because we all can't do it?'

'Si,' says Adolfo, 'something like thees.'

'Aah, whey,' says I, 'an orgy is the answer then, who's game?'

And to my surprise a couple of the very well spoken lasses who had been to public school, and who had joined up with the comrades in Nottingham and were at university there, giggled and shouted 'Us, please!'

'Aah,' I ventured 'three little maids from school are we,' and others joined in. We started to laugh at the whole situation, and take the piss, and make more and more outlandish suggestions. I think actually some of us might have started to get to grips then and there just for the bloody hell of it. But order was restored; the PB made its ruling, females upstairs, males downstairs. There was still much piss-taking, as females in their night clothes encountered males on their way to toilet and made giggly, shy, embarrassed gestures, hiding their knees and pulling their towels over their heads.

Well as if that wasn't bad enough, I slept on Adolfo's new jacket. It was one of those American silk blouse jackets, and in the night I just rolled it up and used it as a pillow. Course it didn't take kindly to being slept on.

'The first jacket I own in fifteen years,' he complained. 'First time I wear.'

'Well, sorry comrade, em, the creases will fall out.' (I think.)

When it comes to the final session of the conference and the review or balance of the leadership and their reports, the Derbyshire comrades propose that Comrade Leam be now elected to the Political Bureau and one of them made a fantastic speech about my standing in the class and power to reach workers; my audacious research in Ireland and contact with the Irish insurgents; my role in Cuba. This was at once supported by the comrades from Nottingham, Newcastle, Hull and Doncaster. The PB then call upon me to respond to the proposal. Which naturally I assumed meant I had been appointed. I concluded that I would not shirk from any task the Party placed upon me. I was being modest. Just as well—the PB stonily responded by slapping down any suggestion that the PB was some sort of popular assembly; some people seemed to think we had slipped into some form of democratic election process. This wasn't a trade union conference, they reminded us. The Political Bureau is a body comrades are appointed to when the political leadership consider they are ready for that role and comrade Leam isn't. He has many lingering illusions with Fidelism, and with the Irish insurgents. Heroic though those comrades are, they do not correspond to the leadership required in this period. Comrade Leam has many strengths and much experience within the working class, but he hasn't yet got the experience within the Party for this position. He will remain on the Central Committee. I felt like I had been stamped on. Comrades got up and walked off shaking their heads. I sat for a long time.

We were soon after to draft a punishing response to the whole segregation foolishness and the earlier disciplining of comrades for the undiscussed baby. They replied, rejecting our criticism, accusing us of 'shallow discussion', telling us it wasn't a matter of embarrassment. 'It is a question of the functioning of the whole international and the class and revolutionary movement.' Claiming the mantle of the Chinese Red Army and Soviet army, they deemed their actions were perfectly as they would have been.

The moment of truth was now here. The break would follow. On the way back in the train we elaborated that the struggle within this Party was futile. We agreed with Posadas but we didn't agree with this party monolithic centralism, this exclusive vanguardism. We began to get excited about breaking away into the wild blue yonder of the class war.

15 February 1974. In a prelude to implementing our ideas of military/physical training for the revolution, I organised, through the auspices of the Red Star Folk Club and at a distance, a big training and social weekend up in Northumberland. [Busy month: strike, party conference, training and social]!Maureen discovered she was the only female on the course and decided to stay instead in Newcastle for the weekend where she had some adventures of her own, with 'Rev' I believe. Having re-established contact with Fred, we discovered he had in fact bought an old ambulance, which was just the job for our training venture. This sort of doubled up as an emergency camper; given the weather, which was increasingly arctic the further north we went, it was just as well. Steve the proto-Scottish ex-RAF banjo-player and now fireman, had his long-wheelbase Land-Rover, which really would be doing its job up in the crags of Northumberland.

With one or two lesser vehicles in tow we set off. We were to have some problems with vehicles that weekend. Off even the minor roads, through dirt tracks, to no tracks, just boulder-ridden sheep paths, with Steve's Land-Rover, his pride and joy, we encountered the first dilemma. It sat wedged, pointing downhill, stuck on a small boulder, a stream flowing underneath it. 'Stuck.' he said, 'I'll have to reverse it and leave it.'

'Nor, man,' says Gordon, 'yee just have to drive it, man.' Getting in, he takes over the wheel, slams the vehicle into reverse, clicks in the four-wheel drive, and wham, slam, bang, bounced the jeep from boulder to boulder up the road, off the road, bounce-bouncing it up to the cottage, while Steve sat, his face deathly white, feeling every bump and bang as if it was his body not his poor Land-Rover's. 'Yee just have to show it whe's gaffer, man,' Gordon instructed. It landed bounced and mud-caked, but looked none the worse for having done the job it was designed for. Trouble was, despite being a fireman, Steve wasn't designed for it and neither, we were to discover almost at mortal peril, were many of the others in 'our team'.

We had met up with Trev Howard, one of our former young RWP members and nephew of Les, now a Geordier-than-Geordie Militant supporter/Jack the Lad. I was given to call him 'the apprentice'. We would doss the neet at Trev's after a historic re-encounter doon the Bridge with many of the old comrades. Maureen would later assure me Trev was no longer an apprentice and was out of his time now! The cheek of it.

Our climbing instructor, and guide really, was big Gordon Thompson. Gordon would warrant a biography of his own. A mate since the early YCND days, an ace banjo and guitar player, he had, God love him, taken on the task of teaching me guitar. We visited and sang together at the Bitter End Folk and Blues Club at the Station Hotel, Hebburn. After which he went off and became a shepherd; although I suspected it was in reaction to my failure as a guitar pupil, he assured me it was not—and I did manage to play 'The Ballad Of Hollis Brown', although really it's only two chords. Gordon's forte was rock-climbing. He came from that breed of Northumbrian Cheviot rock climbers who braved snow-swept blizzards and climbed in their T-shirts without gloves, in their trainers and mostly without ropes too. Gordon was captivated by my talk of revolution and the radical history of Northumbria and determined to lend a hand. He would be our guide and tutor on this adventure. Fred's ambulance proved not up to the hills and mountains of Northumberland, and conked out, finally coming to rest under a tree in a snow drift, where we left it, having pushed it up and down miles of old Roman roads trying to get it to start. We took the gear out of the ambulance and set off trekking up the hills to Spilaw Cottage, which was now an open climbers' bothy. As the snow piled in around the cottage we none the less set off to the pub for an evening drinking. It was perhaps four miles of hard hill walking before we got to the farm road and down to the pub. The crack was ower good, great singing, we nie took over the back room of the pub. Then we set off back. It never occurred to me that there was any danger in this manoeuvre at all. The fog was coming down, the snow was blasting into our faces and out over the silent hills and moors, and laboured breath was the only sound. The thin beams from the pocket torches fell dead after a few feet, and we tramped on, heeds doon into the blizzard looking forward to the roaring wood stoves and feather down sleeping bags at the bothy.

When we landed, we shook off the snow, and pulled oot the carry-oot for final night swag. Some comrades were far from in the mood for that. Steve was at the point of exhaustion, red-faced, sweating, breathing hard, sat in a heap on the floor panting; Gordon went and found a blanket to throw over him. Fred declared himself 'truly knackered but it was exhilarating' which would have been fine commentary at the end of the course, but man, this was just coming from the pub! He leaned against the wall, with the door open, taking great gasps of air, then closing it and shaking a little. He had come through it not too bad, which is what I would have expected from a collier, but the other people were no as fit as I had imagined and had been totally unsuited for this—the walks, the weather, the exertions. It hadn't dawned on me that most of these people had no experience whatsoever in challenging the Earth in its raw state. They had sort of assumed there was some sort of safety net to catch them if it got too tough, but there is no safety net. Worse, four comrades had not arrived back at all. I set off with Gordon to find them, while Fred, administered first aid and made tea for the fallen wounded. Finding the lost comrades, one of them another fireman, and a student, wasn't going to be easy. From here you could wander clear over the border and up into the Scottish mountains, or off over to Cumbria. Not that you would make it that far in these conditions. We shouted, we blew whistles, we waved the big torch from the cottage. At last we retraced our steps almost back to the pub to try and find theirs. Great hoof prints in the drifting snow showed they had gone off the track, then we picked up the trail of abandoned full broon ale bottles. This showed things were bad! They had abandoned any idea of a party, then the drink; what else? At last we found the fireman face down, unconscious, in the snow, or drunk /asleep, dead to the world. A little further on with his gansie over his heed, wedged up against a drift, with his duvet off and covering his feet in what he obviously thought was a survival position was the student. He we slapped some life into and redressed and set him on his feet. The unconscious firemen Gordon slung over his shoulder and we set off. It was hard slog. With the blizzard stopping the snow and visibility about two inches from your eyes, you were forced to put your head down and look at your feet, sneaking a glance up now and then. I took turns to carry the dead weight of Fireman Sam; stumbling over the hidden hollows and dips, it was back-breaking. We got back to the bothy at 4.30 a.m., just clinging on ourselves, frozen to the bones, blinded, feet and knees and locked hands rigid in pain.

We afforded ourselves a little sleep, before organising a search party back onto the hills by 7.30. At length we came across the ambulance and there snug as bugs in rugs were the two missing comrades still abed and still asleep. They had somehow or other found their way to the ambulance and camped up for the night. This was a cock-up that might have been a real disaster; it was good training, though, for all of us. Booze and inexperience and the wild outdoors are a recipe for death. Enforcing the Bolshevik ethos, despite the groans and moans after breakfast we set off through the drifts for some climbing on the crags, no gloves allowed, just wedging your fingers into little cracks in the stone, standing with your full weight on one big toe, curling up your body like giant caterpillar till it stuck out from the crag and into space while your knees dug into the rock's flat surface and your eyes desperately scanned the rock above for the sign of a crack or a gully. Some comrades sat shaking in cold and fear at the bottom of the windswept crags; OK we didn't criticise them, but marked off mentally who would be up for the revolutionary challenge when it came, who had enough courage to force down all fears and have a go? In part this was what this whole manoeuvre was about.[64]

Despite our ever growing discontent the George Hotel at Stainforth hosted another of our public Party meetings on 22 March, on 'How To Implement Labour's Programme'. It was aimed at not just the Young Socialists but all of the Labour Party members from all the local wards, who turned out in surprising numbers to listen and argue their corner. Most of all they were animated by the idea that something was actually on the turn, that something big could be about to happen and they wanted to talk about it, even to us.

THE SEARCH FOR SILENCE

This wasn't helping piece my life together. I struggled to find space, to find something to bring my feet back down to earth and try and steady the pace. I began again to look back, back into the ideas and calmness of Buddhism, began looking in for a wee while, to find some silence.

At the same time, as part of my self-designed rehabilitation programme I had discovered a karate group at the George Hotel, Stainforth and went along to watch. It was terrifying and exciting. It was a class from the Wado Ryu School. At the George it was taught by a bloke known locally as Kung Fu Tommy. Tommy was only actually a green belt, something which had no significance to me at the time. His style of teaching was also not what you would have called authorised or orthodox. It was a kind of make 'em or break 'em regime. People got hurt. I mean really hurt, hospitalised, knocked oot, fractures. At this time training was in the concert room overlooked by the lounge; ironically, Kung Fu Fighting was in the charts and martial arts were in the air. By 1976 there were even adverts in the

Buddhist Society's *Middle Way for Tai Chi Chaun*, also 'Meditation, Philosophy, Self Defence,Weapons, Taoist Health Science, Chi-Kung etc.'[65]

Though most of the Buddhist meditation retreats banned martial arts from their peaceful reflections, Bruce Lee had put a Karate club in almost every hick village across the world along with the corner shop and laundrette. It was damn exciting. I joined. I had reasoned that for two hours at least, throwing myself into training and learning Karate would take my brain out of its spiral of overwork and depression. It was a punishing school; the circuit training was relentless. The brick-smashing techniques looked terrifying, bare feet and fist, on red bricks. Not that I got to do that; I was simply a punchbag, and a cowardly one at that. Cowardly? In the heat of the moment, aroused by oppression or injustice, or charged up on beer and self-righteousness I had thrown myself into many a conflict, but in the cool light of day, in cold blood, standing toe to toe and letting someone try and punch or kick you or knock you down didn't bring out the best of me. I was given no confidence in this class. Fitness, some ideas of what to employ in a real scrap, I suppose, an excuse to start re-looking at Buddhism, but bravery—no. I learned how to cringe in Tommy's class. Maureen did better—she actually gained her yellow belt, as did Lynne. Mind, he had novel training methods. I was on afters waiting to ride when the evening shift came down. A lad shouts 'Hey up, Danny! I just walked past your lass, she's on't tip, fighting in her karate gear.' They were rolling about and knocking each other down on the pit tip. Tommy believed you should learn to fight on uneven and unusual surfaces; mind, he had allowed them trainers on this occasion. Usually, out for a barefoot run, you came back with feet bruised and sometimes bloody as you discover just how much glass there is all over the place, let alone dog shit. He was a strange mixture of things, Tommy. In appearance he was big, imposing, strong-jawed, good-looking, muscular, and in manner jovial. I had asked him once why he had taken up karate. He told me he was at school with Pete Thompson, who was less than half his size, but could knock the bejesus out of him. He didn't like that.

'So you can fight Pete now can you?'

'Can I fuck!' he replied. 'But I can run a lot faster now.'

Tommy liked seeing his karate technique work, liked sinking it in to some unguarded ribs like mine. Liked knocking you in a heap to the floor. It sapped my self-confidence to the point where I think I trembled at the command 'Kemite!' ('Fight!') I was shaking before I tried to spar up to whoever he had chosen I should be matched with. The dojo was like its sensie—unyielding. A concrete floor, walls of fading yellow paint, stuck round with photos of Bruce Lee and other Hollywood exponents of the art. Sombons, the set one-piece or two-piece attacks and responses, I could do; Kata, at least the beginner's ones, I could do; circuits with sweat dripping from my body and every sinew straining, I could do; free fighting I didn't have the knowledge to do and rapidly I had lost the guts to do. The students in the class were mainly younger than me and Maureen and Lynne. They were all hard working-class kids from Stainforth and Dunscroft, who wouldn't have walked from a fight before they started doing karate, and now they had they got stuck into these free fights with vigour. Bloody noses, bloody feet from the concrete floor or slightly missing the bricks, broken bones, bruised ribs and eyes—all went with the gi's (karate suits). We were engaged in one of the more graceful katas, hand in the classic open-hand sweep gesture away from your body, your right foot curled in and toes just touching the floor, while the left leg and foot took the whole body's weight. To the bunch of street-hardened lads who had strolled up the stairs and now blocked the doorway looking in, we looked like a right bunch of pouffs, or so they said. A mix of skinheads and two-tones, they stood in their Doc Martins, or baggy pants, the new descendants of the Ted, with that same perfected pig-ignorant stare. 'We'll fight seven of yourn now!' one of them says walking in with a swagger. 'Boots off, now!' Tommy demanded, imposing his authority on the gang before they got one step further, 'And your best two can have me, and all grades above white belts.' As they took their boots off at the door, Tommy whispered to his students: 'Tha goes in hard and breks summat.'

Meantime we went in hard and brok summat. It was time for a decisive break from the constrictions of the RWP.

16
The Socialist Union

On Sunday 31 March 1974 at 7.30 at the Ingram Arms, Hatfield, we called a meeting of socialist revolutionaries. I opened the meeting and spoke of the need for a revolutionary group in the district, following the break with the RWP, and at the same time to reconsider the role of the Labour Party and trade unions in relation to our revolutionary tasks. It was agreed to form a revolutionary socialist group, although our old comrades Lynne and Jim Shipley withdrew believing there was no need for a revolutionary team. For them the Labour Party was the arena and the vehicle to change society.

We accepted that we had accumulated much already from our past political involvement, but we would open up the question of where we stood on each issue, week by week—the nature of the Labour Party, the nature of the Communist Party, trade union struggle—and develop our perspectives as we developed as an organisation.

A number of names were suggested, but 'The Doncaster Socialist Union' was agreed to.

We drew up a list of the areas in which we would be involved. One of these included a Marxist class to be held in the Miners Welfare on a Sunday afternoon and be open to everyone who was interested, guest speakers being invited to give papers. The work developing the bookshop as an educational, social and political centre was to continue but another was more controversial. It sat in the minutes under the title 'clandestine'.

From the start of this organisation, we had by unanimous agreement decided that the question of armed struggle should be taken seriously, that the preparation for that struggle should occupy a place in our activity alongside all the other areas of political, educational and industrial work.

The meeting of 7 April at the shop amended the previous decision to hold our Marxist classes at the Welfare, as the Club Committee had now sanctioned 'strippers' down in the concert room at the time of our class. We noted that the miners' wives and daughters had drafted a letter to the NUM Branch protesting at this degeneration of the standards in the Welfare and noting it as an insult to the brave women who had supported the NUM and the miners during the last two periods of industrial action.

The Minutes
Item 19: David Douglass was elected secretary.
It was noted that he often has a tendency to be bureaucratic in the sense of not consulting the other comrades before making statements or committing the group to activity. Douglass made a self criticism to this effect and a resolve not to be so impetuous in the future.

The chair was Ken Terry and Maureen elected vice chair 'to give her experience and act as deputy to Mr Terry.'

Under 'reports':

Maureen Douglass made a long exposition on her personal dissatisfaction with the LPYS. The amount of time and effort she puts in it for a very small result in terms of political effect. The few remaining members of LPYS had become very lazy and work was being increasingly left to two members. Maureen was seriously suggesting withdrawing from the LPYS. After a lengthy debate,

Mrs Sharp Secretary of the LPYS was urged to write to all members, ex-members and sympathisers, left members of the labour Party and to include ourselves in a meeting to plan a three month campaign covering all the surrounding districts to build the LPYS. Public meetings, leafleting, door to door sales and loudspeaker vans to be included together with flyposting.

Following this a report was taken from the LPYS, and we discussed the forthcoming LPYS National Conference at Clacton. Four members of the Socialist Union were to attend to support the YS comrades selling socialist literature etc.

A brief discussion took place on the matter of the MP's (Dr Marshall's) surgery ... Since the MP is a liberal paternalist concerned more with parish pump politics it was agreed that we go as a delegation and confront him with political questions.

It was agreed that we take up the question of Noel Jenkinson, an Irishman who was framed on the charge of the Aldershot explosion. It was noted that 'the MP was now attached to the Secretary of State for Northern Ireland [actually his PPS] and therefore was the right bloke to confront on the issue. ..We will prepare a speech and presentation the delegation will make to the MP.

Actually, following my leaving the RWP the LP now had no grounds to exclude me any more, and I was duly reinstated, the NUM at once reinstating me as their representative on the GMC. The reds were back. The planned 'confrontation' with the MP would soon make short work of that.

LPYS NATIONAL CONFERENCE, CLACTON ON SEA (BUTLINS)
Around about now, the comrades of the Nottingham cell of the RWP finally broke too, and rather than join us as we had hoped, decided to concentrate their energies full time within the Labour Party, forming a Labour Left current, with a journal of the same name. We agreed to maintain comradely connections and to sell their paper in part as part of our own perspective on the LP. As time moved on a little we found that we had actually developed along two completely different lines, which is odd given that we sort of came from the same womb.

Our former comrades in 'Labour Left', the comrades at Plumtree in Notts, had had the rare distinction of being expelled from the RWP. Mainly it was Peter and Marie, with Maurice still doing his endless analysis, this time of 'the development of the Labour Party and its perspectives and tasks for the left'. Our hopes to reunite with this team floundered at the first post on the nature of the Labour Party and the struggle of the class for power directly.

They believed the Labour Party was the party for this, albeit after a hard fight to unite the left on the basis of Marxism, but unlike ourselves they saw no need for any other revolutionary instrument, standing independent from that party. Although we took copies of their paper to sell we increasingly took issue with them over popularist terms such as 'anarchy' and 'terrorism', and also, we thought, their general attempt to distance themselves from the far left. They were on a different trajectory than ourselves.

Tom, although he too had now left the RWP, hadn't teamed up with the Labour Left crowd. I was keen to have him on board. I had written to him sending him the manifesto, and inviting him to join. I was a little disappointed when he agreed but only as a Grade 2 member; when I pressed him he responded in typical Kilburn fashion:

Flat 2, 84 Westbourne Ave, Hull

Dear Dave ...

Whether or not it disappoints you, I personally feel that a Grade 2 membership is, at the moment, the most appropriate for me. As, or if, I develop nearer humanity as time goes on (and I do realise that there is precious little time left) then perhaps I may reach Grade 1 level. Also at risk of horrifying and alienating you, life does hold more for me than the struggle for revolution, and moreover always has, even in my most steely-eyed Posadist phase. Perhaps that's when I discovered the full disgusting extent of my degeneracy. But must there always be fixed dichotomy between revolutionary fervour and miserable degeneracy? I believe not.

Tom had gone on to discuss the way state repression would open up against the communist and progressive leadership of the working class and whether an armed militia standing separate from the heart and soul of the mass of the workers would be just wiped out in the first rush. He stressed the need to subvert the armed forces, and win over large sections of the working-class core of the military as being the first objective.

The rather ambiguous phrase 'left wing neddies' was in no way aimed at yourself or any of the Doncaster comrades but at various cretins I have met in the overall left movement who go slightly dewy-eyed and wet-lipped over the prospect of being a real grown-up guerrilla fighter. These poor twisted creatures no doubt go to bed with large pictures of Ché on their walls and have no understanding whatsoever of the political nature of the revolution or on a more mundane level, the horrifying thought of someone shooting back at them.

I have no illusions about the nearness of the repression, even the silliest most respectable middle class 'lefty' can read in the paper the perspectives of David Stirling's paper *GB75*, General Walker's 'Unison' bunch, the baying for blood which now characterises reaction. The time is long overdue to start preparing, but for Gods sake please give some attention to the power of propaganda within the armed-forces ...

RG to all of you

Tom Kilburn

TROOPS OUT

In April we also agreed to affiliate to the Troops Out Movement and attend their conference, on 11 May.

The idea of a Troops Out Movement was at once important, politically attractive, popular and yet full of inherent contradictions. It was to be a widespread campaign aimed at being a mass popular campaign, designed to build the maximum pressure to withdraw the troops from Ireland, 'Immediately and Unconditionally'. It aimed to have but two demands: Troops out of Ireland. Self Determination for the Irish People as a Whole. That meant north and south of the British partition and not just in the selected occupied six counties—self-determination for all people of the whole island of Ireland. It was undoubtedly true that inspiration for this campaign had come from the anti-war movement in the States, the 'bring the boys home' campaign which had linked fathers and mothers, wives and sweethearts, children and grandparents of the troops, to the left politicos and pacifists. For whatever reason, bring the troops home. For some on the left that slogan and that alliance was simply politically incorrect—it was reactionary. The problem for the British Troops Out Movement would be one of being politically correct too; bringing the troops out wasn't enough of a slogan or a demand for some, indeed many a right-wing 'man on the street' would voice the popular sentiment 'We ought to bring the troops out and let the mad bastards kill each other,' or, worse, 'and then drop a bomb on them'. The revolutionary left in Britain wanted to bare its chest and be right-on, which meant you should stand foursquare with the risen masses of occupied Ulster, it meant saying 'Victory to the IRA' . It would be a constant battle within the organisation to try and limit the public demands whatever we all thought politically and outside of Troops Out.

9 April 1974. Otterburn, Northumberland. John Stevenson, the commanding officer at an army training camp at Otterburn, Northumberland, was shot on his doorstep just before 1 a.m. The officer's home was situated next to moorland and the follow-up operation was hampered by dense fog. Around two hours after the killing, two unarmed policemen were wounded at a hotel about a mile from the camp. Three men were later arrested. The man who had stood up in the crowded bar full of leftists at the Bridge Hotel, and cried 'I've ho'rd enough tal'kin lets dey someit' had indeed 'done someit'.

We agreed to work closely with the International Marxist Group on Chile, that we hold our first public meeting on that subject and that we support the national demonstration in London. Maureen undertook to design a banner with the slogan 'Troops Out Of Ireland. Pickets Out Of Jail. Victory To The World Revolutionary Masses.'

Thursday 2 May 1974, 7.30 p.m. Our public meeting 'Against The Gunboats For Chile' , the Nelson, Cleveland Street, Doncaster. This was an issue which excited the left across the board from the revolutionary socialists to the left of the Labour Party, the unions and civil rights proponents. Our upstairs venue at the

Doncaster town centre pub was smokey, and hearty, but full to the doors. These gunboats had been ordered under Dr Allende; now the fascists were running the country, we were outraged that they should be getting sold. The campaign to stop the sale reached every corner of progressive opinion. Some time later, during a meeting with the 'left wing' of the Ulster loyalists, those elements, of which from time to time there was a sizeable faction, who identified with the idea of socialism, I was told that they had held a joint meeting with the Provos with the view to sinking the gunboat as it passed Ireland. They did manage to find a torpedo between them and a means of firing it up, but couldn't come up with a sensible way to aim and launch the damn thing; they reasoned a rowing boat rowed very fast wouldn't be up to the job.

The London demo planned for the 5 May was to include Jack Collins from the NUM, Ken Coates from the Institute for Workers' Control, and Tariq Ali of the International Marxist Group. We would run a coach from Dunscroft down to the demo.

19 May 1974. A one-day strike in Doncaster was called by the Trades Council in support of the nurses and their demo on 29 June. This was believed to be a national one-day strike. It was reported that Hatfield NUM had not been informed, nor the Doncaster Panel. It was resolved that

> We win our NUM branch to the strike: and that they in turn raise it at the panel. That the Trades Council (Thorne and District) send letters out to all union branches in the district. That wherever the official union does not support the strike at our centres of Harvesters, AEI, and Hatfield Colliery the members of this group call unofficial strikes. That we get a nurse and hold factory gate and pit yard meetings. That we utilise banners and the loud speakers. That all members are mandated to strike on that day. (SU(D) minute 74)

Well, grandiose and exciting though that resolution was, its sequel reads a sorry supplement.

2 June. Proletaria Bookshop. Dunscroft

> A report and self criticism was made over the nurses demo, how owing to getting the date wrong we had missed the strike and the demo.
>
> The Doncaster Trades Council supported the nurses demo (which was the biggest outside of London). The biggest section to strike in support was the bus drivers, but factory workers and Brodsworth Colliery also struck, 30 men from Cementation struck—a highly significant section seeing that they are a very conservative subcontracting group very prone to the blacklist and victimisation. British Ropes also struck. Self criticisms were made and accepted—too many comrades had relied on other people for information—however salutes were made to the comrades who participated in the demo without prior notice and to comrade A who had struck and demonstrated.

The Meeting of the 2 June also reports:
Special Point

The point cannot be minuted fully except to say that a series of breeches of discretion and security have occurred arising from this; a very serious accusation was made that a Special Branch infiltrator was currently on the periphery of the group. Action was discussed and agreed—the group closes ranks.

Actually we had faced infiltrators before. The press came from time to time, notably the *Daily Telegraph*— 'How I Infiltrated The Car Workers Secret Trotskyists'; the News of the World— 'Meet the Man Behind the Slogan Seize the Pits'; and the *Doncaster Gazette*— 'NUM and the Take-over Bid Rebels'. The Special Branch man we had had was a right shifty, shit-stirring, fact-gathering disrupter; he lived with us for over a week, but we had been on to him from the third day and strung him along nicely. We had also had a bloke who entered through the Red Star Folk Club and was out of jail on condition he joined us and passed on information; we know because he told us and we vetted what he passed on. There were others, very dodgy from time to time, but we didn't think them actual cops, maybe more in the style of sleepers or grasses.

It must be said, mind, and on reflection, we had one or two nutters, posing as healthy revolutionary workers but up to their necks in some twisted agendas or daydreams of their own, who we had given grand suspicions of being with the state's forces. Actually they were just vulnerable to utility by the state whenever it felt it needed such oddballs for its own purposes. What was the motive of such elements? Inflated senses of themselves, which couldn't come up to the mark, and then turned their failure to success by inventing weakness in us which they had overcome. These are the elements who neybugger knaas but 'on the nod' know everything about everybody else, all the personal scandal, gossip and shite. On occasion one comes across 'organisations' of such people who attack everybody and every organisation within the class despite the fact that they and their reputation are totally unknown, together with any actual contribution to the struggle.

By 8 June Maureen was again complaining of the soul-destroying, mind-boggling, intelligence-killing pointless work in the LPYS and the meeting agreed (87) that 'Comrade "M" be released from entrist work in the YS. That she maintain membership of the LP and do the kind of entrism others members do in the LP, i.e. a general and periodical, issue based intervention.' Meantime our section of the Claimants Union, which was well established in the surrounding area, agreed to kill two birds with one stone, by ensuring the shop was open most days, and by being available to assist and advise claimants. A regular advice and assistance session was organised on Wednesdays for one-parent families.

Around now Dr Rose Dugdale, a spectacular republican socialist activist, is arrested for her part in the multi-million pound Beit Art Robbery. Here was a novel tactic; they had taken hostage, not people, but treasured art works and threatened to destroy them if the demands they put forward were not met. They were not met, and though the art works were not damaged, the outrage of the establishment could hardly have been greater had they been put to the torch. Her eventual sentencing, and the barbarity of her treatment in Limerick jail, in the so-called 'Irish Republic', would have also led you to conclude that.

The Manifesto of the Doncaster Socialist Union, after months of study, debate, brainstorming and work, makes its revolutionary appearance, the front cover designed by Maureen: two hands clasping a hammer and sickle, against a backdrop of a world.

It made its first intervention into the Yorkshire Miners' Gala, selling more than fifty on that day alone, overwhelmingly to miners.

At work, me and Jim in bother again, or me rather than him. We were at our posts, on the big Dosco ripping machine at the tailgate end. Snap time was called, but the coal-cutting machines on the face kept cutting and the dust curled in clouds from under the rip and into the gate, where we had just sat down for snap.

I yelled into the tannoy, 'What yee deying? It's snap time!'

'Aah, look Dave, we're just getting to the gate end, then we can change the picks while we're stood.'

'All right lads, but our snap time starts when your machine finishes, and so does this chain.'

The deputy now gets involved: 'It does not, it goes when snap time's over, yi little bastard.'

'We're entitled to 20 minutes snap in peace!' I yelled.

At last the machine stood. And we sat down to eat. Ten minutes later snap time is over. They start the chain again. I leap up and put the lock- out on. All hell lets loose, and a real set-to, in which the deputy says, 'If you're not going to work get out of the pit.'

So I do. Jim agrees to stay to ensure the rip is safe, after all men have to go in and out under that rip and we can't leave it just hanging. A bitter but small dispute.

The following day, Robinson has me in the office again.

'You've got your pigging way, I see?' he shouts.

'Now what?'

'All that bollocks about snap again.'

'Oh fuck it, I'm off to work.'

'No you're fuckin' not, you're stopping 'ere.'

'How come?'

'Because if you go in the pit all NACODS men are walking out.'

They were all congregated at the shaft bottom, and all had agreed that if I walked down the mine, they would walk out. They were backing up their colleague on our unit.

Just then Tom Mullanny, flushed and red-faced, barges into the office. 'He's going to work!' he yells.

'He ain't: we're still gaffers here, Tom!' And then as an afterthought, 'I'm suspending him on wages, until we can have a meeting about this. This is serious, this is card time this time.'

So a second-stage meeting is convened that very day: Mr White (my old friend); Mr Deeming; Frank Clark; Tom Mullanny; the Area agent, who I think was Sammy Thompson, and me. White opens up: 'So we're here again, back where we said we would be when we tried to talk our way out of this last time, back with the not wanting to work issue, and not accepting supervision contrary to national agreements, playing silly buggers with lock-outs. It's not on. We are drawing a line, and its not just us, the gaffers, Tom. He can't get on with anyone at work. I'm led to believe we had to move men around to stop violence on the main gate rip. We had a string of complaints about him on Keith Sparrow's rip, when he [Sparrow—DD] was one of your members ...'

The case was being built against me, each feature of course explainable and defendable but together the gallows, like in a game of hangman, was being constructed. Frank Clark: 'Would you just like to take a look out of that window?' White stands up. Out the window, hundreds of men are congregated and sitting on the railings and walls. Martin Moffet, shift chargeman, Jimmy Morris, main machine man. The news comes in that men all over the pit are coming out.

'It looks like we've got a dispute Mr White.'

'Then send them back to work, Tom.'

'Nay, lad, its thy dispute. Our men can't work if deputies are hanging round shafts and not carrying out their duties. They are obliged to come out, and while were at it, were not having deputies calling our men "bastards".'

Frank Clark, the Union moderate, chips in: 'You know me, I'm a moderate me, but I would do exactly what Davie Douglass did yesterday—I would bang the button in until we got our 20 minutes snap time. We're entitled to it, and if we need a flexibility at one end to get the job done, then we expect flexibility at the other to eat wa snaps in peace, and if we have to have a strike over that Mr White, then I shall be proposing we have a strike.' Well, well done Frank.

Two days later, it was a Thursday, they caved in. I was reinstated, that deputy was moved, and low and behold we got Keith Sparrow, by now a close personal friend and a man whom both me and Jim had absolute respect for. Keith knew the rip, and knew the code we worked to; after all he had taught me it. We would have no bother with Keith.

But, after a meeting in the paddy station, to discuss where we were and where we had been, we decided that despite the fact it was all settled, we were still going home. 'You can't make a good week from a bad'un' was one rationale, and 'We haven't shown them we mean it enough yet' was another.

Officials tended to approach our shift with some caution from then on. All except Bob Pickles, a comical, bumptious senior overman. Bob had bollocked us about the number of arches set; we 'weren't making enough advance', had to 'Advance! Advance! You've got a pigging machine there Rommel would have given his eye teeth for. Advance! Advance!' he said, braying the machine with his yard stick. Bob reminded me of a pit version of General Patton; he was bumptious and daft, a bit like a working-class Boris Johnson, and we liked him.

In the heat of an argument he accused us of being idle and doing nothing. We nearly ragged up, but instead made a formal complaint to Robinson, who had told us to in future to nip all such blebs in the bud and bring any problems to him. Pickles had been given the Gypsy's warning. Next day, he arrives on the rip. Walks casually along, tapping the arches in turn, obviously silently counting them. Then turns around and starts humming I'm Busy Doing Nothing.

'Bob.'

'What, what's wrong with you?'

We all burst out laughing. 'Actually, Bob, if you count up, even with your fingers' (he had two missing) 'you will see that Dave and I complete and set an arch every shift; nobody else does a whole arch.'

It was true. They didn't understand it, but we actually liked pitwork.

15 June 1974. The Yorkshire Miners' Gala is in Doncaster. Pride of place for a victory procession and an unmatched victory in Labour Movement history. Old Gerry MacDade, the Ulsterman from Dunscroft, was the deputy mayor and he got to do the civic welcome. Tom Mullanny says at the reception the night before at the Mansion House, where Gerry is all decked out in ermine and red satin: 'Our lass genuflected coz she thought it were t' Pope. Ah says deent say daft, lass, its just Gerry MacDade.' Scargill was in the chair, though it might have been a throne, and Len Murray and Lawrence Daly were the guest speakers. In the big marquee, Charles Parker's *The Collier Laddie* was being performed by Birmingham and Midlands Folk Centre: '*The Story of the Coalfield Told in the Words of Miners with Drama, Music and Songs.*' The group are the embryo of what will become Banner Theatre in the living tradition of the *Radio Ballads* as pioneered by McColl and Seeger and Parker. They also play it at the South Wales Miners' Gala of that year.[66]

CLOSURE OF THE SHOP

16 June 1974. The group had now to face the sad fact that the domestic arrangements of the tenants of the upstairs flat having broken down, in the ensuing financial crisis the shop was lost. It wasn't only the income from the flat that had ceased. The claimants' group was supposed to pay for the hire of the shop for their workshops and childcare sessions. The debt mounted week by week, and despite letters and agreements to pay, no money arrived. I was delegated to go an get some money off them. The big guns of the Claimants Union in our area were slightly odd. A gangly thin bloke, with eyes like Marty Feldman which went off in opposite directions, he had worked at Peglers but now was on sick benefit permanently. His wife was a thin, ginger, intense women, full of nervous twitches and strange birdlike head postures.

I arrived at their big council semi, and the bloke (P) led me into the living room where a big little boy sat on the floor. He was rather like Dave Wallace in a distortion mirror—his eyes were huge. It didn't take me too long to work out he was also telepathic. How do I know? Every question I was about to ask him, he answered, including when I was about to say 'Can you always tell what somebody is about to ask you?', to which he replied, before I said a word, 'Sometimes, it just depends.' The hair fair bristled on my neck, this was a rather odd family even by our terms.

No. No money, though it was promised again. It could actually have saved the shop, but we are waiting yet. Worse, they had stopped opening to assist people, and we often had claimants coming down to the house, desperate for assistance. This was not good cred for the organisation as 'an instrument of the masses'.

19 July 1974. Durham Miners' Gala. Old Walt Malt the Durham NUM secretary didn't eat his words at the Gala of that year, and still was preaching the language of moderation despite the flashes of history which shook the chandeliers at Red Hills. He did however bring to the attention of that victorious crowd certain costs along the way, and perhaps in so doing marked the route of the next big clash, not on wages and pay, but on the survival of the industry itself: 'The Labour Government had admitted to closing about 260 pits between 1964 and 1970 ... but the previous five years saw over 200 closures, 460 pit closures in ten or eleven years and our focus was exclusively on what wages would those who survived received.' It was, as Walt had urged, 'raging against the dying of the light'. We too had talked in 1969 of not fearing closures but if the pit were to stay open one more day we wanted decent wages for working in them. We had swallowed too much of the inevitability-of-decline argument. Pit closures and security of a future hadn't struck any real resonances with us, especially the younger miners, but now the gaps were becoming too numerous to ignore.

The following year (1975) I had agreed to meet, at the start of the gala, an American PhD student, who had chosen as his thesis payments systems in the British mining industry. We arranged to meet at the Bridge Hotel, Durham, just down from the railway station. This is also as it happens the main assembly point for the start of the gala, and the starter for ten, at the pub, which was packed to the gunwales. He was quite noticeable, a tall Jewish New Yorker in a leather bomber jacket which could have come off a Flying Fortress. It was Joel Krieger. He tells me, of the occasion of this meeting, 'We met in 1974 and I have never been the same since.' Joel recalls: 'I was astounded by the size and exuberance of the gala, and transfixed by the extraordinary banners—with the range of figures they heralded from Wilson to Lenin.' Me and Joel became close friends and actually colleagues. Other than his work on his massive thesis, we agreed to cooperate in writing a book on the miners, which after much effort we actually seen published (David Douglass and Joel Krieger, *A Miner's Life*, Routledge & Kegan Paul, London 1983). Something we were both immensely proud of, a proper commercial book in proper commercial bookshops. Joel's actual thesis came out in 1979 and is without doubt a milestone in understanding miners' pay systems. The whole thrust of Joel's work was in explaining the movement which took the coal industry toward the development of a national day wages system and away from bonus and incentive payment systems. When the whole thing finally turned round and the contract system was reintroduced Joel suggested you now read the thesis from back to front!

We had taken up a number of cars to the gala, carrying our new Doncaster manifesto, and the inevitable paste table for a selection of our books from the bookshop, and it was I believe wor Emma's first Durham Miners' Gala. I think it was at this gala where Joel agreed to run a series of lectures on the fundamentals of Marxism, back at the Miners Welfare (after the strippers were banned, to many a gloomy face).

One of the guest speakers that year if memory serves was the future prime minister, L. J.Callaghan, whose government, under Wilson, had with the assistance of Gormley just imposed upon us compliance with the 'Social Contract', an integral part of which was the adoption of area incentive schemes, against the teeth of opposition by the miners themselves. The question was to go to ballot and be roundly rejected. But political masters weren't to let it drop. Later the Annual Conference of 1977 passed a resolution reaffirming the national ballot vote of 1974 and the decision to reject any area incentive schemes.

Around this time Kenton High School and other Newcastle and Gateshead schools walk out in protest against uniforms and dress code disciplines; at Kenton the turn out is 100 per cent and brilliantly organised.

Our 14 July meeting records a 'fine letter from the comrades in the USA'. They had sent us a stack of US literature and we were starting to develop our relations with them. Arising from this we agreed to host a special day school on the subject of Peru, the nature of which promoted a heated exchange. Many of us had taken on Posadas's designation of it as a 'revolutionary state'. Now comrades (actually largely Maureen) were challenging whether or not such a description of Peru or anywhere else had any meaning. A letter from Joel at the following meeting raised 'the question of blacks' and women's oppression'. Self-criticisms were made 'for not making women a special section of the manifesto or even their situation. The men admitted they were at fault but it was pointed out that the women comrades would have to be more militant to overcome this.'

Also agreed was that we proceed with full speed to found a Newcastle section of the organisation. It was clear we were beginning to outgrow our 'Doncaster' prefix. In relations with other groups it was agreed to hold a joint open-ended discussion on perspectives and joint areas of work with the Big Flame group at the bookshop. This was a group named after a TV drama-documentary, screened some years before, about an occupation of the Liverpool docks in contemporary times. In preparation for this we had farmed out all of their publications for a solid base of understanding of their founding and positions. Tom was short of impressed:

> I'll be across on Sat for the discussion about the Big Flame Group, but I must say that after having read slightly over half of their documentation they come across as a rather wretched bunch. Anyone who bases their existence on a television pseudo-documentary would benefit from a

horse whipping.

We were still bristling fresh from our formal Posadist backgrounds. We had set the presidium stage up, with the long table for the speakers, draped in the red flag with the hammer and sickle. We set out the water jug and with Maureen in the chair, welcoming the comrades up from Liverpool and Manchester. I rose to present our perspectives with a formal speech. In their response, they didn't remain seated in the audience of the room, neither would they take their place behind the table, but walked up and down the room talking! Worse still, sat on the table and the red flag! They were so informal they almost lay down to speak. They were of the new generation of emerging anarcho-Marxist revolutionaries, Guevarists and situationists. I later tried to explain our cultural difference by saying that this group had been born into the world of the Sixties, the occupation, the sit-in, the street protest and urban guerrilla warfare. Tom as cynically clear as ever remarked that the Sixties were also the era of the cripple boot, the miniskirt, and men in silk polka-dot frilly shirts; it was this aspect of the Sixties to which this group belonged and not the one I had cited. You could rely on Tom to cut through the bullshit. We were infuriated enough to mention in our summary of the group what a great point they made of being 'new', 'very new'—brand new, so new they were still in the box, we mused. They made the point in order to demonstrate that there were no skeletons in their cupboards. Their philosophy was one that suited the Seventies, parodying the Chrysler advert: 'This is the cause you have all been waiting for.' This was a group moulded into the frame of the self-declared 'new left', we thought, an attempt by largely middle-class forces to furnish themselves with an 'independent' political philosophy of the left. People like Marcuse, who concluded that the working class was now bourgeois with the unions absorbed into the state machine. Some of this was reflected in the ideas of Big Flame. They blithely ignored the revolutionary potential of the unions, particularly at shop steward and branch level:

> [T]he shop stewards movement has not met the challenge [of capitalism] successfully. Wedded to the old and inadequate ways of fighting, they have retreated all the way, holding up operations at times, but seldom reversing them. In most places they have few answers to the needs of the struggle, in others they hold it back, forced to act in the new situation as 'policemen' on the shop floor, as a means of ensuring that contracts and agreements are carried out.

Ignoring the class struggle which was everywhere hammering on the doors of the system, largely in and around formal unions and its more informal base, they blithely wrote it all off:

> It means we reject the strategies of electing left leaders, or rank-and-file control of the unions, or at shop floor level electing shop stewards or building left caucuses on the stewards committees ...They will not advance the struggle because they accept the trade union definitions when we need to go beyond the unions.

Similarly had came the prediction that the progressive middle class, and students together with the 'elite's' of the working class would have to challenge the state, forcing it to come down with such ferocity that the kid gloves would come off to expose the iron fist; this would be a revealing moment for the working class as well, who would then understand all.

It was the period when Ché moved from the evergreen onto the wallpaper and the urban guerrilla became the romantic image of the revolutionary. It was within this 'pop politics' that *Big Flame* emerged. With something of the presentation of 'teenagers' in the Fifties, the group little tired of saying how young they are.

The existing groups and parties all claim to be the product of a past revolutionary tradition applying its principles to the present day. We don't claim any such roots in the past ... We are trying to construct a politics that fits advanced capitalism – 1970s style.

The organisation itself, unsurprisingly really, rapidly disappeared, but their core analysis was seized on time and again, by new middle-class theorists thinking they have found some freshly minted holy grail of 'newness'. Thirty years later it is *Subversion* and *Wildcat*, with even less of a readership or their fingers on the pulse than *Big Flame* had. (See my pamphlet *All Power To The Imagination* for a sustained polemic with these and the council communists, et al.)

At the same time we were faced with rising demands for more copies of our manifesto which had clearly struck a chord and was provoking interest nationwide; the other problem was that we were running in quicksand against the debts for the shop. By the following week we were discussing closing it. The minute records: 'Discussion of final shop party, and selling chairs etc. clearing out files and returning books.' It was a sorry end to a great project. We were, remember, a revolutionary team, we seriously considered we were preparing for the forthcoming revolution. Still, the work continued and we got on with it, loss of shop or no. I spent many trips, with Emma perched in the wheelbarrow, going up and down to the shop salvaging what could be salvaged and ensuring there was nothing of value to the cops.

Our physical training programme was being expanded, beyond the initial map-reading courses, to canoeing, with instruction given by John Mason, who had become an associate member as he still retained his loyalty to IMG first and foremost. These became regular extended weekend courses. John was a great canoe enthusiast, which was strange, as politicos rarely if ever had any interest in any sort of physical or sporting activity. Earlier he had taken me to the boathouse where he was building his latest sea-canoe. It took me back at once to my cadet days and I was thrilled by the idea of reliving that experience. I had asked him to make me one, which he agreed to do. John was a physicist, with big bottle-bottom glasses, a shuffling walk, a posh middle-class southern accent, but when you seen him in the wa'ater, doing Eskimo rolls, and charging down a torrent-like stream in slalom it was a different man in the thick of the fight.

July 1974. We launch *The Tractor Worker* on behalf of International Harvester

Joint Shop Stewards Committee; it is edited by Ken Terry, of the AEUW and is printed on the Socialist Union press. All the plant unions are involved in the production and the back page advertises the SU, the Red Star Folk Club, the *Morning Star*, the *Socialist Worker*, *Labour Left*, *Labour Weekly* as well as adverts for garden rollers and second-hand prams. It more or less accurately reflected the leaderships and the readerships, but marked the solid roots in the activist working-class and trade union movement we occupied in the town's industry. Harvesters, after the NCB, was the second-largest employer.

27 July 1974. We announce on huge wall posters and leaflets:

> The Tyneside Irish Folk Group
> The Beggermen
> live at the
> Red Star Folk Club
> The Bentley Hotel, Bentley

2 August. The wall posters read:

> The Red Star Folk Club presents
> The Great Geordie Song Writer and Folk Singer
> Eddie Pickford
> Live at the Spreadeagle Hotel
> St Sepulchregate Doncaster
> (all proceeds to The Proletaria Bookshop and Socialist Centre Rates fund)

7 August. Joel Krieger joins the SUI and becomes our American organiser.

11 August. Joel is accepted as our 'American organiser' but while he remains in Britain his present task will be to help found the Newcastle section.

24 August. Our meetings are held now on the site of our weekend, training and education camp at Pateley Bridge, ten plus three children including Emma. The first item of the meeting was child care and giving the mothers the chance to go out; the names of the other comrades went into the hat. Pateley Bridge was a treasure trove of potholes which revealed a network of caves and holes and tunnels. I was in my element and I loved it, the magic of underground, the peace and tranquility without the roar of production and predatory machines. We clambered and crawled and scrammed around the network of caves. The minutes record that 'some spectacular attempts at underground mountaineering were attempted.'

25 August. Day School on Women's Oppression. Our old comrade Lynne was elected chair of the School with Maureen launching the lead perspective on how she saw the issue. The minute reads:

> The school was opened out to discussion from the floor. All the women comrades (a number of others had arrived during the school) took great part in the discussion particularly two of the observers Lynne and Cath. During the discussion long and continued attacks were made on the Secretary [Who, me?] for his Male Chauvinist attitude toward his wife.
> It was agreed that all the expositions be drafted into a policy statement for the

group as soon as possible.

This was to become the SUI pamphlet *Women: Their Oppression and Their Cause*, a widely sold document on where working-class socialist women stood on this issue of women's oppression as opposed to various middle-class feminist elements. It was none the less scathing on working-class men and the family system in general.

1 September. Tom was accepted as a Grade Two member, on condition he lay off the spirits a bit and commit himself to a process of becoming a full member. True to say Tom didn't like this. He had had a bellyful of the RWP telling him he had to shave his beard off in case it scared the proles and they thought he was beatnik; now we were telling him he should cut down on the whisky. In characteristic style he replied: 'Oh, I see, I can get paralytic drunk on some splendidly proletarian beer, but spirits are anti-social.' Actually it was because we reasoned there was a physical limitation on the volume of beer one could drink before damaging ones brain box permanently, whereas spirits could be consumed to the point of death without needing to take a piss.

It was also reported that we had now sold out of manifestos which were still in demand.

8 September. Agreed we leaflet door to door in all the neighbourhood with a leaflet explaining that the shop was closing, but the group was still here and listing all the books for sale and delivery.

Arising from the big antifascist demo in London, 'That there be no more delegated heroes; if the group decides to support a demo—no matter how violent it may be—the group must go on it. There must be no more volunteers who it is always left to.' (SU, minute 118) This resulted from our agreement to send a delegation to disrupt the big anti-IRA fascist demonstration in London; eventually it had been down to two of us, then the car broke down. I hitched to London. Eventually I got a lift off a couple of young Cockneys who knew absolutely nothing about anything, they heard on the radio about the demo, as we went down, and guessed that's where I was going. My explanations as to what a fascist was came to nought, as they didn't know who or what Hitler had been. They did their public duty by dropping me at some obscure underground station and it took me ages of changes and loads of close encounters with small teams of fascists, who had been positioned at it seemed every station I went to, before I got to Hyde park, just in time to watch our side's Victory Parade having vanquished the NF from the major streets.

15 September. Meeting held at the Nelson, Doncaster. Before the discussion of business a report was given on the state of my health (my nervous breakdown) and the need to ease some of pressure of work from me, which was agreed.

> An observer at the meeting raised doubts on the question of discipline: he felt this was imposed too strictly and that we were too rigid in applying it.
>
> This was answered by several comrades who pointed out that this discipline is not imposed or forced on anyone, but is rather a self-discipline and a sense of responsibility towards other comrades, for the

purpose of making ourselves become a disciplined revolutionary team that can cope with the many difficult and dangerous conditions we might be faced with.

27 October. The first major British demonstration to demand troops out of Ireland is held in London, organised jointly by the Troops Out Movement and the British Peace Committee.

Resistance within the internment camps reaches a new crescendo. Long Kesh, with its 1,400 prisoners housed in wartime-type POW camps, is afire from end to end. Armagh women's prison is completely wrecked. Magilligan camp near Derry is ablaze, Crumlin Road prison witnessed sustained fighting between prisoners and warders and police. Tens of thousands of people have taken to the streets of Belfast, Derry, Strabane and Newry. Roads are blocked across the province by buses, cars, tractors and farm machinery, and lorries. Police and troops wade into the prisoners, hundreds are being injured by the hour and fleets of ambulances ferry the injured to Belfast and Lagan hospitals under guard.

In the later repression against the prisoners, the loyalist political internees were struck down by the same punishment. In a remarkable act of prisoner solidarity, a demonstration demands that the struggle for political prisoner status be extended to both sides of the conflict. The commander of the IRA sends a letters of apology to the UDA 'for inconvenience and suffering' caused by the fires and then by the unwarranted punishment. Dave Moreley, the base commander of the Provo forces, makes it clear that he and his volunteers were entirely responsible for the action and that he has conveyed this to the Northern Ireland Office in an attempt to exonerate the UDA men:

> I have informed them that your men were not responsible for the burning of any huts and so they should not be denied visits and that every effort should be made to ease your conditions before the conditions of the Provos. (*IRIS*, 1 November 1974)

A ground-breaking conference, 'Can Irishmen Find a Common Solution to Their Own Problems?', held in the Speakers Club of Galway Technical College, excluded no party and no viewpoint. Fifty speakers, loyalist and republican, north and south, took part in the debate. Sinn Fein took the assembly seriously, with Ruairi O Bradaigh, Sinn Fein president, speaking for Sinn Fein. Harry Murray, formerly of the loyalist Ulster Workers Council, Sammy Smith of the UDA and many others took part.

> All the sessions, especially the private ones, involving loyalist leaders, the Provisionals and many shades of opinion, provided signs of a large extent of common ground. The delegates taking part were unanimous in a wish to meet again soon. (*IRIS*, 1 November 1974)

It was in my view around this sort of period that we came closest to achieving the main planks of our campaign. Despite all subsequent rewritings of history, the armed ranks of 'loyalism' were at the most subverted by ideas of getting back into the world workers' revolutionary stream. British imperialism was at its most conciliatory. Our side, the socialist wing of revolutionary Irish republicanism, was at its peak. It was under the leadership of Ruari, not a traditional revolutionary Marxist but a man who could read the writing on the wall plain enough, and had enough discipline to quickly fall into line and lead the parade, not the later-acclaimed Gerry Adams. Initially Gerry, a self-proclaimed 'Marxist', was to preside over the biggest betrayal of republican aspirations since partition, but more of that later.

TROTSKYISM AND THE WORKERS' STATES

We had just prior to the split began to develop a number of contacts in the US, and these had developed as we moved toward the establishment of our new group. One was a good revolutionary individual, Peter Anton, and his former group, the Revolutionary Communist League (Internationalist). We had been knocked out when we read their stuff. Their world analysis was contained in the tiny print face of their pamphlet *Whirlwinds of Danger*, a great revolutionary anthem and a great title for the book, coming as it did with the first verse on the red-fronted cover.

> Whirlwinds of danger
> Are whirling around us.
> Overwhelming forces of darkness assail.
> While in the fight see advancing before us,
> The red flags of liberty
> That yet shall prevail.

Posadas's view of the workers' states was at great variance with the rest of the Trotskyist world as we knew it. Our positions were within that mould and likewise far more 'workers-statist' than anyone we encountered. Our condemnation of the so called 'Trotskyist' rebellion in Czechoslovakia and support for the Soviet intervention was at odds even with the CPs of Europe who had, like the rest of the Trots, condemned it. With the RCL we found kindred souls. We couldn't believe how, totally isolated over countries, oceans and decades we had come to much the same conclusions on the entire world and the process developing. Mind, it was true to say the position of RCL on Hungary was unique. Most of the left had seen the Hungarian uprising against the all-embracing hug of Stalin and the USSR as a progressive workers' struggle for an independent, perhaps more democratic workers state. In my old YCL days, we had been told it was a 'fascist uprising' which was trying to rekindle a fascist rebirth in Europe and undermine the USSR. RCL(I), and in a way only intense Trotskyist theorists can do, agreed that it was at base a genuine workers' progressive revolution, but that it wasn't strong enough to succeed in its aim, and would be usurped by the imperialists and restorationists, that Hungary would revert to capitalism as a puppet of the west and springboard against the USSR; and in that event the reluctant conclusion of the genuine revolutionary was to 'defend' the Soviet attack upon the rebellion to overall keep what we had, which was better than what would become when the rebels had failed left to their own volition. The word 'defend' must not be confused with the word 'support'. We do not 'support it' politically, because the USSR is a bureaucratic distortion which exported bureaucratic distortions such as the Hungarian workers' state, and isn't the sort of genuine workers' state we wanted, but we 'defend it' because not to do so would be to undermine the achievements of the revolution and its progressive role. Just how the RCL(I) or we, who went on to accept this formula too, were to actually defend the Red Army was best not put to the test, but, in this instance anyway, meant verbally. Comrade Anton had fallen out with his old RCL(I) team, although we couldn't really tell why; we all asked each other almost at the same time, were these splits really necessary and couldn't you just work together albeit as a faction?, but we each meant the other. We agreed to adopt the RCL(I) paper *Internationalist Worker* and to start to contribute articles and analysis of the British and European situation and start circulating it with our stamped contact details on. So it was copies of the American-produced and priced IW started to appear around the Doncaster and then South Yorkshire coalfield, found down pits and at discos, in libraries and colleges, with the Dunscroft contact address. It had to be exciting and interesting, and for many it was there first step into far-left politics and 'the world revolution'.

Meantime Joel our American organiser, was working to build the New American Movement (NAM), which seemed a very successful project gaining ground far and wide.

We were also a regular Co-circulator of the *Republican Peoples News Service*, and agents for its distribution as the group moved into closer proximity to the Provos as a whole.

We were now organising canoeing weekend schools with John as the instructor and lots of capsizes, in fact many comrades are more often upside down than right way up. John gave me one of his sea canoes, though it scared the rice out of me.

13 October. We moved to our long-term home at the White Hart, Barnby Dun; this would become our meeting place and more often than not our social venue.

20 October. 'It was agreed to attend the next surgery of the MP to demand a date for the withdrawal of troops from Ireland and an end to internment.' (Minute 1)

27 October. 'It was agreed to prepare a statement and that as many comrades as possible should attend. The date will be Saturday 2 November.' That was to be a fateful decision, and one the MP would be unlikely to forget.

The scale of the rebellion and repression in Ireland, given the size of the six counties, was enormous and one which we didn't feel was recognised at home. By 1979, proportionately, if this were a rebellion in Britain three-quarters of a million troops would be in occupation, 73,000 people would have been killed and 100,000 in jail.

By October 1974 Alun Howkins was lecturing in sociology and history at Essex University. He invited me down to give a lecture to the Sociology Society on the 31st. My theme was 'Along the Coally Tyne', which in essence was the chapter of my Durham work which had got edited out. Everyone had heard so much about me, he enthused, everyone was waiting for the lecture and a riproaring, foot-stomping social in the bar that night and a party to follow. The prospect seemed lively. Pete Thompson agreed to drive me down and we would stay over at a lecturer's cottage in the countryside when we got back in. Unfortunately for me, the damn nerve tablets to control my panic got forgot, and as soon as I realised I didn't have them, I was hit with a mini attack, sweating, shaking, fear gripping me belly, total loss of focus. Poor Pete, he couldn't understand it, couldn't understand my condition and how a box of tablets could have such an effect in their absence. I tried like hell to pull it all together, as we drove on. The lecture room was packed, all the groups were there, the IS, the IMG, the daughter of Bob Pennington, leader of the IMG and ex-Derbyshire pitman, was there. Well I set off on autopilot and was soon into it; it went down well. However by the time of the discussion and debate my nerves were starting to go. I had my shirt opened near doon to me belly button, was rubbing my head, and my neck, and started to turn a distinct grey. Pete had been deeply impressed with how I could lecture to students and a couple of lecturers and take them on in debate. He was not too impressed when I had to cry off the evening revelry. I left him on his own, and fled the scene like Cinderella, only by 9 p.m. I was in bed literally by 10 p.m., and only one half of lager to show for it. My body just crashed, and pins and needles ran through its entire length and played electric shocks down the sides of my face.

In the morn I was rested but still had the ferrets in my guts. I hated myself for being out of control, for allowing blind fear to dominate me. I resolved to cure this bastard or be cursed by it the rest of my life.

Raph wrote to me:

> Your letter was very moving and also distressing to read. All the ideas for a year off seem immensely worth while, and of course if there is anything I can do to make them possible I'd be glad to do it.
>
> But I think Maureen and yourself ought to think of the possibility of some more radical change. You gave a painfully vivid description of the way in which things combine to really bash you—the physical strain of pit work in the first place, but then all the political developments you describe: you won't be much help to the miners or anyone else if you allow your health and combativity to be taken from you.
>
> I've been talking about it to one or two people here and have found the name of a very sympathetic head or lecturer at a teachers training college near Wakefield who it seems if he has not already read your stuff would certainly respond to it very enthusiastically and whom we could approach to discuss taking you on if you felt moved to consider it. I think these courses are three years. Despite this they have their advantages. A thesis is included in the work—in fact its more important a part of the course than with a university one; this particular man would be particularly interested in dialect and the whole question of class and language; you get a full grant during the time there and its really close to Doncaster ...
>
> Love to yourself and Maureen and Emma
> Raphael Samuels

The poison chalice? To teach?

In a soldiers stance I aimed my words at the mongrel dogs who teach.

(Bob Dylan)

I toyed with the idea, not for the last time, but the ingrown impact of what teaching was at base, indoctrination of discipline and authority with a bit education on top, shouting at kids, keeping order, all that ran too deep in my veins to become a teacher. Even at the increasingly risk to my health of staying at the pit. That wasn't an option, I had to get out, at least for a break.

October seen a marked increase in our antipathy to the International Socialism group. We hated the IS. It was the antithesis of everything we believed. They were in our view the descendants of Burnham and Schactman, wicked deviationists who contradicted the whole analysis of 'the old man' (Trotsky). For some unexplained reason the IS were known as 'the Trots' by the rest of the Communist and Labour movement, despite the fact that they accepted not one of Trotsky's formulations. Aud Lev' was most famous for his analysis of the process of degeneration of the USSR and by proxy and contamination all the workers' states during and after Stalin. His designation of these developments as 'degenerated workers' states' was the cornerstone of his, and therefore our, world view. The International Socialists, under their leader Tony Cliff, an exiled anti-Zionist Israeli, had turned the clock back by saying the USSR et al. were state-capitalist states. They were simply another form of capitalism.[67]

This altered how they seen the entire world struggle and the motive of the whole 'communist movement' as we would have seen it. Among the real Trots, we called them "State Caps"; the SU went further and branded them counter-revolutionary, in the camp of the enemy. Our hatred of them escalated with the wiping out of the Up Against the Law Collective. These had been a collective of anarchist lawyers, advisers, and folk 'up against the law'. A very well-placed group, who spotlighted the corruption, double speak and dirty deals of the law and all its guises. It was hot stuff and also extremely funny. We enjoyed their journal immensely. It was printed on the IS press, as were a number of left publications. The IS ran a print business; it had two wings, one dealt with purely commercial transactions, printing anything for money regardless of its content, for example '*Blue Jokes*' magazine and other such dross. The other wing printed the leftist papers and journals. The most favourable terms went to the purely commercial outlets; they for example, received credit and received their print on pay-on-delivery terms, or even on sale-or-return. With the left it was money up front or nowt doing. The Up Against the Law Collective duly deposited their draft and their cash paid in full. IS printed the edition, but then decided it was libellous and pulped the whole print run. When the lawyer-anarchists turned up for the magazine, they were told sorry, we pulped it, and when they asked for their money back, they were told sorry, no refunds!

This effectively wiped out the collective: no publication and no money to start again. We were furious, and drafted a resolution condemning the actions of the IS and advocating the occupation of their press building and the seizure and use of their equipment by 'Up Against the Law' and other socialist groups. This we sent off to the collective and every left paper and group in Britain and the world we had an address for. We offered to join the raid and occupation of the building.

You might ask why were the anarchists more acceptable to us than the International Socialists? Well one was just common class justice shown to all class fighters, a kind of Geneva Convention of the left, the other, most of us were still at soul anarchists in our aspirations. More politically, we knew our disagreements with the anarchists, or so we thought at this time. With the IS they traded on being 'Trots', they purported to share our view of the trajectory of history and states and decisions arising from that. Then they opted out of the conclusions but still purported to be part of 'our' movement. They joined the other side of the world argument with imperialism and capitalism, not from the logic of 'non-states' demanded of the anarchist position but of no workers states. Theirs was to us nihilist nonsense. The anarchists we could find time for always, they were, even at the height of our Bolshevism, our soul; the IS we thought of as unprincipled, scabs even.

October. The Proletaria Bookshop on Station Road closes. We decide to run a book order and delivery alternative since we still have a vast stock of books. It is no substitute for the loss of our centre though.

'THE MEN IN BLACK HATS'
2 November 1974. As agreed we were now to confront the MP, who was PPS for Merlyn Rees, the Northern Ireland secretary. We were outraged not only at internment and the general repression on the streets of the occupied six counties, the occupation itself, the institutionalised sectarianism of the 'Ulster' protectorate, but also the savage treatment meted out to the internees. We had posters made up of the beaten and battered faces of men as they were admitted to hospital following the burning of Long Kesh by republican prisoners. I had as instructed prepared a statement to read out. As luck would have it, also up this weekend were the comrades from Cinema Action, Schlacke and Eduardo, and others. They too would come, as would all the comrades doon from the toon. Schlacke agreed to film just on the route plus a statement outside afterwards, for possible use in a forthcoming film on Ireland.

I suppose there ended up fifteen or so of us, in determined mode as we marched down the pavement of Broadway to the St Edwin's Centre, St Lawrence Road, Dunscroft, where Mr Marshall held his surgery. His wife was acting as usher.

'Are you coming in turns?', she asked politely.

'Na, we're a delegation.'

Schlacke, wearing a long trenchcoat, had the camera concealed underneath. When the two old age pensioners came out, we all marched in.

Marshall was shocked. 'Sit down,' he pleaded.

Some of us stood, some sat. After a few exchanges I rose to read the statement, and the blood withdrew in stages from his face. 'Just give me that!' he said, and snatched the notes from my hand. It wasn't meant to be read verbatim, but his eyes focused on the big letters at the bottom of the page: 'Those who support imperialism will pay the price of imperialism, those who make our comrades bleed will be made to bleed.' And just at that point Schlacke draws the big camera from under his trench coat, something like Clint Eastwood pulling out a double-barrelled shotgun. It is clear as Marshall rises limply to his feet that he thinks he is going to get blown away. His wife, pushing open the door, cries 'Whatever is going on?' And Marshall bravely shouts 'Get out dear, get out!' By this time the camera is on Schlacke's shoulder and he is filming, at the same time mouthing, in his heavy German accent: 'You ah fasing zer Britishe trade union movement!' (I don't think he added 'Schweinehund!') Edwardo too, in his Portuguese, shouts 'Justice for the Irish people, or war here!' I grabbed my notes back from the MP. 'You're nice people, aren't you?' he responded in a feeble voice. This hadn't been quite the way I had planned the confrontation but this remark stung, and I flew at him. I was one inch from decking him, and I am glad I didn't, because I think the others would have taken that as a green light to kick him all over the floor. 'You bastards are killing men women and children, you are torturing young boys and old men, and wounded people who cannot defend themselves, you are terrorising oppressed communities. You, you credit yourself with bravery for being in this Ireland Office, well you're going to earn it bonny lad!' I said with eyes blazing, 'Sow the wind and reap the whirlwind!' As we turned and marched out, Schlacker was backing away to the door still filming.

Well, I guessed my stay in the Labour Party would be should-lived, I guessed too that the big knock on the door wouldn't be lang. I ordered the comrades to disperse and leave lest they arrest everyone and throw away the key. We had some frantic clearing away of Irish materials and evidence of links to armed groups, not to mention the guns. Not all went as I had hoped; one Geordie cadre, instructed to hide one of our precious handguns, 'but remember where it is', later admitted with pride he had 'hoyed it in the river'.

Marshall, after speaking to the police on his Home Office link, and after a visit by armed Special Branch to make up his mind what to do, decided not to blow us away, just yet. Instead a long and detailed report was made to the GMC, about 'men in dark hats, dark glasses and disguised accents, and threats to kill'. Dark hats and glasses? Well the image was clear and so was our intention, but dark glasses and berets? That wasn't us. Meantime we spread news of our confrontation and soiled MP underwear to our comrades in Ireland. It was a small enough gesture—our aud mate O'Connail had been a bit more explicit when he shot dead the colonel. Perhaps we actually were not far from the point where we too would take retribution to the MP's head; we were certainly following that trajectory.

In November, and following the success of our Newcastle founding rally, we agreed to change the name of the organisation to Socialist Union (Internationalist), and that our initial manifesto now be improved, expanded and reprinted.

BIRMINGHAM

Birmingham. Bombs ripped through the Tavern in the Town pub, down in the cellar bar. It had been crowded with young people out for a night out en route to the night clubs. Within hours six Irishmen were held as the chief suspects. The press hammered home the horror, the carnage, the mutilation, death, gore and destruction on a normal working-class street. It was on the TV from early morning until evening, the same scenes, hour after hour, day after day, often with Irish rebel music playing in the background; TV screens and newspapers howled for revenge.

'The Irish' in general were now all suspect, were now all guilty and these six especially so. Irish people at large came in for abuse and assault. I suffered a wild clout, down the pit, which snapped me jaw shut and cut me tongue from the back to the front and stopped me chewing properly for days. Amid the clamour of the night shift to 'string them up', to 'shoot the bastards', to 'fly over and bomb Ireland' and other such frenzied outrage, I offered a simple suggestion, that 'The men in question should be afforded the right to a trial first should they not? They might not be guilty.' Of course they were guilty, the police don't arrest people who aren't guilty, why would they have these six instead of someone else?

Me poor Mam. She had been in England thirty years or more but not long enough to save her from the taunts:

Yes David I am still very worried over all the trouble, its a sore thing for me as some people are very nasty to me, even when I go out to the shops they say 'Oh, look in her bag, she might have a bomb!' It might be a joke on their part but its a sore one for me. Yes David I have lots of friends in Birmingham that I went to school with ... half of Kells is in Birmingham.'

And half the pub were Birmingham Irish; a collection tin sat on the bar counter for the children of the prisoners. The daughter of one of the six was in the pub when the bomb went off. If you were going to bomb Birmingham you wouldn't bomb here, especially since the offices of the Conservative and Unionist Party were just round the corner. The IRA never claimed responsibility for the blast, something they had always done on every other occasion—even where bombs had gone wrong. Thirty years down the road, they still haven't.

The six, we now all know, were mercilessly framed in what has become one of the most famous 'miscarriages of justice' in English legal history, but there's more. If these six didn't, and the IRA didn't, who did and why? Of all the original suspects who went to court, only one admitted membership of a military organisation. One of the Littlejohn brothers, who claimed he worked for British special forces, turned Queen's Evidence and was given an amnesty. His brother had been caught as part of the bombing operation in Dublin city centre. The two of them famously engaged in bank robberies and espionage against the republicans, acted as British agents within the ranks of the loyalists and operated with SAS Special Forces. My money is on British forces themselves bombing Birmingham. The Prevention of Terrorism Act went through Parliament on the nod with only a very stifled protest by our usual comrades in the Commons, the police were given their heads, the reputation of the IRA hit the skids, supporters fled to the hills, donations dried up, abroad the voice of militant republicanism was silenced, especially in America, at least for some time. Collusion between loyalist murder squads, the police and British Special Forces was given its head and a 'shoot to kill' policy initiated. Who gained from the bombs, who benefited from the bombs? It was illustrative that in all the books and research uncovering the framing of the Birmingham Six, Littlejohn gets dropped out of the picture.

Our meeting of 24 November at Barnby Dun discussed with serious and grave concern the events in Birmingham. We accepted with relief the republican denial of any involvement in this incident. Later meetings discussed the question of IRA targets in general. We agreed to setting up a branch of Troops Out Movement in Doncaster and to approach all left and progressive groups in the area.

End of November 1974. We are continuing our discussions with the Labor Party League in America, a group dedicated to rebuilding the Fourth International and a Labor Party in the USA. In many ways they are like us, working people, not arrogant, unassuming, young, activist, but politically we don't seem to have a lot in common.

Meantime our ongoing contacts with the International Workers Party, who are arranging for me to visit New York for the founding convention of the Nationwide Unemployed League, reveal some strange predilections. It seems the group in part emerged from the National Caucus of Labor Committees (NCLC). This organisation was obsessed with psychoanalysis and a sort of Psychiatric-Marxist-Leninist fusion. At times this group set up psychological tirades about women and their leadership seemed obsessed with some perverted hatred of them; the IWP while ruthlessly critical of the NCLC seem not to have abandoned the "psycho" connection in their analysis.

Following the Essex lecture the Socialist Union fulfilled one of my ambitions. No, not to become leader of a left group, you cynic—they published my North Durham piece. Maureen illustrated it with pen drawings and copies from *Sketches of the Coal Trade in Northumberland and Durham*, and I added drawings onto the stencil mostly copied from mining textbooks and my experience. Although it was only duplicated, I couldn't have been more proud of it. It was funded between the SU(I) and the Red Star Folk Club. Copies went like hot cakes in the miners' galas, particularly the Big Meeting in July 1975.

Arthur had made a powerful demand about this time: the removal of Wilson and Healey as leaders of the Labour Party! He stated that the Labour Party leaders, together with the unscrupulous alliance between Murray and Jones of the TUC, were marching away from the aspirations and demands of the working class in Britain. He saw them, as did the far left in general, on a collision course with the rank and file, who might never forgive them for their betrayal and set themselves and us down a road of ongoing electoral disasters and victory for the Tories. Whether the NUM had the muscle and direction to halt this process by actually confronting Labour's pay policy only time would tell. There were solidly moderate and right-wing cultures among leaders and areas of the NUM despite everything we had learned in our major strikes. This was soon demonstrated with the apparent approval of a militant-sounding resolution for £100 per week for face workers and £85 for elsewhere underground and £80 on the surface. The resolution, however, only talked of seeking such a rise. The resolution demanding the rise be met by 1 November was withdrawn . The composite was moved powerfully by Arthur, but seconded by the notorious right-wing leader of the Nottingham miners Len Clarke. Clarke insisted that seek didn't mean demand, it meant when 'the country could afford it'. The Communist Party had secretly decided to use its influence in the South Wales and Scotland areas to lean on Arthur and Yorkshire to accept the alternative wording. Mick McGahey had urged Arthur that if put to a vote the Yorkshire resolution would fall, which meant in effect the areas in which they exerted the greatest influence, Scotland, Wales and Kent, had already decided not to support it. It was only the point-blank refusal of the Yorkshire delegation to withdraw the resolution which forced those areas to come clean and admit that if pressed they would vote against. Mick is said to have told Arthur 'Get the best compromise you can. It is better to look responsible than beaten.' Arthur then managed to sell the compromised wording to the delegation, as at least still leaving the question on the agenda.

For themselves, what was the thinking of the CPGB among the miners? Locked into their *British Road To Socialism*, they were quite unable to see how a serious challenge to a Labour government could be mounted; they insisted that were the miners to come into open conflict with this government they would not get the solid backing they had before from the rest of the trade union movement. They were wedded to a strategy of reform, not conflict or revolution. Arthur, I am quite certain, was like the rest of us more than willing to lead the troops over the top against this right-wing, so-called 'Labour' government; that it would pose an enormous challenge within the labour movement, possibly to rival even the conflicts around the 1926 strike, seemed almost certain, with the rank and file making a break and choosing a side in the conflict. This could even see the emergence of an alternative left leadership in the Labour Party, but, more importantly a socialist perspective, an alternative political outlook; it would be a battle right through the labour movement in all its manifestations to seize control and direction of the movement. To be right, Arthur himself had not actually thought through the overall strategy to engage the whole labour movement inside and out in victorious struggle and his own politics were hardly revolutionary at the time. He had no concept of workers' direct control of society. His notions of socialism were based entirely upon 'leaders' running things, and organisations which ran things directed by leaders. Not having an alternative organisation to the existing one, and not really seeing any road outside of it, posed him a political dilemma; unlike his comrades in the Communist Party leadership he did not, however, see that as any good reason not to carry on with the struggle regardless. It was this attitude which the CP leaders most disliked about Arthur.

NOT OUR RAF – THEIR RAF!

End of December 1974. Our Red Star singers were invited to sing at the RAF officers club at Lindholme! True, Steve Walker of the Hogshead was known to them as a folk singer and they wanted something different. We went. We were different, OK. My songs about Christine Keeler, and spies were well received, Paul Barrowcliff's about bombers and burning houses, less so. Steve's Scottish Jacobite songs seemed well received, judging from the ranks of stamping feet and my sea chanties had them rocking like a Munich beer cellar. In the interval I went around the bonny officers' wives and daughters done up in their silk finery selling copies of the *Red Star Song Book*.

I actually sold a few, when one upper-class wife announced: 'Red Star Songs—hardly appropriate to this club.'

I replied laughing, because I was actually only really doing it as a wind-up, 'You don't have to be a Tory to be an RAF officer do you?'

'No' she replied, ' but it helps.'

Then, surprise of my life, a bloke further down the line volunteers to buy one and flicking through the pages starts to sing some of the songs; he was a Communist! He must have overheard my conversation with the RAF lady because he said as he paid me, 'You don't have to be a coal miner to be a communist, do you?' And I replied, likewise, 'No, but it helps.' They paid us for our services, free booze and an invitation to come back socially, which we never did, but I don't recall that being on principle.

Our encounter with the MP was surfacing. The November meeting of the GMC heard a strong letter read from him, and it was being passed on to the EC for action. We planned to circulate the left and trade union movement about the issue, and plan a lobby of the EC. Meantime the new anti- terrorist laws that had sailed through the Commons on the back of the Birmingham outrage and the hysteria fed by the press and TV meant they could bring in just about any repressive measures they wanted. We set our face to the wind and declare

> The Socialist Union sees the so called 'anti-terrorist' laws passed in parliament last week as a clear attack by a capitalist government on the hard won democratic rights of the working people in Britain and Northern Ireland. These laws are intended to divide working class people in an attempt to prop up a crumbling capitalist society.
>
> Therefore we pledge our active support for the people of Ireland in achieving a United Socialist Ireland by whatever means may be made necessary by British Imperialism and instruct all members to campaign for the following wherever and whenever possible:
>
> 1. The Immediate withdrawal of British Troops from Northern Ireland.
>
> 2. The immediate release of internees in Northern Ireland and Irish political prisoners in Britain.
>
> 3. The immediate formation of a free socialist Ireland based upon the programme 'Eire Nua'.

4. The immediate repeal of the new so called 'anti-terrorist' laws and release of anyone imprisoned under it.

Lest there were any confusion still in the minds of the Labour Party where we stood on the war in Ireland, the Young Socialist resolution to the LPYS conference coming up in the new year laid that at rest. After restating much of the above, it goes on:

This conference recognises that the struggle of the Irish republican forces is right and just in fighting militarily and politically for a Socialist 32 county republic, and further pledges its unconditional support for the cause of Irish republicanism and the organisations which struggle for that cause.

Conference totally condemns internment and detention without charge or trial and all that this means—midnight raids, torture, internment after being charged and found not guilty and the atrocious conditions which internees have to suffer. Conference does not recognise the right of British imperialism to jail or detain republican or loyalist people, believing that British imperialism does not have any right to try anybody for anything on Irish soil.

The solution to the problems of Ireland must be found by the Irish people—there is no British military solution, there is no British political solution.

'Believing that the British Government has no right in Ireland, never had any right in Ireland, and never can have any right in Ireland, the presence in any one generation of Irish men or even a respectable minority ready to affirm that truth, makes that government forever a usurpation and crime against humanity. I personally thank God that I have lived to see the day when thousands of Irish men and boys and hundreds of Irish women and girls were ready to affirm that truth and attest to it with their lives if needs be.'—James Connolly.'

Oddly enough it was in this month that the NUM Branch reaffirmed my nomination as one of their members to the GMC of the Constituency Labour Party and the Doncaster Trades Council to which we had now transferred affiliation after the collapse of Thorne. Some joker also put me forward as a justice of the peace. Hey, why Not? Mind, the two spaces for any criminal convictions necessitated that I write 'see attached sheet' on them. I didn't get the position. Pity—that could have been amusing. There was a famous Scottish Communist in the Thirties who was a local sheriff and dispensed justice from the court, and sometimes funds to poor folk instead of sentences. On one occasion he sentenced a miner to come and listen to him address the local May Day rally the following day. On another he ordered the clerk of the court to buy bags of coal for a young girl caught stealing it from the pit to warm her impoverished family home.

DOUBLE STANDARDS?
January 1975. Members of the Oxford University Officer Training Corps carry

out a bombing campaign in Oxford against targets they think are 'Communist, Socialist and Republican or anyway just Irish'. They bomb Blackfriars Catholic Friary, Ruskin College, and the Irish Club. When detected, Michael Skelding, found guilty of criminal damage and recklessly endangering life planting bombs, got just two years. Andrew Grainger, a student at Reading University, got six months, while Roger Moore got fined £300. Nowt for conspiracy to cause explosions which usually carries twenty years, never mind the customary thirty years for actually planting the devices.

> 5 January 1975
> Cinema Action, 35 a Winchester Road, London NW3
> Dear Comrade
> *The Miners' Film* is now finished and we have our first prints ready. The Red Star Club is included in the film, with pictures of the flute player and the sound of your strong singing of 'Farewell Johnny Miner'. We would have liked to have had more pictures of Doncaster in the film (there are a couple of shots of Doncaster at night included) but the old story of lack of funds limited us. But what is included from Doncaster is very strong and is one of the central contributions to the film- thank you very much for your help in this. We hope to be taking the film around the Areas in the next few months and would like very much to bring it to show you all.
>
> We enclose a copy of a letter about the film written by Jack Collins from Kent and will send leaflets about the film as soon as we have them prepared.
>
> Happy New year and all the best to you and your family.
> Yours In Struggle
> Cinema Action"

25 January 1975. Dave and Alison on trial at the GMC of the Labour Party.

At the end of February the Goole Constituency LPYS wound up. Harassment, war-weariness, flogging a dead horse, more exciting things going on outside that decrepit institution, fed up of the rules and restrictions. Any one of these things and all of them had brought about what came as a rather rapid and dramatic decision in the end.

ROTHBURY

Almost from the inception of the group we had grasped the necessity of armed struggle and that the forthcoming revolution in Britain in whatever form it broke would be violent. Violent in the sense that the revolution would be repressed by the state's 'bodies of armed men', and violent in the sense that capitalism and capitalists would be unlikely to simply pack their bags and get on the train without a fight, possibly a war.

We could not see the sense of the revolutionary forces of the left expending their total energies in talking and writing about this revolution without any attention to the mere detail of actually preparing for it. We had started to incorporate various physical and militarist aspects into the life of our team, usually at camps and linked to social settings. Now we decided to set up a military training unit. One which would prepare the revolutionary cadre for the forthcoming clash and if not of the cataclysmic variety than at least the ability to thump a fascist on the nose and defend ourselves.

15 February. The first of a number of training schools up at Rothbury. We have taken advantage of the offer of Bob Hart to use his Berserkers Bothy up in Rothbury; a converted cricket pavilion in a huge abandoned overgrown garden. It is the property of some Lord or other who Bob has beaten for over his grouse moors, and he has given it over scot-free to the use and care and Bob. He knows we will be flying the Red Flag in his bothy and talking up a storm; he is not aware that we carry a Transit full of rifles and intend to train on the moors and cragland of Rothbury.

During the following months Rothbury would host a number of our extended courses. We would teach all forms of military techniques and strategic studies. Karate, unarmed combat, weapon training with sticks, staffs, shooting, map-reading, rock-climbing, first aid, survival. We would throw open our facilities to the left in general to prepare the left and the working class for the forthcoming revolutionary encounter. Although time would show, none—none at all—would ever take us up on our offer, or make any preparation of their own. We issued checklists for all the participants as to what they should bring. Joel wrote from the States translating our stuff: 'I guess a jumper is a sweater, and sand shoes are trainers, but what the hell is a 'ballyclavour'?'

Our 'Embryonic Military Caucus' (EMC) courses were magic – magic in their daring, in the fact we believed, seriously believed, we were preparing for real armed struggle, setting the agenda, building the armed cadres. Magic in that we armed, drilled and trained to shoot. Magic in the star-filled nights over the bitter clear Northumbrian hills and crags where we night-manoeuvred, tried to navigate by star gazing and, often exhausted, in the otherwise pitch black of some cragside, just lay and stared at the stars and enormousness of the universe.

> And its home boys, home,
> Home I'd like to be, laying in the dark with a Provo Company.
> With a comrade on me left and another on me right,
> And meself in the middle with me little Armalite.

DONIEFASH

Receiving reports of a National Front cell established in Doncaster, some of whom attempted intimidation of me and Maureen, we agreed to track down and confront them. This was made a little easier when they started writing to the press. Their main lair was at the Vine, where they met under the guise of a football supporters group. Closing the pub off as a venue was the easiest part of the problem; smashing the group something else. Over the years I received a host of threatening anonymous letters describing all sorts of murder to be done to me. In one I was a 'Geordie-Irish Nigger loving, jew hugging communist pig', which sounded right enough. Hate mail would carry the Battle of Britain commemoration stamps—upside down so the swastika on the Stuka was in the top right hand corner instead of HM. On occasion we found graffiti near the sites of clubs or pubs we visited 'Dave, Ken, Maureen, Alison, we will avenge your race tretchery', or 'Dave and his Reds we will murder you!' I must say, I was suspicious of some of this stuff. AW, who we found to be a dangerous fantasist, always seemed to find the offending slogans in places where we wouldn't otherwise have discovered them. Was it him staging his little world of excitement, or playing for both sides? As time went on we became fairly convinced he was actually working for the Special Branch, and had moved from just being an oddball to collating information for future use, and then at crucial times acting as a purveyor of poisonous rumours and slander. Our mistake was in giving him, time after time, the benefit of the doubt, and because he had been locally recruited with family in the community, and was a convincing conman, we grossly underestimated his later impact. Our humanity saved his life, but later was to cost me in particular untold damage in my local standing in the community.

Friday 28 February 1975. Doncaster Branch of the Troops Out Movement holds a public meeting at the Lord Nelson. The speakers apart from myself were: 'J. Sharp, International Harvesters AUEW, and Paul Barrowcliffe, ICI TGWU.' All of us were members of the SUI; we were however able to build a section independent from our own group with workers from the wider Doncaster community taking part. Not least of these were the Malees from Stainforth, who had married into Irish families from Ulster, all of whose male members worked at the pit. Some of these had had first-hand experience of the British army as an occupation force as well as seeing the loyalist terror first hand.

17 March. Me and Ken catch the train up to Newcastle for St Patrick's night, and swing past me Ma's hoose coz Ah knaa she'll have a big bunch of shamrock for us, which she does. We start off at Pat Foley's in the Bridge, and are soon in the sing and swing of things with Malcolm and some of the other Newcastle comrades. We give out leaflets on Troops Out to all in general and canvass support for Sinn Fein and ourselves among the Tyneside Irish in particular. I need to get some organiser's credentials so I can organise Sinn Fein Cumain among Irish communities here. I think too possibly Sinn Fein might accept the affiliation of the SU(I). We end up at some Catholic college up at Gateshead at a big ceilidh. By the time we cadge a lift to the train we just make it as it is pulling out of the Central. We march up and down the nearly deserted train corridors singing IRA songs and inflicting TOM leaflets on any poor passengers we can find, then flop down in our compartment. We wake up as the train hits Retford. Bloody hell, it's after midnight, cold, and now we have to try and hitch hike back to Doncaster. We manage to walk the way to the A1. Standing by the roadside, bedraggled, in our jackets, no luggage, hitching, swaying.

A squad car pulls up. The cop winds down the window.

'Right lads where you going?'

'Doncaster,' we reply.

'Where have you been?'

'Newcastle,' we reply. 'Newcastle is north of here, as is Doncaster,' he observes.

We are not in the mood to be clever. 'It's St Patrick's night, or it was. We fell asleep on the train.'

He looks at the now crumpled shamrock, bottles of broon ale sticking out of each pocket, the stupid grin. 'OK,' he concludes.

'Any chance of a lift?'

'Piss off!' he says and drives off to our laughter.

Well some way down the road after about four short lifts of folk coming home from the pub, we spy a big motorway service station and decide this is the place for a snack and a lift. We walk into the brightly lit enormous food hall, and the food standing in lines behind its ranks of plastic flaps, but no staff anywhere. Suits us. We get toast and help ourselves to beans and Ken has sausage and bacon. We pour ourselves pop and tea, and sit down for a good forty minutes eating and regaining our composure. Still no staff. We conclude they are asleep somewhere or having a jump. We load up with egg sandwiches and donuts for the journey and walk out. It is a mark to the type of folk we are that we never so much as thought of touching the till. Don't know what that shows, but it's there.

ANTI THE EEC

One of SUI's first campaigns was to mount a workers' opposition to the Common Market. From where we stood it looked as though the overwhelming mass of organised workers were emphatically against the EEC. The decision to go in was taken without reference to anyone. Under mass pressure from its own party, Labour has been forced to call a referendum. All the political forces were split left and right between joining and not joining. The leaders of all the major political parties were in favour, and together were able to launch a mass-media blitz in support. Many national union leaders, even some pro-Chinese Communist parties, were also in favour. By 16 votes to 7 the Labour Cabinet voted to campaign for a 'yes' vote, thus ignoring the views of the Labour Party NEC and the Conference. Against were the far right, and members of all the major political parties, and most unions. Both positions formed united blocks for and against. This we refused point blank to do. We were not going to be party to Popular Frontism, not least because our reasons for opposing entry were nothing to do with the reasons of the far right and 'little Englanders' who basically didn't like 'foreigners'. The formal 'left' in Britain lined up alongside some of the most disgusting right-wing political formations, shared platforms with them, jointly campaigned with them. It wasn't the red flag of socialism this 'left' section marched behind, but the Damned Union Jack, singing the stirring strains of 'Land Of Hope And Glory' while some of the heartfelt pleas for the preservation of 'British Parliamentary Sovereignty' were stomach-churning. We hated all this patriotic bilge: the notion of 'Britishness', the queen, the flag, the empire/commonwealth, the so-called constitution which didn't actually exist, the thousand years of Parliament—without universal adult suffrage in Britain until

1947 and not until 1969 for all Ulster Catholics (although there were extra votes for Oxford and Cambridge graduates until 1950). Everything we hated about the British state, all of its trappings and ruses, our so-called allies loved. A campaign statement of ours issued at the time records: 'We consider it our duty to disrupt and physically attack any platform on which fascists or right-wingers sit Even If It Is An Anti-Common Market Platform Shared With "Left" Leaders'. We had seen nothing to 'defend' in the British parliament, but at the same time see the growth of non-elected, non-accountable governing bodies within the EEC. We believed in some future united Soviet Socialist States of Europe, based upon democratic assemblies of workers and small farmers. We supported our fellow workers in Europe. We saw in the EEC a rich men's club, a block of European employers trying to create a super insurance policy against any nation state adopting socialist policies. We thought we foresaw the creation of a pan-European military and police wing whose members would be deaf to any class appeals by rioting or striking workers in any of the respective countries. We made a focus on the scandalous waste of propping up agricultural prices on the grounds that the prices of food stuffs were otherwise too low! Free market capitalism would in this instance have given us increasingly lower food prices. So instead they spent £21 million buying up fruit and vegetables which they buried or burnt. £7,391,000 spent in one year destroying pears in Italy and £6,956,000 in France trashing apples.

29–31 March 1975. LPYS National Conference, Blackpool. By the end of March 1975 Left Alliances had been formed, one of them in Doncaster whose chief campaign was to be against the EEC. It was reported that some comrades at this meeting had openly said they would work with the extreme right on this issue; even the Communist Party had said they would work with the Tory right-wing Monday Club. We announced at this meeting that we would not. We would be conducting a socialist campaign.

Our campaign covered the whole district with fleets of cars and vans, boasting the anti-EEC message. Loudspeakers mounted on roofs we toured the districts playing socialist songs and tunes and appealing to voters to say NO. Our Geordie blood links with the ancient kingdom of Norway, and the fact that they had just held a successful NO campaign, gave us to wearing Norwegian 'Stem Nee' badges. We even fashioned a few Stem Nee posters, in part to demonstrate that we were not to be confused with the parochial official 'Say No' campaign, who toured their districts playing bloody 'Land Of Hope And Glory'. Indeed one of the leftist arguments, especially offered by our European and some US comrades as to why we should be saying 'Yes', was to take on this chauvinistic British bollocks, to make British workers see themselves in unity and comradeship with the rest of Europe. We didn't think we needed to go that far to learn that lesson. Again at one of our mass meetings, this time in St Edwin's Hall, a massive old wooden communal hall which stood where the supermarket on Station Road now stands, and which we had more or less taken over as our regular campaign building, the radical Left Labour MP Dick Kelly, while urging a 'No' vote, warned the audience in hushed tones to beware of patriotism:

'An Ah wa-arn ahl yee young'uns oot there, be-ware pat-riot-ism. Beware that sinister and cynical bloodthirsty blind torment, pat-riot-ism!'

I thought he underestimated our young and rebellious audience.

'Whey, Dick, man,' I urged in my summing-up of the meeting, 'this is the Woodstock generation, we are the people, we will never be fooled like those young'uns of the first world war, or duped by people like Churchill.'

But Dick wouldn't have it:

'Ah'm tellin yee lad, when they wave that bloody flag, and they bash that drum, and start talking about England, and the British, they'll gaan lad, they'll gaan.'

He was speaking from hindsight of broken visions of the Second International, and the pledges before two world wars that European workers would never again take up arms against each other in conflicts on behalf of their ruling classes and the European capitalists and royalty. But they went, aye they went. Years later I was to tragically see, if not the Woodstock generation, then the beginnings of a new one gaan and gaan again and again and again behind 'that bloody flag'.

Ongoing campaign of mass public Socialist Anti-EEC meetings at the Miners Welfare, Stainforth, and St Edwin's Hall, Dunscroft

27 April. Maureen is congratulated on gaining her 7th Kyu in Wado Karate yesterday. I failed mine; too nervous, got all the stances wrong. Christ, she can beat me up now!

John Sharp resigns from the group:

> having reached a point of suffocation within the limited, rather restricted bounds of the Socialist Union ... this decision is not a direct result of any single issue or disagreement either with the SU(I) policy or its members.
>
> When I first became a member I saw the SU as a means of uniting the Socialist movement, so that we would be ready at any time to move into action immediately on a united front to defend our living standards and to improve life by socialist methods. This has not been the case, all we have done so far is write letters and hold badly attended meetings. We have not made any real progress towards socialist unity, and it is my belief that this is due mainly to the chauvinist attitude of the group i.e. 'This is what we say, we are right, you must change if wish to join us.' The result of this being that we have had very little real response to the SU ... and it does not really exist as a force for uniting the Socialist Movement.

Well I suppose it was true we hadn't swept the country with our new organisation, but we were surely about far more than writing letters and not all our meetings were badly attended, not the public ones anyway.

30 APRIL 1975: THE FALL OF SAIGON

At the end of 1965 the USA had over 100,000 troops in Vietnam. By 1966/7, 300,000; by January 1968 498,000. The Democratic Republic of Vietnam and the NLF meantime had moved from guerrilla attacks to all-out conventional warfare. They had since 1965 been facing the biggest air blitz launched since World War Two, including the two atomic bombs dropped on Japan, but the people remarkably and with superhuman endurance took it on, rebuilt, and continued. With the help of the USSR, DRV did have some air defences, indeed something like 1,400 US planes were shot down during those three years.

The US strategy was to swamp the South with hundreds of thousands of well-equipped soldiers, at the same time launching the biggest ever bombardment and blitz of the North hitherto seen in the history of the world. The brutality and sheer barbarity of the occupation in the South is well recorded and attested to. That anyone could be proud to be a human being let alone an American during this bloodbath of rape, torture and indiscriminate massacre takes some believing. It came therefore as a huge blow to US pride and belief in its own power and omnipotence when in February 1968 the NLF launched its Tet offensive, throughout all the major cities and towns in the occupied territory and against all odds. It was the biggest offensive by either side in the whole war. 80,000 NLF and PAVN insurgents attacked 100 towns, 36 of them provincial capitals. The assault had been repulsed, but the world seen the NLF back in the streets of Saigon and a risen people resisting the greatest power on earth. The armed forces demand a further 200,000 troops to hold the line, or predicted they would start to fail and start to be driven out. At home the antiwar movement was confronting in greater and greater numbers not only the war, but also the whole ideology of American imperialism and capitalism. The draft was being refused by tens of thousands young 'uns lined up, who risked ridicule, the blacklist and a beating to burn their draft cards. A Bulgarian poster of the period shows a US soldier blowing on the embers of a Vietnamese peasant hut, while the flames are igniting on his backside. American veterans of the war, many disabled, were pelting their medals at the White House, were burning the sacred flag. The American state had gone to war in Vietnam to stop the spread of communism through Indochina, but the effect was to spread communist ideas to America, as the process of revulsion against the atrocities started to make working-class and middle-class America challenge the whole basis on which their society was built, and ask why it was so afraid of another set of values and ideas.

They had watched in horror as the US forces at home battened down protesters, even shooting dead their own kids in the fields of their own colleges. From Tet onward the US state sought to find another policy other than blanket assaults and endless piles of US bodies. From 1969 onward numbers of US soldiers started to drop as their place was taken by 'Vietnamisation'. This was an attempt to get more and more puppet forces to take up the strain, by giving them everything war science and technology and money could provide. This didn't stop them continuing the scorched-earth policy; indeed if anything this became more desperate, almost like the mind frame of the Nazis' 'final solution', which in 1944 and 1945 had continued as allied soldiers were knocking on the doors of the extermination camps. Antiwar papers, communist papers, black consciousness papers flooded US military bases across the world. Soldiers joined protests, spoke on rostrums, and, more frighteningly for the US state, started to shoot their own officers in increasing numbers ('fragging', they called it). The US expanded its war into Cambodia and Laos, first in pursuit of Vietnamese insurgents and their bases then quickly against the peoples of those countries too, who it was clear were also contaminated with the alien ideas of national independence and anti-imperialism, not to mention communism. The war would have to continue to be waged throughout Indochina simultaneously if it was to have any chance of winning, but at home it was becoming not meaningless, but precisely its opposite. It was becoming the focus for opposition to the American state per se. Black movements for freedom, armed and certain. White armed working-class resistance, militant feminism, revival of the old American labour movement, growing trade union militancy, and throughout it all, the rock and roll of resistance, the air of defiance, and the sexual resistance. As Dylan had said a little earlier, 'It's going to soon shake your windows and rattle your doors, because the times they are a-changing.' The US state could clearly see and started to predict full-scale insurrection at home; because of the numbers of men and women under arms, and holding arms, it would be a very well-armed insurrection with few or no armed forces to confront it.

Vietnamisation allowed the US state a back door out, and when they signed themselves a cease-fire agreement in January 1973 the last US troops left in March leaving their surrogates, equipped to the gunwales with high-tech death to carry on the fight. The anti-war protesters and the anti- war consciousness however continued at home, and Congress went on to ruthlessly cut the arms bill and military expenditure aid to the Indochina puppet forces. By 1974 they were out of bombs and bullets and by the following year were crushed by a massive joint NLF-DRV offensive which seen puppet soldiers fleeing in all directions tearing off their uniforms. Thousands flocked to the US Embassy and the demarcation centres on the promise of evacuation. Men and women with their children, waving official papers, in convoys of buses and trucks, or walking with their bundled possessions on their backs and the desperate kids at their sides; agents who had worked for the US occupation, from torturers to servants. The Viet girlfriends, and wives of US personnel, the staff, the spies, informers, and playthings of the occupation. The day of reckoning was at hand, poor, hapless, desperate and abandoned like all scabs when the dirty work was over, for whatever reason turns good men and women into class traitors, most of them were to be abandoned by their masters. The taking of Saigon was the crest of the offensive which had begun in January. There had been a lull following the Paris Peace Accord, with both sides regrouping. Thieu and the US had no intention of respecting any treaty. The NLF began its drive south taking northern cities as it came and then the central provinces, then the cities of Da Nang and Hué. The back of the southern puppet forces was broken at Xuan Loc north-east of Saigon. The Vietnamese insurgents entered Saigon to accept the formal surrender in 30 April 1975, although for reasons I do not understand I do not recall that any of us, anywhere, held mass victory parties and celebrations despite this being a victory for the oppressed of the world, on a scale we cannot describe even now. I think there was a worldwide news blackout. Kissinger had appeared on US TV utterly dejected and warned that increased revolutionary activity around the globe would now be a consequence.

Liberation Radio, broadcasting from the former capital, announced the change of name from Saigon to Ho Chi Minh City in honour of the late leader, who had led his people, not always a Mr Nice Guy as far as the folks to his left were concerned, but did so for fifty hard, relentless years. The victory is incalculable. For US imperialism they had spent $350 billion in expenditure and application of the most advanced weapons of mass destruction science and brutality could provide them with. Although I am not suggesting a fully fledged workers democratic socialist system was established in Vietnam, and on the other side means of global oppression and control became both more brutal and more subtle as my story and life evolves. I am jumping ahead of my tale, but this was a remarkable and enduring victory.

May Day 1975. In Doncaster, the Socialist Union (Internationalist) makes its debut appearance. Maureen has once more excelled with the new group banner, this time in black satin and red satin. 'Free at last' we think, we are now our own team with our own direction with our roots firmly in the earth of working class life and labour and our feet squarely on the ground or so it seemed from where we were standing. Workers and their families were far more at ease with us in this organisation than they had been with 'the Party' despite the fact that if anything we were far more radical and revolutionary in physical terms and on questions of legality than we had been with the Posadists, they knew us, worked with us, lived along side us, we were an organisation based upon communities. We had never accepted the inevitability of the nuclear war or its desirability, though we continued to be full of bravado over the pre-emptive strike of the 'degenerated workers states'. We didn't make this a centre of our analysis we thought it a possibility in a range of options, but the central characteristic of the period was revolution not nuclear war.

<

3 May 1975. Larry Lockwood writes for RCL(I):

> In the past two months we have begun to develop very promising discussions with some experienced and very solid black revolutionists. In our workers caucus's progress has been good and we hope soon to accept several candidates. We are carrying on a polemical interchange with a West Coast grouping headed by Arne Swarbeck, a founding member of the Trotskyist movement in the US (he's 84 years old). The West Coast group claims to have developed a "synthesis" between Trotskyism and Maoism, but their positions on China are so "Maoist" that they even uphold China's stance on NATO. Most of their members appear to be in Trade Unions, so we can hope for an interchange and possible united front work can be developed ... This weekend we hope to firm up our strategic perspective toward IWP... with whom we want to begin a very sharp polemic defending Leninism against 'neo-Luxemburgism' (mind

you, we ourselves consider Rosa Luxemburg one of the greatest revolutionaries, but we do not counterpose her to Lenin and Trotsky as some have attempted to do ever since the thirties) ...

Around this time the comrades in America agreed to print professionally the new edition of the manifesto. (In January 1975 we had published Peter Anton's *Puerto Rico: The Graveyard of American Liberalism* as an SUI pamphlet.) Contacts were also being established with the armed and political movements of black people in the USA.

An internal struggle had meantime developed within the NUM at Hatfield, the motive for which seemed hard to pin down but basically the secretary Frank Clark, who was a full-time employee of the Branch, was being pressurised to sign on the NCB's books. Frank came from a tradition of independence from the boss, and fully retained union reps, a tradition which had come from Durham with the various migrations in the Twenties. A faction led by Tom Mullanny was trying to embarrass the secretary, by circulating figures on how much it was costing the Branch and how much could be saved by him signing on with the Coal Board. My political and personal feelings were at once with Frank on this one. The meetings where this matter was discussed were bitter and sickening with earnings and incomes being bandied about the room, and the secretary I thought defending his dignity. The move was defeated, without me ever really understanding the motive.

The women's document which by now was out in its all its glory was going down a bomb. Me Mam had took one look at it and read it out loudly so me Da in the kitchen could hear:

> What price for a woman?
> You can buy her for a ring of gold
> To love and obey
> (Without any pay)
> You get a cook or nurse
> For better or worse
> You don't need a purse when a lady is sold.

– which was a verse from Peggy Seeger's excellent song 'I'm Gonna Be An Engineer'.

She had been thrilled by it and took it everywhere with her in her bag to show her friends. Me Da also read it. He was not so thrilled, in particular the section in praise of women fighters:

> More recently we have Bernadette McAliskey (formerly Devlin) who has fought bravely in defence of her people both on the streets of Belfast and in Parliament; the Price sisters, who have been imprisoned and brutally force-fed for daring to fight for the cause of Irish republicanism; the brave women of the Armagh Jail—both republican and loyalist who took joint militant action including the holding of hostages as a protest against internment.

Na, he wasn't ower pleased with that an muttered about it for some time. Me Ma says she got the full blast of his objections when he read it.

The pamphlet was being sold door to door and in supermarkets and outside bingo halls. It was everywhere striking an impact.

The IMG write to us to complain about the content of some of our songs at our last folk concert. In particular they didn't like Des's excellent country song 'Cuckoo's Nest' which is basically a country anthem in praise of the vagina:

> Some like a girl who is pretty in the face
> Others like a girl who is thin around the waist
> Aye but give me a girl who can wriggle and can twist
> At the bottom of her belly lies the cuckoo's nest.

They didn't like some of sea chanties' rough reference to sex and 'Judies' either. We consider these historic pieces of workers' music, they were written in their time and reflect attitudes then. While we wouldn't sing overtly objectionable racist songs, and might slightly adapt the phraseology, we can see no objection to these songs of sexuality being sung. Some of the black seamen's songs referred to themselves as 'niggers' in the way that some miners' songs referred to themselves as 'pit yaakers', both disparaging terms on anyone else's lips, but with a different meaning when sung by the blokes themselves. These were different and anyway, as the comrades said, 'What's wrong with sexual attraction?'

Received a mint edition of *Behind The Nylon Curtain*, Jerry Zilg's huge research work on the DuPont family. As things turned out this would be one of few surviving copies in the whole world as the DuPonts reacted to its publication.

Public Meetings Against the Common Market with Tom Mullanny from the NUM and Dick Kelly MP.

Around May 1975 came the first plans for the NCB to sell off its housing stock with us in them. The NUM is emphatically against the sale of the houses, to tenants or to the council, never mind private landlords.

Ken wins a place at Ruskin, and like me secures a guarantee of re-employment on the shop floor of Harvesters when he graduates.

17 May. Another disciplinary meeting, before the GMC, most of us on trial.

23–25 May. EMC Training at Rothbury, this time at TC's summer house in the abandoned woods. Karate, stick fighting, knives, survival practice and brick-throwing as urban resistance.

From mid-1975 the direct line of communication from the IRA, the formal one at least, came through the duplicated *Irish Republican Information Service (IRIS)*. We received it regularly; it was published as information required, sometimes twice a week. We digested and reprocessed the information, the tactics, the armed wing's outlook on everything which was being said about them, and also supposedly by them. What they had been engaged in, what the other side had been engaged in. No other news source was as direct and accurate as this, for the most obvious of reasons. We redistributed it through our own publications, we carried out consultation work, and tested the water for them over a range of issues. In this we felt quite honoured.

Thursday 5 June 1975. National referendum on entry into the EEC (the Common Market). We lost. But as it turned out European stormtroopers didn't invade, not yet anyway. The EEC was a godsend for people like me Uncle Peter and most Irish small farmers. From basic cottages they were soon constructing Ponderosa ranches on their bits of land, and the lang walk into Kells was soon eclipsed by the Dukes of Hazard young 'uns zipping up and doon the 'old bog road'. Soon there was little sign of old folks gathering up sticks for the hearth. Peter, who bred a few pigs as a sideline to working on the big farm next door, would sell on the pigs to the big farmer. 'They call me thick,' says Peter. 'Then the man from the Common Market comes and says, "Peter, we'll pay you not to have the pigs," so I take the money not to have the pigs, and I have the pigs anyway.'

Meantime me Mam and Dad are thrilled by *The Miners of North Durham*. Maureen had brought some up in a bag in case me Dad's aud marras in Wardley club might like to have one. As it turned out they were mobbed for them. Me Ma wrote:

> David we think your book is great and wish Maureen had left us about 20. She left 10,some pages came apart as the clips are not long enough to hold them, so we kept that one but I wish they had held a bit better, the pages are very loose. Anyway Dad sold the nine he had and he could have sold more as they all wanted one and I could have sold some at the Summer show in Newcastle. We think that that book is better than the red one [*Pit Talk In Co. Durham*]. How did you remember all the things you have in there, gee I had to laugh at me making the clippie mats ...

For a duplicated and stapled pamphlet this little effort had been a roaring success. I think me folks liked it because it was more folky, about their own lives and their neighbourhoods and our collective history. Pete Elliott of the famous Elliotts of Birtley liked it so much he reproduced it and re-edited it, actually making a much better job than the original.

12 June. Five miners killed in explosion at Houghton Main, Barnsley.

11–13 July. Weekend training, sea survival at Kilnsea. Amid much derision, me and Ken, both non-swimmers, chicken out of most of it. People who are swimmers cannot remember the sheer fear of those not imbued with the simple yet apparently impossible skill.

We are informed that an article about us appears in the July 1975 issue of the *Reader's Digest* no less.

19 July 1975. Durham Miners' Gala. 141 copies of *The Miners of North Durham* sold in one afternoon.

27 July. A big barnstorming concert by the Beggermen. The club record book meantime shows that it was issuing grants for various projects from the funds: printing the SUI manifesto, which was ongoing in the USA; affiliation to the Troops Out Movement; purchase of machetes for EMC courses.

At the end of July we received the first of a litany of complaints from the Revolutionary Communist Group (in Britain) about the function of the Troops Out Movement. The RCG were, well, not to put too fine a point upon it, posh— a few of them quite aristocratic. Their complaints were personal rather than political, although their theme that the IMG and IS were in a manipulative numbers war within the organisation did have some ring of truth in it.

27 November 1975. Ross McWhirter is shown the error of his ways. A member of 'the Balcombe Street Gang', a Provo 'Active Service Unit', knocked on Ross McWhirter's home door and when he answered it, shot him dead. McWhirter, the co-editor of the *Guinness Book of Records*, had just publicly offered £50,000 for information leading to the arrest of the team.

29 November. A big folk concert at the Drum. The record book entry gives us a recollection of that night:

> The room was filled with a lovely red glow from the coal fire— John brought his red lights and it made for a nice atmosphere along with the candles and posters and banners on the walls ... Some from Sheffield IMG came and sold copies of *Red Weekly* in the interval. Two CPGB comrades from the Rossington Branch who enjoyed it.

We were jobbing folk, rentafolk really, we organised folk events for other people, like the folk social for the Sheffield branch of the IMG on Friday 12 December at the Lion, Sheffield. Actually IMG had also asked me to organise a major concert in London for their mass rally at the Roundhouse on 20 February which starred Ernest Mandel, their world leader. As it turned out my opposite number in London with whom I was coordinating the concert had a tragedy in the form of his partner dying unexpectedly of flu at the age of 24 and his devastation left me to sing at the concert on my own. It was terrifying. I think it was the biggest stage I had ever been on in my life. The hall was full, the balconies were full, the stage lights shone right at me, I couldn't see anyone. Just suddenly, boom, you're on. The record says:

> My own intervention went down well. I sang four songs—very poorly I thought. I was dry as bone and sober as me dad—also very nervous, but everyone thought it well. IMG paid me £9 my train fare plus £1 beer money. I met two Ruskin lads who were going back up to Oxford, they asked me to go up and sing for the general Ruskin reunion, which I did.
>
> My intervention at Ruskin went down terrific. I sang four songs, stole

one book and five bottles of pop for me bairne.

I made an overall loss on the whole transport manoeuvre and was forced to draw a subsidy from the Red Star Society, this being a folky intervention. I wrote bitterly in the log of the club:

> We are really desperately poor and I cannot work overtime as my normal five shifts down the mine smashes me to pieces—my nerve tablets help but they could not make up for an extra unnecessary minute. I will climb Everest for the revolution, but work down that filthy mind killer an hour more I cannot do.

16 December 1975. Tony McHugh writes to us on large headed paper bearing the photo inset of the St Basil's Cathedral, Moscow, and in the name of the General Secretary of the Unemployed Workers Action Committee:

> We have now written to you three times, we have also sent you a parcel of leaflets etc. for distribution outside labour exchanges. We have written 34 letters to organisations here and abroad urging them to write to you about NUL [National UnemployedLeague] but until your two phone calls we have received nothing back! We were in Yorkshire for two weeks and wrote to you before our departure to tell you our address but we heard nothing from you and we were not keen on driving to Doncaster on speck ...
> Best Wishes
> Communist Greetings
> Tony McHugh

Needless to say almost, we had received nothing, and the implication was our post was being sabotaged .

December 1975. Ewan and Peggy singing at York University. Fred and I went and they said nice things about us. Fred is studying at York and is in his element. He agrees to link up with us again.

Big Chris Green, my Ruskin marra, lands the job of Trade Unions Studies Information Unit Organiser in Newcastle, the Cockney get. I am happy for him but a bit resentful—that should have been my job. Still Chris has by this time a Ruskin Diploma and a BSc in Economics from Leeds, and I am back on the coalface.

The Founding Convention Of Nationwide Unemployed League took place in New York City on 26–27 December 1975. I stayed on organising and agitating in New York into the new year.

I was the SUI's delegate. Getting there had not been easy. First, all the arrangements were made that end, and as cheaply as could be mustered since we hadn't got a bean and the IWP paid for it all. Second, the arrangements fluctuated constantly as we came up to the deadline for flight times etc., and we did not possess a phone. The whole thing was arranged using the public phone box and reverse charge calls from Station Road, Dunscroft. At times the Americans would ring the phone box, and some kids hanging about on their bikes would answer it, and be sent down to get me, which they did. The ticketing arrangements were bizarre to say the least. I was to pick up the tickets from Brussels from a man standing under the statue at Brussels Central Station. It was some student charter flight. I set off, wary but willing, with actually very little money given what I had before me. I had borrowed money from everybody in the hope the IWP would refund it all.

On the way down to London I 'had a very good discussion with four Scottish people on the nature of the SNP and the subject of the Scottish nation. They confirmed our suspicions that although Scottish people want a free nation, they want it a socialist republic and thought this could only be achieved in conjunction with the rest of the British proletariat's struggle for socialism. Indeed the SNP being in their own words "A Scottish Tory Party" would actually obstruct the passage to a free socialist Scottish Republic by leading the Scottish working class up a blind alley.'

As I waited in the long queue for the boat train, I had my first jab of New Yorkness. A youth was beseeching everyone as to whether this was 'really' the queue for the boat train, and coming upon me asked again in a screeching New York accent 'Say, guy, is this really the queue for the boat train?' I had confirmed this while he held my shoulders with both hands and almost praying asked 'Are you sure? Are You sure?' 'Yes, yes,' I replied but it hardly calmed him. 'But you see I have to get this train to get the boat to get my plane to New York—and if I miss this train, I'll miss the boat and then I can't get to New York and I've got no money.' After he'd repeated this in various ways I confirmed that yes, I too was to catch a plane in Brussels for New York. ' And have you to meet a guy under a statue who has tickets?' 'Yes,' I confirmed. 'But there won't be a guy. Its a ripoff—I bet there isn't even a statue, or a plane for that matter.' 'There will be,' I calmed. 'I'm sure there is a statue and a plane.' 'But the guy must have $900 by now and how much does a guy get paid for standing under a statue?' he reasoned. I told him the company would have the money not the bloke. That fear having been calmed he went back to his original one: 'All these people can't get on that train!' And as the queue moved forward the crowd closed in from both sides and joined the queue. 'Madam!' he screeched, 'If you have one shred of human decency, or one ounce of feeling for the constitution of the United States, you won't go in front of me. If I don't get this plane, I'll blow up the railway and no trains will run in England—I'll sue the company—I'll sue the government.' We both got the train, and we both got seats. However, as we got off at Dover I noticed him rushing madly up and down the corridor begging 'Are you sure this is the stop, what if it isn't? What if the boat has already gone? What if the customs don't like me and I can't get on? Does it carry lifeboats? It's getting pretty windy out there.'

I was berthed onto those airline-style reclining seats in the sleeping area. Suddenly a Dutch boy in a red woolly hat appeared, leading a conga of French, English and Scandinavian young people carrying bottles of wine and beer. 'Everybody alive get up! We are off to make a party in the bar—come you [talking to me], bring that tape machine—we drink, dance, play music—everybody up!!' I joined the parade and we congaed round the boat to my Cuban tapes—round the bottom, up the middle, and onto the windy top open deck where the party began as the blackness of the night and chill of the sea closed round. We drank and danced and talked the whole passage. Everybody was talking 'Revolution, Revolution, Revolution' as I think the Beatles had said. Even a spectacularly attractive public schoolgirl, a Swiss finishing school graduate, who felt personally responsible for the whole plight of the working class, and was soon pledged to overthrowing the entire capitalist system; she would have made a spectacular Tania The Guerilla, I must admit. On the empty commuter train on the French side, she had stretched out while the seats were still empty. Her marvellous bust rose and fell, her angelic face was at peace, her endlessly long legs were draped over three seats. As it became more and more crowded and smoke-filled. I went to wake her, but the crowd of Frenchmen standing holding the straps and hanging onto the walls of the compartment would have none of it. One of them smiled at me and said something in French. I looked puzzled. 'Poetry!' he said.

I left Rome, and I landed in Brussels
With a picture of the Coliseum by my side. (Bob Dylan)

I arrived at Brussels Central three hours early, leaving the girl to continue her journey up to Switzerland I think. She had actually asked me to go with her. Eeh whey, that's what being a revolutionary means, I suppose: sacrifice. I hadn't walked far into the magnificent palatial hall when I heard a failure screech: 'You see, he isn't here, he never existed.' I dragged him off for a tea, and surprised myself by speaking Dutch and even more surprisingly being understood. A little later I lay down on the station bench, and after having been travelling now for 17 hours I was exhausted. I was soon fast asleep. I wasn't long in the deep land of nod when I was prodded awake by a fascist-uniformed, Gestapo-hatted, gun-toting Belgium cop with a club. 'Oh no not these bastards again!' I thought, remembering earlier encounters en-route to Holland in my misspent youth. There were three of them. They addressed me in Dutch, although Belgium cops are never Dutch, I have found. As I responded and handed over my passport, they changed to English. They eyed me all the time. It was only then that I saw my briefcase which was standing on top of my suitcase, prominently displaying a

Belgian Communist sticker which Comrade Tania had given me when she was over in Britain with her comrade Dani before they went off to carry on the struggle in Angola.

At last the man was there, under the statue, and he had tickets. I was pleased to get on board the jumbo with the intention of sleeping like a log, but with the damned Richard Burton film and continuous, or so it seemed, piped music and people toing and froing; it wasn't to be. Soon, too soon for sleep, we were landing.

First major problem: immigration control. I got stopped at the first obstacle, my passport and details all placed in a red envelope, and I was passed to Police Control. I sat in a waiting room full of Italians, Mexicans, blacks, all of whom were being taken away and through the glass I could see were getting serious interrogations. Then it was me. My cop was a real comedian, a caricature of the New York cop, tab in mouth, shirtsleeves, gun holster. 'You've no return ticket here, and you've no money to buy one.' Em, my friends are buying one for me at this side. 'Yeah? Why?' 'Well I'm giving a few talks, you know academic talks.' 'Says here on your Visa application a tourist visit, so why are you coming here?' 'Open the briefcase please.' In the briefcase a stack of notes for preparation of speeches on politics, unions, Ireland, the mines. He takes out a wodge of prepared notes and reads 'To the comrades,' which he pronounces comRADS, 'of radical America.' He looks at me. 'Its an academic history society by that name.' Open the suitcase. It is full of books for sale, on top *Portugal—A Blaze of Freedom*; *Karl Marx, Philosophy of Art*; *Women—Their Oppression and Their Cause*; This one catches his eye.

'You into Women's Lib?'

'Well, it's my wife's pamphlet.'

'So where's your wife?'

'She's back in Britain.'

'Shes back in Britain and you're in New York on Christmas Eve? That's the sort of women's lib I support. If my wife read stuff, she'd be over in England and I'd be stuck here,' he joked.

I had forgotten it was Xmas Eve. 'OK, guy, go with these men.' I followed them into a crowded office, where hot sweating FBI men, all in shirtsleeves, guns in holsters, steamed over desks with those powerful reading lamps that they can shine into your eyes as everyone knows. One of them strolls over to me, looks me straight in the face.

'Take off your jacket, your shoes, your socks, your tie.' He does a quick pat search (I'd just come through half a dozen metal detectors for God's sake).

'Anything up your ass?'

At this I donned my most outraged British Colonial accent: 'I beg your bloody pardon, sir?'

'OK,' he says, 'strip to your underwear, and baby this gives me no kicks, believe me!'

' I believe you, I believe you,' I said trying to relax.

He went through everything I had taken off, while his mate read through the contents of my briefcase; he sat with his feet on the desk and read through my notes on the mines. Then the real questioning started.

'OK, so these folks you're staying with. The IWP? What does IWP stand for?

'I'm not sure,' I said, 'I think its another academic foundation.' I couldn't think of anything to fit the letters.

'Ah-hah?' he says, unconvinced and chewing gum, 'I think maybe, its the International Workers Party!'

The guy gets up from my briefcase, a wadge of my notes in his hand, puts his glasses back up on his head.

'So you're coming here to shoot us all?'

'Wait a minute!' I say, trying to calm him down a bit.

'I've been a vegetarian most of my life!'

'Na, I didn't say are you coming here to eat us all, I said are you coming here to shoot us all?'

'Giv ower!' I replied.

'Giv ower?' They all laughed. 'That jive talk?'

A couple of them had my notes on Ireland, and my Troops Out membership card, and were glancing over them. Another two guys come strolling over now.

'Do you think we've got no beer in the United States?' one of them asks, carrying over my six-pack of Newcastle Broon, which I had humped all the way from Doncaster for the American comrades, who had heard so much about it.

'Not like this,' I replied. 'That's good beer?' 'This,' I said, standing as tall as I could in bare feet and underpants, 'Is the broon dog! This is journey inti space!'

'OK, just leave us the tins and get dressed.'

'Whaat?' I begin to argue, quite forgetting that I am two inches from being booted out of the country. 'Half.'

'OK, four tins and get your clothes on. What you got going here, a strip show? Come on, get dressed get going, out!'

I left them drinking Broon Ale, and toasting a Merry Xmas. I was convinced it was the Irish stuff and the New York Police connection with the 'Dear Ol' Isle', that got me in, that and the broon dog. It surely cannot have been my answers to the questions. [No doubt for the local – outlawed – Stalinists it confirmed their deepest suspicions about Trotskyism.]

Although as I walked through the big plate-glass doors of the airport and out into the wild blue yonder of New York I thought there'd be the rattle of Tommy guns and I would be assassinated, in fact I was in. Me, pitman revolutionary communist, was standing in America, and what's more less intimidated, less threatened, less ill treated than I had been by British cops when I tried to get into Ulster. Actually my interrogation had had nothing whatever to do with me being a red or the bag full of thunderous words; it was because there were strict anti-vagrancy laws in America, and I had no return ticket, and not enough money to buy one. I also didn't actually have a guarantor who would buy me one and vouch for me.

Once in, my first task was the mastery of the New York pay telephone, which cost me lots of dimes and bad temper, but I got through at last to the IWP. It was Christmas Eve but they expected me Boxing Day for some reason, so I was lucky.

They dispatched an estate car and classical Bolshevik women to pick me up and we roared off, into the Christmas decorations of New York and big brash America.

INTERNATIONAL WORKERS PARTY

The IWP HQ was something I wasn't expecting. A huge seventh-story floor, a ballroom of a central meeting hall, with a wall-to-wall map of the world as a background. Around the others, banners and slogans from earlier campaigns, including the ones on Portugal. The doors were made of steel with great iron bars and bolts. The rest of the floor contained nine rooms other than the ballroom and the toilets. These housed Administration, Publicity, Banner Making, Switchboard, Library/Research/Record Office. I had now been up for 36 hours and no sleep and told all the comrades I had to crash. They told me a big Xmas Eve party was planned for all the conference delegates. Well I wasn't that tired, I told myself. The party was a great folky evening of the kind we would have back in Britain, lots of comrades there, from the left and progressive movement, lots of songs lots of friendship. My first impressions of the IWP comrades were that I loved their fraternity and their singing. I met Fred Newman, the leader and chief theorist of the party. Something of an American version of Posadas, although perhaps not quite as high a deity. My first sentence to him as we extended hands to each other was 'You wrote the article in *Critical Practice*, I think number 2, volume 1, but I didn't understand a word of it.' 'OK,' I qualified, 'that's a slight exaggeration, but I have read jargon from Marx to Posadas and that's a fine school, my hobby is the Dutch language, but without exaggeration, I could not understand a sentence.' There was a brief silence fell on the crowd, then a multitude of IWP members leapt in ... and agreed with me! They, it seems, locked in to King's-New-Suit-of-Clothes mode, had never dared to say so, but here, this coal miner, a British prole, said so, now they too could say so. I found that I was the crack in a number of such dams during my stay. I gathered Fred held quite a sway over this team. Although everyone wanted to talk intensely to me, and I was invited to sing, and even dance, my brain was closing down; I could hardly think. I left the party with Julie, Joel's companion, and walked what I always had been told were fatal streets, on the way back to Joel and Julie's flat. They lived on Lower East Side, in fact the only whites on the block. Good God, this was street of slums, worse than any I had seen in Glasgow, Manchester or Edinburgh, although inside there was no water streaming down the walls or mushrooms growing on the stairs. This whole part of the city was something like Old Havana, crumbling and old and neglected, but whereas the Cubans had made a conscious choice to spend what they had on the forgotten countryside this was New York and the richest country in the world. This was a mainly Puerto Rican area, and most of the walls were scrawled with gang symbols and slogans I didn't understand. Korea was a favourite; Kung Fu reflected the American working class's obsession with violence of all sorts. I seen lots of people with tough-looking dogs on spiky chains—Dobermans, Alsatians and pit bulls. The walls advertised Kung Fu, Karate, Tai-Kwan Do, Aikido, Savat and Kendo, schools, fights, gear. Joel survived here, not so much because he was a communist—your average American had not the vaguest idea of what a communist was—but probably because he was eccentric. He never wore a coat, or a jacket, even in the dead of winter with the winds howling through the streets or the hail and snow bouncing off the sidewalks. He would stand in his short-sleeved shirt shivering at the roadside, or walking with his head down, his hair and beard a mass of snow, like an Everest climber. His theory was the more clothes you wore the less heat your own body supplied. So as his bones and teeth chattered and shook from violent non-stop shivers, he reasoned this was his internal body system stoking up the heat. The trouble with his theory was that he was always ravenous; this boiler of his needed filling the whole time and with the amount of money he expended on food, to say nothing of time spent consuming it, he could have bought a large greatcoat.

Also, as mentioned earlier, he was a well-known character, known everywhere as 'Poster Man'. Joel specialised in giant wall posters, elaborating the conspiracy theory (and often conspiracy fact) of the moment, for example:

REAL JFK ASSASSINS IDENTIFIED AS FBI KILLERS !!

Or (later):

JOHN   LENNON's   MURDER   WAS   A   POLITICAL ASSASSINATION!

On the murder of Kennedy, he talked of the 'Slow US Coup d'Etat', and identified the real killers:

'Sturgis under arrest is photographed with muddy boot, indicating that of the arrested 'tramps' Sturgis was most likely the one who fired from the 'grassy knoll'. Sturgis was trained as an expert, experienced and trusted marksman.

The folks on the block, even the cops, read the posters and reasoned that Poster Man often came closer to the likely truth than the kept house media of the American state.

Waking in the wee spare bedroom of Joel and Julie's flat I am first of all aware of the crumbling whitewashed walls, with the lumps out of it, and plaster swelling with damp, the cracked and sagging ceiling. At first, before me eyes focus, I think I am looking at a rather odd, rusty-brown oval pattern all over the walls and ceiling. Then as my eyes clear from their tiredness I realise with horror that the oval brown pattern is an army of cockroaches, just sitting, just twitching, right over the bed, right next to me on the wall. Second thing I become aware of is Joel, groaning in pain, and in mortal anguish. 'Oh God,' he moans, 'Oh no, dear God!' Forgetting the cockroaches I leap from the bed as I think he is being attacked. All sorts of visions of armed vigilantes, the KKK, the American Nazis rush through me heed. Out on the landing, I find Joel in combat with three huge black and bulging bin liners. 'What the fuck's up?' I demand, peering round for the assailants. 'The laundry, Julie leaves me the laundry to take to the laundry shop—fucking heavy man, fucking heavy and ornery.'

The next evening neither Joel nor Julie stay there. I am alone. I decide to sleep in their bed in the hope that the bastard cockroaches haven't invaded that room quite as badly as the spare room. I am awoken by a violent banging on the door.

Joel has the doors protected with iron bars and metal levers and crossbars and a grid. Bang-bang-bang and a muffled shouting from outside the door. I peer through the security spyhole, believing again this is an attack. I see a man in a gasmask with goggles and a rubber diver's suit and a flamethrower. He is shouting from inside the mask 'Extermination!!! Extermination!!' Women and children are being escorted down the stairs, talking loudly in Spanish and complaining as they are ushered from the upstairs flats and past the door. I can't quite grasp this, but grasp clear enough that this man is not in the mood to argue, and I don't fancy being zapped by an animated dalek with a flamethrower. At last I unlock, unbolt, and unpull the door, and he barges past me, shouting "Exterminator!!!" His mate, without the goggles and mask but still in the rubber suit, gets me forcibly by the arm and starts to drag me downstairs, while I get caught up with some big Puerto Rican women with their children. The exterminator enters Joel's apartment and I hear a high-powered flush noise. I hunch my shoulders, hands held up, in a 'What the f—?' gesture. A woman replies in Spanish, 'El exterminador, por cucaracha, cucaracha!' She makes the hand sign of a beetle crawling, but I already knew that word from Cuba. They were the exterminators from the City Hall, come to do battle with the brown creeping oval plagues of my life. 'Viva!' I shouted and everyone laughed.

The exterminator gaans in, sprays everywhere with a thick unbreathable, cloud of poison. As he backs out, like a soldier on a Belfast street, his mate whangs closed the door and seals it with tape and hangs a notice, in Spanish. It shows a dead beetle upside down with its legs in the air, and a dead person also upside down with their legs and arms in the air. The door has a big red X across it, and a sign says 'Prohibida la Entrada'. I get the message. We all go outside into the sun. The men play chess and draughts, the kids play hopscotch and clapping games and the women all stand talking animatedly to each other, laughing and clapping in delight at some piece of news or story. I get the impression the day the exterminator comes is a like a little holiday; it is a communal day, and everyone grumbles that it has knackered their busy schedules, but they soon get into the enforced idleness, and starts to relax. It's like a rag-up at the pit, a bit of light relief.

I had spent the preceding weeks and months reading the founding documents and theoretical works of Fred Newman and the IWP. They had broken from the National Caucus of Labour Committees (NCLC), they being the founding members of the IWP. This group had formed and run what they called 'a revolutionary health service collective' called 'Centre For Change' for six years. The group's theoretical underpinnings were weird, and I knew weird. They were heavily infused with physchoanalytical theories as had been the NCLC, coupled with a Jesuitical analysis which concluded that pure capitalism as such was being eclipsed, especially in the USA and fascism was being developed. Deeper still was the struggle for a real understanding of the real essence of class struggle and class-consciousness.

The practical look of this understanding is the mistaken notion that the modus operandi of working class organisation is to raise the workers awareness of his or her class interests. This is accomplished by laying out programs which are in the class interest of the proletarian class. In fact class interest as defined under the framework of capitalistic cognition is nothing more than the aggregate of the self-interests of the members of the class. As such Olson's theorem holds, from which it follows that organising a worker around class interests is doomed to failure. For, in capitalist fact, it is in his or her self-interest to not act in this class interest thus defined because both self-interest and therefore his class interest are socially determined by the capitalist mode of production.

The point holds true for parochialist forms of programmatic organizing as well as classwide forms of programmatic organizing. For it is no more in the self-interest of the worker to act in accordance with the group interest of a smaller group than it is in his interest to act in accordance with the interests of the class as a whole. Class interested organizing will simply reproduce capitalism. Olson is right. But Marx was righter! Unfortunately, Olson's theorem has application precisely because Marx has been so systematically misunderstood by both bourgeois thinkers and so called Marxist working class organizers.

As Marxists we must organise around historical reality only! Programmatic organizing which reinforces the conception of self-interested man, simply reproduces capitalism. As a plan for changing historical reality, program has its place within working class organising. As a technique for revealing interests to the working class it is counter-revolutionary. It is well to remember Marx's correction to Citizen Weston's banality which argued against supporting workers struggles for wage increases by mistakenly claiming that wage increases would simply produce cost increases which would nullify wage increases. Yet we must also remember that the same document 'Wages, Price and Profit' concludes by saying:

'At the same time and quite apart from the general servitude in the wages system, the working class ought not to exaggerate to themselves the ultimate working of these everyday struggles. They ought not to forget that they are fighting with effects, but not with the causes of those effects: that they are retarding the downward movement, but not changing its direction: that they are applying palliatives, not curing the malady. They ought, therefore, not to be exclusively absorbed in these unavoidable guerrilla fights incessantly springing up from the never-ceasing encroachments of capital or changes of the market. They ought to understand that, with all the miseries it imposes upon them, the present system simultaneously engenders the material conditions and the social forms necessary for an economic reconstruction of society. Instead of the conservative motto: "A fair day's wages for a fair day's work!" They ought to inscribe on their banner the revolutionary watchword: "Abolition of the wages system!"' (Fred Newman, *A Manifesto On Method.* International Workers' Party. New York 1974)

The next day, it being Christmas, we registered for the conference and met the United Front Committee, later to become the Presiding Committee. I phoned round all my contacts and comrades. Joel K was allegedly en route to Britain and we had passed mid-flight. Peter Anton was home, however, and he was delighted to know I was there. We arranged to meet that day.

He turned out to be not at all the erratic and hysterical wild man I had imagined from his literary polemic, but was in person a calm, quietly spoken, round-faced, combat-jacketed, short-haired, American leftist of long experience. Back at his house, I was greeted by his warm and welcoming companion, herself the leader of the Puerto Rican Socialist Party. Their children were the height of normalness too. Jose presented me with one of his favourite trucks 'for Emma', which actually her daughter now plays with. The food at Peter's house was a revelation. I amused Maureen trying to describe the sour black grapes, which turned out to be olives, which I had never seen before ner mind tried to eat. Also the corn. Peter re-established contact recently and still speaks of their family bemusement with my reaction to corn, which I had only seen on cartoons of Woody Woodpecker. I amused kids and parents alike, because I didn't know how you ate it. I ended up much like the crows in the cartoon, with it locked between me paws and chewing it down the side, a sort of sweet potato taste. I managed half a one, though New Yorkers will eat several of these at a sitting. 'Cookies', pretzels and a variety of other strange foodstuffs left me rather like an alien on a strange planet. Of course this was years ago and Britain is far more cosmopolitan as well as having had the middle class promote its own eating options through general society so these things will not be as strange to working-class tables as they were at this time.

Perhaps the most prestigious meeting for me was with the Puerto Rican Socialist Party. Through Peter we had our pamphlet on Puerto Rico among our own literature and high on our agenda. Previously I had been taken on a tour of their massive building; the PSP is a mass party of tens of thousands of Puerto Ricans. On the island itself they were the second biggest political party at this time. It was thought they could maybe become a catalyst for the whole North American revolution itself. The left in America's position toward Puerto Rico is rather like that of the British left toward the Irish struggle and for that reason the PSP was very suspicious of them, or else considered them irrelevant. To actually gain a meeting with their leadership, a member of their Political Commission, was quiet an honour

One of the highlights of this tour and one of my personal ambitions was to preach revolution on the streets of New York. On 27 December we held a rally in Times Square. We had a wagon rigged up as a platform with banks of speakers on it. I was due to speak on the situation in Britain. I had intended to give it some clog, and make a hellfire speech. I was given the mic, and the stage. Cars wound down their windows, joggers stopped to listen, the crowd looked on in interest. I was about five minutes into my speech, when the freezing cold air totally dried out my windpipe. There was no moisture in my throat, my mouth moved, I couldn't swallow, and couldn't speak one word more. Damn. I hadn't counted on the ice-cold New York winter being the only obstruction to my speech.

Ner mind—later I fulfilled the ambition as on another day we set up the lorry on Fifth Avenue beneath the Empire State building. This time the populace would get the full blast. The comrades had made me a banner as a backdrop 'Down With Wilson's Tory Policies—No Return To The Thirties—Full Productive Employment At Union Wages—British Section United Front Committee, Nationwide Unemployed League. That evening 'Keynote Speeches' seen me included at the major evening rally and dinner, and this time they got both barrels. I spoke for nearly an hour to rapt attention. Someone told me later they were as much spellbound by my accent as the content; it was like being at a Dickensian street rally, he told me. Which I supposed was at least out of the ordinary. After the speech the floor was thrown open to the mass crowd for questions and points, a voice rings out in pure Geordie: 'Why Ah knaa wor Davie, but whe's all them buggers wi'im?' It creased me up, I couldn't believe it. This was New York. I should explain to non-Geordies, that there is a longstanding joke, and song, about the exploits of a man called Geordie Broon. In the spirit of the legend, 'wherever yee gaan, ya boond ti find a Geordie', Geordie travels the world, always at once known to Geordies he meets everywhere he gaans. Finally he ends up at the Vatican as a guest of the pope and comes out with the pontiff on the balcony before the mass crowd. A voice shouts: "Whey Ah knaa wor Geordie, but whey's that bugger win him?' The voice in the crowd knew that I would know, and we both knew another Geordie was at large in New York. Whey, dodging most of the crowd after the rally, and still trying to be polite, I peered into the crowd this way and that looking for me marra. At length, a red-faced, blue-eyed, short, blond-haired bloke stood in front of is. I knew at once, we embraced. 'But what? How?' 'Na, Ah'm not telling yee, till ya gaanin' and he whisked me off to a bar. Outside the convention a group of girls, were selling *The Spark*, an 'independent' revolutionary paper. That is, not the organ of any particular party or organisation. 'Why aren't you in the convention?' 'Well,' they explained 'the workers haven't called for such a body yet, when they do we will join.' I suggested that maybe sometimes you had to offer leadership, and if all we did was to follow after whatever the workers were already doing, what was the point of having a separate existence? Besides which, 'Which workers?' I assured them that I was a worker, and there were many more inside from across American industry. 'Yes, but we aren't a vanguardist organisation ...' she began. 'Anyway,' I butted in, now keen to gaan to the bar and find out whe this was I had met, 'I've only got francs.' 'Oh, you're French,' the girl said excitedly, and I looked at her incredulously. 'He's a bliddy Geordie,' my new friend said, 'here's 15 cents,' and took the paper. Then we found the bar and two high stools, and between supping beer we talked the hind legs off. He had been sent a copy of Pit Talk In Co. Durham, he seen that me, the author was speaking down town, so turned out to see me and hev some crack. He resisted all efforts to explain what he was doing here, or what he did. Later, as his taxi, honked outside for him, he slid from the seat, thrust his hand forward, and said 'Reet a'hm gaan.' As he got near the door he said 'I work for the NYPD!' 'Yee twat!' I shouted. 'Ah'm a librarian, man,' he added. 'Me lass lives here, it's a job, and a bliddy gud 'un. It's what Ah dey man an Ah wadn't Ah kna'd yee was here if a hadn't been.' He waved and dived laughing into the taxi. I sat smiling. A librarian. Well, its no se bad, and he'd paid for all the drink.

I should explain that contrary to me description earlier of 'girls' this is regarded as an insult on the American left, as I found to my great discomfiture at the convention, as I rose to support 'the girl over there'. I was told this betrayed a belief that females are small childlike and immature. I pointed out in my defence that mature working class-men call each other 'youth' or 'son' and referred to themselves as 'the lads' or 'the boys', depending which part of Britain you came from. This confirmed their psychoanalysis, demonstrating 'the infantile illusion in everlasting childhood which the British working class had never come to terms with'. Mind, they didn't call the chairwomen a chairperson, which the British left did, always posing me then with the dilemma of whether to refer to 'the chair' as 'it' rather than 'he' or 'she'. This trend was to reach the level of absurdity by the time I came to write this book. Housewives must now be called 'consumers'! Blackboards, chalkboards, anything with 'men' in should be neutralised, I don't know what name was devised for 'manhole cover', only that it's now tantamount to swearing and finally a maternity clinic would ban folk from looking through the windows at new-born babies because 'it infringed their human rights'. All that was to come.

Every day New York City Unemployed Council members board the city's massive subway system armed with bundles of their paper, *Build The Nationwide Unemployed League*, and considerable personal courage and political enthusiasm, given how vexatious that system is in the morning rush hour. In pairs they move systematically from car to car, politely distributing announcements from the convention, then asking the carriage's permission to make announcements about what they are doing and the work of the Unemployed League. Over the loud din of the rumbling metal snake speeding through the black intestines beneath the streets of Manhattan, Brooklyn and Queens, despite the jolts and the swerves, these comrades, straining their voices, talk calmly about the need to organise and the crisis of capitalism. The speakers talk about the campaigns, the limitations and the virtual abandonment by the city employees' unions of any attempt to defend or improve the wages and conditions of their members, who had then left the unions in droves. They address the welfare recipients denied their rights, and urge them to come along to the advice sessions and their front store offices on the Upper West Side of Manhattan and in the neighbourhood of Jamaica in the borough of Queens, across the East River. I had felt a bit guilty at first at an organisation of the unemployed paying my air fare, but then I heard the accounts and seen they were raising half a million dollars a week from the subway collection alone! Their HQ cost a million a year in rent, and they paid organisers and rented two downtown offices and advice centres—'storefronts' they called them.

I have been shocked, shocked to see old folks rooting through the abandoned boxes of old vegetables in Chinatown. As the snowflakes flurry an old lady, surrounded by a woollen black shawl, curls up on a park bench. Her electricity has been cut off and she can't pay the bill; the bailiffs wait for her to return and she has to avoid them. A man with a leg in plaster is laying out in the snow on a park bench. He is homeless and fell and broke his leg. There is no health service, a private ambulance will attend, when all the paying customers are served, he will be brought to whichever hospital isn't seeing someone, and lie with his broken leg, until the paying customers are all seen, then he will be seen to, and returned to the street with his leg in plaster.

The city's giant subway itself is falling apart. Workers and their families burn to death in their homes because the fire service has been slashed to the bone and they have to travel further and further to reach the blaze.

Newman was the visionary of the IWP, its guru. I was urged to actually go his lectures and listen at the workshops to their angle of things. I confessed that after having made a study of their political jurisprudence, I was cautious. Marcus had originated 'Operation MOP UP' and set his NCLC to systematically attack and drive off the streets and out of town the US Communist Party. But more freaky than that, he had come up with a training programme for his members which he openly called 'psychological terror' to steel the membership against anything the state might be able to do to them. After testing out the formulae on European members he returned to the States 'to put leading US members though in-depth psychological sessions, supposedly purging them of all their infantile wishes and hang-ups. The 'psychological terror' process quickly became generalised throughout the organisation, and with devastating effect; any member raising the slightest objection or doubt about official policy was lustily pounced on for his or her 'mother's fears', ' fears of the real world' etc.—with the 'real world' being identified with NCLC's 'real' prospects of winning the New York mayoral election. (Dan Jacobs) This 'mothers fears' feature of the whole psychoanalytic trip took the group down some very dark corridors. This was the supposed fear of the outside world which every mother imparts to her children—as against that of the potent, man-of-the-world father who is the only firm rock and salvation against the suffocation of the mother's coddling. 'Womanhood and witches', 'bitches and female domination' became pathetic crutches of those afraid to meet the challenge.

Marcus located the origin of psychological terror, as the eighth-century church had done, in the image of the witch mother who prevented the individual from acting on the basis of self consciousness by reducing him to an impotent and banalized ego-state. And to this bestialized image of the ego Marcus counterposed himself: for it was never disputed during the course of the session that all true self-consciousness emanated from his own person.

But the image of the witch-mother as a locus for psychological terror was simply a cover. In actuality the terror which the leaders experienced during the session ... was a terror of a depersonalisation imposed upon them by Marcus himself; a depersonalisation, moreover, which was identified by him as true self consciousness; e.g. the phrase 'Step outside of yourself' was used recurringly ... and this phrase epitomizes the extreme form of alienation to which the participants were subjected...

The obsession with shit, and the endless stream of scatalogical and sadistic humour issuing from Marcus around this obsession, successfully and repeatedly reduced all the individuals in the session to the level of animals.

They were forced to concede that a large part of their thinking could be reduced to a preoccupation with shit, and especially to the fear of this preoccupation. Women were hit particularly viciously with this form of reductionism, even to the point of tracing their sexuality to the proximity of the anus and the vagina with only a thin strip the perineum distinguishing between the two. Marcus claimed that this anatomical peculiarity was the origin of women's feelings of degradation, since it gave rise to their confusion of the sexual act with the act of excretion. This was a radical departure from classical Marxism since it located identity not within the matrix of socio-reproductive relations, but in bestialized anatomical reductionism. The degradation of women was further predetermined by the infantile relation a women had to her mother where the first sexual encounter was imprinted on her memory as 'the mother cleaning shit out of her little vagina'. This confusion of sexuality with shit led both men and women to cover up odors associated with love making; according to Marcus this was the reason that women wore perfume and men smoked after making love...[68]

As if not sufficiently off course to begin with, the NCLC crashes to the right, forms tactical alliances with screaming fascists like Barry Goldwater and the KKK, while accusing the entire left of being controlled by the CIA. No strikes could be won under this world climate of recession so the mass strikes of British and US miners taking place at the time were CIA provocations, union leaders and most unions themselves CIA provocations and misleadership. The group next moved on to form the United States Labor Party and run Marcus for US president.

This had been the tradition from which the IWP had escaped. Its current guru was Fred Newman, a psychoanalyst and political theorist. I had been told his core membership was composed of his patients, and he was said to operate a Mormon-style multi-marriage with three or four 'wives', although frankly people's marital arrangements didn't really surprise or bother me; the trouble was rather that there was much of the sect about the whole tradition. The lecture on 'methodology' brought up the question of 'sectarianism', which one of the Newman supporters explained: 'an individual interaction of conflicting psychologies, largely to do with people's pathological fear of each other and "organizations" that sectarian attitudes were struck long before political ideas were expounded to provide "an excuse" for disagreement.' I tried to suggest that this perhaps wasn't the case in Britain, that despite serious and often bitter disagreements, we all went to parties together, drank with them, sang with them, slept with them, lived with them, and actually went out of our way to be near them, whoever they were. They assumed that I must be mistaken. I thought if we had a pathological fear it was of the non-political, uninitiated working class in general. The politicos tended to cling together for company and warmth in an alien environment of people who weren't actually really like them. I was more than a little disturbed by the psychoanalytical sessions. At these, comrades' fears or disagreements or doubts were reduced to a kind of group search through the person's personality, background and subconscious for blocks and obstacles to a clear class and political perception. Eerie.

During the convention I got to meet our close comrades, the Revolutionary Communist League (Internationalist), 'Rickly' for short. We met in Clancy's Bar, over those huge pitchers of beer and minute little beer glasses which you have to aim the beer at from a great height. Larry Lockwood, the group's main theorist, is a hearty lover of the barley, six foot tall plus, with an extraordinary laugh. We debated and discussed till the wee hours of morning, and made outline plans for them to come to Britain and me at some future date to visit them.

Thanks to the Antons, and my credentials as a revolutionary who had worked in Cuba and spoke around Britain and within the unions on the subject, a visit to the home of the chairman of the North American section of the PSP had been arranged. Dixie Bayo was much respected in the Puerto Rican community; usually she was accompanied by armed guards; the PSP is an armed party. Leaders of the independence movement and the socialist movement frequently got assassinated and shot at, Santiago Mari Pesquera, son of the general secretary, being the most recent.

I guessed at 6 p.m. in the evening I was not going to get out of the house for a drink, before it was too late to go anywhere. I supposed I had to admit to myself if no one else that I was a compulsive drinker. I had to have a drink every night. It was something like a daily version of the New Year syndrome.[69] If a day went by and you hadn't been out and got blasted, you had failed somehow. It is an obsession which has blighted my life and made me fidget in whatever otherwise glorious, intellectual, beautiful, religious or sexual experience I was otherwise enjoying; I needed to get out for a drink as well. So that being the case I had bought a six-pack, and with it in one of those marvellous tall brown paper bags they gave you in New York I set off for Dixie's house. Well as I said, in this city you walked directly from A to B, or you didn't always walk far. In this case this was the heart of the Lower East Side. I passed a gang of eight or so Puerto Rican youths standing on the street corner, and walked straight by them, purposefully. Then I realised these numbers were not going the right sequence, so I walked back and passed them again. This time they looked. A little further down the block, I thought, shit, that was the right way and walked towards them again. This time they started crossing the road, in that aimless, slow, arm-hanging, head-flopping way. 'Say, we don't know if you're going to mug us or we're going to mug you,' the big guy says. 'Aye alreet,' Ah says 'Ah'm trying to find the right street.' 'Aye alreet,' they repeat. 'Are you some kind of a Scotsman?' 'Aye, near enough, we're the ones with the brains.' 'OK, dude with the brains, we'll just take the bag and you can carry on looking for your street.' 'Na, I need the bag.' 'Need the bag? Are you crazy we can kill you and take the bag.' 'Well you'd better want it as much as

I do, coz I'm keepin the bag,' I said, with more bravado than sense. 'Where you going anyway in this neighbourhood, this ain't no white man neighbourhood.' So I told them who I was visiting. 'No you ain't,' they challenged. 'No white dude visits that compañera.' I was walking all the while and nearing the house now. 'Aye she does, she's seein' me anyway,' and I started up the stairs to the house while they stood in a clump at the gate watching. I realised afterwards, how stupid I had been not to show them the inside of the bag, it could have been a bomb, or a gun, and this was the leader of a revolutionary working-class party I was trying to get access too. They could have been her guards I was messing with and not just a bunch of street kids. I rang the doorbell and nothing happened. They started to whisper and move around like they were loosening up, then at last she came to the door. First thing she says 'What you got in the bag?' 'Well, I brought some beer.' 'Beer? I got a fridge full of beer for you, English beer too, d'you think we don't have beer?' I walked down the steps and gave the bag to the lads at the gate. 'Its just beer?' they said, mystified. 'You'd die for a bag of beer?' Well, not now anyway.

The meeting was relaxed and detailed. She wanted to know everything about the war in Ireland. About the Provos, about the Officials, about the role of the British Army and the tactics of spies and informers, the response of the community. She gave me a potted history of the Puerto Rican struggle and the long and bloody history of division within the movement and the racism and indifference they had encountered by organised labour in North America. The parallels were very clear. Except their socialism was far more advanced. In the early hours I left the house. At the bottom of steps sat the gang. 'Nuw what?' I said. 'We're your escort. We intend that if you're going to get wasted it don't happen on our turf,' which was reassuring, till they dropped me in Little Italy. I later learned the Mafia doesn't allow street crime so it was probably the safest stretch of NY.

Whilst in New York I visited the crumbling offices of the War Resisters' International. Something of a historic and moving re-encounter for me. It was one of the most impressive organisations of my early conversion to political struggle. The broken rifle badge symbol was in Maureen's coat for much of her early life before being won to armed struggle notions, but she kept it, and now wears it again. In these offices I spoke with David McReynolds, a leader of the American Socialist Party, which is in stamp and history something like the British ILP, and a pacifist-socialist organisation from way back. We had been very impressed by an article he wrote, and I had been instructed to track him down. These offices, were also the home of the anarchists, and the progressive artists, together with the biggest population of cockroaches I had ever seen in my life. They dropped, dived, ran and climbed everywhere. Over glasses of beer and trodden roaches Dave and I discussed 'the peace movement' and I raised with him this whole notion of a nationwide unemployed league. I managed to convince him that the Socialist Party ought to be part of it.

This was also my first encounter with the Spartacist League. They had been a breakaway from the American Socialist Workers Party; originally state cap, they had found their way back to rigid and iron view of the role of the workers' states. They had the stamp of the SLL about them. They had refused to take part in the convention as an affiliate, to work for it or join it, but nonetheless turned up all the time and yelled criticisms throughout the proceedings. They demanded the right to speak on the platform. They mounted unofficial bookstalls and circularised leaflets urging everyone to leave. In frequent discussions I had with them I could see very little room for solidarity or flexibility here.

I was lucky to survive those mean streets, as on a number of occasions I went wondering off down districts and areas no white man treads in. The same black Yellow Cab driver rescued me three times. 'You crazy English guy!' he bellowed. 'You ain't supposed to be down here, they'll just think you're a white guy, yo crazy man!' I sussed out that 'white' had little to do with your actual colour; it was just a characteristic of the force which had given them so much welly over the years. Not being a white American meant I wasn't 'white', least not what they meant by that. I wasn't part of the 'being' they were resentful of and wanted to hit back at. I heard a sympathy expressed by black street kids for Irish folk too, in particular that 'The Irish were the first slaves in the country, man.' I had thought they were speaking figuratively, but they weren't; they knew more about my history than I did. Irish families had been shipped to America literally as slaves, bought and sold.

Joel X Washington was the NUL convenor. He ran the office and advice centre down in Harlem, a big, aggressive, fast-spoken, jive-talking, street-fighting black man. He invited me down to talk at the office, in the big back room. This office, this shop front, was a popular centre for black city youth, and older city workers. This was no white man's talking shop—that they had further up town—this was a Do Something Or Keep Your Mouth Shut advice centre.

Peter was a little apprehensive as he drove me through the streets of Harlem. Peter was white, and clearly Anglo-Saxon and fairly straight-looking. So was his car; although it would take too long to identify the races of cars, they exist apparently. Not content with that, I did the most stupid thing conceivable. I left my tape recorder on the back seat of the car, and draped my coat over it. I only forgot the sign saying 'Come And Steal Me.' Me and Peter were the only white men in the room. I took the stage at the invitation of Comrade X, who had flyposted and stuck up 'bills' as they call them all over the district. I gave them a fairly punchy account of life and labour and work and poverty in Britain, the fight of the unions and the kids on the streets and the war in Ireland and what's really going on, imperialism, the struggle for justice. Ended on a big note. Then sat down, to silence. No clap, no stamping, no cheers, and then worse, no debate. 'Dat's fine Brother Douglass, thanks, you can get going now,' Joel announced and stood up and shook hands and gripped me by the arm. At the same time, a couple of others in the audience leaned over and did the movement, thump and hand twist thing they all do;, one or two others nodded. Then we left. 'Well, that went down like a lead zeppelin,' I said to Peter. 'You're crazy,' he answered. 'You walked out of there on two feet. The fact that you were allowed to walk in there at all, and then speak is enough, walking back out again, intact and alive is real cool, Dave.' he added that I was probably the first white man to speak up at Harlem since the riots.

I suppose it reminded me of the comedian at Westoe Miners' Club at Sooth Shields. Nobody clapped when he finished his routine. He complained to the club secretary as he was being paid: 'Nobody clapped.'

'Yee want clapping and paying?' the secretary replied. 'Neybody claps us when we come oot the pit, lad! Clappin is it?'

Then the clivorness wore off in an instant. Peter's car had the front window smashed completely in, me tape recorder gone off the back seat. This was winter, Xmas, the snow was seething through the city and we had no windscreen. How stupid can you get? The bloody tape recorder was knackered, some old thing I used to rehearse me speeches on, and tape speakers; it was worth nowt, it had caused a front window a hundred times the price to be smashed in. It would have been better to leave the thing on the back seat and the door open. We drove through the city, like two First World War biplane pilots, bundled up with scarves, freezing to death and the snow filling the car up as we drove.

Some controversy arises during the conference when the NUL is called upon to support the People's Party standing in forthcoming elections and endorsing Dr Spock, the child expert, in running for president. Certainly the lessons of unity have to be learned in the States. The left in America is almost exclusively introverted and rarely looks at what's happening outside. For this reason the ordinary member of the American working class has rarely if ever had contact with them and when he does he doesn't know what the hell they are talking about, because by and large they are talking at him, not to him. The Revolutionary Socialist League (a sort of IS grouping) is not amused:

> The IWP is proposing that the NUL implement the seemingly correct call of the official programme for a workers party by supporting Dr Spock's People's Party ... they prefer to have the NUL become the left cover for one of the most pathetic political groupings ever vomited forth from the petty bourgeoisie.

When another delegate came forward to denounce Spock as a 'well-heeled petty-bourgeois politician' Spock corrected them saying he was a 'a thoroughly bourgeois politician'. Then I was asked from the floor what my opinion was, and declared that if it came to a choice of Spocks I preferred the one on Star Trek with the big ears.

Although I think the convention went on to endorse his candidacy, I don't recall that he was elected president, so the RCL need not have worried, although that was never the point; these fine matters of dispute are not about what is practical, but knowing how many angels can stand on the head of a needle.

Irvine Hall, from the Labor Party League, took the opposite track. Irv was clear in his vision that we had to unite all progressive forces and the left into the outline of a Labor Party. He spoke in a Mid-West accent, the kind I had only heard at the pictures, and I think most New Yorkers had too. He wore cowboy boots, and at times one of those Roy Rogers shirts. He was deeply persuasive and talked of 'the good Doctor here' and 'How maybe my kids are little healthier today thanks to his efforts.' The Labor Party League had been a break from the Healyite

'International Committee of the Fourth International', though you would never think so from their demeanour. Most of the group's members were from Southern California, but a number of these had moved to New York to give their work a greater focus on national events. I liked them from word go, I liked the way they talked, and what they said, and I guess the girls reminded me a little of those on Dukes of Hazard, in both dress and speech, which was interesting. They were certainly more proletarian in composition than most delegates I had met. When I went out socially it was with them.

> The New Year's Eve Celebration of Solidarity
> With Suni Paz, Rev. Kirkpatrick
> Film showing – *Lucia*
> Band – Soul Sounds of Abantanna.
> Dancing. Food. Drinks
> Proceeds United Farm Workers Union
> Union Theological Seminary 120th and Broadway (Claremont St Ent)

At the New Year party I was happy to hear Irv getting a Peruvian girl up to dance and say 'You're one hell of a fine looking woman.' It was refreshing; I couldn't imagine most of the left here or in Britain thinking you could still say things as genuine, honest and 'ordinary' as that. On the downside the organisation had a dread of violence, a hatred of it—mass, revolutionary or individual. They were convinced you could smash the state and start the road to socialism without violence. They also had a touching belief in the progressive role the middle class could play in the forthcoming revolution, a little overstated. I stayed with the LPL for New Year. They all got dressed up and ready for the party just as we would have done in the SUI or the YS. I had my eye on one of the young comrades from the League. She was shy, and had that American high-schoolness and a Californian twang. She was fresh-faced, lively, full of energy and white of course. I say that in mock self-rebuke because my taste in girls was fairly predictable. It had scarcely changed since I was 16 and I suppose I found the kinds of girls I would have encountered then attractive now. We didn't know any black girls; I'd scarce ever seen one and I never talked to one until I went to Ruskin, and then only in passing. Somehow they didn't spark any plugs in the sexual engine, and some of the black women in LPL had said something similar about white men—all the turn-ons they found were on and in and of black men. That didn't seem so odd.[70]

We ended up at a big left/progressive/union, dinner the proceeds of which were going to the farm workers' union and its campaign to recruit the mass migratory workers and fight for basic pay and humane working conditions. Most were Mexican migrants, many were illegal, all were oppressed. That night was a magic one. Somehow I just felt the world was so small and the working class just the same everywhere, really; this social, this crack, this endeavour could have been in Britain or Europe or anywhere else. 'Everybody taking about the revolution, revolution, revolution.' After the striking of twelve and the Auld Lang Syne, and the Hokey Kokey, and I think the Madison, least ways that's what I was dancing and before I got too legless and incapable, with the nuzzled warmth of a slender embrace, and feeling the thin outline of her hot little body, listening to that accent. She shyly agreed we should shoot off back to the flat before everyone descended upon us. We whistled through the New Year New York night, the radio playing, on the back seat, her shy little face laughing now and again. I'm one lucky son of a bastard I thought. Mind, it didn't turn out the way I thought—we snogged and got hot, but the clothes weren't coming off. Finally she leaned up and then stood up, and turned round. I was still merry and happy but I suppose had taken for granted a score was the traditional way to usher in the new year.

'I'm not ready for this,' she said, looking right into my eyes.

I was confused.

'Its not you, you're kinda great,' she said.

Still puzzled.

'I ain't never done nothing like this,' she said and still sounded like she was a film star.

'Never?' I asked.

'And nuthin', nuthin' at all.'

My vision of America and High Schools and Cheer Leaders, and hot sex in the back of bright-red convertibles, and rock 'n' roll, just took a reality check. They have virgins in America, teenage virgins, post-school virgins; it never dawned on me.

'So, lets get started on the old education!' I said, jumping up and smacking my hands together in 'Lets get to work' fashion.

'Na, its not right here, Dave. Sorry, have I spoiled your night?'

'God no', I said, although I think selfishly I did feel I should have taken off with one of the other rip-roaring girls at the party who were planning to make a wild, no-holds-barred evening of it. Then I thought, 'Prat. This wee lass had probably been scared shitless coming back with you, had taken her courage in both hands to do the rolling round the couch bit with you.' Mind, she hadn't taken anything else in her hands though.

I gave her a real sincere hug and whispered 'Maybe a little later?'

'Maybe,' she said and then went off to bed.

Fortunately, there was a six-pack in the fridge, which I was sitting supping, musing on the night and the whole trip, in the dark except for the lights on the Christmas tree and outside the window, when the rest of the Labor Party team arrived, and I presumed that they presumed we had done it. New Year is a bugger really. I had come to see it as a kind of sexual test of strength, a trial of achievement and worth; sex was an integral part of a 'Happy New Year'. Still, I hadn't ended up alone; it had been a satisfying sort of an encounter. I felt quite mellow, if not fulfilled.

Out on the streets, New York is a strange and wonderful place. Its a cliché but I fell in love with it, both as a city in abstract and as a living space and its living people. It was wick with down-and-outs, winos, dope fiends—more often than not poor working people and ex-working people—rooting through the restaurant bins for food, groups of teenagers hanging around street corners waiting for some mug to mug, regarding it like we would shoplifting from Woolworths. But the bulk of people are still 'whole people', aren't yet ground down and swallowed by it all, good people, with wit and humour, the most polite people I have ever encountered in the world—in the daytime, and when something hasn't made them snap. Like when the big New York city bus was rammed by a little old lady, who had a passing resemblance to Benny's Mam from *Top Cat* and the big black driver jumps from the cab, hands in the air, 'You don't see a bus? You don't see a bus, lady?' It is a race of races, made up of every nationality and creed and kin in the world with all the traditions and cultural diversity of an Eisteddfod.

A multitude of handshakes, greetings, embraces and kisses. Thousands of diverse ethnic and national restaurants. For every restaurant there was a vegetarian option. New York teams with so many different religions and creeds that a diversity of dietary options is commonplace. New Yorkers rarely eat in; they eat out every day, and try a different place every day.

Pirogi I had at Hungarian and Ukrainian restaurants. On separate occasions I had cheese pirogi and potato pirogi. It is, by the way, impossible for any European to actually eat all the food which is served; even Americans consider these Big meals, and that's big. Other 'meals' are a snack to them: 'a slice' of pizza is actually a whole pizza for us, and cost just 37p. The full-sized one would fill a plastic washing-up bowl in Britain—we don't have plates that size. While dining, New Yorkers eat a whole one of these each, plus a bucketful of 'fries' .

Eve Scott, the Nationwide Unemployed League secretary and an old member of the New York Socialist Party, took me off to the Eagle Tavern on West 14th Street at 9th Avenue, where traditional Irish songs and music were being belted out. Actually I had discovered a Provo paper, *The Irish People*, on one of the subways, and they carried an advert for a seisiun, a traditional Irish music session. Well you got a free pitcher of beer for every song you sang, so up I gets. Stories, songs, jokes, it all went well, even the one about the pope and the Geordie archbishop, but the 'Compañeros' stopped the jollity. 'For a people's free America Fidel has shown the way with Ché Guevara' is the punchline. But Fidel and Cuba were not on the agenda of Irish America. The standard of Irish music was as high as I had heard anywhere outside of Ireland. As the beer flowed and the crack developed, I discovered that in fact most people in this bar were supporters of the Officials. They had been given entirely the wrong story as the reasons for the split. After Eve left, I got plastered and into quite a few rows with the Irish Americans in the bar about Puerto Rico. A hard core of racialism exists in this community, I discovered, and some of the shit they came out with, like 'They only come over here to claim welfare' and 'If we sent them all back the island would sink' and 'We should tow it into the Atlantic and set it adrift', were just the sort of anti-Irish sentences and comments you heard from racists and fascists in England about them. We had a good give and take, loudly arguing, even squaring up from time to time, then downing another drink and getting tore into the music. By the time I left, in the early hours of the morning, we were mates. Except I was lost. Lost is what you never do in New York. You go from A to B in the shortest route, no deviation. Not I, I staggered this way, back down that way, and after about three-quarters of an hour realised this was serious. New York wasn't Gateshead. My plan to walk around until I recognised something wasn't working. So I phoned up Peter. It was the middle of the night, but he grasped the situation at once. For New Yorkers, the city is the most logical in the world, it is laid out in grids and intersecting streets and avenues. Paul talked me from phone booth to phone booth, right across the city, and back to Joel's.

Eve had organised a New Year afternoon party at her Greenwich Village apartment and announced quite unexpectedly that I was the entertainment, and I went through the whole Geordie bit, which went down well. Some were quite upset by the songs and stories from the pits, although Joel Myers was walking around reminding everyone of 'British mines, safest in the world', presumably so comrades didn't get too sympathetic for some reason. Well, the party was quite unprecedented, members of the anarcho-and-gay Red Balloon Collective, the IWP and LPL, the Socialist Party and others sat and drank, sang, kissed each other Happy Noo Year, and danced.

On my birthday, the LPL and some of the IWP people, Joel et al., went with me 'downtown' to a right-on disco. (In those days there was no English equivalent of 'downtown'—it was an entirely North American expression, which it still is but for the little English 'wannabes' who insist on trying to transport everything American to Britain.) The young LPL lass was my date that evening. I was chuffed to wee bits, an American disco, in downtown New York, suppin' Bud' with an American date. As we smooched a bit I began to wonder if she'd changed her mind, sort of like a birthday present like. As the party broke up and we hustled out into the casual sleet of the early morning and her friends drifted into the distance and Joel and Julie had long gone, I asked her if she was going to come back with me. 'Well, gee,' she said, so coyly she reminded me of the little blushing bunny on Bambi, 'how would we get there, how would I get back?' I thought: 'We just jump on the tube, jump on each other, then jump back on the tube in the morning.' A passing cop was flouncing his way by in one of those stagecoach driver's macs, and I said 'Excuse me, how long does it take to get to the subway?' 'Dunno,' he said, without turning round 'I don't know anybody who ever made it that far.' We just looked, then he turned round, his face a mass of smiles. 'You never heard that one, huh? Well, you can just walk round this block, and straight on. I wouldn't recommend waiting on the platform though, that ain't no joke.' 'Well, we could walk and look for a cab.' Suddenly she gripped my arm and said 'Lets do it.' 'Bliddy hell.' At first I thought 'Yippee!' and then as we started to set off I thought, 'Just wait a minute. It's pissing-wet freezing, we may walk for forty five minutes, if we don't get raped, mugged and murdered on the way, we end up in Joel's flat, Lower East Side, wall-to-wall cockroaches, and the exterminator man to give us our alarm call.' Did any of that match up to this young lass's first sexual encounter? We weren't even in the place alone, she's almost bound to bleed, this isn't private, its too dashed to be tender, and 'Wham, bam, thankyou mam' is going to spoil this girl's appreciation of sex for life. So I turned to her, and I could hardly believe it, as I heard myself tell her that was the nicest birthday present anyone had ever offered me, but it wasn't the right time or place.

I waved down a cab and it took her to her friends and then me on to Joel's. It was double the price on the meter and the guy said they were still on New Year rates. I suppose that sounded right, and anyway I was alive and well, though tearing myself apart as to whether I had done the right thing. I suppose I was trying to store up a fund of goodwill and good intention too, by not just dragging her off to bed on the first possible occasion. I thought we might still, some time, some place, be able to do the whole thing right. It was never to happen.

Another highlight of the visit was my encounter with Jerry Zilg. I had been sent his huge, encyclopaedic book *DuPont: Behind the Nylon Curtain*, about the vast, industrial, military and political empire of the DuPont family. As a work of scholarship it was unsurpassed. I imagined Jerry as a sort of Woody Allen intellectual. As it turned out he was an American football player, a mountain of a man and most unlike any academic I ever seen before or since. Come to think of it, he would have had to have been, to have written such a book and faced the obstacles the DuPonts had put in his way. When I first seen Jerry, I was shocked, and held my hand up like a little boy greeting his dad. 'I had no idea you were so big,' I said. 'Gee, I had no idea you were so small,' he countered.

As I flew out of America, I had much to reflect on. We had lots of work to do, too. I kept remembering what Woody Allen had said in one of his films: America might not be the 'land of the free' anymore, but it was still 'the home of the brave'.

The whole experience of the US visit even down to minute details of expenditure on tea and beer in the spirit of total openness, was printed in a report, *Delegate To America*, which we circulated at the pit, and sold elsewhere.

POSTSCRIPT

By February the IWP is expelling the LPL from the Unemployed League against the bitter opposition of every non-aligned affiliate including us. What goes around ... Peter Anton writes to tell us the big Hard Times conference organised by the New York City Crisis Coalition has expelled the IWP from the conference for 'racialism'. Actually they opposed purely black organisation and support class-wide ones instead. We do not consider this 'racialist' it is a perfectly acceptable position of many Marxist organisations, but not one we happen to agree with. We are against the expulsion.

24 March 1976. The International Workers Party formally informs us of the split within their ranks. Something like twenty-four, led by Joel Myers and Myron Jefka (who had joined via the Workers World Party of Sam Marcy), broke away to form the Communist Cadre. The IWP had already expelled the Labour Party League from the Nationwide Unemployed League, which anyway the IWP seemed to be less interested in now. The Communist Cadre caucus now condemned the idea of an NUL and building 'unemployed councils' as 'reformist and sub-economist'. Instead they wanted to see 'increased mobilisations and demonstrations' because the working class would move spontaneously and then take the streets, so it was essential for the vanguard to take the streets first to gain skills and experience to better assist the masses when they came to attempt it. The IWP under the guidance of Myron Jefka from the Central Committee had

reviewed our forthcoming Ireland pamphlet and thought it excellent apart from one or two minor things we had omitted. They agreed to print it, with an international overview from themselves of course. This pamphlet was crucial to our work in Britain. It was, we thought, a revolutionary fusion of Irish republicanism and revolutionary socialism rooted in the working class struggles of both islands engaged with a common enemy. Sadly Jefka left with Myers in the CTC split. Ostensibly the IWP were still offering to print our forthcoming Ireland pamphlet, but we were highly critical of so many of their actions at this period and it was never to be. The pamphlet was never to see the light of day.

August 1976. Larry Lockwood, the lofty, gifted, Russian-speaking theorist of the RCL(I), finds fundamental disagreements and leaves. We meantime will condemn all the expulsions, all the exclusions and maintain relations with everyone we still think is going down the same road as us. In November 1976 the Communist Cadre splits and Communist Cadre (Marxist) is formed. In November 1981 the RCL(I) folds up and they rejoin the Workers World Party from whence they came.

SINN FEIN, BERNADETTE AND MILITARY TRAINING

24 January 1976. Big public meeting at the Miners Welfare: 'Ireland—The Case for British Withdrawal'.

I am appointed as a school governor! On two schools, Hall Cross although the most important is Hungerhill in Edenthorpe which isn't open yet, I get in from beginning to try and ensure no stupid rules and no stupid compulsions. I also get to help appoint the head and heads of departments.

Within Long Kesh, the prisoners develop a Revolutionary Cultural Committee, 'To provide an alternative culture to that provided by the bourgeois media.' This held classes, study, lectures and debates on the nature of imperialism. They taught the Irish language. 'The walls of the huts were decorated with painting and slogans expressing our solidarity with other revolutionary movements and remind us of our principles and polices.' Socialist and Marxist political and economic theory were offered weekly as alternatives to TV time. Aspects of women's oppression were covered, and the necessity to wage 'a cultural revolution' within the movement on this and other fronts was accepted. (Source: *ANS Andersontown News Service*, a republican local news sheet—*International News Shorts*, January 1976.) Within the Provisionals the ideas of Marxism grew, albeit inorganically. The prisoners within the Kesh held Marxist education classes; their library included a dozen copies of Lenin's *State and Revolution*, and numerous more copies of Marx and Engels's *Communist Manifesto*. Revolutionary left theory, without sectarian censure, abounded within the literature used in research and preparation.

Young spokespersons for the Provos talked the language of anti-imperialist class war and talked of a revolutionary socialist Ireland. On the streets and within the communities of occupied Ulster People's Assemblies were up and running. 'The Vindicator' ran a revolutionary socialist column in the Provo paper, *Republican News*, which made the perspectives of this growing current within the movement public and strong. The People's Assemblies were dual power organs of working class power. They would be instruments of administration and democracy after the overthrow of imperialism in the north and semi-colonial Green Toryism in the south.

7 February 1976. I give a public presentation at the Miners Welfare with slide show and discussion: 'Cuba, Island in the Sun'. The branch activists and quite a number from other pits turn out in decent numbers.

Meantime relations with Tony McHugh are getting worse. He writes in reply to a sharp letter from us:

Your letter just received was most uncomradely. Firstly since your letter advising us about the visit did not arrive until THURSDAY we could not let you know about our plans any earlier. I would remind you that we spent two weeks in Yorkshire waiting for you to contact us—a contact that never came.

I am a revolutionary ... active. My life consists more of positive activity than meetings, weekend schools and folk evenings. Quite often I am requested by the International section to undertake specific work and as on this occasion I must go as and when requested. Indeed I am only just back from E. Europe from my visit which lasted 13 days rather than 10 ...

It seems to me that your group do not really understand the true meaning of being a Communist if you cannot grasp this basic fact. There will be no revolution through writing manifestos, only through action ...

Yours Faithfully

Tony McHugh

12 February 1976. Death of Frank Stagg, republican hunger striker. We are deeply upset by the development and question the sense in comrades starving themselves to death. It is principled and heroic and at the same time we consider it an unnecessary loss of life. We do not believe the British state will be moved by it, although the intention clearly is to move British public opinion. Here occurred one of the most shameful episodes of the whole of the current Irish rebellion and one which I believe changed the 'etiquette' of many of the resistance fighters in their choice of targets and attitudes to the war. Frank Stagg was the first of the Irish prisoners to die in an English jail (Wakefield) on hunger strike, defending 'political status'. (Michael Gaughan had died in Parkhurst on hunger strike two years earlier in protest against body searches of family visitors before and after visits). Frank had died a most terrible death after 61 days on hunger strike. When the body was on the way back to the family and the republican movement for burial in accordance with his dying wishes, the Dublin regime stole his body from the family, and arrested Frank's brother George, a member of the Labour Party, who had been accompanying it. The remains, which were destined for Dublin, had landed at Shannon airport by government order whereupon the coffin was seized by armed police and locked in a mortuary, surrounded by one thousand troops and police, who refused to return it to his widow or his mother, kin, or friends, and arranged an unauthorised burial, undertaken by his avowed enemies in the Special Branch, against the outrage and grief of his family. The cemetery workers acting in solidarity with the family had refused to participate in the shameful farce. His widow on arrival in Dublin was kidnapped by detectives and held against her will until during the forced burial, guarded by three carloads of Special Branch, she restated that she had always wanted her husband to be buried in accordance with his wishes and not in this unacceptable manner which she had never agreed to.

Something else died that day—I think the unspoken common courtesies which had prevailed between both sides in this war had now been shamefully torn to shreds. The degree of brutality used in some of armed units of the IRA would harden from now on. They were also outraged at the failure of the British left to mobilise around the whole Frank Stagg affair. It was to get worse. News came through that Troops Out had refused to allow a Sinn Fein speaker on their joint demonstration held by the TOM and the Bloody Sunday Commemoration Committee (BSCC). We wrote, outraged at the decision, and they replied:

In the first instance, we have really no competence to answer for the BSCC. as we represent only TOM which was only one of the component groups of the BSCC

However I was a national TOM delegate to the BSCC and I do know the background to discussions reached.

Firstly it is true that the rally at the end of the demo was a TOM rally and we were opposed to having a Sinn Fein speaker (as a Sinn Fein speaker—or a well known Sinner) on the platform.

This is consistent with the policy of not wishing to identify with the republican movement in this country—recognising one strategic orientation toward the British Labour Movement and the tactical disadvantages that proximity to republicanism would have at this particular conjuncture. We feel that the more responsible elements within the republican movement are in agreement with this policy.

We did not object to Sinn Fein marching on the demo, with their banners—indeed we went to great lengths to urge them to do so and to accommodate them in any way to win their rank and file to support us (short of having a speaker on the platform)—including allowing them to march in the contingent at the head of all other political groups.

That we were unable to reach an agreement was in reality because the emotionalism of the imminence of Frank Stagg's death had left republicans in Britain completely unmoved by any objections from British socialists, against whom they tended to lay much criticism (in my view well deserved) for their almost total apathy on the Stagg issue.

Relations between Sinn Fein and all British left groups (including—but probably leastly—TOM because of the solidarity of London TOM members individually on the pickets) were strained around the time of Stagg's ordeal and eventual murder—but certainly any rifts appear to have been healed now ...

Fraternal Greetings

Peter Maguire

pp. Secretariat.

I first came into contact with Sinn Fein at Ruskin, the runai, whose name I can't recall but I think was Pat Reynalds, was a car worker at Cowley and a shop steward as I recall. I used to take and sell *Republican News* but I can't recall if I actually joined. I thought I had but anyway certainly did so again in 1974 after I wrote to them and suggested we needed to organise Sinn Fein cumann (branches) in all the major northern industrial towns with large Irish centres, and then my membership must have lapsed. (It does if you drop off weekly contact with the organisation.) I then come into national contact with Sinn Fein in March of

1976, although I had forgotten this until I read the minute books of SUI for the period. SUI minute, 21 March 1976:

> One of our comrades has taken the decision to join Sinn Fein. Criticism was raised that the comrade did not bring this matter before the group before this decision was made. However we are quite happy with the comrade's decision and feel it will be a valuable extension to our work. The comrade discussed his plans for work as a member of Sinn Fein.

I joined the London-based cumann, with Michael Holden, one of the leaders of Sinn Fein Britain. From him and with permission from Dublin I was given organiser's credentials, to allow me to go forth and establish Sinn Fein cumann.

At the end of February of the following year I believe I also applied to join the IRA and become an active volunteer in the military wing. It was on the back of a number of things, most of them personal and not political. It was more like the reasons someone joins the French Foreign Legion for. Fortunately my comrades within the republican movement spotted that my motives were more to do with the state my personal life was in at the time and not a considered view of where I could be best use to the movement. P. O'Murchu, from the *Irish Republican Information Service*, instead counselled me to work with them and continue my work within the political wing. He then spoiled it somewhat: 'Remember too, the hold Lord Haw-Haw was able to bring to bear on the English during the last World War. Thank you for your much valued support. Is Mise Le Meas ... ' Some Irish republicans seen the war with Germany less as a noble antifascist campaign by Britain, but a squabble among rich nations of which they should take full advantage in their own cause. For me the comparison with Lord Haw Haw was repulsive not for his 'treachery' to Britain, but his loyalty to the Nazis.

27 February. Workers Institute of Marxism-Leninism–Mao-Tse-Tung Thought thank us for our resolutions in solidarity with their struggle against their repression at the hands of the state, and in particular the arrest of their secretary, Balahrishnan, and 'Comrade Wee', both of whom received prison terms. In response to our inability to understand their blurring of class lines with the invitation of Nixon and Heath to China, they respond:

> Fascism today operates under a different form from that of Hitler's, but the essence is the same, that is brutal suppression of contradictions, anti-communism. The Chinese comrades denounce Soviet revisionist clique as a social-fascist clique, which brutally suppresses the Soviet people ... Heath is one of the architects of the European Union, a union pulling away from the Superpowers to some extent. China invites him over because of his work in this direction. China supports the formation of the EEC as a political union moving away from the superpowers' control because anything that helps to isolate and weaken the main enemy benefits the people. This can be compared with the Communist Party of China, led by Chairman Mao, forming an alliance with the Kuomintang (representatives of the Landlords and Big Bourgeoisie in old China) during the anti-Japanese period, so as to unite with as many people as

possible to isolate the main enemy, Japanese militarism, to the maximum and attack him. In the United Front Chairman Mao maintained the policy of UNITY as well as STRUGGLE. The proletariat maintaining its independence and initiative and giving leadership to the united front. Same is the case today in international front led by China against the two superpowers, United States and Soviet Union. Once the main enemy, the superpowers are wiped out, the rest of imperialist powers as well as third world has to go through reorganisation too. So it is in this context we view Heath's trip to China. The CPC's basic line for the entire period of socialism teaches communists to grasp CLASS STRUGGLE as the key link. So even with Nixon visiting China, the guiding principle of the CPC is never to forget class struggle and never to forget the historic mission of the proletariat to liberate the whole of mankind.

Warmest Revolutionary Greeting, Chanda

The Unemployed Workers Action Committee, which is based down in Great Yarmouth, affiliates to SU(I). It is based around the influence of Tony McHugh, of whom more later. They are closely involved with Maoist politics but we are no sectarians. Unite all who can be united on the highest anti-capitalist programme, is our theme, or as Mao said, let a million blooms blossom let ten thousand schools of thought reign. There's one or two who helped to fertilise the blossoms who wished he had meant it of course. The problem with McHugh and his organisation was despite enthusiastic letters, affiliation, offers to impending visits, joint conferences, speaking tours and whatever, nothing ever came of it. Things got really vexatious after our comrades were booked on coaches and arranged time off work in order to take up offers of meetings and joint activities in Great Yarmouth only to receive a telegram literally as they set off, to say it was all off. The SUI branch meeting in Doncaster on 22 February 1976 was prophetic; the minute reads: 'One comrade voiced suspicions of McHugh since so many meetings had been arranged and then cancelled, always by him. We have written to him on this matter ... '

The explanation we got back was that mail was being interfered with, theirs to us and ours to them, and that this was probably a ploy to cause friction, which it had. They also told us that IS was actively campaigning against the SUI in Yarmouth. In the middle of June 1976 we made arrangement for Comrade McHugh to come and stay, but true to form he never showed up. In September he wrote to us asking for a public phone box number and suggesting a time and date when he would call us on a matter of importance. He was duly given the Abbey number and a comrade posted pint in hand beside the phone on the allotted date and time. Several pints and some hours later the comrade was persuaded the leave his post as McHugh of course didn't phone.

March 1976. The NEC of the NUM calls off the overtime ban which was imposed against the closure of Langwith Colliery; determination to fight closures is very shaky.

SPARTS

Soon the group's missionaries were at work at Britain and becoming a sound nuisance, which seems to be their deliberate role.

21 March. The SUI publicly declares war on the Spartacist League, with the issuing of a public 'Resolution':

> The Socialist Union (Internationalist) aimed at unification of the revolutionary and 'communist' left on a principled fighting programme: aimed at the creation and development of united fronts and comradely 'ad-hoc' organisations for the survival of Marxism in the face of growing fascist repression and state terrorism takes no joy whatever in the 'development' of the so called 'SPARTACIST' tendency in the British Isles.
>
> The Spartacist League is an American shoot-off of the US SWP (Socialist Workers Party—US Section of the IVth International (Mandelista)). As an organisation it reflects the very worse deviations of the US Left, it is elitist, cynical and hostile to a degree of madness toward all and sundry organisations of the left, and progressive movement the world over. It is mortally stricken with 'Stalinophobia' to the degree where it verges and totters on the brink of Schactmanism and anti-workers states reactionism. In terms of sectarianism this group makes the SLL-WRP sound like socialist union members; it is twenty times, thirty times more hysterically sectarian and disruptive than Healy and his team ever have been.
>
> The 'development' of a branch of the Spartacist League in Britain via the transplanting of three or four American students here is just what the British left do not need in this period. Not sufficient with their criminal splitting, smashing role in the USA, where perhaps such behaviour is regarded as 'normal' they have deemed our struggle here too much in contradiction to their line and hope to set the cat among the pigeons, sow confusion in order to point to the resulting chaos and the 'need' for their calming hand ...
>
> There is much on the British left which we of course disagree about, much that we have principled differences on, but overall we, the revolutionary left in general have entered a period of close and sincere co-operation, we have closed ranks against the common class enemy. Our dialogue is no longer the self serving academic sloganising of the past, it is constructive, principled and comradely. The SU (I) salutes and welcomes this development which we in our small way intend to contribute to and further. We also intend to defend it against any agents whose sole role is disruption and the sowing of the seeds of disunity and childish 'infighting'. The Spartacist League is diametrically opposed to the aims and principles of the SU(I). The members and branches of the SU(I) in Britain are urged to adopt a hostile position toward the Spartacists wherever they are encountered until and unless they demonstrate that they are prepared the learn from the British working class and

revolutionary forces. And are seriously trying to develop the struggle here ... our experiences in the USA and recently in Britain where our comrades have been close to physical attack, the receipt and close scrutiny of all their publications, suggest to us that they are on the verge of playing a counter-revolutionary role; and at best are wickedly reactionary on many issues.

We noted though that their politics, if not their social bearing, was better than that of the IS.

The resolution, published in leaflet form, then goes on to invite everyone to march with the SUI at May Day and to come to the May Day Folk Concert at the Drum.

23.3.76 Provisional Sinn Fein
National Co-ordinating Committee (Britain)
Dave A Chara

... I was glad to hear from you again. I don't think you received my last letter sent before St Patrick's Day informing you that our friends in Halifax would forward you a membership card. The reason for this is because I asked them to write back to me and let me know if you had been sent a card but so far I have not heard from them. However I do hope that you had some measure of success at the St Patrick's Day social. I am enclosing for you a Sinn Fein membership card, together with a letter of authorisation for you to form Sinn Fein Cumann or a Republican Political/Social Union in your area or outside of it as you see fit. I wish you every success in this venture, and thank you for your support. No need for me to tell you how grateful we are for this very active participation.

Dave, you have some very progressive ideas on how to get the Republican Message over. We need more ideas like this in Sinn Fein ...

Let me know if there is anything else I can do to help you in any way, just drop me a few lines. All of us here give you our wholehearted support ...

Is Mise Le Maes
Fraternal Greetings and Good Wishes
Michael

This was some authorisation, and some accreditation, the agreement to organise Sinn Fein cumann and to establish links between the SUI and Sinn Fein if I had read that right, although Michael had said 'social' rather than socialist, but later events made it quite clear that was what he, and they, were authorising.

I was abed with Maureen, in the twilight or half sleep that precedes the day shift, my partially conscious mind whiling through fractured dream and nightmare, my body tense and already steeling itself for the shift ahead, when I had become aware of knocking on the front door about 2.30 a.m. I peered from the open bedroom window.

'Compañero!' she greeted me. It was Tania, the beautiful six-foot Russian comrade of the Cuban microbrigadesta, and a large, fur-covered comrade with a big moustache. I was ecstatic, and charged down stairs with Maureen in tow to let them in. Soon the living room was alive with the chatter of debate, and the full-throated laughter at past adventures and new tales. As the Havana Club got aired, all thoughts of day shift vanished to irrelevance. By 6 a.m. we were all beaming and happy and eating breakfast. Dani was Tania's new bloke. Big, Belgian, in an old fur coat with the arms cut out, and a big Cossack-style hat, he looked like a guerrilla down from the hills. Tania was in her beret, a black polo neck with knee-length boots. They were frequent visitors to Cuba and often tied in with whatever international Cuban project was on the go at the time. This time Cape Verde, the next postcard would come from Angola where Tania was deployed as nurse then a teacher. We never lost touch, ever, through the ups and downs of life and changing phases and aspirations of the revolution around the world, though it was a long way from the back seat of that battered old Cuban bus, speeding through the black of night carrying our hopes and dreams.

It was visits like these, the tangible evidence of our worldwide struggle, the physical links of communist struggle comrades from across the globe who just dropped by, that bathed our little pit living-room in the glow of revolution. Well, one day became two and I only started work, much the worse for wear, by Wednesday afternoon having given up on day shift altogether.

Gent, 24 April
Dear Maureen, Dave, lovely little Emma
I apologise we disturbed you those days and I hope you didn't come to difficulties by this and we thank you very much for this kind hospitality ... I think you gave us the very warm feeling to know that everywhere comrades fight the same struggle and we left with new strength and faith.

Dani has to leave very soon on 10th May ... to the Cape Verde islands. I shall follow within a year ... we also made a trip to Italy, where we saw a lot of good comrades Dani met in Cuba; Bologna impressed us very much its really a 'Red City' (60 per cent communists). It was also a good political lesson cause our friends belong to different left groups and we love them all as brothers though they fight and sometimes hate each other on the political scene.

What is wrong with political organisations that they cannot unite and take power as a majority?

I send you a tape with revolutionary and folk songs from Cuba ... With revolutionary greeting and Love from Belgium and hope to see you soon Tania / Dani"

Easter 1976. Extended EMC course. Map-reading and survival. We are not allowed sleeping bags, only a rolled polythene bag and a survival tin. We set off from different points and intend to map-read our way through the Cheviots and meet up at a location described only verbally, among the crags. We will make shelters among the rocks, under great boulders and from trees. We carry water for emergency but are expected to forage for it, boiling it or purifying it on the way. We carry dehydrated packets of soup among our clothes and stuffed down shirts. The object is to live in the Cheviots without detection, to move back and forth and establish contacts and liaison. To plan targets, mock strikes and withdrawal back into hidden locations. Is it our intention to carry the armed revolution to Northumberland? Not really, it's an exercise, but as a one-off it wasn't impossible. Indeed we strayed into army territory and into SAS training grounds on Otterburn, and managed to pull out without getting shot (yet!). A couple of strategic blunders stick in my mind. One, we had stashed a great slab of cheese in the boot of the car, with the intention of dividing this up among the comrades, as a ready source of rich protein which was light and required no preparation. The spare petrol can in the boot however was leaking, ever so slightly. It had soaked through the greaseproof paper round the cheese, and on the extended run from Donny it had produced a marbled bluey effect as it soaked into the body of the cheese. When it was discovered Malc refused to leave it, and cut himself a great wedge of the stuff despite its petrol soaked flavouring. As he tramped along through the course of the day, he broke off lumps of this cheese and happily ate it. It gave him severe heartburn and the burping which accompanied this belched great petrol fumes into his immediate environment. The cheese was welcomed later however; as we sheltered up against an overhanging crag and tried to light a fire we discovered Malc's cheese made excellent firelighters. The rain deluged all day. We tramped through slippery rocks and soaked bracken. Starving at last we made precarious camp in a rocky hollow. We set up the collective pan over the flames and started to boil the water. Just before it started to bubble we added three packets of the soup powder and the meal began to look not only eatable but highly desirable. At this point Alison decided to stand up and move her sitting place. Stumbling past the big pan of soup she slipped and crashed into it, spilling more than half of the precious fluid onto the rocks. We stare in disbelief, and barely suppressed anger. Some of the comrades make the point that in a real revolutionary situation this would be a serious act of revolutionary negligence. Ken wants to execute her on the spot. Alison was a brave and dedicated comrade, she struggled with chronic asthma and found the courses tough but stuck it out. Her forte was the conference platform, where she punched way above her weight.

But back on the course things declined into farce, left to watch the guns hidden in the heather, while the rest of us went to search the surrounding terrain for possible spies and informers, the guards got bored and went for a little walk themselves, leaving the guns, then within less than a hundred yards turned round to see ... a thousand square miles of Northumbrian countryside and not a clue where the guns were. We raged at each other and spread out in all directions combing the bracken and heather foot by foot in search of the revolutionary guns. Of course had THIS been a real situation we'd have been shot down like rats in a bucket, if not by the class enemy than by our own side as punishment.

May Day 1976. Folk social at St Edwin's Hall, which had eighty people attending.

St Edwin's became something of our 'barracks'. With the curtains closed we drilled and marched, staged self-defence classes, did karate, and discussed picket line and demonstration tactics and manoeuvres. Frequently the comrades from our regions, or other groups and countries, slept in the hall and our socials had the old building rocking on its long wooden stilts, it being constructed something like a Malayan river house.

16 May 1976. We discussed the so-called suicide of Comrade Ulrike Meinhoff70, and expressed our deep sympathy and at the same time total disbelief that any suicide took place, rather than a political assassination whilst a captive. We regarded the Red Army Fraction as a sincere and comradely organisation. It hadn't started off as 'individual terrorists' as Militant would have dubbed them, but the armed wing to the mass democratic socialist student movement, and growing workers' movement. Bob Dylan had talked of how 'the waters around you had grown', isolating the old guard, the establishment and the status quo. Unfortunately the waters had while we were preparing our revolutionary cadres started to recede again, leaving some comrades stranded on a rock looking like right idiots. In a way this was our comrades in the Red Army Fraction: the movement upon which and from which they emerged into armed struggle receded, leaving them with little choice but to continue their struggle without a formal milieu to operate from and take their marching orders from. They remained a shining example to the workers of Germany of the vulnerability of the state, for all its high courts and armies of polished boots. The state set out to murder each one of them. Murder? Of course. Having arrested them and imprisoned them, to kill them in cold blood in prison was straightforward murder.[71]

22 May 1976. The Yorkshire Area and Derbyshire Area of the NUM held a fiftieth anniversary of the 1926 strike Commemorative Rally and Meeting, at Sheffield City Hall. There was a short march to the Hall, and Maureen had made a dramatic black banner with gold writing: '1926 General Council TUC, Traitors—1976 General Council TUC, Traitors'. We were advised that our place was at the back of the demonstration but what did we care, all the miners on that march thought the slogan ought to have been at the front. In the chair on the great stage was Arthur Scargill, the speakers were Michael Foot, Leader of the House of Commons, and Will Paynter, former General Secretary of the NUM and famous leader of the South Wales miners. This was to be either a return to the labour movement with his tail between his legs, or else a bid for rehabilitation. Will had disagreed with the CPGB, his party, from the right; he had then resigned in order to sit on the Tory-established Industrial Relations Court set up under the Industrial Relations Bill. He was later to tell me he genuinely thought the court could offer some rights for workers and unions which were long needed. He resigned when he realised the whole set-up was institutionally biased against unions and workers and in favour of employers. Still, it earned him a bob to two in the process, although it lost him his reputation and respect. From this point on

he would try and re-establish himself in the movement he was once such a hero of. We had hung our banner over the balcony, which drew furious gestures from Arthur to take it down, which we ignored, and thumbs up from many in the downstairs audience. Sitting next to me was Billy Matthews, the die-hard member of the Communist Party from Hatfield pit. At the end of Paynter's speech Billy announced him rehabilitated; it had been a tub thumping good speech, and Paynter had much to be proud of in his past. The vote of thanks was made by Peter Heathfield, general secretary of the Derbyshire miners, a great impassioned speaker whose rhythm of voice often near rocked him off his own feet. Mind, Will didn't like me ower much. We got parked together during a Ruskin History Workshop gathering which we were both speaking at. We sat together at dinner, and he chastised me for being 'dour and politically obsessed'. I suggested some might have made that criticism of him when he was my age, but he denied he was ever like me. 'Life's too short,' he concluded, adding that my political obsession, which was I suppose an obsession, was at the expense of being a full human being. 'You don't know me Will,' I had suggested, to which he uncompromisingly replied 'I know all about you.'

23 May.

    Report was given of a meeting and political discussion between one of our comrades and Sinn Fein. It seems that our comrade's individual membership of Sinn Fein has been revoked but he is now being considered for membership as a representative of SU(I). We are in a privileged position to be considered in this way—no other organisation ever has been, and it is an indication of both the correctness of our position on Ireland and the desire of elements of the Provisional Republican movement to embrace the wider socialist ideology which we embody.

This was contradicted a little later when Michael wrote from London (5 June 1976):

    I am glad you met Gerry Cassidy. He wrote to me in fact and told me that he had met you. He is very impressed with what you are doing, didn't say anything about differences of opinion Re building Sinn Fein. Perhaps you can iron them out. He intends to keep in touch with you from what he wrote to me. I hope that together you will be able to get things going in that area. Gerry it seems is on his own in Halifax and was a bit down hearted for a while, but I gather he is game to carry on. Dave, I am certain you are the only person who can help him. It is a pity Eamonn Reilly didn't turn up. I will contact him again and see what is happening ...

    I am sorry about this mix-up with your membership. Of Course you ARE a member Dave. When I signed your membership card I also informed Dublin of what was going on. You needed to be a member because of your plans to organise Sinn Fein activity and this was accepted. I will explain this to Gerry when I write to him. I should perhaps have done it before but I never thought anyone would ever question it—

especially a Sinn Fein member...

Is Mise

Michael

At the end of May Hillary Wainwright, who I had known at Oxford (she was an Oxford undergrad in the IMG and very dolly at the time, with her miniskirt and thigh-high boots, her little gold rimmed glasses on a chain) was now based in the North East and working with the Socialist Centre in Jesmond. She offered me the invite to chair the forthcoming highly prestigious meeting at which Bernadette McAliskey would be the star; there would be an Irish play, and music by the Beggermen, all at the Bridge. Could a better offer be made? It would prove to be the major launch pad for a Tyneside Troops Out Movement, and I considered the embryo of a Sinn Fein Cumann on Tyneside which was lang, lang overdue.

At the beginning of June (1976) I received something of a bombshell of a letter from me Da, though I supposed not surprising really given his working-class patriotism.

23 Joyce Close Bungalows

Wardley

Gateshead

Just a few lines to thank you for the papers, but my main purpose is to tell you that I am disgusted and ashamed to think that my son is to Chair a meeting at which a rebel like Bernadette Devlin will be speaking, you don't seem to consider the feelings of your Mam and Dad over these things it seems to me that you are falling deeper into the mire. I am very upset and can't understand how you come to be in the Chair, living away in Doncaster as you do, unless of course you had anything to do with her coming over here to this meeting. I hate violence from whatever side it comes from. These IRA are cowardly cold-blooded calculating killers, murderers is the correct name for them, with their car bombs, and booby trap bombs, nothing brave or clever about them David, just plain hatred and mark you often catholic people are killed, as happened in London, this Northern Ireland thing will never be settled in this way, indeed the Protestants are only more embittered and moving further away than ever from a United Ireland, which is the main issue. The British Government has stated time and time again if the majority of the people want a United Ireland, the ball is at their feet, of course I know it isn't as simple as that, a lot of good will is required and a change of heart, but violence will not solve the problem, there are over a million Protestants in the North, and most of them would prefer a Republic the same as the south, rather than a United Ireland. This is a very serious complicated problem, and will take some solving, you see if it DID come about, then the Protestants would be in the minority, as Eire has over three million Catholics, and apart from that, the Orangemen are dead against the Pope, and all he stands for, I myself am easy, I can take religion in any form. I could enlarge on this letter, but I just want you to know how I stand, I am dead set against you chairing this meeting, we don't want trouble in Newcastle.

From Dad

Well these are the issues now as they were then. Me Da proved himself to be quite on the button in his understanding of 'Loyalism'. Few people at large were aware that 'an independent' 'loyalist' state was the ultimate alternative to a United Ireland if Britain ever decided to saw them free and concede the principle. He was Jarrow/Hebburn born and bred; those streets were in the days of his youth almost as sectarian at times as Belfast or Glasgow. The Orange Lodge sat cheek by jowl with the Catholic club, over the years the ceilidhs (modern Irish seems to spell the festive night ceilidh these days) had united, at least on the dance floor, people from both camps. But it had been bitter class struggle in Shipyard and mines that had united them as workers and socialists. Core differences still sat under the surface, and I had touched them. Me Da's letter was actually couched respectfully and he had obviously not written it from his all-consuming temper. But it was nie impossible for him to see where we were going in Ireland. He never knew I was a member of Sinn Fein, although me ma did; she kept stumm as certainly the best appeasement policy at home—this was after all an argument which had rocked our house a time or two lang before I arrived in it.

Me Ma wrote on the 29 June:

I am writing this line to tell you I'd love to go to see you and Bernie at the Bridge Hotel, but I am going to hospital on the 3rd June that's a Thursday. But I must tell you I wish to God you had not told your dad about this meeting. You should know your old dad by now and your views, he is driving me mad. He keeps on and on nagging about you coming up to be chairman with Bernadette McAliskey ... and I am coming in for the lot. So for Gods sake if you call here don't say anything about her or the meeting to him. I feel like leaving home he won't let it drop ...

So all the best good luck, Your Mam

Lots of Love to Emma and M XXXX"

Maureen writes on behalf of Doncaster SUI (to me):

We are gaining quite an international reputation for our stand on the analysis of World War Two, i.e. it was a matter of fighting fascism, we do not regard it as an inter-capitalist war.

Well we are rather concerned because the group does not have a stated position and I have many misgivings about what you say. I would like to see your position written down and also Joel's (I'll write to him when he's back in Durham). Neither Alison nor I is very happy about your own personal view being taken as the groups especially on this matter. Can we organise some kind of group exchange of ideas and get a synopsis of all our ideas ... it has just come to our notice in a couple of letters from the US but I do know that it is not a common analysis—which of course does not make it wrong. We would just like it cleared up.

We had arranged to go fly-posting tomorrow night also painting out the NF slogans with two of the IS but I can't get a baby sitter so they'll have to manage with three people. Actually the fourth was only for a look out so it's not too bad.

World War Two was in my mind a very different kind of war than a simple 'inter-imperialist' struggle, although of course the class nature of the states engaging in it didn't alter, they were actually engaged in inter-imperialist struggle. In World War One however we had a classical case of European at first and then other world superpowers fighting for a share-out of the world's plunder, markets, and production. Whoever was the victor, the capitalist per se would win. The socio-political system would not alter one iota, whichever side won; both sides represented exactly the same kind of social system. Indeed this could be seen as a family argument with Queen Victoria's grandchildren in Russia, Germany and Britain arguing which side of the family should reign. They would win whichever the formal outcome of the war and whichever political title and national flags remained flying. The aspirations of a workers' Europe were damned in the conflict as brother worker abandoned brother worker to go and fight each other for their boss's fortunes. So most of us, had we been alive, wouldn't have fought, not on the basis of pacifism but on the basis of socialism and communism.

World War Two was in my view different. At first the 'left', particularly those influenced by the Communist Party and the Comintern and Soviet line, considered the outbreak of war as an inter-imperialist squabble, nothing to dey wi us, we should treat it as the First War. But this wasn't quite right. The political system of Nazi Germany, Mussolini's Italy and, by invasion and war, one which was being goose-stepped across Europe wasn't the same as 'normal' capitalism in Britain or France or elsewhere. Bourgeois democracy was being smashed, the rights of workers, unions, left parties of all descriptions were being destroyed and millions of trade unionists and communists of all sorts were being butchered. One could not say that it didn't matter who won in this war because nothing would change. It would be indescribably worse if the Nazis were successful. As a movement we would be lucky to survive, as individuals most of us assuredly wouldn't. The Nazis had a far-reaching plan for the mass extermination of whole races and peoples. The notions about Jews and Jewish plots, and communism and Jewishness being inseparable from each other, were well known. Less well known was the utter inhumane hatred for Slavs and Russians and Gypsies. Elaborate plans existed for the mass extermination of the bulk of the Russian population; apart from a piece of social engineering in itself it was to free up vast areas of agricultural land to feed the greater Reich. In the opening period of the invasion of the Soviet Union, the Nazi machine pushed all ahead of it; some three million Russian troops surrendered, and within six months two million of them were dead, starved quite deliberately to death. It was crazy to apply the old Bolshevik slogan, 'Your Enemy is at home, fight for the defeat of your own bosses' to this war—it meant supporting a victory for the Nazis. Parliamentary democracy was not our social system, but it was a social system which was an advance and opened up more room for manoeuvre to true social democracy than had tyrannies and dictatorships. There was a particular brand of barbarism loose here; it was in my view absurd to pretend we had no part in that war, albeit with our own agenda.

The argument became less complex for the Stalinists (and presumably the Trotskyists although that is not clear universally), when Hitler stabbed Stalin in the back and invaded the Soviet Union. Now the Communist Party and its fellow travellers joined the war against Hitler in 'defence of the workers states'. Had I been alive I would have sought to organise independent working-class, partisan action against the European fascists. There was for example a famous Greek anarchist tank squadron which coordinated its efforts none the less with 'the allies'; exiled Spanish anarchists and syndicalists drilled and trained independent sections of the Home Guard in bomb-making and guerrilla counter attacks in Hyde Park and although they were increasingly restrained under Churchill's direction, we would have been foolish in the extreme not to co-ordinate resistance (not subordinate it) to the general 'allied' action and support. The class war had to be fought within the world war, against fascism and capitalism. Well, that at least was the way I had worked it all out though that didn't appear to be the common 'Trot' or leftist line: defeatism and war resistance seemed to be the conclusions they had come to.

CTC(M) later homed in on this disagreement in August 1977:

World War II was essentially another inter-imperialist war, but with the Soviet Union caught in the middle, as Comrade Anton points out in his pamphlet *Puerto Rico: The Graveyard Of American Liberalism*. In addition to the complex problem of the Soviet workers state being forced into a military alliance with one bloc of imperialists against the other, World War II contained the additional contradiction of the spread of fascist reaction (as Comrade Douglass' letter to Comrade Anton suggests)— making a correct application of the principle of revolutionary defeatism extremely difficult. Unfortunately in its attempt to grapple with the difficult contradictions presented by World War II, Comrade Douglass' letter fails seriously in our opinion, liquidating the principle of revolutionary defeatism and thus of proletarian internationalism for the duration of World War Two.

Yes 'we would have fought fascism in Spain—we would have fought the rise of fascism in Germany and we would fight the fascist forces in every country'. But we would fight them as members of red armies, not of bourgeois-imperialist armies! Whether the proletariat maintains its class independence makes all the difference in determining the class character of 'antifascist' combat. Trotsky's tactic in the Spanish civil war was for the workers militias to militarily block with the Republican army, but under no condition enter or liquidate into it. He correctly foresaw that the 'republican' bourgeoisie would enthusiastically go over to the Francoites as the struggle intensified and its class content became clearer. Moreover Trotsky was firmly against voting any war credits to the Republic—and here we have the bourgeois democracy of an oppressed and not even imperialist nation! Interestingly, it was Shachtman who disagreed with Trotsky on this, urging voting of war credits to the Republic.

In formulating communist tactics regarding the struggle between fascist imperialism and 'democratic' imperialism, it is first helpful to survey the strategy of the 'democratic' imperialists in the opening phases of World War II. The British and French imperialists consented to German imperial expansion into Eastern Europe. They were more than happy to see their Nazi class ally brutally expand its market eastward, within limits. Britain's strategy was the classical Metternichian ploy of sitting out and balancing the scales in a war between Germany and the Soviet Union, allowing the two nations to bleed each other white, and then mopping up the spoils to strengthen its profit empire. It was only the overtly rapid success of the Nazi armies in the east and the attack on Britain itself that forced the British imperialists into the struggle against Nazi Germany. The US bourgeoisie played an even more cynical, profit-grubbing role. It stage-managed the Pearl Harbour 'surprise attack' to whip the American people up into a chauvinist, racist, hysteria against the Japanese people, and launched a profitable, colony-grabbing war in the Pacific. Meanwhile, it gave only token military support to the besieged Soviet Union. It did not open up the Second Front until the scandalously late date of June, 1944—after the Soviet Union had single-handedly turned the tide against Nazi Germany—and it did this for two interconnected reasons: 1) to prevent the communist-led French resistance from liberating France socially as well as politically, and 2) to race the Soviet Army to Berlin, so as to prevent it from liberating and revolutionising all of Europe east of the Rhine. The US, British and French capitalists went on to resurrect the defeated Nazis in the West German Bundesrepublic.

So actually behind all the verbiage, all of which we knew well, they actually agreed with me, but didn't like the way I said it or failed to emphasise the elements they thought crucial. It wasn't simply an inter-imperialist war.

This was also the time of the History Workshop, and Emma's first memories of it, as 'Long Kresh' and 'pea soup' and being left without parents for hours. A series of disasters meant that neither me nor Maureen came to pick the poor long-suffering bairn up from Headington. We had been told the bairns would be returned down to Walton Street but this wasn't the case. Poor Emma wailed when no one came for her, and we at once dispatched a car to go and get her. In addition, her joy at being the centre of painting and drawing and acting and playing musical instruments had been soured by the apparently compulsory pea soup. These are things she will associate with the History Workshop as long as she lives. Although to be right, she did go off with a Chinese student all day on another occasion and refused to return for dinner with us because she was being so magically and happily entertained.

5 June 1976. Newcastle: launch of Troops Out Movement Branch, Bernadette is the speaker. I am in the chair; Joel and Sean and the SUI organise the security with an elaborate plan of action should the platform or meeting be attacked. A

theatre group provides a realistic cameo of the occupation while the Beggermen play later in the evening. We do not know it at this time, but the police are intensely interested in this meeting. Our comrade Sean has a bad car crash a little later. While he is still in shock the police find much of our Sinn Fein material from our Tyneside cumann, and ostensibly questioning him about the crash they hand over to Special Branch men who interrogate him on the nature of this meeting, and me, Bernadette, the IRA, and the EMC training. At the time we feel Sean has talked too much and we hold a special internal disciplinary meeting to review the facts. We allow Sean, without his knowledge, to drop out of the front frame of our operations, particularly the EMC. Years later while in a noisy, boozy Newcastle night club on the quayside, Sean suggests we are keeping him at arm's length on certain of our activities. He doesn't hear my muffled reasoning, and in response to his 'Eh?' I shout 'We didn't trust you comrade!' He is devastated, deeply hurt, and I don't think he ever forgave me fully for that loss of trust. He had been thoroughly open about the whole issue, but there had been outside forces whispering in our ears about things Sean was supposed to have broadcast. One these sources was the ever malevolent 'Mr Large', who had long since fell from our or any other political circle but still cohabited the Bridge with some of the former comrades.[72] Perhaps we had given too much credence to that crowd. We had been shocked by the fact he had come forth with as much as he did. We were very security-conscious and watching the 'supergrass' activities in Ulster feared we were being set up for a big fall. Sean, with terrific maturity, wrote me on the subject:

> With regard to our earlier discussion—I was not talking about Sinn Fein but Socialist Union Internationalist and the main complaint at that time—muddled by drink though it was—was not that any decision had been made but that it had been made on the basis of information on which I had not been asked to comment and had not even been informed of that decision.
>
> With regard to Sinn Fein I would not expect any close association after my arrest if only on the grounds of the fact that I was known to the police.
>
> As for your point regarding locations—I tell you this only for your own information and reassurance—not to invite discussion of the lies of Large. Only three locations were ever mentioned by me at any time, Rothbury, the Bridge and some where in the south of England. No name ever given for this town. With regard to Rothbury and a hut other than the Beserkers hut first mention of this was made by the fuzz when questioning Tom's wife before I was arrested. The town in the south of England arose when the fuzz wanted to know what letters I had received from Sinn Fein; they suggested one town (the name might be on tape), I offered several others all as possibilities ... A strange tale had reached my ears apparently two drunken Orangemen on their way to my house—with a bottle of petrol were picked up by the fuzz-then released—no charges—no petrol.
>
> Warmest Revolutionary Greetings — Sean

While the rank and file had rightly hailed the miners' victory and the election of a Labour government on the last day of February 1974, notions that this would mark a freeing up of the unions and authority shifting back to the rank and file were soon dispersed as the same bureaucratic team as had acted in unison for an ostensibly progressive victory to the miners now used that same unity of direction to tie down the unions behind Callaghan—who had become prime minister on 5 April 1976 following Wilson's retirement—and his wage restraint programme. Blatant bureaucratic somersaults were performed to pull the votes of the giant unions at a specially convened TUC conference for a maximum 4½ per cent wage increase in the coming round. The T&G, under the direction of Jack Jones, swung 1.8 million votes behind the policy, after just 37 members of his executive had agreed to this, without any consultation of the membership. Suddenly the cry was not 'workers' wages' but 'save the pound'. 'Whose pounds?' we asked. The building union UCAAT's executive had put the proposition to their conference, the delegates had rejected it, and Smith the general secretary announced that he would not carry that mandate to the special conference and would instead abstain. Within the NUM, the left got its first hard knock-back in recent times. Only five areas voted to reject the pay plan, including the trusty alliance of Scotland, Yorkshire, Kent, and Wales.

HEY BIG SUSPENDER

Aah, the suspender becomes suspended! Bill O' Brien, the influential chairman of the Goole Constituency and presider over all the witch-hunts against me and the constituency Labour Party Young Socialists, came to the other side of the table when he was suspended from the NUM. He was banned from holding office in the Union for two years. He had supplied confidential internal NUM documents to the Sheffield Star, in an effort to support their defence against a libel action brought against them by Arthur Scargill. The Yorkshire Area NUM Council had found Bill, who was also chairman of the right-wing Glasshoughton Branch of the NUM, guilty and suspended him. He appealed to Gormley and NEC but even ol' Joe couldn't find any breach of rule on one hand, or appeal mechanism against the decision of the entire NUM Yorkshire Council which represents all the branches in Yorkshire directly on the other.

June 1976. I had been given full charge of all the group's money and all the work which went into The Revolutionary Road to Socialism (Part Two of the SUI manifesto). I had done them on electrostencils, we had wonderful pictures, the text and political analysis brilliant. It was an utter disaster. The capitals of none of the words came out throughout the entire text, portions of the text just faded away and were unreadable. I had tried to correct the missing letters by writing them onto each page in felt tip; the front cover was a dark and black mass. It was and is still an utter disaster. Had this been a revolutionary situation I should almost certainly have been taken outside and shot, and I believe I would have been treated kindly by such an action. The words themselves are brilliantly inspiring, and in particular the sections on armed struggle and armed groups are illuminating, but who but the most curious or dedicated would ever get to read it? I think it can be counted as one of my greatest failures and certainly equal to us losing the shop. I wince even yet when I see it.

Our unlikely comradely contacts with the Marxist-Leninist Organisation of Britain were forcing us both, in the open and honest dialogue, to look again in depth at what was going on in the world, and what had went on in the world. In contrast to the Workers Institute world events were stripping away the illusions:

> [Later] as the Action Centre for Marxist-Leninist Unity and finally as the MLOB we considered that the chief bulwark of opposition in the world to Soviet modern revisionism was represented by the Chinese and Albanian parties. Since then however (more particularly since the 'Great Proletarian Cultural Revolution' of 1966) we consider that a revisionist faction led by Mao Tse-Tung has regained control in China and has incepted policies aimed at establishing an alliance with US Imperialism. We further consider that the faction headed by Liu Shao-chi and Peng Cheng which managed to gain control of sections of the Party apparatus in 1959 and which was powerful enough to force Mao Tse-Tung to resign from the Presidency and to give up all active political life, was the faction which was responsible for the magnificent contribution made by the Chinese CP to the struggle against Soviet modern revisionism from the brief period 1959–60 to 1966.

It would be many years before we ourselves would be so clear-sighted and would come to make any similar revelation about Comrade Trotsky's role in suppressing the soviets and workers' power while he still had a seat at the big table with Lenin and Stalin. We would never do so in this organisation, but that is jumping ahead of my tale.

We agreed to rework and relaunch my earlier disaster, *The Need for Workers' Control in the Mining Industry*, this time without 'worlers' and 'launching sticks' and titled now *The Slaughter of the Miners by the NCB*. I must admit I thought the title fairly clear, but many of the miners thought it highly ambiguous and contentious; they thought of it as a fight between us and the NCB and the NCB had 'slaughtered us'. We actually meant the title literally. Maureen brought her considerable artistic talents to bear on the front cover, something she had done on all our publications, with an adaptation of a Maureen Scott drawing from the (Maoist) Socialist Artists Collective with whom we also worked. It depicted a helmetless miner in a collapsing cavern. This publication brought me none of the earlier embarrassment of the RWP one and still stands the test of time as a statement of our conditions and socialist perspectives. At the Durham Miners' Gala 131 copies were sold in the one afternoon, and it was very well received.

Meantime our ongoing work even with the most honorary of comrades seen us reading the latest pamphlet by the Workers Institute for the Study of Marxism-Leninism–Mao-Tse-Tung-Thought: *The Trade Unions Are the Defensive Weapons of the Fascist Bourgeoisie!* Our contacts with the Marxist-Leninist Organisation of Britain were proving polemical as one would expect given their arch-Stalinism and our Trotskyism, but we were co-operating well on independent workers' activity and antifascist work. We were even reviewing the whole question of Trotsky v. Stalin, and what we seen as the wider anti-Soviet politics and machinations which could have contributed to the splits within the Soviet party.

17 July 1976. Organised a Miners' Gala Folk Music Social for the Durham Miners' Gala at the Bridge.

24 July 1976. Joel Krieger (later Professor Joel Krieger, and dean of faculty at Wellesley College, Cambridge, Massachusetts) starts his series of Saturday afternoon lectures and instruction on Marxism. These were run at the Miners Welfare every fortnight. These were to become immensely popular and not simply with our own members and sympathisers; honest, down-to-earth members of the Communist Party and some other leftist groups also attended. A number of quite 'ordinary'—well, extraordinary really—rank-and-file miners made the effort. The August seminar advertised around the village and on Doncaster streets was on *The 18th Brumaire of Louis Bonaparte*. The following week it was *The State and Revolution*. We sold all the fundamental Marxist literature as we went along with the course, and several houses in the villages of Dunscroft and Stainforth still boast complete sets of *Capital*, all of which have at least been used and studied. It is no exaggeration to say that the politicisation of this community which had taken firm hold by the 1920s was greatly consolidated and built upon by these lectures and general political life and culture which our comrades and their growing numbers on the periphery were generating. The SUI Marxist class upstairs sometimes had as a backdrop the big colliery band practice downstairs, together with the Saturday afternoon drinkers who at times would wander in to the lectures to sup their pints and listen or raise some point that had just, not very helpfully, occurred to them.

We also noted at this time the continued presence of the National Front in Stainforth, who were almost impossible to identify but left their stickers here and there and were clearly around.

The hard core of this nest of vipers was to remain for the coming thirty years, even contesting elections as either the NF or later the BNP. Although we frequently cut back their support in the community even among their core teenage headbangers, total elimination could only have been achieved by political assassination; there was a time when this was seriously weighed and rejected, at least while they posed only an irritation.

August 1976. Got selected for a Labour Party Summer School at Ruskin. I'm up at Headington again—a pleasant re-encounter with the place, where not much seems to have changed. Lots of intense discussion sitting on the lawn and over dinner and within the big lecture halls. Me versus the Militant, both versus the national education officer who I seem to recall was called Doug and was a canny sort of bloke. The whole school is soured by a so called secret report by Reg Underhill on 'infiltration by Trotskyist groups into the Labour Party'; despite all efforts I couldn't get to see a copy of the document.

The same month, I am 'reported' again to the GMC, this time for SUI leaflets having my address them on and suggesting I am a member of a proscribed organisation—the very idea!

Throughout the early 1980s I attended numerous courses at Ruskin organised by the NUM (for 'Section 123' inspectors[73] or the LPYS or the TUC, all of which saw me cruising the patch as a sagely knowledgeable pub and social scene guide for Oxford's drinking establishments). One event greatly sticks in my mind. It was a joint TUC education course, I think on labour law. I fell in with a gang of mostly NEC blokes and the occasional woman from the other unions; one lad in particular was a prominent member of the NUS, who I think modelled himself on Popeye, judging from his walk, his tattoos and the fishy tales of sea and tempest. I had taken them all downstairs in the Mitre which was awash with foreign tourists and students and as usual jammed to the gunwales. Popeye in the course of the evening produced a perfect £10 note—perfect except on closer inspection HM was giving an out-of-shot (no pun intended) punter some head. Near the end of the night, when we came to order the carryoot to take back to the hall, I took possession of the all-but-perfect £10 and strode up to the bar to order three bottles of wine. The barman, poor sod, who had been rushed off his feet all night, directed me to the offsales bar upstairs in the palatial upper-deck establishment. There were one or two getting served, one white-coated barman taking orders from the high and mighty of the town and gown, and one just taking the bills. I duly ordered my three bottles, two white and a red, deposited them in a carrier bag, handed over the £10 to his mate, and set off calmly toward the door. I had all but got there when a shrill voice intoned 'Excuse me, sir!' and I was summoned, suitably mystified, back to the counter where both barmen stood examining the tenner.

'Was it the wrong price?' I asked innocently. 'If its cheaper, I don't mind the mistake.'

'NO, sir,' and handing me the £10, 'I don't think Her Majesty has ever done that, to anyone.'

Well, shock, white ashen face! Those were genuine, the outrage, was all fake.

'Let me tell yee summit bonny lad,' I lapsed into broad offended Geordie, 'I got that £10 downstairs in your cellar bar, and me mates can prove it.'

We all troops down the wooden staircase where me mates are all sitting, wondering what's up.

'Whats happened?' they ask with concern.

'Yee knaa that bliddy £20 I changed to get that last roond in?'

They all nod and confirm.

'They give us a bliddy fake tenner change!'

'What? A respectable place like this? Well I never ... '

At length the barman admits yes, he is sure I changed a £20 and yes, he could well have given me this modified HM tenner in change. 'I don't have time,' he protested to his gaffer, 'to check every note in the till.'

The manager assured him no harm was done, told him to post the fake £10 note behind the till 'to check any more in the pipeline', then rewarded us by insisting we have the wine for free. Our outrage suitably calmed we left, none the worse. Rogues? Mevie. The border marauder and reiver in the blood is hard to knock oot in the flesh.

LABOUR MOVEMENT DELEGATION TO IRELAND, SEPTEMBER 1976

This had been a major achievement of TOM. The campaign had hitherto hit a wall of silence whenever the question of Ireland was raised within the labour and trade union movement. This campaign was to ensure we would break the silence. First we had committed ourselves to months of work, building up sponsor lists of individuals, organisations and unions, trades councils and political groups who would support a fact-finding delegation to Ireland. The delegates would be drawn from across the whole of the British Labour and Trade Union movement. We would visit people, places and organisations though out Ireland and report back. We had been hugely successful in getting people never previously involved with Ireland to become sponsors, including a great many MPs and a large number of trades councils. I had succeeded in winning Doncaster Trades Council not only to sponsoring the delegation but to financing my attendance on it. Hatfield NUM, which had sponsored the idea, when it came to the visit itself refused to support me. A furious row had broken out at the Branch meeting, which was on the occasion the matter was raised packed to the rafters with men who had turned up over an impending dispute at the pit. Some of the Branch committee played to the crowd, went with the anti-Irish sentiment of the gutter press, denounced the 'mad bombers and murderers', supported our boys out there on the streets of Belfast. Then Les Wood (whom I have already mentioned in connection with garden sheds), a militant committee member of North East origins and from one of those strange pit-and-military families prominent in some northern coalfields, rose to make the condemnation more personal. His lad was serving in Ireland, and I had been involved in a riot involving his lad, and part of a skirmish with his regiment. I was speechless, flattered—but I really had no idea what he was talking about. When it came to the vote, we lost it on the casting vote of the chairman Albert Lovell.[74]

Nonetheless the delegation was on. It was to be truly a most eye opening experience and was perhaps the most important achievement of the whole Troops Out Movement. By the time we left for Ireland we had sixty-five representatives from the British trade union movement, and hundreds of more sponsors who would await our report back. This was the first time since 1914 a British Labour delegation would visit the Irish working class with a view to understanding their situation and their struggles.

The national Labour Movement Delegation to Ireland went ahead. This time I flew from Manchester to Dublin and had none of the previous shenanigans on departure. The first session was hosted at the Mansion House, Dublin, and seen a mass array of speakers from the Irish unions, and left and republican political parties. I got into an in-depth discussion with the representatives of the Irish Republican Socialist Party—as already mentioned, a left break from the 'Officials'—and was suddenly shocked into silence by their anti-abortion stance; I hadn't been expecting this from an avowedly 'Marxist' organisation. I met Nora

Connolly, Jim's daughter, a wily though now old republican and now won completely to the Provos, she told me. It was an incredible honour to sit and talk with this woman; she knew all about the Follonsby Lodge, and the banner and George Harvey. It was like meeting a long-lost relative, people and places were so mutually familiar. Twice as many volunteers from the Irish labour and socialist movement turned up to offer beds and accommodation as were needed, and those without 'guests' seemed really disappointed, so keen were they that we actually got to meet and talk and break through the suffocation of British press propaganda. I spent the evenings with the comrades from Sinn Fein, who I felt were disappointed that many of us were already convinced not only of troops out but also their specific struggles and conclusions. They would rather have had 'your average' British worker to show him and her the facts, I felt—this was the interminable failure of Troops Out as a movement. The following morning we assembled at the Mansion House, to hear a variety of speakers. Mr David Thornley, a member of the Irish parliament and a representative of the Irish Transport and General Workers Union, made a speech of welcome to the delegation. On Sunday morning we journeyed across the border by buses up to South Armagh, and the famous Crossmaglen. This was known as 'bandit country' to the British army. 99.9 per cent of the population here is republican and there was no loyalist presence, so if the army was here to keep the peace, who were they keeping apart? There was no way in here for them and only one way out, usually in a zip-up bag. The lonely outpost was nicknamed 'the Alamo' and the troops had painted it on the corrugated fence. Supplies and troops came in out via helicopter. Still, they occasionally ventured forth into the town, tooled up, vandalising republican slogans and monuments and raiding homes and clubs. They were universally hated. There was a kind of compassion nonetheless for 'rats in a trap', the most recent one of whom to die had been given to dressing in an old coat and riding on an abandoned bike down to the paper shop for some fags and a paper, until the poor old bike and him went bang. Crossmaglen was the only place on the visit where I met Protestant republicans. All the Protestants I met in the town, and I met quite a few, were republicans; they had never experienced any hostility to their religion or their right to go to chapel rather than mass.

Our guides took us to the end of the corner, down from which you could see the corrugated tin sheets and barbed-wire entanglements of the fort. 'This is as far as I can take you,' they told us. 'Right!' shouts Pat Arrowsmith, walking stick in hand, Fairisle jumper on her determined wee body, and little woollen hat on her head; she speaks in the most educated and posh of English accents. 'Right, we'll march down there and demand to speak to the commander of the base!' she announces. 'You can't, Pat. Sure they'll just shoot you down.' 'Who's coming?' she demands. 'OK, the women will form a delegation, a delegation of English women wanting to speak to our troops.' The women shuffled about a bit. 'Sorry Pat, we don't think it wise.' 'Very well,' she says, 'I'll go!' And off she strides, faithful walking stick at her side. First we see the gun barrels poke out of the holes, and then we hear Pat's salvo: 'Come out of there! I demand to talk to you at once!' I swear as the guns are pulled back in through the windows they conclude 'Bloody hell! It's Pat Arrowsmith!' Not content with haranguing them outside, she starts walking round the fort, bashing the corrugated tin sheets with her stick and shouting 'I am a British trade unionist, and I want to know what you think you are doing in my name in someone else's country!' Nobody comes out. Finally Pat tells them they have no choice but to leave! One can only reflect on the comments inside that iron vault, at that suggestion.

I am with my Sinn Fein comrades from Dublin and at times outside the main organisation of the delegation. We stay at the home of an old republican widow. She reminds me of my grandma Nelson. When it is time for bed she shows me the downstairs spare room. 'There's some grand fellers slept there in that wee bed so there was,' adding: 'All killed now. Stayed here on their way up yon.' She nodded in the direction of the north. I guess she thought we were an IRA cell en route to armed struggle in the north, like so many of 'the boys' who had slept there previously. It was an odd honour sharing this bed with the ghosts of so many brave lads, and me just a talker.

We next journey up to Belfast, and the occupation hits you like a brick. The buses are pulled over, armed troops board each one, drivers are taken off and questioned, organisers argue with officers. Armoured cars roll by, jeeps with troops carrying machine-guns trace the shoppers as they pass. We stay at Andersontown and hold our first big northern meeting in the club. This club like all the clubs has wire fences to stop bombs, has barricades around the doors to stop car bombs, has barbed-wire enclosures and security gates and antechambers. Folk come here for a night out. I have a go at the SDLP, which is nicknamed 'Stay Down Low, Paddy,' on account of their attitude to resistance, and there is a marvellous shot of me on me hind legs doing just that, but for the fact that one of the female delegates in the background is sound asleep. Well it was a late and hectic and boozy set of nights, and early mornings, I suppose.

I take time to meet 'progressive' elements of the loyalist militia. This isn't part of the tour or the delegation; it is eye-opening and shocking, but we must find some resonance within the loyalist community, must start to rediscover the progressive and revolutionary wings of the Protestant community in the North, and there was a proud tradition of course, until it was ruthlessly suppressed, as it still is. IRA–UDA, IRA–UVF meetings do take place, there is a dialogue if only to discover who really shot who, and why, and who has been killed by the British army posing as one side or the other. This was particularly true during the first IRA ceasefire when political progress with the government was making real advances: elements of the special forces tried on a number of occasions to start 'tit-for-tat' sectarian killing, by assassinating members of the respective communities and implying it had been one side or the other, and joint meetings effectively identified which killings were coming from 'the third force'.

On the third evening (19 September) of the visit, while we were enjoying a social at Andersonstown Social Club, the army raided the Michael Sloan Working Men's Club at Ballymurphy. They marched in guns in hand saying they were looking for members of the IRA. The club committee members advised everyone to stay seated and not be provoked. The troops marched around the tables, kicking chairs, abusing everyone, swearing at everyone for a full 30 minutes but got no response. The working population of this community knew to bite their tongue. The troops then, walking backwards in a permanent challenge as they do, headed towards the door as if to leave. Meantime people had come into the club, but because of the raid and not knowing quite what else to do were just standing by the door. The troops didn't like them standing there and started without warning to batter people out of the way with their rifle butts. A number went to the floor with head injuries and broken limbs before the crowd started to fight back. In a matter of minutes troops had fired first plastic bullets and then live rounds into the unarmed people at the door and then sprayed the room with gunfire as people fell to the floor. The poor old club cocker-spaniel running around barking in fear and confusion was sprayed with bullets in an act of pure vindictiveness and lay splattered on the floor. As a delegation we were in time to see the mayhem and the blood and the wounded and the poor dead dog. The army offered the delegation no explanation for its actions other than that some of their men had been hurt that evening, but declined to comment on whether that was after they started battering people, or even whether it had been before they entered the club. It crossed my mind that this was a raid for our benefit, to show they couldn't give a monkey's what we thought.

When we reconvened to discuss the whole picture and everything we had seen and heard, as if by way of further illustration our bus was overhauled by two light tanks and an army Land-Rover bristling with automatic weapons pointed up at us. A tank at the rear, a tank at the front, the open-topped Land-Rover pulled up on the pavement side of the road next to the door of the bus. Two big commandos get on with blackened faces and little Sten-gun things at the ready. We are questioned and told, 'People on this bus have been seen taking photos. Taking photos is not allowed in Belfast!'

We agreed there were three solutions to the war in Ireland. One, leave things as they are. Two, allow the loyalist majority in the one and a half or two counties of Ulster to secede from Britain and Ireland but maintain a special relationship, something more than Gibraltar, with Britain. Or three, recognise Ireland as a sovereign, indivisible nation of thirty-two counties, comprising Protestant and Catholic, believer and non-believer, north and south, from loyalist and republican traditions. It was our unanimous decision that only the third option was really viable and sensible and just. Truthfully, for nearly all of us this had been a reinforcing of that conviction rather than some new-found revelation, although for some, including a former British Army general, it was.

4 October 1976. We staged a showing of Cinema Action's *The Miners' Film* at the Drum. We advertised it in all the local press, and followed the screening with a folk social the guest star of which was Charles Parker, who as mentioned earlier had been the co-inventor of the Radio Ballads with MacColl and Seeger. He had given a performance at the Miners' Gala of his stage performance '*A Miner's Story*',

both of which were greatly taken by the mining families in the audience.

December 1976. I start the first of a series of *Republican News* Readers' Meetings at the Bridge in Newcastle as a sounding board to establish a Sinn Fein Cumann in the region. It becomes the James Connolly Cumann—what else?

Sinn Fein were advancing their vision of a future island of Ireland in the radical and socialist programme Eire Nua:

> [D]ividing Ireland into four provinces with strong regional parliaments is confronting the problem face to face. One of the facts we have got to face is that no citizen of the six counties of the north, whether he is orange or green, Catholic or Protestant is going to accept the Dublin government thrust upon them in a governing capacity. The northern people would resent being passed from one domineering system to another—with the new authorities being as unfamiliar with local problems as the government across the Irish Sea. For this reason the republican movement have never claimed to want 'Irish Unity' if by that one means joining the six counties to the twenty six counties. Republicans fully realise that a new Ulster, like a new Ireland, requires creative government. This eliminates the government of Dublin as it presently exists. There they have had one-party government similar to that of one-party domination in the north with the one exception that the 'republic' has had an opposition that was able to interrupt its rule twice over the last forty years of its power. The government of Dublin is as stale as that of Stormont was before being brought down and deep down as indifferent as that of London. The indifference of both London and Dublin has prolonged the agony of the north. There has never been any real pressure from either government to have a settlement—only guarded words.

Their idea was to bring along with them the people of the four-county loyalist tradition, into a united nine-county Ulster Province, where together they would exercise an autonomy and control over their futures within a federal Ireland. For a time, sections of the loyalist movement, particularly those who would describe themselves as socialists, toyed with this notion. At joint meetings both sides agreed they had probably more in common, even with their mutual adversity with each other, than those 'down south', and that together they could speak truly for Ulster as a whole. I believe that during this period we all actually came closer to a principled and just solution to the Irish war than at any time before or since.

Despite widespread and indiscriminate murder of Catholic men, women and children, in a purely sectarian targeting of the Catholic population, the Provos struggled hard to keep their sights set, not against 'Protestants' or people from the loyalist communities in general, but on their guerrilla war against the occupation forces and British commerce.

The republican movement was maturing and perhaps hardening a little against what it might consider either 'hostile borders' on the inside or self-appointed alternative leaders on the outside. Certainly later years of industrial struggle would lead us to adopt a similar caution with our comrades who had come to take their self-assured position as our leaders. We ourselves in Doncaster Troops Out Movement had been more than annoyed by the ad-hoc character of the way TOM had worked. At first it was an alliance of organisations and individuals, but then it linked itself extraneously to other groups too. Doncaster's resolution to the National Delegate Conference, 23 April 1977, moved by Maureen, set our position straight:

The TOM is an organisation made up of groups and individuals who agree on the two principles of TOM:

A. Withdrawal of troops immediately.

B. Self determination for the Irish people.

but may disagree strongly on other issues. Joint rallies and meetings do not mean that in order to advertise the TOM event, propaganda for the other participating organisations has to be distributed by comrades who may disagree with that organisation. Conference does not accept 'special relationships' within TOM.

Conference recognises that reasons of finance were involved in making a decision for the joint Bloody Sunday Rally with the SWP, but believes that finance should not sway the TOM into 'special alliances' and that TOM should maintain its independent organisational intentions.

It was passed 9 to 1 following a walkout, but they knew we would pass it if they had stayed.

Other important resolutions were that we aim to put a TOM branch in every union at every level, and that we send representatives to Ireland to explain the dispute with 'the groups'.

In among all this, a little time later United TOM was started by the dissident groups. SUI decided it couldn't ignore this development and affiliated to both 'old' TOM and UTOM. They couldn't really exclude 'old' TOM so they affiliated too, saying 'If there are some new initiatives out there we haven't thought of yet, by all means lets have them.'

April 1977. We produce *Egypt: The January Events* written by our 'Egyptian Caucus' and marking the explosion of wrath among the Egyptian working class in response to government announcements of price rises on all the basic necessities of life, hitherto actually subsidised; this a direct instruction from the IMF to President Sadat.

Easter 1977. Extended arms training course in Rothbury. We have the use of the big old farm labourer's cottage in an abandoned wood. A great old coal fire, which we bank up with logs chopped from the fallen trees. I discover an ancient bell pit, and with a little howkin aboot in the burn gully I find a thin coal seam, about three inches thick. I manage to 'mine' about three big sacks; it fair deadens the fire, but keeps its heart red and hot while were out on manoeuvres or at the pub. A poke when we return causes a great rush of flame and heat to be released. In the grounds and woods we practice karate, pole fighting, stick fighting, mass attacks and defence. Up on the moors a dozen guns blaze away at targets as we dive for cover and advance on our targets. We shoot for hours per day. Were we observed? At least once a police squad car surged by and looked surprised at the line of advancing guerrillas with their red and black neckerchiefs and bandoliers, but we thought they thought we were a clay pigeon club or the local toffs out for grouse-shooting. A few times we heard the ominous flatter-flatter of a police helicopter but we always went to ground before it spotted us. Actually we had guns trained on it as it hovered just above the ground; we could have brought it down, but what would have been the point at this stage in the struggle? It would have been simple bravado and served no tactical purpose. We completed extensive search-and-find programmes which involved heavy map-reading skills, not always mastered as I recall. With us on the course was Andy, a Belfast Protestant socialist, a city kid who had done no training of any kind. He had never climbed a mountain, never trekked thirty miles through wet heather, never slept out under a rock, or depended upon his map-reading skills to get him to pub before closing. The day we met up at the Bridge before the start of the course, in came Andy. His face was a mass of pepper shot, his skin cut in a thousand places, his eye red and swollen, his cheek blue with deep bruising.

'What the fuck?'

'Your IRA bastards blew me up!' he announced, none too pleased.

He had been walking down the high street on an afternoon, when a shop was suddenly blown up; he caught the blast across the road. Andy, seen the politics of the IRA struggle, couldn't see the route through their current armed struggle for Protestant workers like himself. I was at pains to explain the strategy behind his poor face. I thought at first it couldn't be the boys, not without any warning or anything. Warning or no, it had been them.

That he well 'stuck to his guns' and came on the course spoke volumes for his courage and dedication. The course had included hand-to-hand fighting, karate, staffs, sticks, knives. Maureen trying to batter me with a stick caused much amusement with Malc her brother, until it was his turn. The theory class, with the fire and newly mined duff roaring up the chimney, was Ché's *Urban Guerrilla Warfare* and *The strategy, politics and tactics of the Red Army Fraction.*[75]

The conclusion of the course was to be a forced march from Rothbury to Seahouses; I announced it on the evening of the night before. One of our erstwhile comrades bottled out, but unable to take it, and unable to admit it, invented the most tragic story, after we got to the local pub, that he had been on the phone, that his kid was dying, that he had to get home. We went into overdrive and pulled together all our wit, not to mention what scarce cash and petrol we had, to get him back there.

Had I believed it? At first, but as this cadre buckled under pressure and started to show strange ambivalent signs towards the group in general and me in particular I doubted it, then disbelieved it. The courses were meant to do just this; trouble was, once they were rejected some former cadres become poisoned and untrustworthy, even going over to the other side. In a real revolutionary situation that is the time to part company in a permanent fashion with such elements, as had been the case over the water in Ireland.

July we establish contact with the Free Wales Army.[76]

To our view the United Kingdom isn't a country, it is a state which dominates the different nationalities and people of this island, it is the alliance of the 'British' ruling class aimed at subjugating all the people of the island. The dominant nationality within the ruling class is 'English' and it is the English section of that alliance which does best out of and is most favoured. As revolutionaries we wanted the utter destruction of 'the United Kingdom' as a political concept and ruling-class instrument. We supported all efforts of the peoples of the older Celtic nations to break free of this kingdom, whether that was Ireland, or Scotland or Wales, or even distinct and self-conscious sections such as Cornwall or Northumbria. Self-determination for the Irish people as a whole was our principle, we could do no other than extend that same principle to the people of Wales and Scotland, or any of the regions. Of course we favoured a socialist Wales, and a socialist Ireland, but this wasn't a precondition. We had earlier staged a dynamic conference in Newcastle to determine our position towards the developing independence struggle in Scotland. Gavin Kennedy had spoken for the Scottish National Party, a big branch of which, we were surprised to find existed at Morpeth. Old Tom Murray from the Workers Party of Scotland told us he had first visited 'the toon' in 1919. The presentation which coincided with the May Day march, and was held at the Bridge, drew furious debate, not least from Jim Murray, the famous militant joint convenor of Vickers factories and yards, who launched a furious attack against what he seen as forces 'splitting the unity of the British working class' and 'tartan Toryism'.

2–3 July. The 'NEW' Troops Out Movement, United TOM, holds its founding conference and as a part of the conscious decision the leftists within Sinn Fein had decided to take the socialist message of the organisation into the British working class and address the British left and trade union movement. Jim Reilly, the most influential and respected leader of Sinn Fein Britain, made a draft address to the Troops Out Movement. It took head-on all the resolutions being advanced at the United Troops Out conference, and presented Sinn Fein's view. To the best of my knowledge that had never been done before. There is not really the space nor perhaps the need to reproduce that whole document, and it is available in the archives for those who wish to see it, but one question which was to become more vexed as time has gone on can do, for clarity, with reproducing— namely Marxism and the republican movement. Jim needless to say was an Irish industrial Marxist and socialist worker.

That the Republican Movement Neglects the Marxist Philosophy in the Socialist Struggle

It has never been denied that Marx played a part in Ireland's fight from British domination in the nineteenth century. His help particularly in respect of the Fenian prisoners has been well chronicled. Although his involvement didn't produce the desired effects, it did introduce an international flavour into the Irish struggle. If any fault lies in Marxism, it is that very little effort has been made to update the teachings of Marx to the present day environment. We feel that Marxism has been allowed to stand still for too long, allowed to 'mature'. When anything matures for too long it begins to rot. Had Marx come to England during the reign of Elizabeth 2 rather than Victorian Regina, the Communist Marx-festo would have never been written. However no sane republican would deny the genius of Karl Marx. His expose of capitalism would be ignored at our peril. We accept he predicted the changing face and increasing menace of capitalism. We accept that capitalism and the greed of individuals, which capitalism breeds, to be the underlying cause for Ireland's plight.

Some of the papers submitted for the Troops Out Open Conference explain the situation admirably. The rundown of investment in the north, increased British investment in the 'Republican' (sic) South. No wonder the loyalist is bewildered.

It is not the purpose of this paper to pontificate on the good or otherwise of Marx on capitalism. Suffice to say that any republican worth his salt holds fast to the teaching of the great socialist and republican James Connolly, leader of the Irish Citizens Army, who was executed by the British for his part in the 1916 uprising. Connolly was a Marxist, a man of his own time, and a man of our time. Connolly formed the first Workers' Militia in Europe, because he knew that political action alone would not be enough. The ruling classes would not give up without a struggle. Connolly knew he would get justice, out of the barrel of a gun.

The Easter Rebellion was the most successful failure of recent times. It brought the common man into the Freedom Struggle, it restored his dignity, the dignity of nationhood. It taught our people 'Better to die on your feet than live on your knees.' Connolly died but his spirit lives on. The words and teachings of Connolly live on:

"If you remove the English army tomorrow and hoist the green flag over Dublin castle, unless you set about the organisation of the Socialist Republic, your efforts would have been in vain. England would still rule you through her capitalists, through her landlords, through her financiers, through the whole array of commercial and industrial institutions they have planted in this country and matured with the tears of our mothers and the blood of our martyrs. England would still rule you to your ruin, even while your lips offered hypocritical homage at the shrine of that Freedom whose cause you betrayed.'

This is the teaching of a man who is our guiding principle. That is the teaching which was ignored in 1921 and again in 1969/70/71 by the stickies/Officials and again in 1972/3 by Gerry Fitt and his SDLP crew. 'Hypocritical homage at the shrine of that Freedom whose cause you betrayed.' Connolly betrayed by political opportunists whose idea of Socialism is more free handouts on the dole.

It is any wonder that the defenders of the principles of Connolly are selective in membership intake. We and we alone hold fast to the ideal, a free united Socialist Republic, we will have no less.

... The Eire Nua document is available for all to read. Our policy has been stated and restated time and time again. Perhaps it's the case of 'There are none so blind as those who will not see.'

Provisional Sinn Fein.

7 August 1977. Sinn Fein public rally in London. I have the great privilege of speaking at the rally for Sinn Fein. I had done this twice at major rallies in Glasgow and one in Edinburgh at a rally organised by the First of May team, but this was the first truly national open-air platform for the movement I had spoken on. I remember because there was a lack of anywhere to put spent notes; I just let them blow away as I finished with them, which was not a good idea as people in the crowd thought they were the notes I needed and set off retrieving them. The speech itself was greatly appreciated. The bulk of the 300 people on the demonstration were members or families of Sinn Fein members; only about 75 of the so-called 'left' bothered to intervene into this demonstration, showing the lack of commitment and understanding they have of the process. We consciously discuss the growth of socialist ideas and election of socialist leaders to key positions within the movement. One of the comrades who has been in since its inception tells me it was scarcely possible before to think like a caucus, although actually we aren't that organised, we aren't a tendency, we see the struggle as for the whole organisation and believe we are anyway pushing at an open door. When I spoke at that rally I spoke clearly as a revolutionary Marxist member of Sinn Fein, as an official PSF speaker at an official Sinn Fein rally and on a Sinn Fein platform. I spoke to the British left and slated them on their failure of Marxism; I spoke of the struggle with the republican movement as part of the overall workers movement in the world. No big hook at any time came from stage right to pull me off, there were no disapproving shakes of the head or tut-tuts. It never dawned on me that I needed to formally acknowledge that Sinn Fein wasn't a Marxist organisation as such; from my point of view and the view of the group that had bugger all to do with it at this stage.

Meantime we are honoured by a letter from Michael Holden at the end of August:

There certainly seems to be a real break through everywhere on the question of Ireland. I must say Dave you and your wife are really involved in a big way and doing a great job at every opportunity. If we could only get more of our members involved in this work there is no end to what could be accomplished.[77]

The Seventh Cavalry, it is said, boasted a Geordie scout. Charging back to the column, Custer asks, 'Are those war drums?', to which he replied, 'Ah diviknaa to be sure, but Ah think they're their buggers.' Bob Hart was that Geordie scout! Always crouched up some rock chimney, bivouacked out in thick bracken or wriggling along some hole in a rock, he was bold, red-faced from howling gales and blistering sun. He worked oil rigs, sank pit shafts, steeplejacked, dug up roads, navvied on building-sites or worked as a tunneller. Always around the scene, never at the centre of it, politically at any rate, his views were those which pragmatically occurred to him. He had no time for anything which didn't relate to his common-sense evaluation of things he had experienced, hated theory, hated intellectuals and the middle class.

A nicer man when sober one couldn't hope to meet. Generous to a fault, he would give you the shirt off his back and share with you his last pound so long as you were drinking it. But Bob could be a different man when drunk. When the broon was in, Bob was a bull at a gate, on any subject he could lock his horns into.

We were sitting in the front bar of the Bridge one sunny dinner time, Bob already flushed with the broon dog and pulling faces as he tried with great difficulty to work out some mental equation, when into the bar comes a pack of bikers. At this stage the bikers were going through their transition from being Teds on wheels to becoming hippies on wheels, and greased-back hair and white socks still cut a dash. So did the aura of impending violence and rock-hardness. The air resounded to loud laughter and bike-speech. Bob sets his glare upon them, listens to the crack for ten minutes or so, then rocks to his feet.

'Bob, man, fuck's sake, Bob, man!' I try to distract him, too late.

'Ah bet yees, nen o' yees, could set ya bike away, ower the High Level, then stand up straight.'

'Aah, and fucking lumberjack man, yee can?'

'Aye, and fucking torn roond.'

As they all turned to each other with sarcastic laughs and open-handed appeals to unseen umpires, Bob walks past the table at which some are sitting, snatches up a set of bike keys and strides to the door.

'Huw, huw', the lad whose bike is about to be seized jumps to his feet, while the others follow on through the door, shouting 'Let him gaan, let him splatter hisell!' Bob is nearly fallin' ower the bike as he kick starts. It is suddenly roaring up in a wide semicircle past the keep, oot onto the road and off ower the High Level, where incredibly, beyond belief, he stands bolt upright, then does a spin and faces back toward us, waving in a slow rhythmic bon voyage gesture, as he resquats the bike and revs off out of sight. For a moment there is stunned silence. It crosses my mind he's nicked the bike and I should start departing stage left, when suddenly in the distance a roaring speck is bouncing back ower the bridge towards us, fortunately sitting down this time. He leans expertly into a curve and skids to a halt, hoying the keys to the gob-smacked bike-owner while jumping from the bike. A genuine and hearty round of applause breaks from the assembly of black leather and heads shek in sheer disbelief. Mine too. He puts his arms roond me shoulder as we reach the bar door.

'Didn't yee knaa I was in the Royal Corps of Signals display team?'

As we swept away from a raggy-arsed working-class hippyism and sort of love-everyone quasi-pacifism towards the 'oil the rifles and pass the ammunition' working-class revolutionism, but love (almost) everybody, well shag (almost) everybody as well, Bob stayed where he was. The trouble with arguing with Bob about the need for armed insurrection was that he'd get mad and punch ya heed in, crying as oft as no: 'Whey, ahl yee need is love, man.' While we lost contact with Bob, only once a flood seeing him at Christmas doon the Bridge as the dispersed tribes of Northumbria rebel youth from factories, pits, colleges and trekking the world came together in drunken embraces and Peggy Garden, one o' Bob's favourite songs, and doing a sort of hokey-kokey to the Internationale, fifty strang underneath the keep at New Year's Eve, to the accompaniment of clanking broon-ale bottles and breaking glass, deep-throat necking and the odd puke-up, everything was fine. But in later years some of us came off the drawing-board and started to train actively, guns in hand, for the forthcoming revolutionary encounter. Bob, when he got wind of this, would not like it. It would have been enough to keep his reed jaunty face chuntering in his broon many a neet. But word was we were training in his bonny Northumberland Cheviots! In the Sierra Mestra that might be fine and dandy, but the Cheviots! Bob, the Geordie scout bar nen, set off te find the secret guerrillas.

It was not without a little humour, as we literally cleared the bolts on the rifles and ran through the maps to locate wa target areas, that Bob descended upon wi like a bliddy aud Geordie bloodhoond.

This was a dilemma, and an ideological tautology. This was a for-real military manoeuvre. These cadres were training for working-class revolution and resistance to the armed repression we expected from the state, and in defence of fully active military units of the world revolution. This was Bob, in his lumberjack-red tartan shirt and braces, his corduroy pants and woolly hat, yanking a rifle from a cadre's hands and hoyin' it away. Oh aye, he was pissed. The week-lang search through freezing mists and driving rain, searching the night skyline for signs of smoke, and under rocks for fresh cacks, hadn't sobered him up any. The broon was undeniably in and his blood was up. For a moment or two, while we were in the steely-eyed Bolshevik mode, he was nearly shot right there.

Two things saved him. First, this wasn't a revolutionary situation. We weren't in the revolution, we were a training unit, an embryonic team preparing for revolution. This was insulting, fucking awkward, a bit humiliating, an' downright counter-revolutionary, but Bob bending all the barrels of the rifles as he had threatened wasn't actually going to alter the fate of the revolution. Second, this was fucking Bob, man!

As Bob made to grab for another gun, we spotted his armoury of a dozen broon-ale bottles bulging from his rucksack, and started redistributing them. He couldn't hold onto his broon and grab the guns, not now we were back in focus. A rough and tumble and wrestling match ensued in the mud and snow while we hurriedly gathered back the guns, leaving a couple of Bob's closer compadres to crack a few jars and angrily argue the route of the revolution against Bob's attempts to thump them, heed them and deck them while slugging as much of his broon as he could.

The armed caucus meantime withdrew to a distant venue to continue the course. A process of elimination would in time have disclosed us afresh, but Bob had made his point. He had, he thought dispersed and disarmed us. And in any case, coming face to face with so many of his old comrades, whom he had not hitherto known were involved, disheartened him. Neither he nor we slept easily as to the choices we had made in this dilemma.

The Ard Feis this year (1977) was the best yet since the foundations of the Provisional movement. It followed big debates within the pages of *An Phoblacht* about the need to advance socialist policies within the movement. Jammy Drumm at the Bodenstown funeral address this year had talked of the revolutionary socialist nature at the heart of the struggle and the need to develop strong links with the working class and radical trade unionists.

Gerry Cassidy (Sinn Fein—Yorkshire) was to respond to our proposition for a joint internal meeting with a view to some sort of fusion on 23 March (1978):

Your venue for the meeting looks interesting and promising and could very well form the foundation for stronger links with provisional Sinn Fein. I will let Jim Reilly the Ard Comhairle representative see your letter on Sunday. Jim for your information is a Marxist Socialist but his stature as militant republican is beyond challenge. You will find that you and him have a lot in common.

In fact a month later Jim was telling me:

You are no doubt aware of the differences of opinion between Sinn Fein and IMG/SWP. This is due to a change on their part. We are coming to a stage in the Revolution when support groups must totally commit themselves. So far we are doing OK grassroots wise. (Letter from Jim Reilly, 13 April 1978)

Both IMG and IS had simultaneously though separately come to the decision that their main objective was to build their own organisations. They would no longer spend time and energy on joint, ad-hoc, broad-front campaigns.

This they started to apply to Ireland and in particular the Troops Out Movement. *Red Weekly*, the IMG paper, had as a policy decision stopped covering and publicising our events and stopped participating in them or even publishing formal letters from us to their letters page. This followed a bust-up with 'the groups' led in the main by our old sparring partners Big Flame. Big Flame had charged that we didn't do mass work with the working class, but spent our time in lobby work of Parliament, the Labour Party and the Unions. Big Flame through its distorted mirror couldn't see that actually they were a tiny sect who probably thought about 20 was 'mass' and didn't realise initiatives like the Labour Movement Delegation to Ireland had engaged the trade union movement the length and breadth of Britain in debate and arguing the questions posed by Ireland and where the British Labour movement would stand. They called this 'lobbying', so the Tribunal on War Crimes, aimed as it was at securing as many 'big' names from the world of international politics and justice and science and as well as from other areas of influence, was politically anathema. IMG, which had been a lukewarm supporter of TOM as time went by, joined this walkout, as did IS, though to be right they had only kept a watching presence for some time.

Early on, members of International Marxist Group Irish Commission had left TOM; they concluded that a Troops Out Movement could not in fact be built and they announced that from now on they would provide an independent initiative. We are still waiting for it to come. They at first opposed the Labour Movement Delegation but then joined it again when they seen the success it was having; however they caused problems within the visiting teams when they tried to change the agenda and itinerary in order to meet members of the UDA and other loyalist groups.

By August relations with the left were on the skids. The Prisoners Aid Committee in particular was outraged at the wall of silence from our erstwhile comrades on the left and those liberal conscience. They began a programme of exposure, picketing the SWP bookshop, the offices of the CPGB's *Morning Star* and offices of Amnesty International (AI), which we now retitled Amnesia Ireland. For the SWP to have a noisy prisoners' picket at their HQ was quite an embarrassment.[78]

With regards our SUI/Sinn Fein political proximity it is not ultimately clear what happened to this process. In fact it was confirmed by subsequent correspondence from the leadership of the organisation that my membership was not revoked and was firmly accepted. I think Sinn Fein was debating whether it could accept an organisation such as ours as an affiliate, or sympathetic body. The politics of Sinn Fein were highly fluid at this period, and nobody had asserted a repressive grip or 'a line' on who could be in and out and which politics were 'in' or 'out'. Republican politics were never just what appeared on paper. The political wing had been highly confused in the beginning as to what its politics were and were not, and the translation of everyday meanings into political jargon hadn't helped. The different geopolitical locations and traditions across provisional politics produced what was at first a confused alliance. The politics of the north by and large were in sharp revolutionary socialist contrast to the 'green' and Catholic politics of the south. But this was a movement;, it was responding to all the influences around it and to the conditions of civil war it had been born into and was growing in. During this time the left was certainly on the ascendancy; this was due to its own internal process as well as the interesting 'second front' of socialist ideas and influence coming from the cumann in Britain. The London cumann and those based in solidly industrial trade union Irish communities with strong socialist ideas and culture, who seen socialism and republicanism as obvious and synonymous, were also either influential in the colouration or else perhaps at least symptomatic of it. The policies of the party at this time included work in the unions of both islands, and a recognition of the centrality of the working class now and for the future shape of a new Ireland. Winning support— genuine, in-its-own-right support—from the revolutionary left, as an agent of influence and information for the British working class, was a recognised task of the movement within three years of its formation. Gerry Adams, I am sure, once confided to me that he too was a 'a Marxist', and certainly as time went on he spoke like one, and talked publicly and at internal rallies of the need to build a revolutionary alternative. 'We must ensure that the cause of Ireland becomes the cause of Labour, a task neglected since Connolly's time and we must also ensure that the cause of labour become the cause of Ireland' (*An Phoblacht*, 23 June

1979). This had been Connolly's phrase; Adams was calling for nothing short than the implementation of its direction, a direction which as he said had been subservient to the 'cause of Ireland' per se. As it happened we considered our party in Ireland to be Sinn Fein, we urged that all Irish workers join that party and fight for an anti-capitalist programme within it. We likewise began to see that all British–Irish communities here should see Sinn Fein as their party and urge all Irish and mixed-Irish workers within those communities to join. To this end I had been cleared to organise Sinn Fein Cumann directly, so the question of our actual physical affiliation as an organisation withered on the vine. We would soon have joint members anyway, arguing our programme within Sinn Fein. We had matured enough to recognise long ago that class consciousness and revolutionary political programmes were processes, they did not come ready made tied up with a pink ribbon. Provisional Sinn Fein represented a genuine anti-imperialist struggle and was composed of thousands of Irish workers many of whom were developing a stark understanding of the world revolutionary process, and where they fitted into it, and a deeper understanding of class struggle as it manifested itself in this Irish liberation struggle. There were many other less-enlightened attitudes, cultures and tendencies. All we demanded was the right to fight for our perspectives within the overall movement. As the political struggle within that body developed some of our more right-leaning and conservative fellow members of the republican movement would see this as too strong a plank for the left, and more particularly too open to outside influence by other leftist organisations.

30 March 1979. House of Commons, London. Airey Neave, then Conservative spokesperson on Northern Ireland, was killed by a bomb attached to his car as he left the car park at the House of Commons. It went off just after 3 p.m. on a Friday afternoon as he drove his Vauxhall Cavalier up a ramp from the Commons underground car park. The Irish National Liberation Army (INLA) claimed responsibility. If he had lived Neave would have been highly likely to become Secretary of State for Northern Ireland in the new Conservative government. Neave was a secret planner of 'the shoot to kill' policy where the SAS or others just go out and shoot the people who they believe are in the IRA. The bombing, wonderfully executed and we thought at the time a shining example of very particular targeted armed struggle should be, none the less reaped a whirlwind. British special forces shot dead a leading IRSP member, Miriam Daly, and two highly placed officers of the INLA, Ronnie Bunting and Noel Lyttle. Bunting interestingly enough was a Protestant socialist, the son of a leading Paisleyite. His wife was severely wounded in the assassination too. John Turnley, also assassinated, was another leading Protestant republican, leader of the National H Blocks Committee and a founder member of the constitutionalist Irish Independence Party. Coincidentally he was killed at Carnlough where me and Maureen and Emma had been on holiday just the year before. At the time, the movement thought the killings were the UDA, but as time passed it became clear the targets were too specific and it had probably been the SAS.

Back on the mental health front it was clear that to get myself free of this drug dependency and my mental straitjacket a long break from the pit and perhaps some of the political work was necessary. Dr Waters had suggested in a throwaway comment, 'Why don't you return to your studies?' It struck and resonated a chord. A word or two with Raph and I had a list of all the university courses in Britain, and narrowed that down to history, industrial relations and law. Only three had that as a sort of combination, and one of them was Strathclyde University in Glasgow. Well, my Dad had always maintainéd that if you had to move, always go north, 'because the north of anywhere is always better than the south of anywhere' and I have always found that to be the case.

Strathclyde became my university. I started in October 1976. I was privileged as 'a mature student' and one from 'away' to get one of the much sought-after student residences—13b, 105 Birkbeck Court, Cathedral Road, Glasgow. This first year I share the accommodation with: Jeff, a classic old beatnik, now hippie, jazz bass-player vegetarian from doon sooth. An Egyptian Arab who shouts the Koran throughout the day. A Saudi student who tells me off for joining in each time he lets rip; I think it hilarious fun and fall aboot laughing, but he thinks it very disrespectful. A young Indian and an old Indian. I think the university accommodation folk had judged that we all were vegetarians, or somehow had similar diets, and could live in close proximity to each other in harmony. It was not to be, though not in any way you might imagine.

This time at the student fair I would throw myself in lock, stock and barrel and partake of all the amusements of student life which I had forsaken at Ruskin. I joined the Business Administration Club; the Athletics Club, citing karate, aikido and rifle as my interests; the Scottish Arab Friendship Society; the Broad Left; the Scottish Republican Socialist Club. I later formed and was president of the Industrial Relations Study Group. I became the life and soul of every party at the Union, particularly after being elected a member to the Student Council. I was always on tap and always running things. There weren't many discos I missed most nights of the week. I was strutting my stuff. I intended to actually sit these exams and pass them, dedicated myself to eight hours per day of study, come what may. The hub of the whole Union was the Trade and Finance Committee. I was elected to sit on it, a rare privilege for a first year. I sat with the vice president Steve Kelly, a 'bough' Yorkshire lad, and the administration officer, a full-time staff member, quiet, intellectual and incidentally Catholic. I mention that because relations with staff were not always harmonious and I discovered the shop steward was a heart-and-soul Orangeman, who never wasted an opportunity to snipe away at the admin officer. Steve more often than not was up to his armpits in running the Union and I almost invariably came to chair the finance meetings, for the three years. With a budget of £1.5 million per annum, driving this big and complex machine became one of the joys of my life.

I burst upon the Strathclyde student scene with something of a crash. My views were already fully formed and forceful. I swatted down the arguments of the student right and doubters, I proclaimed the common sense of the revolutionary road to socialism. I chided the moderate, the liberal, the middle-of-the-roader socialist, and appeared unassailable at least from the point of view of my working-class credentials. Most of these students were straight from school, although among the left many had come from strong working-class and socialist traditions. This university was an industrial study centre. It rested upon the granite proletarian rock of Glasgow and sat in its heart. The 'kids' here didn't speak with plummy English accents, they were Scots. This was my kind of university and my kind of town. Mind, it took only a few weeks before I started to detect the difference in twang between working-class and middle-class Glaswegian. The 'Kelvinside' Miss Jean Brodie voice of the middle-class Scot and the middle-class Glaswegian was soon quite audible to me.

I couldn't believe it: the left and the reds of all descriptions would sit and booze with the young Tories. Tories! I had never ever really met a Tory in my life; drink with one? I was consumed with hatred for such scum, except it was hard to tell who was who. They didn't sound like Tories, they spoke by and large with Glasgow accents, they dressed just like students, they went to the discos, they told jokes and got off with one another. I was soon ushered into the 'Ents' office. One of the semi-autonomous sections of the Union enterprise, the Entertainments Committee was the engine-room of the Union. The biggest section was the Athletic Society and most students joined at least one section of that; it was the biggest expenditure, it was the 'loss leader', but the bread and butter of the organisation was this Entertainments Committee.

Wee Dave was the chairman. He sat behind his desk and rolled a big magnificent joint on his big blotting paper pad. He had a funny sort of crinkled face, he was small and dressed like the youngster he was but he looked prematurely old, a fast-talking Glaswegian, always joking, always laughing. He put his feet up on the desk, took a lang toke, then passed it over to me. 'Ah want te explain things Davie,' he started. Amid great gulps and slow releases of smoke, he explained he was a prominent member of the Strathtory group! He had realised that to me, from my background, such folk as him would be extraterrestrial. He offered 'Ah dinnet suppose yiv sat and smoked dope wi a Tory before?' Well, a lang lang, chinwag at least led me not to want to hit him on the nose anymore, but that didn't stop me being the main spokesperson against any policy or position coup they attempted. But as luck would have it, the trend was moving in our direction;, the student body as a whole was marching left, though not entirely.

Soon after I got there I addressed a meeting of thousands of Strathclyde students at their AGM in support of a resolution to send buses and money down to the Grunwick strikers. This was a battle royal, with the Tories getting up denouncing the unions, and me in full flight along with the Labour Club and Communist Club students, but we lost. Despite this, my performance made me something of a star of the left scene, not that that stopped violent argument and sometimes battles within the left as my revolutionism tested their more liberal boundaries. I was counterposed to the leader of the Strathclyde Tory Students, Paul Moston, a rather pathetic, big mumbling upper-English-accented balding Tory prone to childish little fits in which he would run about screaming his head off and trying to hit folk. So I start off my big speech by saying I'm not going to say anything about him at all, and just let that sit:

Nothing at all ... if he ... yee knaa?

But that character couldn't stand on his own two feet for more than five minutes without people helping him ... But that's OK, that's what we're about, looking after each other, keeping it together ... we live in the real world and there's no way we can lock the big doors and shut the big bad world outside, leaving us all safe and coddled and classless and political-less and snuggled up warm and apathetic in the womb.

We have to break out into the real world. We've got to have the right to decide on big issues which effect these islands, the state of politics, the state of industrial relations.

Where are we going? 150 years of toil and struggle, blood and bitterness, of jails and transportation to win what? The right of working people to a voice.

What century are we in that Mr Moston and Mr Ward think they can disenfranchise us industrially? Do they think we're going to let the working people have their tongues cut out to please the wild and paranoid machinations of autocratic bosses? You're not on!

Get it right. This man wants working people to have no say whatever ... isn't that the most extreme thing you ever heard?

'It's his factory'—IT'S OUR LIVES!

Working people invest their lives, their families' lives, the education of their children, their standards of life. Theirs is a total investment—and you say they can't even have voice?

The Grunwick strikers are not fighting for a closed shop. They don't want a closed shop, and they have agreed a guarantee that they will not press for one ... all they want is the right to form a union for those that want one. Now that sounds like a hell of a moderate request to me, and if you moderates don't agree that it is, you ought to tend to your mooring because you've slipped into some far, far, right-wing waters.

By the way, we have a closed shop here. If Mr Moston thinks we should be talking about things that directly effect the students—why is he pissing about with this resolution, why hasn't he got a resolution before us ending the closed shop here? I'll tell you why. Because he enjoys the benefits of it—because it would weaken us not to have it—because it would limit our resources, that's why, and that's why Mr Moston and the movers of this motion are flaming hypocrites because there denying something to somebody else that they've got.

Just imagine if we didn't have a union. Everywhere else has got one but we don't. A bunch of us get together and start to collect names of students who want to form a union. We approach the university authorities and tell them we are starting a union. 'No you're not—we run this place, you're just students—this is our university, you go back to your seats—shut your mouths—sit still! 'But ...' we say. Right, you're expelled—the lot you's out!! And as is the wont of certain yellow-livered crawling things at this university, some of our colleagues say 'Serves you right! Teacher knows best!' and carry on going in while we are outside month after month trying to reason our case—a simple case after all,   a reasonable case. Meantime our places are being filled by others, new students.

Does that detract from the justice of our case? We only want a union like all the other colleges? Why pick on us? And suppose we go to the trade unions and say 'Can you donate £50 to our strike fund? It's for the students who are married and for the ones with children.' How would you feel if they turned round and said 'Na—go on, on your bike ... Bugger off, bloody communist Trotskyist students, this is Our Money—it's for us so we can have more booze in the president's drink cabinet or for the council's Christmas Ball. Na—off you go!

IT WOULD STINK!

But that is exactly what we are being asked to do in reverse.

Let's call a spade a spade and a selfish bastard a selfish bastard.

Over one and half million pounds we take in this union. We lavish tens of thousands of pounds on booze-ups, discos, bands, aye and I enjoy it ... this lavish banquet of privilege. But can't we even allow a few measly morsels of crumbs to fall from the table onto the laps of these Asian lasses who've been standing there bravely in their saris for 19 months?

What sort of people are we? £50 is nothing more than a gesture, just a wave of friendship. We've got a union, and if we didn't have one, we'd demand it and cause such an uproar they'd think Scotland had got its oil back.

We'd expect other colleges and universities unions to support our call.

We'd even expect trade unions to ... and that would be justice.

What we'd do for ourselves, lets do for others, what we'd expect for ourselves.

Lets show Mr Moston and the far-right Tories that if they're petty-minded, selfish toadies the rest of us have still got hearts ... Reject their motion.

It took a wee while to find me feet. First off, I hadn't recognised the cultural difference of this milieu and the one I had graduated from. In Scotland bright kids could go to university at 16. Our first year seen a plethora of bright-eyed, fresh-as-daisy-skinned young things in their new denim and thrusting sweaters. Scotland, even a city like Glasgow, hadn't embraced the sexual revolution of the Sixties and Seventies quite so enthusiastically as England; there was a strong moral impediment to carefree sex. For a time I deemed this place the 'last bastion of bourgeois morality'. Virginity seemed to be far more widespread here than any place I had ever encountered before, but then other than at school I had never been in the middle of so many people so much younger than me. Probably ten or twelve years different. Girls were more cautious here about jumping in and out of bed, and I suppose it frustrated me at first. Many girls seemed to be in a sort of 1950s moral code of not going beyond 'first base' unless you loved the bloke, not going beyond 'second base' unless you were going to marry the bloke and had been going out with him for years. Here a girl would ask 'Why me?' And mean, "Why do you want to have sex with me in particular.' How special was she? Sex as a thing in and for itself was an immoral concept here by and large. Ower the border it hadn't really mattered if she knew the bloke, or even, sometimes, if she liked the bloke. I didn't make things easy by, within the first two-minute conversation with some brand-new undergrad, telling her I was married, with a child, but we had an open relationship, and casual sex was OK, so don't worry about it. And the girl, taken aback, would suggest I tell her my name first. It was all a bit to take in at one glance. It wasn't ower long though before we got to know each other, me and this student body, this body of students as a whole explosive and vibrant force. I have never ever before or since felt such a love, aye love, for a whole body of people at one time. We were a living community, vast yet intimate. At mass rock gigs on the top floor of the union, on a Saturday neet, in a throng of 2000, a moving, writhing body, we resonated the music, we were the chords they struck, we pulsed as one, as if the whole throng was one single instrument, a pulsing moving entity driven by sound.

On dreamy Sunday afternoons, recovering from the sex and drugs and rock 'n' roll, the adventures of the weekend, we crashed out together, en masse, watching films together on the big screen. At times we would stick something like *Emmanuelle* on 'as a stocking filler' and the beautifully shot scene of the Arab dhow, drifting across the Nile, brought forth a mass chorus of 'We Are Sailing', a song which somehow became an anthem for the Strathclyde students. During a Dracula film, as the vampire homes in on the young exposed female neck, someone shouts 'Why me?', which drew knowing laughs from the lads. Friday evenings it was full-length, general release films we watched, like a huge extended family sitting together in a huge common living-room. It was something of the mass moving demonstration, the permanent party that had been my Tyneside youth. It was a communal and belonging feeling. Helping to run this Union, driving it with the satisfaction some folk do a big truck, was an immensely satisfying and rewarding skill.

Initial reluctance, or my own big-gobbed incompetence, was initially and gradually overcome. First, I think, Julie, a big-haired, sweet-faced rather plump Welsh girl from a public school. Her air of the schoolgirl dormitory and sexual enthusiasm made her quite impervious to any qualms her Scottish dorm mates had about me being married. She got this sexual revolution bit ney problem, borrowed my room when I was away to shag boys she met at the Union discos, my flat being in the student residence, just a quick grope and stagger from the Union. Sex with Julie wasn't my best. Short and plumpish, if bonny. I had to psych myself up for it, and because of my endeavour that the girl always must come first, usually before penetration, I was usually struggling to keep aroused by the time I did, and then I had to hurry it up for fear of loosing the erection mid-flight. So I knew my performances weren't great with her; the only one she regarded as any good was when I skipped the formalities and the protocol and just shagged her raw and hungry. How do I know? Because a sexlet, first-year sexy-as-hell wee thing who I fancied the knickers off asked Julie what I was like in bed, it being her first time, and Julie told her 'Crap except the last time.' Needless to say she chose someone else to test the water with. 'But it wouldn't have been like that with you,' I whimpered in the background.

One of Julie's flatmates was a small Indian girl called Nina. We were soon seeing each other almost every night. Nina was not only virginal but already a bride-to-be, a family-arranged marriage having been secured some time ago. Nina was going through with it, education or no, because she loved her parents, not the bloke, who she had met on occasion but never without a chaperone, and in any case that sort of contact just didn't arrive in the context of India and home. With me? Well it was odd; she didn't know exactly what the rules were here for normal people, ner mind one who was betrothed and another already married. We were close friends, we danced the nights away, we laughed a lot, snogged and well almost everything you could touch was OK, but no oral and no intercourse, oh and she didn't touch me either! It was all a bit like being thirteen again; she would get all hot and sweaty and panting and I would try and get her undressed without loosing the heat or momentum but she always cried halt and I of course always did. But it was great fun having a sort of girlfriend. The Christmas ball was preceded by an Executive/Council dinner. Everyone gets dressed up formally for both—a bit of college tradition and an excuse to get out of jeans and dross and look a million dollars. I invited Maureen up for the Ball and dinner, which left Nina a bit in the cold, but she came up with her friends and they all met Maureen who blushed like a schoolgirl herself. They all thought she was stunning and they weren't being polite. The lads too, knowing our relationship, tried to home in for a date with Maureen, but that wasn't on, not while we were both there, and hadn't seen each other for ages. Truth was we actually preferred each other still, to anyone of our extra relationships. Sex with Maureen was still hot, as the lads in the residence noted by the endless banging of the bloody bed against the wall and the door.

Another first I suppose was when I dated briefly the secretary of the Engineering Society. Yes, a girl, Susan, small, rosy cheeks, cherry red lips, big frizzy hair, thin waist, large bust. She was the only female engineering student in the second year. Like most of 'the plumbers', as the science students were nicknamed, she was working-class through and through. Practical, science-based, an engineer. I fancied her for all of that, but also her girlyness. She hung about with her female mates, and they gossiped and danced together and linked each other's arms as they walked about the place. They knew this wasn't a student style of behaviour, which is another reason why they did it; they looked liked the lasses oot on the toon from the works or the scheme. Sometimes, though, you'd swear they were modeling a scene from *Grease*, hanging with their folders in front of them, their little cardies slung round their shoulders. Susan was on and off, she'd say yes to a date, then not turn up, or just pretend we didn't have one. The married bit got to her too, although one extended summer, as we studied together prior to the exams, she took me through an indulgence I thought I never would repeat after being 15. We lay out on the grass in front of the Andersonian Library, in the sun, amid the collapsed piles of students, and snogged, her laying on top of me, her hair cascading over my face like the leaves on a benevolent tree, smelling the clean strands and fragrance of shampoo and feeling the sunbeams dive here and there through its canopy. The pubic bone under her hot little knickers under her tight denim jeans lay just across my erect penis wedged up against the underpants and zipper of my jeans as she rolled ever so slightly and moved her head as her mouth covered mine. 'Don't wake me now, Mother, I'm in heaven!' I wasn't this 15 when I was 15. She would let the guilt take care of itself, for a few afternoons. But that was as far as it got, and I've still never had an engineer, but the memory of those hot and sweaty public affections have never left me.

My fortnightly jaunts doon yem te Geordieland to meetings of the Tyneside Irish republicans were also occasions for neets roond the clubs and night-time venues. I had ended up at the Guildhall where some blues and R&B and Geordiefolk and Irish folky rock bands were on. Lad, was I in me element and cruising. Mind, I recall I had me jacket nicked and then the janitor said he knew where it was, sitting on the back of a chair in a room where I never had been; me Phoenix was still in the lapel but me money and stuff had gone. Fortunately I remembered I was carrying very little anyway, as I was expecting some expenses back. I accused the caretaker of being a thieving bastard and in me drunken state threatened that this wasn't over. Before I left he gave me £20 and said he had caught the lass who admitted she stole it from me after putting me jacket on and walking up stairs. I think I remember strongly believing this tale and even of giving him £5 as repayment for me bad faith earlier. I shared a lift back to Tony Corcoran's place. He was carrying a number of folk and the band back to various hooses en route among whom a bonny Irish lass. She too was high as kite and invited me in when we stopped at her place. I intended still to make it alang to Tony's later. We had rolled a joint or two, then got engaged in one those dreamy, sex-driven, everything-off-and-everything-is-on sexual spectaculars. To add to the surrealist quality she had a small child who sleepwalked through the living room as we bucked away naked on the living room floor, and appeared and disappeared through doors, amid the legs in the air and frantic demands to 'fuck the fuckin' arse off me'. We shagged all night, literally all night. I do not know where the erections kept coming from—I think it was her freckly face her pert little tits and that sexual crudity. I left the next morning in total confusion as to where I was, or what the hell I was doing in Newcastle.

The Strathclyde Telegraph was my muse. For almost my entire three-year period I was to be found in lengthy news, political, and historical pieces, always controversial. My attacks upon the academic institutions, the teaching methods and the right-wing bias in the curriculum all produced angry responses from the staff. My polemical pieces on China, the Soviet Union and armed revolution rattled most of the left who held public meetings with invited speakers to combat my 'assertions'. The politics of the Student Union, the struggle for a Scottish Union of Students against Trevor Phillips and the NUS, produced alliances of Scottish nationalists and republican Clubs, Scottish liberals and the odd Tory. But the NUS campaign was the fight that united all the potential bureaucrats regardless of political persuasion. Our AGM's, our Council meetings went on for hours, as we clashed, all sides against all sides on all subjects. I don't know what other university student unions were like, but we had a great spread of characters and brilliant speakers and comic performers. A composite, a unity of opposites. My attempts at parody were well received, and this one was the Union favourite (to Bob Dylan's tune 'Stuck Inside Of Mobile With The Memphis Blues'):

> I was walking down John Street, feeling most alone.
> I had just about decided that I should just go home,
> When all of a sudden, came a shout out from the hall
> Saying 'David Douglass needed up in the Assembly Hall.'
> So I rushed up the flights of stairs to see what was to do
> Steve Kelly he was standing there he says 'I have a job for you.'
> Me, I just shrugged my shoulders I figured I was pretty slick ... then
> He handed me a plastic bag and a great big pointed stick.
> Oh Mamma, can this really be the end?
> To be stuck in Strathclyde Union, with Steve Kelly and his friends?
> I was walking past the Doolittle, when I heard another noise
> It was drunkin bumkin Duncan, saying 'Has anyone seen Joyce?'
> Then something funny happened just after the dormouse spoke.
> Dave Patterson walked by me, with a big glass full of smoke.
> Then it all started to go crazy but me I didn't care,
> Till Alastair minced by me, with a rosebud in his hair.
> Me I expected it to happen, ever since the time
> He was stuck in his office with Nicky and a big bottle of wine.
> Well I thought I heard the dustbin men a rattling the bins,
> But it was just Miles going to the disco with a wheelbarrow full of tins.
> He was followed up by Stewart Grey, a tall guy you'll agree.
> He walks into The Macintyre saying 'The High Balls are on me.'
> Well I thought I heard some banging, then I knew I heard a scream.
> I thought it was the vandals at the cigarette machine.
> So I rushed down the landing the crooks all for to nab,
> But I just caught Terri Colpi going crazy for a fag.

I had missed out on an NUM grant for Ruskin, but had applied for a supplementary grant from the Coal Industry Social Welfare Organisation—Education Fund. It was a one-off grant but would make an enormous difference to my financial position. The other advantage was that they paid all sorts of expenses to get down to the interview. My rail fare from Glasgow Central of course to London, but I was warned to keep all receipts. I got the buffet man to write me one for sandwiches, and pop and crisps. I was to be put up in hotel near Kings Cross, a bit sleazy but with a bar and everything. Unfortunately I wasn't alone; I was booked in with another candidate who was studying at Lancashire or somewhere. Well, the two of us set off to the Baked Spud/Pizza place near Kings Cross and ordered a slap-up meal knowing the expenses would be paid. I was flying high, and felt like the world was my oyster as we strolled over to the nearest bar with the intention of having a grand night on the city. Well, people who know me, and most of the folk who read this book will know me fairly well by the end, know that I am not the kind of bloke who can give out a quickfire, witty, female-impressing bar chat. I'm much more likely to launch off on a conversation about the news, but on this occasion it was different and my spirits were flying.

There were two girls down by the end of the bar. Laughing and pushing each other around but looking at us every now and again. 'C'mon,' I says to my new-found mate, 'lets gaan an chat up these two' (I couldn't believe I had actually said that). I thought I'd take on the role Larch used to when we were out on the Oxford circuit. I tried to think myself nearer six foot as we approached the girls. Mine, well, the one I had made a beeline for, was small and dark, wore a tiny mini skirt and had a real nice face. I noticed also she had big breasts but that wouldn't have influenced my judgement in any way—I'm a face-led person rather than any other part of the anatomy but yee knaa, they do pose a certain fascination. We were soon laughing and joking and telling each other the story of our lives, well almost, and had paired up without complication. The girls didn't want to move on as they stayed just across the road and weren't bothered about walking round London or going anywhere else. I couldn't believe it when the other one suggested we get a pile of cans and go back over to their place. Ney bother. We sat on the floor and played records, and my new flatmate was getting into a necking session on the couch with the other girl.

Out of the blue I thought I'd just cut to the chase. 'D'yee want to come back to my hotel? We can get a drink there and you could stay if you wanted?' 'OK,' she says and stands up, just like that. For some stupid reason we think maybe she won't get in, so will pretend to be the other bloke. She borrows his blouse jacket and we set off back. It's a different night shift staff than when we booked in, and all they know is there are two people in the room. So we sit and have a drink at the bar, chat away to the barman then head off to the room. As soon as I get through the door, wham, she sends me flying onto the bed and starts to snog the face off me, already breathing hard. As we get down to the nakedness, except for the mini skirt which looks fantastic pulled right up around her thighs with her legs splayed out, my cock is making its own way home. Then she moans 'no'. I stop dead, she looks up at me and then starts necking with me again, rubbing my cock up and down her vagina and breathing short quick breaths. I'm just sliding into her when she says louder 'No, no, no!' Well, OK, that's me, if its no then it's no, so I just kiss her on the forehead and say 'OK' and turn over to go to sleep, pulling the sheet off the floor where everything has fallen and sweeping it over us.

She sat up and looked at me, panting and annoyed 'What's the bleedin matter?' 'Eh? You said to stop.' 'Stupid,' she says and rolls over onto me, the cock has gone off the hard slightly but she straddles me and starts rubbing it up and down her cunt again, then slides it in, bucking me and holding onto my shoulders, the head board knocking hell out of the wall and the bed bouncing like crazy. Her thrusts are getting so wild I'm scared I'm going to slide out again. She starts to fuck me wildly, saying 'No, no!', and this time she has no intention of me stopping or going away; she has me pegged to the bed and is riding me to a furious orgasm. It was her turn-on thing, but I must say it wasn't mine: 'no' means NO to me; I can't judge if 'no' means maybe or in fact yes, although in this case it was hard not to get the impression 'no' didn't mean 'no' to this lass. Personally I don't want to shag someone who doesn't want sex; she obviously got turned on by the idea of being reluctantly shagged, although she could have worked a little harder on the reluctance if that's the role. Maybe her other partners just ignored her 'noes' and carried on; it must have been a bucket of cold water when I actually stopped. We lay flaked out for a minute or two, then I turned to her and said: 'Actually, I like girls who like it and who really want it. When you said "no" I thought you meant no.' 'Shurrup you stupid northerner,' she said with a little bit too much meaning, and slid herself right over my face and on top of me. 'I like it all right!' I never argue with me mouth full. I guess we made it three times, including the morning session before breakfast.

Breakfast was to be more alarming than the confusing features of the night before.

We sat opposite each other at breakfast and chatted and laid into the toast and jam. Somehow the conversation got round to what she called 'the niggers'. 'Niggers?' I charged, 'that's a bit racialist isn't it?' 'Yeah, well I am a racialist see?' she responds. I start to reason out how stupid such a reaction is to whatever problems she thinks there are in London, but she cuts me short: 'You sahnd like one of them fucking reds to me.' 'Aye,' I says, putting me knife down and looking her in the eyes, still noticing how beautiful they are in the full light of day. 'Well I am a red; what are you, a fucking Nazi?' And to my utmost surprise she says 'Yis, I is as a matter of fact,' and pulls out a membership card with a bold black swastika in the middle and 'NSM' on the top. She picks her knife up and points it like she will stab me in the eye. I try to grab it but she pulls it away, laughing. Other people are starting to notice now. 'I think our date is over,' I suggest. 'Your bleedin life is over,' she says pointing the knife at my head before tossing it down noisily on the table, and walking out. 'Wow!' I thought, flopping back into my seat. 'Fuckin' hell!'

Well I went back to the room to pack, and there was my nice suit, and my white shirt, but no bloody shoes. I hadn't packed any. I was forced to wear me trainers with the suit. The education committee discussed my financial situation, and one kindly aud lad says 'He' yee no got any better shoes than those lad?' 'Not nuw,' I lied. 'The others fell apart and I can't really afford a new pair just nuw.'

One way or the other, the interview went well; they were to extend me a one-off award of £180—not bad really. I split it with Maureen. That should be the end of the story. Really it should, but after the interview I had two or three hours to kill before the train, and well, the girls did live in the vicinity, and I wondered if my fellow applicant was still at their flat. I wondered if he had had his interview and how things went with the other lass. I convinced myself I would just pop round and see if he was there. As I walked up the stairs to the flat I wondered what I would do if Eva Braun flew at me again. I reasoned, 'Look, you never tried to talk this out politically, never asked her how she came to her conclusions, should at least give her the chance to explain and me to explain.' By the time I was knocking on the door, I had forgotten any idea of finding the other student.

She opens the door just an inch and sees it's me; then she opens it wide. The room is in darkness, the curtains are closed, she is stark naked. She stands aside. I don't speak, I just look at her, she puts both hands round my throat but doesn't squeeze, then launches me backwards onto her bed. 'Stupid northern geezer!' she says as she rips my pants open and drags my dick from my underpants. OK, I admit I didn't actually do any conversion work, we didn't get around to talking politics at all, but I gave her bed springs a good work out. By the time I left I was knackered and had fifteen minutes to catch me train. 'Red cunt!' she shouted out of the door at me. 'Fascist bastard!' I responded. She thrust her naked crotch in my direction standing on the landing, still naked. That was the last I seen of her. So there, that's my confession: I shagged a Nazi, first time in ignorance, second time in her room. Years later I was to end up digging a scab's garden, which is just about the same gravity of sin I suppose, but that's a story I have yet to come to.

Wee Dave wasn't the only Tory student to try fraternisation. By the second year, I had stirred the interest of the very prim and proper Ms C, the president of the Strathclyde Conservative Students. She was in her honours year (Scottish Universities don't do honours until after the basic degree is taken) but planning to go straight on to the PhD. She was quiet, tall, her hair in a bun, thin and dressed like a secretary in pencil skirts and white shirts. She was canvassing round the dorms for one their candidates in a student election when she came upon my room. I was lying on the bed, pretending to read, thinking of the disco later that night, when the door was knocked. It was a pleasant surprise. She stood there beaming. I brought her in and she sat on the bed beside me, and explained all about the candidate, then how she had heard me speak, and was fascinated that I had worked down coalmines, written books, been on riots, and she was still 'just a student'. Actually by this time she was 20, but she had never been linked to any boys and tended not to make the scene down at the disco nights. I explained that she was the first Tory ever to sit on my bed, indeed the first Tory I had ever really talked to, certainly the first Tory I had ever fancied. 'Oh!' she said quietly, then took her glasses off and looked me hard in the face. I smiled and thought 'What the hell?' and moved a little closer to her. She welcomed my kiss and flung her arms around my neck, but we landed with me lying half over and her half kneeling with me knees sticking in her belly. The blood was draining from my calves but I didn't want to move in case she took flight. Then I thought 'I will take charge of this,' said 'Just a minute,' got up, put the pillow under her head, changed the tape on the recorder and then lay down beside her. She started to get up. 'This is silly,' she said. 'How come?' 'You're married!' 'I don't want to marry you, Terry,' I replied, moving in to start the snog again, which she accepted half-heartedly. 'You're a wee communist.' 'No that wee,' I replied but she got up. 'Everyone will make fun of us.' I didn't know about the gossip machine which fed the piss-taking culture of the students and at least part of the paper, the *Telegraph*. She turned at the door, and kissed me with a passionate kiss, then said 'We'll see,' which sounded promising. 'I love your Geordie accent,' she said.

'I love yours,' I replied with honesty. She was shocked rigid. 'You mean to say' she said in the Jean Brodie, Kelvinside Glaswegian equivalent, 'you think I have an accent?' Terry believed she spoke normal English 'Whey, aye, you've a soft lilting Scottish accent.' 'Not Glasgow?' 'Emm, no, not really.' 'Guid.' I was redeemed. I lay on the bed after she had gone and thought whether I should have in fact risked gangrene and just carried on snogging while we had the chance. Was it a betrayal of class principles to seek the seduction of a leading Tory student? Na, I assured myself, it was re-education, maybe subversion. This young lady was obviously an entrenched virgin, not a feature of the female development process I find endearing, but she was a smouldering volcano. I could tell she wanted to be freed, and I think, had decided I would be the fizz to uncork the genie in the bottle.

We seen each other from time to time, but kept it a secret—well my flatmates all knew of course, but kept their peace. For her twenty-first birthday her Dad bought her a car; it marked her Ph.D. years. A few weeks later she rang the door bell; all the lads were in the kitchen and leaned out of the window. It was Terry; she climbed the stairs to the kitchen.

'Where's the wee car?' they ask. Terry in her posh Scottish accent replies: 'I have a huge crack.' They all fall about laughing, which she doesn't understand. 'So we imagine, but where's the car?' they persist. 'It blew up.' 'Blew up?' they all said in unison. 'I didn't know you put oil in'. These lads, mining engineers, mechanical engineers, chemists, fall silent. 'Well,' she says, 'I kenned fine about the petrol, I knew about that, but I didn't know about oil.' Silently the kitchen emptied. Being a middle-class Tory spoiled bitch was one thing, but destroying an engine out of sheer practical ignorance—that was another.

Some time later we had been at a big party late into the early evening, the cocktails had flowed, and she was very matey. We took a taxi back to my flat at Birkbeck; I resolved not to try and hustle her down to my bedroom as that would put the anchors on. So knowing most of the lads were away for the weekend, and John the chemist would be fast asleep my now, we sat in the moonlight-filled kitchen on the big comfy seats. We started to snog with passion. I slowly undid every button on her shirt and her white and full- filled breasts stood out from her chest. She didn't know! She looked down and seeing her breasts exposed was genuinely shocked 'Mr Douglass!' She demanded 'A man of your principles!' I was dumbstruck, mystified, but it was a natural progression of events since I was twelve years old, and I had never ever had this response, and anyway I hadn't actually touched them yet. 'I'm away,' she said getting up. 'Na, wait, I'll get you a taxi.' Which I did, and made her a cup of coffee while we waited. 'That wasn't disrespectful,' I tried to explain. 'Why do you think I brought us up here? Didn't you think necking would lead on? Wouldn't you have thought I didn't fancy you if it hadn't and we'd shook hands at the door?' No, sex wasn't on her agenda; I don't think it was just me.

Well, that was that with Terry. She got the highest mark ever for a geographer and wrote the first PhD ever on tourism, and landed a top job last off as Britain's senior tourism consultant and toured the world. Whether the breasts were still untouched and unseen by human eye and hand in the end I do not know. I learned the real meaning of 'conservatism' with T.

British Anti-Zionist Organisation–Palestine Solidarity was one of the most serious organisations I joined when I reached Glasgow. Strathclyde had many Arab students and the cities long left-wing traditions ensured that the college left groups all adopted to various degrees the cause of Palestinian liberation. The University group was led by Dr George Mitchell, a postgrad and PhD who did what I'm not sure of but spent much of his time in and around the University campus and student union. He was the hub of the Scottish-Arab Society and BAZO, and his frequent visits to the Middle East and almost constant company of Arab students and activists caused him to adopt the accent of an Arab speaking with a Scottish accent—most peculiar. More so when I discovered George Galloway, nicknamed 'Gorgeous George', 'the 'member for Baghdad West'. A Labour MP, the spit of Dr George, who spoke in an identical mock Arab/Scottish accent. The SUI had a cell operating in Egypt and had in fact, as mentioned already, produced a small pamphlet on the Egyptian January events of 1977, when workers and students demanded progressive, socialist and democratic change. The Posadist group had had a preoccupation with the Middle East process and we too were keen to expand both our knowledge and contacts into what was for us one of the front lines against imperialism in the world. BAZO was to soon win a major libel case against the *Scottish Daily Record*, which had accused the organisation of anti-Semitism; it was the first refuge of the Zionists, but utterly flawed, as BAZO was able to demonstrate in court through witnesses, including Anti-Zionist Jews, both orthodox and secular, Anti-Zionist atheists of Jewish ethnicity, as well of course the even more basic and obvious fact, that the Palestinians are in fact Semitic people themselves.

Judaism and Zionism Are Utterly Incompatible

The Zionists have usurped for their nationalistic and militaristic state the holy name of Israel. Zionism has always endeavoured to estrange Jews from the observance of the laws of their faith and has offered instead the twin curses of atheism and National Socialism. Jews, who are faithful to the Torah, have nothing to do with Zionist pressure politics, national boycotts, and 'punitive' expeditions or sneak attacks. Zionists do not and cannot represent the Jewish people or speak in the name of millions of Jews who are non-Zionists or active anti-Zionists.

The Establishment of the Zionist state notwithstanding, the Jewish people is patiently and confidently awaiting the coming of the true Messiah, The Jewish people has seen many pseudo-messianic movements, false prophets and alien idols come and go. The Zionist episode too will pass but the Jewish people will live.[79]

There was no racial difference between a Palestinian 'Oriental' Jew and a Palestinian Muslim, Christian or atheist. The paper lost when the judge rules Anti-Zionism does not and has not meant anti-Semitism or anti-Jewishness. The paper published the correction to its designation. However that slander goes on, even against the anti-Zionist Jews who get called 'self-haters'.

One of the first projects I was involved with was a delegation and conference to take place in Lebanon, around the subject of peace in the Middle East, and a united front against Zionism for Palestinian liberation. The conference was to be hosted in Beirut. After deep reflection I nominated Maureen to go on behalf of the SUI; she was now the general secretary and was feeling somewhat left out of things with me up at Strathclyde and Ken down at Ruskin. She was over the moon, and certainly made a big impact while she was there. She visited from 11 to 22 July and took part in intense study and meetings with the people. She was along with another twenty six people mainly members of other leftist group's guests of the PLO. She tells us:

> One of the things which was particularly requested by members of the delegation was to meet with the five political groups which go to make up the Executive Committee of the PLO. Fatah, the Popular Democratic Front for the Liberation of Palestine, Saiga, the Arab Liberation Front, the Popular Front for the Liberation of Palestine ...

The last, however, the group we as an organisation were drawn closest to, was now no longer on the EC, and they met them separately. They also asked and met the different factions of the Lebanese left:

> The existence of different and also often conflicting groups within the umbrella organisation of the PLO was of particular interest, probably because of the western experience of left organisations and the sectarianism and inability to work together which exists among them ... it was felt that discussion and political polemic is a vital and lively force within the PLO but that it is a surrounding feature (at that time) to the central aim of the PLO which is the achieving of a secular democratic state of Palestine ...The PLO obviously wanted to stress to us that the Palestinian revolution is not merely a military one and I was very much impressed by what we saw. The Palestinians are creating a social revolution alongside a revolutionary war and all this in exile!
>
> We visited the refugee camps of Shateela, Sabra Damour and Burj-el-Barajneh where I was appalled by the poverty and bad conditions of the people living there but despite the conditions I was amazed by the spirit of the people towards their revolution ... The PLO also took us to the

South of Lebanon (Tibnin) where fighting is still taking place between the Palestinians revolutionary forces (Fedayeen) and the Isolationists (Lebanese rightists) and where the Israelis are still shelling over the border, which we observed while in the south—so much for Israeli denials!

She just fell in love with the city, and the people, and the movement:

To have the personal experience of seeing a revolution in action, socially, politically and militarily is an inspiration for our continued struggle against Imperialism here. It's hard to explain the kind of personal attachment which one develops to the Palestinian revolution and the commitment I now feel to support and defend the Palestinians in their very just and correct struggle.

Maureen was destined to become a star of BAZO and its national chairwoman.

Back at university I had conquered all fear and started talking to the most beautiful Jewish student in the world. She was a girl greatly desired among the male student populace. She was sort of light olive coloured, with golden brown hair, about the same height as me, with deep brown eyes. He teeth were whiter than white and straight and level. She wore shirts without a bra and her cleavage, exposed through the open buttons on her shirt, rose and fell as she breathed very deeply from time to time. I know all of this because before talking to her I had sat opposite her across the desk in the library for days. At length she looked up smiled at me and said 'Do you want to go for coffee?' Aah no, this wasn't 'coffee' as in when you come up, after taking someone to their flat. This was coffee like doonstairs in the refractory bar. She lived from time to time in Israel, she had toured America, she was worldly wise, sharp as a knife blade. She seemed utterly unobtainable, then she said, 'Here, some gum,' offering a strange round toffee sort of shape. 'Its cum gum,' she said. I hadn't a clue what she meant, until after sucking it for a while the liquid inside burst into your mouth. I laughed, she smiled, I thought … She agreed to come out with me; we spent the whole evening discussing and then arguing about the state of Israel. Zionism, anti-Zionism, socialism, Palestine, until drunk and a bit annoyed with each other; any suggestion of cosying down into my bed seemed out of the question. She agreed finally to come to the lecture given by a Jewish socialist from the Jewish Socialist Party; she didn't come. She told me the next day that, on reflection, Zionism and being a Jew were the same thing, so she must be both too; there was no more point in arguing about it. Actually that hadn't really been the intention, but such obvious differences were bound to come up. From time to time I would see her; she wore sort of army fatigues, like army-issue desert shorts, rolled shorter, army-issue shirts opened further. She looked like a Jewish settler. I hated her politics, wanted to get close to her, speak to her. We smiled, we waved, we said 'Hi'. That was all.

Met Karen. Small, thin, punk-haired girl with a pixy face and cheeky grin, a southerner with a sort of Cockney accent though she had come from well-bred stuff, and been the wealthy daughter of well-heeled British colonials abroad. Photos of her in her pre-punk days showed the most devastatingly beautiful girl with waist-length hair, in a floor-length, white off-the-shoulder dress. All that had come off, the hair cropped into spiky boy length, bovver boots and rolled-up jeans, a little fawn jacket with a little collar also spiky and turned up. She wanted to consume the far left, wanted to make revolution her cause. If I had signed her up for the RAF she would have drawn her Oozie then and there and gone off to shoot a judge or a bank director. We rolled onto her bed, back at Birkbeck, though I made her leave her little jacket on, shagging her with her collar turned up and her neck silhouetted against its border. Her neck, I didn't say, was long and thin and swanlike. My rough working-class revolutionary street cred fell a little when she went out to the toilet and I took the occasion to clean my teeth. I don't like the idea of having smelly breath. When she came back in, as I finally removed her jacket, she smelt the toothpaste and accused me of 'cheating'. When the jacket came off, and the torn T-shirt was pulled over her head, the most gorgeously pointing, thrusting, large breasts leapt out from her body. You would never have suspected that under that jacket and camouflage a body models would kill for was being disguised. I think we had a few more encounters of the bouncy variety before the whole university adventure was over, as I recall her legs each side of my head, her arms laid dormant at her sides. She lets her tits take on a shuddering, bouncing vibration mesmerism as I stuff as much momentum into her curled up pelvis pubes assisted by my arms and hands under her shoulders drawing her relentlessly back and forwards into me, leaning back to watch her breasts move and shake, her nipples like tight little rocks.

She broke her leg and was on crutches for ages—not in bed of course, we weren't that pneumatic, though her bed did collapse one night, causing us to be rendered totally unsexual from laughter and happiness and maybe a few ower many tokes of 'the old Bob Hope' as the Glasgow workers called it. Karen joined the SUI, and after graduation did a lot of work for us all over the country before seeking the actual revolution in faroff countries of Africa and the Middle East.

Up at Sthrathclyde I had joined the 'Broad Left'. Militant, the CP, the left Nationalists and Irish Labour Party were in there; mainly it was CP-dominated. I soon discovered it wasn't broad enough for me, in fact it was a broad right from my perceptive. The greatest point of conflict was armed struggle and the armed groups. Whereas they, the BL, never wasted an opportunity to condemn them and distance themselves from their actions and politics, I loudly defended and even supported them. Resolutions to the area council condemning the armed organizations put forward by the student right were happily supported by the BL so long as they could add, 'the British Army', 'the CIA' etc. and nicely condemn them all. Not so me, who rose in defence of the BLA, SLA, RAF, and of course the IRA, although the IRA were not really in the same category as the others, being an armed forced based upon a mass working-class base. The pages of the *Telegraph* and the minutes of the Council reflect these deep divisions. Ireland however was the biggest test of our comradeship. Without exception all the participants of the Broad Left heartily condemned the Provisional IRA, whereas I was a member of Sinn Fein, now working with the huge Donegal Cumain which was dually based in Glasgow. I had also started writing for *Republican News* under the name of (among others) Provo Student. I sold the paper round the university and student union and my comrades from the BL had tried to have it and me banned from doing so.

My last encounter with them came when they agreed to host a 'Real Facts On Ireland' platform and invite 'all parties'—this would of course include LPYS, SDLP, and both the major bourgeois 'Eire' parties, the CPI, the Connolly Association and even the Peace People. I insisted that since that whole platform would simply be there to condemn the IRA a spokesperson from Sinn Fein should also be invited. They might have thought such a platform would blow the Provos out of the water, or even that they wouldn't show up. But on the contrary. I had already arranged for Jim Reilly, Belfast born and bred, leader of Sinn Fein Britain, to come up and speak and he was straining at the leash. I also knew that although the 'left' and nationalist organisations to a person condemned the Provos, a great bulk of the ordinary Glasgow students supported them; although they didn't orientate it in political terms very well, I knew from the sale of the paper what a cord they struck. This would be a public roasting for our opponents. As it turned out none of their great platform speakers agreed to come, only wor Jim. I insisted they cobble together a platform of opponents from their own ranks which they frequently did when publicly confronting me, and that the meeting go ahead. News sped round the college that 'The Provos' were coming. The Tory students started to organise a picket—'They Shall Not Pass' they ironically suggested—and bomb threats were made ostensibly by the UDA in Glasgow. The day before the meeting, they announced that the university had taken legal advice and if Jim was allowed to speak the officers of the Union could be prosecuted under the Prevention Of Terrorism Act.

'So?' I demanded, 'What about a stand for free speech? What about opposing repressive laws no matter who they are aimed at?'

Kelly and Evans the leaders of the BL demanded that they wouldn't let me make martyrs of them. Actually they had gone fleeing to the University authorities looking for a way out and this was the brainstorm solution they came up with. It wasn't subject to debate or a vote; the meeting was banned as illegal. So that was me and the Broad Left.

Actually my support for the Provos was becoming general knowledge around the student population. I was called to account for each and every action blamed on them or claimed by them. I had forgotten I think how real the division in Glasgow is and how seriously they take Irish politics. I was at a crowded party across from Cathedral Street, when two big Ulster lads collared me: 'Yee'r the fucking Provie aren't yee?' The pushing started first then the furious argument about murders and outrage, but it didn't take long to sus out that these two were UDA supporters, and returned them the charge in full measure. The music stopped and a number of students from both communities in Ulster joined in the argument, though they were talking rationally and calmly and pointing out certain facts of things they saw happening and could speak of from first hand experience. Stories of relatives and friends being blown away, stories of sectarian murders, stories of horror and fear, it calmed us both down. We were neither of us saints here. The argument subsided.

The following early morning I was rolling over in bed, when a huge explosion, or what sounded to me like a huge exlosion, went off outside the window at Birkbeck Court, a shower of soil and flowers splattered against the glass and there was a sizeable hole in the ground outside. As I rushed downstairs and outside I heard feet running and laughter. It was still dark and I had no torch. My flatmates came out and one of them picks a notice off the front door: 'Beware MAD Geordie Provo Bastard.' 'Friends of yours?' they enquire. Well the UDA supporters from Belfast actually lived in Birkbeck too, and were only two blocks up from me. They were ordinary working-class lads, much more so than most students. Saturday afternoons they'd be with their mates in the common room at their apartment, watching the racing on the telly, drinking cans of beer, phoning in bets and smoking; they stood on their chairs and cheered and shouted the horses on, race after race. My turn, I think. With a couple of volunteers from my flat we sneak into their block, unwind the coiled-up fire hose, and with my mate on the tap, I kick the door in and let them have it. I had no idea how powerful that fire hose would be, it knocked them clean off their seats and washed the telly smack against the opposite wall where it exploded. As we ran out I tied up the front door with tie bands and hung a large sign: 'Beware Of Ginger Orange Bastards!' (They both had bright ginger hair.) Well it went on, back and forth, and involved mass water fights with the fire hose, hostage-taking of clothes in the ironing room, ambushes with fireworks and buckets of water, but it wasn't all good-natured. At times the arguments were serious and heated and I thought it might get to physical harm, even murder.

I couldn't go on like this, always looking over my shoulder. One of the lads was quite amenable to live and let live, at least while at college, but his mate was a real militant Orangeman with a grudge. Finally we agreed to go out and talk it all over in the pub and if we couldn't settle it, fight the fucker out toe to toe, 'a square go' as they call it in Glasgow. We adjourned to a real-ale pub on the corner; although I was confined to bottled beer they both were great lovers of real ale and this was the real ale pub of the city. They were impressed, although actually I hadn't known and had just picked it for being out of the road. We sat, drank, joked and talked over the situation, past, present and future, we outlined our respective histories, our thoughts, our dreams, our bottom lines. They ended up back at my flat drinking and listening to The Dubliners, who they enjoyed 'except all that political Fenian bollocks'. We joked about the bomb outrage; they had put the concoction together in the kitchen, not realising it would be so powerful. They had thought they'd actually blown the side of the building out. They had lain low for two days but incredibly nobody had come to investigate. There was more fuss over the water damage from my response. At length and weel drunk, I offered them my famous stew which was sitting in the pan waiting for visitors. 'Look, he's so fucking republican he even dyes his stew green!' We all laugh at the dreaded tin of peas in the stew phenomenon for which I was becoming famous. 'I'm not eating that,' decides my main assassin, 'I'll be wearing shamrock next.' We agree to differ, but the war, between us anyway, was over. Was I relieved.

GEORDIE'S 300-FOOT TREES: THE ORIGIN OF COAL

In the second year at Birkbeck, I am in residence on my floor with a joint little kitchen common room, with a chemist, a mechanical engineer, and a mining engineer. The discussions were illuminating, not least when I put forth the polemic of Geordie Summerson, my old colliery linesman at Wardley, against coal coming from trees upon the mining engineer. He blustered as I had, but using Geordie's impeccable argument and maths I argued him to total silence. None of the others had any answers either. In turn, the engineer laid the theory out on his professor of mining, who aahed and ummed and observed that this was a 'quite fascinating empirical observation and a rude challenge to assumptions'. But what WAS the true reason why all the coal cleats the world over run in the same geological and geographical direction and regardless of millions of years of separate formation, a factor which had made the old pitmen think they were being asked to believe all the trees in prehistory had fallen in the same direction, time and time again, over millions of years? Actually, the truth was not just then in real time; attempts to create coal in a laboratory, by applying increasing amounts of pressure to carbon, like wood, also produced a 'cleat' in the mineral which runs in the same direction as its natural brethren. Fact is the wood under extreme pressure crystallises, and 'sets' into those lines, that 'make' as we call it, regardless of what shapeless and un-uniform mass it has originally fallen into. As for the 'inch of coal coming from 30 foot of tree', so 300-foot coal seams would require 3600-foot trees—we now knew it didn't have to have been all from the same tree; they got squashed together and remoulded into a crystallised fusion which became coal. It had taken me thirteen years to discover the answer to Geordie's conundrum.

Katie lived across the quad, at Berkbeck Court. She was blond, a little taller than me, a smouldering sexual face and the figure of a movie star. We got it on at the beginning of the second year; she was exciting but all-consuming. I liked sexy girls, but Katie was predatory; she went off in a wisp of smoke with anyone she fancied, just then and there. You had to know this about Katie. She was some chick on your arm, but get a photo quick because she didn't stay there long. She was the archetypal hippie chick, vegetarian, mystical, sexually totally free and unchained. She was the 'groovy Tuesday' the song was about. She would flop on my bed and roll a giant joint, her lovely legs tucked underneath her and sing along loudly to Dylan on my tape. She had a passion, but on deeper enquiry I discovered it wasn't all laid-back freedom. None of Katie's lovers had ever succeeded in giving her an orgasm. It was linked somehow with the will-o-the-wisp nature of her flirtations and breathless conquests. She explained this to me once; when maybe I was coming on a bit ower heavy about taking off when we were oot. This was a challenge. I wasn't so stupid as to think this thing would work just by simple technique, although I used every trick in the book, and she was willing to let me try, anytime of the day or night or mid afternoon. My jaw locked into contortions, the string on my tongue was strained to snapping point, my fingers refused to operate any further and wherever I wanged my prick, in whatever formation, rhythm or degree, it didn't work. You would think I would have just enjoyed trying, but I didn't. It was a challenge; I couldn't believe I couldn't bring her to climax. If that frustrated me, it obsessed her. We drifted apart; she thought I was getting too heavy—I think I told her I loved her. How could I say that? She needed more than me and anyway liked classy company at the jazz lounges and casinos where she cut a cultured dash in her red satin dress and flowing blond hair and magnificent breasts. I must say that with her as my 'partner' to the big Irish meeting in Glasgow where I spoke as Sinn Fein's representative, I felt like a star that had cornered the leading lady.

She gave me a tiny wee wooden bowl of flowers, which I still have. She used to drop over with stir fry from her freshly grown jam jar bean sprouts, eat, chat, kiss me and leave. We stopped trying the other thing, but I think her search for a physically compatible partner continued apace.

Dawn was my first sort of 'right-on' encounter at university. Fascinating, middle-class, intellectual, a nationalist, beautiful. It hadn't 'dawned on me' yet (yes *The Telegraph* gossip columns were full of such witticisms), as our relationship became obvious, but Dawn too was a virgin. I couldn't understand why she would jump up and go just as she was getting all hot and exposed. She had fascinatingly sexual feet, those naked, writhing tell-tale signs of her pleasure, blood-red toenails, tight and neat belly button, a thrusting twisting baring of hips and whispering passion in my ears. She had a most beautiful body, she visited my room almost daily and I couldn't wait to get her out of those clothes of hers which were always 'just so', and suited her like they were made for her, but best of all was her body which was made for her. She went onto the pill specifically, deliberately choosing the time, the hour, when it would go all the way. She became I suppose my girlfriend sort of, she came with me to lectures, the kind I was giving, and socials, the kind I sang at, history expositions and demonstrations. *The Telegraph* had a field-day: 'Three Nights On The Trot Dawn!' and 'Dave—Up At The Crack Of Dawn?' It was awkward; Dawn treated me like her previous boyfriends, and I picked her up from her house, came over and had dinner with her Mam and Dad, helped her old man move furniture out of his shed, watched every word I said in case I mentioned the fact that I too had a family. Her Dad and Mam and family watched me on *Light of Experience*; they were not quite sure, asked all the time if I was really only thirty— I 'seemed so much older some how'. I think I was growing fonder of Dawn the whole time, I think it was mutual, and so she ended it. 'I'm 17 Dave. I shouldn't be involved with a married man with weans; where will it lead us?'

STRIPPERS FOR THE UNION?
The Student Union AGM of May 1977 heralded a mass meeting crowded to

capacity. For agendaed by Steve Kelly, the Yorkshire vice president, was the propostion that we should allow paid strippers into the Union. It was to be somewhat of a celebrity debate, proposed by the bluff and rough-and-ready Steve, who argued that stripping was just a job, no more exploitative than working behind the bar, only better paid. Dave Cruickshanks, the Strathtory dwarf and hemp smoker, contrasted the boring politics of the Broad Left and opposers of the motion with fun, having a laugh and strippers. I was the principal speaker in opposition and they got both barrels. I pointed out that this was a motion moved by those who came to university and after three years hadn't seen anyone naked except themselves, that I believed in free love and if everyone or anyone wanted to get up and take their clothes off I would applaud them, but I wasn't going to pay someone to do it, or force through poverty some hapless lass to do it. I suggested all the girls who wanted male strippers and all the blokes who wanted female strippers get together, 'And take your clothes off. It's easy!' The hall filled with laughter throughout the debate and it was quite clear we had humiliated the movers of the motion, who appeared fairly inept voyeurs. Then Harry Mullen, a born-again 'Christian Communist', with a passing resemblance to Ian Paisley in voice and manner took to the stage and nearly blew it. 'You'd have these young girls, getting up here and exposing their young nubile bodies, taking off their brassieres and knickers!' The crowd cheered at his every image, and at one point I felt like voting for the motion myself. 'For God's sake, get him off!' I yelled. When I retook the stage I insisted Harry had not in fact been speaking for the motion although it was the best speech in favour we had heard. The motion was lost 3 to 1.

Close-up and in class with the general student populace—not the rockers, ravers, sexers, drug takers and politicos of all hues—I am regarded I suppose as a pain up the arse. Most of these students are retired schoolkids, indeed have simply moved class from school to university. They are used to sitting in a trancelike state, writing on autopilot, the girls writing, receiving and transmitting by talking to each other at the same time. In the first year many classes are base mass classes of hundreds upon hundreds of students. Business Admin. of all descriptions includes Industrial Relations One, which it seems everyone from typists to business managers and accountants must attend.

I am parked somewhere near the front, and the lecturer is in full flight, when I just up and say 'Na, I can't agree with that!'

'What?' he says, suddenly quite alert, 'What?'

'I don't agree with that, that's not objective commentary, its just a-priori justification for the existence of social classes.'

Three hundred students look at each other through the corners of their eyes, or giggle, or go loudly 'A hem!' meaning 'Let's get on shall we, embarrassing wee person?'

At the end of the class as the students troop down the isles and stairs and out into the sunshine, the tutor calls me over.

'Dave, isn't it?'

'Aye.'

'Dave, don't do that again please.'

'What, you can't take a bit of free discussion? What about academic freedom and debate?'

'Nothing to do with that, Dave. I have stood there for ten years and given a lecture twice a week and nobody has ever so much as said good morning. I had quite forgotten anybody else was in the room. You nearly gave me a heart attack—I thought for a moment I was in the real world.'

He went on to tell me how when he was new and keen he used to stick the odd joke in and anecdote, only to have the students write it down without realising what he said, never mind what he meant; he knew this because they started to be re-quoted in essays back him to him which were verbatim recordings of pieces of his lectures.

Tutorials with a group of six or seven students were even more annoying for those who wanted a quiet life, or who were just trying to piece together some bit of philosophy of the world, when in would wade this horny-handed son of toil with the gospel of Marxism ready and applicable to every question and situation.

By the second year, as the industrial relations class became more specialist and refined, there were about six of us 'mature students', men and women from work and industry and unions, and interventions became thick and frequent. I was forced to produce an '*Open Letter to the Industrial Relations Dept* and *Students On The Study of Industrial Relations*'. These I ran off by the hundred and circulated at every class and every tutorial and then round the entire business school. The students recognised a bit of interesting mischief when they seen it and pounced upon it to read it avidly. The academic staff were not amused. One of the law lecturers told me, 'You have created quite a fuss downstairs' while year-two tutors accused me of 'Marching into Poland unannounced without warning'.

So it has come somewhat half way though the course that we students come to face the tired old question of 'academic neutrality'. In the interests of academic (to say nothing of moral) understanding, and so my fellow students will understand my class and tutorial battles I feel it necessary to present another side of the question.

1) Neutrality

It would seem reasonable that a tutor charged with instructing young and inexperienced students should present all sides of the subject. The students hovering over this selection box of ideology and idealism can freely pick the angle of his/her choice.

Critique

Trouble is all angles are not equally presented, the reading list, the choice and more particularly the wording of essay titles, the solution to exam problems are not non-biased. They are chosen by tutors and the dept to urge students in one consistent direction. Consider if you will the space devoted to Marxist interpretations of Industrial relations. Not more than 2 per cent of the reading list (in the 2nd year) can possibly be regarded as a Marxist view. Indeed it could be argued that there are no

Marxist authors on the list with the exception of Hyman. Marxism is not Marxism but 'radicalism' (a dead eighteenth century political creed of philanthropic and extraordinary landlords). What percentage of lecturers has been given over to this 'radical' view never mind a straight Marxist view? The weight of course pushes toward pluralism and pluralist literature.

2) Method of Analysis

We consider this view and that and the other—criticise all in turn and draw a little from each.

Critique

Hedge your bets; be all things to all men, a good academic is vague and undecided. There is no objective place to stand in such an assessment. What view does one occupy while so reviewing the scope of ideas? It is inconceivable in any science, social science included, that elements can be reviewed at random and without a platform to subject such features. What is clearly required is a hypothesis, i.e. A valued statement—which is set up and then plummeted with countless facts and sets of evidence to see how it stands up. Certain hypothesis will be in this way demolished— but others will stand the test i.e. There are some facts. Some things are provable. The notion so posed by tutors is that only a critical selection of all theories is objective. This is scientific nonsense—if we asses a wide variety of subjects surely some must be eliminated at some stage. We do not expect at the end of two years to have the same subjects standing before us as at the inception of the study.

3) We are being presented with a choice.

From all this medley of selection one can choose a view of one's own and stick to it and use it analysing industrial relations.

Critique

This is not true, for although we are told 'this is unitary' 'this is pluralist' 'this is radical' one is never allowed to occupy any of these positions—if we do we are told it is dogmatism. Non analytical. This is presented as a neutral view, but actually it is a view in itself, which says all theories are wrong. If one rejects the Marxist theory of class war and irreconcilable class forces one is automatically occupying another position. This 'neutrality' (so called) is a view easily adopted by academics because it does not require a theory and therefore there is nothing of literally substance that one can come back on to attack. It is also non-neutral, when by force of essay marks and exam results one is failed for taking up any alternative position. (Odd that well qualified men and women who have written the literature to which we are referred are recommended reading and yet if we present an argument supporting their views are marked down by tutors who have never put pen to paper themselves.)

ALL THE QUESTIONS ARE THE SAME

There are different titles but actually when it comes down to it we are being asked the self same question. For e.g. 'What is the role of the law in British Industrial relations?' 'How far are strikes damaging to Britain's economy?' 'How far should the state intervene into industrial relations?' Straightforward it might seem BUT the questions are actually asking what is the unitary, pluralist, radical view of the role of the state, strikes, law etc. Having mulled round the three views one must conclude with a vague and ambiguous answer that nobody has it right. But these are simply conceptualisations of something which actually in reality does exist outside of men's minds i.e. The state does have a role, the law does have a role, but if one has the audacity to answer the questions straight and say what this role is, one is marked down as being dogmatic. It matters not how many facts and statistics one brings forth to support the argument, if it is an argument from a Marxist premise only, it is automatically 'non analytical'. Is there a real world or is there only a world as seen through someone's else's eyes? I would argue (as a Marxist) that the world is not amorphous and mysteriously vague, that Marxism as a science makes sense of history and current reality and sees them not a load of separated and isolated events but as a continuing process, linked one to the other and interacting.

DOES THIS MEAN NO OTHER VIEWS SHOULD BE CONSIDERED?

All other views must be considered, every angle of the question must be considered—but for what purpose? Surely not just to say 'here is one view. there is another. and look over there is yet another' but to say 'does this view correspond to the fact?' Having developed a table on which to analyse the forces in society one submits all theories to it, for the purpose of rejecting some and proving others. By this method as Marxists we can study the unitary theory, pluralism or black magic for that matter. What we are offered instead is a nowhere land in which no view may reign. This is not science; it is a despairing cry of someone lost in a maze of facts they do not know what to do with and daren't reject any route for fear that was the one. (Actually it is only by a process of elimination that one could get out of such a maze)

I submit this paper to open up a dialogue with my long suffering fellow students who wonder why I simply can't do what I'm told and like with the Kings New Clothes see what I am told is there. I hope the dept tutors will reply to this.

He who holds the mark pen dictates what reality is. But does the real outside world correspond to the vision of the outside as seen by middle-class scholars and academics? Or is it a perpetual mirror image of their own confusion and social indecision?

Ooh, ouch, that must have stung. Well it set the place buzzing but it cleared some things up for me. Management Science, and Management Techniques lecturers started their lectures by saying: 'This field of study will start from the premises that Capitalism is the social and economic model we will be working with. It could be there are other social systems either now or in the future, but we will be working from the proposition of how this one sees itself working. I am sure Mr Douglass will tell us, even supposed rival social systems use a great deal of this system in their supposed alternatives.' Well I could live with that. I didn't have to agree with it, but the fact they offered that this was a value judgement based upon a particular premises and not some immutable fact of life made it easy for me to get down to the mechanics of business administration without further disruption and challenges. Industrial relations never altered though. I don't think they ever forgave me.

STRATHCLYDE AND UNIVERSITY CHALLENGE

Our team sets off with a busload of supporters down to Manchester to take part in the live contest. Steve Kelly the vice president is aboard, as are crates of beer and packs of lager supplied buckshee from the Union. We aren't sure how other university teams supporters prepare but this is how we do it. The journey down is boisterous and joyful. The quiz team, mainly 'plumbers' (as the electrical, mechanical and mining students are known) and scientists, don't overindulge. The bus was late setting off while the lads loaded up their carryoots, and had also stopped three or four times for a piss on the way down, and at one point the lads were having a game of pool. The bus arrived on the wire of the programme going out and the big doors to the studio were opened and the bus drove in. The Strathclyde supporters poured off the bus, almost literally and straight into the studio, still carrying their cans and bottles. If things had went well, the night would have been little more than noisy. As it turned out, all the questions were arty farty questions; Strathclyde is an industrial university and the team didn't have a clue. 'William Shakespeare' was the only answer they could come up with for some question on the arts; this was then taken up by the supporters in the audience every time a similar question was posed and the team fell downcast and silent. Bamber Gascoigne the question-asker had to demand that the supporters stop shouting out and then threatened to have them removed. One suspects booing the other side (Lancaster) wasn't the usual way this game is played. It got worse as one of the lads leaned forward and with his lighter set fire to Lancaster's mascot 'gonk'. The fizz of beer cans being opened echoed across the question desks and ringpulls could be seen flying across the TV screen and landing on the floor area. Some of our more serious and highly embarrassed female students, livid at the whole thing, later complained in *The Telegraph*, concluding:

> However the piece de resistance of the whole trip is still to come.
> The time the bus was to leave had been altered (to suit certain individuals' drunken habits) to 11 p.m. Previously it has been advertised as 9.30 p.m. We were told about the change after the programme. We arrived for departure at 10.30 p.m. Not long afterwards the drunks started to roll on!! Only to be followed by two CID men, two constables and the landlord of a pub, who proceeded to pick out certain people. These people were then taken to the police station where 10 supporters were taken off the bus. Finally we left Manchester at 12.15 a.m. leaving two of our 'supporters'

behind to face charges and arrived back at 5.15 a.m.

BLONDIE

February 1978. I get to meet 'Blondie'. One of the perks of helping to run the Student Union and take charge of its security was I often came into contact with the stars of our Saturday night big bashes. Debbie arrived with the band and two great fairground wagons of gear. It was early afternoon and the Union was scarce deserted. Debbie was walking about in an old brown boiler suit helping direct roadies and band here there and everywhere; on her head she had a woollen hat. Dozens of students just walked past her, and didn't realise they were in the presence of a rock goddess. She was chatty and unaffected. God know who fitted this band into the 'punk' mode; even by US standards they were never that. She told me that although they thought of their genre as 'new wave' they didn't have a clue what 'punk' was all supposed to be about until really reaching Britain. Her attempts at a bit of a pogo on stage looked frankly silly. As the mass Glasgow crowds of punk rockers cram our huge concert hall to capacity and over-capacity, there is a sort of embarrassed contrast, the punks in their grot and the oh-so-pretty Debbie. Mind, once she came out with the crocheted little string dress, and the body stocking which made it look even from close up like she was wearing nothing underneath, few of the blokes seemed to care what her musical definition was. The crowd crammed into the front third of the room and serious crush injuries were pending. Their roadies were going down like ninepins and ours were shitting a brick. She sat backstage terrified at the hysteria being unleashed out front. Then she just let it rip and got tore into her act. As the night went on the crowd eased back a little, anyway enough to carry the bodies out. 'Gee!' she gurgled, 'I didn't know you Scottish had so much Latin blood in you!' I thought nope, its whisky and lager. At the end of the show, when the crowd had all but gone, she came out to thank us for our efforts, and she invited me back to a party with her and the band! Can you believe I didn't go? I was with Dawn, my heartthrob at the time, and she was feeling ill, so I felt I had to do the decent thing and leave with her. I didn't even get my photo took with Debs. Actually, she told me they had had very little; they had signed disastrous contracts which had taken most of everything they earned and the rest was spent saving up to buy the things out, which when they succeeded in doing it the companies blocked them from tours, starved them of publicity and stifled their distribution. They never did make it big time financially for themselves. Today their music is warm and nostalgic to me and I am glad they managed to carry on working—Debbie still cutting a dash and creating a crush.

Motorhead was the firm, cheap favourite of the union. We could get them almost anytime for £500. They never failed to fill the room and crash through the night like they were still on their motorbikes. In addition to the £500 they got free booze. They would arrive in the middle of the afternoon and Lemmie would usually be found upstairs in our lounge, decking pints of lager. I could never understand his physical capacity to absorb beer. He could down ten to fifteen pints, right up to the final call for him on stage. I have seen him be still downing his pint while the band were already into the first number and he strides from the lounge straight on stage, head back straight into the thrust and violence of the song. He would stay in this position right through the gig, and beyond, because while ever there was a crowd there Motorhead would play, for the sheer joy of performing. They would often go an hour over their spot, but the point was, what did he dey with the booze? He never had to piss and I never ever seen a pool of liquid on stage where he had been standing. It baffled me. As did a couple of other things. Like I had been chatting to him at the bar, while he stood there in his grot, swastikas and Iron Crosses hanging from his denim. 'Can I ask you something, Lemmie?' I began. He eyed me with a sideways glance and replied, 'Do I look like a Nazi?' I looked again. The wild unkempt hair, the Hell's Angel garb, the wild spirit of freedom pulsing through his body. 'Na,' I replied 'Then what were you going to ask me?' 'Er, nothing, it doesn't matter,' I responded somewhat sheepishly. That had been what I was going to ask him and he knew it— I suppose from the frequency people like me asked him. He wasn't actually overtly political in anyway, he was part of a generation, a rock 'n' roll movement which had an energy and agenda of its own, on which the folk like him and the Stones for example didn't see any further need of political statement or elaboration.[80]

I am invited by Jon Smith from York University Socialist History Group to speak, sing, and tell the tale at the University Vanbrough College, on the history of the miners' union, the oral history and musical traditions of the miners. They offer me expenses and to put me up at one of their sedate residences, so I invite Dawn along with me. It is a memorable and happy weekend in the leafy glades of York University in the snow. Playing snowball fights, walking hand in hand, in bed together in a snug eighteenth-century cottage which the students had use of. I recall the delicate scent of her body spray, her subdued and quiet panting as she came. I recall her perfume .... her painted toenails ... even now. My lecture was well attended, and questions overflowed into the JCR. Dawn had to tell them a time or two not to presume she was a revolutionary socialist, rather she was a revolutionary nationalist.

In March our excellent pamphlet *Whither Scotland* makes its appearance, the ninth publication since the inception of the SUI. It reads very powerfully and Maureen inscribes it throughout with excellent Celtic pen drawings, mainly of Gaelic symbols. As I proudly sell the pamphlet in the lounge bar I am surprised to be regaled as a 'racialist' by a group of black African students. After ludicrous cross-purpose exchanges and mutual non-comprehension, they demand to know why with my credentials I am selling a pamphlet called '*Whiter Scotland*'. (No, this time it wasn't a Posadist spangle problem or my bad spelling – it was, thankfully, their misreading of the title.)

30 April 1978. Mass Irish and Scottish Republican Rally, Carnegie Hall Glasgow. This is raw working-class republican Scottish, republican Irish working-class, red and green Glasgow. This is where the 'rammie' will start in earnest if the Orangies decided to attack. Odd isn't it, that wherever you get the genuine, bedrock, proletarian great 'unwashed' turning out to add their political voices and add their brain and muscle, suddenly the ranks of paper-sellers and revolutionary vanguards

are all absent? I think the revolutionary left, so called, is actually afraid, physically afraid of the working class and with no resonance to strike with them, is nervous and ill at ease. None of the well-rehearsed gospels and text seem relevant anymore. So they are conspicuous by their absence. But this was red Glasgow, masses of young workers and older workers, men and women, a forest of lang hair or flat caps, or as in the pit communities both, Celtic football shirts, and a cloud of thick smoke. I am here to speak for Sinn Fein; actually Jim Reilly, Sinn Fein Ard Comharlie Britain, was due to speak but couldn't, so delegated me to read his speech, which of course I did, following to the letter his instructions on pauses, and applause and emphasis. It should be recalled that I am here speaking to the existing Cumann in Glasgow, and the newly emerging James Connolly Cumann Glasgow (a more youthful socialist branch than the established Cumann, which is actually a section of the Donegal Cumann over the wee bit water), on behalf of the Ard Comharlie—boy was that an honour. Jim had written me out a formal letter of authorisation saying I 'was authorised to carry out work on behalf of the Provisional Republican Movement, approved by the Ard Comharlie Britain Jim Reilly, through Kevin Street.'

A famous photographer who pictures guerrilla fighters and conflicts all over the world asks me to arrange for him to tour with the IRA and photograph actions and organisation! I have to ask him if he's crazy or he thinks we are. But no, he is adamant that this sort of thing is very good publicity. Although he is a wee bit over-romantic, he is 100 per cent trustworthy, and if he isn't, 'You'll know where I am.' So I pass on his request. I don't recall his name, or know if he ever got to do his 'shoot of shoots' so to speak. I was more sorry not to stay in touch because he took some ace professional photos of me and Kathy, 'because you look so colourful,' which was odd because we both happened to be both dressed in black.

May 1978. John O'Connel (some called him Davie)—he himself had gone back to the Gaelic spelling and redesignated the name Sean O Conaill—our Geordie-Irish freedom fighter dies in agony in prison. He has stomach cancer, though they wouldn't give him hospital treatment until the last few days and then mainly to prevent him dying in prison. He had not been a member of the IRA or any Irish armed group, he was a member of our raggy-lad cadre of internationalist revolutionary Geordies. He was well liked by all the Irish prisoners though; they were exchanging Irish lessons for Geordie lessons.

Ard Chomharlie Report:
>Recently we have seen attacks upon the Republican Movement in Left Wing Journals.
>
>In this country there has been a deliberate attempt to play down the role of Sinn Fein. The Journals concerned amongst others *Socialist Challenge*, *Socialist Worker*, *Leveller* and *Inprecor*. It is hoped that comrades in London will use their common sense in this matter ...

Somehow the 'left' wished to support the action on the street, but not the team organising the action, to support 'the people' but not how and where they were actually organising. Like somehow pretend the republican movement didn't exist, and the rebel masses were just vacuous, politically virginal and heroic if naive waiting only for the arrival of the revolutionary vanguard from over the water to come and give the real direction and analysis to the struggle.

Unofficial strike action sweeps through the Yorkshire coalfield in May. It is actually a dying shot in a crucial battle against the implementation of the new incentive scheme. The scheme is a strategically placed plan to divide the miners and break their national unity. It is not an accident nor is it some incidental development. It is Labour's central plan to disarm the miners. Its impact wasn't felt until the whole structure of the union was shaken by a head-on clash years later; the divisions sown in this period were to send cracks right through the union's structure, in its most decisive hour.

BOTTLE O' BROON FOR CHARLIE

Prince Charles visits Newcastle and receives a bottle of broon, unfortunately for him it is thrown against the window of his car and smashes with an awful waste of its content. A well-placed local journalist gets a shot of a startled Big Ears peering through the shattered impact ring of the side window of his car. It had been thrown by an unemployed Geordie determined that his Highness's PR stunt doesn't work. The man is chased by motorcycle cops through the streets before being felled by one of the bikes and run over. Worse, he is then assaulted by a number of old Geordie royalist housewives who batter him with their handbags.

5 June 1978. My best mate at school, my very best friend Billy Bell, dies when his car hurtles 30 feet off a cliffside at Seaham Harbour, hits the rocks and bursts into flames. Bill had just landed the position of club steward at the new Leam Lane Estate Social Club. A position he had dreamed of, at the centre of the community he had grown up in and which all his friends were now making a point of visiting. His wife Eileen and his two kids Karen, eight, and John, ten, had just moved into the club's accommodation and were looking forward to a settled future.

The impact of Bill's death has never left me. I think of him still, his big smiling face, his 'meedman' expressions. I still refer me 'scores' and deyins to Bill, to check his much-esteemed approval or hear his mockery. I still visit his graveside almost every Boxing Day as I call to see my sister Marina's grave on her birthday. Me and Emma had called almost every year since she was born, to see me Mam and Dad, dropping off at the cemetery on the way. Two little bundles of red carnations, one for Tommy Hepburn, the founder of the Miners' Union, and one for Marina. Emma had heard me each year tell Tommy what the Union was up to and speculate on just what he would have made of it all now. With Marina, my thoughts were silent, but Emma always just hugged my arm, or put her arm around my shoulder as I crouched to tend the grave. She would be looking up at me with deep sympathy as I wiped the tears away, and we set off hand in hand to see me Mam and have one of her favourite teas. Now I had started taking three solitary red carnations, one of them for Bill. My yarns and exploits retold to Bill, as we would in the school yard, or outside the pub, as we met by chance on odd occasions afterwards, were not the sort little Emma would have understood. The grave is always well attended. There is always a big bunch of flowers every year when I call, as I suppose his kids, now grown up, have lived without the magic of their magical Dad. My best mate. Those bloody coast rocks always got us in trouble, lad. Remember Pedro's shoe?

20–22 June 1978. The Revolutionary Communist Group attempt big public meetings in Glasgow at the Langside Public Hall and Edinburgh Trade Council Club, with Terry Marlow from their group and me on behalf of Provisional Sinn Fein.

July 1978. RCL (I) come over from America for a period of joint work. We set up a reception for them at the Abbey.

RACHAEL SWEET

At the beginning of November I am struck down with instant love on seeing the star of the Stiff Tour, Rachel Sweet, sweet little sixteen, a ball of rock 'n' roll fire. As a person charged with security issues I get access to the entourage and to buy her a Coke and sit and chat. I think we are getting along fine, although under the distant scrutiny of her roadies. She sits there flinging her head and hair about in her Firestone High School sweatshirt and talks about Akron where she comes from and a lifetime, literally, in song and dance since the age of five—although she insists, in her lyrical little Ohio voice, that her folks weren't the pushy sort. I am sat right next to her on the long back seat of the upstairs TV room, her little bum is snuggled right up close to mine in her ice-blue jeans with brass studs on, and then I go and blow it. I suggest we go down to the disco which is already in full flight. 'Hey you got a disco?' she says excitedly. 'Gee!' she says and jumps up doing a little 'get down boogie' jive. 'Lets go!' 'Great!' I think, 'bliddy great, dancing with Rachael Sweet.' 'Where you going?' one of the roadies shouts. 'Down to the disco, boys. 'No you ain't.' She shrugs. 'He thinks he's my dad.' 'We've work to do,' the roadie says, and gives me an 'Oh, yeah?' look. She invites me to follow them up to Edinburgh with the tour and for a second or so I think of dropping everything and trailing after her like a groupie, but I've been in these sort of 'not-really-on' situations before, where you don't really know why you're there and the other person isn't making too strong a suggestion that you're anything to do with them really. I had in the back of my mind the words of the student journalist who had got to do a full-page interview piece in *Strathclyde Telegraph* with Rach':

> I ask her if she thinks people will regard her as a sex symbol. She falls about laughing. I suspect much more at me than the question, and answers 'maybe— to 15 year old boys'. Fair enough—I'll stick my head on the chopping block …

So I am aware she really is aware she has sexual pull .When she comes on stage with the rest of band, she is wearing sparkling little hot pants and is tiny, but anything but 'sweet' in her country rock power, a dynamo. She quite eclipses Lovitch the punk starlet also on stage with her, knocking about and chatty, who I virtually ignore, until many too many years later I realise she had been strikingly sexy, too,. The Stiff Tour announced on its publicity 'If It Ain't Stiff It Ain't Worth A W…' The tour and Rachael's fame was rapidly over and true to say I don't think she ever got bigger than this in commercial terms. She was going back to school after the tour and planned to finish her other two years before deciding what to do. I thought she was so unaffected, a bundle of laughs and drop-dead gorgeous. Half of the male population of Strathclyde fell for her too so I wasn't alone in my admiration

10–12 November 1978. History Workshop 'In Our Time—Britain 1945–1978'. I address two sessions, one on the impact of the unofficial strike of 1969 and the other on the Tyneside Committee of 100 which together with my earlier pieces, one on childhood and the other on the Tyneside Irish communities, become the starting blocks for this whole work. My great friend and comrade Phillip Donellan, in his grand, cultured and Shakespearean-actor voice, gives a session on 'The BBC in the 1950s' and later sings some hilarious risqué songs at our mid-afternoon social. Ray Challinor, a man I first will not countenance because of his 'third campism', as I would have put it, wins me over to a position of utmost admiration in respect of his ruthlessly efficient and amazing historical research on early workers' movements and particularly those of the miners. Ray's piece is on 'British Trotskyism 1953–1978' and despite my pre-existing suspicions is utterly enthralling and informative.

17 November 1978. London: History Workshop Benefit Social—McColl, Seeger, Alun Howkins and me!

I am on stage on the same platform as Ewan MacColl and Peggy Seeger and Alun Howkins. Unfortunately they put me on last, after McColl and Seeger, and after a barn dance and after Alun, then it's me, by which time I was a three sheets to the wind. Peggy had bollocked me at half time, about drinking before going on, and normally I wouldn't have except, being last, I was going to end up at the whole concert and ceilidh without a drink. I felt guilty too because they paid my fare down, which ended up the most expensive expenses of everyone, including Peggy and Ewan, and I only told two jokes and did three songs. They were well received but I know the organisers thought me a bit of an unnecessary extravagance, which I was—but they invited me.

PUBLIC IMAGE OR PUBIC IMAGE?
November 1978: The History Workshop, Oxford. Since my interests and studies straddle three broad areas— history, the law and industrial relations—I likewise belong to all three University societies and manage to successfully lobby among all three disciplines for a joint delegation to the Workshop over the long weekend. It's unusual for three societies to gain financial assistance from the General Student Union funds to go to the same event, but we succeed. I was chuffed to

bits with the Glasgow students, who knocked spots off their Oxford colleagues and some of the lecturers, pointing out how this law or that law didn't apply in Scotland, how this 'right' or that Act didn't apply. A Scottish slant on some of the southcentric historic givens was also quite refreshing. Raph was ecstatic at the size of the Scottish contingent and their vocal participation. Maureen and Emma and the comrades from Doncaster came down, and joined up with our emigré Oxford cell. Quite a reunion but it was the return trip which was to be memorable.

It was one of them balmy sunny Oxford days, with sunlight streaming through the trees, and happiness swimming through our bodies. We were setting off back to Glasgow, a team, camaraderie, intelligent, knowledgeable but pointedly working-class, Geordie and Glaswegian. We boarded the train, and found ourselves sitting in the buffet section, the kind with tables. As we left the station and waved everyone off we uncorked the first of the big bottles of white wine and began to relax. It had been a wonderful weekend. We felt we had done ourselves and Strathclyde proud, a little better than our University Challenge team, although in way they too had upheld a Strathclyde tradition. We chattered and laughed, debated and sang, as the miles sped by and the bottles were drained. We then started buying the wee bottles from the buffet—an expensive way to drink, but we were merrily carefree now. By the time we cruised into Glasgow Central there was time for one mad charge to the bar counter before time was called, but by now we were all in full flight and the day was too full, too happy to end yet. Aileen announces that she has a horde of cans at her flat but we can't stay there. Nae problem: we gather up two carrier bags of tins and head for my place where I have recalled I have a nice wee lump of Nepalese Black. With the Dylan up lood, and my huge langjoints circulating the room, we sit on the floor, in a big circle, smoking, toking, drinking, and blathering. I am half sitting, half lying next to Maggie, a classmate with huge breasts who I have never particularly noticed in a sexual sense until now. We are in the centre of the gang, people are talking across each other, individually or all at once, to all and to each. Then I am sliding my hand up Maggie's back under her sweater, I feel the thin valley of her spine, the shape of her shoulders, the thin straining strap of her bra. She is still for a minute, everyone is still talking, and I no longer see them. My hand is up through the top of her sweater stroking her neck, her head, her hair, then sliding back down to her bum and round the top of her knickers, fingers following their line around to her belly. She turns and looks at me, then she is lying on me, and we are snogging with a passion as her jumper comes off over her head and I have freed the breasts and their round pink nipples flop towards my mouth and which I plunge round them and try to swallow them whole. My fly is being torn open; the erect eager thrust of my penis is now free too and in search of a partner. In seconds we are absolutely naked, I am in an oral engagement and Maggie is rubbing my cock round her face and tits. For a few minutes not everyone in the room has noticed, then they all are struck speechless and silent and a shocked immobility falls over them all. We were totally and utterly oblivious of them. Someone puts the light off, and they go off in search of beds and chairs to doss down in. We haven't bothered with a bed and roll about the floor. Maggie is whispering the most passionate and crude things in my ears, but the erotic impact of this is now and again lost in translation. 'Just fuck me fast' sounded like 'Just fuck me first.' I, puzzled, suddenly stop and shake my head into semiconsciousness. 'Why what deyee want ti dey after?' 'Eh?' 'What yee say?' 'Fuckin' fuck me fast and fucking shut up!' We fell into a pause of helpless laughter when I explained what I thought she'd said, as the laughter subsided, me dick was still standing untamed, and uncum, the effect of booze and dope. I stood up and pulled her to her feet and started to fuck standing up, then rammed against the wall, holding her off the floor with her legs up in the crooks of my arms and her tits bouncing and slapping up and down. The poor sods trying to sleep, and hiding under their sleeping bags couldn't possibly have missed the floor show.

As morning broke, I realised I was now lying on the mattress in the corner of the room, which I used as bed. I felt Maggie next to me, naked. She turned to me. 'Dave, tell me we didnae dey what I think we did last night?' Oh no, oh no. As we peered from the blankets, the other students, who had been up and about washing, cleaning teeth, tidying up, making breakfast, gave forth with a round of applause as we sheepishly got out of bed. I held a sheet in front in me as I walked to find me claes. 'A wadne bother noo!' they shout. 'Bit late for modesty, Davie.'

Well, we were the talk of the Union for the rest of the year. I never really got to know Maggie; it was just one of those things. We said 'Hi' when we passed between classes.

December 1978–January 1979. SUI/EMC start to make serious efforts to recruit serving soldiers and start to hold meetings with groups of them near various barracks. York becomes a national centre for this work. We have quite a number on board but cannot be sure how many of these are working for the state to penetrate us. We are attempting to utilise their military training in association with ours to test how far we can trust them and work with them. All express sympathy with the IRA, some ask to join. We are highly cautious about any attempt to expose members of either wing of the Provos to direct soldier connection and will pass information over to them, to make the judgement and call directly. We also pull off the most dangerous and daring EMC operation with the Glasgow team. The Officer Training Corps has been on a big Scottish exercise with the Territorial Army, among whom are the part-time NCOs of the SAS. Believe me, they have them—men who work in normal life but are trained SAS operatives.

They have got use of part of the Student Union building. The officials seeing it as their civic duty to assist the forces of the crown, earn lots of money for the Union and gain themselves some Brownie points for their future careers.

Andy, working as white-jacketed waiter, nicks the briefcase with all the operational plans in it, passes it to me and I am away. The briefcase had been shackled to the right hand of some little upstart officer caddy, but the young bigwig impressing the ladies in their long frocks decided to undo it to let him get in a big tray of drinks. Then, following their reception, their grand dinner, their speeches, their presentations, their back-slapping, the brandy was being supped and they were well pissed. The briefcase? The Briefcase!! The shit well and truly hit the fan. Staff recalled and questioned, squaddies called in to search on their hands and knees, waste baskets and dustbins combed through, taxis halted, buses stopped, passengers questioned. Police roadblocks, stop and search. You name it. The officials came under intense pressure to give a breakdown of the student activists their affiliations, their addresses. It got rough. A couple of days later, we returned the by now well read and copied bulging briefcase to a little-used toilet in the back stairs, used by the stars en route to and from the stage. The cleaners found it. The officials looked at me sideways for some time. They were suspicious but I hadn't been there—I was over at Dennistoun now and I wouldn't come near an army do. The officers couldn't be sure which toilets they had used, and couldn't rule out either them or the batman having taken it with them for safety and then in their stupor put it down and forgot where they had been. That was, as far as I am assured, the result of the resulting joint police/army inquiry. Was it any use? I don't know. Would our penetration and subversion of the army have impacted?

We had every reason to believe that in the situation of an anti-labour coup, sections of the armed forces would have joined the workers. Six years later, the biggest civil unrest since the General Strike hits Britain, the army cannot be relied upon to break the miners' blockades of coal stocks. We have contacts within the barracks, Class War produces the most subversive propaganda of the revolt aimed at subverting the troops, it is quite clear our efforts were far from futile, though obviously not self-sufficient.

In my final Strathclyde year, just when I need the security and certainty of a roof over my head in the run-up to the final exams, I am forced to give up the Birkbeck residence. Boy, has it been a hot and eventful two years, but now I'm out on the cobbles. For a time I sleep on people's floors. I take up residence with the good Doctor for Bagdad, up at Maryhill but in the end, I find a flat up at Denniston. Roebank Street—I share it with one of the mining engineers, Peter Sillars. We take the flat in the evening. I haven't had a chance to look round the neighbourhood. I am woken on the Sunday morning by the sound of the big bass drum and I think for a moment I am back at hyme and it's Gala day. I open the sash window and past the house marches the big bass drum and pipe band of the bliddy Denniston Orange Lodge. I am about to shout 'Up the IRA!' when I notice in large letters on the wall opposite: 'One Bible, One Crown, No Pope in Dennistoun'.

A SCOTTISH UNION OF STUDENTS

Strathclyde Student Union was not affiliated to the 'National' Union of Students. In some earlier period there had been an attempt to form a Scottish Union of Students but this had ended with only one affiliate, Edinburgh. Most of the small colleges were in the NUS. Glasgow, Strathclyde and most others were not in any 'national' student union other than their college-based ones. This hadn't prevented them participating in campaigns and protests and joint meetings . All through my time at the university there had been a growing campaign among the 'Broad Left' for affiliation to the NUS. By the end of 1978 it was agreed we should hold a referendum of the all the 6,000 students on and off campus. In line with our political current I was forcibly in favour of a Scottish Union of Students and quickly became one of its major advocates. Politics aside, autonomy aside, there were loads of practical reasons for why. Mainly, though, to start with, the laws relating to almost everything which affected Scottish students were different from those attending students south of that border. This did not stop the NUS sending up packs of totally irrelevant material on housing, rent acts, sexual rights, grants, exams, and legal rights, none of which applied to Scotland. Even more stupidly, these were often given out at advice centres and student fairs all over Scotland. The second major reason was that the NUS was an established career route for budding politicians, media commentators and media stars and had developed an all-consuming bureaucracy with a life and agenda all of its own, and was consuming vast sums of student money on the pet enterprises of the self-serving clique at the top of the career trail. That in brief was my opposition to it. Scotland was a nation, Scottish students—and that included me, and the other 'foreign' students studying in Scotland—needed a voice which was relevant to us, not exclusive to the campaigns over the border against a common government in London, but autonomous from them and targeted at our specific constituency. The prospect of Strathclyde going over to the SUS camp and joining Edinburgh sent alarm bells ringing down in London. They sent up all the NUS bigwigs and the president to actively campaign against us. It wasn't all our own way either; a large, piss-taking, rather narrow-minded and selfish clique was lining up behind 'The Tea Pot Party' to campaign for a 'Neither' vote. This was to be a single transferable vote scheme and was somewhat of a Mexican stand-off, with the SUS supporters advocating their second votes go reluctantly to an NUS alternative, and the NUS proposing the same for an SUS alternative, but with the 'Neither camp' actually proposing a vote for the NUS rather than us. The campaign, taking place at the worse possible time for me, during my finals, got quite heated, with the NUS top brass demanding on stage 'What's a bleeding Geordie doing leading a campaign for a Scottish Union of Students?' And me just in time to catch the remark rushing to the platform to respond 'Because all my life and the lives of other Geordie folk, people like you a lang lang away in London have thought it your God-given right to decide what's best for us. In any case I wouldn't expect a bliddy Cockney to know anything of the relationship between Scotland and Newcastle—fucking hell, man, we share a brewery!' I announced to cheers and stomping. Ner mind the enthusiastic singing of 'Scots Wa Hae' and a bagpiper who paraded around the colleges and libraries with our banner 'Build A Scottish Union Now', the intervention of Malc up from Newcastle to give us a leg up, and at least half the African students, ZANU in particular, who came over to us and toi-toied outside, clapping and swaying in the wind—we lost, the bliddy 'Neither' wing swinging it for the NUS. The 'Build A Scottish Union' sticker stood large as life in my old army coat for twenty years afterwards; I didn't feel it right to remove it. As predicted, the costs and positions spiralled, the essential conferences escalated, the full-time paid sabbaticals escalated, the escape route was torn up. In the end the Union lost its independence and allowed the University to bail it out, the students shackling themselves to the control of academic masters and their olders and betters for all time—something we would have considered shameful in those long-gone days of our super-efficient, super-profitable, highly independent and totally autonomous student Union. The rot began with the NUS, I have to say. Another of my magnificent failures on which I can none the less say, as with much else, 'Telt yee se!'

April 1979. Me Ems comes up to Glasgow to spend some time with me. I take her to all my classes, where she sits with her big drawing sketchpad and happily draws and writes through Professor Gavin's criminology lecture. In the afternoon she skips along to the Union to moan about the chips and cheese pasty along with the other students and in the evening she makes herself known round the student union bar, telling jokes about 'Dave' and his exploits, despite my efforts to shush her up. The students have religiously been collecting crisp packets with 'Flutterbye' coupons for her. The student bars on a night time are full of empty packets and my fellow Council members collect them in their hundreds. She succeeds in getting the whole set and the big wall display which goes with it.

6 July 1979. I graduate at Strathclyde. Veronica comes up as she is so proud of me, but is a little stricken when the woman in the canteen asks 'Is this your wee mum?' I have a final farewell and congratulations fling with Aileen, a small, slightly plump second-year who I had met at the beginning of the year. She is full of Glasgow humour and a mass of energy. A virgin who had made up her mind no longer to be and decided I would be the one. She knew I was married of course, but had tested me to see what I would say. 'Do you live with your mum in Geordieland?' she asked. When I started the whole ritual explanation about an open relationship, she cut me short and laughing said 'Everybody in the Union knows you Dave, we all know you're married.' We had ended up back at the Dennistoun flat, and got more and more passionate on the floor. As usual I hadn't thought, given her virginity, we were going to go that far, so unceremoniously continued the roll around the floor until she sat up and said 'Have yee no got a bed or what?' I just loved her Glaswegian working lass humour and sense of fun. I recall once us running for a late-night bus, and she was wearing one of those (horribly named) 'boob tubes'. We were running toward the bus, and her top wriggled its way down and her breasts were flying aboot in public. She just stood helpless with laughter and so did I. The bus driver couldn't drive for laughing either and when we got on she, pulling her top back up, received a cheer from the passengers . She was part of that, somehow belonging.

Few people get the chance to relive their youth, indeed to live a youth they missed the first time round. Glasgow and Strathclyde will always be the city of my rebirth, of unbounded happiness and unmatched memories.

PRAISE MARX AND PASS THE AMMUNITION

January 1977. We are in action against National Front meetings at the Vine (Doncaster), where they pose as a football supporters club. We disperse them from this venue, and some disappear from political life while others dig in.

THE BATTLE AT GRUNWICK

These were explosive years of widespread strike action across the board, but by and large these were battles to stand still as inflation ate into wages in real terms. Of course that was no accident—inflation isn't something like flu which just happens along: governments can use it as a device to lower wages, while increasing productivity. The workers kenned this fine and fought to rise above the tide. Grunwick was, though, a 'watershed', a sort of parting of the ways for the working class in Britain. Government direct control over the working class through the social contrick, as we called it, had been driven onto the rocks by rank-and-file obstinacy and refusal to play the game with 'their' government despite the efforts by many top union officials. Heath's outright confrontation had failed. Now there were signs of what looked like a counter-offensive by the employers directly. Nowhere was this better shown than down at Grunwicks, a large photo-processing firm, which took your photos through the post, in packets labelled Truprint and other catchy titles. The firm was situated in a North London suburb on the Bakerloo Line, Dollis Hill. It employed mainly Pakistani and Indian women workers, many of them deeply traditional. In the social climate which pervaded 'the workers' at large in those times, even these unlikely toilers, with no previous experience, decided to strike. This they did by forming a strike committee of their own; they had no union and hadn't known how to go about joining one. After the start of the strike in August 1976 APEX (Association of Professional, Executive, Clerical and Computer Staff) signed them up.

The conditions in the factory, although structurally it was modern, were, in human terms, abysmal, with pathetically low pay. Many worked for £0.75 per hour; a 50-hour week would allow you come out at the end of the week with £36. Poverty wages and lousy conditions betrayed the fact that most of these women were living in poverty; many wouldn't or couldn't strike.

The owner, a feature perhaps of things to come, was George Ward. A 'self-made', no-nonsense businessman, he would not recognise any union or any interference in what he seen as 'his' business. Without union recognition, there was deadlock and this issue tended to push the conditions and wages aside as the strike went on and became bitterer. The TUC was supposed to be on the crest of a wave. Unions hadn't been stronger, the miners had fronted two amazing victories and were undefeated, workers standing together could surely defeat a narrow-minded little jumped-up gaffer like this? That was the general feeling as the big guns of the TUC and even the Labour government itself lined up alongside the women in their saris standing on the picket line. Grunwick became a line in the sand. From the left's point of view, here was a strike in their backyard:

in the city, not up north, on the doorstep. They flooded in to stand with the women and earn some real picket credentials.

22 June 1977. An army of buses from all over Britain headed for Grunwick—workers, leftists, students; this was a fight we must not loose., Alison, from our Socialist Union Internationalist, boarded the early-morning buses from Doncaster along with the miners. As they sped toward the conflict, her belly turned over, but I recall that she said that, as she looked from the windows at the volumes of sleeping houses, the words 'Arise yee starvelings from your slumber' stuck in her head. She wanted to shout out the windows 'Get up! Your comrades need you!' It was a common sentiment. The streets around Dollis Hill were blockable, scabs were ambushable, we could rally here the strength of the trade union and labour movement and crush this employer's offensive before it got off the ground. With great ceremony Arthur Scargill arrived, at the head of our miners' contingent. In the front row stand Owen Briscoe, general secretary of the Yorkshire miners; Arthur Scargill, president of the Yorkshire miners; Tom Mullanny, Executive member and Branch delegate at my pit, shirt open, tie off ready for the fight; Dick Kelly, miners' MP for Doncaster; Percy Riley, Communist Area executive member; and Dinger Bell—who? Well, Dinger was actually only a back ripper at Hatfield and had made his way into the front rank just to cadge a tab off Mullanny, and found himself immortalised in the famous picture. Arthur, arms outstretched at the head of the throng, looking like he has just been beamed down, or even more like Jesus at the last supper, comes face to face with the guardians of law and order. The scene got transferred to one of the Yorkshire Area NUM banners, and Dinger became probably the only back ripper with no union position whatever to appear on a miners' banner—quite a distinction; years later admiring faces would ask, 'And who's the feller to the left of Arthur?' to shrugs all round. As the crowd blocked the streets the scab bus, a London double-decker bus was halted and led away elsewhere. The crowd chanted 'Easy! Easy!' as Arthur led the whole assembly on a victory march to Parliament, which just happened to occur to him on the hoof I think. The police, mad as hell they had been thwarted, waded in and some very violent scenes followed. The cops, for really the first time in a labour dispute since the Twenties and Thirties, waded in, making free with their truncheons and horses, driving the crowd into walls and underfoot, the crowd replying with milk bottles and a flurry of fists and boots. Arthur was arrested in the melee, and as he sat in the back of the police wagon a young cop says to him, 'We've got him.' 'Who?' asks Arthur. 'I've just heard we've got that leader of yours, Arthur Scargill.' ' Really?' replies Arthur, 'You'd better take firm hold of him he's a slippery character.' But the 'Easy! Easy!' chants soon died away, as the marching victory parade made its way back to the factory. In the absence of the crowd the police had run the scab bus through the depleted pickets, knocking aside women and families who had stayed behind.

Throughout the long and bitter dispute the women themselves had come under terrific pressure not simply from the employer but from their families, particularly the menfolk; this was unseemly stuff for women to be involved with. Others made the break with tradition and the oppression of the mullahs, and supported the women in the stand. Peggy and Ewan did some great interviews and wrote some great songs based upon the experiences of the women strikers.

The police were different in this dispute than almost any previous one. They had been given their head: they had been told not to play their previous good old British game of push and shove, but to wade in hard, use batons, use the horses to charge the crowds, injure people, frighten people, make them disperse. It seemed almost personal, as though previous picketing defeats had scratched a line in the sand for them too—this time the pickets will not win. It was a sign that things had changed and were changing, though few noticed it at the time.

The postal workers, not on the gate, but at work, held the key to the dispute. They blacked the mail, so films couldn't go into the factory because the posties wouldn't touch them coming in or going out. The company now turned to the courts to force the postal workers to process the films. Tom Jackson, the comic leader of the postal workers, with a passing resemblance to the equally comic Tory MP Gerald Nabarro, a giant of a moderate, quite notorious for his strike-breaking, rushed to the scene and threatened greater action against the posties than the courts could make to stick: cutting off bonuses already earned, dismissal from the union, the blacklist. The furious and utterly betrayed postmen backed off. The workers, taking the employers through the industrial relations court to enforce recognition, discovered the full impartiality of the courts. Prosecute striking solidarity workers. Instruct the employer to recognise the union. They had won, but then Mr Ward basically told the court "Bollocks!"—he didn't recognise its judgement and the law had no means of enforcing it. The strike quietly collapsed. The strikers were never reinstated and the union never recognised.

June 1977. The Workers Institute For Marxism-Leninism Mao-Tse-Tung Thought forecasts the successful world wide revolution presided over by revolutionary China this year!

THE TYNEMOUTH CONFERENCE

The NUM conference at Tynemouth in July 1977 was a hugely important one. The battle between ostensible 'moderates' and the 'militants' was perhaps classic. Closer inspection will find few actual moderate resolutions or demands being made—the differences were of emphasis not quality. The conference was thoroughly militant in its objectives. First they voted 'NO' to further wage restraint, and to set a target of £135 per week for face workers. A composite from Nottingham, South Wales and South Derbyshire rejected any further extension of the 'Social Contract' and demanded a return to 'free collective bargaining'. However this wasn't an immediate demand; it called for this position to be adopted after Phase Two of the 'Contract' ended, and was aimed to buy the government enough time to change its mind voluntarily without facing a conflict, especially given the growing opposition to the scheme. The wage claim from Nottingham and others gazumped Yorkshire, Scotland and Wales, who had demanded a lower figure of £110, but demanded it be met by November. The

Nottingham alternative aimed higher but again sought only to seek to achieve it by then. However when push came to shove both resolutions called for a special conference to be convened to discuss possible forms of industrial action were the demands not met. The key difference was that Yorkshire tied the NEC negotiating team to accept nothing less than the demand or consult the membership; it tied them solely to the demand of conference. The Nottingham demand was to seek to achieve a higher figure than Yorkshire was looking for, but to come back with the best offer they could get, which if it failed to satisfy would result in a special conference being convened. A further difference was the demand from Nottingham et al. that the gap between face workers and elsewhere underground be widened as it had closed too far too fast; Yorkshire's demand was to maintain the narrowed differential. The Yorkshire alliance was outvoted twice on a card vote.

However the Tynemouth Conference issue which was really the Trojan horse of government strategy towards the strength of the miners was the notion of an 'incentive scheme', that is, a bonus scheme. This idea had been first submitted in November 1974. Clear-sighted members of the Union could see this plan as the result of Labour think tanks, which had drawn up a strategy on how to derail the collective strength of the miners' union. The effect of the National Power Loading Agreement had been to weld together the divergent cultures and moods of the diverse areas into a nationally orientated body through the achievement of the national day wage system. It had at once united all the miners nationwide to a collective interest in a single wage system and a single pay negotiation. An incentive/bonus scheme, it was feared from our point of view, would break this unity by introducing diverse payments, and re-establish regional identities and interests. Many of us could see that this was just what it was intended it should do. The question of allowing area incentive schemes to be developed was put to individual ballot and was rejected by the membership en masse by 63 per cent to 37 per cent. Despite this South Derbyshire had forwarded a resolution calling for the introduction of an incentive scheme. It said that if a national scheme couldn't be negotiated (a national scheme would effectively have killed the government's strategy of divide-and-conquer, and therefore the NCB on their behalf were not interested in it) then areas should be given permission to negotiate their own. This was narrowly defeated, and an alternative resolution from South Wales adopted reaffirming the decision of 1974. The breakdown on this issue was clearly that of militant and moderate, government-inclined politics versus the left. Those against the local schemes: Cokemen, Derbyshire, Kent, Scotland, South Wales, Yorkshire and Group No. 2. Those in favour: Cumberland, Durham, North Western, Leicester, Midlands, Northumberland, North Wales, Nottinghamshire, South Derbyshire, Group No. 1, COSA. Power Group and Power Group 2.

Gormley, the NUM president, had made his own support for the schemes clear in his opening presidential address:

> As for some of the statements which have been made that it would—if it had been successful—break down the united front we have shown these last few years, I tell these people they are talking a load of poppycock. ...

History will prove the critics of the incentive schemes wrong in the future. When the issues are right, the miners will be completely united whatever the wages pattern which exists in the industry.

That year's Durham Miners Gala saw the struggle come to the platform in veiled and not-so-veiled references from the stage. The argument took centre and angry stage, with Daly, Scargill and Prime Minister James Callaghan arguing their respective corners before tens of thousands of rank and file miners and their families in the blazing sunshine, amid some audience participation from the field, myself included. Daly spoke of a cautious joint return by the TUC to free collective bargaining. Scargill stated:

I am arguing for £135 a week for miners from November as a positive claim. I want the whole Trade Union Movement, and my own Union in particular, to ignore the advice and pleas of the government for a further wage restraint policy.

Arthur had been a dangerous guest speaker for the moderate Durham Area. In letting him loose directly on the crowds of Durham and Northumberland miners and their families, they risked exposing his own reasonable militancy in the cause of the miners, and their own reluctance. Among the miners, particularly young miners like myself, his speech was electrifying.

Callaghan, who succeeded Wilson as prime minister in the spring of 1976, had sat on the same stage seething. It was him and his policies Arthur was directly confronting, and before the eyes and ears of tens of thousands of northern miners and visitors from other coalfields. Callaghan had taken the mic before tens of thousands of rank-and-file miners to spread the government's theme that only the strong survive in free wage bargaining, the weak stay poor and the powerful command the best terms.

The lions can command the lions' share under a system of free collective bargaining. But the Labour movement and the socialist movement is about more than lions. It is about the weak and the sick and about those whose bargaining power is not so strong.

However, The TUC was drifting away from the Social Contract and Healey as chancellor. This conference was also of vital importance to future events when yet further attempts were made by North Western and South Derbyshire to have an 'Incentive Scheme' introduced. Gormley had made it the centrepiece of his presidential address and the question though defeated at previous conferences had enjoyed his continued support and was a crucial part of a bigger government picture we perhaps none of us were aware of. When the NEC had put it out to individual ballot it was rejected by 63 per cent to 37 per cent. At the conference arms were being fearfully twisted to get the scheme through but it was still defeated by three (card) votes (137 to 134). Of the areas voting in favour, some like Cumberland, barely hanging on by their fingertips to survival, voted with astonishing shortsightedness. (It would be the big productive coalfields that would win in the dog-eat-dog world of area incentives, not small traditional mines like Cumberland's. Plus the fact if they needed back-up in a fight to stay in the ring, it would have to be from the areas they were now allied against.) Others, like COSA, the massive white-collar section, also voted in favour, in the full knowledge that they would not need to sweat one bean extra to receive enhanced wages on the back of speed-up, danger and job losses among the men underground.[81] However, despite the conference votes, the card votes and the ballot the issue had not gone away. It was a cancerous seed which had been planted by external forces and nourished by internal ones acting as a fifth column to blunt the effectiveness of their own union, in the interests of what they seen as higher political interests.

BLACK LIBERATION

Our old comrade Larry Lockwood, formerly of the Revolutionary Communist League (Internationalist), a towering Russian linguist, Marxist theorist of frighteningly precise and detailed insights, described this organisation thus, and fortunately on this occasion in language we can understand:

> The Black Liberation Army was originally created as the armed section of the Black Panther Party (1971). When the BPP split into two wings, most of the members assigned to the BLA declared their support for Eldridge Clever, whom you may have heard of. They then went underground and in 1972 declared armed action as their course, releasing a series of documents on urban guerrilla warfare in the US. Since February 1973 we have insistently declared our willingness to defend the BLA against the state in spite of our political disagreements ... I wish to point out that the New Haven Three (who are still being tried and who are likely to receive total sentences of 100 years apiece) would be greatly encouraged if they were to receive a message from proletarian fighters in Britain.

2 August 1977. We establish contact with Anthony Bottom, one of the most important black activists in the United States, a founder member of the Black Liberation Army, and leading theorist of black armed struggle and political resistance. He writes to us from jail in California. First off this is on the issue of class war prisoners of war, and human rights issues. Later our contact becomes deeper and more sustained. Anthony is unknown in Britain, possibly in Europe. We soon develop firm political links with Anthony, circulating and reproducing his For the Liberation of North America, which was his manifesto for armed struggle,

> Offered as a treatise for revolutionary nationalists and internationalists to discuss and develop in direct relationship to their own levels of resistance in struggle. Undoubtedly, it is not the last word on revolutionary armed struggle in North America but it is hoped it will provide a beacon for the future course of politico-military action in the American Revolution.

This one was written in Auburn State Prison, New York. In some ways we, pure white working-class British folk, became a wing of his black revolutionary movement, circulating his material, printing it, bringing it for the first time to the attention of black people in cities and regions where we could reach them. Later we were to stand at the ready to house, shelter and 'lose' comrades on the run from the States, and that too posed the question of their physical defence. Our training perspective was being forced by real events to at least contemplate action before we were ready. Our friendship with Anthony developed from simply political exchanges to sincere personal ones, with wee Emma, bless her, writing to him in jail and sending him drawings and stories. These he much appreciated and wrote back to her explaining the nature of the American state and his incarceration. He had written to me early on in our correspondence:

Yes! Comrade Dave, maybe one day we will be able to meet outside of the walls of these dungeons, but for me that day will have to be as a course being liberated since, I'm doing time for political activities in this country and being a member of the Black Liberation Army. I've been in prison for the last 6 years and will soon be transferred to New York state institution to serve another 25 years for the assassination of two NY Police officers in May of 1971, I'm also serving time for the armed (expropriation) bank robbery, among other political (crimes?) Activity against the so called established state apparatus. So you see David our meeting will be based on our ability to develop our socialist internationalist movement towards complete victory! ...

In Unity and Arms
Anthony Bottom

The BLA had by this time really ceased to exist as an operating unit; most of its comrades had been liquidated by the state or were banged up for the rest of their naturals. The BLA was the centre of one side of a break of direction and perspective within the Black Panther Party, the other wing really having become an adjunct to the Democratic Party and seeing the way forward in courting respectable constitutional political directions.

A big internal row broke loose within the SUI in the summer of 1977. It had to do with the uneven application of disciplined work and commitment within the organisation. Some comrades were at the very heart of revolutionary struggles as we seen them, not just in Britain and Ireland but the Middle East and elsewhere. Many of us risked everything and were precious close at times to serious collision with the state and its law machine. At the same time we had other members who just didn't get either the level of commitment required or the need for it. It reached critical mass with the Northern branch.

A major national mobilisation for the Durham Miners' Gala, at which we always made a strong and expected intervention, was missed by the failure of the branch and a couple of delegated members to make up copies of our hot-off-the-press manifesto which was due to be launched and had been widely publicised for the gala. Jim, the comrade against whom much of the criticism was lodged, and who lived in Durham City along with Joel, and who had all of the uncompleted manifestos at his flat, turned up with his hands in his pockets and simply announced he had forgotten to do any. For the first time in seven years we were unable to present our politics to our fellow miners and their families at the Gala.

More non-attendance and lackadaisical behaviour followed. This led to a major disciplinary meeting. Jim actually had produced a document, a polemic almost, which he titled 'a discussion paper', and was to some extent his defence got in first.

I have reproduced the bulk of my contribution at that meeting, which I attended in the capacity of the general organiser and therefore almost 'the prosecution' in order to demonstrate the seriousness with which we took the revolutionary nature of the organisation and the tasks before us. It is not an exaggeration that a number of us at times risked our lives in the political work we did, and we seriously expected that the whole organisation might strategically or just by pull of events be drawn into armed conflict and illegal operations with the state. We could not afford therefore to have anybody close enough to us to be an actual member who wasn't serious. If it appears the comrade's skin was being flayed off, it is because we considered such loose behaviour to be downright dangerous not just to the organisation in some romantic lefty political sense, but in terms of flesh of blood and life and death.

This was a serious disciplinary meeting addressed first to the lack of disciplined functioning in the branch as a whole, and also individually within that. Jim was the main chargee.

3 August 1977. General Organiser's address to Extraordinary Meeting of Socialist Union Internationalist. I asked first for a collective response from the branch as whole, before going on to the individual response I had had to charges by Jim – essentially his dropping out of all activity and correspondence since 13 April this year:

> Amazingly the comrade claims to be an innocent member of an identity parade who is picked out by an eye witness as being involved in a crime. The humour of it is of course that he's right—how can he guilty of something when he hasn't done anything? Trouble is Jim, it's not doing anything which is the crime ...
>
> I will repeat this to all comrades—members of this group are not free agents. They belong to a disciplined Bolshevik team—they will act in such a manner. We will not accept will-o-the-wisp, fly-by-night, flash-in-the-pan ... Menshevism. We will not accept woolly behaviour. The widest possible diversity of ideas—yes. Different tactics- yes. But sleepy, apathetic members no. We are too small a team with too great a work load for that.
>
> 'Loss of addresses', comrade? I think it quite astounding how a person sitting on 500 copies of our addresses should say he doesn't know what they are. A person who must have at least one copy each of our publications all of which have our addresses on. Not withstanding the telephone book, the car, the bus, and our local pub which we all gravitate to. This excuse is so lame I'm amazed the comrade wrote it down....
>
> Firstly I will ask for an explanation on the failure of Jim to attend the Troops Out Founding meeting in Newcastle. To which I traveled 150 miles at my own not inconsiderable expense and prepared a lengthy speech.
>
> Secondly on the Whither Scotland meeting, an official meeting of the

SUI, Malc, did you write and inform the comrade? ... & I will swear before witnesses that I phoned your home—and your dept. and received an answer on the Friday. Malc phoned, Sean phoned, and we left messages at the dept., so there are no 'non existent messages.' In any case we should not have to do this to a member—that member should be in contestant touch and in physical activity.

Jim I want you to be honest, and to an extent you have been—quite boldly you outline in-between the lines the fact that you simply either do not understand the role of the SUI or you are not convinced of it, or your position in it.

This organisation is deeply, very deeply involved in leadership and directional questions within the Irish Struggle, the British Anti-Zionist Organisation and the Palestinian struggle, the Scottish Independence Struggle and the Scottish Republican Socialist Clubs, the Troops Out Movement and the revolutionary left, in the Trade Unions and the Labour Party.

But we don't just link these struggles by our physical connection to all of them, no we aren't a 'rent a person' to swell the amorphous ranks—nor yet a 'rent a hand to sell a programme or even elevated programmes'. Our programme, our perspective, our intervention without the branch, without organisation, one is simply practising bourgeois liberalism. The comrade says he failed to see the reason to report back to any meeting. Without coordination you are an individual not linked to the world struggle, your actions are unconnected with our perspective.

'I certainly felt at the time I could do more useful work with the evening saved ... ' Yet this 'usefulness' didn't even include the production of half a dozen manifestos.

Questions for the future. Jim brings out so clearly his absolute failure to understand the perspectives of the SUI.

Republican News. Selling *RN* is an act of solidarity with the anti-imperialist forces; it is a confrontation with social chauvinism and social imperialism. It is an immediate link with the English struggle. This is done by members and supporters of the SUI who have a world perspective. Ireland must be seen as part of the world struggle that is our specific role.

Ireland is THE major contradiction of British Imperialism. The I.R. Movement is the vanguard of the revolutionary struggle in the whole islands. Selling *Republican News* is a part of a whole perspective and tactic on Ireland. Failure to grasp the absolute indispensable nature of our work on Ireland is quite simply failure to understand the nature of class war in Britain in this period.

We intervene into the Socialist Centre, Chile Solidarity, Portuguese Solidarity etc. with a plan with a programme with an overall global perspective sitting each of these fronts in the world- and struggle for leadership. It is precisely because Jim doesn't see the point of organisation that he says he can do it all without the SUI, but we don't intervene as individuals. We intervene as disciplined cadres, cells, leaders with a firm base in the international class war.

In the USA we have directly stimulated the development of a Troops Out Of Puerto Rico movement. We are listened to and respected within that organisation.

We have held meetings with the Executive Committee of the Puerto Rican Socialist Party, we have spoken to members of the IRA Army Council and the leadership of Sinn Fein, our pamphlets are read, with members of the NEC of the Labour Party, or NUPE and of numerous other union leaderships.

We didn't gain those ears and that reputation by being amorphous individuals, but by being a consistent team organised around a revolutionary programme and perspective for years.

The selling of '*Socialist Challenge*' has shades of liquidationism in it—that aside for now—we have more specific documents to sell, like our own Manifesto—which is carrying all our funds by the way apart from an unmatched socialist perspective. We have the *Troops Out Movement Report Back* document and the *Document on The Prevention of Terrorism Act*.

We will work with IMG—if they'll bother to do anything, like build a Troops Out Movement, like unemployed work, like anti-fascist work, they didn't even come to our Scottish conference – nor any of the times when we are selling *Republican News*, we've not seen them do any of that.

Socialist Challenge has no answers—we will make an intervention into IMG, or IMG initiatives but not just swelling the woolly ranks, but with our own programme and ideas. Without being SUI cadres with all that means then, yes, the role of any individual radical will be the same.

13 August 1977. Folk Concert, Bentley Hotel, (The Drum). Log entry reads:
Very good concert especially when one considers that we've not held one for a long time. Quite a few singers arrived and the crowd filled out. Lots of old friends and comrades, lots and lots new people who also seen the posters and advert in the press. Lots of people joined the club. Members of the SUI were down from Newcastle and over from America and from the base—there were members of SWP and YCL, and CP. Lots of singers, me, Paul (Barrowcliffe), Dave Ash who was here last time and our group The Hogshead, and an old man of 65, an Irishman, who sang two great songs. An Irish lad called Tay, who sang last time. Also a new lad Dave Williams played and sang.

Posters on Grunwick, Ireland and Cuba and the Black Liberation Army and the Middle East decorated the walls. Banners of Stainforth, Dunscroft and Hatfield Tenants Association, Clay Lane Tenants Association, Goole Constituency Labour Party Young Socialists, Doncaster Socialist Women's Action Group. Full Employment Under Workers Control.

20 September. The Miners Welfare at Stainforth hosted our public meeting 'A People In Exile: The Struggle of the Palestinians'. It was addressed by Maureen who gave a detailed report of her visit to Lebanon. The meeting was supported by the NUM and Tom Mullanny, who was a regular visitor and contributor to many of our meetings these days, chaired it. My early antagonism to Tom and his mini vexious struggle against me had long ago given way to mutual respect, and we were by this time comrades and close family friends.

9 November 1977. John Mason resigns from SUI as a sympathising member. He now declares that we are political upstarts, too inexperienced to be a tendency, certainly not worldly wise enough to be a national organisation let alone an international one. We have no analysis, we don't understand complex processes, etc. We think that he has never recovered from having been made to peel potatoes on one of our exercises. He had grumbled and moaned but finally got his hands into the dish and started to peel them, staring at each spud with utter contempt. Then finally he snapped, throwing the knife into the water and refusing to continue. We had challenged him and he had responded, 'I just don't see the point.' We soon demonstrated the point as when dinner time came he had only a very much diminished share of tatties on his galvie plate.

PALESTINE AND IRAQ

20 October. Maureen addresses a public meeting at The Nelson (Doncaster) on 'A People In Exile: The Struggle Of The Palestinians' which attracts a lot of people with no connection to us at all and some older LP types.

As chairwoman she goes on to visit Baghdad on four occasions and falls in love with Iraq and its people. We are none of us in love with Saddam but as rulers in the Middle East go, he is 'progressive' and the society is secular, with large socialised features throughout the economic system. The Ba'ath Party was in theory a socialist, pan-Arab formation rooted in the idea of working-class freedom and anti-imperialism. Saddam's belief in a secular Iraq fits squarely with his Sunni muslem traditions; it puts him profoundly at odds with those of non-secular Shias. These internal political and cultural divisions align roughly with the external political enemies in Iran. This causes a tight grip and at times the repressive suppression of Shia political and religious expression, which he sees as allied to Iran and the alternative political gravity of fundemantalism as expressed by the Khomani. The reality of the regime was not too evident at this period; it was somewhat more brutal and tyrannical, but certainly far less than most others. Maureen's deep move into Arab politics led us to in-depth study of Middle East situation and all of its players, particularly the ones we deemed progressive states: Libya, Syria and Iraq.

22 October 1977. Folk Concert, Bentley Hotel (The Drum), with Alun Howkins.

The concert itself was a great success. Singers were Alun Howkins, Hogshead, Jeff (the Accordion Kid) and Kathy Davin. Alun conducted some dancing in the 2nd half to music from Jeff and The Hogshead and it was greatly enjoyed by all.

16 December 1977. Folk Benefit Concert For the Fire-fighters' Strike Fund.

19 December 1977. I'm on In *The Light Of Experience*, on BBC2-TV. I suppose they needed a non-religious presentation for a change. I'm quite pleased with the whole thing, I scrap the pan music at the end of the piece, though, as I don't think that's appropriate. Incidentally I am having dinner at the TV studio in their guest dining-room, with a Rabbi who is filming for his part on the programme. Having particular diets, we have both ordered quiche. We are eating and arguing furiously over the table about the nature of the Israeli state and Zionism and the Palestinians, when suddenly I observe, 'You know rabbi, I could swear this quiche tastes of bacon!' It is the first time he agrees with me, and we form a solid front to storm back to the food counter where the chef is sent for.

A very jolly and obviously gay and very camp chef comes out waving his hands about saying 'I always put bacon in my quiche, nobody told me about Rabbis and communist vegetarians!'

'I can request forgiveness and better focus in future; how about you?' the Rabbi asks me.

'Me? I'm going to be sick!' —and I was too, nearly spoiled my shot.

Mind, the programme was seen by many of my friends when it was broadcast on 18 January 1978, late at night. Some I had lost contact with including Bob Hart, who told me he was in a bedsit, while working with contractors in London, 'And who should come on but Davie Douglass, lang hair and yellow teeth an'ahl!' I suppose teeth were not a high priority to people in general in those days, and I think I indulged in cigs, pipes and dope a little too freely then. It made me self-conscious about me teeth for years afterwards, although I have never been able to track down a copy of the film to see just how 'non-white' they are in it. Still, loads of folk wrote to me in praise of the film so it can't have been too distracting. It was on again on BBC1 on 13 August in the early evening.

ICEBERG DEAD AHEAD

Christmas Eve 1977. We were as usual staying with Maureen's Mam and Dad, had been out back doon the Bridge, had a great reunion with everyone, supped, sang, cracked-on, walked back through the drizzle, arm in arm and helped prepare all the mountains of presents and things with her folk for the arrival of Sante Claes.

That night the passage of our love and relationship through the dark depths of time and space struck a hidden submerged object and holed us below the waterline; from now on our love, our trust, our future was doomed. We were slowly foundering, our unshakeable, unsinkable love on the way to the bottom of the murky depths.

I wretched my insides out, cried pitilessly, felt hopeless and dejected. Before long poor Emma was trotting around the landing asking 'Has he been yet?' and her nana and grandad were lining up to go downstairs and greet the Christmas morn with all its surprise and promise. I was red-eyed, and shaking, Maureen was ashen, we pulled on what bright smiles we could and joined the line down for Emma's Christmas morning. She knew, though; she could feel the sadness, though she tried to ignore it, poor wee soul.

The details now no longer matter. It was long ago, but the subject is raw and we are keen that it doesn't impact on our children and their children. This history is not aimed to generate further upset guilt or blame. Suffice it say a major error of judgement in Maureen's extramarital relations threw us irrecoverably off course and onto the rocks.

For readers aware of my descriptions of my own extramarital sexual relations, all of this must seem very confusing—or, worse, must seem the very height of hypocrisy—but there was a world of difference, no not between me having extra relations and her having extra relations, that had always been mutual and cool and accepted. Maureen having sex with some sexy bloke she met while I was away, a one-night stand at a conference, or a party, was nowt. It was a turn-on actually; we mutually consented to sexual freedom and having fun with other people. For the whole thing to work though meant no one was ever under any circumstances taken instead of each other or in contempt of each other's feelings.

This one though had been a secret ongoing relationship outside the rules. It had been a very short-lived affair and was rapidly concluded but the impact was mortal. I left and walked, walked and thought to keep on walking and not come back.

But I had to go back, had to go back for Emma's Christmas, had to try and not spoil her holiday, at least. I went back to university to mull things over. I was in the depth of depression. Actually volunteered to join the IRA; really, however, it was a death wish and—as already mentioned earlier—they soon spotted it.

Me and Maureen decided to try and stay together for Emma, and just see how it went. Our relationship would be unspecified. We remained as companions, husband and wife, comrades, through more turbulent years and encounters. Sometimes I forgot we had had a problem, sometimes we seemed to be back as normal. We experienced much in this intervening period but always that gaping hole below the waterline was drawing us down.

Christmas Day 1977: Charlie Chaplin dies. A great human being, socialist and Cockney who never lost sight of his roots or despite his money his class origins. His films, he made 50 of them in the two years between 1916 and 1918, highly explosive years—were subversively funny, they take the side of the poor, the foreigner the outsider and mock the high and mighty, lampoon authority and the law. Taking his antifascism onto the screen was far from popular among certain sectors of the American ruling class (*The Great Dictator*, 1940); they set their dogs at his heels throughout his career. In particular Charlie's attraction to younger women set the FBI hunting high and low to discredit and jail him, always to be confounded by Charlie's predilection to marry them. Their real chance came with the founding of the rabidly anti-Communist, ultra-patriotic 'un-American Activities League'. Banished from the US, he went to live in Switzerland where he spent the bulk of the rest of his life; from there he issued a retaliatory salvo in the shape of *A King In New York* (1957), a biting satire on US society.

'All I need to make a comedy is a park, a policeman and a pretty girl.' (*My Autobiography*, 1964)

9 January 1978. The Organization for Solidarity with the People of Asia, Africa and Latin America (OSPAAAL), the nearest thing we had to a functioning Communist International, issued a resolution to Kampuchea and Vietnam to fraternally end their military dispute and unite against world imperialism. We endorsed this call and submitted an amendment calling for the same position to be taken in the Eritrea/Ethiopia conflict, a war between two ostensibly socialist forces which seemed to have Cuban assistance at both ends. Actually, when we issued our 'appeal for Cambodia and Vietnam to dissolve their differences in a communist spirit as two sister socialistic states' we were chronically ignorant of what was happening in Cambodia. After having fought alongside their Vietnamese comrades to oust the United States, Pol Pot had come to power at the head of the immensely popular Khmer Rouge. The two countries and others of the region had actually been one country, Indochina, until the vacillations of warring imperialism had divided the countries along ethnic lines, or as far as was possible given the ethnic mix particularly along the so-called borders. This had worked to the good for the Vietcong resistance and in the end the USA, unable to distinguish where was where and who was who, simply invaded Cambodia too and took the war into that landmass as well, bombing the economy back to medieval conditions in the process.

Pol Pot had been in the same Indochinese Communist Party with Ho Chi Minh. His anti-imperialist 'communist' guerrillas were described as 'pro-Chinese'. Prince Sihanouk, the playboy monarch, had been largely anti-American and pro-independence; oddly he was also a relative of Pol Pot—though I never really worked out how that worked—who overthrew him in 1976. The people welcomed Pol Pot and his team into the capital in the belief that liberation and justice had arrived. Pol Pot however, who ran his Central Committee in the style of Joe Stalin, had a grossly distorted and obsessive vision of the future for Kampuchea, as the country was now called having reverted to its pre-imperialist name. The cities were the harbinger of reaction and capitalism, they were the source of jealousy and useless consumerism, they consumed pointless objects, they lived in luxury, the people in them resented the peasants and did no work. At gunpoint and with mass summary executions the cities were emptied and people forced to work and live in the countryside. The entire economy was to be based upon basic peasant agriculture. It was a return to nature, a return to some ancient agrarian system based solely on backbreaking toil without science or machinery. Books and scientific equipment were burned and wrecked. Universities and colleges were closed and students and professors put to planting the fields with their bare hands. Was this some sort of cultural revolution of the kind we had so admired in China? Perhaps Pol Pot genuinely thought it was, but this was not progressive, this was a kind of mystical belief that the outside world and all its science and technology was reactionary and that only the old traditional peasant methods of scrub paddy-field economics would cleanse the soul and led on to a shinny socialist future. Money was abandoned, and blew around the wrecked, burned-out, smashed cities. But money can only be abandoned if there is an abundance of wealth and production which renders it unnecessary. Everywhere the rice production and production of basic foodstuffs was failing. Pol Pot swore it was being sabotaged by the city folk who had contaminated the peasants, and more mass executions were performed all over the country—men, women and little children. The peasants were next accused of stealing produce and hiding it; torture and further executions followed. The Communist Party leaders were 'discovered' to be at the root of the opposition and the 'sabotage' of the country; they were massacred along with every member of their families and often their neighbours too. Many of the people of the border regions were ethnically and culturally Vietnamese or were interrelated across whole swathes of the south. Many of these people were in the Kampuchean armed forces guarding the vague borders. They were the next victims for mass indiscriminate murder. With tens of thousands of desperate people flooding into Vietnam to escape, Vietnam's forces had no choice, in the interests of their common revolution and basic humanity, but to invade across the borders and liberate the country in January 1979. We and OSPAAAL had been wrong not to take a side: the Vietnamese were right although a trifle late. OSPAAAL as well as us would perhaps not have believed what was going on. Something more than two million people had been ruthlessly killed. Pol Pot took his guerrillas to the mountains where he continued a massively destructive campaign against attempts by the new government to restore the country and start to reconstruct a modern society. In a blinding flash of capitalist immorality the USA and Britain then started to equip and fund his Khmer Rouge. China, in an endgame only it comprehended and with utter, reactionary contempt, also backed Pol Pot's forces to the hilt, with arms, sanctuary and training. They blocked every move to have the new government recognised and allowed only Pol Pot's representatives to sit in the United Nations representing Kampuchea. The liberation forces were denounced by the west as illegal occupation forces, even after the Vietnamese pullout and handover to anti-Pol-Pot forces. It wasn't until 1996 that a split emerged within the Khmer Rouge and this faction effectively ended the war of terror. The UN under the sway of the USA and Britain only ended their blockade and non-recognition of the country when this faction was allowed back to take seats in government. Pol Pot was placed under house arrest in 1997 and died, I think in 1999, unrepentant, still believing internal reactionary forces had killed his beautiful vision of rural, agrarian, communist Kampuchea. Ironically but unsurprisingly it was Pol Pot's version of 'communism' which would be rammed down our throats—though this time only metaphorically—as an example of what happened to 'communism'. On the contrary, Pol's vision was a forcible rejection of communism, certainly any Marxist version of that development. For Marx the whole basis for his optimism in the triumph of communism was that capitalism had provided the necessary stage of human development to get there. That is, the technological and economic forces necessary to meet all human needs. The most complete and total forms of democracy and control by the working class directly would be necessary at all stages of the transition from capitalism to socialism and communism. Pol Pot had abandoned both of these elemental features. After his overthrow, his forces were in fact seen by US Imperialism as 'the front line against the spread of communism' through the region.

21 January 1978. British Anti Zionist Organisation National Conference at UMIST.

I am home working at the pit over the Christmas break (other than the seasonal pit holiday of course) when Hatfield Branch agrees to send a bus full of pickets down to Sanderson Forklift Ltd, Skegness, whose T&GWU members are on strike against victimisation of union officials and for recognition. This little hick firm out in the sticks was quite surprised when the little huddle of pickets at the gates is joined by a regiment of the crack battalion. We soon kick this little game of gentlemen into touch and surge up the drive toward the works, where a young spotty-looking manager with a long neck and a couple of typists are working in the offices. He runs outside like someone doing an impersonation of a chicken and tries to close the little fence gate. I ask him, in what he would call 'brutish language' I suppose, if he thought a little wooden gate would stop us getting in if we wanted, I also questioned his intelligence and legitimacy, I seem to recall. A little while later I have found my way to the back of the building and encouraged one of the girls to come out and talk to me, which she does. She's rather nice, and tells me she's just started there. Should she come out on strike?

'Well, what are you actually doing?'

'Hm, just making tea and answering the telephone,' she says.

'Well, don't make very nice tea, leave the phone to ring or pick it up and put it down again or say wrong number, and when the men start back work, join the union.'

I hoped the picket would be arranged for some longer period of days in order to discuss tactics with the young worker comrade in more detail, but it was a one-off gesture. I think they won the dispute though.

17 February 1978. The Provos carry out one of their most irrational bombings to date. A firebomb planted in the La Mon restaurant in Belfast, which gutted the building and killed 12 diners and maimed 32. They had given a nine-minute warning, not enough to get everyone out in time given the scale of the bomb, and anyway what a plainly stupid and counter-productive target. Why it had been picked, with what purpose, I never yet understood.

Tony McHugh writing for his organisation, the Maoist Institute for Marxism-Leninism–Mao-Tse-Tung Thought, from his Great Yarmouth address, tells us how they are forging forward with leafleting, by people who had never previously done any work before, 'interacting with the masses ... we go door knocking asking workers and unemployed workers if they need help or advice, such as knowing their rights for supplementary benefits, whether they have housing problems or need help with industrial or security tribunals.' 'Myself and one other comrade will be coming to Doncaster on a date early in October as we are en route to a political meeting in Glasgow.'

6 April 1978. Tony writes from the Great Yarmouth Maoist Institute:

All our comrades in London Mao-Tse-Tung Memorial Centre have been arrested by the British Fascist police and remanded in prison. They were raided at 5 a.m. one morning and dragged from their centre. The Centre has been closed down and boarded up by police, seen only by a *Morning Star* photographer who happened past at an early hour.

Many Communists in this country have to grasp what is going on and now the notion is being nurtured and prepared for the advent of a fully fledged fascist dictatorship. You will witness as each day goes by many more Communists and revolutionaries will be put out of action (one way or another). Watch the by-elections and you'll know what we mean. Time for the left in Britain is running out unless they can unite now. When the general election comes which will probably be in October the Tory party will march into parliament with a very comfortable majority. The right will then strike against us with all the fury it can unleash.

April 1978. The Spartacists launch themselves as a national tendency in Britain with their paper *Workers Hammer*. They headline with 'The Rebirth of British Trotskyism' because of course there had been none until their arrival.

We at once regarded them as 'the left cover of the American imperialist state'. We had been outraged at the stance taken by this group towards the comrades of the Symbionese Liberation Army and of the Black Liberation Army. They cheer-led the police in shooting down and imprisoning those comrades. In the case of the SLA their last stand in a blazing house, which had been set on fire as a result of so many bullets fired into it, while the five young occupants died heroically defending themselves, the bodies were hardly cold when the Sparts were ridiculing them as 'the left wing of the Salvation Army'.

They had set themselves the task in Britain of breaking the left from the Irish Republican Movement, echoing the weasel words of the so-called British and Irish Communist Organisation. They too had come to the conclusion that the loyalist population of the six counties of Ireland constituted 'a nation' distinct from the rest of the population, and therefore the struggle for a single island Irish republic was unfounded and reactionary.

'A correct approach to the immediate question in Ireland must begin with the recognition of the simply fact that there is no single Irish nation [*Spartacist Britain*, no. 1, April 78] ... there is no sense in which we can speak of the Irish people as a whole' (ibid. p. 12). They go on to conclude that religion constitutes the core of these different nations, ignoring the fact that the earliest founders of Irish republicanism were all Protestant. Ignoring too the international support of the republicans for armed liberation fighters at war with Catholic-based organisations like the phalange in Lebanon or their opposition to the twenty-six-county statelet, which was thoroughly Catholic. 'The Protestants are clearly not at this time part of the Irish Catholic nation but a separate people.' The republican movement we were told was violating the rights of the Protestant people with its demand for thirty-two-county independence. They ignored everything the Provisionals wrote and said on this matter and simply made up agendas and perspectives which they had never shared.

The Provos summed up their own position as follows:

> The IRA is an organisation seeking to overthrow British power in Ireland by the only means possible, it owes its allegiance to no puppet government based upon six counties or twenty-six counties ... Sinn Fein does not ask the people of the six counties to join the 26 county state. It seeks to replace both states with a democratic Socialist Republic of all 32 counties in which church and state would be separate. (*Ireland. The Facts*)
>
> ... I don't blame them (the loyalists) for having nothing to do with The South; we are not very enamored by the south either, if we are speaking of the Southern Establishment, because our objective is to see that the establishment go by the board. We believe in a new Ireland and the creation of new institutions of government for the whole of Ireland ... We are not trying to bomb Protestants into the 26 counties. We are trying to get ourselves out of it. (Daithi O Conaill, TV interview)

The Sparts made it quite clear where they stood on this Ireland war issue and the stance of most of the British left:

> The goal of our regroupment policy has always been to decisively split the cadre of the Centrist organisations. [That being the left in general as they seen it.]
>
> The right to self determination does not imply support to the revisionists advocacy of the supposed 'right' of each nation to completely determine its own future. [Spartacist Britain] ... We must reject slogans such as 'No British Plans for Ireland ...' as expressions of petit-bourgeois romanticism. [Ibid.]

Such a downright reactionary posture in an area where the class was at war put the Sparts on collision course with us. They had wisely stated that they wouldn't be actually entering into Ireland north or south as they feared physical attack. It was their only correct reflection on the whole situation.

7 June 1978. We organised our traditional Miners' Gala Folk Concert, this time at the Corporation Taps. The gala was held in Doncaster on the Town Fields and this was our day. The parade boasted 22 colliery brass bands, three pipe bands and 17 junior brass and seven children's jazz bands; these last ranged in ages from the toddlers done out like little tin soldiers who act as drum mascots, to busty pubescent Lolitas, stripping brazenly into their uniforms in front of the bus windows as they enter the field, which seems to have become something of a custom among the juvenile band girls.

The chairman was Arthur Scargill, guest speakers Mick McGahey and

Norman Atkinson MP. Votes of thanks were moved by Briscoe the general secretary and Dick Kelly our local Old Left MP. For our part, this being Donie, we had a great day with Malc and Sean down from Newcastle. The social seen Tom Gilfellon, our old mate from the High Level Ranters and much else, as the guest singer. The sun blazed until early evening and we had the side doors of the pub open. Most of the audience were colliers and Gillfellon went down great.

The Communist Cadre (Marxist) split has now become Class War, with their paper *Scarlet Letter*. It's basically Dan Jacobs and his mate, who were 'forced to leave' by Peter Anton and Joel Myers. They send us a detailed demolition of our manifestos and what they call our

> One sided, non polemical approach to the rest of the left; a pronounced tendency to accommodate to the reformist leadership of the existing mass-based workers parties under the guise of 'pressuring from below'; a largely non-dialectical analysis of the bureaucratically-deformed workers states such as the USSR; and a lack of a perspective on the oppressed nationalities, the Labor aristocracy and racism in England. We find that the *Manifesto* (parts 1 and 2) is on the whole an unholy amalgam of revolutionary Marxism and reformism politically and of dialectics and mechanical evolutionism methodologically.

For groups like this there is an obsessive, all-consuming preoccupation with 'the correct analysis'. It renders them virtually housebound and immobile, with each step requiring the care of a Jaine monk, not in fear of treading on a small creature but for fear of breaching some sacred Marxist-Leninist encyclical or rule. Our approach of 'getting down and dirty' in among the class and fighting our corner from within the mass movements was politically and socially repugnant to them, yet still they took sheer delight in disseminating line by line our published positions.

> An electoral combination of two or more workers parties around a common program, is absolutely antithetical to the concept and practice of the united front, as by definition this involves the subordination of the revolutionary program to a reformist program.

The following day we have an all-day conference at the White Hart, Barnby Dun, on 'Bolshevism and Its Meaning for Our Movement Worldwide Today', myself as the speaker then the RCL (I) addresses itself to the same issue. There was an enthusiastic crowd, some old leftist workers, and young revolutionaries apart from our normal members and periphery.

10 September 1978. 'AW' was deemed to have resigned from the group. He was increasingly oddball and had failed to meet the rigors of the EMC course; this was not of itself enough to deny him membership of the group, but his fantasies and lies made him more and more a liability.

He re-emerges years later, ostensibly 'hail fellow well met', then we track him down as the source of some ugly and dangerous rumours being spread about me in particular. On reflection he had come from a family of oddballs, the male populace of which was nicknamed 'The Wheelies' since they all had wheelchairs. A veritable wagon train of wheelchairs would roll up for family occasions, every pubescent in the family seeing it as his birthright to get around in this fashion, though medical reports rarely if ever advised this method of transport and all of them had been purchased privately. it was before the advent of Little Britain's 'Yeah, Ah Know', but surely he was based on one of these guys? Alison went in February, exhausted and spent, and we were steadily using up or dispensing with cadres as they fell by the wayside.

October 1978. Tony McHugh, in the guise of the Workers Institute for Marxism-Leninism–Mao-Tse-Tung Thought, arrives at our Doncaster meeting, coincidentally at the same time as a Hull representative of the 'Tricontinental' (OSPAALA). The minute reads:

> Most of the discussion centred around the Institute's claim that the British State is a fascist state and that the only thrust of their political activity is to build a new revolutionary workers party. There was much disagreement on these points, both from SUI and Tri-Con. It appears that Cde McHugh is touring the country looking for a suitable base from which to launch 'the new party'. It became obvious that Doncaster was not that place.

We loose all contact with the suspicious Tony until the winter of 1997, where he emerges 'playing for the other side' in more ways than one! One wonders how long he had been in the enemy camp, and reflects that we were either too keen or just plain lucky not to have been 'penetrated' by him.

In September I take Emma off fossiling. It has become a dad-and-daughter thing. We scour old pit tips across Northumberland and Durham, rock outcrops, seashores and quarries. She is accumulating quite an interesting collection and gets to display it at school on 'What I Did During My Holidays' presentations. It is something uniquely ours, the fossils and the time we spent collecting them are more precious than were the collected precious stones. Mind, through her grandad Hill's wonderful jewellery making she also is picking up a knowledge of precious and semi-precious stones and what they look like in their bland and dull state. These she carries off back to him, who washes them, tumbles them and turns them into shining and colourful pieces for rings and pendants.

7–8 October 1978. South Yorkshire History Workshop. 'The Miners and The Class Struggle In South Yorkshire 1844-1972'. Sheffield.[82]

21 November 1978, 4.55 a.m. Down Bentley pit the night shift was on its way outbye, when the loco which was pulling the manriding set ran out of control down a 1 in 16 gradient, killing 7 men and seriously injuring 19 others. The train jumped the tracks when its speed was too great to get round the turn and the coaches impacted with the arch girders supporting the roadway. Anyone who saw the accident report photos of the crushed and overturned coaches can only

wonder how any of the riders survived. A number of men, never ever returned to the mines and who could blame them? It made you wonder every time you got back aboard a manrider diving down the steep gradients or twisting round an awkward turn if this was where you would meet your doom.[83]

MURDER OF A MINER

Phil Parphet was what I have called 'a moors miner'. Something of a 'hillbilly'. A moors man; always out across the vast expanses of the moors which surrounded Hatfield and Thorne Colliery, this latter sunk in Moorends. They were of that tradition of miner, men who worked in the depth of the mines but whose souls were out on the moors. They tended to wear wellies and combat gear, were totally relaxed and non-excitable. Whey aye, they poached, rabbit, salmon, pheasant, grouse, anything. They didn't call it poaching, it was as much their right to take from the land as that of the rich who claimed to own it. They shot animals but only ever 'fo' t' pot', never for 'sport' or 'fun'. They respected nature, knew it intimately. But these same lads, the pre-and post-Kes generations, fused pit work and wild life, down pit and moors. They might come to work with a pair of dead grouse down their jumpers, having been out over the bog since the night but would not understand cruelty and meaningless killing. They railed against the introduction of 'mixi' aimed at 'controlling' the wild rabbit population. In arguments which could have descended from the anti-enclosure struggle, they seen it as a ruling-class ploy to deprive 'wo'kin man of fuud'. It was an endeavour to prevent the worker having an alternative source of livelihood and sustenance, to make him more subservient and likely to buckle down to the factory discipline of the nineteenth-century mill and mine. Additionally it was unnecessarily cruel; they often shot rabbits who were dying of mixi, just to save their suffering. Phil was all that, but a likely lad too, into everything and anything going.

We were riding up off night shift one morning and I was standing next to Phil.

'Hey-up,' he says, 'tha's a revolutionary in't tha, Danny?'

'Aye,' I reply.

'Does tha, want to buy some guns?'

It was rumoured Phil had found some large army stockpile somewhere. We got that impression because he tended to poach salmon with hand-grenades. Making a dam, then hoying in a grenade and collecting the stunned and dead fish as they floated to the surface. Sometimes he would try fishing on a much larger scale and nick a fishing boat. He kidded Chick on that he had hired it from Brid'. Later he would explain his navigational skills, as he cruised past Whitby and Chick shouted 'Tha's missed it marra'. But Phil knew somehow that to gain entrance to the harbour you have to go past it and come back in an arc. Chick got suspicious when Phil tested a number of red diesel tanks before finding one with the connectors still on. He 'borrowed boat from mate, like,' he assured Chick, who remained none too sure, but they caught wheelbarrowfuls of fish and sold them up and down the coast before mooring the boat somewhere, getting a sick note to cover their absences and restarting work, bronzed, weatherbeaten and strong.

'Well, we weren't exactly planning on starting the revolution tomorrow,' I had responded, 'but what yi got?'

'Bazookas, mortars, grenades,' he replies as the cage gates open and the crowd surges out. 'Ler is knaa,' he yells as he runs off.

He and Chick had found rich hunting grounds on the lands of some relative to the Queen and regularly went out poaching. It was November 1978. They were walking quietly across a dark field when suddenly shots rang out and they scattered. Chick heard shots off in the distance as he ran to get away.

The following night it was bonfire night and Chick was in the garden with the blazing fire and the kids and lighting the fireworks while their lass did the roast tatties and everyone drank cans of beer and lager. Suddenly two squad cars pulled up and out jumped half a dozen cops. Chick assumed they had come about the poaching and fained total ignorance. They took him down to the station and into a back room.

A stern-looking detective looked him in the face and said 'You don't know, do you? Your mate's dead!'

The gamekeeper had shot Phil and everything becomes murky after that. We were sure they had been ambushed, but the keeper's story was he tried to disarm Phil but he had tried to grab the keeper's gun and they wrestled with it and it went off. The court however heard the police switchboard record of the conversation with the desk sergeant after the killing.

'Tha knaas them poachers that's been coming round?,

'Yes?'

'Ah'v got one of them.'

When the prosecution got to cross-examine the keeper they asked if his story was true, how come there were no finger prints on either gun anywhere?

'Because,' came the reply, 'I cleaned them.'

'You had just shot a man, you say by accident, and you sit down to clean the guns involved, leaving the man to bleed in the field?'

'I always clean guns after shooting,' he replied without sarcasm.

Chick sat in court waiting to give evidence. He was sure they had been ambushed, but mysteriously he wasn't called. A verdict of misadventure was recorded. Chick was boiling with anger and welled up with tears of grief and frustration. He grabbed a police inspector who happened to be leaving the court the same time as he.

'There's nowt short of murder gone on, and its all covered up here,' he said.

The cop took from under his arm a big paper file, 'I had all this to present, kid. I never got the chance either. Some things are more powerful than me and thee,' he said.

I was studying law up at university. I was determined to get the case reopened and sent Chick to ask Phil's widow if she would agree. The answer was she'd got three kids to bring up, no money, no dad, and nothing can bring him back. The 'Crown Estates' had offered her a pension (ex-gratia of course) to help her get by on condition the matter was let rest. She couldn't afford to be idealistic, besides which my novice enthusiasm would be unlikely to unravel whatever strings had been pulled behind the scenes.

Word came through that down in the keeper's pub a wild celebration party had been arranged; pride of place on the bar was a pitman's helmet upside down filled with earth from which daisies were growing. It was fortunate I was hundreds of miles away in Glasgow, and unable to organise the anger which was bubbling among the miners. I am led to believe they went down to the pub in convoy but the cops had got word and thrown up a road block on a country lane and given public warnings to those most likely to. Plus the fact Phil's wife made a public appeal to let him and it rest. We never have forgotten it.

Jim was something of a moors man too, always over the fields with his gun, always bringing home huge field mushrooms and jars full of berries. A keen pitman at work, he repeated the miner's mantra in the midst of the dust and the bucking boring machine, eyes smarting from sharp stone fragments and nostrils filled with coal and rock: 'By, there has to be someit better than this bugger ae knaa.' So he always, ducking and diving, tried to find some safety net, some escape route. While I was at university, he took to helping one the local characters scrap buses. Driving a big tractor, to pick 'em up and scrap 'em and make bit money on the side. I don't know quite what they thought they were doing, but he and his mate Haemison attempted to put one over on a Gypsy scrap merchant, which would leave them with a significant amount of burning equipment and a couple of buses buckshee. He wasn't too pleased and put out the word to 'get Shipley'. I mean 'get' as in dispose of. I am told the price for the hit was £275, but for that money you don't get the Get Carter sharpshooter, more a sledgehammer in the back of the skull. Jim went seriously to ground, his mate got caught but paid off what he owed and with no Jim to argue, blamed the whole scam on Jim.

Jim's story would rival this one. He escaped first to France where he roughnecked for a circus, then made his way back to England, living among the travellers as a traveller, picked up their twang and spoke fifty to the dozen. He lived even faster on his feet, wheeling and dealing. This experience was to be priceless later when we came to cover and hide members of various armed teams who we were committed to 'defending'. Jim got to go to a big peace pow- wow with the Gypsy scrapper, and despite paying off his debt, apologising most humbly, still took a kicking for the audacity. Finally he had to pay off the debt to the hit man who cared not whether Jim lived or died so long as he got paid once the warrant was issued.

A little time later Raph sought my assistance in helping a member of the Red Brigades who was on the run, but still making the scene with the middle-class 'in-crowd' liberals round London. Raph needed him out of the house and moving on. We arranged via Jim's connections to get the man an entirely new identity and bona fide credentials. It would however require the Brigada Rossa compadre to work, actually in a coal yard shoveling coal eight hours per day.

Now this bloke, for a revolutionary, was the immaculate conception. Not a hair moved out of place which was carefully styled, his pure white cotton trousers didn't have a crease, his silk blouse shirt impeccable. How he killed people was beyond me, but the concept of getting into the struggle with the masses and actually working was beyond him. He was horrified. It reminded me of something someone wrote of the defeated and tribeless clan leaders after Culloden, who made the scene in the French court and had become caricatures of themselves, from warriors to 'popinjays'. Our comrade announced he would sooner take his chance back in Milan than in the coal yard, which is where we think he went. Other comrades on the run were not so fussy or ungrateful.

Jim meantime rather than contemplate going back to the pit launched a home coal business.

December 1978. James Connolly Cumann, Tyneside, founded with great enthusiasm at the Bridge Hotel, Castle Garth, Newcastle Upon Tyne. We bring together the revolutionary socialist comrades of the Tyneside Irish community with the older, more established cultural community based around music, and dancing and the Tyneside Irish Club. The Tyneside Irish are an established cultural section with a strong self identity and culture, despite many being third, fourth or even longer generation Irish. They are in many respects like the Irish American community in New York.

March 1979. Dan Jacobs is coming over from 'The States'. Dan, a veteran of the early *Workers World* days, had been room mates at university with the other RCL(I) leading lights. His trajectory had led him to the IWP, then *Communist Cadre* and to his own publication *Scarlet Letter* and a number of serious politico-anthropological works. Peter Anton describes him as a cop; RCL(I) defends him against this unsubstantiated accusation, and then is denounced by Jacobs on another matter, which draws RCL(I) to attack him for his unprincipled and un-Bolshevik approach to political work. 'Meantime life goes on outside all around you' (Bob Dylan).

May 1979. The first man dies in the new Selby Coalfield. He was a shaft sinker, 111 metres from the surface and 2–3 metres from the shaft bottom when he was struck by falling equipment as he stood on the sinking platform suspended in the shaft.

June 1979. I return to Doncaster from Glasgow and run for NUM Branch delegate position. There are five candidates and I am second; Len Caven, former president and currently Labour councillor for Stainforth third; Brian Robson,[84] secretary of Thorne and District Communist Party, fourth; Billy Matthews, a member of Stainforth Communist Party, comes last. The position is won by Roy Bolton, just a rank-and-file member of the committee and the only non-politico in the race, with 237 votes. I received 216 so I wasn't disgraced.

I have slain the dragon. I no longer view the pit with terror and those dark memories and possession have been exorcised. I am stronger, and fitter. I slide back into pit work like a long walk down a familiar lane. The community draws me back in, back into its all-absorbing embrace, meaning, security, belonging. I am invigorated by the priceless sabbatical I have just enjoyed and the infusion of new ideas and ways of living. But this is *my* culture, this hard rock, this living, breathing subterranean effort. Another world, dually inhabited with the surface world, one in which your surface self is marked by your underground worth. Comradeship deeper than blood relatives. I stand totally engaged holding both handles of the boring machine, eyes in concentration, holding firm the weight of the machine and the long length of whirling rod, refusing its efforts to twist from my grasp, rimming and boring its way into the rock. My marra stands behind me. He is my eyes; he looks up and scans the rock above for the slightest sign of movement, his hand rests gently on my naked back. He will convey to me as quickly as he sees it himself: danger, serious injury or death. I do not need to look up, we are one person. I do not ask him to do this, I do not thank him that he does. We are miners.

NOTES

1: Ee Aye Ah Cud Hew – Eddie Pickford.

2: The old lads could smell the probable presence of firedamp. While the experts will tell you methane, the explosive component of firedamp, is odourless, and that's a fact, in firedamp it never occurs alone but is always accompanied by other gases which do have both a distinct smell and, given enough quantities, a distinct effect on your body. Now its also true these other gases often occur without the methane, so the aud lads' sense of smell could sometimes be wrong, but in the days when armies of men were blown to kingdom come by this gas, it was a canny skill to develop nen the less. Truth was our trusty Davy lamp also on occasion fibbed and was far from faultless, but I for one was never without it; it was the most accessible, dynamic instrument the miners had. Its presence and our possession of it was backed up by unique banks of laws which conferred on the pitman the power to decide when to leave off work, leave a district and even when to unilaterally turn off all power and production, based upon the evidence collected in his lamp.

3: A roll is an unexpected intrusion of rock into the coal seam. A fault is a major intrusion or a displacement of the coal.[3]

4: See the section on organisations at the end of this book.

5: At times of action, mass movements of peoples demand that all pure theories get laid aside, and the communists join the battles which the workers are engaged in for their own survival. At times of dormancy and calm, when all resistance seems to have gone, the pure theorists will re-emerge and question why we watered down the theory. Sometimes, with the heat of the moment and the movement gone, we will scarce remember, or, in the cold and calm of the ebb tide, our explanations will not be understood. This is so of many points of history when communists joined the mass movement and seemed to loose their specific direction and political theoretical purity. National struggles, even national liberation struggles strike little resonance today, especially among the simon-pure tiny sects of Marxist-Leninist-Anarcho Immaculate Conceptions. Class struggle is surely the only struggle we engage in?

The 'Anti-Imperialist, National Liberationist Front' perspective which many of us shared in the Sixties and Seventies, though, had reasoned that US imperialism represented imperialism per se in the world. It had subsumed all other mini imperialisms and potential imperialisms. The class struggle on a world scale was represented on the one hand by US imperialism and on the other the so-called workers' states. Though these might be seen as degenerated, bureaucratic, or by any other designation, they were still, on the scale of things, forced to represent the interests of the workers of the world even despite and against their sectional bureaucratic interests. There were inter-imperialist rivalries and hostilities, but none which would distract US imperialism from its prime objective, namely confronting and defeating the world movement of the workers and oppressed.

Regarding the national liberation struggles, we deemed they had only one way to go. Their path as emerging capitalist states was extremely limited; they could never now get to the big table of the world and could only at best be a very junior partner of major world capitalist powers. To strike such an accommodation with the global forces which had supported their national domination and subjugation would be a contradiction to their aspirations of national freedom and independence. The struggle to achieve national independence would force them into the 'socialist' camp and into objective and often military alliance with 'the workers' states' or the global forces of socialist revolution.

We also held that the only true independence they could achieve for the peoples of those countries was a socialist path which freed people economically and socially from all forms of capitalism, native and imperialist. Many saw Cuba as a classical example of this trajectory. The pressure for imperialism to soak up and control the world's resources made it very reluctant to share any part of that with some upstart independent capitalist economy. This would leave the independence movement no choice but to swing toward socialism and the socialist camp.

Were we naive? Nothing at that time would have suggested this was anything other than a principled and accurate analysis of the balance of forces and how we should play it, not just as a cynical exercise, but as a principle of isolating the major enemy of progress for the world's peoples. Few of us had any illusions in the ruling castes and bureaucracies of those countries, although Ché and Fidel did appear for a time to be of a different mettle than the men in grey overcoats. As it turned out, and true to form, unless control and direction of the revolution is kept under the direct control of the working class, through democratic committees and councils and assemblies, with recallable delegates and popular mass decision-making, 'leaders', whether charismatic or brutal or both, will assume power over the masses and derail the very point of the revolution. I'm sure we were aware of that maxim at the time, but we considered the whole world revolution a process which was still unfolding both numerically and in depth and quality.

6: [N]PLA The National Power Loading Agreement was introduced in 1966. I was aimed at achieving a standard day wage for the whole country. It aimed at ensuring a coalface worker in Wales or Scotland earned the same wage as a man in Nottingham or Kent. PLA was the face workers rate, but local lodges negotiated a rate protection so workers coming off face work because of injury or infirmity kept the wage.

7: Taps, tapman: Yorkshire terms for the man who pulls the button out and pushes it in to start the conveyor belt. He was charged with clearing obstructions and spillages also. Probably the least demanding work underground.

8: A caravan and holiday park at Cleethorpes almost entirely occupied by Yorkshire miners and their families.

9: A great war memorial in the centre of Amsterdam. It became the night and day 'scene' for the hippies; see *Geordies—Wa Mental*.

10: Recent disclosures from secret state papers, revealed under the Freedom of Information Act, show that our movement shook them to the core, with Special Branch and counter-terrorist police in widespread operation against demonstrations and organisations. Healey and Callaghan actively and seriously discussed the circumstances in which they would use troops on the streets in 1968. See the *Morning Star*, 20 June 2008, p. 7. The article notes however: 'The Cabinet Office, Home Office and Metropolitan Police have all refused freedom of information requests to open their files on the unruly protest outside the American Embassy in Grosvenor Square in March 1968.'

11: Not without justification of course, although the Trotskyists in Vietnam were among the first affiliates to The Fourth International under Lev himself, and they had joined the National Liberation Movement, Ho was determined to eliminate them. From July 1940 Ho and the Communist Party of Indochina (PCI) publicly denounced the Trots as 'fascist agents', reporting to the Comintern that alliances and concessions to them were out of the question, and advocating their 'political extermination'. Between 1945 and 1951 Trotskyists were ruthlessly and determinedly assassinated.

During this period the reason stated was that they were calling for fully arming the people and breaking the national front by splitting the peasants and workers from the sympathetic landlords within the movement. (*Co giai phong*, 23 October 1945; see also Vietnam and the Us Armed Forces Revolt, *Weekly Worker*, 5 June 2008, pp. 10–11.)

12: The Free Wales Army was founded in around 1965 by Julian Cayo Evans, one of that blend of Argentinean-Welsh, a horse breeder of "wild gaucho Argentinean stock" according to my fellow anarchist Ian Bone.

13: Rudi Dutschke was the political/pen name of Sebastian Bloomberg, he wrote for *Gewait* (*Violence*) and was a revolutionary socialist in the main stream of student and youth politics of that period.

14: The term wasn't being used lightly in Germany; the new German 'democratic' state was virulently anti-communist and its offices were staffed with ex-Nazis.

15: I don't believe that I've mentioned my talented sister was a world Irish Dance champion and the founder of a number of schools of Irish dancing, whose pupils were to go on to found their own highly professional Irish Dance schools. Many years later she was to graduate as an Irish Dance Adjudicator, an extremely senior position in the field of Dance and Culture, requiring as it does enough Gaelic to conduct the whole proceedings of a *fheis*, marking and commenting in Irish, and have enough left over for the odd native Irish-speaker or precocious dancer who might ask, unrehearsed, something in Irish.

16: Mandel and Pablo were leaders of the European bureau of the Fourth International, Healy of the British section.

17: The closures began really after the collapse of the miners' determined resistance in 1926, following their betrayal by the TUC leadership. From a million and a quarter miners in 1920, in 3,020 pits the number of miners would be reduced by a third and the number of pits by a half by the start of World War II. In 1947 the newly created National Coal Board took over 980 pits; ten years later there were 822. by 1968 only 317 pits remained open.

18: See *News Line*, Friday 14 May 1982, p. 5. There is also a photo.

19: Cambodia along with Vietnam and Laos had been part of 'French Indochina'. The struggle for liberation against the French and then the Japanese had been fought across the whole of the 'protectorate' by an ungrateful Indochinese population who didn't want protecting by French imperialism any more than they wanted the Japanese variety. Following the end of World War Two, with the Japanese imperial army fought to a standstill by the mostly communist-led Viet Minh, the 'allies' launched a renewed offensive against the peoples anti-imperialist forces. Britain moved its troops across Indochina to fight under French command, and Japanese prisoners of war were drafted into the French forces to take up where they had left off. With the UN busily dividing the world among the superpowers, the Geneva Convention co-hosted by Britain and the USSR in 1954 agreed to divide the whole of Indochina up again. Cambodia and Laos were re-established, but Vietnam was divided into two countries.

20: The ability of the US state to win over the United Nations to armed intervention in support of 'South Korea' was achieved only by the absence of the USSR who could otherwise have exercised its Secuity Council veto. The huge international US-led military coalition swept through South Korea and on through North Korea with no sign of stopping at the Chinese border. In these circumstances China marched to meet its US led foe in what remained of North Korea. The coalition commander MacArthur, for the US military and that wing of the US state which wanted to launch the nuclear war against the so-called 'Communist States', made it clear and public that he envisaged a devastating nuclear strike against China. During all of this time, the USSR sat on its hands.

21: Nogbad the Bad was the wicked uncle of Noggin the Nog, a Viking prince in a TV cartoon in the 1970s co-created by Oliver Postgate. Oliver's father was Raymond Postgate, the joint author with G.D.H. (Desmond) Cole of *The Common People*.

22: The little red shiny cover, though, had been a traditional folder in which extended Chinese families gave each other gifts of money, for birthdays, weddings, celebrations of all sorts; it had deep social and historic connotations in Chinese society. Whoever chose to dress Mao's works, then those of Lin and of the party in these covers was a clever tactician. The 'book' cover at least was magic before the book was ever written.

23: Jim Moody writing many years later in *Weekly Worker*, 16 October 2008, alleges that the training lasted only two months, the Fatah instructors loosing patience with the teams 'indiscipline; and infighting'. (p. 10, 'Substitute For Mass Action'). I take issue with the whole critical and frankly ignorant tone of the critique (of the RAF) and submit a letter in their posthumous defence. What actually happened was a stark culture clash. Fatah though secular and socialist was steeped individually in Islam and strict Arab social mores, the young Germans were typical of our generation, sexual, uninhibited and anti-authoritarian, in so far as a military expression of that culture can be. Politically allied, they were socially and culturally worlds apart. Better to march (and sleep) separately but strike together.

24: See conference report for July 1970, also *Evening Chronicle*, Newcastle

Upon Tyne, Monday 6 July 1970, p. 3.

25: Actually, 'the Deils Danger'.

26: Milldown Burn.

27: The state's secret service agents, as it turned out, weren't finished yet, and before they had done, they had also put into place a scheme which would knobble Wilson, the Liberals and Ted Heath, who they didn't think was made of the sort of hard right metal needed. I explain a little of this later when it comes to Ted's turn at running the country.

28: Alexandra Maria Lara.

29: Peter Cox describes the first encounter between them. She had been recruited by Alan Lomax along with Ewan and other folk /theatre worthies to stage a BBC version of the play *Dark of the Moon*. 'He found her in a Danish youth hostel, and over 24 wearying hours later she arrived at Waterloo Station to a reassuring Lomax bear hug. She was dishevelled and unwashed, with little more than the banjo and the clothes she stood up in. The clothes would have stood up of their own accord. Lomax's then girlfriend was a model, and she sluiced her down and spruced her up, put her long hair up in a lacquered beehive creation, and stood her in unfamiliar high heels. At 10.30 on 25 March 1956 she tottered into Alan Lomax's basement flat in Chelsea, and all heads turned. One head in particular.' Peter Cox, *Set Into Song*, Labatie Books, Cambridge, 2008.

30: By the time she had just turned teenage, she played piano, guitar and banjo. In 1956 Alan Lomax the great American folk archivist and researcher had called her 'the best banjo player in Europe' (she had made a tortuous journey through her teenage years and landed in Copenhagen at the age of 21). It is impossible to overplay the role Peggy Seeger played in the working-class women's and socialist feminist movement. Working-class women were coming into their own, leading massive strike movements, kicking their way into the trade union movement, taking back sections of the unions which were supposed to be theirs in the first place. Stamping working women's demands on union demands. Equal pay, at work yes, but dignity and recognition of women's work in the home. Taking back the term 'housewife' and 'mother' and demanding their recognition as priceless skills and proud careers. Demanding wages for housework. Kicking chauvinism in the arse of every socialist and union platform which women in increasingly rising temper were now mounting. In the van of all of this and orchestrating each and every new battle front for 'bread and roses' were Peggy's songs. The men in the movement, myself included, could not ignore even if we wanted to these songs which penetrated your soul and conscience and made you examine your role and attitude. My little Emma was raised from the cradle to teenage and beyond against a background of Peggy's humour wit and strength, her and Maureen sang duets of Peggy's most biting and often very funny and pithy songs. Some of my most tearfully happy memories are of these two sitting with their recorders and the New City Songster learning Peggy's latest musical commentary. See Peggy's *The Peggy Seeger Songbook: Forty Years of Songmaking* (New York: Music Sales Corporation. US International Standard Book Number 0.8256.0344.7; UK International Standard Book Number 0.7119.9140.

31: Tom Kilburn was supporting the PORT(O) Belgian section of the International in their election campaign. Foreigners are prohibited by law from taking part in the election process, however, and he was promptly arrested, protesting 'Je suis belge' (I am Belgian) in his schoolboy French—which didn't convince. Later on he was escorted to a train for deportation. The police boarded with him and escorted him to a small compartment where they pulled down the blinds. Tom was expecting a thumping, Gestapo-style, but was instead surprised when they offered him a cigarette and asked him to explain the possible difference between the Mandel Fourth International and that of Posadas.

32: Abbie emerged into the Civil Rights Movement as a fairly straight-laced middle-class American with a conscience. By 1967 he was in the leadership of the anti-war movement and embryonic revolutionary movement emerging. He was later to comment looking back on the slaughter the US state unleashed on Vietnam Indochina and its own dissident rebel population 'No one can image any of this unless they've lived through it.' I think perhaps that's probably true; Abbie became a victim of the Federal FBI CointelPro (counter-intelligence programme). This was a counterinsurgency scheme, set up by anti-communist, anti-union witchhunter J. E. Hoover, the head of the FBI. though Hoover was usually a law unto himself, this particular programme had been commissioned by Nixon. Originally the programme had been a CIA device, to discredit and undermine and bring down foreign political movements and governments. It dealt in disinformation, slander, rumour, lies, and personal character assassination. As we know CIA moved outside this method to direct coups and physical assassinations as circumstances required. CointelPro wasn't simply deployed in Africa, Asia and Latin America, but to Europe, Eastern and Western. Some of my tale will suggest it was deployed here in Britain—against Wilson, against Thorpe and Heath. Strings would be pulled, facts on the ground manipulated, events set up, mud-slinging, dirty tricks, all the trade of the extortionist and blackmailer, deployed however not to exert money but to destroy the leader and his/her movement. Hoover brought the scheme home, probably both aspects of it. Direct assassination, and in the case of Abbie, character assassination. (While the physical assassination rests on circumstantial evidence and to an extent patent common-sense empirical evidence.) The deployment of spies, plants, and setups by Hoover is on public record. Look around today in Britain: who is running the panic press, whence comes the terror and fear of perverts, killers, teenagers, hoodies, black men, Muslims and paedophiles?

A bolt on- attachment following the CIA/FBI programme was the Chaos Programme. The aim is to instil a need for state protection, a fear of the enemies without and within, hence support for the state's agents of law and order, its bodies of armed men and its 'values'. I would guess someone is still operating the system—or is that paranoia?

33: See the section on organisations at the end of this book.

34: When the pit gallowas (ponies) were bought out of the pit during the holiday, or a strike shutdown, they went wild with excitement at seeing the daylight and breathing the fresh air, galloping around in the meadow, free at last—at least for a time.

35: Granville Williams, of the Doncaster Socialist Alliance, a teacher and later a prominent member for some decades of the Campaign For Press and Broadcasting Freedom if my memory serves me right.

36: I wanted to be on the stage,
> And now my ambitions I've gottem!
> In my grey pantaloons I'm the rage
> I'm the hole in the elephant's bottom!
> My friends all think I'm a wit,
> In their seats in the stalls I can spot 'em!
> And I wink at the girls in the pit
> Through the hole in the elephant's bottom!
> Last night I had some bad luck,
> The manager said I was rotten!
> Cos I happened to get my head stuck
> Through the hole in the elephant's bottom!

37: The origins and practice of this system, an early example of miners' job control, can be found in my History Workshop pamphlet, *Pit Life in Co. Durham*.

38: I think we little understood what they had in mind: a mass destruction of the heartlands of the European Proletariat, a tearing out by the roots of settled, highly class-conscious, heavily politicised concentrations of traditional manufacture, heavy engineering, mining, shipbuilding, docks, the lot. It was the breaking of an identity, the breaking of class rooted to location and history and production. Economic mass migration, alienation of migrant and local. The creation of 'super-state' bureaucracy so remote from controls and popular constraints as to be almost self-governing quasi-dictatorships.

39: In September of 2007 the local *Berwickshire Gazette Office News Window* is announcing the 'closure of the Coldingham YHA'. Sad, sad. Fond memories.

40: I don't think I seen Art again until the midst of the big coalfield battle of 84/85 when he leapt onto the stage of a giant Sheffield charity rock night to tell the heavy throng what was going on in the pit villages and to urge them to get their hands in their pockets and support 'our lads'. Next time I seen him he passed me in Doncaster and I'd been to some big NUM executive meeting, wearing as I did a three-piece suit and watch and chain, in the style of the old-time Union leaders. He roared with irreverent laughter "Danny the Red in the suit!" He had more often than not seen me spaced out in the field of a rock festival or making the scene at an all night party.

41: Being made secretary of Thorne and District Trade Union Council was my first real promotion in the labour movement. Thorne TUC had seen better days, but Legay and some stalwarts had persisted. He had pestered me for years about the Hatfield NUM Branch not having representatives on the Council, so I had raised it at the Branch, and me and Jim were duly elected. We switched the Council meetings to the Proletaria Bookshop and started to smarten the organisation up again, raising issues affecting trade unionists and working people in the area. We started to regain affiliates, from Goole and Finningly, Thorne and Moorends. It was surprising how many trade unions there were in the immediate area.

42: If you were suspended pending expulsion you had the right to appeal first to the Constituency General Management Committee, then the Executive Committee, then the National Executive Committee, then finally to Conference.

43: It should be recognised that very few black people lived among us. In 1971 there were only 1.4 million 'non-white' people of all descriptions on the island. At the start of my teenage tale in 1961 there were only 400,000 nationally, living down south or in the Midlands; very very few per capita lived in 'the North' generally. (*Race For Change*, Commission For Racial Equality report, based upon national census figures, quoted in *The Guardian* 26 September 2007).

44: Children's liberation, children's rights, children's freedoms were all aimed at recognising the independence and individuality of children, recognising children as simply smaller people to whom as far as possible the right to participate in democratic decisions should be granted. The *Children's Rights* magazine and group of this period stand in utter contrast and contradistinction to the weight of repression and misrepresentation of children in today's society. People claiming to be the guardians of children today would have been considered their physical social mental and spiritual jailers back then. Today's social service 'experts' would have been howled down during this period, while the progressive and visionary experts of that time would now be given the same treatment. Of course none of this has as much to do with science or facts, as it has with finding the evidence to fit the already entrenched and deeply held value judgements underpinning the two wholly conflictual outlooks and philosophies. Many of the laws and restrictions and practices touted by the government today as 'child protection' would have been clearly seen in the Seventies as simply means to repress children's rights and liberties under the guise of paternalism. (The magazine *Children's Rights*, subsequently retitled *Kids*, was a spin-off from the book by Paul Adams, A.S. Neill, Robert Ollendorff and others, *Children's Rights – Towards the Liberation of the Child* (London: Elek Books, 1971), which had appeared, coincidentally, during the run-up to the Old Bailey prosecution of the editors of *Oz*, the hippie paper, for supposedly corrupting the morals of young people (the convictions were quashed on appeal). *Children's Rights* magazine folded after a few issues owing to editorial disputes and lack of funds. In 2000, almost thirty years after the Oz trial, as part of the Blair government's attempt to corral childhood, David Blunkett the Education Secretary attempted to close down Summerhill School, which had been in continuous existence pioneering child-centred education in voluntarily attended classes since being founded by A.S. Neill in 1921; the best efforts of Blunkett's inspectors were soundly defeated in court by a home-grown legal team led by a boy of fifteen.)

45: Silent rig' is the drill adoptd by submarines being stalked by surface vessels with listening devices.

46: It was just as incredible that in 1960, 30 states in the USA banned (i.e. declared illegal) 'mixed-race' marriages. No less than 16 of these states jailed men and women for the 'offence'. John F. Kennedy had personally asked Sammy Davis, not to marry his girlfriend Mai Britt, who was white, because it was prior to the presidential elections and the backlash would mean he was put on the spot to comment and this could cost him the presidency. He didn't marry her and stopped seeing her. Something tells me it was more than the Kennedy charm broke Sammy from his love, and adjacent to the request lurked some large lumpen characters with big sticks. Poor Marilyn Monroe had wound up dead in circumstances, which are clearly related to not only to her affairs with the Kennedy boys, but more importantly her long association with American communists and her sympathy for Cuba and the Mexican revolutions. Marilyn was far from the 'dumb blonde' history would try to make her. (An unlikely source of information comes in the *Daily Mail* feature 'Was Marilyn murdered because she was a communist?', 29 April 2006, p. 45, based upon FBI files released under the Freedom of Information Act. We were to see more examples of the Land of the Free and its hold on democracy as the Sixties unfolded.)

47: Ian Bone tells us that Cayo's marching column and explosive salute outside the Dublin GPO cut such a dash with the former insurgents of the old rusty guns of the 'Official IRA' that they delivered a big consignment of Thompson machine-guns direct to his farmhouse in Lampeter. This was not 'the banner strand' however and since a number of Welsh Free bombs were exploding across Wales with few other likely suspects, Cayo promptly dumped the lot into Tregaron bog. As it turned out he and his number two the Welsh pitman Denis Coslett, who had boasted perhaps a little too grandly that they now had an airforce, well one plane, and Gethyn ap Iestyn were jailed in 'a show trial' in 1969. (See *Bash the Rich*, pp. 48–50.) There was too, though, a lot of bullshit, with the FWA claiming actions which it didn't in fact carry out. At the same time as Cayo was dumping the machine-guns, another team, Mudiad Amddiffyn Cymru, was actually already engaged in multiple bombing raids. Bone says: 'As the investiture of the Prince of Wales at Caernarfon in 1969 drew closer, the bombings intensified with an attempt to blow up the Royal Train at Abergele resulting in the bombers George Taylor and Alwyn Reese losing their lives.' The founder of the movement, John Barnard Jenkins, was later arrested and jailed for ten years. In 1983 he was jailed again for his involvement with the Workers Army of the Welsh Republic. During all these operations, Ian tells us, Cayo 'would appear on television claiming responsibility for the bombing on behalf of FWA and promising further more daring acts ... But of course there was no evidence because no one in FWA had any connection with the bombings or even knew who was doing them. Cayo and his band of merry men continued to strut about West Wales with impunity as the bombing campaign intensified giving credence to his claims as a skilled urban guerrilla leader.' (Bash the Rich, pp. 52–3.)

48: Joe was a wonderful combination of Irish wit and politics with pit talk and crack. His accent merged into a sort of Liverpudlian despite working in Nottingham.

49: Joe had entered the industry at the age of 14 and graduated his way through every task and skill in underground mining. He was elected to the NEC of the NUM in 1958, acting for the North Western Area, and became general secretary of that area in 1961. Elected to the Labour Party's NEC in 1963 he became national president of the NUM in a vigorously fought contest in 1971. He received an OBE in 1969 and was elected to the TUC General Council in 1973.

50: We shared a number of 'regular' and established local folk singers, including Tony Capstick, John Lennard and some we had set on their feet from being young dewy-eyed boys. Steve Womack cut his teeth in our Red Star Club and a hard school it was too. He went on to become a halarious singer-songwriter and stand up comedian in the Capstick tradition: 'I'm from Doncaster, centre of the South Yorkshire coalfield. Me Dad coming back black from work ... and you know I never knew why because he worked at the bank.' See Steve Womack, *Turn The Other Cheek* (CD), Available from New Wave International (phone: 01302 881117).

51: The Royal Antiquarian Order of Buffaloes—a sort of poor man's Freemasons; nicknamed the Buffs.

52: We were being sarcastic; it couldn't have come from anywhere but the roof of course.

53: Actually the Blair government's attempt to manipulate courts and trials and outcomes forced through a whole range of changed definitions of 'rape' in order to make lesser crimes more serious. From a clear definition of forcing some one to have intercourse against their will either through force or bribery or threats, it was widened to almost any unlawful sexual act whether or not both parties were consenting and even in the case of underage girls, where no intercourse took place, and where the participants in minor sexual acts were of the same age and both fully consensual. This in turn led to the vast majority of trials failing to convict as juries refused to recognise the events as 'rape'. This then led to a widespread campaign by women's groups suggesting that the law was biased against women, refusing to recognise that the trivialisation of the term and the penalisation of non crimes under the law was what lay behind the not guilty verdicts and not some blind eye to violence against women. The biggest area of 'failed' rape prosecutions seems to be those where previously willing sexual partners, wives, girlfriends etc. claim not to have consented on an occasion. Juries have found it difficult to identify the conflicting facts of the (obviously) unwitnessed and unsubstantiated claim, especially where time has passed and the claim is made retrospectively. The jury has after all has to satisfy itself beyond reasonable doubt and this is often impossible to do within an existing or previous sexual relationship and no evidence other than what the parties say. This is not to suggest many of these women have not been raped, only that in such cases it is very difficult to prove simply on the basis of conflicting individual stories. In November 2008 the Solicitor General on the basis of a ruling from the High Court come up with two major shifts in legal practice in order to try and achieve more convictions for rape. One, the judge is allowed to instruct the jury that a long passage of time between the alleged incident and the complaint doesn't mean the complainant has made it up, but simply may be suffering mental and social trauma, which prevented immediate reporting of the offence when the evidence was fresh and testable. Two, that people wrongly accused of rape, falsely accused of rape, will not be allowed to sue the person making the false or malicious allegation. The courts further ruled that people accused of rape cannot have anonymity during the period when they are untried and legally innocent. One can only conclude that in this area an accused person is indeed guilty until proven innocent and subject to the abuse and social ostracism that accompanies guilt for such a crime.

54: Cuban Posadists went on to claim that Castro had had Guevara killed when, it turned out, he was actually in Bolivia fighting with the guerrilla movement there. Conversely, after Bolivian authorities executed Guevara, Posadas claimed in 1967 that Ché wasn't actually dead but was being kept in prison by Castro's government.

55: The truth was that the Cuban people supported the vision and outlined by Fidel and the party. Other insights, other socialist versions and visions were suppressed, so true socialist, pluralist, workers' democracy was never allowed to take root. Thus at this stage Fidel and the Cuban state, having taken control of the ideology, were confident that the Cuban people could be trusted with the guns.

56: The neutron bomb was a device which would kill the citizens but leave the infrastructure of the buildings standing. Miron's 'bomb' was devised to wipe out the union but leave the industry standing.

57: While this may well be true, either in concert with this or acting independently, another branch of the 'secret state' was moving against Heath. He was the target in the last in a line of publicity coups against the leaders of the major political parties, aimed at bringing about a hard right-wing, free-market, anti-union, pro-American, up-front imperialist foreign policy. Ted didn't match up in their view. The way the land lay to this team, Wilson was a proto-Soviet agent, who had a far-left agenda, and he was helped to office by the Liberal Party and Jeremy Thorpe in particular, who were winning votes from the Tories and conducting a high-profile campaign against apartheid and the South African state. First it was needed to set the political scene through manipulation of the press and scandal to bring them down or severely weaken them. The next step was to undermine and sink Heath as leader of the Conservative Party in order to pave the way for a much more right-wing Tory political leader (already waiting in the wings was the "Iron Lady", Mrs Thatcher with a political agenda in line with the emerging US hawks). Additionally there is much to suggest apartheid South Africa had its own secret service (the Bureau of State Security, or BOSS) in operation working in conjunction with sections of the British state. The young and dynamic Peter Hain, leader of the radical Young Liberals of the time, had been heading up a powerful campaign against South Africa and inflicting deep PR damage to that state. He was soon to be set up for a major criminal offence. Meanwhile, Ted's 'softness' on the Palestinian question made him enemies in the powerful Israeli ops teams, and their own agents directly.

Thorpe was dispatched in a homosexual sex scandal which tottered on accusations of attempted murder, then came his chief whip Cyril Smith. The young sexual partner pointing the finger turned out to be Colin Wallace, a state agent working for Psychological Operations with the Ministry of Defence. Part of the plan seems to have been to bump the unsuspecting Wallace off (to stop him disclosing his sexual encounters) and really finish any political credibility the Liberals and their leaders had. While Wallace seems either to have been up for the public scandal bit, or else was set up and used by his 'handlers', no not Jeremy in this case, he obviously balked at the notion of becoming a martyr to the cause of the Liberals' humiliation. In 1987 he gave left-wing journalist Paul Foot a top-secret plan of the wider operation. It was called Clockwork Orange and was the blueprint of an MI5 operation. The file sets out the terms of reference, as follows:

Every effort should be made to exploit character weaknesses in 'target' subjects and in particular:

(a) Financial misbehaviour.

(b) Sexual misbehaviour.

(c) Political misbehaviour.

Alongside this 'the targets' are listed :

Heath. Wilson. Benn. Thorpe. Smith. Castle.

While Thorpe, Smith and Heath are to be tarred with the homosexual brush, Wilson would be sloshed with all three, (a)–(c), but more particularly financial misdealings, while Benn and Castle would get political misbehaviour (far-left links and activity).

The notes on Heath are explicit:

The Conservative Party … cannot win the next the election under Edward Heath's leadership. The key issue … is whether there should be cosmetic treatment to help elect a weak government under Heath or major surgery to bring about change of leadership before the next election.

Much of the evidence of these dirty tricks can be found in *Who Framed Colin Wallace?* by the late Paul Foot (1989) and a review of the whole situation can be found in 'Was Cyril Smith set up—Rochdale MP in seventies sex scandal', *Northern Voices*, no. 8, Winter 2007/8, p. 6.

58: Mary Holland, 'No doubts In Arthur Horner's Little Moscow', *Observer* (?) 5 January 1974.

59: NUM Annual Conference Report, 1 July 1968, p. 174. As it turned out the resolution was passed near unanimously with a surprising impassioned speech in support by Joe Gormley, who was speaking, one supposes, for himself and not the NEC, although there is no record of an NEC recommendation on the resolution and clearly NEC members, including Joe, had been allowed to speak freely on the issue.

60: Tony had been one our team of long-haired bearded hippy pitmen bikers, his garb was identical to Jim Shipley's and my own at that time, raggy jeans, denim shirt, over white T-shirt, mostly with steel toecap boots, denim badge-covered jacket or leather biker jacket. Tony had become politicised and like Jim and the rest of that team become more focused and less spontaneously wild. Tony and his sidekick Steve Lancaster had been quite the Wild West men. Given to sudden explosion of violence, one scene at the Winning Post in Moorends concluded with Steve tossing pint glasses to Tony, who, rounders style, smashed them across the room with a broken chair leg. Tony gravitated toward our Mineworker tendency but never lost his strong leaning to anarchism, while Steve continued to be a colourful character. We would stay in proximity almost the entire duration of this story.

61: Susan started a tradition of McQuire baby-sitters, with her sisters Sharon, Kathleen and then Mary all taking up the family pitch looking after Emma. Pete did have one son, little Pete, though they were both heavily outnumbered in the sex war. The McQuires were one of those big interconnected families, linked to the Youngs who seemed to occupy half of Abbeyfield Road at one time, one and all good and caring neighbours from generations of pit folk, many of them active in the union or community resistance throughout this period.

62: Although we operated a 'free' relationship, it had strict rules. The first rule in all cases was that if an extramarital sex romp was likely to cause hurt, resentment, pain, embarrassment or whatever to either other, you didn't do it. This was an unconditional rule, no argument, no explanation necessary. The second and joint rule was that you didn't have sex on the doorstep, with people who you shared your daily lives with and who were likely to get in the way of your main relationship. You didn't have sex with regular, close and mutual friends and comrades. Such encounters were likely to impact on the real relationship, and the position could become damaging and untenable. So they were banned.

63: The Hull fishing community like its neighbouring mining communities lived in each others pockets. Nothing much passed without soon everyone knowing about it. So it is that we know the Royal Navy spy recruitment officer at Hull was J. J. Brooks DSC. Although formally he'd left the RN in the early Sixties he was recruited to SIS (the State Intelligence Service), better known as MI6. He operated a briefing and recruitment office on St Andrews Fish Dock. Vessels were paid £20,000 a trip whether they caught fish or not, and since this was often share fishing the crew got a portion of this too. Barmaids would joke to crews about them going off spying on this trip, as news of who got the shore catch this time would soon spread around the fishing crews. The whole fishing boat spy operation was codenamed Operation Hornby.

64: The fearful climbers got sweet revenge when those not so challenged had trembled in fear at the later water survival course.

65: *The Middle Way, Journal of the Buddhist Society*, August 1976, p. 83.

66: Charles was giant of a man, not simply in his tall ganglyness, but as a radio pioneer, producer, historian, and human archaeologist. I had met him through Philip Donnellan, but actually knew him by reputation since the age of 14 from the Radio Ballads and in particular the famous, almost sacred 'Big Hewer'. A bearded man with a red face and a tendency to stoop. When singing on stage he bent in strange contortions as if to resonate or prolong a note. I knew him from the TV studios in Birmingham where I met Philip on more than a few occasions, and at that time he was still knee-deep in work on the culture of the Gypsies and travelling people. People said he had developed his stoop when working in submarines during the war and kept crouched rather than smack his head on the deckheads. What I didn't know was that he was a wartime submarine commander, and had been involved in towing the X-craft that succesfully attacked the German battleship *Tirpitz*, which had been sinking merchant ships on the Arctic convoys to Russia. A recent book by Peter Cox, a contemporary of Donnellan and the whole Radio Ballad team, is revealing: 'The tense and protracted operation involved snaking through fiercely defended Norwegian fjords at night. This action and others won him the DSC... the following year.' (Peter Cox, *Set Into Song: Ewan MacColl, Charles Parker, Peggy Seeger and The Radio Ballads*. Labatie Books, Cambridge 2008.) I was to meet Charles quite a bit after that, especially when he took over a workers' educational programme in Derbyshire and he invited me down to speak or comment on his ongoing work on the pits.

67: Decades later the IS group, now the SWP, began to adopt a similar 'defence and non-critical' position toward the Islamists and Islamic regimes.

68: Christine Berle, ex NEC Member;, both quotes from IWP's *Critical Practice*, Fall 1975 article by Dan Jacob.

69: My New Year syndrome was fear of thorough demoralisation and anticlimax which results from a New Year's Eve in which I do not end up in bed with a sexy chick. Since schooldays the one evening in the year in which nobody can fail is New Year's Eve when everyone, everyone is looking to end the night with sex. You can't not score, to do so is to be utterly useless and an unwanted, unfulfilled failure. Letting the evening pass away without being drunk was a mini version of the same wasted night. While New Years steadily would decline in expectations to a point where I dreaded them as impending colossal disappointments, I could always do something about having a drink.

70: Mind, that's up to now; my genes may yet surprise me. I was later to develop a relationship with my first Indian girl, and found her quite absorbing and utterly attractive, and I have long drooled over girls of Indochinese and 'oriental' appearance, neither of which I had shared my formative years with, so perhaps that formula needs reworking. Whatever the reasons, and I didn't choose this orientation, my sexual needle is certainly stuck firmly in an endless and unchanging 'true to form' groove. Something of Nabakov's opening paragraphs in Lolita, explaining his early teen encounter with an angelette nymphet who haunted his brain and every waking and sleeping moment ever after, and a search to re-encounter its sacred brilliance which walked by his side and in his spirit like a possession. Though I hasten to add, straightening up to my full height and regaining my composure, my own attraction is at the late teens and twenty end of the scale, your honour, and not the pubescent end. Not now anyway. M'lord and members of the jury. Of late, too, women in their thirties have started to focus my attention so perhaps my sexual taste is starting to mature.

71: Ulrike was found hanged in her cell, from a rail she couldn't possibly reach on her own, with nothing to stand on, with her hands tied behind her back facing AWAY from the wall. Ulrike had been fiendishly tortured over a long period by sensory deprivation using sound-absorbing equipment in her solitary cell, rendering her effectively deaf, and utterly isolated. Jean-Paul Sartre wrote after finding a similar set-up on a visit to Andreas Baader in prison late in 1974:

And there's something he's missing: sound. Apparatuses in the interior of the cell select sounds, weaken them and render them perfectly inaudible within the cell itself.

We know that sound is indispensable to a human body and consciousness. There must be an atmosphere surrounding a person.

Sounds, which we call silence — but which carry to us, for example, the sound of a passing tram, that of a passer-by on the street, warning sirens — are connected to human conduct; they mark human presence.

This absence of communication with others through sound creates profound problems — circulatory problems of the body, and problems of consciousness. These latter destroy thought by rendering it increasingly difficult. Little by little, it provokes blackouts, then delirium, and, obviously, madness.

So even if there is no 'torturer,' there are people who squeeze certain levers on another level. This torture provokes deficits in the prisoner; it leads him to stupefaction or to death.

Baader, who is a victim of this torture, speaks quite appropriately, but from time to time he stops, as if he has lost his train of thought. He takes his head in his hands in the middle of a sentence and then starts up again two minutes later.

(From *www.marxists.org/reference/archive/sartre/1974/baader.htm* – *Libération*, 7 December 1974; more at the website.)

During the 1970s there were outrages against prisoners in Brtish jails too. Following the introduction of internment in Northern Ireland in 1971, 14 prisoners were interrogated by the army after being subjected to sleep deprivation, standing for hours spread-eagled against a wall and suffering sensory deprivation in the form of hooding and loud, droning noise. They were also beaten in various ways, and, blindfolded, were thrown from grounded or almost grounded helicopters which they had thought were airborne at altitude so they imagined they were plunging to their deaths. A subsequent official inquiry (behind closed doors) stopped short of naming these abuses as torture—which they very clearly were.

72: Mr Large was on the turn. I next saw him six or seven years later. He was centre of a crowd of noisy football supporters, in the bar of the Bridge Hotel, giving it large licks on the issue of Newcastle United. He had lost some weight and looked formidable in a clean white shirt and reed galluses. Problem was his speech which was now littered with references to 'niggers yee knaa'. I had long ago parted company with Large and this current display persuaded me he had gone to the bad. Twenty-eight years later I re-encounter Bob Davies, who had been something of his mentor. I relate the above story to him and he tells me:- [I've altered the man's real name] 'I am a bit disappointed but not too surprised about Large. His father was in Mosley's National Union of Fascists before the war and

Large was involved with a fascist group when I first met him. I persuaded him to join the Young Socialists and he married Pauline — from Prudhoe Young Socialists.' So we have it; was he already drifting to the far right when he put the finger on Sean? The revelations remain dangerous but the spin put on them by Large clearly put them in an even worse light, and certainly opened up suspicions.

73: S.123 of the 1954 Mines and Quarries Act provides for workmen to elect and pay their own safety inspectors with rights to inspect, unimpeded, the whole mine and make written reports to the HMI.

74: Les Wood was an extremely funny man, both consciously and without knowing it; he was known also to fly off at a tangent from time to time. He was a dedicated militant member of Hatfield Main NUM Branch Committee as well a leading light both in the Home Coal Scheme, which he helped run, and in the Labour Party. His lads were all likewise – Vinny and especially Jimmy with whom I had worked for years and who was my constant comrade in the Branch and enthusiastic supporter of our later publication *Hot Gossip*. Both were fearless pickets in the battles of the Union and the Branch. His other lads after army service became active trade unionists in NUPE then UNISON I believe.

75: The RAF at its inception bore many similarities to where we found ourselves now. As previously noted, they became an armed expression of a popular movement; they hadn't actually set off to become do-or-die full-time armed insurgents, but were left in that role as the popular movement later receded. We needed to learn lessons and not be drawn into premature armed engagements in the heat of any moments.

76: The Free Wales Army was founded in around 1965/66 by Julian Cayo Evans, one of that blend of Argentinean-Welsh, a horse breeder of 'wild gaucho Argentinean stock' according to my fellow anarchist Ian Bone. The Breton Liberation Army we shall come upon later in this tale, while the Scottish Republican Army members had all been rounded up and jailed just prior to me breaking upon the Scottish scene. There was too briefly a Cornish Republican Army, nicknamed by the disrespectful 'The Oo – Ar – A'.

77: Later, as things turned out, the comrades of the Glasgow Cumann were not always so understanding; they couldn't understand my commitment to actually study and not abandon my then place at the University of Strathclyde, but that was the perspective I went up there for. Unlike at Ruskin I intended to actually complete the course, while carrying out a strong political intervention too. Control and balance was the key. I was in this for the long haul, I needed to make coordinated and measured use of my time, without by any means becoming a monk. At Ruskin, the battle had been academic and had been part of the student movement protests on exams and the principles of free education and methods of study. Since we were a trade union college, this was linked to the class struggle and the agenda we were fighting for in the wider labour and trade union movement. But I hadn't gone to Strathclyde to drop out or particularly to engage in that same field of combat. I was actually committed to sharpening my skills and gaining knowledge for the industrial fight in the mines and the mine communities. Law, rent acts, health and safety, sex discrimination, union representation, welfare, common law, industrial relations etc. It meant study, it meant passing exams. I hadn't gone to Glasgow to take up root and branch the republican struggle there, and drop everything else I was engaged with. Many in the Cumann though thought that's exactly why I had come, with such glowing references from Dublin and London. I was however now planning what I did, and picking out priorities for my time and attention. My past health problems had demonstrated how much I needed to do that for my own sanity. But politically I also had to have a scale and programme of involvement too. Sinn Fein was my major political field of work, but in a context of the class struggle in Britain.

78: See *PAC News* August–September 1978, p. 4–5.

79: Statement of orthodox Jewish Neturei Karta, *New York Times*, 5 December 1978.

80: To be right, if World War II had been fought on the catwalk the Nazis would have won it hands down. They had the gear. All the insignia and black and jackboots and caps, it was damn powerful stuff. Like most kids born into the war or just at the end of it I had collected lots of Nazi costume Jewellery, the Iron Cross—I had a silver one of those, my mate had a Gestapo bayonet. The German U-Boat ensign was my pride and joy. Even into my years as a young Anarchist, I used to keep it rolled in a bottom drawer and sneak up to look at it, like my mates furtively took out dirty books. I suppose in a way it was all pornography, but Lemmie and Motorhead and tens and thousands of bikers didn't give a fuck about censorship anyway. Flirting with the imagery didn't mean embracing the politics of what it stood for. Although to be perfectly honest I never felt that relaxed about the Mod craze for wearing the Union Jack. We have to look behind the symbol and see what people really feel and think rather than what they are wearing on their sleeve or lapel, as it may not be their heart.

81: *The Miner*, July–August 1977, Conference Reports.

82: Among the contributors apart from myself talking about the 1969 unofficial action, which I illustrate singing songs between the text, is Jim MacFarland. Jim is a Doncaster miner, who becomes a lecturer at Sheffield University following Ruskin. His forte is Denaby and Conisbrough, his paper *The Bag Muck Strike 1902* becomes a little pamphlet. Jim goes on to become leader of the Doncaster Council during the great coal strike of 1984–5 when he does everything legally possible to support the miners' families. Nick Howard, the IS bloke from Sheffield who first gave *The Mineworker* so much encouragement but then recoiled in horror as the RWP(T) exposed itself, spoke on post World War Two, and Arthur Scargill gave a paper on the 1972 strike. I had quite forgotten, until I chanced upon a report on the conference I had written in *The Strathclyde Telegraph*, about how barbed and controversial the session on 1939–45 had been. The workshop, being in Yorkshire in the heart of the coalfields as well as being star-studded with Arthur and a number of well-known local union characters, had attracted a good lump of men and their wives from the pits. The controversy had its origins in the vexed question of the nature of World War Two, and whether it was indeed 'a people's war' or 'bosses' war' or something of both.

It had impacted hard in the pit communities for a variety of reasons; one was their exempt status from military service, their special place in the war economy, another the political character of the miners as a vanguard section of the working class, and their extreme reluctance to set aside struggles in their own cause for those of the state.

Tempers flared a number of times as ageing CP miners' leaders confronted equally elderly rank-and-file members who had never forgiven them for crossing the class lines and supporting the employers, stopping strike pay and sacking miners right through the war ... the miners could have comprised no more than one twentieth of the working population in the inter-war period (actually one fifteenth is more reasonable) yet their strike propensity against a unitary government, against the Labour Party, against the NUM (MFGB) leadership, the TUC bigwigs and against the Communist Party 'theory and leadership' were truly dynamic.

(Actual totals)

1938—41.5% of all strikes **1939**—43% **1942**—40.4% **1944**—57.1% **1945**—56.9%

Weighted in numbers of workers, those totals would mean that something in the region of two thirds of all strikes through the war years were by miners.

Later enquiry into this fact showed me two things further. One was that within these overall figures was an even greater concentration of activity in specific unruly coalfields, not least Scotland overall. The second thing was that CPGB membership among miners in the Scottish coalfield, for example, demonstrated that many members of the CPGB themselves followed their class instincts and despite the official 'anti-strike' party line engaged in rag-ups and walkouts along with everybody else.

83: *NUM Annual Reports*, 1979, pp. 187–206.

84: Brian, who had worked with me in headings, and with whom we had long debates about politics and power, initially had a bad stammer at public meetings, but at length he struggled and totally eliminated it with great willpower and perseverance. He gained confidence from joining the Thorne and District Communist Party, a branch with deep roots and traditions within that mining community; he was by the time of the great strike in 1984/85 president of the NUM Branch and an accomplished public speaker. Brian was in the lead of the Branch's struggles throughout that momentous year and into the thick of the turmoil that followed. He had been a skilled S.123 inspector and often was seen as a voice of calm reason during the periods when raised voices and fury held sway. He stayed active in politics after ill health forced him out of the industry, and remained a close friend and comrade throughout this story.

A

aal. All. But meant to pronounce the long aa sound; the sang is a bairnie dandling sang.

a had. A hold.

aah. It's just a noise. An oral expression, it means in this case 'Oh, yes?'

aalreet. All right.

aan. Own.

aboot, aboon. About.

AEI. Engineering company.

Ah. I.

Ah'm. I am.

Ahad. A hold,

aheed. Ahead.

ahint. Behind.

ain. Own.

alain. Alone.

alang. Along.

alreet, aalreet. All right.

amang. Among.

an'ahl, anarl. And all, as well.

An Ard Comhairle (Irish). Executive Committee.

Ard Fheis (Gaelic). Grand Meeting /National Conference).

Arthur (Scargill). For most this story president of the NUM, although initially Yorkshire Area president, and ultimately honorary president of the NUM.

aud/auld. Old.

audfarand. Wise beyond their years.

av. The Yorkshire shortened version of 'have'.

aye. Always.

B

baccy. Smoking or chewing tobacco.

bairn(e). Child.

bang. Literally to strike, but actually to excel, be better than.

bank. The surface of the mine, but also the middle of the coalface in Yorkshire.

banksman. The man at the top of the pit shaft in charge of the loading and lowering and rising of the cage with men or materials.

banty. Small version of.

bareback (riding). Unprotected sexual intercourse.

belang. Belong.

bla, blae. Blow; it means to strike a blow, but also 'get a blow' – take a breath of air and cool down.

blare. Shouting of children, or drunks, or blast from an instrument.

blather. Pointless talking.

blinns, blinds. Glasses.

boards. Wooden planks used underground for lagging.

boody. A precious child object of currency, normally recognised throughout Northumbria, Tyne, Tees, Wear and Tweed, though probably not by adults. The true form was broken real bone china items, though with the expansion of northern populations and the diminution of real bone china tea sets, any china pieces became currency too. In every child community expert children could distinguish the ever-smaller items of real bone china 'bonny bits' from the lesser varieties.

bords. Birds/girls.

bowk (1). Be sick.

bowk (2). Used to describe the sound of the earth crashing down in higher seams, or falling in overhead cavities, while underground – the sound was thought to resemble someone being persistently sick.

boxhole. A sort of rudimentary underground 'office' much more in common with a cave, in which the overman deploys his deputies and gets reports from off going officials. It is a source of kists and desks, picks and tools, and when no one is around flaked-out diesel drivers and fitters grabbing a quiet kip.

brae. A little hill.

brass. Money.

bray. To hit something hard. So called, it is said, because the Ancient Brits had swords of weaker metal than the invading Romans, and had perfected a technique of attacking in waves, so that when their swords became bent they would retreat with one wave to the crest of a brae to hammer straight their swords while the next wave engaged the enemy.

brek. Break.

Brid. Bridlington.

broon. Newcastle Brown Ale (high-alcohol-content bottled beer brewed by Scottish and Newcastle Breweries).

burn. Stream.

C

cacks. Shit.

cannie, cannit. Can not.

canny. Cute, quite.

cardies. Cardigans.

carryoot. The drink brought from bars or off-licences to take away with you and continue drinking after the bars are closed.

caunch, canch. The stone face of a tunnel or working coalface. (Likewise 'rip', Yorkshire.)

caunchmen. The 'stoneworkers' who work the caunch.

ceilidh. Celtic music, song and dance social for the whole family.

chow. Chewing baccy.

Cla's, Santie. Father Christmas.

claes. Clothes.

clarts. Mud.

clarty. Muddy.

clout. Cloth.

clout. Smack.

cowp. To hit in a sweeping motion by an object or circular blow.

crêche. A place where babies and young children are taken care of.

cuddie. Horse (also nickname for someone from Durham).

cumann, cumainn (Irish). Branch, branches.

D

de'e. Die.

de'el. Devil.

dee (1). Do.

dee (2). Die.

deent, daint (Yorkshire). Don't.

der (Netherlands). The.

dey. Do.

dinnet. Divind, don't.

dit (Netherlands). This.

divind, dinnet, deen'd. Do not, don't.

divinknaawhat/Ahdivinknaawhat. Don't know what/ I don't know what. Usually accompanied with 'yeknaa': 'Ahdivinknaawhatyeknaa'.

doot. Doubt.

dook. Duck (lower your head).

doon. Down.

Dosco. The big brother of the boom ripper, a tunnelling machine of various 'marks' and types.

dunch. Collide.

E

eerste (Netherlands). First.

eiyt. Eight.

F

fall back (rate). Face and heading men, available for work on their own job and therefore capable of earning the top A1 power loader rate, who are held off that work for reasons beyond their control were entitled to be paid 'fall back rate' or the rate for their normal job.

feller. Fellow.

fernant/fernance. Directly opposite.

firedamp. The explosive mixture found in underground coal workings: methane and smaller gases in combination.

flee. Fly.

fleein. Flying.

follies. Follows.

foond/fund. Found.

forbye. That aside.

foya. For you.

frau (Netherlands). Women.

G

gaan. Go.

gaanan/gaanin. Going.

gaaninboard. Track underground which links the board and wall headings, gaanins and the main roadway (gate).

gaanins. Alleyways.

gallis/gallus (Glaswegian). Cocky, boastful.

galvie. Galvanised.

gate. Road.

geet/greet /gret. Great.

Geordie(s). Originally the inhabitants of Newcastle Upon Tyne. Geordies were the supporters of King George during the Jacobite rebellions of 1715 and 1745. Actually the 'Geordies' were not really Geordies, as the vast majority of the region, not least Newcastle and Tyneside overall, supported the Jacobites in both rebellions and the period in between. The name fell upon them because Newcastle was a garrison town and the largest centre for George's soldiers in the north. People have speculated that the name came from the mines and the northern pitmen's preference for the Geordie lamp rather than the Davie lamp; they did, but that is not where the name originates. Likewise, it was a widespread custom to call marras or workmates 'Geordie' in absence of their proper name, so everyone was 'Geordie' at work; true, but again incidental to the origin. All Tynesiders rather than just the folk o the toon now acclaim themselves Geordies.

gud. Good.

gud'un. Good one.

H

ha'way, haweh. Come on.

had on. Hold on.

had. Hold.

hadaway. Go away.

hadawaycumback. Kevin Gartland's description of the slide trombone which has become a part of my language ever since, and remarkably now finds it way into glossaries of Tyneside dialect.

hade. A rather complicated mining concept which is difficult to explain if you haven't seen it. Basically it is an unplanned hole which occurs in the strata above the area in which you are mining, and is usually composed of crushed minerals which continue to run out in small or large sizes. The hole can run forward in advance of the area you are working and to unlimited heights above your supports. It often accompanies geological faults and intrusions, and is a very volatile environment in which to work, with the risk of being buried alive or struck by boulders falling from very high.

hadin. Holding.

hail. (Netherlands). Very.

heed. Head.

het. Have.

hev. Have.

hing, hingin. Hang, hanging.

hinger. Name for various clinging metal supports attached to last girder set which support the running girders as above.

hoor. Hour.

hoose. House.

horseheed/head. A metal box attached to the last girder set, through which forepollings or girders are run in line with the tunnel and upon which the middle section of the arch girder will rest. Or a square metal box which attached to the adjacent girder on the coalface, which the adjacent girder will sit in and be supported by when the props are withdrawn from beneath it and it is advanced.

hoss. Horse.

hoyed. Thrown.

hoying. Throwing.

hoys. Throws.

hyme (La'lands Northumbrian). Home. (The 'h' is silent; in La'lands Scots it is pronounced yem.)

I

in't (Doncaster twang). Isn't.

inbye. In toward the face and away from the shafts.

J

ja (Netherlands). Yes.

K

keek (Netherlands). Look (verb).

keeker. Colliery 'viewer' on the surface who supervised the tubs coming to bank for the quality and quantity of the coal in each tub or corf.

ken'd. Understood, known.

kiddha. Kid, children. Used to address an adult it can be threatening, seriously or as mock rebuke.

kijker (Netherlands). A look.

kipping. Napping.

kist. Box, usually deputies' kist, at the corner of a mine district in which the reports of off going and oncoming shifts are made out and stored and men are deployed or assembled before and at the end of shifts.

kleiner (Netherlands). A little.

knaa(s). Know(s).
knad. Knew.

L

la'r. The pitman's self-gained knowledge.
lang. Long.
lang'uns. Long ones – the trousers pitmen wear when not on the coalface, in outbye regions which tend to be cold or even freezing.
langjoint. A greet lang joint – 'Art' had taught me how to make a 26-skinner.
langsyne. Long time since.
lavie. Lavatory.
leds. Lads.
leets. Lights.
leng (Northumbrian). Long.
les (Netherlands). Lesson.
lig'ht (Netherlands). Lie, lay.
loco. Locomotive, either electric or diesel.
lol. Rest.
lope. Bound.
loppin. Bounding.
lowse. Knock-off time at the pit, meaning literally to 'lowse' or loose the coal-bearing corfs and gear from the pit winding rope to accommodate loops or baskets or skips to carry the workers out of the mine.
luek, luekin. Look, looking.
lurn. Learn.

M

ma. Mother, also shortened version of 'marra'.
mak. Make. (Usually the Wearside variant, alang wi 'tak', which gives the Wearside folk the oft misunderstood tag of 'makums'. The Tyneside pronunciation by distinction is 'mek' and 'tek'.)
manrider. Means of conveying men underground, either on a manriding belt, or manriding set of vehicles pulled by a loco (a paddy in Yorkshire) or by rope.
marra. Workmate. In the nineteenth century northern coalfields the marraship was a highly prised and important relationship, touching on life and death and level of income. See my *Pit Life In Co. Durham*, History Workshop, Oxford, 1972.
Meedmen/man, Madmen/man. Name we gave our adolescent gang.
meg. Make fun of.
mek. Make. Scots/Tyneside variant, alang wi 'tek', which differentiates from wa Wearside comrades' 'mak'.
mel. Big hammer.
mer. More.
mevie. Maybe.
mickle (La'lands: Scots /Northumbrian). Few.

mit. (Netherlands). With.

mixi. Mixamatosis – a disease deliberately spread by the government postwar to control the numbers of rabbits, now war-starved populations were no longer eating them in such numbers. It causes blindness (among the rabbits) and an extremely painful death.

mo (Netherlands; pronounced 'moo'). Tired.

muckle (La'lands: Scots/Northumbrian). Many.

mun. Must.

N

na. No.

nae (Netherlands). No.

nay. No, nothing. (Modern infusion of La'lands.)

neet. Night.

nen. None.

netty. Toilet.

neverlerim (Scouse). Never let him.

ney. No/nothing.

neybody. Nobody.

neybugger. Nobody.

nie. Near.

nivor. Never.

noggin (men). A noggin is a bout of overtime at the end of the shift, the noggin men those working the overtime.

nouce (Yorkshire). Pitman's self-gained knowledge.

nowt. Nothing.

O

on't (Yorkshire). On top of.

onsetter. The man at the bottom of the pit shaft who is in charge of the riding of materials and men up and down the shaft.

oot. Out.

ootbye. Away from the coalface toward the shaft.

oss (Yorkshire). Horse.

Ouseburn. One-time self -contained industrial community on the way to Byker from Newcastle. Its surviving meandering river and abandoned condition ensured it would be 'redeveloped' largely by Yuppies, but also cheek by jowl by the Star and Shadow, and the nuevo hippies along with a number of artists and academics. Features of the old community survive and the folkies too have adopted its four pubs for ceilidhs and impromptu sessions. The overall effect, despite the upper-class accents, and the presence of students and woolly middle-class folk, is a pleasant one.

overmans, overman. A colliery official under the under-manager.

oversman. Scottish pronunciation of above.

ower. Over.

P

Padmasana (Sanskrit). Lotus sitting position.

pinners. Wooden wedges used in tightening supports.

pneumo. Pneumoconiosis: the miner's often fatal lung disease, nicknamed by American miners 'Black Lung'.

pricker. The wire 'thread' that fits in the centre of the oil lamp base and makes connection with the wick to adjust its height for testing for gas levels.

R

R&B. A music genre intermingling basic blues with jazz. It was originally associated with the poor rural black Southern states but spread to the urban black population. It was the root of rock 'n' roll and then experienced a resurgence among the hip generation of Sixties Britain, in particular in Liverpool and on Tyneside. It became the adopted motive force of the Rolling Stones, the Beatles and the Animals among many others. The term in the today covers a far wider and non-specific field and the music so termed today is to Sixties ears now unrecognisable as 'true' R&B.

rammle. Bits of abandoned tackle: ropes and wires etc.

reet. Right.

retelt. Retold.

roon/roond. Round.

runai (Irish). Secretary of an organisation.

S

Sand Dancer. A resident of South Shields. A mix of the sandy shores and long-time presence of Arabs has given the seafaring coalmining town's residents the name. Legend has it that the Arabs were the first real inhabitants of the town while modern research says they came with the invention of the steamship as stokers from mainly Aden and Yemen. Seafarers and coalminers were often the same blokes, switching from one trade to the other seasonally or in accordance with their age and marital status. Early Durham Miners certificates and membership diplomas clearly show Arab coal hewers in their cameos, so at least from the time of the Durham Miners Association in the 1860s, Arab coalminers worked Shields coal seams along with their more Nordic Tynesiders. Who knows? But the Romans called the local fort 'Fort Arbeia'; my Latin isn't too good since leaving the Catholic church but that sounds like 'Fort of the Arabs' to me.

sark. Shirt.

schlafsacken (Netherlands). Sleeping bag.

scrat. Poke about in the dirt, sand or soil.

shelt. Shalt, shall have.

shoot. Shout.

shooted. Shouted.

slooter (probably Tyneside Irish). To walk with the soles of one's footwear scraping or sliding along the ground.

snadgies. Turnips 'snadged' or nicked from a farmer's field.

sook. Groveller, toady (short for 'sook-up'). Not to be confused with the American 'sucks' which seems to be describing something completely different.

soond. Sound.

sprag (Yorkshire). Tell tales on someone.

spragged. Propped up.

sprags. Small props wedged under nicked jud prior to blasting at the coalface. (A space is dug out from below the coal seam, the width and depth of the jud or portion of coal to be felled; it is supported by sprags prior to firing. The shot for maximum impact must have a space in which to absorb the blast through the coal seam, otherwise it would tend to fire back out of the shot hole and do little damage to the coal seam.)

sprake (Netherlands). Speak.

spraken (Netherlands). Speaking.

stot. Bounce ('being on the stot': having an erection).

strags. Strays.

swallie (Northumbria), swillie (Yorkshire). A dip in an underground roadway.

T

taities/tatties. Potatoes.

tart. At one time a fairly common expression in the north for a young female companion or potential companion, a girlfriend sort of but less serious, potentially sexual, and potentially casually regular but ney strings. Someone decided then to class 'tarts' as easy, and from that prostitutes, or loose women, so 'tarty' like you were dressed up for it and cheap. It became number one on the middle-class feminist's hit list of working-class bloke's expressions for girls; though it is doubtful we ever meant the things they thought the word meant. So there's a surprise.

tatty. A bit threadbare.

te, tey. Too.

Teds, Teddy Boys. Teens and twenties working-class lads, who dressed in Edwardian style clothes, or so it was said. They were the postwar rock 'n' roll generation, given to lots of violence, the head-butt, the flick-knife, gang fights, some murders and a snog and a touch of breast before they were married if they were lucky. The music was far cooler than they were, unless you were a middle-class American in a red Ford Thunderbird with whitewall tyres making out overlooking the ocean. (Newcastle Teds were not like that.)

tellitale. Child who informs on other children, a sneak.

telt. Told.

tha. Their.

thiv. They have.

thorty. Thirty.

thou, tha, thee. You (singular).

thowt. Thought.

thy. Your.

ti'vis. To me.

toi-toi. A Southern African mining community dance of defiance and celebration, a sort of African Knees Up Mother Brown.

toking. Taking a toke is taking a long, deeply inhaled draw of a marijuana cig or joint.

twe. Two.

U

up't'tash (Yorkshire). Sexual analogy for the drill being right at the end of its length up to the face of the stone or coal, as with a penis being fully inserted 'up to the tash' or pubic hair of the vagina, 'tash' being a shortened version of moustache. (That's really ower much information, I agree.).

us (Yorkshire). Our.

V

vloer (Netherlands). Floor.

vornie. Very nearly.

W

wa/wa. We/we are.

wa'ater. Water spelt like that to demonstrate the long waa sound at the beginning of the word.

wa'llers. Wallers, big rocks used in construction of 'dry stone walls' underground.

wa-arn. Warn.

wadn't. Wouldn't.

Wado-Ryu. One of the (three) branches of the Shito-Ryu school of Karate, along with Shukokai and Shotokan.

wasells. Ourselves.

wasens (Yorkshire). Ourselves.

water notes. Locally based agreements that allow men to ride out of the pit early when they have been working in excess water. The note is written out by the deputy, the mine official on the job, and shown to the onsetter who operates the cage to the surface at the bottom of the shaft.

wee. Small.

weel. Well.

wes. Was.

whee's. Whose.

whey aye. Of course. When I first attended at Strathclyde University Scottish students would comment in surprise, 'So you really do say "Whey aye,"' and I would likewise observe that they really did say 'Och aye.'

whey. Who.

while (Yorkshire). Until.

wi (1). With.

wi (2). Us.

wick. Thick with,

wifie. Wife, older women.
wo'ord. Word.
woorm. Snake, sea-serpent, or worm.
wor. Our.
workie-ticket. Someone who pushes their luck in testing people's patience.
workin ya ticket. Trying others' patience with provocative behaviour.
wors. Ours.

Y

ya mooth. Your mouth.
yaakers. Sometimes derogatory term for young face workers.
yasell, yersell. Yourself.
yee/yee's, ye/ye's. You, youse.
yee'r, yer. Your.
yem, hyme. Home.
yensen (Yorkshire). Yourself.
yi/yi's. You, youse.
yourn (Doncaster twang). Yours

ORGANISATIONS

Anarchist Communist Federation. Old sparing partners of mine who initially adopted an anti-union, council communist position but then in the light of experience and contact with workers came down to a more practical understanding of the nature of class struggles in the unions themselves as well as through the unions.

Anarchist Federation. Renamed from the Anarchist Communist Federation, a bit presumptuously I thought since it doesn't actually federate all anarchists, even all class struggle anarchists, just basically the people who were in the ACF. Good comrades for all that.

Big Flame. Libertarian Marxist group founded in 1970 on Merseyside, taking their name from a fictitious TV docu-drama about the seizure of the Liverpool Docks by the dockers. They modelled themselves on Italian organisations of the same informal, libertarian traditions, claiming not to be The Party, or the embryo of that Party, but believed in the necessity for A Party all the same. Their paper *Big Flame* was big and colourful and attractive, however it began to spend a great deal of time and space on self analysis and where it stood in relation to the rest of the left. They moved in Troops Out circles and Irish solidarity and although they came to describe their politics as libertarian Marxist, though they never renounced Leninism as far as we recall. In 1978 they joined the election coalition Socialist Unity founded by the IMG. In 1980 they were joined by the anarchist Libertarian Communist Group, and the Revolutionary Marxist Current. However the struggle within the Labour Party and LPYS by 1982 and the growth of revolutionary tendencies within it, posed a platform which seemed more relevant than the one many of their members were operating in, and most of their members bled away into that milieu, we think for a time operating a short-lived left tendency though the name of that current is now lost. The organisation wound up in 1983.

British Anti Zionist Organisation – Palestine Solidarity. Mostly Scottish based organisation campaigning around Palestine and the Middle East. Aimed equally at breaking the identity of Zionism with the Semitic peoples or the Jewish religion and regarding Zionism as a form of racism.

British Socialist Party. 1911 split from the Independent Labour Party on the basis that it wasn't independent enough of liberal and parliamentary influences.

CGT. Confederation Général du Travail: communist-inspired mass union.

Class War Federation. Class struggle anarchist organisation.

CND. Campaign for Nuclear Disarmament.

COSA. Colliery Officials and Staff Association: the NUM's white-collar and colliery officer's section.

CPB. Communist Party of Britain.

CPBML. Communist Party Britain, Marxist-Leninist.

CPGB. Communist Party of Great Britain

Fedayeen (Iran). Beginning in 1971, as an insurgency against the Shah, but also against the line of official 'Communism' represented by the Tudeh Party, it was formed of two main factions, broadly Maoist and politically in line with the Chinese wing of the Sino-Soviet world split in the state communist movement. Its base MO was guerrillaism. As China's stance became more hostile to the USSR which it deemed 'social imperialist', the Fed' and other leftist Iranian groups distanced themselves from formal Maoism and announced themselves independent of either Moscow or Peking, though still clearly heavily Stalinist in orientation. Following the mass uprising of 79 when the bulk of the leadership was freed from the Shah's jails, the movement effectively split between the guerrillas and those who wished for some national common front. Both wings were short on organisation and theory with basically Lenin's *What Is To Be Done* written in a different time frame in another country and set of circumstances becoming the guiding text for action and theory. The first public rally of the Fedayeen called in Tehran in 1979 attracted 500,000 people, and they stood in the 'revolutionary' constituent elections, returning 2 million votes. The major split following on 1979 was what attitude to adopt toward the Mullahs and the Islamic revolution. The majority wing favoured a common front and 'bide our time' position with the minority adopting a hostile, pro-secular democratic position. While the minority were hunted almost to extinction, the majority were able to maintain an office in the capital until 1983. By 1988 the Ayatollah Khomeini had moved to the final solution for the leftist and secular opposition and unleashed a bloodbath against all non-Islamic forces, with up to 20,000 murdered in his first sweep. See the article by Fedayeen militant Yassamine Mather, 'Learn the lessons', *Weekly Worker*, 11 September 2008, pp. 8–9.

Fedayeen. Other political organisations of the Middle East also adopt the name Fedayeen. It is a prominent tendency within the PLO.

ILP. Independent Labour Party.

International Marxist Group. One of the splits within European and world Trotskyism; this one is loyal to Ernest Mandel, and the United Secretariat of IVth International.

IWP. International Workers Party: US socialist revolutionary Marxist-Leninist-Luxemburgist Tendency, greatly influenced by its founder Fred Newman, his theories of social psychology and variations on Freudianism.

Mujahedin. Afghan resistance/united front of mainly fundamentalist Islamist tribesmen against the 'socialist government', then their Soviet allies. Backed by the west to stop any Afghan socialist experiment succeeding, they were armed, trained and financed by the USA in co-ordination with NATO and the Saudis. The Mujahedin government was short-lived with a more fundamentalist and medievalist current the Taliban defeating them and forming a government which was politically allied to Al Qaeda and the cause of a universal Islamic republic. Following Al Qaeda's attack upon the USA, Britain and other major nations, NATO invaded Afghanistan and set up a 'popular' though thoroughly ineffective government, and waged war, unsuccessfully against its own offspring the Taliban.

Mujahedin. Resistance organisation/ united front, against the Shah in Iran, then those forces against the Mullah's Islamic Republic.

NACODS. National Association of Colliery Overmen, Deputies and Shotfirers.

NCP. New Communist Party.

NLF. National Liberation Front: the Vietcong.

Northern Anarchist Network. Make the best cooked meals of the whole left at their conferences and their politics aren't half bad either.

NUM. National Union of Mineworkers.

Parliament. The political wing of the British Army.

PCF. Parti Communiste Français – French Communist Party: had 250,000 members at the time of the May 1968 events, and over 1 million voters. It dominated the CGT.

Provisional Sinn Fein. Political wing of the Provisional IRA

Provos (Dutch). 1960s hippy anarchist movement, creators of 'the happening'.

Revolutionary Communist Group. Originally expelled from Tony Cliff's 'third camp' International Socialists (1973), they developed as a tendency and formed as the RCG, firmly in the defence of the workers' states and the third world anti-imperialist struggle. Following their bad experiences within the IS and now totally confused about Trotsky and the nature of the bureaucratic states/ degenerated workers' states/state capitalist states, they decide not to endorse Trotsky or Stalin but enthusiastically defend the states as more or less workers' states. They developed a tendency toward 'third world struggles first' and struggles of minorities, gradually coming to see less and less importance in the traditional working class of the imperialist states and implicitly at least seeing them as in part collaborators or 'labour aristocrats'. Their paper *Fight Imperialism, Fight Racialism* has been none the less an important tool in the class war, and I have on occasion over the years written for it, and stood on their platforms.

Revolutionary Communist Tendency. This formed at the same time a RCG following their joint expulsion from IS or split from RCG soon afterwards. Firstly they developed highly sectarian 'holier-than-thou' attitudes toward the rest of the left and ultra-pure positions on the war in Ireland which excluded most initiatives being taken at the time, even by those doing the fighting. The group's political arrogance was only matched by its social composition; frequently middle class and even upper class and at times aristocratic, its members were often from yuppie backgrounds and careers. They soon started to develop strange refracted right-wing and reactionary perspectives. While most of the left stood against nuclear energy and for clean coal technology as a bridge to more green, self-sustaining energy sources RCT advocated nuclear power. Their paper *The Next Step* became infamous during the 1984/5 miners' strike for condemning the strike, its leaders and its union for not having had a ballot, staged joint meetings with the scabs and became the left face of the blacklegs. They were hounded from the strike-bound coalfields and miners' demonstrations. They went on to develop a harder rejection of the British working class than their erstwhile RCG compatriots, concluding us to be non-revolutionary, and virtually all campaigns and movements of the class to be reformist and reactionary. Somewhere along the line they transformed themselves into the Revolutionary Communist Party and in 1987 entered an alliance, the Red Front, with the Revolutionary Democratic Group and Red Action, neither of which they shared anything at all with really, to stand in the 1987 elections. Since they had long ago written off the British working class it is hard to see why they thought the workers would vote for them; they didn't. They then turned away from the working class altogether and went after the bright young things of their own social milieu, launching an upmarket glossy mag *Living Marxism*, which they later smoothed down to *LM*. The politics got weirder and weirder with demonstrations in support of the Argentinean invasion of the Falklands/Malvinos, and support for the Serbs in the Yugoslavian conflict (as against opposition to all sides and for 'No War But The Class War'). Its social milieu ensured that they penetrated influential areas of the academic world, science and the media, effectively running their own TV programme *Against Nature* in 1997. Politically the group was moving toward bourgeois 'market' libertarianism and taking 'issues' into global corporations. Hardly surprising they end up backing and promoting GM foods, the rights of smokers, debunking climate change, and supporting the Countryside Alliance. The cherry on the cake was when they came out in support of the Tory candidate for mayor of London, Boris Johnson, against Ken Livingstone or any of the alternative left slates. Despite this they have raised some important rebukes on Green liquidationism and medievalism, challenged some of the taken-for-granteds on climate change and stood out against the acceptance of multiculturalism and anti-secularist trends on the left. Positions I would largely agree with, though probably from a different political pole.

Revolutionary Workers Party. The old Latin American Bureau of the IVth International split under Comrade Posadas, to form the International Secretariat and found national sections. The RWP was the British section.

RUC. Royal Ulster Constabulary.

SLL. Socialist Labour League: one of the British splits of Trotskyism, this one loyal to Gerry Healy. It transformed itself into the Workers' Revolutionary Party, British Section of the International Committee of the 1Vth International.

Socialist Labour Party. Originally a break from the British Socialist Party, and closely linked to the early days of the IWW. The SLP was refounded by Arthur Scargill in the late 1990s, although with an entirely different programme and political history.

Tudah Party. Communist Party of Iran.

Tyneside Anarchist Federation. There have probably been numerous such federations but ours was started in 1964 and dominated the youth political scene on Tyneside and Northumberland basically until 1970/1, when Trotskyist politics became dominant for a time.

Tyneside Anarchist Group. Seems to have emerged in the mid 1980s and was highly active and successful for a few years.

Tyneside Committee of 100. Direct action movement against the bomb and war. At its peak had sub-committees throughout the region including those at Wardley, Felling, Heaton and Gateshead.

Tyneside Direct Action Movement. The early 1960s predecessor of the Committee of 100, mainly composed of anarchists, old ILP members and Buddhist-influenced pacifists.

Weatherpeople (previously Weathermen). A violent and heroic resistance organisation in USA who later became full-time armed urban guerrillas. They took their name from a line in a Bob Dylan song, 'You don't need a weatherman to know which way the wind blows.'

WPPE. Working People's Party of England. One of the breaks from the CPGB in support of Stalin and China.

WPPS. Working People's Party of Scotland:, similar to the above although the two organisations fell out almost at their inception.

YCL. Young Communist League: youth section of the CPGB.

YCND. Youth CND.

YHA. Youth Hostels Association.

Youth Against The Bomb. 'The Geordie Cong': Tyneside anti-bomb, anti-war, alliance. It adopted a generally anarchist with some Trotskyist-influenced political perspectives and campaigned fairly much on everything anti-capitalist and anti-imperialist.

PLACES

The Abbey, Dunscroft, Doncaster. The first 'home' of the revolutionary caucus in the Hatfield Colliery area. Here was the base of the Revolutionary Workers Party, the Labour Party Young Socialists and the Troops Out Movement. The landlord frequently equipped us with crates of beer to take away on conferences and rallies as we assembled in his car park, with flags and banners. Later the home base of the Socialist Union Internationalist, and their large milieu. Regular scene of Morris's heavy metal disco and second favourite waterhole for the Donny bikers and heavy metal freaks. It was also the home of the local footballers, pigeon flyers, darts players, vegetable and flower growers and had a quiet upmarket lounge where folk in their best clothes could have a drink and a bar meal of an evening. Our revolutionary caucus and regular influx of European and American revolutionaries was taken 'on the nod'. Footballers and pigeon flyers came to our folk and disco socials and parties and we came to theirs, even turning out to cheer them on the touchline. It was no great surprise given that mostly we all worked together down the pit anyway, and shared the same streets.

Beetham's. Market-place cellar bar in Doncaster, a sort of born-again Sixties hippie pub but frequented by many bikers, most of whom were actually coalminers. We adopted it as a movement pub and fused with the pub's heavy metal freaks, pot smokers, bikers and hippies. Its heyday was the Seventies through to about the late Eighties.

The Bridge. The Bridge Hotel, Newcastle Upon Tyne. Stands on the Newcastle side of the High Level Bridge just in the lee of the Keep. A traditionally Irish cultural and political centre for decades, it became the home of the High Level Ranters and the Folk Song and Ballad Club, as well as the left in all its hues and forms. It punctuates this story almost from start to finish.

The Broadway Hotel. Miners' pub on Broadway, Dunscroft. For the duration of this story mainly under the management of Pete Thompson. The source of numerous rallies, folk music socials, and meetings. In the later period of the strike also home to one of Hatfield Main's three food kitchens.

Delector Hall, Raby Street, Byker. Big upstairs hall and venue for the left and alternative movement for all sorts of events in the Sixties, as well as a conventional community centre for the local population.

Doonbeat. Legendary R&B nightclub in Newcastle in the Sixties, housed in an old converted warehouse.

Fifteen. A pub at the bottom of Doncaster High Street, the favourite of people in their forties through to their seventies, by the look. It plays Sixties/Seventies rock, and is frequented by the people who were the in-scene of those years. It is packed to the gunwales, with the survivors of that generation still cool and still looking for sexual encounters.

The Fox. Ancient pub in what was once Stainforth Market Square, venue for a number of revolutionary meetings since the late Sixties, folk socials and for a time the branch meetings of Hatfield Main NUM Branch, Doncaster Class

War, and IWW national conference. Now renamed.

The George Hotel, Stainforth. Huge pub and centre for much village activity since the Forties and through much of this story. Centre for our Young Mineworkers Committee in the late Sixties, and our folk socials in support of Vietnam. Mass meetings of the LPYS, and the RWP(T) and incidentally Kung Fu Tommy's Karate classes. Closed and converted into flats in the Nineties.

ILP Hall, Shields Road, Byker. The traditional offices of the ILP on Tyneside, subsequently taken over by the anarchists and the Committee of 100, as a social centre, crash pad, bar, and generally the centre of alternative youth Tyneside in the mid Sixties. The hall itself is still there above some small shop at the time of writing.

The Madge. The Majestic Ballroom; was the ace dance-hall of the Fifties and Sixties for conventional rock 'n' roll and rock'n'rollers – teds and their teddy girls.

Newcastle Socialist Centre. Formed in 1911. Corner of Leazes Park and Percy Street. Had developed within the offices of the British Socialist Party formed that year and the Clarion Fellowship as a general social centre of the left. It became so successful it moved to much larger premises in the prestigious Royal Arcade. It occupied two floors, downstairs the meeting room and library and café, and upstairs the theatre and social rooms. There have been a number of Tyneside Socialist Centres since, one of which was based at Jesmond in the late Seventies.

Ouseburn. One-time self-contained industrial community on the way to Byker from Newcastle, its surviving meandering river and abandoned condition ensured it would be 'redeveloped' largely by Yuppies, but also cheek by jowl by the Star and Shadow, and the nuevo hippies along with a number of artists and academics. Features of the old community survive and the folkies too have adopted its four pubs for ceilidhs and impromptu sessions. The overall effect, despite the upper-class accents, and the presence of students and woolly middle-class folk, is a pleasant one.

Palette. Underground in the sense of being down some steps and under another building, café/coffee bar on Pilgrim Street, Newcastle. Now gone in the Eldon Square development, it was the meeting place for 'ordinary' shoppers as well as the mods and beats and politicos.

The People's Bookshop. The Communist Party Bookshop which stood midway up Westgate Hill and was for decades a centre of 'The Party's' industrial and youth work. Now a dwelling.

The Pit Club, Stainforth. At the top of the pit lane, witnessed many pickets and battles since the Twenties through to the Nineties.

Proletaria Bookshop. Station Road. Dunscroft. Our famous bookshop and social centre, home of the revolutionary pitmen and women and their wild all-night folk music socials.

Silver Link. Downstairs cellar bar in Doncaster off the High Street, the haunt of the emerging 'Scene' in Doncaster in the late Sixties, dope smokers, free sexers, progressive teens and twenties, and increasingly revolutionary socialists.

Star and Shadow. Alternative anarcho film centre, socialist centre and bar on the Newcastle side of Byker Bridge.

Strathclyde University Student Union. John Street, Glasgow.

Tyneside Irish Club. Gallowgate, Newcastle. Four-storey super club opposite St James Park.

The Welfare, Stainforth Miners Welfare. A massive ballroom/meeting room which housed a long bar. The centre of village life and scene of mass miners' meetings as well as the usual club turns, though not usually on at the same time. (Although at sombre times, as the room packed with grave faces waited our deliberation from the Branch Committee room, we on occasion were seen to side-step, arms linked, onto the big stage, singing 'There's no business like show business, like no business ...' which tended to lighten the atmosphere. It was the venue for Hatfield Main Brass Prize Band, practice and performances. It was the scene for the annual retired miners tea, where thousands of men sat down to a regal spread with free drinks and a host of free raffle prizes. It was, during the time of the great coal strike, the main food kitchen serving thousands of cooked meals. Its upstairs committee rooms became the venue for Marxist lessons, pit 123 inspector's courses, and political meetings of the left. The bar was home to any number of village characters. Following the final closure programme of the Nineties it went into steep decline. It was sold to a private owner as a private club, and was then abandoned. Village vandals burnt it out and it was demolished in the mid Nineties. Now an open space.

The Welfare, Thorne. Very similar to the above in every aspect, suffering the same ultimate fate. (The British Legion Club and The Archers Club in Stainforth were also burned out and demolished, as was The Regal on Broadway, Dunscroft).